Jesse Liberty
Siddhartha Rao
Bradley Jones

Sams **Teach Yourself**

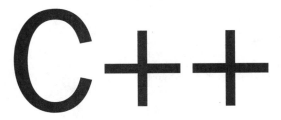

in **One Hour** a Day

 800 East 96th Street, Indianapolis, Indiana 46240

Sams Teach Yourself C++ in One Hour a Day

Copyright © 2009 by Sams Publishing

All rights reserved. No part of this book shall be reproduced, stored in a retrieval system, or transmitted by any means, electronic, mechanical, photocopying, recording, or otherwise, without written permission from the publisher. No patent liability is assumed with respect to the use of the information contained herein. Although every precaution has been taken in the preparation of this book, the publisher and author assume no responsibility for errors or omissions. Nor is any liability assumed for damages resulting from the use of the information contained herein.

ISBN-13: 978-0-672-32941-8

ISBN-10: 0-672-32941-7

Library of Congress Cataloging-in-Publication Data

Liberty, Jesse.

   C++ in one hour a day / Jesse Liberty, Siddhartha Rao, Bradley Jones. — 6th ed.

     p. cm.

   Includes bibliographical references and index.

   ISBN 978-0-672-32941-8 (pbk.)

   1. C++ (Computer program language) I. Rao, Siddhartha. II. Jones, Bradley. III. Title.

QA76.73.C153L528 2008

005.13′3—dc22

               2008024283

Printed in the United States of America

Fifth Printing December 2010

Trademarks

All terms mentioned in this book that are known to be trademarks or service marks have been appropriately capitalized. Sams Publishing cannot attest to the accuracy of this information. Use of a term in this book should not be regarded as affecting the validity of any trademark or service mark.

Warning and Disclaimer

Every effort has been made to make this book as complete and as accurate as possible, but no warranty or fitness is implied. The information provided is on an "as is" basis. The authors and the publisher shall have neither liability nor responsibility to any person or entity with respect to any loss or damages arising from the information contained in this book or from the use of the CD or programs accompanying it.

Bulk Sales

Sams Publishing offers excellent discounts on this book when ordered in quantity for bulk purchases or special sales. For more information, please contact

   U.S. Corporate and Government Sales
   1-800-382-3419
   corpsales@pearsontechgroup.com

For sales outside of the U.S., please contact

   International Sales
   international@pearson.com

This Book Is Safari Enabled

The Safari® Enabled icon on the cover of your favorite technology book means the book is available through Safari Bookshelf. When you buy this book, you get free access to the online edition for 45 days.

Safari Bookshelf is an electronic reference library that lets you easily search thousands of technical books, find code samples, download chapters, and access technical information whenever and wherever you need it.

To gain 45-day Safari Enabled access to this book:

- Go to http://www.informit.com/onlineedition
- Complete the brief registration form
- Enter the coupon code ETR3-REFQ-5UBU-SLQ5-TYNC

If you have difficulty registering on Safari Bookshelf or accessing the online edition, please email customer-service@safaribooksonline.com.

Acquisitions Editor
Mark Taber

Development Editor
Songlin Qiu

Managing Editor
Patrick Kanouse

Project Editor
Seth Kerney

Copy Editor
Mike Henry

Indexer
WordWise Publishing
Services, LLC

Proofreader
Kathy Ruiz

Technical Editors
Jon Upchurch
Dr. Mark S. Merry

**Publishing
Coordinator**
Vanessa Evans

Book Designer
Gary Adair

Contents at a Glance

Table of Contents

PART II: Fundamentals of Object-Oriented Programming and C++

LESSON 10: Classes and Objects   265

PART IV: More STL

LESSON 22: Understanding Function Objects — 553

LESSON 23: STL Algorithms — 569

Appendixes

Lead Author, Sixth Edition

Siddhartha Rao is a Microsoft Most Valuable Professional for Visual C++ and a moderator at one of the Internet's most vibrant online development communities, CodeGuru. "Sid," as he is popularly known, is an expert in the Windows programming domain, and is experienced in the architecture and development of driver and application software using C++ and other modern programming languages. Currently employed by a German software giant, he specializes in software landscape management and best practices in software development. With the international experience of having lived and worked in three countries behind him, he believes that the travel bug has bit him, and firmly so! Sid speaks many languages that have nothing to do with programming, and when he's not working, you will find him discovering new places on the planet, or shooting—using his Canon, of course!

Contributing Authors

Jesse Liberty is the author of numerous books on software development, including best-selling titles in C++ and .NET. He is the president of Liberty Associates, Inc., where he provides custom programming, consulting, and training.

Bradley Jones, Microsoft MVP, Visual C++, can be referred to as a webmaster, manager, coding grunt, executive editor, and various other things. His time and focus are on a number of software development sites and channels, including Developer.com, CodeGuru.com, DevX, VBForums, Gamelan, and other Jupitermedia-owned sites.

Acknowledgments

Siddhartha Rao: I am thankful to the editors—Songlin Qiu, Seth Kerney, and Mark Taber—for their prompt and professional involvement that helped make this book a reality. I am deeply endowed to my loved ones for their unconditional support, for tolerating me spending my vacations on this project, and for helping me out with every little chore that I could concentrate on this book, which I consider so important. I hope you enjoy reading it!

Jesse Liberty: A new edition is another chance to acknowledge and to thank those folks without whose support and help this book literally would have been impossible. First among them remain Stacey, Robin, and Rachel Liberty.

Bradley Jones: I would also like to thank Mark Cashman, David Corbin, Songlin Qiu, and a number of readers from the previous editions.

We Want to Hear from You!

As the reader of this book, *you* are our most important critic and commentator. We value your opinion and want to know what we're doing right, what we could do better, what areas you'd like to see us publish in, and any other words of wisdom you're willing to pass our way.

You can email or write me directly to let me know what you did or didn't like about this book—as well as what we can do to make our books stronger.

Please note that I cannot help you with technical problems related to the topic of this book, and that due to the high volume of mail I receive, I might not be able to reply to every message.

When you write, please be sure to include this book's title and author as well as your name and phone or email address. I will carefully review your comments and share them with the author and editors who worked on the book.

Email: webdev@samspublishing.com

Mail: Mark Taber
           Associate Publisher
           Sams Publishing
           800 East 96th Street
           Indianapolis, IN 46240 USA

Reader Services

Visit our website and register this book at informit.com/register for convenient access to any updates, downloads, or errata that might be available for this book.

Introduction

This book is designed to help you teach yourself how to program with C++. Just as you can learn to walk one step at a time, you can learn to program in C++ one hour at a time. Each lesson in this book has been designed so that you can read the entire lesson in just an hour a day. It lays emphasis on the practical usage of the language, and helps you get up-to-speed with concepts that are most important in writing C++ applications for real-world usage.

By focusing for just an hour a day at a time, you'll learn about such fundamentals as managing input and output, loops and arrays, object-oriented programming, templates, using the standard template library, and creating C++ applications—all in well-structured and easy-to-follow lessons. Lessons provide sample listings—complete with sample output and an analysis of the code—to illustrate the topics of the day.

To help you become more proficient, each lesson ends with a set of common questions and answers, a quiz, and exercises. You can check your progress by examining the quiz and exercise answers provided in Appendix D, "Answers."

Who Should Read This Book

You don't need any previous experience in programming to learn C++ with this book. This book starts you from the beginning and teaches you both the language and the concepts involved with programming C++. You'll find the numerous examples of syntax and detailed analysis of code an excellent guide as you begin your journey into this rewarding environment. Whether you are just beginning or already have some experience programming, you will find that this book's clear organization makes learning C++ fast and easy.

Organization of This Book

This is a book that appeals as much to a beginner in the language as it does to someone who wishes to understand C++ again, but from a more practical perspective. It is hence divided into five parts:

- Part I, "The Basics," introduces C++, and its syntactical details. This is very useful for absolute beginners who would first like to understand the basics of programming in C++.

- Part II, "Fundamentals of Object-Oriented Programming and C++," introduces the object-oriented features of C++—those that set it apart from its predecessor C. This section lays the foundation for a more practical view of the language and one of its most powerful utilities, the standard template library.

- Part III, "Learning the Standard Template Library (STL)," gives you a close look at how C++ is used in real-life practical applications where quality of your application can be vastly improved by using readily available, standard-compliant constructs.

- Part IV, "More STL," introduces you to algorithms such as sort and other STL constructs that help streamline your application and increase its reliability.

- Part V, "Advanced C++ Concepts," discusses details and features of the programming language that not every application built using it needs to have, yet, knowing them can help in error analysis or in writing better code.

Conventions Used in This Book

Within the lessons, you'll find the following elements that provide additional information:

TIP

> These boxes highlight information that can make your C++ programming more efficient and effective.

NOTE

> These boxes provide additional information related to material you just read.

> **FAQ**
>
> **What do FAQs do?**
>
> **Answer:** These Frequently Asked Questions provide greater insight into the use of the language and clarify potential areas of confusion.

CAUTION

> These focus your attention on problems or side effects that can occur in specific situations.

These boxes provide clear definitions of essential terms.

DO	DON'T
DO use the "Do/Don't" boxes to find a quick summary of a fundamental principle in a lesson.	**DON'T** overlook the useful information offered in these boxes.

This book uses various typefaces to help you distinguish C++ code from regular English. Actual C++ code is typeset in a special `monospace` font. Placeholders—words or characters temporarily used to represent the real words or characters you would type in code—are typeset in *`italic monospace`*. New or important terms are typeset in *italic*.

Sample Code for This Book

The code samples in this book are available online for download from the publisher's website.

PART I:
The Basics

LESSON 1
Getting Started

Welcome to *Sams Teach Yourself C++ in One Hour a Day*! You will get started on your way to becoming a proficient C++ programmer.

In this lesson, you will learn

- Why C++ is a standard in software development
- The steps to develop a C++ program
- How to enter, compile, and link your first working C++ program

A Brief History of C++

Computer languages have undergone dramatic evolution since the very first electronic computers. Early on, programmers worked with the most primitive computer instructions: machine language. These instructions were represented by strings of ones and zeros. Assembly soon became the standard in programming as it replaced (or mapped) the cumbersome binary strings by human-readable and -manageable mnemonics such as ADD and MOV.

However, as the tasks performed by software applications being developed became more complex (for example, in the computation of missile trajectories), programmers felt the need for a language that could perform relatively complex mathematical instructions that in turn would be a combination of many assembly codes; that is, many machine language instructions. Thus, FORTRAN was born: the first high-level programming language optimized for numeric and scientific computation that introduced, among other things, subroutines, functions, and loops to the programming arena. In time, higher-level languages such as BASIC and COBOL evolved that let programmers work with something approximating words and sentences (referred to as *source code*), such as Let I = 100.

C itself came into being as an evolutionary improvement over a previous version called B (sounds too obvious, doesn't it?), which was an improved version of a language called BPCL (Basic Combined Programming Language). Although C was invented expressly to help programmers use features that new hardware (in those days) presented, it owes its popularity largely to its portability and speed. C was a procedural language, and as computer languages evolved into the object-oriented domain, Bjarne Stroustrup invented C++ (1981) that continues to be one of the most evolved and widely used programming languages. In addition to introducing features such as operator overloading and inline functions, C++ also implemented object-oriented concepts such as inheritance (allowing multiple inheritance), encapsulation, abstraction, and polymorphism—terms that will be explained later in this lesson. The implementation of templates (generic classes or functions) in C++ and the sophistication of that concept were until recently not available in newer programming languages such as Java and C#.

After C++, Java was the next revolution in the programming world. It became popular on the promise that a Java application could be run on many popular platforms. Java's popularity stemmed also from its simplicity, which was created by not supporting many features that make C++ a powerful programming language. In addition to not allowing pointers, Java also managed memory and performed garbage collection for the user. After Java, C# was one of the first languages developed to be based on a framework (the Microsoft .NET Framework). C# derived ideologically and syntactically from both Java and C++, in addition to differing in some respects from both of these. A managed version of C++ (called *Managed C++*) is the .NET Framework equivalent of the C++ language, which brings the advantages of the Framework (such as automated memory management and garbage collection) to C++ programmers, and promises a faster execution than other framework-based languages such as C#.

C++ continues to be the programming language of choice for many applications not only because newer languages still don't cater to many application's requirements, but also because of the flexibility and power it places in the hands of the programmer. C++ is regulated by the ANSI standard and continues to evolve as a language.

Interpreters and Compilers

An *interpreter* translates and executes a program as it reads it, turning the program instructions, or source code, directly into actions. A *compiler* translates source code into an intermediary form. This step is called *compiling*, and it produces an object file. A linking application called a *linker* runs after the compiler and combines the object file into an executable program containing machine code that can directly be run on the processor.

Because interpreters read the source code as it is written and execute the code on the spot, interpreters can be easier for the programmer to work with. Today, most interpreted programs are referred to as *scripts*, and the interpreter itself is often called a *script engine*.

Compilers introduce the extra steps of compiling the source code (which is readable by humans) into object code (which is readable by machines). This extra step might seem inconvenient, but compiled programs run very fast because the time-consuming task of translating the source code into machine language has already been done once, at compile time. Because the translation is already done, it is not required when you execute the program.

Another advantage of compiled languages such as C++ is that you can distribute the executable program to people who don't have the compiler. With an interpreted language, you must have the interpreter installed to run the program on any computer.

Some high-level languages, such as Visual Basic 6, call the interpreter the runtime library. Other languages, such as C#, Visual Basic .NET, and Java have another component, referred to as a *virtual machine* (VM) or a *runtime*. The VM is also an interpreter. However, it is not a source code interpreter that translates human-readable language into computer-dependent machine code. Rather, it interprets and executes a compiled computer-independent virtual machine language or intermediary language. These languages, therefore, still feature a compiler or a compilation step during which the source code written by a programmer is first translated; that is, compiled into content that can be *interpreted* by the virtual machine or runtime library.

C++ is typically a compiled language, although there are some C++ interpreters. Like many compiled languages, C++ has a reputation for producing fast and powerful programs.

NOTE

> The word *program* is used in two ways: to describe individual instructions (or source code) created by the programmer and to describe an entire piece of executable software. This distinction can cause enormous confusion, so this book tries to distinguish between the source code, on one hand, and the executable, on the other.

Changing Requirements, Changing Platforms

The problems programmers are asked to solve today are totally different from the problems they were solving twenty years ago. In the 1980s, programs were created to manage and process large amounts of raw data. The people writing the code and the people using the program were computer professionals. Today, computers are in use by far more people, and many know very little about how computers and programs really work. Computers are tools used by people who are more interested in solving their business problems than struggling with the computer.

Ironically, as programs are made easier for this new audience to use, the programs themselves become far more sophisticated and complex. Gone are the days when users typed in cryptic commands at esoteric prompts, only to see a stream of raw data. Today's programs use sophisticated, user friendly interfaces involving multiple windows, menus, dialog boxes, and the myriad of metaphors with which we've all become familiar.

With the development of the Web, computers entered a new era of market penetration; more people are using computers than ever before, and their expectations are very high. The ease at which people can use the Web has also increased the expectations. It is not uncommon for people to expect that programs take advantage of the Web and what it has to offer.

In the past few years, applications have expanded to different devices as well. No longer is a desktop PC the only serious target for applications. Rather, mobile phones, personal digital assistants (PDAs), Tablet PCs, and other devices are valid targets for modern applications.

As programming requirements change, both languages and the techniques used for writing programs evolve to help programmers manage complexity. Although the complete history is fascinating, this book focuses only briefly on the key part of this evolution: the transformation from procedural programming to object-oriented programming (OOP).

Procedural, Structured, and Object-Oriented Programming

Until recently, computer programs were thought of as a series of procedures that acted on data. A *procedure*, also called a *function* or a *method*, is a set of specific instructions executed one after the other. The data was separate from the procedures, and the trick in programming was to keep track of which functions called which other functions, and what data was changed. To make sense of this potentially confusing situation, *structured programming* was created.

The principal idea behind structured programming is the concept of "divide and conquer." A computer program can be thought of as consisting of a set of tasks. Any task that is too complex to be described simply is broken down into a set of smaller component tasks until the tasks are sufficiently small and self-contained enough that each is easily understood.

As an example, computing the average salary of an employee of a company is a rather complex task. You can, however, break it down into the following subtasks:

1. Count how many employees you have.
2. Find out what each employee earns.
3. Total all the salaries.
4. Divide the total by the number of employees you have.

Totaling the salaries can be broken down into the following steps:

1. Get each employee's record.
2. Access the salary.
3. Add the salary to the running total.
4. Get the next employee's record.

In turn, obtaining each employee's record can be broken down into the following:

1. Open the file of employees.
2. Go to the correct record.
3. Read the data.

Structured programming remains an enormously successful approach for dealing with complex problems. By the late 1980s, however, some of the deficiencies of structured programming had become all too clear.

First, a natural desire is to think of data (employee records, for example) and what you can do with that data (sort, edit, and so on) as a single idea. Unfortunately, structured programs separate data structures from the functions that manipulate them, and there is no natural way to group data with its associated functions within structured programming. Structured programming is often called *procedural programming* because of its focus on procedures (rather than on objects).

Second, programmers often found themselves needing to reuse functions. But functions that worked with one type of data often could not be used with other types of data, limiting the benefits gained.

Object-Oriented Programming

Object-oriented programming responds to these programming requirements, providing techniques for managing enormous complexity, achieving reuse of software components, and coupling data with the tasks that manipulate that data. The essence of object-oriented programming is to model objects (that is, things or concepts) rather than data. The objects you model might be onscreen widgets, such as buttons and list boxes, or they might be real-world objects, such as customers, bicycles, airplanes, cats, and water.

Objects have characteristics, also called *properties* or *attributes*, such as age, fast, spacious, black, or wet. They also have capabilities, also called *operations* or *functions*, such as purchase, accelerate, fly, purr, or bubble. It is the job of object-oriented programming to represent these objects in the programming language.

C++ and Object-Oriented Programming

C++ fully supports object-oriented programming, including the three pillars of object-oriented development: encapsulation, inheritance, and polymorphism.

Encapsulation

When an engineer needs to add a resistor to the device she is creating, she doesn't typically build a new one from scratch. She walks over to a bin of resistors, examines the colored bands that indicate the properties, and picks the one she needs. The resistor is a "black box" as far as the engineer is concerned—she doesn't much care how it does its work, as long as it conforms to her specifications. She doesn't need to look inside the box to use it in her design.

The property of being a self-contained unit is called *encapsulation*. With encapsulation, you can accomplish data hiding. *Data hiding* is the highly valued characteristic that an object can be used without the user knowing or caring how it works internally.

Similarly, when the engineer uses the resistor, she need not know anything about the internal state of the resistor. All the properties of the resistor are encapsulated in the resistor object; they are not spread out through the circuitry. It is not necessary to understand how the resistor works to use it effectively. Its workings are hidden inside the resistor's casing.

C++ supports encapsulation through the creation of user-defined types, called classes. You'll see how to create classes in Lesson 10, "Classes and Objects." After being created, a well-defined class acts as a fully encapsulated entity—it is used as a whole unit. The actual inner workings of the class can be hidden. Users of a well-defined class do not need to know how the class works; they just need to know how to use it.

Inheritance and Reuse

When the engineers at Acme Motors want to build a new car, they have two choices: They can start from scratch, or they can modify an existing model called Star. Perhaps their Star model is nearly perfect, but they want to add a turbocharger and a six-speed transmission. The chief engineer prefers not to start from the ground up, but rather to say, "Let's build another Star, but let's add these additional capabilities. We'll call the new model a Quasar." A Quasar is a kind of Star, but a specialized one with new features.

C++ supports inheritance. With inheritance, you can declare a new type that is an extension of an existing type. This new subclass is said to *derive* from the existing type and is sometimes called a *derived type*. If the Quasar is derived from the Star and, thus, inherits all the Star's qualities, the engineers can add to them or modify those qualities as needed. Inheritance and its application in C++ are discussed in Lesson 11, "Implementing Inheritance."

Polymorphism

A new Quasar might respond differently than a Star does when you press down on the accelerator. The Quasar might engage fuel injection and a turbocharger, whereas the Star simply lets gasoline into its carburetor. A user, however, does not have to know about these differences. He can just floor it, and the right thing happens, depending on which car he's driving.

C++ supports the idea that different objects can be treated similarly and still do the right thing through what is called *function polymorphism* and *class polymorphism*. *Poly* means many, and *morph* means form. Polymorphism refers to the same name taking many forms, and it is discussed in Lesson 12, " Polymorphism."

How C++ Evolved

As object-oriented analysis, design, and programming began to catch on, Bjarne Stroustrup took the most popular language for commercial software development, C, and extended it to provide the features needed to facilitate object-oriented programming. Although it is true that C++ is a superset of C and that virtually any legal C program is a legal C++ program, the leap from C to C++ is very significant. C++ benefited from its relationship to C for many years because C programmers could ease into their use of C++. To really get the full benefit of C++, however, many programmers found they had to unlearn much of what they knew and learn a new way of conceptualizing and solving programming problems.

Should I Learn C First?

The question inevitably arises: "Because C++ is a superset of C, should I learn C first?" Stroustrup and most other C++ programmers agree that not only is it unnecessary to learn C first, it might be advantageous not to do so.

C programming is based on structured programming concepts; C++ is based on object-oriented programming. If you learn C first, you'll have to unlearn the bad habits fostered by C.

This book does not assume that you have any prior programming experience. If you are a C programmer, however, the first few days of this book will largely be review. Starting in Lesson 10, you will begin the real work of object-oriented software development.

Microsoft's Managed Extensions to C++

With .NET, Microsoft introduced Managed Extensions to C++ ("Managed C++"). This is an extension of the C++ language to allow it to use Microsoft's new platform and libraries. More importantly, Managed C++ allows a C++ programmer to take advantage of the advanced features of the .NET environment. Should you decide to develop specifically for the .NET platform, you will need to extend your knowledge of standard C++ to include these extensions to the language.

The ANSI Standard

The Accredited Standards Committee, operating under the procedures of the American National Standards Institute (ANSI), has created an international standard for C++. The C++ Standard is also referred to as the *ISO* (International Organization for Standardization) *Standard*, the *NCITS* (National Committee for Information Technology

Standards) *Standard*, the *X3* (the old name for NCITS) *Standard*, and the *ANSI/ISO Standard*. This book continues to refer to ANSI standard code because that is the more commonly used term.

> **NOTE** — ANSI is usually pronounced "antsy" with a silent "t."

The ANSI standard is an attempt to ensure that C++ is portable—ensuring, for example, that ANSI-standard–compliant code you write for Microsoft's compiler will compile without errors using a compiler from any other vendor. Further, because the code in this book is ANSI compliant, it should compile without errors on a Macintosh, a Windows box, or an Alpha.

For most students of C++, the ANSI standard is invisible. The most recent version of the standard is ISO/IEC 14882-2003. The previous version, ISO/IEC 14882-1998, was stable and all the major manufacturers support it. All the code in this edition of this book has been compared to the standard to ensure that it is compliant.

Keep in mind that not all compilers are fully compliant with the standard. In addition, some areas of the standard have been left open to the compiler vendor, which cannot be trusted to compile or operate in the same fashion when compiled with various brands of compilers.

> **NOTE** — Because the Managed Extensions to C++ apply to only the .NET platform and are not ANSI standard, they are not covered in this book.

Preparing to Program

C++, perhaps more than other languages, demands that the programmer design the program before writing it. Most of the problems and scenarios discussed in this book are generic and don't require much design. Complex problems, however, such as the ones professional programmers are challenged with every day, do require design, and the more thorough the design, the more likely it is that the program will solve the problems it is designed to solve, on time and on budget. A good design also makes for a program that is relatively bug-free and easy to maintain. It has been estimated that fully 90% of the cost of software is the combined cost of debugging and maintenance. To the extent that good design can reduce those costs, it can have a significant impact on the bottom-line cost of the project.

The first question you need to ask when preparing to design any program is, "What is the problem I'm trying to solve?" Every program should have a clear, well-articulated goal, and you'll find that even the simplest programs in this book do so.

The second question every good programmer asks is, "Can this be accomplished without resorting to writing custom software?" Reusing an old program, using pen and paper, or buying software off the shelf is often a better solution to a problem than writing something new. The programmer who can offer these alternatives will never suffer from lack of work; finding less expensive solutions to today's problems always generates new opportunities later.

Assuming that you understand the problem and it requires writing a new program, you are ready to begin your design. Fully understanding the problem (analysis) and creating a plan for a solution (design) form the necessary foundation for writing a world-class commercial application.

Your Development Environment

This book assumes that your compiler has a mode in which you can write directly to a console (for instance, an MS-DOS/command prompt or a shell window) without worrying about a graphical environment, such as the ones in Windows or on the Macintosh. Look for an option such as *console* or *easy window* or check your compiler's documentation.

Your compiler might be part of an integrated development environment (IDE), or might have its own built-in source code text editor, or you might be using a commercial text editor or word processor that can produce text files. The important thing is that whatever you write your program in, it must save simple, plain-text files, with no word processing commands embedded in the text. Examples of safe editors include Windows Notepad, the DOS Edit command, Brief, Epsilon, Emacs, and vi. Many commercial word processors, such as WordPerfect, Word, and dozens of others, also offer a method for saving simple text files.

The files you create with your editor are called *source files*, and for C++ they typically are named with the extension `.cpp`, `.cp`, or `.c`. This book names all the source code files with the `.cpp` extension, but check your compiler for what it needs.

NOTE

> Most C++ compilers don't care what extension you give your source code, but if you don't specify otherwise, many use .cpp by default. Be careful, however—some compilers treat .c files as C code and .cpp files as C++ code. Again, please check your compiler's documentation. In any event, it is easier for other programmers who need to understand your programs if you consistently use .cpp for C++ source code files.

DO	DON'T
DO use a simple text editor to create your source code, or use the built-in editor that comes with your compiler.	**DON'T** use a word processor that saves special formatting characters. If you do use a word processor, save the file as ASCII text.
DO save your files with the .c, .cp, or .cpp extension. The .cpp extension is recommended.	**DON'T** use a .c extension if your compiler treats such files as C code instead of C++ code.
DO check your documentation for specifics about your compiler and linker to ensure that you know how to compile and link your programs.	

The Process of Creating the Program

The first step in creating a new program is to write the appropriate commands (statements) into a source file. Although the source code in your file is somewhat cryptic, and anyone who doesn't know C++ will struggle to understand what it is for, it is still in what we call *human-readable form*. Your source code file is not a program and it can't be executed, or run, as an executable program file can.

Creating an Object File with the Compiler

To turn your source code into a program, you use a compiler. How you invoke your compiler and how you tell it where to find your source code varies from compiler to compiler; check your documentation.

After your source code is compiled, an object file is produced. This file is often named with the extension `.obj` or `.o`. This is still not an executable program, however. To turn this into an executable program, you must run your linker.

Creating an Executable File with the Linker

C++ programs are typically created by linking one or more object files (`.obj` or `.o` files) with one or more libraries. A *library* is a collection of linkable files that were supplied with your compiler, that you purchased separately, or that you created and compiled. All C++ compilers come with a library of useful functions and classes that you can include in your program. You'll learn more about functions and classes in great detail in lessons 6 and 10.

The steps to create an executable file are

1. Create a source code file with a `.cpp` extension.
2. Compile the source code into an object file with the `.obj` or `.o` extension.
3. Link your object file with any needed libraries to produce an executable program.

NOTE

> If programming using an IDE, you might be presented with an option called Build that will perform steps 2 and 3 for you and supply the executable output.

The Development Cycle

If every program worked the first time you tried it, this would be the complete development cycle: Write the program, compile the source code, link the program, and run it. Unfortunately, almost every program, no matter how trivial, can and will have errors. Some errors cause the compile to fail, some cause the link to fail, and some show up only when you run the program (these are often called *bugs*).

Whatever type of error you find, you must fix it, and that involves editing your source code, recompiling and relinking, and then rerunning the program. This cycle is represented in Figure 1.1, which diagrams the steps in the development cycle.

FIGURE 1.1
The steps in the
development of a
C++ program.

1

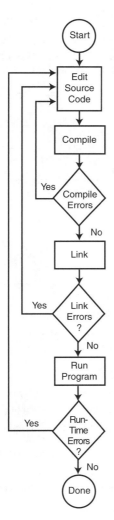

HELLO.cpp—Your First C++ Program

Traditional programming books begin by writing the words Hello World to the screen, or a variation of that statement. This time-honored tradition is carried on here.

Type the source code shown in Listing 1.1 directly into your editor, exactly as shown (excluding the line numbering). After you are certain you have entered it correctly, save the file, compile it, link it, and run it. If everything was done correctly, it prints the words Hello World to your screen. Don't worry too much about how it works; this is really just to get you comfortable with the development cycle. Every aspect of this program is covered over the next couple of lessons.

CAUTION

> The following listing contains line numbers on the left. These numbers are for reference within the book. They should not be typed into your editor. For example, on line 1 of Listing 1.1, you should enter
>
> ```
> #include <iostream>
> ```

LISTING 1.1   `HELLO.cpp`, the Hello World Program

```
1:  #include <iostream>
2:
3:  int main()
4:  {
5:    std::cout << "Hello World!\n";
6:    return 0;
7:  }
```

Be certain you enter this exactly as shown. Pay careful attention to the punctuation. The << on line 5 is the redirection symbol, produced on most keyboards by holding the Shift key and pressing the comma key twice. Between the letters std and cout on line 5 are two colons (:). Lines 5 and 6 each end with semicolon (;).

Also check to ensure that you are following your compiler directions properly. Most compilers link automatically, but check your documentation to see whether you need to provide a special option or execute a command to cause the link to occur.

If you receive errors, look over your code carefully and determine how it is different from the preceding listing. If you see an error on line 1, such as cannot find file iostream, you might need to check your compiler documentation for directions on setting up your include path or environment variables.

If you receive an error that there is no prototype for main, add the line int main(); just before line 3 (this is one of those pesky compiler variations). In that case, you need to add this line before the beginning of the main function in every program in this book. Most compilers don't require this, but a few do. If yours does, your finished program needs to look like this:

```
#include <iostream>
int main();            // most compilers don't need this line
int main()
{
    std::cout <<"Hello World!\n";
    return 0;
}
```

NOTE

It is difficult to read a program to yourself if you don't know how to pronounce the special characters and keywords. You read the first line "Pound include" (some say hash-include, others say sharp-include) "eye-oh-stream." You read the fifth line "ess-tee-dee-see-out Hello World or standard-see-out Hello World."

On a Windows system, try running HELLO.exe (or whatever the name of an executable is on your operating system; for instance, on a UNIX system, you run HELLO because executable programs do not have extensions in UNIX). The program should write

```
Hello World!
```

directly to your screen. If so, congratulations! You've just entered, compiled, and run your first C++ program. It might not look like much, but almost every professional C++ programmer started out with this exact program.

Some programmers using IDEs (such as Visual Studio or Borland C++ Builder) will find that running the program flashes up a window that promptly disappears with no chance to see what result the program produces. If this happens, add these lines to your source code just prior to the return statement:

```
char response;
std::cin >> response;
```

These lines cause the program to pause until you type a character (you might also need to press the Enter key). They ensure that you have a chance to see the results of your test run. If you need to do this for hello.cpp, you will probably need to do it for most of the programs in this book.

Using the Standard Libraries

If you have a very old compiler, the program shown previously will not work—the new ANSI standard libraries will not be found. In that case, please change your program to look like this:

```
1:  #include <iostream.h>
2:
3:  int main()
4:  {
5:      cout << "Hello World!\n";
6:      return 0;
7:  }
```

> Notice that the library name ends in `.h` (dot-h) and that we no longer use `std::` in front of `cout` on line 5. This is the old, pre-ANSI style of header files. If your compiler works with this and not with the earlier version, you have an antiquated compiler. You should update your compiler, or download one of the many free IDEs that come packaged with a modern C++ compiler to be able to compile samples presented in this book.

Getting Started with Your Compiler

This book is *not* compiler specific. This means that the programs in this book should work with *any* ANSI-compliant C++ compiler on any platform (Windows, Macintosh, UNIX, Linux, and so on).

That said, the vast majority of programmers are working in the Windows environment, and the vast majority of professional programmers use the Microsoft compilers. The details of compiling and linking with every possible compiler is too much to show here; however, we can show you how to get started with Microsoft Visual C++ 6, and that ought to be similar enough to whatever compiler you are using to be a good head start. Compilers differ, however, so be certain to check your documentation.

Building the Hello World Project

To create and test the Hello World program, follow these steps:

1. Start the compiler.
2. Choose File, New from the menus.
3. Choose Win32 Console Application and enter a project name, such as `hello`, and click OK.
4. Choose An Empty Project from the menu of choices and click Finish. A dialog box is displayed with new project information.
5. Click OK. You are taken back to the main editor window.
6. Choose File, New from the menus.
7. Choose C++ Source File and give it a name, such as `hello`. You enter this name into the File Name text box.
8. Click OK. You are taken back to the main editor window.
9. Enter the code as indicated previously.
10. Choose Build, Build `hello.exe` from the menus.

11. Check that you have no build errors. You can find this information near the bottom of the editor.

12. Run the program by pressing Ctrl+F5 or by selecting Build, Execute hello from the menus.

13. Press the spacebar to end the program.

FAQ

I can run the program, but it flashes by so quickly I can't read it. What is wrong?

Answer: Check your compiler documentation; there ought to be a way to cause your program to pause after execution. With the Microsoft compilers, the trick is to use Ctrl+F5.

With any compiler, you can also add the following lines immediately before the return statement (that is, between lines 5 and 6 in Listing 1.1):

```
char response;
std::cin >> response;
```

This causes the program to pause, waiting for you to enter a value. To end the program, type any letter or number (for example, 1) and then press Enter (if necessary).

The meaning of `std::cin` and `std::cout` will be discussed in Lessons 2 and 27, but for now, just use it as if it were a magical incantation.

Compile Errors

Compile-time errors can occur for any number of reasons. Usually, they are a result of a typo or other inadvertent minor error. Good compilers not only tell you what you did wrong, they point you to the exact place in your code where you made the mistake. Great compilers even suggest a remedy!

You can see this by intentionally putting an error into your program. If HELLO.cpp ran smoothly, edit it now and remove the closing brace on line 7 of Listing 1.1. Your program now looks like Listing 1.2.

LISTING 1.2   Demonstration of Compiler Error

```
1:  #include <iostream>
2:
3:  int main()
4:  {
5:    std::cout << "Hello World!\n";
6:    return 0;
```

Recompile your program and you should see an error that looks similar to the following:

```
Hello.cpp(7) : fatal error C1004: unexpected end of file found
```

This error tells you the file and line number of the problem and what the problem is (although I admit it is somewhat cryptic). In this case, the compiler is telling you that it ran out of source lines and hit the end of the source file without finding the closing brace.

Sometimes, the error messages just get you to the general vicinity of the problem. If a compiler could perfectly identify every problem, it would fix the code itself.

Summary

After reading today's lesson, you should have a good understanding of how C++ evolved and what problems it was designed to solve. You should feel confident that learning C++ is the right choice for anyone interested in programming. C++ provides the tools of object-oriented programming and the performance of a systems-level language, which makes C++ the development language of choice.

Today, you learned how to enter, compile, link, and run your first C++ program, and what the normal development cycle is. You also learned a little of what object-oriented programming is all about.

Q&A

Q What is the difference between a text editor and a word processor?

A A text editor produces files with plain text in them. No formatting commands or other special symbols are used that might be required by a particular word processor. Simple text editors do not have automatic word wrap, bold print, italic, and so forth.

Q If my compiler has a built-in editor, must I use it?

A Almost all compilers will compile code produced by any text editor. The advantages of using the built-in text editor, however, might include the ability to quickly move back and forth between the edit and compile steps of the development cycle. Sophisticated compilers include a fully integrated development environment, enabling the programmer to access help files, edit, and compile the code in place, and to resolve compile and link errors without ever leaving the environment.

Q Can I ignore warning messages from my compiler?

A Compilers generally give warnings and errors. If there are errors, the program will not be completely built. If there are just warnings, the compiler will generally go ahead and still create the program.

Many books hedge on this question. The appropriate answer is No! Get into the habit, from day one, of treating warning messages as errors. C++ uses the compiler to warn you when you are doing something you might not intend. Heed those warnings and do what is required to make them go away. Some compilers even have a setting that causes all warnings to be treated like errors, and thus stop the program from building an executable.

Q What is compile time?

A *Compile time* is the time when you run your compiler, in contrast to *link time* (when you run the linker) or *runtime* (when running the program). This is just programmer shorthand to identify the three times when errors usually surface.

Workshop

The Workshop provides quiz questions to help you solidify your understanding of the material covered and exercises to provide you with experience in using what you've learned. Try to answer the quiz and exercise questions before checking the answers in Appendix D, and be certain that you understand the answers before continuing to the next lesson.

Quiz

1. What is the difference between an interpreter and a compiler?
2. How do you compile the source code with your compiler?
3. What does the linker do?
4. What are the steps in the normal development cycle?

Exercises

1. Look at the following program and try to guess what it does without running it:

```
 1: #include <iostream>
 2: int main()
 3: {
 4:    int x = 5;
 5:    int y = 7;
 6:    std::cout << std::endl;
 7:    std::cout << x + y << " " << x * y;
 8:    std::cout << std::endl;
 9:    return 0;
10:}
```

2. Type in the program from Exercise 1, and then compile and link it. What does it do? Does it do what you guessed?

3. Type in the following program and compile it. What error do you receive?

```
1: include <iostream>
2: int main()
3: {
4:     std::cout << "Hello World \n";
5:     return 0;
6: }
```

4. Fix the error in the program in Exercise 3 and recompile, link, and run it. What does it do?

LESSON 2
The Anatomy of a C++ Program

C++ programs consist of classes, functions, variables, and other component parts. Most of this book is devoted to explaining these parts in depth, but to get a sense of how a program fits together, you must see a complete working program.

In this lesson, you will learn

- The parts of a C++ program
- How the parts work together
- What a function is and what it does

A Simple Program

Even the simple program HELLO.cpp from Lesson 1, "Getting Started," had many interesting parts. This section reviews this program in more detail. Listing 2.1 reproduces the original version of HELLO.cpp for your convenience.

LISTING 2.1   HELLO.cpp Demonstrates the Parts of a C++ Program

```
1:  #include <iostream>
2:
3:  int main()
4:  {
5:      std::cout << "Hello World!\n";
6:      return 0;
7:  }
```

Output ▼

```
Hello World!
```

Analysis ▼

On the first line, the file iostream is included into the current file. Here's how that works: The first character is the # symbol, which is a signal to a program called the *preprocessor*. Each time you start your compiler, the preprocessor is run first. The preprocessor reads through your source code, looking for lines that begin with the pound symbol (#) and acts on those lines before the compiler runs. The preprocessor is discussed in further detail in Lesson 15, "An Introduction to Macros and Templates," and in Lesson 29, "Tapping Further into the Preprocessor."

The command #include is a preprocessor instruction that says, "What follows is a filename. Find that file, read it, and place it right here." The angle brackets around the filename tell the preprocessor to look in all the usual places for this file. If your compiler is set up correctly, the angle brackets cause the preprocessor to look for the file iostream in the directory that holds all the include files for your compiler. The file iostream (input-output-stream) is used by cout, which assists with writing to the console. The effect of line 1 is to include the file iostream into this program as if you had typed it in yourself.

NOTE

The preprocessor runs before your compiler each time the compiler is invoked. The preprocessor translates any line that begins with a pound symbol (#) into a special command, getting your code file ready for the compiler.

2

> **NOTE**
>
> Not all compilers are consistent in their support for #includes that omit the file extension. If you get error messages, you might need to change the include search path for your compiler or add the extension to the #include.

The actual program starts with the function named main(). Every C++ program has a main() function. A function is a block of code that performs one or more actions. Usually, functions are invoked or called by other functions, but main() is special. When your program starts, main() is called automatically.

main(), like all functions, must state what kind of value it returns. The return value type for main() in HELLO.cpp is int, which means that this function returns an integer to the operating system when it completes. In this case, it returns the integer value 0. A value may be returned to the operating system to indicate success or failure, or using a failure code to describe a cause of failure. This may be of importance in situations where an application is launched by another. The application that launches can use this "exit code" to make decisions pertaining to success or failure in the execution of the application that was launched.

> **CAUTION**
>
> Some compilers let you declare main() to return void. This is no longer legal C++, and you should not get into bad habits. Have main() return int, and simply return 0 as the last line in main().

> **NOTE**
>
> Some operating systems enable you to test the value returned by a program. The informal convention is to return 0 to indicate that the program ended normally.

All functions begin with an opening brace ({) and end with a closing brace (}). Everything between the opening and closing braces is considered a part of the function.

The meat and potatoes of this program is in the usage of std::cout. The object cout is used to print a message to the screen. You'll learn about objects in general in Lesson 10, "Classes and Objects," and cout and cin in detail in Lesson 27, "Working with Streams." These two objects, cin and cout, are used in C++ to handle input (for example, from the keyboard) and output (for example, to the console), respectively.

cout is an object provided by the standard library. A *library* is a collection of classes. The standard library is the standard collection that comes with every ANSI-compliant compiler.

You designate to the compiler that the cout object you want to use is part of the standard library by using the namespace specifier std. Because you might have objects with the same name from more than one vendor, C++ divides the world into namespaces. A namespace is a way to say, "When I say cout, I mean the cout that is part of the standard namespace, not some other namespace." You say that to the compiler by putting the characters std followed by two colons before the cout.

Here's how cout is used: Type the word cout, followed by the output redirection operator (<<). Whatever follows the output redirection operator is written to the console. If you want a string of characters written, be certain to enclose them in double quotes ("), as visible in Listing 2.1.

NOTE

> You should note that the redirection operator is two greater-than signs with no spaces between them.

A text string is a series of printable characters. The final two characters, \n, tell cout to put a new line after the words Hello World!

The main() function ends with the closing brace (}).

A Brief Look at cout

In Lesson 27, you will see how to use cout to print data to the screen. For now, you can use cout without fully understanding how it works. To print a value to the screen, write the word cout, followed by the insertion operator (<<), which you create by typing the less-than character (<) twice. Even though this is two characters, C++ treats it as one.

Follow the insertion character with your data. Listing 2.2 illustrates how this is used. Type in the example exactly as written, except substitute your own name where you see Jesse Liberty (unless your name *is* Jesse Liberty).

LISTING 2.2   Using cout

```
1:  // Listing 2.2 using std::cout
2:  #include <iostream>
3:  int main()
4:  {
5:      std::cout << "Hello there.\n";
```

LISTING 2.2 Continued

```
 6:     std::cout << "Here is 5: " << 5 << "\n";
 7:     std::cout << "The manipulator std::endl ";
 8:     std::cout << "writes a new line to the screen.";
 9:     std::cout <<   std::endl;
10:     std::cout << "Here is a very big number:\t" << 70000;
11:     std::cout << std::endl;
12:     std::cout << "Here is the sum of 8 and 5:\t";
13:     std::cout << 8+5 << std::endl;
14:     std::cout << "Here's a fraction:\t\t";
15:     std::cout << (float) 5/8 << std::endl;
16:     std::cout << "And a very very big number:\t";
17:     std::cout << (double) 7000 * 7000 << std::endl;
18:     std::cout << "Don't forget to replace Jesse Liberty ";
19:     std::cout << "with your name...\n";
20:     std::cout << "Jesse Liberty is a C++ programmer!\n";
21:     return 0;
22: }
```

Output ▼

```
Hello there.
Here is 5: 5
The manipulator endl writes a new line to the screen.
Here is a very big number:      70000
Here is the sum of 8 and 5:     13
Here's a fraction:              0.625
And a very very big number:     4.9e+007
Don't forget to replace Jesse Liberty with your name...
Jesse Liberty is a C++ programmer!
```

CAUTION

Some compilers have a bug that requires that you put parentheses around the addition before passing it to cout. Thus, line 13 would change to

```
cout << (8+5) << std::endl;
```

Analysis ▼

The statement #include <iostream> causes the iostream file to be added to your source code. This is required if you use cout and its related functions.

The program starts with the the simplest use of cout by printing a string; that is, a series of characters. The symbol \n is a special formatting character. It tells cout to print a newline character to the screen; it is pronounced "slash-n" or "new line."

Three values are passed to `cout` in this line:

```
std::cout << "Here is 5: " << 5 << "\n";
```

In here, each value is separated by the insertion operator (<<). The first value is the string `"Here is 5: "`. Note the space after the colon. The space is part of the string. Next, the value 5 is passed to the insertion operator and then the newline character (always in double quotes or single quotes) is passed. This causes the line

```
Here is 5: 5
```

to be printed to the console. Because no newline character is present after the first string, the next value is printed immediately afterward. This is called concatenating the two values.

Note the usage of the manipulator `std::endl`. The purpose of `endl` is to write a new line to the console, thus presenting an alternative to '\n'. Note that `endl` is also provided by the standard library; thus, `std::` is added in front of it just as `std::` was added for `cout`.

> **NOTE**   `endl` stands for **end *l*ine** and is end-ell rather than end-one. It is commonly pronounced "end-ell."
>
> The use of `endl` is preferable to the use of \n because `endl` is adapted to the operating system in use, whereas \n might not be the complete newline character required on a particular operating system or platform.

The formatting character \t inserts a tab character. Other lines in the sample demonstrate how `cout` can display integers, decimal equivalents, and so on. The terms (`float`) and (`double`) tell `cout` that the number is to be displayed as a floating-point value. All this will be explained in Lesson 3, " Using Variables, Declaring Constants," when data types are discussed.

You should have substituted your name for `Jesse Liberty`. If you do this, the output should confirm that you are indeed a C++ programmer. It must be true, because the computer said so!

Using the Standard Namespace

You'll notice that the use of `std::` in front of both `cout` and `endl` becomes rather distracting after a while. Although using the namespace designation is good form, it is tedious to type. The ANSI standard allows two solutions to this minor problem.

The first is to tell the compiler, at the beginning of the code listing, that you'll be using the standard library cout and endl, as shown on lines 5 and 6 of Listing 2.3.

LISTING 2.3 Using the using Keyword

```
1:  // Listing 2.3 - using the using keyword
2:  #include <iostream>
3:  int main()
4:  {
5:      using std::cout;  // Note this declaration
6:      using std::endl;
7:
8:      cout << "Hello there.\n";
9:      cout << "Here is 5: " << 5 << "\n";
10:     cout << "The manipulator endl ";
11:     cout << "writes a new line to the screen.";
12:     cout <<  endl;
13:     cout << "Here is a very big number:\t" << 70000;
14:     cout <<  endl;
15:     cout << "Here is the sum of 8 and 5:\t";
16:     cout << 8+5 << endl;
17:     cout << "Here's a fraction:\t\t";
18:     cout << (float) 5/8 << endl;
19:     cout << "And a very very big number:\t";
20:     cout << (double) 7000 * 7000 << endl;
21:     cout << "Don't forget to replace Jesse Liberty ";
22:     cout << "with your name...\n";
23:     cout << "Jesse Liberty is a C++ programmer!\n";
24:     return 0;
25: }
```

Output ▼

```
Hello there.
Here is 5: 5
The manipulator endl writes a new line to the screen.
Here is a very big number:    70000
Here is the sum of 8 and 5:    13
Here's a fraction:            0.625
And a very very big number:    4.9e+007
Don't forget to replace Jesse Liberty with your name...
Jesse Liberty is a C++ programmer!
```

Analysis ▼

You will note that the output is identical to the previous listing. The only difference between Listing 2.3 and Listing 2.2 is that on lines 5 and 6, additional statements inform the compiler that two objects from the standard library will be used. This is done with the keyword using. After this has been done, you no longer need to qualify the cout and endl objects.

The second way to avoid the inconvenience of writing std:: in front of cout and endl is to simply tell the compiler that your listing will be using the entire standard namespace; that is, any object not otherwise designated can be assumed to be from the standard namespace. In this case, rather than writing using std::cout;, you would simply write using namespace std;, as shown in Listing 2.4.

LISTING 2.4   Using the namespace Keyword

```
1:  // Listing 2.4 - using namespace std
2:  #include <iostream>
3:  int main()
4:  {
5:      using namespace std;  // Note this declaration
6:
7:      cout << "Hello there.\n";
8:      cout << "Here is 5: " << 5 << "\n";
9:      cout << "The manipulator endl ";
10:     cout << "writes a new line to the screen.";
11:     cout <<  endl;
12:     cout << "Here is a very big number:\t" << 70000;
13:     cout <<  endl;
14:     cout << "Here is the sum of 8 and 5:\t";
15:     cout << 8+5 << endl;
16:     cout << "Here's a fraction:\t\t";
17:     cout << (float) 5/8 << endl;
18:     cout << "And a very very big number:\t";
19:     cout << (double) 7000 * 7000 << endl;
20:     cout << "Don't forget to replace Jesse Liberty ";
21:     cout << "with your name...\n";
22:     cout << "Jesse Liberty is a C++ programmer!\n";
23:     return 0;
24:  }
```

Analysis ▼

Again, the output is identical to the earlier versions of this program. The advantage to writing using namespace std; is that you do not have to specifically designate the objects you're actually using (for example, cout and endl;). The disadvantage is that you run the risk of inadvertently using objects from the wrong library.

Purists prefer to write `std::` in front of each instance of `cout` or `endl`. The lazy prefer to write `using namespace std;` and be done with it. In this book, most often the individual items being used are declared, but from time to time each of the other styles are presented just for fun.

Commenting Your Programs

When you are writing a program, your intent is always clear and self-evident to you. Funny thing, though—a month later, when you return to the program, it can be quite confusing and unclear. No one is ever certain how the confusion creeps into a program, but it nearly always does.

To fight the onset of bafflement, and to help others understand your code, you need to use comments. Comments are text that is ignored by the compiler, but that can inform the reader of what you are doing at any particular point in your program.

Types of Comments

C++ comments come in two flavors: single-line comments and multiline comments. Single-line comments are accomplished using a double slash (`//`). The double slash tells the compiler to ignore everything that follows, until the end of the line.

Multiline comments are started by using a forward slash followed by an asterisk (`/*`). This "slash-star" comment mark tells the compiler to ignore everything that follows until it finds a "star-slash" (`*/`) comment mark. These marks can be on the same line or they can have one or more lines between them; however, every `/*` must be matched with a closing `*/`.

Many C++ programmers use the double-slash, single-line comments most of the time and reserve multiline comments for blocking out large blocks of a program. You can include single-line comments within a block commented out by the multiline comment marks; everything, including the double-slash comments, is ignored between the multiline comment marks.

NOTE The multiline comment style has been referred to as *C-style* because it was introduced and used in the C programming language. Single-line comments were originally a part of C++ and not a part of C; thus, they have been referred to as *C++-style*. The current standards for both C and C++ now include both styles of comments.

Using Comments

Some people recommend writing comments at the top of each function, explaining what the function does and what values it returns. Functions should be named so that little ambiguity exists about what they do, and confusing and obscure bits of code should be redesigned and rewritten so as to be self-evident. Comments should not be used as an excuse for obscurity in your code.

This is not to suggest that comments ought never be used, only that they should not be relied upon to clarify obscure code; instead, fix the code. In short, you should write your code well, and use comments to supplement understanding. Listing 2.5 demonstrates the use of comments, showing that they do not affect the processing of the program or its output.

LISTING 2.5   Demonstrates Comments

```
 1:  #include <iostream>
 2:
 3:  int main()
 4:  {
 5:      using std::cout;
 6:
 7:      /* this is a comment
 8:      and it extends until the closing
 9:      star-slash comment mark */
10:      cout << "Hello World!\n";
11:      // this comment ends at the end of the line
12:      cout << "That comment ended!\n";
13:
14:      // double-slash comments can be alone on a line
15:      /* as can slash-star comments */
16:      return 0;
17:  }
```

Output ▼

```
Hello World!
That comment ended!
```

Analysis ▼

The comment on lines 7–9 is completely ignored by the compiler, as are the comments on lines 11, 14, and 15. The comment on line 11 ended with the end of the line. The comments on lines 7 and 15 required a closing comment mark.

NOTE — A third style of comment is supported by some C++ compilers. These comments are referred to as *document comments* and are indicated using three forward slashes (///). The compilers that support this style of comment allow you to generate documentation about the program from these comments. Because these are not currently a part of the C++ standard, they are not covered here.

A Final Word of Caution About Comments

Comments that state the obvious are less than useful. In fact, they can be counterproductive because the code might change and the programmer might neglect to update the comment. What is obvious to one person might be obscure to another, however, so judgment is required when adding comments. The bottom line is that comments should not say *what* is happening, they should say *why* it is happening.

Functions

Although main() is a function, it is an unusual one. To be useful, a function must be called, or *invoked*, during the course of your program. main() is invoked by the operating system.

A program is executed line-by-line in the order it appears in your source code until a function is reached. Then the program branches off to execute the function. When the function finishes, it returns control to the line of code immediately following the call to the function.

A good analogy for this is sharpening your pencil. If you are drawing a picture and your pencil point breaks, you might stop drawing, go sharpen the pencil, and then return to what you were doing. When a program needs a service performed, it can call a function to perform the service and then pick up where it left off when the function is finished running. Listing 2.6 demonstrates this idea.

NOTE — Functions are covered in more detail in Lesson 6, "Organizing Code with Functions." The types that can be returned from a function are covered in more detail in Lesson 3, "Using Variables, Declaring Constants." The information provided in the current lesson is to present you with an overview because functions will be used in almost all of your C++ programs.

LISTING 2.6   Demonstrating a Call to a Function

```
 1:  #include <iostream>
 2:
 3:  // function Demonstration Function
 4:  // prints out a useful message
 5:  void DemonstrationFunction()
 6:  {
 7:      std::cout << "In Demonstration Function\n";
 8:  }
 9:
10:  // function main - prints out a message, then
11:  // calls DemonstrationFunction, then prints out
12:  // a second message.
13:  int main()
14:  {
15:      std::cout << "In main\n" ;
16:      DemonstrationFunction();
17:      std::cout << "Back in main\n";
18:      return 0;
19:  }
```

Output ▼

```
In main
In Demonstration Function
Back in main
```

Analysis ▼

The function `DemonstrationFunction()` is defined on lines 6–8. When it is called, it prints a message to the console screen and then returns.

Line 13 is the beginning of the actual program. On line 15, `main()` prints out a message saying it is in `main()`. After printing the message, line 16 calls `DemonstrationFunction()`. This call causes the flow of the program to go to the `DemonstrationFunction()` function on line 5. Any commands in `DemonstrationFunction()` are then executed. In this case, the entire function consists of the code on line 7, which prints another message. When `DemonstrationFunction()` completes (line 8), the program flow returns to from where it was called. In this case, the program returns to line 17, where `main()` prints its final line.

Using Functions

Functions either return a value or they return `void`, meaning they do not return anything. A function that adds two integers might return the sum, and thus would be defined to return an integer value. A function that just prints a message has nothing to return and would be declared to return void.

Functions consist of a header and a body. The header consists, in turn, of the return type, the function name, and the parameters to that function. The parameters to a function enable values to be passed into the function. Thus, if the function were to add two numbers, the numbers would be the parameters to the function. Here's an example of a typical function header that declares a function named Sum that receives two integer values (first and second) and also returns an integer value:

```
int Sum( int first, int second)
```

2

A *parameter* is a declaration of what type of value will be passed in; the actual value passed in when the function is called is referred to as an argument. Many programmers use the terms *parameters* and *arguments* as synonyms. Others are careful about the technical distinction. The distinction between these two terms is not critical to your programming C++, so you shouldn't worry if the words get interchanged.

The body of a function consists of an opening brace, zero or more statements, and a closing brace. The statements constitute the workings of the function.

A function might return a value using a return statement. The value returned must be of the type declared in the function header. In addition, this statement causes the function to exit. If you don't put a return statement into your function, it automatically returns void (nothing) at the end of the function. If a function is supposed to return a value but does not contain a return statement, some compilers produce a warning or error message.

Listing 2.7 demonstrates a function that takes two integer parameters and returns an integer value. Don't worry about the syntax or the specifics of how to work with integer values (for example, int first) for now; that is covered in detail in Lesson 3.

LISTING 2.7   FUNC.cpp Demonstrates a Simple Function

```
 1:  #include <iostream>
 2:  int Add (int first, int second)
 3:  {
 4:      std::cout << "Add() received "<< first << " and "<< second <<
➡ "\n";
 5:      return (first + second);
 6:  }
 7:
 8:  int main()
 9:  {
10:      using std::cout;
11:      using std::cin;
12:
13:
```

LISTING 2.7 Continued

```
14:        cout << "I'm in main()!\n";
15:        int a, b, c;
16:        cout << "Enter two numbers: ";
17:        cin >> a;
18:        cin >> b;
19:        cout << "\nCalling Add()\n";
20:        c=Add(a,b);
21:        cout << "\nBack in main().\n";
22:        cout << "c was set to " << c;
23:        cout << "\nExiting...\n\n";
24:        return 0;
25:    }
```

Output ▼

```
I'm in main()!
Enter two numbers: 3 5

Calling Add()
In Add(), received 3 and 5

Back in main().
c was set to 8
Exiting...
```

Analysis ▼

The function Add() is defined on line 2. It takes two integer parameters and returns an integer value. The program itself begins on line 8. The program prompts the user for two numbers (line 16). The user types each number, separated by a space, and then presses the Enter key. The numbers the user enters are placed in the variables a and b on lines 17 and 18. On line 20, the main() function passes the two numbers typed in by the user as arguments to the Add() function.

Processing branches to the Add() function, which starts on line 2. The values from a and b are received as parameters first and second, respectively. These values are printed and then added. The result of adding the two numbers is returned on line 5, at which point the function returns to the function that called it—main(), in this case.

On lines 17 and 18, the cin object is used to obtain a number for the variables a and b. Throughout the rest of the program, cout is used to write to the console. Variables and other aspects of this program are explored in depth in the next lesson.

Methods Versus Functions

A function by any other name is still just a function. It is worth noting here that different programming languages and different programming methodologies might refer to functions using a different term. One of the more common words used is *method*. Method is simply another term for functions that are part of a class.

Summary

The difficulty in learning a complex subject, such as programming, is that so much of what you learn depends on everything else there is to learn. Today's lesson introduced the basic parts of a simple C++ program.

2

Q&A

Q **What does `#include` do?**

A This is a directive to the preprocessor that runs when you call your compiler. This specific directive causes the file in the <> named after the word `#include` to be read in as if it were typed in at that location in your source code.

Q **What is the difference between `//` comments and `/*` style comments?**

A The double-slash comments (`//`) expire at the end of the line. Slash-star (`/*`) comments are in effect until a closing comment mark (`*/`). The double-slash comments are also referred to as *single-line comments*, and the slash-star comments are often referred to as *multiline comments*. Remember, not even the end of the function terminates a slash-star comment; you must put in the closing comment mark or you will receive a compile-time error.

Q **What differentiates a good comment from a bad comment?**

A A good comment tells the reader *why* this particular code is doing whatever it is doing or explains what a section of code is about to do. A bad comment restates what a particular line of code is doing. Lines of code should be written so that they speak for themselves. A well-written line of code should tell you what it is doing without needing a comment.

Workshop

The Workshop provides quiz questions to help you solidify your understanding of the material covered and exercises to provide you with experience in using what you've learned. Try to answer the quiz and exercise questions before checking the answers in Appendix D, and be certain that you understand the answers before continuing to the next lesson.

Quiz

1. What is the difference between the compiler and the preprocessor?

2. Why is the function `main()` special?

3. What are the two types of comments and how do they differ?

4. Can comments be nested?

5. Can comments be longer than one line?

Exercises

1. Write a program that writes `I love C++` to the console.

2. Write the smallest program that can be compiled, linked, and run.

3. **BUG BUSTERS:** Enter this program and compile it. Why does it fail? How can you fix it?

```
1: #include <iostream>
2: main()
3: {
4:     std::cout << Is there a bug here?";
5: }
```

4. Fix the bug in Exercise 3 and recompile, link, and run it.

5. Modify Listing 2.7 to include a subtract function. Name this function `Subtract()` and use it in the same way that the `Add()` function was called. You should also pass the same values that were passed to the `Add()` function.

LESSON 3
Using Variables, Declaring Constants

Programs need a way to store the data they use or create so that it can be used later in the program's execution. Variables and constants offer various ways to represent, store, and manipulate that data.

In this lesson, you will learn

- How to declare and define variables and constants
- How to assign values to variables and manipulate those values
- How to write the value of a variable to the screen

What Is a Variable?

In C++, a *variable* is a place to store information. A variable is a location in your computer's memory in which you can store a value and from which you can later retrieve that value.

Notice that variables are used for temporary storage. When you exit a program or turn the computer off, the information in variables is lost. Permanent storage is a different matter. Typically, the values from variables are permanently stored either to a database or to a file on disk. Storing to a file on disk is discussed on Lesson 27, " Working with Streams."

Storing Data in Memory

Your computer's memory can be viewed as a series of cubbyholes. Each cubbyhole is one of many, many such holes all lined up. Each cubbyhole—or memory location—is numbered sequentially. These numbers are known as *memory addresses*. A variable reserves one or more cubbyholes in which you can store a value.

Your variable's name (for example, `myVariable`) is a label on one of these cubbyholes so that you can find it easily without knowing its actual memory address. Figure 3.1 is a schematic representation of this idea. As you can see from the figure, `myVariable` starts at memory address 103. Depending on the size of `myVariable`, it can take up one or more memory addresses.

FIGURE 3.1
A schematic representation of memory.

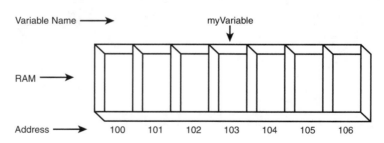

NOTE

> *RAM* stands for *random access memory*. When you run your program, it is loaded into RAM from the disk file. All variables are also created in RAM. When programmers talk about memory, it is usually RAM to which they are referring.

Setting Aside Memory

When you define a variable in C++, you must tell the compiler what kind of variable it is (this is usually referred to as the variable's *type*): an integer, a floating-point number, a character, and so forth. This information tells the compiler how much room to set aside and what kind of value you want to store in your variable. It also allows the compiler to warn you or produce an error message if you accidentally attempt to store a value of the wrong type in your variable (this characteristic of a programming language is called *strong typing*).

Each cubbyhole is one byte in size. If the type of variable you create is four bytes in size, it needs four bytes of memory, or four cubbyholes. The type of the variable (for example, integer) tells the compiler how much memory (how many cubbyholes) to set aside for the variable.

There was a time when it was imperative that programmers understood bits and bytes; after all, these are the fundamental units of storage. Computer programs have gotten better at abstracting away these details, but it is still helpful to understand how data is stored. For a quick review of the underlying concepts in binary math, please take a look at Appendix A, "Working with Numbers: Binary and Hexadecimal."

> **NOTE** If mathematics makes you want to run from the room screaming, don't bother with Appendix A—you won't really need it. The truth is that programmers no longer need to be mathematicians, although it is important to be comfortable with logic and rational thinking.

Size of Integers

On any one computer, each variable type takes up a single, unchanging amount of room. That is, an integer might be two bytes on one machine and four on another, but on either computer it is always the same, day in and day out.

Single characters—including letters, numbers, and symbols—are stored in a variable of type char. A char variable is most often one byte long.

> **NOTE** There is endless debate about how to pronounce char. Some say it as "car," some say it as "char"(coal), others say it as "care." Clearly, car is correct because that is how *I* say it, but feel free to say it however you like.

For holding smaller integer numbers, a variable can be created using the short type. A short integer is two bytes on most computers, whereas a long integer is usually four bytes, and an integer (without the keyword short or long) can be either of two or four bytes.

You'd think the language would specify the exact size that each of its types should be; however, C++ doesn't. All it says is that a short must be less than or equal to the size of an int, which, in turn, must be less than or equal to the size of a long. That said, you're probably working on a computer with a two-byte short and a four-byte int, with a four-byte long.

The size of an integer is determined by the processor (16 bit, 32 bit, or 64 bit) and the compiler you use. On a 32-bit computer with an Intel Pentium processor, using modern compilers, integers are *four* bytes.

CAUTION	When creating programs, you should never assume that you know the amount of memory being used for any particular type.

signed **and** unsigned

All integer types come in two varieties: signed and unsigned. Sometimes you need negative numbers and sometimes you don't. Any integer without the word unsigned is assumed to be signed. signed integers can be negative or positive. unsigned integers are always positive.

Integers, whether signed or unsigned, are stored in the same amount of space. Because of this, part of the storage room for a signed integer must be used to hold information on whether the number is negative or positive. The result is that the largest number you can store in an unsigned integer is twice as big as the largest positive number you can store in a signed integer.

For example, if a short integer is stored in two bytes, an unsigned short integer can handle numbers from 0 to 65,535. Alternatively, for a signed short, half the numbers that can be stored are negative; thus, a signed short can only represent positive numbers up to 32,767. The signed short can also, however, represent negative numbers giving it a total range from –32,768 to 32,767. For more information on the precedence of operators, read Appendix C, "Operator Precedence."

Fundamental Variable Types

Several variable types are built in to C++. They can be conveniently divided into integer variables (the type discussed so far), floating-point variables, and character variables.

Floating-point variables have values that can be expressed as fractions—that is, they are real numbers. Character variables hold a single byte and are generally used for holding the 256 characters and symbols of the ASCII and extended ASCII character sets.

NOTE The ASCII character set is the set of characters standardized for use on computers. ASCII is an acronym for *American Standard Code for Information Interchange*. Nearly every computer operating system supports ASCII, although many support other international character sets as well.

3

The types of variables used in C++ programs are described in Table 3.1. This table shows the variable type, how much room the type generally takes in memory, and what kinds of values can be stored in these variables.

TABLE 3.1 Variable Types

Type	Size	Values
bool	1 byte	True or false
unsigned short int	2 bytes	0 to 65,535
short int	2 bytes	−32,768 to 32,767
unsigned long int	4 bytes	0 to 4,294,967,295
long int	4 bytes	−2,147,483,648 to 2,147,483,647
int (16 bit)	2 bytes	−32,768 to 32,767
int (32 bit)	4 bytes	−2,147,483,648 to 2,147,483,647
unsigned int (16 bit)	2 bytes	0 to 65,535
unsigned int (32 bit)	4 bytes	0 to 4,294,967,295
char	1 byte	256 character values
float	4 bytes	1.2e–38 to 3.4e38
double	8 bytes	2.2e–308 to 1.8e308

> **NOTE**
>
> The sizes of variables on your system might be different from those shown in Table 3.1, depending on the compiler and the computer you are using. You should consult your compiler's manual for the values that your variable types can hold.

Defining a Variable

Up to this point, you have seen a number of variables created and used. Now it is time to learn how to create your own.

You create or *define* a variable by stating its type, followed by one or more spaces, followed by the variable name and a semicolon. The variable name can be virtually any combination of letters, but it cannot contain spaces. Legal variable names include x, J23qrsnf, and myAge. Good variable names tell you what the variables are for; using good names makes it easier to understand the flow of your program. The following statement defines an integer variable called myAge:

```
int myAge;
```

> **NOTE**
>
> When you declare a variable, memory is allocated (set aside) for that variable. The *value* of the variable will be whatever happened to be in that memory at that time. You will see in a moment how to assign a new value to that memory.

As a general programming practice, avoid such horrific names as J23qrsnf, and restrict single-letter variable names (such as x or i) to variables that are used only very briefly. Try to use expressive names such as myAge or howMany. Such names are easier to understand three weeks later when you are scratching your head trying to figure out what you meant when you wrote that line of code.

Try this experiment: Guess what these programs do, based on the first few lines of code:

Example 1

```
int main()
{
    unsigned short x = 10;
    unsigned short y = 11;

    unsigned short z = x * y;

    return 0;
}
```

Example 2

```
int main()
{
    unsigned short Width = 10;
    unsigned short Length = 11;

    unsigned short Area = Width * Length;

    return 0;
}
```

> **NOTE**
> You will note that the short-integer values Width and Length have been assigned values 10 and 11 in the line where they have been declared. This is called variable-initialization, and will be discussed further in this lesson.

3

Clearly, the purpose of the second program is easier to guess. The inconvenience of having to type the longer variable names is more than made up for by how much easier it is to understand, and thus maintain, the second program.

Case Sensitivity

C++ is case sensitive. In other words, uppercase and lowercase letters are considered to be different. A variable named age is different from Age, which is different from AGE.

> **CAUTION**
> Some compilers allow you to turn case sensitivity off. Don't be tempted to do this; your programs won't work with other compilers, and other C++ programmers will be very confused by your code.

Naming Conventions

Various conventions exist for how to name variables, and although it doesn't much matter which method you adopt, it is important to be consistent throughout your program. Inconsistent naming will confuse other programmers when they read your code.

Many programmers prefer to use all lowercase letters for their variable names. If the name requires two words (for example, my car), two popular conventions are used: my_car or myCar. The latter form is called camel notation because the capitalization looks something like a camel's hump.

Some people find the underscore character (my_car) easier to read, but others prefer to avoid the underscore because it is more difficult to type. This book uses camel notation, in which the second and all subsequent words are capitalized: myCar, theQuickBrownFox, and so forth.

Many advanced programmers employ a notation style referred to as *Hungarian notation*. The idea behind Hungarian notation is to prefix every variable with a set of characters that describes its type. Integer variables might begin with a lowercase letter i. Variables of type long might begin with a lowercase l. Other notations indicate different constructs within C++ that you will learn about later, such as constants, globals, pointers, and so forth.

NOTE

It is called Hungarian notation because the man who invented it, Charles Simonyi of Microsoft, is Hungarian. You can find his original monograph at http://www.strangecreations.com//library/c/naming.txt.

Microsoft has moved away from Hungarian notation recently, and the design recommendations for C# strongly recommend *not* using Hungarian notation. Their reasoning for C# applies equally well to C++.

Keywords

Some words are reserved by C++, and you cannot use them as variable names. These keywords have special meaning to the C++ compiler. Keywords include if, while, for, and main. A list of keywords defined by C++ is presented in Table 3.2 as well as in Appendix B, "C++ Keywords." Your compiler might have additional reserved words, so you should check its manual for a complete list.

TABLE 3.2 The C++ Keywords

asm	else	new	this
auto	enum	operator	throw
bool	explicit	private	true
break	export	protected	try
case	extern	public	typedef
catch	false	register	typeid
char	float	reinterpret_cast	typename
class	for	return	union
const	friend	short	unsigned

TABLE 3.2   Continued

const_cast	goto	signed	using
continue	if	sizeof	virtual
default	inline	static	void
delete	int	static_cast	volatile
do	long	struct	wchar_t
double	mutable	switch	while
dynamic_cast	namespace	template	

In addition, the following words are reserved:

And	bitor	not_eq	xor
and_eq	compl	or	xor_eq
bitand	not	or_eq	

DO	DON'T
DO define a variable by writing the type, and then the variable name.	**DON'T** use C++ keywords as variable names.
DO use meaningful variable names.	**DON'T** make assumptions about how many bytes are used to store a variable.
DO remember that C++ is case sensitive.	**DON'T** use unsigned variables for negative numbers.
DO understand the number of bytes each variable type consumes in memory and what values can be stored in variables of that type.	

3

Determining Memory Consumed by a Variable Type

The programmer should not make an assumption on the amount of memory occupied by a particular type. Although type int probably occupies four bytes on your computer and on most computers out there, you would be wise to not take this for granted because processor types and compilers can potentially play with the actual amount of bytes assigned to a particular type (which is, however, constant for one particular computer). Therefore, C++ specifies an operator called sizeof that helps compute the amount of space required by a type at program execution time—so that you, as a programmer, don't need to make assumptions. Compile and run Listing 3.1 and it will tell you the exact size of each of these types on your computer.

LISTING 3.1 Determining the Size of Variable Types on Your Computer

```
1:  #include <iostream>
2:
3:  int main()
4:  {
5:      using std::cout;
6:
7:      cout << "The size of an int is:\t\t"
8:          << sizeof(int)    << " bytes.\n";
9:      cout << "The size of a short int is:\t"
10:          << sizeof(short)  << " bytes.\n";
11:      cout << "The size of a long int is:\t"
12:          << sizeof(long)   << " bytes.\n";
13:      cout << "The size of a char is:\t\t"
14:          << sizeof(char)   << " bytes.\n";
15:      cout << "The size of a float is:\t\t"
16:          << sizeof(float)  << " bytes.\n";
17:      cout << "The size of a double is:\t"
18:          << sizeof(double) << " bytes.\n";
19:      cout << "The size of a bool is:\t"
20:          << sizeof(bool)   << " bytes.\n";
21:
22:      return 0;
23:  }
```

Output ▼

```
The size of an int is:        4 bytes.
The size of a short int is:   2 bytes.
The size of a long int is:    4 bytes.
The size of a char is:        1 bytes.
The size of a float is:       4 bytes.
The size of a double is:      8 bytes.
The size of a bool is:        1 bytes.
```

NOTE | On your computer, the number of bytes presented might be different.

Analysis ▼

Most of Listing 3.1 should be pretty familiar. The lines have been split to make them fit for the book; so, for example, lines 7 and 8 could really be on a single line. The compiler ignores whitespace (spaces, tabs, line returns) and so you can treat these as a single line. That's why you need a ; at the end of most lines.

The new feature in this program to notice is the use of the `sizeof` operator on lines 7–20. The `sizeof` is used like a function. When called, it tells you the size of the item you pass to it as a parameter. On line 8, for example, the keyword `int` is passed to `sizeof`. You'll learn later in today's lesson that `int` is used to describe a standard integer variable. Using `sizeof` on a Pentium 4, Windows XP machine, an `int` is four bytes, which coincidentally also is the size of a `long int` on the same computer.

Creating More Than One Variable at a Time

You can create more than one variable of the same type in one statement by writing the type and then the variable names, separated by commas. For example:

```
unsigned int myAge, myWeight;    // two unsigned int variables
long int area, width, length;    // three long integers
```

As you can see, both `myAge` and `myWeight` are declared as `unsigned` integer variables. The second line declares three individual `long` variables named `area`, `width`, and `length`. The type (`long`) is assigned to all the variables, so you cannot mix types in one definition statement.

Assigning Values to Your Variables

You assign a value to a variable by using the assignment operator (`=`). Thus, you would assign 5 to `width` by writing

```
unsigned short width;
width = 5;
```

> **NOTE** `long` is a shorthand version of `long int`, and `short` is a short-hand version of `short int`.

You can combine the steps of creating a variable and assigning a value to it. For example, you can combine these two steps for the `width` variable by writing:

```
unsigned short width = 5;
```

This initialization looks very much like the earlier assignment, and when using integer variables like `width`, the difference is minor. Later, when `const` is covered, you will see that some variables must be initialized because they cannot be assigned a value at a later time.

3

Just as you can define more than one variable at a time, you can initialize more than one variable at creation. For example, the following creates two variables of type `long` and initializes them:

```
long width = 5, length = 7;
```

This example initializes the `long` integer variable `width` to the value 5 and the `long` integer variable `length` to the value 7. You can even mix definitions and initializations

```
int myAge = 39, yourAge, hisAge = 40;
```

This example creates three type `int` variables, and it initializes the first (`myAge`) and third (`hisAge`).

Listing 3.2 shows a complete, ready-to-compile program that computes the area of a rectangle and writes the answer to the screen.

LISTING 3.2   A Demonstration of the Use of Variables

```
 1:  // Demonstration of variables
 2:  #include <iostream>
 3:
 4:  int main()
 5:  {
 6:      using std::cout;
 7:      using std::endl;
 8:
 9:      unsigned short int Width = 5, Length;
10:      Length = 10;
11:
12:      // create  an unsigned short and initialize with result
13:      // of multiplying Width by Length
14:      unsigned short int Area  = (Width * Length);
15:
16:      cout << "Width:" << Width << endl;
17:      cout << "Length: "  << Length << endl;
18:      cout << "Area: " << Area << endl;
19:      return 0;
20:  }
```

Output ▼

```
Width:5
Length: 10
Area: 50
```

Analysis ▼

As you have seen in the previous listing, line 2 includes the required `include` statement for the `iostream`'s library so that `cout` will work. Line 4 begins the program with the `main()` function. Lines 6 and 7 define `cout` and `endl` as being part of the standard (`std`) namespace.

On line 9, the first variables are defined. `Width` is defined as an `unsigned short` integer, and its value is initialized to 5. Another `unsigned short` integer, `Length`, is also defined, but it is not initialized. On line 10, the value 10 is assigned to `Length`.

On line 14, an `unsigned short` integer, `Area`, is defined, and it is initialized with the value obtained by multiplying `Width` times `Length`. On lines 16–18, the values of the variables are printed to the screen. Note that the special word `endl` creates a new line.

Creating Aliases with `typedef`

It can become tedious, repetitious, and, most important, error-prone to keep typing `unsigned short int`. C++ enables you to create an alias for this phrase by using the keyword `typedef`, which stands for *type definition*.

In effect, you are creating a synonym, and it is important to distinguish this from creating a new type. `typedef` is used by writing the keyword `typedef`, followed by the existing type, and then the new name, and ending with a semicolon. For example:

```
typedef unsigned short int USHORT;
```

creates the new name `USHORT` that you can use anywhere you might have written `unsigned short int`. Listing 3.3 is a replay of Listing 3.2, using the type definition `USHORT` rather than `unsigned short int`.

LISTING 3.3 A Demonstration of `typedef`

```
1:  // Demonstrates typedef keyword
2:  #include <iostream>
3:
4:  typedef unsigned short int USHORT;    //typedef defined
5:
6:  int main()
7:  {
8:
9:      using std::cout;
10:     using std::endl;
11:
12:     USHORT  Width = 5;
13:     USHORT Length;
```

3

LISTING 3.3   Continued

```
14:    Length = 10;
15:    USHORT Area  = Width * Length;
16:    cout << "Width:" << Width << endl;
17:    cout << "Length: "  << Length << endl;
18:    cout << "Area: " << Area <<endl;
19:    return 0;
20:  }
```

Output ▼

```
Width:5
Length: 10
Area: 50
```

NOTE   An asterisk (*) indicates multiplication.

Analysis ▼

On line 4, USHORT is typedefined (some programmers say "typedef'ed") as a synonym for unsigned short int. The program is very much like Listing 3.2, and the output is the same.

When to Use short and When to Use long

One source of confusion for new C++ programmers is when to declare a variable to be type long and when to declare it to be type short. The rule, when understood, is fairly straightforward: If any chance exists that the value you'll want to put into your variable will be too big for its type, use a larger type.

As shown in Table 3.1, unsigned short integers, assuming that they are two bytes, can hold a value only up to 65,535. signed short integers split their values between positive and negative numbers, and thus their maximum value is only half that of the unsigned version.

Although unsigned long integers can hold an extremely large number (4,294,967,295), it is still quite finite. If you need a larger number, you'll have to go to float or double, and then you lose some precision. floats and doubles can hold extremely large numbers, but only the first seven or nine digits are significant on most computers. This means that the number is rounded off after that many digits.

Shorter variables use up less memory. These days, memory is cheap and life is short. Feel free to use int, which is probably four bytes on your machine.

Wrapping Around an unsigned Integer

That unsigned long integers have a limit to the values they can hold is only rarely a problem, but what happens if you do run out of room? When an unsigned integer reaches its maximum value, it wraps around and starts over, much as a car odometer might. Listing 3.4 shows what happens if you try to put too large a value into a short integer.

LISTING 3.4   A Demonstration of Putting Too Large a Value in an unsigned short Integer

```
 1:  #include <iostream>
 2:  int main()
 3:  {
 4:     using std::cout;
 5:     using std::endl;
 6:
 7:     unsigned short int smallNumber;
 8:     smallNumber = 65535;
 9:     cout << "small number:" << smallNumber << endl;
10:     smallNumber++;
11:     cout << "small number:" << smallNumber << endl;
12:     smallNumber++;
13:     cout << "small number:" << smallNumber << endl;
14:     return 0;
15:  }
```

Output ▼

```
small number:65535
small number:0
small number:1
```

Analysis ▼

On line 7, smallNumber is declared to be an unsigned short int, which on a Pentium 4 computer running Windows XP is a two-byte variable, able to hold a value between 0 and 65,535. On line 8, the maximum value is assigned to smallNumber, and it is printed on line 9.

On line 10, `smallNumber` is incremented; that is, 1 is added to it. The symbol for incrementing is ++ (as in the name C++—an incremental increase from C). Thus, the value in `smallNumber` would be 65,536. However, `unsigned short` integers can't hold a number larger than 65,535, so the value is wrapped around to 0, which is printed on line 11.

On line 12, `smallNumber` is incremented again, and then its new value, 1, is printed.

Wrapping Around a `signed` **Integer**

A `signed` integer is different from an `unsigned` integer, in that half of the values you can represent are negative. Instead of picturing a traditional car odometer, you might picture a clock much like the one shown in Figure 3.2, in which the numbers count upward moving clockwise and downward moving counterclockwise. They cross at the bottom of the clock face (traditional 6 o'clock).

FIGURE 3.2
If clocks used signed numbers.

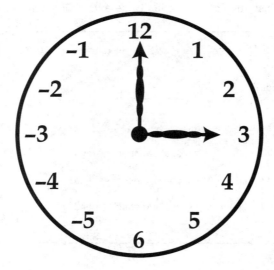

One number from 0 is either 1 (clockwise) or –1 (counterclockwise). When you run out of positive numbers, you run right into the largest negative numbers and then count back down to 0. Listing 3.5 shows what happens when you add 1 to the maximum positive number in a `short` integer.

LISTING 3.5   A Demonstration of Adding Too Large a Number to a `signed` `short` Integer

```
1:  #include <iostream>
2:  int main()
3:  {
```

LISTING 3.5 Continued

```
 4:     short int smallNumber;
 5:     smallNumber = 32767;
 6:     std::cout << "small number:" << smallNumber << std::endl;
 7:     smallNumber++;
 8:     std::cout << "small number:" << smallNumber << std::endl;
 9:     smallNumber++;
10:     std::cout << "small number:" << smallNumber << std::endl;
11:     return 0;
12: }
```

Output ▼

```
small number:32767
small number:-32768
small number:-32767
```

3

Analysis ▼

On line 4, `smallNumber` is declared this time to be a `signed short` integer (if you don't explicitly say that it is `unsigned`, an integer variable is assumed to be `signed`). The program proceeds much as the preceding one, but the output is quite different. To fully understand this output, you must be comfortable with how `signed` numbers are represented as bits in a two-byte integer. The bottom line, however, is that just like an `unsigned` integer, the `signed` integer wraps around from its highest positive value to its highest negative value. This is also called an *overflow*.

Working with Characters

Character variables (type `char`) are typically 1 byte, enough to hold 256 values (see Appendix C). A char can be interpreted as a small number (0–255) or as a member of the ASCII set. The ASCII character set and its ISO equivalent are a way to encode all the letters, numerals, and punctuation marks.

NOTE

Computers do not know about letters, punctuation, or sentences. All they understand are numbers. In fact, all they really know about is whether a sufficient amount of electricity is at a particular junction of wires. These two states are represented symbolically as a 1 and 0. By grouping ones and zeros, the computer is able to generate patterns that can be interpreted as numbers, and these, in turn, can be assigned to letters and punctuation.

In the ASCII code, the lowercase letter a is assigned the value 97. All the lowercase and uppercase letters, all the numerals, and all the punctuation marks are assigned values between 1 and 128. An additional 128 marks and symbols are reserved for use by the computer maker, although the IBM extended character set has become something of a standard.

NOTE   ASCII is usually pronounced "Ask-ee."

Characters and Numbers

When you put a character, for example, the letter a, into a char variable, what really is there is a number between 0 and 255. The compiler knows, however, how to translate back and forth between characters (represented by a single quotation mark and then a letter, numeral, or punctuation mark, followed by a closing single quotation mark) and the corresponding ASCII values.

The value/letter relationship is arbitrary; there is no particular reason that the lowercase letter a is assigned the value 97. As long as everyone (your keyboard, compiler, and screen) agrees, no problem occurs. It is important to realize, however, that a big difference exists between the value 5 and the character 5. The character 5 actually has an ASCII value of 53, much as the letter a is valued at 97. This is illustrated in Listing 3.6.

LISTING 3.6   Printing Characters Based on Numbers

```
1:  #include <iostream>
2:  int main()
3:  {
4:     for (int i = 32; i<128; i++)
5:        std::cout << (char) i;
6:     return 0;
7:  }
```

Output ▼

```
!"#$%&'()*+,-./0123456789:;<=>?@ABCDEFGHIJKLMNOPQRSTUVWXYZ[\]^_`abcdefghijklmno
pqrstuvwxyz{|}~?
```

Analysis ▼

This simple program prints the character values for the integers 32 through 127. This listing uses an integer variable, i, on line 4 to accomplish this task. On line 5, the number in the variable i is forced to display as a character. A character variable could also have been used as shown in Listing 3.7, which has the same output.

LISTING 3.7   Printing Characters Based on Numbers, Take 2

```
1:  #include <iostream>
2:  int main()
2:  {
4:      for (unsigned char i = 32; i<128; i++)
5:          std::cout <<  i;
6:      return 0;
7:  }
```

As you can see, an unsigned character is used on line 4. Because a character variable is being used instead of a numeric variable, the cout on line 5 knows to display the character value.

Special Printing Characters

The C++ compiler recognizes some special characters for formatting. Table 3.3 shows the most common ones. You put these into your code by typing the backslash (called the escape character), followed by the character. Thus, to put a tab character into your code, you enter a single quotation mark, the slash, the letter t, and then a closing single quotation mark:

```
char tabCharacter = '\t';
```

This example declares a char variable (tabCharacter) and initializes it with the character value \t, which is recognized as a tab. The special printing characters are used when printing either to the screen or to a file or other output device.

The escape character (\) changes the meaning of the character that follows it. For example, normally the character n means *the letter n*, but when it is preceded by the escape character, it means *new line*.

3

TABLE 3.3   The Escape Characters

Character	What It Means
\a	Bell (alert)
\b	Backspace
\f	Form feed
\n	New line
\r	Carriage return
\t	Tab
\v	Vertical tab
\'	Single quote
\"	Double quote
\?	Question mark
\\	Backslash
\000	Octal notation
\xhhh	Hexadecimal notation

Constants

Like variables, *constants* are data storage locations. Unlike variables, and as the name implies, constants don't change—they remain constant. You must initialize a constant when you create it, and you cannot assign a new value later. C++ has two types of constants: literal and symbolic.

Literal Constants

A *literal constant* is a value typed directly into your program wherever it is needed. For example:

```
int myAge = 39;
```

myAge is a variable of type int; 39 is a literal constant. You can't assign a value to 39, and its value can't be changed.

Symbolic Constants

A *symbolic constant* is a constant that is represented by a name, just as a variable is represented. Unlike a variable, however, after a constant is initialized, its value can't be changed.

If your program has an integer variable named `students` and another named `classes`, you could compute how many students you have, given a known number of classes, if you knew each class consisted of 15 students:

```
students = classes * 15;
```

In this example, 15 is a literal constant. Your code would be easier to read, and easier to maintain, if you substituted a symbolic constant for this value:

```
students = classes * studentsPerClass
```

If you later decided to change the number of students in each class, you could do so where you define the constant `studentsPerClass` without having to make a change every place you used that value.

Two ways exist to declare a symbolic constant in C++. The old, traditional, and now obsolete way is with the preprocessor directive `#define`. The second, and appropriate, way to create them is using the `const` keyword.

Defining Constants with `#define`

Because a number of existing programs use the preprocessor `#define` directive, it is important for you to understand how it has been used. To define a constant in this obsolete manner, you would enter this:

```
#define studentsPerClass 15
```

Note that `studentsPerClass` is of no particular type (`int`, `char`, and so on). The preprocessor does a simple text substitution. In this case, every time the preprocessor sees the word `studentsPerClass`, it puts in the text 15.

Because the preprocessor runs before the compiler, your compiler never sees your constant; it sees the number 15.

CAUTION   Although `#define` looks very easy to use, it should be avoided because it has been declared obsolete in the C++ standard.

Defining Constants with `const`

Although `#define` works, a much better way exists to define constants in C++:

```
const unsigned short int studentsPerClass = 15;
```

This example also declares a symbolic constant named `studentsPerClass`, but this time `studentsPerClass` is typed as an `unsigned short int`.

3

This method of declaring constants has several advantages in making your code easier to maintain and in preventing bugs. The biggest difference is that this constant has a type, and the compiler can enforce that it is used according to its type.

NOTE   Constants cannot be changed while the program is running. If you need to change `studentsPerClass`, for example, you need to change the code and recompile.

DO	DON'T
DO watch for numbers overrunning the size of the integer and wrapping around incorrect values.	**DON'T** use keywords as variable names.
DO give your variables meaningful names that reflect their use.	**DON'T** use the #define preprocessor directive to declare constants. Use const.

Enumerated Constants

Enumerated constants enable you to create new types and then to define variables of those types whose values are restricted to a set of possible values. For example, you could create an enumeration to store colors. Specifically, you could declare COLOR to be an enumeration, and then you could define five values for COLOR: RED, BLUE, GREEN, WHITE, and BLACK.

The syntax for creating enumerated constants is to write the keyword enum, followed by the new type name, an opening brace, each of the legal values separated by a comma, and finally, a closing brace and a semicolon. Here's an example:

```
enum COLOR { RED, BLUE, GREEN, WHITE, BLACK };
```

This statement performs two tasks:

- It makes COLOR the name of an enumeration; that is, a new type.
- It makes RED a symbolic constant with the value 0, BLUE a symbolic constant with the value 1, GREEN a symbolic constant with the value 2, and so forth.

Every enumerated constant has an integer value. If you don't specify otherwise, the first constant has the value 0, and the rest count up from there. Any one of the constants can be initialized with a particular value, however, and those that are not initialized count upward from the ones before them. Thus, if you write

```
enum Color { RED=100, BLUE, GREEN=500, WHITE, BLACK=700 };
```

RED has the value 100; BLUE, the value 101; GREEN, the value 500; WHITE, the value 501; and BLACK, the value 700.

You can define variables of type COLOR, but they can be assigned only one of the enumerated values (in this case, RED, BLUE, GREEN, WHITE, or BLACK). You can assign any color value to your COLOR variable.

It is important to realize that enumerator variables are generally of type unsigned int, and that the enumerated constants equate to integer variables. It is, however, very convenient to be able to name these values when working with information such as colors, days of the week, or similar sets of values. Listing 3.8 presents a program that uses an enumerated type.

3

LISTING 3.8   A Demonstration of Enumerated Constants

```
1:  #include <iostream>
2:  int main()
3:  {
4:      enum Days { Sunday, Monday, Tuesday,
5:                  Wednesday, Thursday, Friday, Saturday };
6:
7:      Days today;
8:      today = Monday;
9:
10:     if (today == Sunday || today == Saturday)
11:         std::cout << "\nGotta' love the weekends!\n";
12:     else
13:         std::cout << "\nBack to work.\n";
14:
15:     return 0;
16:  }
```

Output ▼

```
Back to work.
```

Analysis ▼

On lines 4 and 5, the enumerated constant Days is defined, with seven values. Each of these evaluates to an integer, counting upward from 0; thus, Monday's value is 1 (Sunday was 0).

On line 7, a variable of type Days is created—that is, the variable contains a valid value from the list of enumerated constants defined on lines 4 and 5. The value Monday is assigned to the variable on line 8. On line 10, a test is done against the value.

The enumerated constant shown on line 8 could be replaced with a series of constant integers, as shown in Listing 3.9.

LISTING 3.9   Same Program Using Constant Integers

```
 1:  #include <iostream>
 2:  int main()
 3:  {
 4:      const int Sunday = 0;
 5:      const int Monday = 1;
 6:      const int Tuesday = 2;
 7:      const int Wednesday = 3;
 8:      const int Thursday = 4;
 9:      const int Friday = 5;
10:      const int Saturday = 6;
11:
12:      int today;
13:      today = Monday;
14:
15:      if (today == Sunday || today == Saturday)
16:          std::cout << "\nGotta' love the weekends!\n";
17:      else
18:          std::cout << "\nBack to work.\n";
19:
20:      return 0;
21:  }
```

Output ▼

```
Back to work.
```

CAUTION   A number of the variables you declare in this program are not used. As such, your compiler might give you warnings when you compile this listing.

Analysis ▼

The output of this listing is identical to Listing 3.8. Each of the constants (Sunday, Monday, and so on) was explicitly defined, and no enumerated Days type exists. Enumerated constants have the advantage of being self-documenting—the intent of the Days enumerated type is immediately clear.

Summary

This lesson discussed numeric and character variables and constants, which are used by C++ to store data during the execution of your program. Numeric variables are either integral (char, short, int, and long int) or they are floating point (float, double, and long double). Numeric variables can also be signed or unsigned. Although all the types can be of various sizes among different computers, the type specifies an exact size on any given computer.

You must declare a variable before it can be used, and then you must store the type of data that you've declared as correct for that variable. If you put a number that is too large into an integral variable, it wraps around and produces an incorrect result.

This lesson also presented literal and symbolic constants as well as enumerated constants. You learned two ways to declare a symbolic constant, using #define and using the keyword const, but you learned that using const is the appropriate way.

3

Q&A

Q If a short int can run out of room and wrap around, why not always use long integers?

A All integer types can run out of room and wrap around, but a long integer does so with a much larger number. For example, a two-byte unsigned short int wraps around after 65,535, whereas a four-byte unsigned long int does not wrap around until 4,294,967,295. However, on most machines, a long integer takes up twice as much memory every time you declare one (such as four bytes versus two bytes), and a program with 100 such variables consumes an extra 200 bytes of RAM. Frankly, this is less of a problem than it used to be because most personal computers now come with millions (if not billions) of bytes of memory.

Using larger types than you need might also require additional time for your computer's processor to processes.

Q What happens if I assign a number with a decimal point to an integer rather than to a float? Consider the following line of code:

```
int aNumber = 5.4;
```

A A good compiler issues a warning, but the assignment is completely legal. The number you've assigned is truncated into an integer. Thus, if you assign 5.4 to an integer variable, that variable will have the value 5. Information will be lost, however, and if you then try to assign the value in that integer variable to a float variable, the float variable will have only 5.

Q Why not use literal constants; why go to the bother of using symbolic constants?

A If you use a value in many places throughout your program, a symbolic constant allows all the values to change just by changing the one definition of the constant. Symbolic constants also speak for themselves. It might be hard to understand why a number is being multiplied by 360, but it's much easier to understand what's going on if the number is being multiplied by `degreesInACircle`.

Q What happens if I assign a negative number to an `unsigned` variable? Consider the following line of code:

```
unsigned int aPositiveNumber = -1;
```

A A good compiler issues a warning, but the assignment is legal. The negative number is assessed as a bit pattern and is assigned to the variable. The value of that variable is then interpreted as an `unsigned` number. Thus, −1, whose bit pattern is 11111111 11111111 (0xFF in hex), is assessed as the `unsigned` value 65,535.

Q Can I work with C++ without understanding bit patterns, binary arithmetic, and hexadecimal?

A Yes, but not as effectively as if you do understand these topics. C++ does not do as good a job as some languages at protecting you from what the computer is really doing. This is actually a benefit because it provides you with tremendous power that other languages don't. As with any power tool, however, to get the most out of C++, you must understand how it works. Programmers who try to program in C++ without understanding the fundamentals of the binary system often are confused by their results.

Workshop

The Workshop provides quiz questions to help you solidify your understanding of the material covered and exercises to provide you with experience in using what you've learned. Try to answer the quiz and exercise questions before checking the answers in Appendix D, and be certain that you understand the answers before continuing to the next lesson.

Quiz

1. What is the difference between an integer variable and a floating-point variable?
2. What are the differences between an `unsigned short int` and a `long int`?
3. What are the advantages of using a symbolic constant rather than a literal constant?

4. What are the advantages of using the `const` keyword rather than `#define`?

5. What makes for a good or bad variable name?

6. Given this `enum`, what is the value of `BLUE`?

   ```
   enum COLOR { WHITE, BLACK = 100, RED, BLUE, GREEN = 300 };
   ```

7. Which of the following variable names are good, which are bad, and which are invalid?

   A. `Age`

   B. `!ex`

   C. `R79J`

   D. `TotalIncome`

   E. `__Invalid`

Exercises

1. What would be the correct variable type in which to store the following information?

   A. Your age

   B. The area of your backyard

   C. The number of stars in the galaxy

   D. The average rainfall for the month of January

2. Create good variable names for this information.

3. Declare a constant for pi as 3.14159.

4. Declare a `float` variable and initialize it using your pi constant.

LESSON 4
Managing Arrays and Strings

In previous lessons, you declared a single int, char, or other object. However, you may want to declare a collection of objects, such as 20 ints or a litter of Cats.

In this lesson, you will learn

- What arrays are and how to declare them
- What strings are and how to use character arrays to make them

What Is an Array?

An *array* is a sequential collection of data storage locations, each of which holds the same type of data. Each storage location is called an *element* of the array.

You declare an array by writing the type, followed by the array name and the subscript. The subscript is the number of elements in the array, surrounded by square brackets. For example:

```
long LongArray[25];
```

declares an array of 25 `long` integers, named `LongArray`. When the compiler sees this declaration, it sets aside enough memory to hold all 25 elements. If each `long` integer requires four bytes, this declaration sets aside 100 contiguous bytes of memory, as illustrated in Figure 4.1.

FIGURE 4.1
Declaring an array.

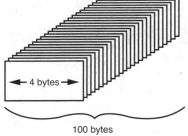

← 4 bytes →

100 bytes

Accessing Array Elements

You access an array element by referring to its offset from the beginning of the array. Array element offsets are counted from zero. Therefore, the first array element is referred to as `arrayName[0]`. In the `LongArray` example, `LongArray[0]` is the first array element, `LongArray[1]` is the second array element, and so forth.

This can be somewhat confusing. The array `SomeArray[3]` has three elements. They are `SomeArray[0]`, `SomeArray[1]`, and `SomeArray[2]`. More generally, `SomeArray[n]` has *n* elements that are numbered `SomeArray[0]` through `SomeArray[n-1]`. Remember that this is because the index is an offset, so the first array element is zero storage locations from the beginning of the array, the second is one storage location from the beginning of the array, and so on.

Therefore, `LongArray[25]` is numbered from `LongArray[0]` through `LongArray[24]`. Listing 4.1 shows how to declare an array of five integers and fill each with a value.

NOTE

> The line numbers for code samples in this lesson will start with zero. This is to help you remember that in C++, elements in an array start from offset position zero!

LISTING 4.1   Using an Integer Array

```
0:  //Listing 4.1 - Arrays
1:  #include <iostream>
2:
3:  int main()
4:  {
5:      int myArray[5];      // Array of 5 integers
6:      int i;
7:      for ( i=0; i<5; i++)  // 0-4
8:      {
9:          std::cout << "Value for myArray[" << i << "]: ";
10:         std::cin >> myArray[i];
11:     }
12:     for (i = 0; i<5; i++)
13:         std::cout << i << ": " << myArray[i] << std::endl;
14:     return 0;
15: }
```

Output ▼

```
Value for myArray[0]:  3
Value for myArray[1]:  6
Value for myArray[2]:  9
Value for myArray[3]:  12
Value for myArray[4]:  15
0: 3
1: 6
2: 9
3: 12
4: 15
```

Analysis ▼

Listing 4.1 creates an array, has you enter values for each element, and then prints the values to the console. In line 5, the array, called myArray, is declared and is of type int. You can see that it is declared with 5 in the square brackets. This means that myArray can hold five integers. Each of these elements can be treated as an integer variable.

4

In line 7, a `for` loop is started that counts from zero through four. This is the proper set of offsets for a five-element array. The user is prompted for a value on line 9, and on line 10 the value is saved at the correct offset into the array.

Looking closer at line 10, you see that each element is accessed using the name of the array followed by square brackets with the offset in between. Each of these elements can then be treated like a variable of the array's type.

The first value is saved at `myArray[0]`, the second at `myArray[1]`, and so forth. On lines 12 and 13, a second `for` loop prints each value to the console.

> **NOTE**
>
> Arrays count from zero, not from one. This is the cause of many bugs in programs written by C++ novices. Think of the index as the offset. The first element, such as `ArrayName[0]`, is at the beginning of the array, so the offset is zero. Thus, whenever you use an array, remember that an array with 10 elements counts from `ArrayName[0]` to `ArrayName[9]`. `ArrayName[10]` is an error.

Writing Past the End of an Array

When you write a value to an element in an array, the compiler computes where to store the value based on the size of each element and the subscript. Suppose that you ask to write over the value at `LongArray[5]`, which is the sixth element. The compiler multiplies the offset (5) by the size of each element—in this case, 4 bytes. It then moves that many bytes (20) from the beginning of the array and writes the new value at that location.

If you ask to write at `LongArray[50]`, most compilers ignore the fact that no such element exists. Rather, the compiler computes how far past the first element it should look (200 bytes) and then writes over whatever is at that location. This can be virtually any data, and writing your new value there might have unpredictable results. If you're lucky, your program will crash immediately. If you're unlucky, you'll get strange results much later in your program, and you'll have a difficult time figuring out what went wrong.

The compiler is like a blind man pacing off the distance from a house. He starts out at the first house, `MainStreet[0]`. When you ask him to go to the sixth house on Main Street, he says to himself, "I must go five more houses. Each house is four big paces. I must go an additional 20 steps." If you ask him to go to `MainStreet[100]` and Main Street is only 25 houses long, he paces off 400 steps. Long before he gets there, he will, no doubt, step in front of a truck. So, be careful where you send him.

Listing 4.2 writes past the end of an array. You should compile this listing to see what error and warning messages you get. If you don't get any, you should be extra careful when working with arrays!

CAUTION	Do not run this program; it might crash your system!

LISTING 4.2   Writing Past the End of an Array

```
0: Listing 4.2 demonstrates what writing past the bounds of an array is!
1:
2: #include <iostream>
3: using namespace std;
4:
5: int main()
6: {
7:     long TargetArray[25]; // array to fill
8:
9:     int i;
10:     for (i=0; i<25; i++)
11:         TargetArray[i] = 10;
12:
13:     cout << "Test 1: \n";  // test current values (should be 0)
14:     cout << "TargetArray[0]: " << TargetArray[0] << endl;        // lower
➥bound
15:     cout<<"TargetArray[24]: "<<TargetArray[24]<<endl<<endl; // upper bound
16:
17:     cout << "\nAttempting at assigning values beyond the upper-bound...";
18:     for (i = 0; i<=25; i++)          // Going a little too far!
19:     TargetArray[i] = 20; // Assignment may fail for element [25]
20:
21:     cout << "\nTest 2: \n";
22:     cout << "TargetArray[0]: " << TargetArray[0] << endl;
23:     cout << "TargetArray[24]: " << TargetArray[24] << endl;
24:     cout<<"TargetArray[25]: "<<TargetArray[25]<<endl<<endl; // out of bounds^
25:
26:     return 0;
27: }
```

4

Output ▼

```
<Program may terminate in a stack-corruption warning>
Test 1:
TargetArray[0]: 10
TargetArray[24]: 10


Attempting at assigning values beyond the upper-bound...
Test 2:
TargetArray[0]: 20
TargetArray[24]: 20
TargetArray[25]: 20
```

Analysis ▼

This simple program does something very dangerous. You see that the array of long integers TargetArray has been filled with sample values twice. However, on the second instance as visible in line 18, the for-loop actually crosses the bounds of the array and assigns a value at offset position 25. Note that arrays in C++ have elements starting at offset position 0. Hence, TargetArray that is 25 elements long contains elements in the offset range 0 – 24. To write a value at offset position 25 is a violation. Similarly to read from that position as visible in line 24 is a violation too. This is called a "buffer overflow" error, and this program is not guaranteed to work (even if you see it work on your development environment).

> **NOTE**
>
> Note that because all compilers use memory differently, your results might vary. In any case, accessing or writing elements beyond the bounds of an array can result in an "access violation" and should be avoided at all costs.

Fence Post Errors

It is so common to write to one past the end of an array that this bug has its own name. It is called a *fence post error*. This refers to the problem in counting how many fence posts you need for a 10-foot fence if you need one post for every foot. Most people answer 10, but of course you need 11. Figure 4.2 makes this clear.

FIGURE 4.2
Fence post errors.

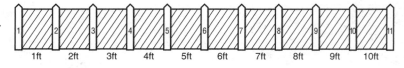

This type of "off by one" counting can be the bane of any C++ programmer's life. Over time, however, you'll get used to the idea that a 25-element array counts only to element 24, and that everything counts from 0.

> **NOTE**
>
> Some programmers refer to ArrayName[0] as the *zeroth element*. Getting into this habit is a mistake. If ArrayName[0] is the zeroth element, what is ArrayName[1]? The oneth? If so, when you see ArrayName[24], will you realize that it is not the twenty-fourth element in the array, but rather the twenty-fifth? It is far less confusing to say that ArrayName[0] is at offset zero and is the first element.

Initializing Arrays

You can initialize a simple array of built-in types, such as integers and characters, when you first declare the array. After the array name, you put an equal sign (=) and a list of comma-separated values enclosed in braces. For example:

```
// An array of 5 integers, all elements initialized to 0

int IntegerArray[5] = {0};
```

declares an integer array of five elements that are all initialized to a value 0. This is just another way of initializing individual elements to 0, as shown in this example:

```
// An array of 5 integers initialized to zero

int IntegerArray[5] = { 0, 0, 0, 0, 0 };
```

which is equivalent to the previous one but different in the sense that every element here is explicitly initialized to 0. Thus, if the requirement needs elements in an array to be initialized to different number, that would be possible as seen here:

```
// An array of 5 integers with 5 different initial values

int IntegerArray[5] = { 10, 20, 30, 40, 50 };
```

where the first element IntegerArray[0] is initialized to the value 10, IntegerArray[1] the value 20, and so forth.

If you omit the size of the array, an array just big enough to hold the initialization is created. Therefore, if you write

```
// The size is not specified, yet 5 initialization values

// tell the compiler to create an array of 5 integers

int IntegerArray[] = { 10, 20, 30, 40, 50 };
```

4

you will create the same array as you did in the previous example, an array that holds five elements.

You cannot initialize more elements than you've declared for the array. Therefore,

```
// Array of 5 integers get assigned 6 initial values --> error!
int IntegerArray[5] = { 10, 20, 30, 40, 50, 60};
```

generates a compiler error because you've declared a five-member array and initialized six values. It is legal, however, to write

```
int IntegerArray[5] = {10, 20};
```

In this case, you have declared a five-element array and only initialized the first two elements, `IntegerArray[0]` and `IntegerArray[1]`.

DO	DON'T
DO remember to initialize arrays or else the elements will contain unknown values until first assigned.	**DON'T** write past the end of the array.
DO remember that the first member of the array is at offset 0.	**DON'T** get goofy with naming arrays. They should have meaningful names just as any other variable would have.

Declaring Arrays

Arrays can have any legal variable name, but they cannot have the same name as another variable or array within their scope. Therefore, you cannot have an array named `myCats[5]` and a variable named `myCats` at the same time.

The code in listing 4.2 uses "magic numbers" such as 25 for the size of `TargetArray`. It is safer to use constants so that you can change all these values in one place. In Listing 4.2, literal numbers were used. If you want to change the `TargetArray` so that it holds only 20 elements instead of 25, you have to change several lines of code. If you used a constant, you have to change only the value of your constant.

Creating the number of elements, or dimension size, with an enumeration is a little different. Listing 4.3 illustrates this by creating an array that holds values—one for each day of the week.

LISTING 4.3   Using consts and enums in Arrays

```
0:  // Listing 4.3
1:  // Dimensioning arrays with consts and enumerations
2:
```

LISTING 4.3 Continued

```
3:   #include <iostream>
4:   int main()
5:   {
6:       enum WeekDays { Sun, Mon, Tue,
7:               Wed, Thu, Fri, Sat, DaysInWeek };
8:       int ArrayWeek[DaysInWeek] = { 10, 20, 30, 40, 50, 60, 70 };
9:
10:      std::cout << "The value at Tuesday is: " << ArrayWeek[Tue];
11:      return 0;
12:  }
```

Output ▼

```
The value at Tuesday is: 30
```

Analysis ▼

Line 6 creates an enumeration called WeekDays. It has eight members. Sunday is equal to 0 and DaysInWeek is equal to 7. On line 8, an array called ArrayWeek is declared to have DaysInWeek elements, which is 7.

Line 10 uses the enumerated constant Tue as an offset into the array. Because Tue evaluates to 2, the third element of the array, ArrayWeek[2], is returned and printed on line 10.

4

Arrays

To declare an array, write the type of object stored, followed by the name of the array and a subscript with the number of objects to be held in the array.

Example 1

```
int MyIntegerArray[90];
```

Example 2

```
long * ArrayOfPointersToLongs[100];
```

To access members of the array, use the subscript operator.

Example 1

```
// assign ninth member of MyIntegerArray to theNinthInteger
int theNinthInteger = MyIntegerArray[8];
```

Example 2

```
// assign ninth member of ArrayOfPointersToLongs to pLong.
long * pLong = ArrayOfPointersToLongs[8];
```

Arrays count from zero. An array of *n* items is numbered from 0 to *n-1*.

Multidimensional Arrays

Arrays that we have seen so far have been unidimensional. We can talk of the length of the array in a sense similar to the length of a string (a string is also unidimensional), and array elements can be located by a single subscript parameter the same way that points on a string can be identified by their distance from the beginning.

Arrays can, however, get multidimensional too. That is, just as points on a string can be represented by a unidimensional array, points in a rectangular area can be represented by a multidimensional one. This array-based representation of points in a rectangular area would need two subscript parameters, x and y (two dimensions), which are necessary to locate a point within an area. Arrays programmed in C++ exist in a virtual world and are not limited by two dimensions alone. You can create an array of any number of dimensions, and that is what makes multidimensional arrays an interesting topic from mathematical points of view.

Declaring Multidimensional Arrays

Each dimension in an array is represented as a subscript in the array. Therefore, a two-dimensional array has two subscripts; a three-dimensional array has three subscripts; and so on. Arrays can have any number of dimensions.

A good example of a two-dimensional array is a chess board. One dimension represents the eight rows; the other dimension represents the eight columns. Figure 4.3 illustrates this idea.

Suppose that every square on the board was represented by a pair of integers, one that supplied the x-position (in the horizontal direction) and another that supplied the y-position (in the vertical direction). The declaration of an array that would represent the board, as a collection of squares would be

```
int Board[8][8];
```

You could also represent the same data with a one-dimensional, 64-square array (that is, all squares along the x-axis only). For example:

```
int Board[64];
```

This, however, doesn't correspond as closely to the real-world object as a two-dimensional array. When the game begins, the king is located in the fourth position in the first row; that position corresponds to

```
Board[0][3];
```

assuming that the first subscript corresponds to row and the second to column.

FIGURE 4.3
A chess board and
a two-dimensional
array.

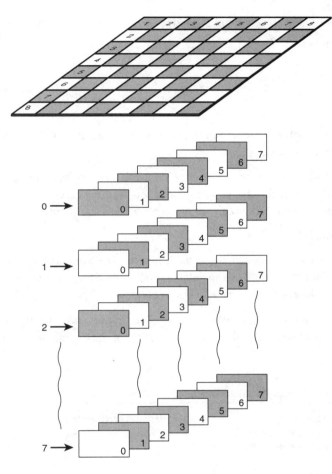

4

Initializing Multidimensional Arrays

You can initialize multidimensional arrays. You assign the list of values to array elements in order, with the last array subscript (the one farthest to the right) changing while each of the former holds steady. Therefore, if you have an array

```
int theArray[5][3];
```

the first three elements go into theArray[0]; the next three into theArray[1]; and so forth.

You initialize this array by writing

```
int theArray[5][3] = { 1,2,3,4,5,6,7,8,9,10,11,12,13,14,15 };
```

For the sake of clarity, you could group the initializations with braces. For example:

```
int theArray[5][3] = {  {1,2,3},
    {4,5,6},
    {7,8,9},
    {10,11,12},
    {13,14,15} };
```

The compiler ignores the inner braces, but they do make it easier to understand how the numbers are distributed.

When initializing elements of an array, each value must be separated by a comma, without regard to the braces. The entire initialization set must be within braces, and it must end with a semicolon. Initializing all elements to zero could not be any simpler:

```
int theArray[5][3] = {0},
```

The compiler assigns all elements in the array, starting from position [0, 0] and ending at position [4, 2] with 0. Note that the element positions or indexes are zero-based, whereas the array definition specifies the number of elements in the array and hence starts at 1.

Listing 4.4 creates a two-dimensional array. The first dimension is the set of numbers from zero to four. The second dimension consists of the double of each value in the first dimension.

LISTING 4.4 Creating a Multidimensional Array

```
0:   // Listing 4.4 - Creating a Multidimensional Array
1:   #include <iostream>
2:   using namespace std;
3:
4:   int main()
5:   {
6:       int SomeArray[2][5] = { {0,1,2,3,4}, {0,2,4,6,8}};
7:       for (int i = 0; i<2; i++)
8:       {
9:           for (int j=0; j<5; j++)
10:          {
11:              cout << "SomeArray[" << i << "][" << j << "]: ";
12:              cout << SomeArray[i][j]<< endl;
13:          }
14:      }
15:      return 0;
16:  }
```

Output ▼

```
SomeArray[0][0]: 0
SomeArray[0][1]: 1
SomeArray[0][2]: 2
SomeArray[0][3]: 3
SomeArray[0][4]: 4
SomeArray[1][0]: 0
SomeArray[1][1]: 2
SomeArray[1][2]: 4
SomeArray[1][3]: 6
SomeArray[1][4]: 8
```

Analysis ▼

Line 6 declares SomeArray to be a two-dimensional array. The first dimension indicates that there will be two sets; the second dimension consists of five integers. This creates a 2×5 grid, as Figure 4.4 shows.

FIGURE 4.4
A 2×5 array.

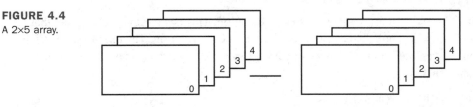

SomeArray [5] [2]

4

The values are based on the two sets of numbers. The first set is the original numbers; the second set is the doubled numbers. In this listing, the values are simply set, although they could be computed as well. Lines 7 and 9 create a nested for loop. The outer for loop (starting on line 7) ticks through each member of the first dimension, which is each of the two sets of integers. For every member in that dimension, the inner for loop (starting on line 9) ticks through each member of the second dimension. This is consistent with the printout. SomeArray[0][0] is followed by SomeArray[0][1]. The first dimension is incremented only after the second dimension has gone through all of its increments. Then counting for the second dimension starts over.

> **A Word About Memory**
>
> When you declare an array, you tell the compiler exactly how many objects you expect to store in it. The compiler sets aside memory for all the objects, even if you never use it. This isn't a problem with arrays for which you have a good idea of how many objects you'll need. For example, a chessboard has 64 squares, and cats have between 1 and 10 kittens. When you have no idea of how many objects you'll need, however, you must use more advanced data structures.
>
> In Lesson 18, "STL Dynamic-Array Classes," this book discusses dynamic arrays in the form of `std::vector` and `std::deque`. The behavior of these entities is specified by the C++ Standards Committee. They provide the programmer with a ready and generic implementation of dynamic arrays that should solve most requirements and address issues, such as memory management, copying, and so forth.

char **Arrays and Strings**

There is a type of array that gets special attention. This is an array of characters that is terminated by a null. This array is considered a C-style string. The only C-style strings you've seen until now have been unnamed C-style string constants used in `cout` statements, such as

```
cout << "hello world";
```

You can declare and initialize a C-style string the same as you would any other array. For example:

```
char Greeting[] =
{ 'H', 'e', 'l', 'l', 'o', ' ', 'W','o','r','l','d','\0' };
```

In this case, `Greeting` is declared as an array of characters and it is initialized with a number of characters. The last character, `'\0'`, is the null character, which many C++ functions recognize as the terminator for a C-style string. Although this character-by-character approach works, it is difficult to type and admits too many opportunities for error. C++ enables you to use a shorthand form of the previous line of code. It is

```
char Greeting[] = "Hello World";
```

You should note two things about this syntax:

- Instead of single-quoted characters separated by commas and surrounded by braces, you have a double-quoted C-style string, no commas, and no braces.
- You don't need to add the null character because the compiler adds it for you.

When you declare a string, you need to ensure that you make it as large as you will need. The length of a C-style string includes the number of characters including the null character. For example, Hello World is 12 bytes. Hello is 5 bytes, the space is 1 byte, World is 5 bytes, and the null character is 1 byte.

You can also create uninitialized character arrays. As with all arrays, it is important to ensure that you don't put more into it than there is room for. Listing 4.5 demonstrates the use of an uninitialized buffer.

LISTING 4.5   Filling an Array

```
0:   //Listing 4.5 char array buffers
1:
2:   #include <iostream>
3:
4:   int main()
5:   {
6:        char buffer[80] = {'\0'};
7:        std::cout << "Enter the string: ";
8:        std::cin >> buffer;
9:        std::cout << "Here's the buffer: " << buffer << std::endl;
10:       return 0;
11:  }
```

4

Output ▼

```
Enter the string: Hello World
Here's the buffer: Hello
```

Analysis ▼

On line 6, a character array is created to act as a buffer to hold 80 characters all of which are initialized to \0, the null character. This array is large enough to hold a 79-character C-style string and the terminating null character.

On line 7, the user is prompted to enter a C-style string, which is entered into the buffer on line 8. cin writes a terminating null to the buffer after it writes the string.

Two problems occur with the program in Listing 4.5. First, if the user enters more than 79 characters, cin writes past the end of the buffer. Second, if the user enters a space, cin thinks that it is the end of the string, and it stops writing to the buffer.

To solve these problems, you must call a special method on `cin` called `get()`. `cin.get()` takes three parameters:

- The buffer to fill
- The maximum number of characters to get
- The delimiter that terminates input

The delimiter defaults to a newline character. Listing 4.6 illustrates the use of `get()`.

LISTING 4.6   Filling an Array with a Maximum Number of Characters

```
0:   //Listing 4.6 using cin.get()
1:
2:   #include <iostream>
3:   using namespace std;
4:
5:   int main()
6:   {
7:       char buffer[80] = {'\0'};
8:       cout << "Enter the string: ";
9:       cin.get(buffer, 79);        // get up to 79 or newline
10:      cout << "Here's the buffer:  " << buffer << endl;
11:      return 0;
12:  }
```

Output ▼

```
Enter the string: Hello World
Here's the buffer:  Hello World
```

Analysis ▼

Line 9 calls the method `get()` of `cin`. The buffer declared on line 7 is passed in as the first argument. The second argument is the maximum number of characters to get. In this case, it must be no greater than 79 to allow for the terminating null. No need exists to provide a terminating character because the default value of newline is sufficient.

If you enter spaces, tabs, or other whitespace characters, they are assigned to the string. A newline character ends the input. Entering 79 characters also results in the end of the input. You can verify this by rerunning the listing and trying to enter a string longer than 79 characters.

Using the `strcpy()` and `strncpy()` Methods

A number of existing functions are available in the C++ library for dealing with strings. C++ inherits many of these functions for dealing with C-style strings from the C language. Among the many functions provided are two for copying one string into another: `strcpy()` and `strncpy()`. `strcpy()` copies the entire contents of one string into a designated buffer. The other, `strncpy()`, copies a number of characters from one string to another. Listing 4.7 demonstrates the use of `strcpy()`.

LISTING 4.7 Using `strcpy()`

```
0:   //Listing 4.7 Using strcpy()
1:
2:   #include <iostream>
3:   #include <string.h>
4:   using namespace std;
5:
6:   int main()
7:   {
8:       char String1[] = "No man is an island";
9:       char String2[80] = {'\0'};
10:
11:      strcpy(String2,String1);
12:
13:      cout << "String1: " << String1 << endl;
14:      cout << "String2: " << String2 << endl;
15:      return 0;
16:  }
```

Output ▼

```
String1: No man is an island
String2: No man is an island
```

Analysis ▼

This listing is relatively simple. It copies data from one string into another. The header file `string.h` is included on line 3. This file contains the prototype of the `strcpy()` function. `strcpy()` takes two character arrays—a destination followed by a source. On line 11, this function is used to copy `String1` into `String2`.

You have to be careful using the strcpy() function. If the source is larger than the destination, strcpy() overwrites past the end of the buffer. To protect against this, the standard library also includes strncpy(). This variation takes a maximum number of
characters to copy. strncpy() copies up to the first null character or the maximum number of characters specified into the destination buffer. Listing 4.8 illustrates the use of
strncpy().

LISTING 4.8   Using strncpy()

```
0:   //Listing 4.8 Using strncpy()
1:
2:   #include <iostream>
3:   #include <string.h>
4:
5:   int main()
6:   {
7:       const int MaxLength = 80;
8:       char String1[] = "No man is an island";
9:       char String2[MaxLength+1] = {'\0'};
10:
11:      strncpy(String2, String1, MaxLength);    // safer than strcpy
12:
13:      std::cout << "String1: " << String1 << std::endl;
14:      std::cout << "String2: " << String2 << std::endl;
15:      return 0;
16:  }
```

Output ▼

```
String1: No man is an island
String2: No man is an island
```

Analysis ▼

Once again, a simple listing is presented. Like the preceding listing, this one simply
copies data from one string into another. On line 11, the call to strcpy() has been
changed to a call to strncpy(), which takes a third parameter: the maximum number of
characters to copy. The buffer String2 is declared to take MaxLength+1 characters. The
extra character is for the null, which both strcpy() and strncpy() automatically add to
the end of the string.

String Classes

C++ inherited the null-terminated C-style string and the library of functions that includes strcpy() from C, but these functions aren't integrated into an object-oriented framework. Like all arrays, character arrays are static. You define how large they are. They always take up that much room in memory, even if you don't need it all. Writing past the end of the array is disastrous.

As you've seen in previous code samples, using C-style functions such as strcpy() puts the onus of memory management on the programmer. For example, before using strcpy, you need to be sure that the destination buffer is allocated to the right capacity to be able to hold the string being copied in to it; otherwise you would write past the end of the buffer and cause serious problems. This constraint presents a big disadvantage in storing user input (for example) that can be of variable lengths. The programmer would need to dynamically allocate the destination buffer (which would require you to determine the length of the source and allocate appropriately) or use a statically allocated buffer (such as an array) whose length is an optimistic estimate—that might still prove inadequate at run-time. An activity such as copying strings, which ought to be trivial, is therefore fraught with the danger of being flawed and can bring the application down in the worst of cases.

To address these frequently occurring requirements, the C++ standard library includes a string class that makes working with strings easy by providing an encapsulated set of data, and functions for manipulating that string data. std::string, as this class is known, handles memory allocation details and makes copying strings, or assigning them, an easy activity. See Listing 4.9.

4

LISTING 4.9 Initializing, Assigning (Copying), and Concatenating Strings Using std::string

```
0: #include <string>
1: #include <iostream>
2:
3: int main ()
4: {
5:     // A sample string
6:     std::string str1 ("This is a C++ string! ");
7:
8:     // display on the console / screen
9:     std::cout << "str1 = " << str1 << std::endl;
10:
11:     // a second sample string
12:     std::string str2;
13:
```

LISTING 4.9   Continued

```
14:    // assign to make a copy of the first in the second
15:    str2 = str1;
16:
17:    // display the copy
18:    std::cout << "Result of assignment, str2 = " << str2 << std::endl;
19:
20:    // change (overwrite) the second string with a new value
21:    str2 = "Hello string!";
22:
23:    std::cout << "After over-writing contents, str2 = " << str2;
24:    std::cout << std::endl << std::endl;
25:
26:    std::string strAddResult;
27:
28:    // Add the two std::strings (concatenate) and store in a third
29:    strAddResult = str1 + str2;
30:
31:    std::cout << "The result of str1 + str2 is = " << strAddResult;
32:
33:    return 0;
34: }
```

Output ▼

```
str1 = This is a C++ string!
Result of assignment, str2 = This is a C++ string!
After over-writing contents, str2 = Hello string!

The result of str1 + str2 is = This is a C++ string! Hello string!
```

Analysis ▼

Without going deep into the concepts behind the workings of the string class, a quick look at its usage tells you that it made copying strings almost as intuitive and easy as copying integers. Similarly, concatenating two strings was done by simply adding them, just as we would do with any integer. The std::string class managed the memory handling and the copying of data for the programmer behind the scenes, making for a quick, clean, and stable implementation. A prerequisite here is inclusion of the header <string>, as you see in the first line of code.

To learn the various functions of std::string in detail, take a quick look at Lesson 17, "The STL string Class." Because you have still not covered classes and templates, ignore sections that seem unfamiliar in that lesson and concentrate on understanding the gist of the samples.

Summary

In this lesson, you learned how to create arrays in C++. An array is a fixed-size collection of objects that are all the same type.

Arrays don't do bounds checking. Therefore, it is legal—even if disastrous—to read or write past the end of an array. Arrays count from 0. A common mistake is to write to offset *n* of an array of *n* members.

Arrays can be one dimensional or multidimensional. In either case, the members of the array can be initialized as long as the array contains either built-in types, such as `int`, or objects of a class that has a default constructor.

Strings are arrays of characters, or `char`s. C++ provides special features for managing `char` arrays, including the capability to initialize them with quoted strings.

The C++ standard library also provides the programmer with `std::string` via the header `<string>`, which makes copying strings and manipulating them an easy activity. After gaining an understanding of how C-style strings are declared and used, you should base your practical implementations on C++ string classes such as `std::string`.

Q&A

4

Q What is in an uninitialized array element?

A Whatever happens to be in memory at a given time. The results of using an uninitialized array member without assigning a value can be unpredictable. If the compiler is following the C++ standards, array elements that are static, nonlocal objects will be zero initialized.

Q Can I combine arrays?

A Yes. With simple arrays, you can use pointers to combine them into a new, larger array. With strings, you can use some of the built-in functions, such as `strcat`, to combine strings.

Q What are the advantages of dynamic array classes like the `std::vector`?

A The advantage is that when using dynamic arrays, the programmer does not need to know the number of items the array can contain at compile-time. The dynamic arrays resize themselves automatically to suit the requirement of the application. Additionally, the utility functions that these classes supply the programmer with can be an incentive too.

Q Must a string class use an internal `char` buffer to hold the contents of the string?

A No. It can use any memory storage the designer thinks is best.

Q Must a string class use an internal `char` buffer to hold the contents of the string?

A No. It can use any memory storage type the designer thinks is apt for the situation.

Workshop

The Workshop provides quiz questions to help you solidify your understanding of the material covered and exercises to provide you with experience in using what you've learned. Try to answer the quiz and exercise questions before checking the answers in Appendix D, and be certain that you understand the answers before continuing to the next lesson.

Quiz

1. What are the first and last elements in `SomeArray[25]`?
2. How do you declare a multidimensional array?
3. Initialize all members of an array declared as `SomeArray[2][3][2]` to zero.
4. How many elements are in the array `SomeArray[10][5][20]`?
5. How many characters are stored in the string "Jesse knows C++"?
6. What is the last character in the string "Brad is a nice guy"?

Exercises

1. Declare a two-dimensional array that represents a tic-tac-toe game board.
2. Write the code that initializes all the elements in the array you created in Exercise 1 to the value `0`.
3. Write a program that contains four arrays. Three of the arrays should contain your first name, middle initial, and last name. Use the string-copying function presented in today's lesson to copy these strings together into the fourth array, full name.
4. **BUG BUSTERS:** What is wrong with this code fragment?
   ```
   unsigned short SomeArray[5][4];
   for (int i = 0; i<4; i++)
       for (int j = 0; j<5; j++)
           SomeArray[i][j] = i+j;
   ```
5. **BUG BUSTERS:** What is wrong with this code fragment?
   ```
   unsigned short SomeArray[5][4];
   for (int i = 0; i<=5; i++)
       for (int j = 0; j<=4; j++)
           SomeArray[i][j] = 0;
   ```

LESSON 5

Working with Expressions, Statements, and Operators

At its heart, a program is a set of commands executed in sequence. The power in a program comes from its capability to execute one or another set of commands, based on whether a particular condition is true or false.

In this lesson, you will learn

- What statements are

- What blocks are

- What expressions are

- How to branch your code based on conditions

- What truth is and how to act on it

Starting with Statements

In C++, a statement controls the sequence of execution, evaluates an expression, or does nothing (the null statement). All C++ statements end with a semicolon and nothing else. One of the most common statements is the following assignment statement:

```
x = a + b;
```

Unlike in algebra, this statement does not mean that x is equal to a+b. Rather, this is read, "Assign the value of the sum of a and b to x," or "Assign to x, a+b," or "Set x equal to a plus b."

This statement is doing two things. It is adding a and b together, and it is assigning the result to x using the assignment operator (=). Even though this statement is doing two things, it is one statement, and thus has one semicolon.

NOTE   The assignment operator assigns whatever is on the right side of the equal sign to whatever is on the left side.

Using Whitespace

Whitespace is the invisible characters such as tabs, spaces, and new lines. These are called *whitespace characters* because if they are printed on a piece of white paper, you see only the white of the paper.

Whitespace is generally ignored in statements. For example, the assignment statement previously discussed could be written as

```
x=a+b;
```

or as

```
x                       =a
+              b        ;
```

Although this last variation is perfectly legal, it is also perfectly foolish. Whitespace can be used to make your programs more readable and easier to maintain or it can be used to create horrific and indecipherable code. In this, as in all things, C++ provides the power; you supply the judgment.

Blocks and Compound Statements

Any place you can put a single statement, you can put a compound statement, also called a block. A block begins with an opening brace ({) and ends with a closing brace (}).

Although every statement in the block must end with a semicolon, the block itself does not end with a semicolon, as shown in the following example:

```
{
    temp = a;
    a = b;
    b = temp;
}
```

This block of code acts as one statement and swaps the values in the variables a and b.

DO	DON'T
DO end your statements with a semicolon.	**DON'T** forget to use a closing brace any time you have an opening brace.
DO use whitespace judiciously to make your code clearer.	

Expressions

Anything that evaluates to a value is an expression in C++. An expression is said to *return* a value. Thus, the statement 3+2; returns the value 5, so it is an expression. All expressions are statements.

The myriad pieces of code that qualify as expressions might surprise you. Here are three examples:

```
3.2                  // returns the value 3.2
PI                   // float constant that returns the value 3.14
SecondsPerMinute     // int constant that returns 60
```

Assuming that PI is a constant created that is initialized to 3.14 and SecondsPerMinute is a constant equal to 60, all three statements are expressions.

The slightly more complicated expression

```
x = a + b;
```

not only adds a and b and assigns the result to x, but returns the value of that assignment (the value of x) as well. Thus, this assignment statement is also an expression.

As a note, any expression can be used on the right side of an assignment operator. This includes the assignment statement just shown. The following is perfectly legal in C++:

```
y = x = a + b;
```

5

This line is evaluated in the following order:

1. Add a to b.

2. Assign the result of the expression a + b to x.

3. Assign the result of the assignment expression x = a + b to y.

If a, b, x, and y are all integers, and if a has the value 9 and b has the value 7, both x and y will be assigned the value 16. This is illustrated in Listing 5.1.

LISTING 5.1 Evaluating Complex Expressions

```
 1:  #include <iostream>
 2:  int main()
 3:  {
 4:      using std::cout;
 5:      using std::endl;
 6:
 7:      int a=0, b=0, x=0, y=35;
 8:      cout << "a: " << a << " b: " << b;
 9:      cout << " x: " << x << " y: " << y << endl;
10:      a = 9;
11:      b = 7;
12:      y = x = a+b;
13:      cout << "a: " << a << " b: " << b;
14:      cout << " x: " << x << " y: " << y << endl;
15:      return 0;
16:  }
```

Output ▼

```
a: 0 b: 0 x: 0 y: 35
a: 9 b: 7 x: 16 y: 16
```

Analysis ▼

On line 7, the four variables are declared and initialized. Their values are printed on lines 8 and 9. On line 10, a is assigned the value 9. On line 11, b is assigned the value 7. On line 12, the values of a and b are summed and the result is assigned to x. This expression (x = a+b) evaluates to a value (the sum of a + b), and that value is, in turn, assigned to y. On lines 13 and 14, these results are confirmed by printing out the values of the four variables.

Working with Operators

An *operator* is a symbol that causes the compiler to take an action. Operators act on operands, and in C++ any expression can be an operand. In C++, several categories of operators exist. The first two categories of operators that you will learn about are

- Assignment operators
- Mathematical operators

Assignment Operators

You saw the assignment operator (=) earlier. This operator causes the operand on the left side of the assignment operator to have its value changed to the value of the expression on the right side of the assignment operator. The expression

```
x = a + b;
```

assigns the value that is the result of adding a and b to the operand x.

---

l-values and r-values

An operand that legally can be on the left side of an assignment operator is called an *l-value*. That which can be on the right side is called (you guessed it) an *r-value*.

You should note that all l-values are r-values, but not all r-values are l-values. An example of an r-value that is not an l-value is a literal. Thus, you can write

```
x = 5;
```

but you cannot write

```
5 = x;
```

x can be an l-value or an r-value, 5 can only be an r-value.

NOTE | Constants are r-values. Because they cannot have their values changed, they are not allowed to be on the left side of the assignment operator, which means they can't be l-values.

Mathematical Operators

A second category of operators is made up of the mathematical operators. Five mathematical operators are addition (+), subtraction (–), multiplication (*), division (/), and modulus (%).

5

Addition and subtraction work as you would expect: Two numbers separated by the plus or minus sign are added or subtracted. Multiplication works in the same manner; however, the operator you use to do multiplication is an asterisk (*). Division is done using a forward slash operator. The following are examples of expressions using each of these operators. In each case, the result is assigned to the variable `result`. The comments to the right show the value of `result`:

```
result = 56 + 32    // result = 88
result = 12 - 10    // result = 2
result = 21 / 7     // result = 3
result = 12 * 4     // result = 48
```

Subtraction Troubles

Subtraction with `unsigned` integers can lead to surprising results if the result is a negative number. You saw something much like this in Lesson 4, "Managing Arrays and Strings," when variable overflow was described. Listing 5.2 shows what happens when you subtract a large unsigned number from a small unsigned number.

LISTING 5.2   A Demonstration of Subtraction and Integer Overflow

```
 1:  // Listing 5.2 - demonstrates subtraction and
 2:  // integer overflow
 3:  #include <iostream>
 4:
 5:  int main()
 6:  {
 7:      using std::cout;
 8:      using std::endl;
 9:
10:      unsigned int difference;
11:      unsigned int bigNumber = 100;
12:      unsigned int smallNumber = 50;
13:
14:      difference = bigNumber - smallNumber;
15:      cout << "Difference is: " << difference;
16:
17:      difference = smallNumber - bigNumber;
18:      cout << "\nNow difference is: " << difference <<endl;
19:      return 0;
20:  }
```

Output ▼

```
Difference is: 50
Now difference is: 4294967246
```

Analysis ▼

The subtraction operator is invoked for the first time on line 14, and the result is printed on line 15, much as you might expect. The subtraction operator is called again on line 17, but this time a large unsigned number is subtracted from a small unsigned number. The result would be negative, but because it is evaluated and printed as an unsigned number, the result is an overflow, as described in Lesson 3, "Using Variables, Declaring Constants." This topic is reviewed in detail in Appendix C, "Operator Precedence."

Integer Division and Modulus

Integer division is the division you learned when you were in elementary school. When you divide 21 by 4 (21/4), and you are doing integer division, the answer is 5 (with a remainder).

The fifth mathematical operator might be new to you. The modulus operator (%) tells you the remainder after an integer division. To get the remainder of 21 divided by 4, you take 21 modulus 4 (21%4). In this case, the result is 1.

Finding the modulus can be very useful. For example, you might want to print a statement on every tenth action. Any number whose value is 0 when you modulus 10 with that number is an exact multiple of 10. Thus 1%10 is 1, 2%10 is 2, and so forth, until 10%10, whose result is 0. 11%10 is back to 1, and this pattern continues until the next multiple of 10, which is 20. 20%10 = 0 again. You'll use this technique when looping is discussed in Lesson 7, "Controlling Program Flow."

FAQ
When I divide 5/3, I get 1. What is going wrong?

Answer: If you divide one integer by another, you get an integer as a result.

Thus, 5/3 is 1. (The actual answer is 1 with a remainder of 2. To get the remainder, try 5%3, whose value is 2.)

To get a fractional return value, you must use floating-point numbers (type `float`, `double`, or `long double`).

5.0/3.0 gives you a fractional answer: 1.66667.

If either the divisor or the dividend is a floating point, the compiler generates a floating-point quotient. However, if that quotient is assigned to an l-value that is an integer, the value is once again truncated.

5

Combining the Assignment and Mathematical Operators

It is common to want to add a value to a variable and then to assign the result back to the same variable. If you have a variable myAge and you want to increase the value stored in it by two, you can write

```
int myAge = 5;
int temp;
temp = myAge + 2;    // add 5 + 2 and put it in temp
myAge = temp;        // put it back in myAge
```

The first two lines create the myAge variable and a temporary variable. As you can see in the third line, the value in myAge has two added to it. The resulting value is assigned to temp. In the next line, this value is then placed back into myAge, updating it.

This method, however, is terribly convoluted and wasteful. In C++, you can put the same variable on both sides of the assignment operator; thus, the preceding becomes

```
myAge = myAge + 2;
```

which is much clearer and much better. In algebra, this expression would be meaningless, but in C++ it is read as "add two to the value in myAge and assign the result to myAge."

Even simpler to write, but perhaps a bit harder to read is

```
myAge += 2;
```

This line is using the self-assigned addition operator (+=). The self-assigned addition operator adds the r-value to the l-value and then reassigns the result into the l-value. This operator is pronounced "plus-equals." The statement is read "myAge plus-equals two." If myAge had the value 24 to start, it would have 26 after this statement.

Self-assigned subtraction (-=), division (/=), multiplication (*=), and modulus (%=) operators exist as well.

Incrementing and Decrementing

The most common value to add (or subtract) and then reassign into a variable is 1. In C++, increasing a value by 1 is called *incrementing*, and decreasing by 1 is called *decrementing*. Special operators are provided in C++ to perform these actions.

The increment operator (++) increases the value of the variable by 1, and the decrement operator (--) decreases it by 1. Thus, if you have a variable, `Counter`, and you want to increment it, you would use the following statement:

```
Counter++;              // Start with Counter and increment it.
```

This statement is equivalent to the more verbose statement

```
Counter = Counter + 1;
```

which is also equivalent to the moderately verbose statement

```
Counter += 1;
```

NOTE As you might have guessed, C++ got its name by applying the increment operator to the name of its predecessor language: C. The idea is that C++ is an incremental improvement over C.

Prefixing Versus Postfixing

Both the increment operator (++) and the decrement operator (--) come in two varieties: prefix and postfix. The prefix variety is written before the variable name (++myAge); the postfix variety is written after the variable name (myAge++).

In a simple statement, it doesn't matter which you use, but in a complex statement when you are incrementing (or decrementing) a variable and then assigning the result to another variable, it matters very much. The prefix operator is evaluated before the assignment; the postfix operator is evaluated after the assignment. The semantics of prefix is this: Increment the value in the variable and then fetch or use it. The semantics of postfix is different: Fetch or use the value and then increment the original variable.

This can be confusing at first, but if x is an integer whose value is 5 and using a prefix increment operator you write

```
int a = ++x;
```

you have told the compiler to increment x (making it 6) and then fetch that value and assign it to a. Thus, a is now 6 and x is now 6.

If, after doing this, you use the postfix operator to write

```
int b = x++;
```

you have now told the compiler to fetch the value in x (6) and assign it to b, and then go back and increment x. Thus, b is now 6, but x is now 7. Listing 5.3 shows the use and implications of both types.

5

LISTING 5.3   A Demonstration of Prefix and Postfix Operators

```
1:  // Listing 5.3 - demonstrates use of
2:  // prefix and postfix increment and
3:  // decrement operators
4:  #include <iostream>
5:  int main()
6:  {
7:      using std::cout;
8:
9:      int myAge = 39;      // initialize two integers
10:     int yourAge = 39;
11:     cout << "I am: " << myAge << " years old.\n";
12:     cout << "You are: " << yourAge << " years old\n";
13:     myAge++;             // postfix increment
14:     ++yourAge;           // prefix increment
15:     cout << "One year passes...\n";
16:     cout << "I am: " << myAge << " years old.\n";
17:     cout << "You are: " << yourAge << " years old\n";
18:     cout << "Another year passes\n";
19:     cout << "I am: " << myAge++ << " years old.\n";
20:     cout << "You are: " << ++yourAge << " years old\n";
21:     cout << "Let's print it again.\n";
22:     cout << "I am: " << myAge << " years old.\n";
23:     cout << "You are: " << yourAge << " years old\n";
24:     return 0;
25: }
```

Output ▼

```
I am      39 years old
You are   39 years old
One year passes
I am      40 years old
You are   40 years old
Another year passes
I am      40 years old
You are   41 years old
Let's print it again
I am      41 years old
You are   41 years old
```

Analysis ▼

On lines 9 and 10, two integer variables are declared, and each is initialized with the value 39. Their values are printed on lines 11 and 12.

On line 13, myAge is incremented using the postfix increment operator, and on line 14, yourAge is incremented using the prefix increment operator. The results are printed on lines 16 and 17, and they are identical (both 40).

On line 19, myAge is incremented as part of the printing statement, using the postfix increment operator. Because it is postfix, the increment happens after the printing, so the value 40 is printed again, and then the myAge variable is incremented. In contrast, on line 20, yourAge is incremented using the prefix increment operator. Thus, it is incremented before being printed, and the value displays as 41.

Finally, on lines 22 and 23, the values are printed again. Because the increment statement has completed, the value in myAge is now 41, as is the value in yourAge.

Understanding Operator Precedence

In the complex statement

```
x = 5 + 3 * 8;
```

which is performed first, the addition or the multiplication? If the addition is performed first, the answer is 8*8, or 64. If the multiplication is performed first, the answer is 5+24, or 29.

The C++ standard does not leave the order random. Rather, every operator has a precedence value, and the complete list is shown in Appendix C. Multiplication has higher precedence than addition; thus, the value of the expression is 29.

When two mathematical operators have the same precedence, they are performed in left-to-right order. Thus,

```
x = 5 + 3 + 8 * 9 + 6 * 4;
```

is evaluated multiplication first, left to right. Thus, 8*9 = 72, and 6*4 = 24. Now the expression is essentially

```
x = 5 + 3 + 72 + 24;
```

Now, the addition, left to right, is 5+3 = 8; 8+72 = 80; 80+24 = 104.

Be careful with this. Some operators, such as assignment, are evaluated in right-to-left order!

In any case, what if the precedence order doesn't meet your needs? Consider the expression

```
TotalSeconds = NumMinutesToThink + NumMinutesToType * 60
```

5

In this expression, you do not want to multiply the `NumMinutesToType` variable by 60 and then add it to `NumMinutesToThink`. You want to add the two variables to get the total number of minutes, and then you want to multiply that number by 60 to get the total seconds.

You use parentheses to change the precedence order. Items in parentheses are evaluated at a higher precedence than any of the mathematical operators. Thus, the preceding example should be written as

```
TotalSeconds = (NumMinutesToThink + NumMinutesToType) * 60
```

Nesting Parentheses

For complex expressions, you might need to nest parentheses one within another. For example, you might need to compute the total seconds and then compute the total number of people who are involved before multiplying seconds times people:

```
TotalPersonSeconds = ( ( (NumMinutesToThink + NumMinutesToType) * 60) *
(PeopleInTheOffice + PeopleOnVacation) )
```

This complicated expression is read from the inside out. First, `NumMinutesToThink` is added to `NumMinutesToType` because they are in the innermost parentheses—that sum is then multiplied by 60. Next, `PeopleInTheOffice` is added to `PeopleOnVacation`. Finally, the total number of people found is multiplied by the total number of seconds.

This example raises an important related issue. This expression is easy for a computer to understand, but very difficult for a human to read, understand, or modify. Here is the same expression rewritten, using some temporary integer variables:

```
TotalMinutes = NumMinutesToThink + NumMinutesToType;
TotalSeconds = TotalMinutes * 60;
TotalPeople = PeopleInTheOffice + PeopleOnVacation;
TotalPersonSeconds = TotalPeople * TotalSeconds;
```

This example takes longer to write and uses more temporary variables than the preceding example, but it is far easier to understand. If you add a comment at the top to explain what this code does and change the 60 to a symbolic constant, you will have code that is easy to understand and maintain.

DO	DON'T
DO remember that expressions have a value. **DO** use the prefix operator (`++variable`) to increment or decrement the variable before it is used in the expression. **DO** use the postfix operator (`variable++`) to increment or decrement the variable after it is used. **DO** use parentheses to change the order of precedence.	**DON'T** nest too deeply because the expression becomes hard to understand and maintain. **DON'T** confuse the postfix operator with the prefix operator.

The Nature of Truth

Every expression can be evaluated for its truth or falsity. Expressions that evaluate mathematically to zero return `false`; all others return `true`.

In previous versions of C++, all truth and falsity was represented by integers, but the ANSI standard introduced the type `bool`. A `bool` can only have one of two values: `false` or `true`.

> **NOTE**   Many compilers previously offered a `bool` type, which was represented internally as a `long int` and, thus, had a size of four bytes. Now, ANSI-compliant compilers often provide a one-byte `bool`.

Evaluating with the Relational Operators

The relational operators are used to compare two numbers to determine whether they are equal or if one is greater or less than the other. Every relational statement evaluates to either `true` or `false`. The relational operators are presented later, in Table 5.1.

> **NOTE**   All relational operators return a value of type `bool`; that is, either `true` or `false`. In previous versions of C++, these operators returned either 0 for false or a nonzero value (usually 1) for true.

If the integer variable myAge has the value 45, and the integer variable yourAge has the value 50, you can determine whether they are equal by using the relational "equals" operator (==):

```
myAge == yourAge;   // is the value in myAge the same as in yourAge?
```

This expression evaluates to false because the variables are not equal. You can check to see whether myAge is less than yourAge using the expression,

```
myAge < yourAge;   // is myAge less than yourAge?
```

which evaluates to true because 45 is less than 50.

CAUTION

Many novice C++ programmers confuse the assignment operator (=) with the equals operator (==). This can lead to a nasty bug in your program.

The six relational operators are equals (==), less than (<), greater than (>), less than or equal to (<=), greater than or equal to (>=), and not equals (!=). Table 5.1 shows each relational operator and a sample code use.

TABLE 5.1   The Relational Operators

Name	Operator	Sample	Evaluates
Equals	==	100 == 50;	false
		50 == 50;	true
Not equals	!=	100 != 50;	true
		50 != 50;	false
Greater than	>	100 > 50;	true
		50 > 50;	false
Greater than or equal to	>=	100 >= 50;	true
		50 >= 50;	true
Less than	<	100 < 50;	false
		50 < 50;	false
Less than or equal to	<=	100 <= 50;	false
		50 <= 50;	true

DO	**DON'T**
DO remember that relational operators return the value `true` or `false`.	**DON'T** confuse the assignment operator (=) with the equals relational operator (==). This is one of the most common C++ programming mistakes—be on guard for it.

The `if` **Statement**

Normally, your program flows along line-by-line in the order in which it appears in your source code. The `if` statement enables you to test for a condition (such as whether two variables are equal) and branch to different parts of your code, depending on the result. The simplest form of an `if` statement is the following:

```
if (expression)
    statement;
```

The *expression* in the parentheses can be any expression, but it usually contains one of the relational expressions. If the *expression* has the value `false`, the statement is skipped. If it evaluates `true`, the statement is executed. Consider the following example:

```
if (bigNumber > smallNumber)
    bigNumber = smallNumber;
```

This code compares `bigNumber` and `smallNumber`. If `bigNumber` is larger, the second line sets its value to the value of `smallNumber`. If `bigNumber` is not larger than `smallNumber`, the statement is skipped.

Because a block of statements surrounded by braces is equivalent to a single statement, the branch can be quite large and powerful:

```
if (expression)
{
    statement1;
    statement2;
    statement3;
}
```

Here's a simple example of this usage:

```
if (bigNumber > smallNumber)
{
    bigNumber = smallNumber;
    std::cout << "bigNumber: " << bigNumber << "\n";
    std::cout << "smallNumber: " << smallNumber << "\n";
}
```

5

This time, if bigNumber is larger than smallNumber, not only is it set to the value of smallNumber, but an informational message is printed. Listing 5.4 shows a more detailed example of branching based on relational operators.

LISTING 5.4   A Demonstration of Branching Based on Relational Operators

```
1:  // Listing 5.4 - demonstrates if statement
2:  // used with relational operators
3:  #include <iostream>
4:  int main()
5:  {
6:     using std::cout;
7:     using std::cin;
8:
9:     int MetsScore, YankeesScore;
10:    cout << "Enter the score for the Mets: ";
11:    cin >> MetsScore;
12:
13:    cout << "\nEnter the score for the Yankees: ";
14:    cin >> YankeesScore;
15:
16:    cout << "\n";
17:
18:    if (MetsScore > YankeesScore)
19:       cout << "Let's Go Mets!\n";
20:
21:    if (MetsScore < YankeesScore)
22:    {
23:       cout << "Go Yankees!\n";
24:    }
25:
26:    if (MetsScore == YankeesScore)
27:    {
28:       cout << "A tie? Naah, can't be.\n";
29:       cout << "Give me the real score for the Yanks: ";
30:       cin >> YankeesScore;
31:
32:       if (MetsScore > YankeesScore)
33:          cout << "Knew it! Let's Go Mets!";
34:
35:       if (YankeesScore > MetsScore)
36:          cout << "Knew it! Go Yanks!";
37:
38:       if (YankeesScore == MetsScore)
39:          cout << "Wow, it really was a tie!";
40:    }
41:
42:    cout << "\nThanks for telling me.\n";
43:    return 0;
44:  }
```

Output ▼

```
Enter the score for the Mets: 10

Enter the score for the Yankees: 10

A tie? Naah, can't be
Give me the real score for the Yanks: 8
Knew it! Let's Go Mets!
Thanks for telling me.
```

Analysis ▼

This program asks for the user to input scores for two baseball teams; the scores are stored in integer variables, MetsScore and YankeesScore. The variables are compared in the if statement on lines 18, 21, and 26.

If one score is higher than the other, an informational message is printed. If the scores are equal, the block of code that begins on line 27 and ends on line 40 is entered. The second score is requested again, and then the scores are compared again.

Note that if the initial Yankees score is higher than the Mets score, the if statement on line 18 evaluates as false, and line 19 is not invoked. The test on line 21 evaluates as true, and the statement on line 23 is invoked. Then the if statement on line 26 is tested and this is false (if line 18 is true). Thus, the program skips the entire block, falling through to line 41. This example illustrates that getting a true result in one if statement does not stop other if statements from being tested.

Note that the action for the first two if statements is one line (printing Let's Go Mets! or Go Yankees!). In the first example (on line 19), this line is not in braces; a single-line block doesn't need them. The braces are legal, however, and are used on lines 22–24.

5

Avoiding Common Errors with if Statements

Many novice C++ programmers inadvertently put a semicolon after their if statements:

```
if(SomeValue < 10);     // Oops! Notice the semicolon!
   SomeValue = 10;
```

What was intended here was to test whether SomeValue is less than 10, and if so, to set it to 10, making 10 the minimum value for SomeValue. Running this code snippet shows that SomeValue is always set to 10! Why? The if statement terminates with the semicolon (the do-nothing operator).

Remember that indentation has no meaning to the compiler. This snippet could more accurately have been written as

```
if (SomeValue < 10)  // test
;  // do nothing
SomeValue = 10;  // assign
```

Removing the semicolon makes the final line part of the `if` statement and makes this code do what was intended.

To minimize the chances of this problem, you can always write your `if` statements with braces, even when the body of the `if` statement is only one line:

```
if (SomeValue < 10)
{
    SomeValue = 10;
};
```

Indentation Styles

Listing 5.4 shows one style of indenting `if` statements. Nothing is more likely to create a religious war, however, than to ask a group of programmers what is the best style for brace alignment. Although dozens of variations are possible, the following appear to be the most popular three:

- Putting the initial brace after the condition and aligning the closing brace under the `if` to close the statement block:

```
if (expression){
    statements
}
```

- Aligning the braces under the `if` and indenting the statements:

```
if (expression)
{
    statements
}
```

- Indenting the braces and statements:

```
if (expression)
    {
    statements
    }
```

This book uses the middle alternative because it is easy to understand where blocks of statements begin and end if the braces line up with each other and with the condition being tested. Again, it doesn't matter which style you choose, so long as you are consistent with it.

The else Statement

Often, your program needs to take one branch if your condition is true or another if the condition is false. In Listing 5.4, you wanted to print one message (Let's Go Mets!) if the first test (MetsScore > YankeesScore) evaluated true, and another message (Go Yankees!) if it evaluated false.

The method shown so far—testing first one condition and then the other—works fine but is a bit cumbersome. The keyword else can make for far more readable code:

```
if (expression)
     statement;
else
     statement;
```

Listing 5.5 demonstrates the use of the keyword else.

LISTING 5.5   Demonstrating the else Keyword

```
 1:   // Listing 5.5 - demonstrates if statement
 2:   // with else clause
 3:   #include <iostream>
 4:   int main()
 5:   {
 6:       using std::cout;
 7:       using std::cin;
 8:
 9:       int firstNumber, secondNumber;
10:       cout << "Please enter a big number: ";
11:       cin >> firstNumber;
12:       cout << "\nPlease enter a smaller number: ";
13:       cin >> secondNumber;
14:       if (firstNumber > secondNumber)
15:           cout << "\nThanks!\n";
16:       else
17:           cout << "\nOops. The first number is not bigger!";
18:
19:       return 0;
20:   }
```

5

Output ▼

```
Please enter a big number: 10

Please enter a smaller number: 12
Oops. The first number is not bigger!
```

Analysis ▼

The if statement on line 14 is evaluated. If the condition is true, the statement on line 15 is run and then program flow goes to line 18 (after the else statement). If the condition on line 14 evaluates to false, control goes to the else clause and so the statement on line 17 is run. If the else clause on line 16 was removed, the statement on line 17 would run regardless of whether the if statement was true.

Remember, the if statement ends after line 15. If the else were not there, line 17 would just be the next line in the program. You should also note that either or both of the if and the else statements could be replaced with a block of code in braces.

The if Statement

The syntax for the if statement is as follows:

Form 1

```
if (expression)
    statement;
next_statement;
```

If the *expression* is evaluated as true, the *statement* is executed and the program continues with the *next_statement*. If the *expression* is not true, the *statement* is ignored and the program jumps to the *next_statement*.

Remember that the statement can be a single statement ending with a semicolon or a block enclosed in braces.

Form 2

```
if (expression)
    statement1;
else
    statement2;
next_statement;
```

If the *expression* evaluates as true, the *statement1* is executed; otherwise, the *statement2* is executed. Afterward, the program continues with the *next_statement*.

Example 1
```
Example
if (SomeValue < 10)
    cout << "SomeValue is less than 10");
else
    cout << "SomeValue is not less than 10!");
cout << "Done." << endl;
```

Advanced if Statements

It is worth noting that any statement can be used in an if or else clause, even another if or else statement. Thus, you might see complex if statements in the following form:

```
if (expression1)
{
    if (expression2)
        statement1;
    else
    {
        if (expression3)
            statement2;
        else
            statement3;
    }
}
else
    statement4;
```

This cumbersome if statement says, "If expression1 is true and expression2 is true, execute statement1. If expression1 is true but expression2 is not true, and then if expression3 is true, execute statement2. If expression1 is true but expression2 and expression3 are false, execute statement3. Finally, if expression1 is not true, execute statement4." As you can see, complex if statements can be confusing! Listing 5.6 gives an example of one such complex if statement.

LISTING 5.6   A Complex, Nested if Statement

```
1:  // Listing 5.6 - a complex nested
2:  // if statement
3:  #include <iostream>
4:  int main()
5:  {
6:      // Ask for two numbers
7:      // Assign the numbers to bigNumber and littleNumber
8:      // If bigNumber is bigger than littleNumber,
```

LISTING 5.6   Continued

```
 9:     // see if they are evenly divisible
10:     // If they are, see if they are the same number
11:
12:     using namespace std;
13:
14:     int firstNumber, secondNumber;
15:     cout << "Enter two numbers.\nFirst: ";
16:     cin >> firstNumber;
17:     cout << "\nSecond: ";
18:     cin >> secondNumber;
19:     cout << "\n\n";
20:
21:     if (firstNumber >= secondNumber)
22:     {
23:         if ( (firstNumber % secondNumber) == 0) // evenly divisible?
24:         {
25:             if (firstNumber == secondNumber)
26:                 cout << "They are the same!\n";
27:             else
28:                 cout << "They are evenly divisible!\n";
29:         }
30:         else
31:             cout << "They are not evenly divisible!\n";
32:     }
33:     else
34:         cout << "Hey! The second one is larger!\n";
35:     return 0;
36: }
```

Output ▼

```
Enter two numbers.
First: 10

Second: 2
They are evenly divisible!
```

Analysis ▼

The user is prompted for two numbers, one at a time, and they are compared. The first if statement, on line 21, checks to ensure that the first number is greater than or equal to the second. If not, the else clause on line 33 is executed.

If the first if is true, the block of code beginning on line 22 is executed, and a second if statement is tested on line 23. This checks to see whether the first number divided by the second number yields no remainder. If so, the numbers are either evenly divisible or equal. The if statement on line 25 checks for equality and displays the appropriate message either way. If the if statement on line 23 fails (evaluates to false), the else statement on line 30 is executed.

Using Braces in Nested if Statements

Although it is legal to leave out the braces on if statements that are only a single statement, and it is legal to nest if statements, doing so can cause enormous confusion. The following is perfectly legal in C++, although it looks somewhat confusing:

```
if (x > y)          // if x is bigger than y
    if (x < z)      // and if x is smaller than z
        x = y;      // set x to the value in y
    else            // otherwise, if x isn't less than z
        x = z;      // set x to the value in z
else                // otherwise if x isn't greater than y
    y = x;          // set y to the value in x
```

Remember, whitespace and indentation are a convenience for the programmer; they make no difference to the compiler. It is easy to confuse the logic and inadvertently assign an else statement to the wrong if statement. Listing 5.7 illustrates this problem.

LISTING 5.7   Demonstrates Why Braces Help Clarify Which else Statement Goes with Which if Statement

```
1:  // Listing 5.7 - demonstrates why braces
2:  // are important in nested if statements
3:  #include <iostream>
4:  int main()
5:  {
6:      int x;
7:      std::cout << "Enter a number less than 10 or greater than 100: ";
8:      std::cin >> x;
9:      std::cout << "\n";
10:
11:     if (x >= 10)
12:         if (x > 100)
13:             std::cout << "More than 100, Thanks!\n";
14:     else                          // not the else intended!
15:         std::cout << "Less than 10, Thanks!\n";
16:
17:     return 0;
18: }
```

5

Output ▼

```
Enter a number less than 10 or greater than 100: 20

Less than 10, Thanks!
```

Analysis ▼

The programmer intended to ask for a number less than 10 or greater than 100, check for the correct value, and then print a thank-you note.

When the `if` statement on line 11 evaluates true, the following statement (line 12) is executed. In this case, line 12 executes when the number entered is greater than 10. Line 12 contains an `if` statement also. This `if` statement evaluates true if the number entered is greater than 100. If the number is greater than 100, the statement on line 13 is executed, thus printing out an appropriate message.

If the number entered is less than 10, the `if` statement on line 11 evaluates false. Program control goes to the line following the `if` statement, which in this case is line 16. If you enter a number less than 10, the output is as follows:

```
Enter a number less than 10 or greater than 100: 9
```

As you can see, no message printed. The `else` clause on line 14 was clearly intended to be attached to the `if` statement on line 11, and thus is indented accordingly. Unfortunately, the `else` statement is really attached to the `if` statement on line 12, and thus this program has a subtle bug.

It is a subtle bug because the compiler. will not complain. This is a legal C++ program, but it just doesn't do what was intended. Further, most of the times the programmer tests this program, it will appear to work. As long as you enter a number greater than 100, the program will seem to work just fine. However, if you enter a number from 11 to 99, you'll see that there is obviously a problem! Listing 5.8 fixes the problem by putting in the necessary braces.

LISTING 5.8   A Demonstration of the Proper Use of Braces with an `if` Statement

```
1:  // Listing 5.8 - demonstrates proper use of braces
2:  // in nested if statements
3:  #include <iostream>
4:  int main()
5:  {
6:      int x;
7:      std::cout << "Enter a number less than 10 or greater than 100: ";
```

LISTING 5.8   Continued

```
 8:      std::cin >> x;
 9:      std::cout << "\n";
10:
11:      if (x >= 10)
12:      {
13:          if (x > 100)
14:              std::cout << "More than 100, Thanks!\n";
15:      }
16:      else                              // fixed!
17:          std::cout << "Less than 10, Thanks!\n";
18:      return 0;
19: }
```

Output ▼

```
Enter a number less than 10 or greater than 100: 9
Less than 10, Thanks!
```

Analysis ▼

The braces on lines 12 and 15 make everything between them into one statement, and now the `else` on line 16 applies to the `if` on line 11, as intended.

If the user types 9, the `if` statement on line 11 is true; however, the `if` statement on line 13 is false, so nothing would be printed. It would be better if the programmer put another `else` clause after line 14 so that errors would be caught and a message printed.

5

TIP

You can minimize many of the problems that come with `if...else` statements by always using braces for the statements in the `if` and `else` clauses, even when only one statement follows the condition.

```
if (SomeValue < 10)
{
    SomeValue = 10;
}
else
{
    SomeValue = 25;
};
```

NOTE

> The programs shown in this book are written to demonstrate the particular issues being discussed. They are kept intentionally simple; no attempt is made to bulletproof the code to protect against user error. Ideally, in professional-quality code, every possible user error is anticipated and handled gracefully.

Using the Logical Operators

Often, you want to ask more than one relational question at a time. "Is it true that x is greater than y, and also true that y is greater than z?" A program might need to determine that both of these conditions are true—or that some other set of conditions is true—to take an action.

Imagine a sophisticated alarm system that has this logic: "If the door alarm sounds AND it is after 6:00 p.m. AND it is NOT a holiday, OR if it is a weekend, call the police." C++'s three logical operators are used to make this kind of evaluation. These operators are listed in Table 5.2.

TABLE 5.2   The Logical Operators

Operator	Symbol	Example
AND	&&	*expression1* && *expression2*
OR	||	*expression1* || *expression2*
NOT	!	*!expression*

The Logical AND Operator

A logical AND statement uses the AND operator to connect and evaluates two expressions. If both expressions are true, the logical AND statement is true as well. If it is true that you are hungry, AND it is true that you have money, it is true that you can buy lunch. Thus,

```
if ( (x == 5) && (y == 5) )
```

evaluates as true if both x and y are equal to 5, and it evaluates as false if either one is not equal to 5. Note that both sides must be true for the entire expression to be true.

Note that the logical AND is two && symbols. A single & symbol is a different operator, called the 'bitwise' AND.

The Logical OR Operator

A logical OR statement evaluates two expressions. If either one is true, the expression is true. If you have money OR you have a credit card, you can pay the bill. You don't need both money and a credit card; you need only one, although having both is fine as well. Thus,

```
if ( (x == 5) || (y == 5) )
```

evaluates true if either x or y is equal to 5, or if both are equal to 5.

Note that the logical OR is two || symbols. A single | symbol is a bitwise OR operator, which is discussed in Lesson 29.

The Logical NOT Operator

A logical NOT statement evaluates to true if the expression being tested is false. Again, if the expression tested is false, the value of the test is true! Thus,

```
if ( !(x == 5) )
```

is true only if x is not equal to 5. This is the same as writing

```
if (x != 5)
```

Short Circuit Evaluation

When the compiler is evaluating an AND statement, such as

```
if ( (x == 5) && (y == 5) )
```

the compiler evaluates the truth of the first statement (x==5), and if this fails (that is, if x is not equal to 5), the compiler does *NOT* go on to evaluate the truth or falsity of the second statement (y == 5) because AND requires both to be true.

Similarly, if the compiler is evaluating an OR statement, such as

```
if ( (x == 5) || (y == 5) )
```

if the first statement is true (x == 5), the compiler never evaluates the second statement (y == 5) because the truth of *either* is sufficient in an OR statement.

Although this might not seem important, consider the following example:

```
if ( (x == 5 )|| (++y == 3) )
```

If x is not equal to 5, (++y == 3) is not evaluated. If you are counting on y to be incremented regardless, it might not happen.

5

Relational Precedence

Like all C++ expressions, the use of relational operators and logical operators each return a value: true or false. Like all expressions, they also have a precedence order (see Appendix C) that determines which relationship is evaluated first. This fact is important when determining the value of statements such as the following:

```
if ( x > 5 && y > 5 || z > 5)
```

It might be that the programmer wanted this expression to evaluate true if both x and y are greater than 5 or if z is greater than 5. On the other hand, the programmer might have wanted this expression to evaluate true only if x is greater than 5 and if it is also true that either y is greater than 5 or z is greater than 5.

If x is 3, and y and z are both 10, the first interpretation is true (z is greater than 5, so ignore x and y), but the second is false (it isn't true that x is greater than 5, and thus it doesn't matter what is on the right side of the && symbol because both sides must be true).

Although precedence determines which relation is evaluated first, parentheses can both change the order and make the statement clearer:

```
if ( (x > 5) && (y > 5 || z > 5) )
```

Using the values from earlier, this statement is false. Because it is not true that x is greater than 5, the left side of the AND statement fails, and thus the entire statement is false. Remember that an AND statement requires that both sides be true—something isn't both "good tasting" AND "good for you" if it isn't good tasting.

TIP	It is often a good idea to use extra parentheses to clarify what you want to group. Remember, the goal is to write programs that work and that are easy to read and to understand. Parentheses help to clarify your intent and avoid errors that come from misunderstanding operator precedence.

More About Truth and Falsehood

In C++, zero evaluates to false, and all other values evaluate to true. Because an expression always has a value, many C++ programmers take advantage of this feature in their if statements. A statement such as

```
if (x)          // if x is true (nonzero)
    x = 0;
```

can be read as "If x has a nonzero value, set it to 0." This is a bit of a cheat; it would be clearer if written

```
if (x != 0)        // if x is not zero
    x = 0;
```

Both statements are legal, but the latter is clearer. It is good programming practice to reserve the former method for true tests of logic, rather than for testing for nonzero values.

These two statements also are equivalent:

```
if (!x)            // if x is false (zero)
if (x == 0)        // if x is zero
```

The second statement, however, is somewhat easier to understand and is more explicit if you are testing for the mathematical value of x rather than for its logical state.

DO	DON'T
DO put parentheses around your logical tests to make them clearer and to make the precedence explicit. **DO** use braces in nested `if` statements to make the `else` statements clearer and to avoid bugs.	**DON'T** use `if(x)` as a synonym for `if(x != 0)`; the latter is clearer. **DON'T** use `if(!x)` as a synonym for `if(x == 0)`; the latter is clearer.

The Conditional (Ternary) Operator

The conditional operator (`?:`) is C++'s only ternary operator; that is, it is the only operator to take three terms. The conditional operator takes three expressions and returns a value:

```
(expression1) ? (expression2) : (expression3)
```

This line is read as "If *expression1* is true, return the value of *expression2*; otherwise, return the value of *expression3*." Typically, this value is assigned to a variable. Listing 5.9 shows an `if` statement rewritten using the conditional operator.

5

LISTING 5.9   A Demonstration of the Conditional Operator

```
1:  // Listing 5.9 - demonstrates the conditional operator
2:  //
3:  #include <iostream>
4:  int main()
5:  {
6:     using namespace std;
7:
8:     int x, y, z;
9:     cout << "Enter two numbers.\n";
10:    cout << "First: ";
11:    cin >> x;
12:    cout << "\nSecond: ";
13:    cin >> y;
14:    cout << "\n";
15:
16:    if (x > y)
17:       z = x;
18:    else
19:       z = y;
20:
21:    cout << "After if test, z: " << z;
22:    cout << "\n";
23:
24:    z =  (x > y) ? x : y;
25:
26:    cout << "After conditional test, z: " << z;
27:    cout << "\n";
28:    return 0;
29: }
```

Output ▼

```
Enter two numbers.
First: 5

Second: 8

After if test, z: 8
After conditional test, z: 8
```

Analysis ▼

Three integer variables are created: x, y, and z. The first two are given values by the user. The if statement on line 16 tests to see which is larger and assigns the larger value to z. This value is printed on line 21.

The conditional operator on line 24 makes the same test and assigns z the larger value. It is read like this: "If x is greater than y, return the value of x; otherwise, return the value of y." The value returned is assigned to z. That value is printed on line 26. As you can see, the conditional statement is a shorter equivalent to the if...else statement.

Summary

In this lesson, you have learned what C++ statements and expressions are, what C++ operators do, and how C++ if statements work. You have seen that a block of statements enclosed by a pair of braces can be used anywhere a single statement can be used.

You have learned that every expression evaluates to a value, and that value can be tested in an if statement or by using the conditional operator. You've also seen how to evaluate multiple statements using the logical operator, how to compare values using the relational operators, and how to assign values using the assignment operator.

You have explored operator precedence. And you have seen how parentheses can be used to change the precedence and to make precedence explicit, and thus easier to manage.

Q&A

Q Why use unnecessary parentheses when precedence will determine which operators are acted on first?

A It is true that the compiler will know the precedence and that a programmer can look up the precedence order. Using parentheses, however, makes your code easier to understand, and therefore easier to maintain.

Q If the relational operators always return true or false, why is any nonzero value considered true?

A This convention was inherited from the C language, which was frequently used for writing low-level software, such as operating systems and real-time control software. It is likely that this usage evolved as a shortcut for testing if all the bits in a mask or variable are 0.

The relational operators return true or false, but every expression returns a value, and those values can also be evaluated in an if statement. Here's an example:

```
if ( (x = a + b) == 35 )
```

This is a perfectly legal C++ statement. It evaluates to a value even if the sum of a and b is not equal to 35. Also note that x is assigned the value that is the sum of a and b in any case.

5

Q What effect do tabs, spaces, and new lines have on the program?

A Tabs, spaces, and new lines (known as *whitespace*) have no effect on the program, although judicious use of whitespace can make the program easier to read.

Q Are negative numbers true or false?

A All nonzero numbers, positive and negative, are true.

Workshop

The Workshop provides quiz questions to help you solidify your understanding of the material covered and exercises to provide you with experience in using what you've learned. Try to answer the quiz and exercise questions before checking the answers in Appendix D, and be certain that you understand the answers before continuing to the next lesson.

Quiz

1. What is an expression?

2. Is x = 5 + 7 an expression? What is its value?

3. What is the value of 201/4?

4. What is the value of 201%4?

5. If myAge, a, and b are all int variables, what are their values after
    ```
    myAge = 39;
    a = myAge++;
    b = ++myAge;
    ```

6. What is the value of 8+2*3?

7. What is the difference between if(x = 3) and if(x == 3)?

8. Do the following values evaluate to true or false?

    A. 0

    B. 1

    C. -1

    D. x = 0

    E. x == 0 // assume that x has the value of 0

Exercises

1. Write a single `if` statement that examines two integer variables and changes the larger to the smaller, using only one `else` clause.

2. Examine the following program. Imagine entering three numbers, and write what output you expect.

```
1:    #include <iostream>
2:    using namespace std;
3:    int main()
4:    {
5:        int a, b, c;
6:        cout << "Please enter three numbers\n";
7:        cout << "a: ";
8:        cin >> a;
9:        cout << "\nb: ";
10:       cin >> b;
11:       cout << "\nc: ";
12:       cin >> c;
13:
14:       if (c = (a-b))
15:           cout << "a: " << a << " minus b: " << b <<
16:                              _" equals c: " << c;
17:       else
18:           cout << "a-b does not equal c: ";
19:    return 0;
20: }
```

3. Enter the program from Exercise 2; compile, link, and run it. Enter the numbers 20, 10, and 50. Did you get the output you expected? Why not?

4. Examine this program and anticipate the output:

```
1:    #include <iostream>
2:    using namespace std;
3:    int main()
4:    {
5:        int a = 2, b = 2, c;
6:        if (c = (a-b))
7:            cout << "The value of c is: " << c;
8:        return 0;
9:    }
```

5. Enter, compile, link, and run the program from Exercise 4. What was the output? Why?

5

LESSON 6
Organizing Code with Functions

Although object-oriented programming has shifted attention from functions and toward objects, functions nonetheless remain a central component of any program. Global functions can exist outside of objects and classes, and member functions (sometimes called *member methods*) exist within a class and do its work.

In this lesson, you will learn

- What a function is and what its parts are
- How to declare and define functions
- How to pass parameters into functions
- How to return a value from a function

You'll start with global functions in this lesson, and in Lesson 10, "Classes and Objects," you'll see how functions work from within classes and objects as well.

What Is a Function?

A function is, in effect, a subprogram that can act on data and return a value. Every C++ program has at least one function: main(). When your program starts, the main() function is called automatically. main() might call other functions, some of which might call still others.

Because these functions are not part of an object, they are called *global*—that is, they can be accessed from anywhere in your program. For today, you will learn about global functions unless it is otherwise noted.

Each function has its own name, and when that name is encountered, the execution of the program branches to the body of that function. This is referred to as *calling* the function. When the function finishes (through encountering a return statement or the final brace of the function), execution resumes on the next line of the calling function. This flow is illustrated in Figure 6.1.

FIGURE 6.1
When a program calls a function, execution switches to the function and then resumes at the line after the function call.

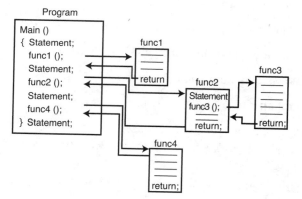

Well-designed functions perform a single, specific, and easily understood task, identified by the function name. Complicated tasks should be broken down into multiple functions, and then each can be called in turn.

Functions come in two varieties: user-defined and built-in. Built-in functions are part of your compiler package—they are supplied by the manufacturer for your use. User-defined functions are the functions you write yourself.

Return Values, Parameters, and Arguments

As you learned on Lesson 2, "The Anatomy of a C++ Program," functions can receive values and can *return* a value. When you call a function, it can do work and then send back a value as a result of that work. This is called its *return value*, and the type of that return value must be declared. Thus, if you write

```
int myFunction();
```

you are declaring a function called myFunction that will return an integer value. Now consider the following declaration:

```
int myFunction(int someValue, float someFloat);
```

This declaration indicates that myFunction will still return an integer, but it will also take two values.

When you send values *into* a function, these values act as variables that you can manipulate from within the function. The description of the values you send is called a *parameter list*. In the previous example, the parameter list contains someValue that is a variable of type integer and someFloat that is a variable of type float.

As you can see, a parameter describes the type of the value that will be passed into the function when the function is called. The actual values you pass into the function are called the *arguments*. Consider the following:

```
int theValueReturned = myFunction(5,6.7);
```

Here you see that an integer variable theValueReturned is initialized with the value returned by myFunction, and that the values 5 and 6.7 are passed in as arguments. The type of the arguments must match the declared parameter types. In this case, the 5 goes to an integer and the 6.7 goes to a float variable, so the values match.

Declaring and Defining Functions

Using functions in your program requires that you first declare the function and that you then define the function. The declaration tells the compiler the name, return type, and parameters of the function. The definition tells the compiler how the function works.

No function can be called from any other function if it hasn't first been declared. A declaration of a function is called a *prototype*.

6

Three ways exist to declare a function:

- Write your prototype into a file, and then use the `#include` directive to include it in your program.
- Write the prototype into the file in which your function is used.
- Define the function before it is called by any other function. When you do this, the definition acts as its own prototype.

Although you can define the function before using it, and thus avoid the necessity of creating a function prototype, this is not good programming practice for three reasons. First, it is a bad idea to require that functions appear in a file in a particular order. Doing so makes it hard to maintain the program when requirements change.

Second, it is possible that function `A()` needs to be able to call function `B()`, but function `B()` also needs to be able to call function `A()` under some circumstances. It is not possible to define function `A()` before you define function `B()` and also to define function `B()` before you define function `A()`, so at least one of them must be declared in any case.

Third, function prototypes are a good and powerful debugging technique. If your prototype declares that your function takes a particular set of parameters or that it returns a particular type of value, and then your function does not match the prototype, the compiler can flag your error instead of waiting for it to show itself when you run the program. This is like double-entry bookkeeping. The prototype and the definition check each other, reducing the likelihood that a simple typo will lead to a bug in your program.

Despite this, the vast majority of programmers select the third option. This is because of the reduction in the number of lines of code, the simplification of maintenance (changes to the function header also require changes to the prototype), and the order of functions in a file is usually fairly stable. At the same time, prototypes are required in some situations.

Function Prototypes

Many of the built-in functions you use will have their function prototypes already written for you. These appear in the files you include in your program by using `#include`. For functions you write yourself, you must include the prototype.

The function prototype is a statement, which means it ends with a semicolon. It consists of the function's return type and signature. A function signature is its name and parameter list.

The parameter list is a list of all the parameters and their types, separated by commas. Figure 6.2 illustrates the parts of the function prototype.

FIGURE 6.2
Parts of a function prototype.

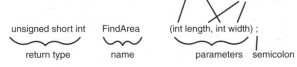

The function prototype and the function definition must agree exactly about the return type and signature. If they do not agree, you receive a compile-time error. Note, however, that the function prototype does not need to contain the names of the parameters, just their types. A prototype that looks like this is perfectly legal:

```
long Area(int, int);
```

This prototype declares a function named `Area()` that returns a `long` and that has two parameters, both integers. Although this is legal, it is not a good idea. Adding parameter names makes your prototype clearer. The same function with named parameters might be

```
long Area(int length, int width);
```

It is now much more obvious what this function does and what the parameters are.

Note that all functions have a return type. If none is explicitly stated, the return type defaults to `int`. Your programs will be easier to understand, however, if you explicitly declare the return type of every function, including `main()`.

When you don't want your function to return a value, you declare its return type to be `void`, as shown here:

```
void printNumber( int myNumber);
```

This declares a function called `printNumber` that has one integer parameter. Because `void` is used as the return type, nothing is returned.

Defining the Function

The definition of a function consists of the function header and its body. The header is like the function prototype except that the parameters must be named, and no terminating semicolon is used.

The body of the function is a set of statements enclosed in braces. Figure 6.3 shows the header and body of a function.

Listing 6.1 demonstrates a program that includes a function prototype for the `Area()` function.

6

FIGURE 6.3
The header and
body of a function.

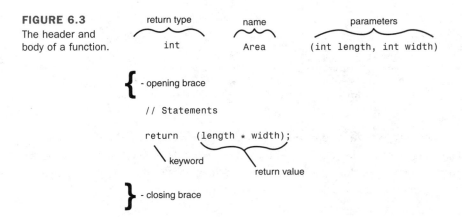

LISTING 6.1   A Function Declaration and the Definition and Use of That Function

```
1:  // Listing 6.1 - demonstrates the use of function prototypes
2:
3:  #include <iostream>
4:  int Area(int length, int width); //function prototype
5:
6:  int main()
7:  {
8:      using std::cout;
9:      using std::cin;
10:
11:     int lengthOfYard = 0;
12:     int widthOfYard = 0;
13:     int areaOfYard = 0;
14:
15:     cout << "\nHow wide is your yard? ";
16:     cin >> widthOfYard;
17:     cout << "\nHow long is your yard? ";
18:     cin >> lengthOfYard;
19:
20:     areaOfYard= Area(lengthOfYard, widthOfYard);
21:
22:     cout << "\nYour yard is ";
23:     cout << areaOfYard;
24:     cout << " square feet\n\n";
25:     return 0;
26:  }
27:
28:  int Area(int len, int wid)
29:  {
30:      return len * wid;
31:  }
```

Output ▼

```
How wide is your yard? 100
How long is your yard? 200
Your yard is 20000 square feet
```

Analysis ▼

The prototype for the Area() function is on line 4. Compare the prototype with the definition of the function on line 28. Note that the name, the return type, and the parameter types are the same. If they were different, a compiler error would have been generated. In fact, the only required difference is that the function prototype ends with a semicolon and has no body.

Also note that the parameter names in the prototype are length and width, but the parameter names in the definition are len and wid. As discussed, the names in the prototype are not used; they are there as information to the programmer. It is good programming practice to match the prototype parameter names to the implementation parameter names, but as this listing shows, this is not required.

The arguments are passed in to the function in the order in which the parameters are declared and defined, but no matching of the names occurs. Had you passed in widthOfYard, followed by lengthOfYard, the FindArea() function would have used the value in widthOfYard for length and lengthOfYard for width.

NOTE	Braces always enclose the body of the function, even when it consists of only one statement, as in this case.

Execution of Functions

6

When you call a function, execution begins with the first statement after the opening brace ({). Branching can be accomplished by using the if statement. (The if and other related statements will be discussed on Lesson 7, "Controlling Program Flow.") Functions can also call other functions and can even call themselves (see the section "Recursion," later in this lesson).

When a function finishes executing, control returns to the calling function. When the main() function finishes, control returns to the operating system.

Determining Variable Scope

A variable has scope, which determines how long it is available to your program and where it can be accessed. Variables declared within a block are scoped to that block; they can be accessed only within that block's braces and go out of existence when that block ends. Global variables have global scope and are available anywhere within your program.

Local Variables

Not only can you pass in variables to the function, but you can also declare variables within the body of the function. Variables you declare within the body of the function are called *local* because they only exist locally, within the function itself. When the function returns, the local variables are no longer available; they are marked for destruction by the compiler.

Local variables are defined the same as any other variables. The parameters passed in to the function are also considered local variables and can be used exactly as if they had been defined within the body of the function. Listing 6.2 is an example of using parameters and locally defined variables within a function.

LISTING 6.2   The Use of Local Variables and Parameters

```
 1:  #include <iostream>
 2:
 3:  float Convert(float);
 4:  int main()
 5:  {
 6:     using namespace std;
 7:
 8:     float TempFer;
 9:     float TempCel;
10:
11:     cout << "Please enter the temperature in Fahrenheit: ";
12:     cin >> TempFer;
13:     TempCel = Convert(TempFer);
14:     cout << "\nHere's the temperature in Celsius: ";
15:     cout << TempCel << endl;
16:     return 0;
17:  }
18:
19:  float Convert(float TempFer)
20:  {
21:     float TempCel;
22:     TempCel = ((TempFer - 32) * 5) / 9;
23:     return TempCel;
24:  }
```

Output ▼

```
Please enter the temperature in Fahrenheit: 212

Here's the temperature in Celsius: 100

Please enter the temperature in Fahrenheit: 32

Here's the temperature in Celsius: 0

Please enter the temperature in Fahrenheit: 85

Here's the temperature in Celsius: 29.4444
```

Analysis ▼

On lines 8 and 9, two `float` variables are declared, one to hold the temperature in Fahrenheit and one to hold the temperature in Celsius. The user is prompted to enter a Fahrenheit temperature on line 11, and that value is passed to the function `Convert()` on line 13.

With the call of `Convert()` on line 13, execution jumps to the first line of the `Convert()` function on line 21, where a local variable, also named `TempCel`, is declared. Note that this local variable is not the same as the variable `TempCel` on line 9. This variable exists only within the function `Convert()`. The value passed as a parameter, `TempFer`, is also just a local copy of the variable passed in by `main()`.

This function could have named the parameter and local variable anything else and the program would have worked equally well. `FerTemp` instead of `TempFer` or `CelTemp` instead of `TempCel` would be just as valid and the function would have worked the same. You can enter these different names and recompile the program to see this work.

The local function variable `TempCel` is assigned the value that results from subtracting 32 from the parameter `TempFer`, multiplying by 5, and then dividing by 9. This value is then returned as the return value of the function. On line 13, this return value is assigned to the variable `TempCel` in the `main()` function. The value is printed on line 15.

The preceding output shows that the program was run three times. The first time, the value `212` is passed in to ensure that the boiling point of water in degrees Fahrenheit (`212`) generates the correct answer in degrees Celsius (`100`). The second test is the freezing point of water. The third test is a random number chosen to generate a fractional result.

6

Local Variables Within Blocks

You can define variables anywhere within the function, not just at its top. The scope of the variable is the block in which it is defined. Thus, if you define a variable inside a set of braces within the function, that variable is available only within that block. Listing 6.3 illustrates this idea.

LISTING 6.3   Variables Scoped Within a Block

```
1:  // Listing 6.3 - demonstrates variables
2:  // scoped within a block
3:
4:  #include <iostream>
5:
6:  void myFunc();
7:
8:  int main()
9:  {
10:     int x = 5;
11:     std::cout << "\nIn main x is: " << x;
12:
13:     myFunc();
14:
15:     std::cout << "\nBack in main, x is: " << x;
16:     return 0;
17:  }
18:
19:  void myFunc()
20:  {
21:     int x = 8;
22:     std::cout << "\nIn myFunc, local x: " << x << std::endl;
23:
24:     {
25:        std::cout << "\nIn block in myFunc, x is: " << x;
26:
27:        int x = 9;
28:
29:        std::cout << "\nVery local x: " << x;
30:     }
31:
32:     std::cout << "\nOut of block, in myFunc, x: " << x << std::endl;
33:  }
```

Output ▼

```
In main x is: 5
In myFunc, local x: 8

In block in myFunc, x is: 8
Very local x: 9
Out of block, in myFunc, x: 8
Back in main, x is: 5
```

Analysis ▼

This program begins with the initialization of a local variable, x, on line 10, in main(). The printout on line 11 verifies that x was initialized with the value 5. On line 13, MyFunc() is called.

On line 21 within MyFunc(), a local variable, also named x, is initialized with the value 8. Its value is printed on line 22.

The opening brace on line 24 starts a block. The variable x from the function is printed again on line 25. A new variable also named x, but local to the block, is created on line 27 and initialized with the value 9. The value of this newest variable x is printed on line 29. The local block ends on line 30, and the variable created on line 27 goes out of scope and is no longer visible.

When x is printed on line 32, it is the x that was declared on line 21 within myFunc(). This x was unaffected by the x that was defined on line 27 in the block; its value is still 8.

On line 33, MyFunc() goes out of scope, and its local variable x becomes unavailable. Execution returns to line 14. On line 15, the value of the local variable x, which was created on line 10, is printed. It was unaffected by either of the variables defined in MyFunc(). Needless to say, this program would be far less confusing if these three variables were given unique names!

6

Parameters Are Local Variables

The arguments passed in to the function are local to the function. Changes made to the arguments do not affect the values in the calling function. This is known as passing *by value*, which means a local copy of each argument is made in the function. These local copies are treated the same as any other local variables. Listing 6.4 illustrates this important point.

LISTING 6.4   A Demonstration of Passing by Value

```
1:  // Listing 6.4 - demonstrates passing by value
2:  #include <iostream>
3:
4:  using namespace std;
5:  void swap(int x, int y);
6:
7:  int main()
8:  {
9:      int x = 5, y = 10;
10:
11:     cout << "Main. Before swap, x: " << x << " y: " << y << endl;
12:     swap(x,y);
13:     cout << "Main. After swap, x: " << x << " y: " << y << endl;
14:     return 0;
15: }
16:
17: void swap (int x, int y)
18: {
19:     int temp;
20:
21:     cout << "Swap. Before swap, x: " << x << " y: " << y << endl;
22:
23:     temp = x;
24:     x = y;
25:     y = temp;
26:
27:     cout << "Swap. After swap, x: " << x << " y: " << y << endl;
28: }
```

Output ▼

```
Main. Before swap, x: 5 y: 10
Swap. Before swap, x: 5 y: 10
Swap. After swap, x: 10 y: 5
Main. After swap, x: 5 y: 10
```

Analysis ▼

This program initializes two variables in main() and then passes them to the swap() function, which appears to swap them. When they are examined again in main(), however, they are unchanged!

The variables are initialized on line 9, and their values are displayed on line 11. The swap() function is called on line 12, and the variables are passed in.

Execution of the program switches to the swap() function where, on line 21, the values are printed again. They are in the same order as they were in main(), as expected. On lines 23–25, the values are swapped, and this action is confirmed by the printout on line 27. Indeed, while in the swap() function, the values are swapped. Execution then returns to line 13, back in main(), where the values are no longer swapped.

As you've figured out, the values passed in to the swap() function are passed by value, meaning that copies of the values are made that are local to swap(). These local variables are swapped on lines 23–25, but the variables back in main() are unaffected.

In Lesson 8, "Pointers Explained," you'll see alternatives to passing by value that will allow the values in main() to be changed.

Global Variables

Variables defined outside any function have global scope, and thus are available from any function in the program, including main(). Local variables with the same name as global variables do not change the global variables. A local variable with the same name as a global variable *hides* the global variable, however. If a function has a variable with the same name as a global variable, the name refers to the local variable—not the global—when used within the function. Listing 6.5 illustrates these points.

LISTING 6.5   Demonstrating Global and Local Variables

```
1:  #include <iostream>
2:  void myFunction();          // prototype
3:
4:  int x = 5, y = 7;          // global variables
5:  int main()
6:  {
7:     using namespace std;
8:
9:     cout << "x from main: " << x << endl;
10:    cout << "y from main: " << y << endl << endl;
11:    myFunction();
12:    cout << "Back from myFunction!" << endl << endl;
13:    cout << "x from main: " << x << endl;
14:    cout << "y from main: " << y << endl;
15:    return 0;
16:  }
17:
18:  void myFunction()
19:  {
20:     using std::cout;
21:
22:     int y = 10;
23:
24:     cout << "x from myFunction: " << x << std::endl;
25:     cout << "y from myFunction: " << y << std::endl << std::endl;
26:  }
```

6

Output ▼

```
x from main: 5
y from main: 7

x from myFunction: 5
y from myFunction: 10

Back from myFunction!

x from main: 5
y from main: 7
```

Analysis ▼

This simple program illustrates a few key, and potentially confusing, points about local and global variables. On line 4, two global variables, x and y, are declared. The global variable x is initialized with the value 5, and the global variable y is initialized with the value 7.

On lines 9 and 10 in the function main(), these values are printed to the console. Note that the function main() defines neither variable; because they are global, they are already available to main().

When myFunction() is called on line 11, program execution passes to line 18. On line 22, a local variable, y, is defined and initialized with the value 10. On line 24, myFunction() prints the value of the variable x, and the global variable x is used, just as it was in main(). On line 25, however, when the variable name y is used, the *local* variable y is used, hiding the global variable with the same name.

The function call ends and control returns to main(), which again prints the values in the global variables. Note that the global variable y was totally unaffected by the value assigned to myFunction()'s local y variable.

Global Variables: A Word of Caution

In C++, global variables are legal, but they are almost never used. C++ grew out of C, and in C, global variables are a dangerous but necessary tool. They are necessary because at times the programmer needs to make data available to many functions, and it is cumbersome to pass that data as a parameter from function to function, especially when many of the functions in the calling sequence only receive the parameter to pass it on to other functions.

Globals are dangerous because they are shared data, and one function can change a global variable in a way that is invisible to another function. This can and does create bugs that are very difficult to find.

Considerations for Creating Function Statements

Virtually no limit exists to the number or types of statements that can be placed in the body of a function. Although you can't define another function from within a function, you can *call* a function, and of course, `main()` does just that in nearly every C++ program. Functions can even call themselves, which is discussed soon in the section on recursion.

Although no limit exists to the size of a function in C++, well-designed functions tend to be small. Many programmers advise keeping your functions short enough to fit on a single screen so that you can see the entire function at one time. This is a rule of thumb often broken by very good programmers, but it is true that a smaller function is easier to understand and maintain than a larger one.

Each function should carry out a single, easily understood task. If your functions start getting large, look for places where you can divide them into component tasks.

More About Function Arguments

Any valid C++ expression can be a function argument, including constants, mathematical and logical expressions, and other functions that return a value. The important thing is that the result of the expression matches the argument type expected by the function.

It is even valid for a function to be passed as an argument. After all, the function will evaluate to its return type. Using a function as an argument, however, can make for code that is hard to read and hard to debug.

As an example, suppose that you have the functions `myDouble()`, `triple()`, `square()`, and `cube()`, each of which returns a value. You could write

```
Answer = (myDouble(triple(square(cube(myValue)))));
```

You can look at this statement in two ways. First, you can see that the function `myDouble()` takes the function `triple()` as an argument. In turn, `triple()` takes the function `square()`, which takes the function `cube()` as its argument. The `cube()` function takes the variable, `myValue`, as its argument.

Looking at this from the other direction, you can see that this statement takes a variable, `myValue`, and passes it as an argument to the function `cube()`, whose return value is passed as an argument to the function `square()`, whose return value is in turn passed to `triple()`, and that return value is passed to `myDouble()`. The return value of this doubled, tripled, squared, and cubed number is assigned to `Answer`.

6

It is difficult to be certain what this code does (was the value tripled before or after it was squared?), and if the answer is wrong, it will be hard to figure out which function failed. An alternative is to assign each step to its own intermediate variable:

```
unsigned long myValue = 2;
unsigned long cubed   = cube(myValue);      // cubed = 8
unsigned long squared = square(cubed);      // squared = 64
unsigned long tripled = triple(squared);    // tripled = 192
unsigned long Answer  = myDouble(tripled);  // Answer = 384
```

Now each intermediate result can be examined, and the order of execution is explicit.

CAUTION

> C++ makes it really easy to write compact code like the preceding example used to combine the cube(), square(), triple(), and myDouble() functions. Just because you *can* make compact code does not mean you *should*. It is better to make your code easier to read, and thus more maintainable, than to make it as compact as you can.

More About Return Values

Functions return a value or return void. void is a signal to the compiler that no value will be returned.

To return a value from a function, write the keyword return followed by the value you want to return. The value might itself be an expression that returns a value. For example:

```
return 5;             // returns a number
return (x > 5);       // returns the result of a comparison
return (MyFunction()); // returns the value returned by calling another
➥function
```

These are all legal return statements, assuming that the function MyFunction() itself returns a value. The value in the second statement, return (x > 5), will be false if x is not greater than 5 or it will be true. What is returned is the value of the expression, false or true, not the value of x.

When the return keyword is encountered, the expression following return is returned as the value of the function. Program execution returns immediately to the calling function, and any statements following the return are not executed.

It is legal to have more than one return statement in a single function. Listing 6.6 illustrates this idea.

LISTING 6.6   A Demonstration of Multiple return Statements

```
1:   // Listing 6.6 - demonstrates multiple return
2:   // statements
3:   #include <iostream>
4:
5:   int Doubler(int AmountToDouble);
6:
7:   int main()
8:   {
9:      using std::cout;
10:
11:     int result = 0;
12:     int input;
13:
14:     cout << "Enter a number between 0 and 10,000 to double: ";
15:     std::cin >> input;
16:
17:     cout << "\nBefore doubler is called... ";
18:     cout << "\ninput: " << input << " doubled: " << result << "\n";
19:
20:     result = Doubler(input);
21:
22:     cout << "\nBack from Doubler...\n";
23:     cout << "\ninput: " << input << "   doubled: " << result << "\n";
24:
25:     return 0;
26:  }
27:
28:  int Doubler(int original)
29:  {
30:     if (original <= 10000)
31:        return original * 2;
32:     else
33:        return -1;
34:     std::cout << "You can't get here!\n";
35:  }
```

Output ▼

```
Enter a number between 0 and 10,000 to double: 9000

Before doubler is called...
input: 9000 doubled: 0

Back from doubler...

input: 9000    doubled: 18000

Enter a number between 0 and 10,000 to double: 11000
```

6

```
Before doubler is called...
input: 11000 doubled: 0

Back from doubler...
input: 11000  doubled: -1
```

Analysis ▼

A number is requested on lines 14 and 15 and printed on lines 17 and 18, along with the local variable `result`. The function `Doubler()` is called on line 20, and the `input` value is passed as a parameter. The result will be assigned to the local variable, `result`, and the values will be reprinted on line 23.

On line 30, in the function `Doubler()`, the parameter is tested to see whether it is less than or equal to 10,000. If it is, the function returns twice the original number. If the value of `original` is greater than 10,000, the function returns –1 as an error value.

The statement on line 34 is never reached because regardless of whether the value is less than or equal to 10,000 or greater than 10,000, the function returns on either line 31 or line 33—before it gets to line 34. A good compiler warns that this statement cannot be executed, and a good programmer takes it out!

FAQ

What is the difference between int `main()` and void `main()`; which one should I use? I have used both and they both worked fine, so why do I need to use int `main(){ return 0;}`?

Answer: Both may work on most compilers, but only int `main()` is ANSI compliant, and thus only int `main()` is correct and guaranteed to continue working.

Here's the difference: int `main()` returns a value to the operating system. When your program completes, that value can be captured by, for example, batch programs or an application that invokes your application to check its return value (that is, exit code) for success or failure.

Although programs in this book don't use the return value from `main`, the ANSI standard requires us to declare the main function returning an int, and we consciously chose to remain compliant!

Default Parameters

For every parameter you declare in a function prototype and definition, the calling function must pass in a value. The value passed in must be of the declared type. Thus, if you have a function declared as

```
long myFunction(int);
```

the function must, in fact, take an integer variable. If the function definition differs or if you fail to pass in an integer, you receive a compiler error.

The one exception to this rule is if the function prototype declares a default value for the parameter. A *default value* is a value to use if none is supplied. The preceding declaration could be rewritten as

```
long myFunction (int x = 50);
```

This prototype says, "myFunction() returns a long and takes an integer parameter. If an argument is not supplied, use the default value of 50." Because parameter names are not required in function prototypes, this declaration could have been written as

```
long myFunction (int = 50);
```

The function definition is not changed by declaring a default parameter. The function definition header for this function would be

```
long myFunction (int x)
```

If the calling function did not include a parameter, the compiler would fill x with the default value of 50. The name of the default parameter in the prototype need not be the same as the name in the function header; the default value is assigned by position, not name.

Any of or all the function's parameters can be assigned default values. The one restriction is this: If any parameter does not have a default value, no previous parameter can have a default value.

If the function prototype looks like

```
long myFunction (int Param1, int Param2, int Param3);
```

you can assign a default value to Param2 only if you have assigned a default value to Param3. You can assign a default value to Param1 only if you've assigned default values to both Param2 and Param3. Listing 6.7 demonstrates the use of default values.

6

LISTING 6.7   A Demonstration of Default Parameter Values

```
1:  // Listing 6.7 - demonstrates use
2:  // of default parameter values
3:  #include <iostream>
4:
5:  int AreaCube(int length, int width = 25, int height = 1);
6:
7:  int main()
8:  {
9:      int length = 100;
10:     int width = 50;
11:     int height = 2;
12:     int area;
13:
14:     area = AreaCube(length, width, height);
15:     std::cout << "First area equals: " << area << "\n";
16:
17:     area = AreaCube(length, width);
18:     std::cout << "Second time area equals: " << area << "\n";
19:
20:     area = AreaCube(length);
21:     std::cout << "Third time area equals: " << area << "\n";
22:     return 0;
23:  }
24:
25:  int AreaCube(int length, int width, int height)
26:  {
27:
28:      return (length * width * height);
29:  }
```

Output ▼

```
First area equals: 10000
Second time area equals: 5000
Third time area equals: 2500
```

Analysis ▼

On line 5, the AreaCube() prototype specifies that the AreaCube() function takes three integer parameters. The last two have default values.

This function computes the area of the cube whose dimensions are passed in. If no width is passed in, a width of 25 is used and a height of 1 is used. If the width but not the height is passed in, a height of 1 is used. It is not possible to pass in the height without passing in a width.

On lines 9–11, the dimension's length, height, and width are initialized, and they are passed to the `AreaCube()` function on line 14. The values are computed, and the result is printed on line 15.

Execution continues to line 17, where `AreaCube()` is called again, but with no value for height. The default value is used, and again the dimensions are computed and printed.

Execution then continues to line 20, and this time neither the width nor the height is passed in. With this call to `AreaCube()`, execution branches for a third time to line 25. The default values are used and the area is computed. Control returns to the `main()` function where the final value is then printed.

DO	DON'T
DO remember that function parameters act as local variables within the function.	**DON'T** try to create a default value for a first parameter if no default value exists for the second.
DO remember that changes to a global variable in one function change that variable for all functions.	**DON'T** forget that arguments passed by value cannot affect the variables in the calling function.

Overloading Functions

C++ enables you to create more than one function with the same name. This is called *function overloading*. The functions must differ in their parameter list with a different type of parameter, a different number of parameters, or both. Here's an example:

```
int myFunction (int, int);
int myFunction (long, long);
int myFunction (long);
```

`myFunction()` is overloaded with three parameter lists. The first and second versions differ in the types of the parameters, and the third differs in the number of parameters.

The return types can be the same or different on overloaded functions. However, overloaded versions of functions cannot differ only in return type; that is, they should also accept a uniquely different set of arguments:

```
int myFunction (int);
void myFunction (int);          // illegal - as it differs only in return type
void myFunction (long);      // OK!
void myFunction (long, long);    // OK!
int myFunction (long, long);     // illegal - as it differs only in return type
int myFunction (long, int);      // OK!
int myFunction (int, long);      // OK!
```

6

As you can see, it is important that an overloaded version of a function presents a unique signature in terms of the type of arguments it accepts.

NOTE   Two functions with the same name and parameter list, but different return types, generate a compiler error. To change the return type, you must also change the signature (name and/or parameter list).

Function overloading is also called *function polymorphism*. *Poly* means many, and *morph* means form: A polymorphic function is many-formed.

Function polymorphism refers to the capability to overload a function with more than one meaning. By changing the number or type of the parameters, you can give two or more functions the same function name, and the right one will be called automatically by matching the parameters used. This enables you to create a function that can average integers, `doubles`, and other values without having to create individual names for each function, such as `AverageInts()`, `AverageDoubles()`, and so on.

Suppose that you write a function that doubles whatever input you give it. You would like to be able to pass in an `int`, a `long`, a `float`, or a `double`. Without function overloading, you would have to create four function names:

```
int DoubleInt(int);
long DoubleLong(long);
float DoubleFloat(float);
double DoubleDouble(double);
```

With function overloading, you make this declaration:

```
int Double(int);
long Double(long);
float Double(float);
double Double(double);
```

The second version is easier to read and easier to use. You don't have to worry about which one to call; you just pass in a variable, and the right function is called automatically. Listing 6.8 illustrates the use of function overloading.

LISTING 6.8   A Demonstration of Function Polymorphism

```
1:  // Listing 6.8  - demonstrates
2:  // function polymorphism
3:  #include <iostream>
4:
```

LISTING 6.8   Continued

```
 5:  int Double(int);
 6:  long Double(long);
 7:  float Double(float);
 8:  double Double(double);
 9:
10:  using namespace std;
11:
12:  int main()
13:  {
14:     int     myInt = 6500;
15:     long    myLong = 65000;
16:     float   myFloat = 6.5F;
17:     double  myDouble = 6.5e20;
18:
19:     int     doubledInt;
20:     long    doubledLong;
21:     float   doubledFloat;
22:     double  doubledDouble;
23:
24:     cout << "myInt: " << myInt << "\n";
25:     cout << "myLong: " << myLong << "\n";
26:     cout << "myFloat: " << myFloat << "\n";
27:     cout << "myDouble: " << myDouble << "\n";
28:
29:     doubledInt = Double(myInt);
30:     doubledLong = Double(myLong);
31:     doubledFloat = Double(myFloat);
32:     doubledDouble = Double(myDouble);
33:
34:     cout << "doubledInt: " << doubledInt << "\n";
35:     cout << "doubledLong: " << doubledLong << "\n";
36:     cout << "doubledFloat: " << doubledFloat << "\n";
37:     cout << "doubledDouble: " << doubledDouble << "\n";
38:
39:     return 0;
40:  }
41:
42:  int Double(int original)
43:  {
44:     cout << "In Double(int)\n";
45:     return 2 * original;
46:  }
47:
48:  long Double(long original)
49:  {
50:     cout << "In Double(long)\n";
51:     return 2 * original;
52:  }
53:
```

6

LISTING 6.8 Continued

```
54:  float Double(float original)
55:  {
56:     cout << "In Double(float)\n";
57:     return 2 * original;
58:  }
59:
60:  double Double(double original)
61:  {
62:     cout << "In Double(double)\n";
63:     return 2 * original;
64:  }
```

Output ▼

```
myInt: 6500
myLong: 65000
myFloat: 6.5
myDouble: 6.5e+20
In Double(int)
In Double(long)
In Double(float)
In Double(double)
DoubledInt: 13000
DoubledLong: 130000
DoubledFloat: 13
DoubledDouble: 1.3e+21
```

Analysis ▼

The Double() function is overloaded with int, long, float, and double. The prototypes are on lines 5–8, and the definitions are on lines 42–64.

Note that in this example, the statement using namespace std; has been added on line 10, outside of any particular function. This makes the statement global to this file, and thus the namespace is used in all the functions declared within this file.

In the body of the main program, eight local variables are declared. On lines 14–17, four of the values are initialized, and on lines 29–32, the other four are assigned the results of passing the first four to the Double() function. When Double() is called, the calling function does not distinguish which one to call; it just passes in an argument, and the correct one is invoked.

The compiler examines the arguments and chooses which of the four Double() functions to call. The output reveals that each of the four was called in turn, as you would expect.

Special Topics About Functions

Because functions are so central to programming, a few special topics arise that might be of interest when you confront unusual problems. Used wisely, inline functions can help you squeak out that last bit of performance. Function recursion is one of those wonderful, esoteric bits of programming, which, every once in a while, can cut through a thorny problem otherwise not easily solved.

Inline Functions

When you define a function, normally the compiler creates just one set of instructions in memory. When you call the function, execution of the program jumps to those instructions, and when the function returns, execution jumps back to the next line in the calling function. If you call the function 10 times, your program jumps to the same set of instructions each time. This means only one copy of the function exists, not 10.

A small performance overhead occurs in jumping in and out of functions. It turns out that some functions are very small, just a line or two of code, and efficiency might be gained if the program can avoid making these jumps just to execute one or two instructions. When programmers speak of efficiency, they usually mean speed; the program runs faster if the function call can be avoided.

If a function is declared with the keyword `inline`, the compiler does not create a real function; it copies the code from the inline function directly into the calling function. No jump is made; it is just as if you had written the statements of the function right into the calling function.

Note that inline functions can bring a heavy cost. If the function is called 10 times, the inline code is copied into the calling functions each of those 10 times. The tiny improvement in speed you might achieve might be more than swamped by the increase in size of the executable program, which might in fact actually slow the program!

The reality is that today's optimizing compilers can almost certainly do a better job of making this decision than you can, so it is generally a good idea not to declare a function as inline unless it is only one or, at most, two statements in length. When in doubt, leave `inline` out. Some compilers might deliberately not inline a function marked by the programmer as inline if the function is way too big and making it inline would result in a significant bloating of the executable being built.

6

NOTE

Performance optimization is a difficult challenge, and most programmers are not good at identifying the location of performance
problems in their programs without help.

The correct way to optimize performance is by studying the behavior of the application using profilers, which can present a variety of
statistics ranging from time spent in a particular function to the
number of times it was invoked. These statistics help programmers focus their efforts on parts of the code that really need
attention rather than using intuition and spending time on code
artifacts that bring little gain.

For this reason, it is always better to write code that is clear and
understandable than to write code that contains your guess about
what will run fast or slow, but is harder to understand. It is often
easier to make understandable code run faster.

Listing 6.9 demonstrates an inline function.

LISTING 6.9   A Demonstration of an Inline Function

```
 1:  // Listing 6.9 - demonstrates inline functions
 2:  #include <iostream>
 3:
 4:  inline int Double(int);
 5:
 6:  int main()
 7:  {
 8:      int target;
 9:      using std::cout;
10:      using std::cin;
11:      using std::endl;
12:
13:      cout << "Enter a number to work with: ";
14:      cin >> target;
15:      cout << "\n";
16:
17:      target = Double(target);
18:      cout << "Target: " << target << endl;
19:
20:      target = Double(target);
21:      cout << "Target: " << target << endl;
22:
23:      target = Double(target);
24:      cout << "Target: " << target << endl;
25:      return 0;
26:  }
27:
```

LISTING 6.9 Continued

```
28:   int Double(int target)
29:   {
30:       return 2*target;
31:   }
```

Output ▼

```
Enter a number to work with: 20

Target: 40
Target: 80
Target: 160
```

Analysis ▼

On line 4, `Double()` is declared to be an inline function taking an `int` parameter and returning an `int`. The declaration is just like any other prototype except that the keyword `inline` is prepended just before the return value. This compiles into code that is the same as if you had written

```
target = 2 * target;
```

everywhere you entered

```
target = Double(target);
```

By the time your program executes, the instructions are already in place, compiled into the `.obj` file. This saves a jump and return in the execution of the code at the cost of a larger program.

NOTE

The `inline` keyword is a hint to the compiler that you want the function to be inlined. The compiler is free to ignore the hint and make a real function call.

6

Recursion

A function can call itself. This is called *recursion*, and recursion can be direct or indirect. It is *direct* recursion when a function calls itself; it is *indirect* recursion when a function calls another function that then calls the first function.

Some problems are most easily solved by recursion, usually those in which you act on data and then act in the same way on the result. Both types of recursion, direct and indirect, come in two varieties: those that eventually end and produce an answer, and those that never end and produce a runtime failure. Programmers think that the latter is quite funny (when it happens to someone else).

It is important to note that when a function calls itself, a new copy of that function is run. The local variables in the second version are independent of the local variables in the first, and they cannot affect one another directly any more than the local variables in main() can affect the local variables in any function it calls, as was illustrated in Listing 6.3.

To illustrate solving a problem using recursion, consider the Fibonacci series:

1,1,2,3,5,8,13,21,34...

Each number, after the second, is the sum of the two numbers before it. A Fibonacci problem might be to determine what the twelfth number in the series is.

To solve this problem, you must examine the series carefully. Each of the first two numbers is a 1. Each subsequent number is the sum of the previous two numbers. Thus, the seventh number is the sum of the sixth and fifth numbers. More generally, the nth number is the sum of n−2 and n−1, as long as n > 2.

Recursive functions need a stop condition. Something must happen to cause the program to stop recursion or it will never end. In the Fibonacci series, n < 3 is a stop condition (that is, when n is less than 3, the program can stop working on the problem).

An *algorithm* is a set of steps you follow to solve a problem. One algorithm for the Fibonacci series is the following:

1. Ask the user for a position in the series.
2. Call the fib() function with that position, passing in the value the user entered.
3. The fib() function examines the argument (*n*). If n < 3, the function returns 1; otherwise, fib() calls itself (recursively) passing in n-2. It then calls itself again passing in n-1, and returns the sum of the first call and the second.

If you call fib(1), it returns 1. If you call fib(2), it returns 1. If you call fib(3), it returns the sum of calling fib(2) and fib(1). Because fib(2) returns 1 and fib(1) returns 1, fib(3) returns 2 (the sum of 1 + 1).

If you call fib(4), it returns the sum of calling fib(3) and fib(2). You just saw that fib(3) returns 2 (by calling fib(2) and fib(1)) and that fib(2) returns 1, so fib(4) sums these numbers and returns 3, which is the fourth number in the series.

Taking this one more step, if you call `fib(5)`, it returns the sum of `fib(4)` and `fib(3)`. You've seen that `fib(4)` returns 3 and `fib(3)` returns 2, so the sum returned is 5.

This method is not the most efficient way to solve this problem (in `fib(20)` the `fib()` function is called 13,529 times!), but it does work. Be careful: If you feed in too large a number, you'll run out of memory. Every time `fib()` is called, memory is set aside. When it returns, memory is freed. With recursion, memory continues to be set aside before it is freed, and this system can eat memory very quickly. Listing 6.10 implements the `fib()` function.

CAUTION   When you run Listing 6.10, note that the input of a bigger number will result in more recursive function calls, and hence in greater memory consumption.

LISTING 6.10   A Demonstration of Recursion Using the Fibonacci Series

```
1:  // Fibonacci series using recursion
2:  #include <iostream>
3:  int fib (int n);
4:
5:  int main()
6:  {
7:
8:      int n, answer;
9:      std::cout << "Enter number to find: ";
10:     std::cin >> n;
11:
12:     std::cout << "\n\n";
13:
14:     answer = fib(n);
15:
16:     std::cout << answer << " is the " << n;
17:         std::cout << "th Fibonacci number\n";
18:     return 0;
19:  }
20:
21:  int fib (int n)
22:  {
23:      std::cout << "Processing fib(" << n << ")... ";
24:
25:      if (n < 3 )
26:      {
27:          std::cout << "Return 1!\n";
28:          return (1);
29:      }
```

6

LISTING 6.10   Continued

```
30:      else
31:      {
32:         std::cout << "Call fib(" << n-2 << ") ";
33:            std::cout << "and fib(" << n-1 << ").\n";
34:         return( fib(n-2) + fib(n-1));
35:      }
36:  }
```

Output ▼

```
Enter number to find: 6

Processing fib(6)... Call fib(4) and fib(5).
Processing fib(4)... Call fib(2) and fib(3).
Processing fib(2)... Return 1!
Processing fib(3)... Call fib(1) and fib(2).
Processing fib(1)... Return 1!
Processing fib(2)... Return 1!
Processing fib(5)... Call fib(3) and fib(4).
Processing fib(3)... Call fib(1) and fib(2).
Processing fib(1)... Return 1!
Processing fib(2)... Return 1!
Processing fib(4)... Call fib(2) and fib(3).
Processing fib(2)... Return 1!
Processing fib(3)... Call fib(1) and fib(2).
Processing fib(1)... Return 1!
Processing fib(2)... Return 1!
8 is the 6th Fibonacci number
```

NOTE   Some compilers have difficulty with the use of operators in a cout statement. If you receive a warning on line 32, place parentheses around the subtraction operation so that lines 32 and 33 become

```
std::cout << "Call fib(" << (n-2) << ") ";
   std::cout << "and fib(" << (n-1) << ").\n";
```

Analysis ▼

The program asks for a number to find on line 9 and assigns that number to n. It then calls fib() with n. Execution branches to the fib() function, where, on line 23, it prints its argument.

The argument n is tested to see whether it is less than 3 on line 25; if so, fib() returns the value 1. Otherwise, it returns the sum of the values returned by calling fib() on n-2 and n-1.

It cannot return these values until the call (to fib()) is resolved. Thus, you can picture the program diving into fib repeatedly until it hits a call to fib that returns a value. The only calls that return a value are the calls to fib(2) and fib(1). These values are then passed up to the waiting callers, which, in turn, add the return value to their own, and then they return. Figures 6.4 and 6.5 illustrate this recursion into fib().

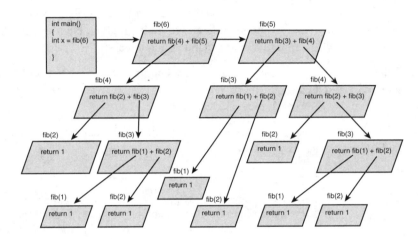

FIGURE 6.4
Using recursion.

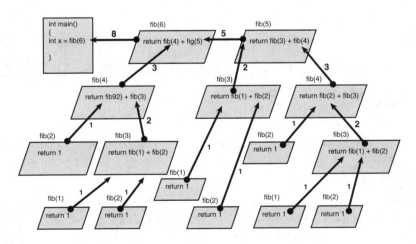

FIGURE 6.5
Returning from recursion.

In the example, n is 6 so fib(6) is called from main(). Execution jumps to the fib() function, and n is tested for a value less than 3 on line 25. The test fails, so fib(6) returns on line 34 the sum of the values returned by fib(4) and fib(5). Look at line 34:

```
return( fib(n-2) + fib(n-1));
```

From this `return` statement a call is made to `fib(4)` (because `n == 6`, `fib(n-2)` is the same as `fib(4)`) and another call is made to `fib(5)` (`fib(n-1)`), and then the function you are in (`fib(6)`) *waits* until these calls return a value. When these calls return a value, this function can return the result of summing those two values.

Because `fib(5)` passes in an argument that is not less than 3, `fib()` is called again, this time with 4 and 3. `fib(4)` in turn calls `fib(3)` and `fib(2)`. The output traces these calls and the return values. Compile, link, and run this program, entering first 1, and then 2, and then 3, building up to 6, and watch the output carefully.

This would be a great time to start experimenting with your debugger. Put a break point on line 21 and then trace *into* each call to `fib`, keeping track of the value of *n* as you work your way into each recursive call to `fib`.

Recursion is not used often in C++ programming, but it can be a powerful and elegant tool for certain needs.

NOTE   Recursion is a tricky part of advanced programming. It is presented here because it can be useful to understand the fundamentals of how it works, but don't worry too much if you don't fully understand all the details.

How Functions Work—A Peek Under the Hood

When you call a function, the code branches to the called function, parameters are passed in, and the body of the function is executed. When the function completes, a value is returned (unless the function returns `void`), and control returns to the calling function.

How is this task accomplished? How does the code know where to branch? Where are the variables kept when they are passed in? What happens to variables declared in the body of the function? How is the return value passed back out? How does the code know where to resume?

The explanation requires a brief tangent into a discussion of computer memory. You can choose to revisit this section later, and continue with the next lesson.

Levels of Abstraction

One of the principal hurdles for new programmers is grappling with the many layers of intellectual abstraction. Computers, of course, are only electronic machines. They don't know about windows and menus, they don't know about programs or instructions, and they don't even know about ones and zeros. All that is really going on is that voltage is being measured at various places on an integrated circuit. Even this is an abstraction: Electricity itself is just an intellectual concept representing the behavior of subatomic particles, which arguably are themselves intellectual abstractions(!).

Few programmers bother with any level of detail below the idea of values in RAM. After all, you don't need to understand particle physics to drive a car, make toast, or hit a baseball, and you don't need to understand the electronics of a computer to program one.

You do need to understand how memory is organized, however. Without a reasonably strong mental picture of where your variables are when they are created and how values are passed among functions, it will all remain an unmanageable mystery.

Partitioning RAM

When you begin your program, your operating system (such as DOS, Linux/UNIX, or Microsoft Windows) sets up various areas of memory based on the requirements of your compiler. As a C++ programmer, you'll often be concerned with the global namespace, the free store, the registers, the code space, and the stack.

Global variables are in global namespace. You'll learn more about global namespace and the free store in coming days, but here, the focus is on the registers, code space, and stack.

Registers are a special area of memory built right into the CPU. They take care of internal housekeeping. A lot of what goes on in the registers is beyond the scope of this book, but what you should be concerned with is the set of registers responsible for pointing, at any given moment, to the next line of code. These registers, together, can be called the *instruction pointer*. It is the job of the instruction pointer to keep track of which line of code is to be executed next.

6

The code itself is in the *code space*, which is that part of memory set aside to hold the binary form of the instructions you created in your program. Each line of source code is translated into a series of instructions, and each of these instructions is at a particular address in memory. The instruction pointer has the address of the next instruction to execute. Figure 6.6 illustrates this idea.

FIGURE 6.6
The instruction
pointer.

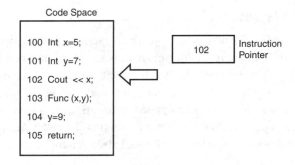

The *stack* is a special area of memory allocated for your program to hold the data required by each of the functions in your program. It is called a stack because it is a last-in, first-out queue, much like a stack of dishes at a cafeteria, as shown in Figure 6.7.

FIGURE 6.7
A stack.

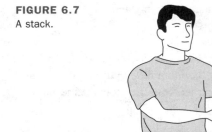

Last-in, first-out means that whatever is added to the stack last is the first thing taken off. This differs from most queues in which the first in is the first out (like a line at a theater: the first one in line is the first one off). A stack is more like a stack of coins: If you stack 10 pennies on a tabletop and then take some back, the last three you put on top are the first three you take off.

When data is *pushed* onto the stack, the stack grows; as data is *popped* off the stack, the stack shrinks. It isn't possible to pop a dish off the stack without first popping off all the dishes placed on after that dish.

A stack of dishes is the common analogy. It is fine as far as it goes, but it is wrong in a fundamental way. A more accurate mental picture is of a series of cubbyholes aligned top to bottom. The top of the stack is whatever cubby the stack pointer (which is another register) happens to be pointing to.

Each cubby has a sequential address, and one of those addresses is kept in the stack pointer register. Everything below that magic address, known as the *top of the stack*, is considered to be on the stack. Everything above the top of the stack is considered to be off the stack and invalid. Figure 6.8 illustrates this idea.

FIGURE 6.8
The stack pointer.

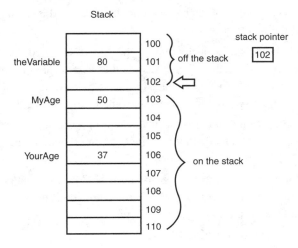

When data is put on the stack, it is placed into a cubby above the stack pointer and the stack pointer is moved to the new data. All that really happens when data is popped off the stack is that the address of the stack pointer is changed by moving it down the stack. Figure 6.9 makes this rule clear.

The data *above* the stack pointer (off the stack) might or might not be changed at any time. These values are referred to as *garbage* because their value is no longer reliable.

FIGURE 6.9
Moving the stack pointer.

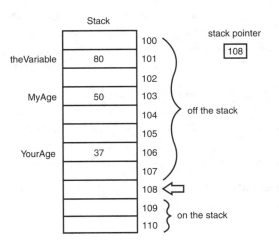

6

The Stack and Functions

The following is an approximation of what happens when your program branches to a function. (The details will differ depending on the operating system and compiler.)

1. The address in the instruction pointer is incremented to the next instruction past the function call. That address is then placed on the stack, and it will be the return address when the function returns.

2. Room is made on the stack for the return type you've declared. On a system with two-byte integers, if the return type is declared to be `int`, another two bytes are added to the stack, but no value is placed in these bytes (that means that whatever garbage was in those two bytes remains until the local variable is initialized).

3. The address of the called function, which is kept in a special area of memory set aside for that purpose, is loaded into the instruction pointer, so the next instruction executed will be in the called function.

4. The current top of the stack is now noted and is held in a special pointer called the *stack frame*. Everything added to the stack from now until the function returns will be considered local to the function.

5. All the arguments to the function are placed on the stack.

6. The instruction now in the instruction pointer is executed, thus executing the first instruction in the function.

7. Local variables are pushed onto the stack as they are defined.

When the function is ready to return, the return value is placed in the area of the stack reserved at step 2. The stack is then popped all the way up to the stack frame pointer, which effectively throws away all the local variables and the arguments to the function.

The return value is popped off the stack and assigned as the value of the function call itself, and the address stashed away in step 1 is retrieved and put into the instruction pointer. The program thus resumes immediately after the function call, with the value of the function retrieved.

Some of the details of this process change from compiler to compiler, or between computer operating system or processors, but the essential ideas are consistent across environments. In general, when you call a function, the return address and the parameters are put on the stack. During the life of the function, local variables are added to the stack. When the function returns, these are all removed by popping the stack.

In Lesson 8 you will learn about other places in memory that are used to hold data that must persist beyond the life of the function.

Summary

This lesson introduced functions. A function is, in effect, a subprogram into which you can pass parameters and from which you can return a value. Every C++ program starts in the `main()` function, and `main()`, in turn, can call other functions.

A function is declared with a function prototype that describes the return value, the function name, and its parameter types. A function can, optionally, be declared inline. A function prototype can also declare default values for one or more of the parameters.

The function definition must match the function prototype in return type, name, and parameter list. Function names can be overloaded by changing the number or type of parameters; the compiler finds the right function based on the argument list.

Local function variables, and the arguments passed in to the function, are local to the block in which they are declared. Parameters passed by value are copies and cannot affect the value of variables in the calling function.

Q&A

Q Why not make all variables global?

A At one time, this was exactly how programming was done. As programs became more complex, however, it became very difficult to find bugs in programs because data could be corrupted by any of the functions—global data can be changed anywhere in the program. Years of experience have convinced programmers that data should be kept as local as possible, and access to changing that data should be narrowly defined.

Q When should the keyword `inline` be used in a function prototype?

A If the function is very small, no more than a line or two, and won't be called from many places in your program, it is a candidate for inlining.

Q Why aren't changes to the value of function arguments reflected in the calling function?

A Arguments passed to a function are passed by value. That means that the argument in the function is actually a copy of the original value. This concept is explained in depth in the section "How Functions Work—A Peek Under the Hood."

Q If arguments are passed by value, what do I do if I need to reflect the changes back in the calling function?

A In Lesson 8, pointers will be discussed and in Lesson 9, "Exploiting References," you'll learn about references. Use of pointers or references will solve this problem, as well as provide a way around the limitation of returning only a single value from a function.

6

Q What happens if I have the following two functions?

```
int Area (int width, int length = 1); int Area (int size);
```

Will these overload? A different number of parameters exist, but the first one has a default value.

A The declarations will compile, but if you invoke `Area` with one parameter, you will receive this error: `ambiguity between Area(int, int) and Area(int)`.

Workshop

The Workshop provides quiz questions to help you solidify your understanding of the material covered and exercises to provide you with experience in using what you've learned. Try to answer the quiz and exercise questions before checking the answers in Appendix D, and be certain that you understand the answers before continuing to the next lesson.

Quiz

1. What are the differences between the function prototype and the function definition?

2. Do the names of parameters have to agree in the prototype, definition, and call to the function?

3. If a function doesn't return a value, how do you declare the function?

4. If you don't declare a return value, what type of return value is assumed?

5. What is a local variable?

6. What is scope?

7. What is recursion?

8. When should you use global variables?

9. What is function overloading?

Exercises

1. Write the prototype for a function named `Perimeter()`, which returns an `unsigned long int` and takes two parameters, both `unsigned short ints`.

2. Write the definition of the function `Perimeter()` as described in Exercise 1. The two parameters represent the length and width of a rectangle. Have the function return the perimeter (twice the length plus twice the width).

3. **BUG BUSTERS:** What is wrong with the function in the following code?

```
#include <iostream>
void myFunc(unsigned short int x);
int main()
{
    unsigned short int x, y;
    y = myFunc(int);
    std::cout << "x: " << x << " y: " << y << "\n";
    return 0;
}

void myFunc(unsigned short int x)
{
    return (4*x);
}
```

4. **BUG BUSTERS:** What is wrong with the function in the following code?

```
#include <iostream>
int myFunc(unsigned short int x);
int main()
{
    unsigned short int x, y;
    x = 7;
    y = myFunc(x);
    std::cout << "x: " << x << " y: " << y << "\n";
    return 0;
}

int myFunc(unsigned short int x);
{
    return (4*x);
}
```

5. Write a function that takes two unsigned short integer arguments and returns the result of dividing the first by the second. Do not do the division if the second number is zero, but do return –1.

6. Write a program that asks the user for two numbers and calls the function you wrote in Exercise 5. Print the answer, or print an error message if you get –1.

7. Write a program that asks for a number and a power. Write a recursive function that takes the number to the power. For example, if the number is 2 and the power is 4, the function will return 16.

6

LESSON 7
Controlling Program Flow

Programs accomplish most of their work by branching and looping. In Lesson 5, "Working with Expressions, Statements, and Operators," you learned how to branch your program using the *if* statement.

In this lesson, you will learn

- What loops are and how they are used

- How to build various loops

- An alternative to deeply nested *if...else* statements

Programming Loops

Many programming problems are solved by repeatedly acting on the same data. Two ways to do this are recursion (discussed in Lesson 6, "Organizing Code with Functions") and iteration. *Iteration* means doing the same thing again and again. The principal method of iteration is the loop.

The Roots of Looping: `goto`

In the primitive days of early computer science, programs were nasty, brutish, and short. Loops consisted of a label, some statements, and a jump that went to the label.

In C++, a label is just a name followed by a colon (`:`). The label is placed to the left of a legal C++ statement. A jump is accomplished by writing `goto` followed by the name of a label. Listing 7.1 illustrates this primitive way of looping.

LISTING 7.1   Looping with the Keyword goto

```
1:  // Listing 7.1
2:  // Looping with goto
3:  #include <iostream>
4:
5:  int main()
6:  {
7:      using namespace std;
8:      int counter = 0;        // initialize counter
9:  loop:
10:     counter ++;             // top of the loop
11:     cout << "counter: " << counter << endl;
12:     if (counter < 5)        // test the value
13:         goto loop;          // jump to the top
14:
15:     cout << "Complete. Counter: " << counter << endl;
16:     return 0;
17: }
```

Output ▼

```
counter: 1
counter: 2
counter: 3
counter: 4
counter: 5
Complete. Counter: 5.
```

Analysis ▼

On line 8, `counter` is initialized to zero. A label called `loop` is on line 9, marking the top of the loop. `counter` is incremented and its new value is printed on line 11. The value of `counter` is tested on line 12. If the value is less than 5, the `if` statement is `true` and the `goto` statement is executed. This causes program execution to jump back to the `loop` label on line 9. The program continues looping until `counter` is equal to 5, at which time it "falls through" the loop and the final output is printed.

Why `goto` Is Shunned

As a rule, programmers avoid `goto`, and with good reason. `goto` statements can cause a jump to any location in your source code, backward or forward. The indiscriminate use of `goto` statements has caused tangled, miserable, impossible-to-read programs known as *spaghetti code*.

The `goto` Statement

To use the `goto` statement, you write `goto` followed by a label name. This causes an unconditioned jump to the label.

Example

```
if (value > 10)
    goto end;
if (value < 10)
    goto end;
cout << "value is 10!";
end:
    cout << "done";
```

To avoid the use of `goto`, more sophisticated, tightly controlled looping commands have been introduced: `for`, `while`, and `do...while`.

Using while Loops

A `while` loop causes your program to repeat a sequence of statements as long as the starting condition remains true. In the `goto` example in Listing 7.1, the counter was incremented until it was equal to 5. Listing 7.2 shows the same program rewritten to take advantage of a `while` loop.

7

LISTING 7.2   while Loops

```
 1:  // Listing 7.2
 2:  // Looping with while
 3:  #include <iostream>
 4:
 5:  int main()
 6:  {
 7:    using namespace std;
 8:    int counter = 0;        // initialize the condition
 9:
10:    while(counter < 5)      // test condition still true
11:    {
12:        counter++;          // body of the loop
13:        cout << "counter: " << counter << endl;
14:    }
15:
16:    cout << "Complete. Counter: " << counter << endl;
17:    return 0;
18:  }
```

Output ▼

```
counter: 1
counter: 2
counter: 3
counter: 4
counter: 5
Complete. Counter: 5.
```

Analysis ▼

This simple program demonstrates the fundamentals of the while loop. On line 8, an integer variable called counter is created and initialized to zero. This is then used as a part of a condition. The condition is tested, and if it is true, the body of the while loop is executed. In this case, the condition tested on line 10 is whether counter is less than 5. If the condition is true, the body of the loop is executed; on line 12, the counter is incremented, and on line 13, the value is printed. When the conditional statement on line 10 fails (when counter is no longer less than 5), the entire body of the while loop (lines 11–14) is skipped. Program execution falls through to line 15.

It is worth noting here that it is a good idea to always use braces around the block executed by a loop, even when it is just a single line of code. This avoids the common error of inadvertently putting a semicolon at the end of a loop and causing it to endlessly repeat—for instance:

```
int counter = 0;
while ( counter < 5 );
    counter++;
```

In this example, the counter++ is never executed.

The while Statement

The syntax for the while statement is as follows:

```
while ( condition )
  statement;
```

condition is any C++ expression, and statement is any valid C++ statement or block of statements. When condition evaluates true, statement is executed and then condition is tested again. This continues until condition tests false, at which time the while loop terminates and execution continues on the first line below statement.

Example

```
// count to 10
int x = 0;
while (x < 10)
  cout << "X: " << x++;
```

Exploring More Complicated while Statements

The condition tested by a while loop can be as complex as any legal C++ expression. This can include expressions produced using the logical && (AND), ¦¦ (OR), and ! (NOT) operators. Listing 7.3 is a somewhat more complicated while statement.

LISTING 7.3   Complex while Loops

```
1:  // Listing 7.3
2:  // Complex while statements
3:  #include <iostream>
4:
5:  int main()
6:  {
7:      using namespace std;
8:      unsigned short small;
9:      unsigned long  large;
10:     const unsigned short MAXSMALL=65535;
11:
12:     cout << "Enter a small number: ";
13:     cin >> small;
```

7

LISTING 7.3 Continued

```
14:     cout << "Enter a large number: ";
15:     cin >> large;
16:
17:     cout << "small: " << small << "...";
18:
19:     // for each iteration, test two conditions
20:     while (small < large  && small < MAXSMALL)
21:     {
22:        if (small % 5000 == 0)  // write a dot every 5k lines
23:           cout << ".";
24:
25:        small++;
26:        large-=2;
27:     }
28:
29:     cout << "\nSmall: " << small << " Large: " << large << endl;
30:     return 0;
31:  }
```

Output ▼

```
Enter a small number: 2
Enter a large number: 100000
small: 2.........
Small: 33335 Large: 33334
```

Analysis ▼

This program is a game. Enter two numbers, one small and one large. The smaller number will count up by ones, and the larger number will count down by twos. The goal of the game is to guess when they'll meet.

On lines 12–15, the numbers are entered. Line 20 sets up a while loop, which will continue only as long as two conditions are met:

1. small is not bigger than large.

2. small doesn't overrun the size of a small integer (MAXSMALL).

On line 22, the value in small is calculated modulo 5,000. This does not change the value in small; however, it returns the value 0 only when small is an exact multiple of 5,000. Each time this happens, a dot (.) is printed to the screen to show progress. On line 25, small is incremented, and on line 26, large is decremented by 2. When either of the two conditions in the while loop fails, the loop ends and execution of the program continues after the while loop's closing brace on line 27.

> **NOTE**
>
> The modulus operator (%) and compound conditions were covered in Lesson 5, "Working with Expressions, Statements, and Operators."

Introducing continue and break

At times, you'll want to return to the top of a while loop before the entire set of statements in the while loop is executed. The continue statement jumps back to the top of the loop.

At other times, you might want to exit the loop before the exit conditions are met. The break statement immediately exits the while loop, and program execution resumes after the closing brace.

Listing 7.4 demonstrates the use of these statements. This time, the game has become more complicated. The user is invited to enter a small number and a large number, a skip number, and a target number. The small number will be incremented by 1, and the large number will be decremented by 2. The decrement will be skipped each time the small number is a multiple of the skip. The game ends if small becomes larger than large. If the large number reaches the target exactly, a statement is printed and the game stops. The user's goal is to put in a target number for the large number that will stop the game.

LISTING 7.4   break and continue

```
1:  // Listing 7.4 - Demonstrates break and continue
2:  #include <iostream>
3:
4:  int main()
5:  {
6:     using namespace std;
7:
8:     unsigned short small;
9:     unsigned long  large;
10:    unsigned long  skip;
11:    unsigned long target;
12:    const unsigned short MAXSMALL=65535;
13:
14:    cout << "Enter a small number: ";
15:    cin >> small;
16:    cout << "Enter a large number: ";
17:    cin >> large;
18:    cout << "Enter a skip number: ";
19:    cin >> skip;
20:    cout << "Enter a target number: ";
```

7

LISTING 7.4   Continued

```
21:     cin >> target;
22:
23:     cout << "\n";
24:
25:     // set up 2 stop conditions for the loop
26:     while (small < large && small < MAXSMALL)
27:     {
28:        small++;
29:
30:        if (small % skip == 0)  // skip the decrement?
31:        {
32:           cout << "skipping on " << small << endl;
33:           continue;
34:        }
35:
36:        if (large == target)    // exact match for the target?
37:        {
38:           cout << "Target reached!";
39:           break;
40:        }
41:
42:        large-=2;
43:     }                        // end of while loop
44:
45:     cout << "\nSmall: " << small << " Large: " << large << endl;
46:     return 0;
47: }
```

Output ▼

```
Enter a small number: 2
Enter a large number: 20
Enter a skip number: 4
Enter a target number: 6

skipping on 4
skipping on 8

Small: 10 Large: 8
```

Analysis ▼

In this play, the user lost; small became larger than large before the target number of 6 was reached. On line 26, the while conditions are tested. If small continues to be smaller than large and if small hasn't overrun the maximum value for a small int, the body of the while loop is entered.

On line 30, the small value is taken, modulo the skip value. If `small` is a multiple of skip, the `continue` statement is reached and program execution jumps to the top of the loop back at line 26. This effectively skips over the test for the target and the decrement of `large`.

On line 36, `target` is tested against the value for `large`. If they are the same, the user has won. A message is printed and the `break` statement is reached and executed. This causes an immediate break out of the `while` loop, and program execution resumes on line 44.

NOTE

Both `continue` and `break` should be used with caution. They are the next most dangerous commands after `goto`, for much the same reason. Programs that suddenly change direction are harder to understand, and liberal use of `continue` and `break` can render even a small `while` loop unreadable.

A need for breaking within a loop often indicates that the terminating condition of the loop has not been set up with the appropriate Boolean expression. It is often better to use an `if` statement within a loop to skip some lines than to use a breaking statement.

The `continue` Statement

`continue;` causes a while, do...while, or for loop to begin again at the top of the loop. See Listing 7.4 for an example of using `continue`.

The `break` Statement

`break;` causes the immediate end of a while, do...while, or for loop. Execution jumps to the closing brace.

Example

```
while (condition)
{
    if (condition2)
        break;
    // statements;
}
```

7

Examining while(true) Loops

The condition tested in a while loop can be any valid C++ expression. As long as that condition remains true, the while loop continues. You can create a loop that never ends by using the value true for the condition to be tested. Listing 7.5 demonstrates counting to 10 using this construct.

LISTING 7.5 while(true) Loops

```
1:  // Listing 7.5
2:  // Demonstrates a while true loop
3:  #include <iostream>
4:
5:  int main()
6:  {
7:      int counter = 0;
8:
9:      while (true)
10:     {
11:         counter ++;
12:         if (counter > 10)
13:             break;
14:     }
15:     std::cout << "Counter: " << counter << std::endl;
16:     return 0;
17: }
```

Output ▼

```
Counter: 11
```

Analysis ▼

On line 9, a while loop is set up with a condition that can never be false. The loop increments the counter variable on line 11, and then on line 12 it tests to see whether counter has gone past 10. If it hasn't, the while loop iterates. If counter is greater than 10, the break on line 13 ends the while loop, and program execution falls through to line 15, where the results are printed.

This program works, but it isn't pretty. This is a good example of using the wrong tool for the job. The same thing can be accomplished by putting the test of counter's value where it belongs—in the while condition.

CAUTION | Eternal loops such as while (true) can cause your computer to hang if the exit condition is never reached. Use these with caution and test them thoroughly.

C++ gives you many ways to accomplish the same task. The real trick is picking the right tool for the particular job.

DO	DON'T
DO use while loops to iterate using a conditional statement.	**DON'T** use the goto statement.
DO exercise caution when using continue and break statements.	**DON'T** forget the difference between continue and break. continue goes to the top; break exits the loop.
DO ensure that your loop will eventually end.	

Implementing do...while Loops

It is possible that the body of a while loop will never execute. The while statement checks its condition before executing any of its statements, and if the condition evaluates false, the entire body of the while loop is skipped. Listing 7.6 illustrates this.

LISTING 7.6   Skipping the Body of the while Loop

```
1:  // Listing 7.6
2:  // Demonstrates skipping the body of
3:  // the while loop when the condition is false.
4:
5:  #include <iostream>
6:
7:  int main()
8:  {
9:      int counter;
10:     std::cout << "How many hellos?: ";
11:     std::cin >> counter;
12:     while (counter > 0)
13:     {
14:         std::cout << "Hello!\n";
15:         counter--;
16:     }
17:     std::cout << "Counter is OutPut: " << counter;
18:     return 0;
19: }
```

7

Output ▼

```
How many hellos?: 2
Hello!
Hello!
Counter is OutPut: 0

How many hellos?: 0
Counter is OutPut: 0
```

Analysis ▼

The user is prompted for a starting value on line 10. This starting value is stored in the integer variable counter. The value of counter is tested on line 12 and decremented in the body of the while loop. In the output, you can see that the first time through, counter was set to 2, and so the body of the while loop ran twice. The second time through, however, the 0 was entered. The value of counter was tested on line 12 and the condition was false; counter was not greater than 0. The entire body of the while loop was skipped, and Hello was never printed.

What if you want to ensure that Hello always prints at least once? The while loop can't accomplish this because the if condition is tested before any printing is done. You can force the issue with an if statement just before entering the while loop

```
if (counter < 1)  // force a minimum value
    counter = 1;
```

but that is what programmers call a *kludge* (pronounced klooj to rhyme with *stooge*), an ugly and inelegant solution.

Using do...while

The do...while loop executes the body of the loop before its condition is tested, thus ensuring that the body always executes at least one time. Listing 7.7 rewrites Listing 7.6 using a do...while loop.

LISTING 7.7   Demonstrating a do...while Loop

```
1:  // Listing 7.7
2:  // Demonstrates do while
3:
4:  #include <iostream>
5:
6:  int main()
7:  {
```

LISTING 7.7   Continued

```
8:      using namespace std;
9:      int counter;
10:     cout << "How many hellos? ";
11:     cin >> counter;
12:     do
13:     {
14:        cout << "Hello\n";
15:        counter--;
16:     } while (counter >0 );
17:     cout << "Counter is: " << counter << endl;
18:     return 0;
19: }
```

Output ▼

```
How many hellos? 2
Hello
Hello
Counter is: 0
```

Analysis ▼

Like the previous program, Listing 7.7 prints the word *Hello* to the console a specified number of times. Unlike the preceding program, however, this program will always print at least once.

The user is prompted for a starting value on line 10, which is stored in the integer variable counter. In the do...while loop, the body of the loop is entered before the condition is tested, and, therefore, the body of the loop is guaranteed to run at least once. On line 14, the hello message is printed; on line 15, the counter is decremented; execution jumps to the top of the loop on line 13—otherwise, it falls through to line 17.

The continue and break statements work in a do...while loop exactly as they do in a while loop. The only difference between a while loop and a do...while loop is when the condition is tested.

The do...while Statement

The syntax for the do...while statement is as follows:

```
do
   statement
while (condition);
```

7

statement is executed, and then *condition* is evaluated. If *condition* is true, the loop is repeated; otherwise, the loop ends. The statements and conditions are otherwise identical to the `while` loop.

Example 1

```
// count to 10
int x = 0;
do
   cout << "X: " << x++;
while (x < 10)
```

Example 2

```
// print lowercase alphabet.
char ch = 'a';
do
{
   cout << ch << ' ';
   ch++;
} while ( ch <= 'z' );
```

DO	DON'T
DO use do...while when you want to ensure that the loop executes at least once.	**DON'T** use break and continue with loops unless it is clear what your code is doing. There are often clearer ways to accomplish the same tasks.
DO use while loops when you want to skip the loop if the condition is false.	**DON'T** use the goto statement.
DO test all loops to be certain they do what you expect.	

Looping with the `for` Statement

When programming `while` loops, you'll often find yourself going through three steps: setting up a starting condition, testing to see whether the condition is true, and incrementing or otherwise changing a variable each time through the loop. Listing 7.8 demonstrates this.

LISTING 7.8 `while` Reexamined

```
1:  // Listing 7.8
2:  // Looping with while
3:
```

LISTING 7.8   Continued

```
 4:  #include <iostream>
 5:
 6:  int main()
 7:  {
 8:      int counter = 0;
 9:
10:      while(counter < 5)
11:      {
12:          counter++;
13:          std::cout << "Looping!   ";
14:      }
15:
16:      std::cout << "\nCounter: " << counter << std::endl;
17:      return 0;
18:  }
```

Output ▼

```
Looping!  Looping!  Looping!  Looping!  Looping!
Counter: 5.
```

Analysis ▼

In this listing, you can see that three steps are occurring. First, the starting condition is set on line 8: counter is initialized to 0. On line 10, the test of the condition occurs when counter is tested to see whether it is less than 5. Finally, the counter variable is incremented on line 12. This loop prints a simple message at line 13. As you can imagine, more important work could be done for each increment of the counter.

A for loop combines the three steps into one statement. The three steps are initializing, testing, and incrementing. A for statement consists of the keyword for followed by a pair of parentheses. Within the parentheses are three statements separated by semicolons:

```
for( initialization; test ; action )
{
   ...
}
```

The first expression, *initialization*, is the starting conditions or initialization. Any legal C++ statement can be put here, but typically this is used to create and initialize a counting variable. The second expression, *test*, is the test, and any legal C++ expression can be used here. This test serves the same role as the condition in the while loop. The third expression, *action*, is the action that will take place. This action is typically the

7

increment or decrement of a value, although any legal C++ statement can be put here. Listing 7.9 demonstrates a for loop by rewriting Listing 7.8.

LISTING 7.9   Demonstrating the for Loop

```
 1:  // Listing 7.9
 2:  // Looping with for
 3:
 4:  #include <iostream>
 5:
 6:  int main()
 7:  {
 8:     int counter;
 9:     for (counter = 0; counter < 5; counter++)
10:        std::cout << "Looping! ";
11:
12:     std::cout << "\nCounter: " << counter << std::endl;
13:     return 0;
14:  }
```

Output ▼

```
Looping!  Looping!  Looping!  Looping!  Looping!
Counter: 5.
```

Analysis ▼

The for statement on line 9 combines into one line the initialization of counter, the test that counter is less than 5, and the increment of counter. The body of the for statement is on line 10. Of course, a block could be used here as well.

The for Statement

The syntax for the for statement is as follows:

```
for (initialization; test; action )
   statement;
```

The initialization statement is used to initialize the state of a counter or to otherwise prepare for the loop. test is any C++ expression and is evaluated each time through the loop. If test is true, the body of the for loop is executed and then the action in the header is executed (typically the counter is incremented).

Example 1

```
// print Hello ten times
for (int i = 0; i<10; i++)
   cout << "Hello! ";
```

Example 2

```
for (int i = 0; i < 10; i++)
{
    cout << "Hello!" << endl;
    cout << "the value of i is: " << i << endl;
}
```

Advanced for Loops

for statements are powerful and flexible. The three independent statements (*initialization*, *test*, and *action*) lend themselves to a number of variations.

Multiple Initialization and Increments

It is common to initialize more than one variable, to test a compound logical expression, and to execute more than one statement. The initialization and the action can be replaced by multiple C++ statements, each separated by a comma. Listing 7.10 demonstrates the initialization and increment of two variables.

LISTING 7.10   Demonstrating Multiple Statements in for Loops

```
 1:  //Listing 7.10
 2:  // Demonstrates multiple statements in
 3:  // for loops
 4:  #include <iostream>
 5:
 6:  int main()
 7:  {
 8:
 9:      for (int i=0, j=0; i<3; i++, j++)
10:          std::cout << "i: " << i << " j: " << j << std::endl;
11:      return 0;
12:  }
```

7

Output ▼

```
i: 0  j: 0
i: 1  j: 1
i: 2  j: 2
```

Analysis ▼

On line 9, two variables, i and j, are initialized with the value 0. A comma is used to separate the two separate expressions. You can also see that these initializations are separated from the test condition by the expected semicolon.

When this program executes, the test (i<3) is evaluated, and because it is true, the body of the for statement is executed, where the values are printed. Finally, the third clause in the for statement is executed. As you can see, two expressions are here as well. In this case, both i and j are incremented.

After line 10 completes, the condition is evaluated again, and if it remains true, the actions are repeated (i and j are again incremented), and the body of the loop is executed again. This continues until the test fails, in which case the action statement is not executed and control falls out of the loop.

Null Statements in for Loops

Any or all the statements in a for loop can be left out. To accomplish this, you use a null statement. A *null statement* is simply the use of a semicolon (;) to mark where the statement would have been. Using a null statement, you can create a for loop that acts exactly like a while loop by leaving out the first and third statements. Listing 7.11 illustrates this idea.

LISTING 7.11   Null Statements in for Loops

```
1:  // Listing 7.11
2:  // For loops with null statements
3:
4:  #include <iostream>
5:
6:  int main()
7:  {
8:      int counter = 0;
9:
10:     for( ; counter < 5; )
11:     {
12:         counter++;
13:         std::cout << "Looping!   ";
14:     }
15:
16:     std::cout << "\nCounter: " << counter << std::endl;
17:     return 0;
18: }
```

Output ▼

```
Looping! Looping! Looping! Looping! Looping!
Counter: 5.
```

Analysis ▼

You might recognize this as exactly like the `while` loop illustrated in Listing 7.8. On line 8, the `counter` variable is initialized. The `for` statement on line 10 does not initialize any values, but it does include a test for `counter < 5`. No increment statement exists, so this loop behaves exactly as if it had been written

```
while (counter < 5)
```

You can once again see that C++ gives you several ways to accomplish the same thing. No experienced C++ programmer would use a `for` loop in this way shown in Listing 7.11, but it does illustrate the flexibility of the `for` statement. In fact, it is possible, using `break` and `continue`, to create a `for` loop with none of the three statements. Listing 7.12 illustrates how.

LISTING 7.12   Illustrating an Empty for Loop Statement

```cpp
 1:  //Listing 7.12 illustrating
 2:  //empty for loop statement
 3:
 4:  #include <iostream>
 5:
 6:  int main()
 7:  {
 8:     int counter=0;      // initialization
 9:     int max;
10:     std::cout << "How many hellos? ";
11:     std::cin >> max;
12:     for (;;)            // a for loop that doesn't end
13:     {
14:        if (counter < max)      // test
15:        {
16:           std::cout << "Hello! " << std::endl;
17:           counter++;           // increment
18:        }
19:        else
20:           break;
21:     }
22:     return 0;
23:  }
```

7

Output ▼

```
How many hellos? 3
Hello!
Hello!
Hello!
```

Analysis ▼

The for loop has now been pushed to its absolute limit. Initialization, test, and action have all been taken out of the for statement on line 12. The initialization is done on line 8, before the for loop begins. The test is done in a separate if statement on line 14, and if the test succeeds, the action, an increment to counter, is performed on line 17. If the test fails, breaking out of the loop occurs on line 20.

Although this particular program is somewhat absurd, sometimes a for(;;) loop or a while (true) loop is just what you'll want. You'll see an example of a more reasonable use of such loops when switch statements are discussed later in this lesson.

Empty for Loops

Because so much can be done in the header of a for statement, at times you won't need the body to do anything at all. In that case, be certain to put a null statement (;) as the body of the loop. The semicolon can be on the same line as the header, but this is easy to overlook. Listing 7.13 illustrates an appropriate way to use a null body in a for loop.

LISTING 7.13   Illustrates the Null Statement in a for Loop

```
1:  //Listing 7.13
2:  //Demonstrates null statement
3:  // as body of for loop
4:
5:  #include <iostream>
6:  int main()
7:  {
8:     for (int i = 0; i<5; std::cout << "i: " << i++ << std::endl)
9:        ;
10:    return 0;
11: }
```

Output ▼

```
i: 0
i: 1
i: 2
i: 3
i: 4
```

Analysis ▼

The `for` loop on line 8 includes three statements: The initialization statement establishes the counter `i` and initializes it to `0`. The condition statement tests for `i<5`, and the action statement prints the value in `i` and increments it.

Nothing is left to do in the body of the `for` loop, so the null statement (`;`) is used. Note that this is not a well-designed `for` loop: The action statement is doing far too much. This would be better rewritten as

```
8:          for (int i = 0; i<5; i++)
9:              cout << "i: " << i << endl;
```

Although both do the same thing, this example is easier to understand.

Nesting Loops

Any of the loops can be nested within the body of another. The inner loop will be executed in full for every execution of the outer loop. Listing 7.14 illustrates writing marks into a matrix using nested `for` loops.

LISTING 7.14   Illustrating Nested for Loops

```
 1:  //Listing 7.14
 2:  //Illustrates nested for loops
 3:  #include <iostream>
 4:
 5:  int main()
 6:  {
 7:      using namespace std;
 8:      int rows, columns;
 9:      char theChar;
10:      cout << "How many rows? ";
11:      cin >> rows;
12:      cout << "How many columns? ";
13:      cin >> columns;
14:      cout << "What character? ";
15:      cin >> theChar;
16:      for (int i = 0; i<rows; i++)
17:      {
18:          for (int j = 0; j<columns; j++)
19:              cout << theChar;
20:          cout << endl;
21:      }
22:      return 0;
23:  }
```

7

Output ▼

```
How many rows? 4
How many columns? 12
What character? X
XXXXXXXXXXXX
XXXXXXXXXXXX
XXXXXXXXXXXX
XXXXXXXXXXXX
```

Analysis ▼

In this listing, the user is prompted for the number of rows and columns and for a character to print. The first for loop, on line 16, initializes a counter (i) to 0, and then the body of the outer for loop is run.

On line 18, the first line of the body of the outer for loop, another for loop is established. A second counter (j) is initialized to 0, and the body of the inner for loop is executed. On line 19, the chosen character is printed, and control returns to the header of the inner for loop. Note that the inner for loop is only one statement (the printing of the character). The condition is tested (j < columns) and if it evaluates true, j is incremented and the next character is printed. This continues until j equals the number of columns.

When the inner for loop fails its test, in this case after 12 Xs are printed, execution falls through to line 20 and a new line is printed. The outer for loop now returns to its header, where its condition (i < rows) is tested. If this evaluates true, i is incremented and the body of the loop is executed.

In the second iteration of the outer for loop, the inner for loop is started over. Thus, j is reinitialized to 0 and the entire inner loop is run again.

The important idea here is that by using a nested loop, the inner loop is executed for each iteration of the outer loop. Thus, the character is printed columns times for each row.

NOTE	As an aside, many C++ programmers use the letters i and j as counting variables. This tradition goes all the way back to FORTRAN, in which the letters i, j, k, l, m, and n were the only counting variables.
	Although this might seem innocuous, readers of your program can become confused by the purpose of the counter and might use it improperly. You can even become confused in a complex program with nested loops. It is better to indicate the use of the index variable in its name—for instance, CustomerIndex or InputCounter.

Scoping in for Loops

In the past, variables declared in the for loop were scoped to the outer block. The American National Standards Institute (ANSI) standard changes this to scope these variables only to the block of the for loop itself; however, not every compiler supports this change. You can test your compiler with the following code:

```
#include <iostream>
int main()
{
    // i scoped to the for loop?
    for (int i = 0; i<5; i++)
    {
        std::cout << "i: " << i << std::endl;
    }

    i = 7;  // integer 'i' should not be in scope!
    return 0;
}
```

If this compiles without complaint, your compiler does not yet support this aspect of the ANSI standard. If your compiler complains that i is not yet defined (in the line i=7), your compiler does support the new standard. You can write code that will compile on either compiler by declaring i outside of the loop, as shown here:

```
#include <iostream>
int main()
{
    int i; //declare outside the for loop
    for (i = 0; i<5; i++)
    {
        std::cout << "i: " << i << std::endl;
    }

    i = 7;  // now this is in scope for all compilers
    return 0;
}
```

Summing Up Loops

In Lesson 6, "Organizing Code with Functions," you learned how to solve the Fibonacci series problem using recursion. To review briefly, a Fibonacci series starts with 1, 1, 2, 3, and all subsequent numbers are the sum of the previous two:

1,1,2,3,5,8,13,21,34...

7

The nth Fibonacci number is the sum of the n–1 and the n–2 Fibonacci numbers. The problem solved in Lesson 6 was finding the value of the nth Fibonacci number, and this was done with recursion. Listing 7.15 offers a solution using iteration.

LISTING 7.15   Solving the nth Fibonacci Number Using Iteration

```
 1:  // Listing 7.15 -  Demonstrates solving the nth
 2:  // Fibonacci number using iteration
 3:
 4:  #include <iostream>
 5:
 6:  unsigned int fib(unsigned int position );
 7:  int main()
 8:  {
 9:     using namespace std;
10:     unsigned int answer, position;
11:     cout << "Which position? ";
12:     cin >> position;
13:     cout << endl;
14:
15:     answer = fib(position);
16:     cout << answer << " is the ";
17:     cout << position << "th Fibonacci number. " << endl;
18:     return 0;
19:  }
20:
21:  unsigned int fib(unsigned int n)
22:  {
23:     unsigned int minusTwo=1, minusOne=1, answer=2;
24:
25:     if (n < 3)
26:        return 1;
27:
28:     for (n -= 3; n != 0; n--)
29:     {
30:        minusTwo = minusOne;
31:        minusOne = answer;
32:        answer = minusOne + minusTwo;
33:     }
34:
35:     return answer;
36:  }
```

Output ▼

```
Which position? 4
3 is the 4th Fibonacci number.
Which position? 5
5 is the 5th Fibonacci number.
Which position? 20
6765 is the 20th Fibonacci number.
Which position? 100
3314859971 is the 100th Fibonacci number.
```

Analysis ▼

Listing 7.15 solves the Fibonacci series using iteration rather than recursion. This approach is faster and uses less memory than the recursive solution.

On line 11, the user is asked for the position to check. The function `fib()` is called, which evaluates the position. If the position is less than 3, the function returns the value 1. Starting with position 3, the function iterates using the following algorithm:

1. Establish the starting position: Fill variable `answer` with 2, `minusTwo` with 1, and `minusOne` with 1. Decrement the position by 3 because the first two numbers are handled by the starting position.

2. For every number, count up the Fibonacci series. This is done by

   A. Putting the value currently in `minusOne` into `minusTwo`

   B. Putting the value currently in `answer` into `minusOne`

   C. Adding `minusOne` and `minusTwo` and putting the sum in `answer`

   D. Decrementing `n`

3. When `n` reaches 0, return the answer.

This is exactly how you would solve this problem with pencil and paper. If you were asked for the fifth Fibonacci number, you would write

1, 1, 2,

and think, "two more to do." You would then add 2+1 and write 3, and think, "one more to find." Finally, you would write 3+2 and the answer would be 5. In effect, you are shifting your attention right one number each time through and decrementing the number remaining to be found.

Note the condition tested on line 28 (`n != 0`). Many C++ programmers use the following for line 28:

```
for ( n-=3; n; n-- )
```

7

You can see that instead of using a relational condition, just the value of n is used for the condition in the for statement. This is a C++ idiom, and n is considered equivalent to n != 0. Using just n relies on the fact that when n reaches 0, it will evaluate as false because 0 has been considered as false in C++. In keeping with the current C++ standards, it is better to rely on a condition to evaluate to the value of false than to use a numeric value.

Compile, link, and run this program, along with the recursive solution offered in Lesson 6. Try finding position 25 and compare the time it takes each program. Recursion is elegant, but because the function call brings a performance overhead, and because it is called so many times, its performance is noticeably slower than iteration. Microcomputers tend to be optimized for the arithmetic operations, so the iterative solution should be blazingly fast.

Be careful how large a number you enter. fib grows quickly, and even unsigned long integers will overflow after a while.

Controlling Flow with switch Statements

In Lesson 5, "Working with Expressions, Statements, and Operators," you saw how to write if and if...else statements. These can become quite confusing when nested too deeply, and C++ offers an alternative. Unlike if, which evaluates one value, switch statements enable you to branch on any of several values. The general form of the switch statement is

```
switch (expression)
{
    case valueOne: statement;
                   break;
    case valueTwo: statement;
                   break;
    ....
    case valueN:   statement;
                   break;
    default:       statement;
}
```

expression is any legal C++ expression, and the statements are any legal C++ statements or block of statements that evaluate (or can be unambiguously converted to) an integer value. Note, however, that the evaluation is for equality only; neither relational operators nor Boolean operations can be used here.

If one of the case values matches the expression, program execution jumps to those statements and continues to the end of the switch block unless a break statement is encountered. If nothing matches, execution branches to the optional `default` statement. If no `default` and no matching `case` value exist, execution falls through the `switch` statement and the statement ends.

> **TIP**
>
> It is almost always a good idea to have a `default` case in switch statements. If you have no other need for the default, use it to test for the supposedly impossible case, and print out an error message; this can be a tremendous aid in debugging.

It is important to note that if no `break` statement is at the end of a `case` statement, execution falls through to the next `case` statement. This is sometimes necessary, but usually is an error. If you decide to let execution fall through, be certain to put a comment indicating that you didn't just forget the `break`. Listing 7.16 illustrates use of the `switch` statement.

LISTING 7.16   Demonstrating the `switch` Statement

```
1:  //Listing 7.16
2:  // Demonstrates switch statement
3:  #include <iostream>
4:
5:  int main()
6:  {
7:      using namespace std;
8:      unsigned short int number;
9:      cout << "Enter a number between 1 and 5: ";
10:     cin >> number;
11:     switch (number)
12:     {
13:       case 0:   cout << "Too small, sorry!";
14:                 break;
15:       case 5:   cout << "Good job! " << endl; // fall through
16:       case 4:   cout << "Nice Pick!" << endl; // fall through
17:       case 3:   cout << "Excellent!" << endl; // fall through
18:       case 2:   cout << "Masterful!" << endl; // fall through
19:       case 1:   cout << "Incredible!" << endl;
20:                 break;
21:       default:  cout << "Too large!" << endl;
22:                 break;
23:     }
24:     cout << endl << endl;
25:     return 0;
26:  }
```

7

Output ▼

```
Enter a number between 1 and 5: 3
Excellent!
Masterful!
Incredible!

Enter a number between 1 and 5: 8
Too large!
```

Analysis ▼

The user is prompted for a number on lines 9 and 10. That number is given to the switch statement on line 11. If the number is 0, the case statement on line 13 matches, the message Too small, sorry! is printed, and the break statement on line 14 ends the switch. If the value is 5, execution switches to line 15 where a message is printed, and then falls through to line 16, another message is printed, and so forth until hitting the break on line 20, at which time the switch ends.

The net effect of these statements is that for a number between 1 and 5, that many messages are printed. If the value of number is not 0 to 5, it is assumed to be too large and the default statement is invoked on line 21.

The switch **Statement**

The syntax for the switch statement is as follows:

```
switch (expression)
{
    case    valueOne: statement;
    case    valueTwo: statement;
    ....
    case    valueN: statement;
    default: statement;
}
```

The switch statement allows for branching on multiple values of expression. The expression is evaluated, and if it matches any of the case values, execution jumps to that line. Execution continues until either the end of the switch statement or a break statement is encountered.

If expression does not match any of the case statements, and if there is a default statement, execution switches to the default statement, otherwise the switch statement ends.

Example 1

```cpp
switch (choice)
{
    case 0:
        cout << "Zero!" << endl;
        break;
    case 1:
        cout << "One!" << endl;
        break;
    case 2:
        cout << "Two!" << endl;
    default:
        cout << "Default!" << endl;
}
```

Example 2

```cpp
switch (choice)
{
    case 0:
    case 1:
    case 2:
        cout << "Less than 3!";
        break;
    case 3:
        cout << "Equals 3!";
        break;
    default:
        cout << "greater than 3!";
}
```

Using a `switch` **Statement with a Menu**

Listing 7.17 returns to the `for(;;)` loop discussed earlier. These loops are also called *forever loops* because they will loop forever if a break is not encountered. In Listing 7.17, the forever loop is used to put up a menu, solicit a choice from the user, act on the choice, and then return to the menu. This continues until the user chooses to exit.

NOTE

Some programmers like to write:

```cpp
#define EVER ;;
for (EVER)
{
    // statements...
}
```

7

A forever loop is a loop that does not have an exit condition. To exit the loop, a break statement must be used. Forever loops are also known as *eternal* or *infinite loops*.

LISTING 7.17 Demonstrating a Forever Loop

```
1:  //Listing 7.17
2:  //Using a forever loop to manage user interaction
3:  #include <iostream>
4:
5:  // prototypes
6:  int menu();
7:  void DoTaskOne();
8:  void DoTaskMany(int);
9:
10: using namespace std;
11:
12: int main()
13: {
14:     bool exit = false;
15:     for (;;)
16:     {
17:         int choice = menu();
18:         switch(choice)
19:         {
20:           case (1):
21:               DoTaskOne();
22:               break;
23:           case (2):
24:               DoTaskMany(2);
25:               break;
26:           case (3):
27:               DoTaskMany(3);
28:               break;
29:           case (4):
30:               continue;  // redundant!
31:               break;
32:           case (5):
33:               exit=true;
34:               break;
35:           default:
36:               cout << "Please select again! " << endl;
37:               break;
38:         }              // end switch
39:
40:         if (exit == true)
41:             break;
42:     }                  // end forever
43:     return 0;
44: }                      // end main()
45:
```

LISTING 7.17 Continued

```
46:  int menu()
47:  {
48:     int choice;
49:
50:     cout << " **** Menu **** "    << endl << endl;
51:     cout << "(1) Choice one. "    << endl;
52:     cout << "(2) Choice two. "    << endl;
53:     cout << "(3) Choice three. " << endl;
54:     cout << "(4) Redisplay menu. " << endl;
55:     cout << "(5) Quit. "    << endl << endl;
56:     cout << ": ";
57:     cin >> choice;
58:     return choice;
59:  }
60:
61:  void DoTaskOne()
62:  {
63:     cout << "Task One! " << endl;
64:  }
65:
66:  void DoTaskMany(int which)
67:  {
68:     if (which == 2)
69:        cout << "Task Two! " << endl;
70:     else
71:        cout << "Task Three! " << endl;
72:  }
```

Output ▼

```
**** Menu ****

(1) Choice one.
(2) Choice two.
(3) Choice three.
(4) Redisplay menu.
(5) Quit.

: 1
Task One!
 **** Menu ****
(1) Choice one.
(2) Choice two.
(3) Choice three.
(4) Redisplay menu.
(5) Quit.
```

7

```
: 3
Task Three!
**** Menu ****
(1) Choice one.
(2) Choice two.
(3) Choice three.
(4) Redisplay menu.
(5) Quit.

: 5
```

Analysis ▼

This program brings together a number of concepts from this lesson and previous lessons. It also shows a common use of the switch statement.

The forever loop begins on line 15. The menu() function is called, which prints the menu to the screen and returns the user's selection. The switch statement, which begins on line 18 and ends on line 38, switches on the user's choice.

If the user enters 1, execution jumps to the case (1): statement on line 20. Line 21 switches execution to the DoTaskOne() function, which prints a message and returns. On its return, execution resumes on line 22, where the break ends the switch statement, and execution falls through to line 39. On line 40, the variable exit is evaluated to see whether it is true. If it evaluates as true, the break on line 41 is executed and the for(;;) loop ends; but if it evaluates false, execution resumes at the top of the loop on line 15.

Note that the continue statement on line 30 is redundant. If it were left out and the break statement were encountered, the switch would end, exit would evaluate as false, the loop would reiterate, and the menu would be reprinted. The continue does, however, bypass the test of exit.

DO	**DON'T**
DO carefully document all intentional fall-through cases.	**DON'T** use complex if...else statements if a clearer switch statement will work.
DO put a default case in switch statements, if only to detect seemingly impossible situations.	**DON'T** forget break at the end of each case unless you want to fall through.

Summary

This lesson started with a look at the `goto` command that you were told to avoid using. You were then shown different methods that don't require a `goto` to cause a C++ program to loop.

The `while` statement loops check a condition, and if it is true, execute the statements in the body of the loop. `do...while` loops execute the body of the loop and then test the condition. `for` loops initialize a value, and then test an expression. If the expression is true, the body of the loop executes. The final expression in the `for` header is then executed and the condition is then checked again. This process of checking the condition, executing the statements in the body, and executing the final expression in the `for` statement continues until the conditional expression evaluates to false.

You also learned about `continue`, which causes `while`, `do...while`, and `for` loops to start over, and `break`, which causes `while`, `do...while`, `for`, and `switch` statements to end.

Q&A

Q How do I choose between `if...else` and `switch`?

A If more than just one or two `else` clauses are used, and all are testing the same value, consider using a `switch` statement.

Q How do I choose between `while` and `do...while`?

A If the body of the loop should always execute at least once, consider a `do...while` loop; otherwise, try to use the `while` loop.

Q How do I choose between `while` and `for`?

A If you are initializing a counting variable, testing that variable, and incrementing it each time through the loop, consider a `for` loop. If your variable is already initialized and is not incremented on each loop, a `while` loop might be the better choice. Experienced programmers look for this usage and will find your program harder to understand if you violate this expectation.

Q Is it better to use `while (true)` or `for (;;)`?

A No significant difference exists; however, it is best to avoid both.

Q Why shouldn't a variable be used as a condition, such as `while(n)`?

A In the current C++ standard, an expression is evaluated to a Boolean value of `true` or `false`. Although you can equate `false` to 0 and `true` to any other value, it is better—and more in line with the current standards—to use an expression that evaluates to a Boolean value of true or false. However, a variable of type `bool` can be used in a condition without any potential problems.

7

Workshop

The Workshop provides quiz questions to help you solidify your understanding of the material covered and exercises to provide you with experience in using what you've learned. Try to answer the quiz and exercise questions before checking the answers in Appendix D, and be certain that you understand the answers before continuing to the next lesson.

Quiz

1. How do you initialize more than one variable in a `for` loop?
2. Why is `goto` avoided?
3. Is it possible to write a `for` loop with a body that is never executed?
4. What is the value of x when the `for` loop completes?
   ```
   for (int x = 0; x < 100; x++)
   ```
5. Is it possible to nest `while` loops within `for` loops?
6. Is it possible to create a loop that never ends? Give an example.
7. What happens if you create a loop that never ends?

Exercises

1. Write a nested `for` loop that prints a 10×10 pattern of 0s.
2. Write a `for` statement to count from 100 to 200 by twos.
3. Write a `while` loop to count from 100 to 200 by twos.
4. Write a `do...while` loop to count from 100 to 200 by twos.
5. **BUG BUSTERS:** What is wrong with this code?
   ```
   int counter = 0;
   while (counter < 10)
   {
       cout << "counter: " << counter;
   }
   ```

6. **BUG BUSTERS:** What is wrong with this code?
   ```
   for (int counter = 0; counter < 10; counter++);
       cout << counter << " ";
   ```

7. **BUG BUSTERS:** What is wrong with this code?

```cpp
int counter = 100;
while (counter < 10)
{
    cout << "counter now: " << counter;
    counter--;
}
```

8. **BUG BUSTERS:** What is wrong with this code?

```cpp
cout << "Enter a number between 0 and 5: ";
cin >> theNumber;
switch (theNumber)
{
    case 0:
          doZero();
    case 1:            // fall through
    case 2:            // fall through
    case 3:            // fall through
    case 4:            // fall through
    case 5:
          doOneToFive();
          break;
    default:
          doDefault();
          break;
}
```

7

LESSON 8
Pointers Explained

One of the powerful but low-level tools available to a C++ programmer is the ability to manipulate computer memory directly by using pointers. This is an advantage that C++ has over some other languages, such as Java, C#, and Visual Basic.

Pointers present two special challenges when you're learning C++: They can be somewhat confusing, and it isn't immediately obvious why they are needed. This lesson explains how pointers work, step-by-step. You will fully understand the need for pointers, however, only as the book progresses.

In this lesson, you will learn

- What pointers are

- How to declare and use pointers

- What the free store is and how to manipulate memory

What Is a Pointer?

A *pointer* is a variable that holds a memory address. That's it. If you understand this simple sentence, you know the core of what there is to know about pointers.

A Bit About Memory

To understand pointers, you must know a little about computer memory. Computer memory is divided into sequentially numbered memory locations. Each variable is located at a unique location in memory, known as its *address*. Figure 8.1 shows a schematic representation of the storage of an unsigned long integer variable named theAge.

FIGURE 8.1
A schematic representation of theAge.

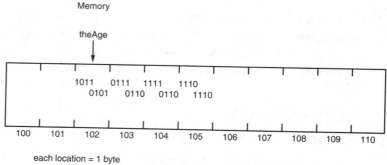

> NOTE
>
> The capability to use pointers and manipulate memory at a low level is one of the factors that makes C++ the language of choice for embedded and real-time applications.

Getting a Variable's Memory Address

Different computers number this memory using different complex schemes. Usually, as a programmer, you don't need to know the particular address of any given variable because the compiler handles the details. If you want this information, though, you can use the address-of operator (&), which returns the address of an object in memory. Listing 8.1 is used to illustrate the use of this operator.

LISTING 8.1   Demonstrating the Address-of Operator

```
 1:  // Listing 8.1 Demonstrates address-of operator
 2:  // and addresses of local variables
 3:  #include <iostream>
 4:
 5:  int main()
 6:  {
 7:      using namespace std;
 8:      unsigned short shortVar=5;
 9:      unsigned long  longVar=65535;
10:      long sVar = -65535;
11:
12:      cout << "shortVar:\t" << shortVar;
13:      cout << "\tAddress of shortVar:\t";
14:      cout <<  &shortVar << endl;
15:
16:      cout << "longVar:\t"  << longVar;
17:      cout  << "\tAddress of longVar:\t" ;
18:      cout <<  &longVar  << endl;
19:
20:      cout << "sVar:\t\t"     << sVar;
21:      cout << "\tAddress of sVar:\t" ;
22:      cout <<  &sVar       << endl;
23:
24:      return 0;
25:  }
```

Output ▼

```
shortVar:      5       Address of shortVar:    0012FF7C
longVar:       65535   Address of longVar:     0012FF78
sVar:          -65535  Address of sVar:        0012FF74
```

(Your printout might look different, especially the last column.)

Analysis ▼

Three variables are declared and initialized: an unsigned short on line 8, an unsigned long on line 9, and a long on line 10. Their values and addresses are printed on lines 12–22. You can see on lines 14, 18, and 22 that the address-of operator (&) is used to get the address of the variable. This operator is simply placed on the front of the variable name to have the address returned.

Line 12 prints the value of shortVar as 5, which is expected. In the first line of the output, you can see that its address is 0012FF7C when run on a Pentium (32-bit) computer. This address is computer-specific and might change slightly each time the program is run. Your results will be different.

When you declare a variable, the compiler determines how much memory to allow based on the variable type. The compiler takes care of allocating memory and automatically assigns an address for it. For a `long` integer that is typically four bytes, for example, an address to four bytes of memory is used.

> **NOTE**
>
> Note that your compiler might insist on assigning new variables on four-byte boundaries. (Thus, `longVar` was assigned an address four bytes after `shortVar` even though `shortVar` needed only two bytes!)

Storing a Variable's Address in a Pointer

Every variable has an address. Even without knowing the specific address, you can store a variable's address in a pointer.

Suppose, for example, that `howOld` is an integer. To declare a pointer called `pAge` to hold its address, you write

```
int *pAge = 0;
```

This declares `pAge` to be a pointer to an `int`. That is, `pAge` is declared to hold the address of an integer.

Note that `pAge` is a variable. When you declare an integer variable (type `int`), the compiler sets aside enough memory to hold an integer. When you declare a pointer variable such as `pAge`, the compiler sets aside enough memory to hold an address (on most computers, four bytes). A pointer, and thus `pAge`, is just a different type of variable.

Pointer Names

Because pointers are just another variable, you can use any name that is legal for other variables. The same naming rules and suggestions apply. Many programmers follow the convention of naming all pointers with an initial p, as in `pAge` or `pNumber`.

In the example,

```
int *pAge = 0;
```

`pAge` is initialized to zero. A pointer whose value is zero is called a *null* pointer. All pointers, when they are created, should be initialized to something. If you don't know what you want to assign to the pointer, assign 0. A pointer that is not initialized is called a *wild* pointer because you have no idea what it is pointing to—and it could be pointing to anything! Wild pointers are very dangerous.

For a pointer to hold an address, the address must be assigned to it. For the previous example, you must specifically assign the address of howOld to pAge, as shown in the following example:

```
unsigned short int howOld = 50;    // make a variable
unsigned short int * pAge = 0;     // make a pointer
pAge = &howOld;                    // put howOld's address in pAge
```

The first line creates a variable named howOld—whose type is unsigned short int—and initializes it with the value 50. The second line declares pAge to be a pointer to type unsigned short int and initializes it to zero. You know that pAge is a pointer because of the asterisk (*) after the variable type and before the variable name.

The third and final line assigns the address of howOld to the pointer pAge. You can tell that the address of howOld is being assigned because of the address-of operator (&). If the address-of operator had not been used, the value of howOld would have been assigned. That might or might not have been a valid address.

At this point, pAge has as its value the address of howOld. howOld, in turn, has the value 50. You could have accomplished this with one fewer step, as in

```
unsigned short int howOld = 50;       // make a variable
unsigned short int * pAge = &howOld;  // make pointer to howOld
```

pAge is a pointer that now contains the address of the howOld variable.

Getting the Value from a Variable

Using pAge, you can actually determine the value of howOld, which in this case is 50. Accessing the value stored in a variable by using a pointer is called *indirection* because you are indirectly accessing the variable by means of the pointer. For example, you can use indirection with the pAge pointer to access the value in howOld.

Indirection means accessing the value at the address held by a pointer. The pointer provides an indirect way to get the value held at that address.

With a normal variable, the variable type tells the compiler how much memory is needed to hold the value. With a pointer, the pointer variable type does not do this; all pointers hold addresses in the memory, and hence are the same size—usually four bytes on a machine with a 32-bit processor and eight bytes on a machine with a 64-bit processor.

The type tells the compiler how much memory is needed for the object at the address, which the pointer holds!

In the declaration

```
unsigned short int * pAge = 0;      // make a pointer
```

pAge is declared to be a pointer to an unsigned short integer. This tells the compiler that the pointer (which needs four bytes to hold an address) will hold the address of an object of type unsigned short int, which itself requires two bytes.

Dereferencing with the Indirection Operator

The indirection operator (*) is also called the *dereference* operator. When a pointer is dereferenced, the value at the address stored by the pointer is retrieved.

Normal variables provide direct access to their own values. If you create a new variable of type unsigned short int called yourAge, and you want to assign the value in howOld to that new variable, you write

```
unsigned short int yourAge;
yourAge = howOld;
```

A pointer provides *indirect* access to the value of the variable whose address it stores. To assign the value in howOld to the new variable yourAge by way of the pointer pAge, you write

```
unsigned short int yourAge;
yourAge = *pAge;
```

The indirection operator (*) in front of the pointer variable pAge means "the value stored at." This assignment says, "Take *the value stored at* the address in pAge and assign it to yourAge." If you didn't include the indirection operator, as in the following line:

```
yourAge = pAge;   // bad!!
```

you would be attempting to assign the value in pAge, a memory address, to YourAge. Your compiler would most likely give you a warning that you are making a mistake.

8

Different Uses of the Asterisk

The asterisk (*) is used in two distinct ways with pointers: as part of the pointer declaration and also as the dereference operator.

When you declare a pointer, the * is part of the declaration and it follows the type of the object pointed to. For example:

```
// make a pointer to an unsigned short
unsigned short * pAge = 0;
```

When the pointer is dereferenced, the dereference (or indirection) operator indicates that the value at the memory location stored in the pointer is to be accessed, rather than the address itself.

```
// assign 5 to the value at pAge
*pAge = 5;
```

Also note that this same character (*) is used as the multiplication operator. The compiler knows which operator to call based on how you are using it (context).

Pointers, Addresses, and Variables

It is important to distinguish between a pointer, the address that the pointer holds, and the value at the address held by the pointer. This is the source of much of the confusion about pointers. Consider the following code fragment:

```
int theVariable = 5;
int * pPointer = &theVariable ;
```

theVariable is declared to be an integer variable initialized with the value 5. pPointer is declared to be a pointer to an integer; it is initialized with the address of theVariable. pPointer is the pointer. The address that pPointer holds is the address of theVariable. The value at the address that pPointer holds is 5. Figure 8.2 shows a schematic representation of theVariable and pPointer.

FIGURE 8.2
A schematic representation of memory.

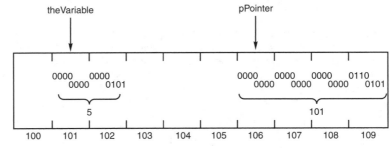

Address location

In Figure 8.2, the value 5 is stored at address location 101. This is shown in the binary number

```
0000 0000 0000 0101
```

This is two bytes (16 bits) whose decimal value is 5. The pointer variable is at location 106. Its value is

```
000 0000 0000 0000 0000 0000 0110 0101
```

This is the binary representation of the value 101, which is the address of theVariable, whose value is 5. The memory layout here is schematic, but it illustrates the idea of how pointers store an address.

Manipulating Data by Using Pointers

In addition to using the indirection operator to see what data is stored at a location pointed to by a variable, you can also manipulate that data. After the pointer is assigned the address, you can use that pointer to access the data in the variable being pointed to.

Listing 8.2 pulls together what you have just learned about pointers. In the listing, you see how the address of a local variable is assigned to a pointer and how the pointer can be used along with the indirection operator to manipulate the values in that variable.

LISTING 8.2   Manipulating Data by Using Pointers

```
1:  // Listing 8.2 Using pointers
2:  #include <iostream>
3:
4:  typedef unsigned short int USHORT;
5:
6:  int main()
7:  {
8:
9:      using namespace std;
10:
11:     USHORT myAge;          // a variable
12:     USHORT * pAge = 0;     // a pointer
13:
14:     myAge = 5;
15:
16:     cout << "myAge: " << myAge << endl;
17:     pAge = &myAge;        // assign address of myAge to pAge
18:     cout << "*pAge: " << *pAge << endl << endl;
19:
20:     cout << "Setting *pAge = 7... " << endl;
21:     *pAge = 7;             // sets myAge to 7
22:
```

LISTING 8.2 Continued

```
23:     cout << "*pAge: " << *pAge << endl;
24:     cout << "myAge: " << myAge << endl << endl;
25:
26:     cout << "Setting myAge = 9... " << endl;
27:     myAge = 9;
28:
29:     cout << "myAge: " << myAge << endl;
30:     cout << "*pAge: " << *pAge << endl;
31:
32:     return 0;
33: }
```

Output ▼

```
myAge: 5
*pAge: 5

Setting *pAge = 7...
*pAge: 7
myAge: 7

Setting myAge = 9...
myAge: 9
*pAge: 9
```

Analysis ▼

This program declares two variables: an unsigned short, myAge, and a pointer to an unsigned short, pAge. myAge is assigned the value 5 on line 14; this is verified by the printout on line 16.

On line 17, pAge is assigned the address of myAge. On line 18, pAge is dereferenced—using the indirection operator (*)—and printed, showing that the value at the address that pAge stores is the 5 stored in myAge.

On line 21, the value 7 is assigned to the variable at the address stored in pAge. This sets myAge to 7, and the printouts on lines 23 and 24 confirm this. Again, you should notice that the indirect access to the variable was obtained by using an asterisk—the indirection operator in this context.

On line 27, the value 9 is assigned to the variable myAge. This value is obtained directly on line 29 and indirectly (by dereferencing pAge) on line 30.

Examining the Address

Pointers enable you to manipulate addresses without ever knowing their real value. After today, you'll take it on faith that when you assign the address of a variable to a pointer, it really has the address of that variable as its value. But just this once, why not check to be certain? Listing 8.3 illustrates this idea.

LISTING 8.3   Finding Out What Is Stored in Pointers

```
 1:  // Listing 8.3
 2:  // What is stored in a pointer.
 3:  #include <iostream>
 4:
 5:  int main()
 6:  {
 7:     using namespace std;
 8:
 9:     unsigned short int myAge = 5, yourAge = 10;
10:
11:      // a pointer
12:     unsigned short int * pAge = &myAge;
13:
14:     cout << "myAge:\t" << myAge
15:        <<  "\t\tyourAge:\t" << yourAge << endl;
16:
17:     cout << "&myAge:\t" << &myAge
18:        << "\t&yourAge:\t" << &yourAge << endl;
19:
20:     cout << "pAge:\t" << pAge << endl;
21:     cout << "*pAge:\t" << *pAge << endl;
22:
23:
24:     cout << "\nReassigning: pAge = &yourAge..." << endl << endl;
25:     pAge = &yourAge;        // reassign the pointer
26:
27:     cout << "myAge:\t" << myAge <<
28:        "\t\tyourAge:\t" << yourAge << endl;
29:
30:     cout << "&myAge:\t" << &myAge
31:        << "\t&yourAge:\t" << &yourAge << endl;
32:
33:     cout << "pAge:\t" << pAge << endl;
34:     cout << "*pAge:\t" << *pAge << endl;
35:
36:     cout << "\n&pAge:\t" << &pAge << endl;
37:
38:     return 0;
39:  }
```

Output ▼

```
myAge:   5                yourAge:        10
&myAge:  0012FF7C         &yourAge:       0012FF78
pAge:    0012FF7C
*pAge:   5

Reassigning: pAge = &yourAge...

myAge:   5                yourAge:        10
&myAge:  0012FF7C         &yourAge:       0012FF78
pAge:    0012FF78
*pAge:   10

&pAge:   0012FF74
```

(Your output might look different.)

Analysis ▼

On line 9, myAge and yourAge are declared to be variables of type unsigned short integer. On line 12, pAge is declared to be a pointer to an unsigned short integer, and it is initialized with the address of the variable myAge.

Lines 14–18 print the values and the addresses of myAge and yourAge. Line 20 prints the *contents* of pAge, which is the address of myAge. You should notice that the output confirms that the value of pAge matches the value of myAge's address. Line 21 prints the result of dereferencing pAge, which prints the value at pAge—the value in myAge, or 5.

This is the essence of pointers. Line 20 shows that pAge stores the address of myAge, and line 21 shows how to get the value stored in myAge by dereferencing the pointer pAge. Be certain that you understand this fully before you go on. Study the code and look at the output.

On line 25, pAge is reassigned to point to the address of yourAge. The values and addresses are printed again. The output shows that pAge now has the address of the variable yourAge and that dereferencing obtains the value in yourAge.

Line 36 prints the address of pAge itself. Like any variable, it has an address, and that address can be stored in a pointer. (Assigning the address of a pointer to another pointer will be discussed shortly.)

Pointers and Array Names

In C++, an array name is a constant pointer to the first element of the array. Therefore, in the declaration

```
int Numbers [5];
```

Numbers is a pointer to &Numbers[0], which is the address of the first element of the array Numbers.

It is legal to use array names as constant pointers and vice versa. Therefore, Numbers + 4 is a legitimate way of accessing the integer at Numbers [4].

The compiler does all the arithmetic when you add to, increment, and decrement pointers. The address accessed when you write Numbers + 4 isn't four bytes past the address of Numbers, it is four objects; that is, four integers. Because an integer is typically four bytes long, Numbers + 4 is 16 bytes past the start of the array. This relationship between pointers and arrays is illustrated in Listing 8.4, which uses a pointer to print the contents of an array.

LISTING 8.4   Array Pointer Relationship

```
0: #include <iostream>
1: const int ARRAY_LENGTH = 5;
2:
3: int main ()
4: {
5:    using namespace std;
6:
7:    // An array of 5 integers initialized to 5 values
8:    int Numbers [ARRAY_LENGTH] = {0, 100, 200, 300, 400};
9:
10:    // pInt points to the first element
11:    const int *pInt = Numbers;
12:
13:    cout << "Using a pointer to print the contents of the array: " << endl;
14:
15:    for (int nIndex = 0; nIndex < ARRAY_LENGTH; ++ nIndex)
16:        cout << "Element [" << nIndex << "] = " << *(pInt + nIndex) << endl;
17:
18:    return 0;
19: }
```

Output ▼

```
Using a pointer to print the contents of the array:
Element [0] = 0
Element [1] = 100
Element [2] = 200
Element [3] = 300
Element [4] = 400
```

Analysis ▼

We created an array of five integers called Numbers and accessed its elements using the pointer pInt. Because an array name (Numbers in our case) is a pointer to the first element, pInt does just the same. Thus (pInt + 1) is a pointer to the second element, (pInt + 2) is a pointer to the third element, and so on. Dereferencing these pointers helps fetch the values being pointed at. So, *pInt returns the first value, *(pInt + 1) the second value, and so on.

The preceding example indicates the similarity between pointers and arrays. In fact, in line 16, we could have simply used pInt [nIndex] instead of *(pInt + nIndex) and still received the same output.

A Pointer to an Array Versus an Array of Pointers

Examine the following three declarations:

```
int    NumbersOne[500];

int * NumbersTwo[500];

int * NumbersThree = new int[500];
```

NumbersOne is an array of 500 int objects. NumbersTwo is an array of 500 pointers to int objects. NumbersThree is a pointer to an array of 500 int objects.

You have already studied that an array name such as NumbersOne is actually a pointer to the first element in the array. It hence becomes apparent that the first and last declarations (that is, NumbersOne and NumbersThree) are most similar. NumbersTwo, however, stands out in being an array of pointers that point to integers; that is, it contains 500 addresses that can point to integers in memory.

DO	DON'T
DO use the indirection operator (*) to access the data stored at the address in a pointer.	**DON'T** confuse the address in a pointer with the value at that address.
DO initialize all pointers either to a valid address or to null (0).	

Using Pointers

To declare a pointer, write the type of the variable or object whose address will be stored in the pointer, followed by the pointer operator (*) and the name of the pointer. For example:

```
unsigned short int * pPointer = 0;
```

To assign or initialize a pointer, prepend the name of the variable whose address is being assigned with the address-of operator (&). For example:

```
unsigned short int theVariable = 5;
unsigned short int * pPointer = &theVariable;
```

To dereference a pointer, prepend the pointer name with the dereference operator (*). For example:

```
unsigned short int theValue = *pPointer
```

Why Would You Use Pointers?

So far, you've seen step-by-step details of assigning a variable's address to a pointer. In practice, though, you would never do this. After all, why bother with a pointer when you already have a variable with access to that value? The only reason for this kind of pointer manipulation of an automatic variable is to demonstrate how pointers work. Now that you are comfortable with the syntax of pointers, you can put them to good use. Pointers are used, most often, for three tasks:

- Managing data on the free store
- Accessing class member data and functions
- Passing variables by reference to functions

The remainder of this lesson focuses on managing data on the free store and accessing class member data and functions.

The Stack and the Free Store (Heap)

In the section "How Functions Work—A Peek Under the Hood" in Lesson 6, "Organizing Code with Functions," five areas of memory are mentioned:

- Global namespace
- The free store
- Registers

- Code space
- The stack

Local variables are on the stack, along with function parameters. Code is in code space, of course, and global variables are in the global namespace. Registers are used for internal housekeeping functions, such as keeping track of the top of the stack and the instruction pointer. Just about all the remaining memory is given to the free store, which is often referred to as *the heap*.

Local variables don't persist; when a function returns, its local variables are destroyed. This is good because it means the programmer doesn't have to do anything to manage this memory space. But is bad because it makes it hard for functions to create objects for use by other objects or functions without generating the extra overhead of copying objects from stack to return value to destination object in the caller. Global variables solve that problem at the cost of providing unrestricted access to those variables throughout the program, which leads to the creation of code that is difficult to understand and maintain. Putting data in the free store can solve both of these problems if that data is managed properly.

You can think of the free store as a massive section of memory in which thousands of sequentially numbered cubbyholes lie waiting for your data. You can't label these cubbyholes, though, as you can with the stack. You must ask for the address of the cubbyhole that you reserve and then stash that address away in a pointer.

One way to think about this is with an analogy: A friend gives you the 800 number for Acme Mail Order. You go home and program your telephone with that number, and then you throw away the piece of paper with the number on it. If you push the button, a telephone rings somewhere, and Acme Mail Order answers. You don't remember the number, and you don't know where the other telephone is located, but the button gives you access to Acme Mail Order. Acme Mail Order is your data on the free store. You don't know where it is, but you know how to get to it. You access it by using its address—in this case, the telephone number. You don't have to know that number; you just have to put it into a pointer (the button). The pointer gives you access to your data without bothering you with the details.

The stack is cleaned automatically when a function returns. All the local variables go out of scope and they are removed from the stack. The free store is not cleaned until your program ends, and it is your responsibility to free any memory that you've reserved when you are done with it. This is where destructors are absolutely critical: They provide a place where any heap memory allocated in a class can be reclaimed.

The advantage to the free store is that the memory you reserve remains available until you explicitly state you are done with it by freeing it. If you reserve memory on the free store while in a function, the memory is still available when the function returns.

The disadvantage of the free store is also that the memory you reserve remains available until you explicitly state you are done with it by freeing it. If you neglect to free that memory, it can build up over time and cause the system to crash.

The advantage of accessing memory in this way, rather than using global variables, is that only functions with access to the pointer (which has the appropriate address) have access to the data. This requires the object containing the pointer to the data, or the pointer itself, to be explicitly passed to any function making changes, thus reducing the chances that a function can change the data without that change being traceable.

For this to work, you must be able to create a pointer to an area on the free store and to pass that pointer among functions. The following sections describe how to do this.

Allocating Space with the new Keyword

You allocate memory on the free store in C++ by using the new keyword. new is followed by the type of the object that you want to allocate, so that the compiler knows how much memory is required. Therefore, new unsigned short int allocates two bytes in the free store, and new long allocates four bytes, assuming that your system uses a two-byte unsigned short int and a four-byte long.

The return value from new is a memory address. Because you now know that memory addresses are stored in pointers, it should be no surprise to you that the return value from new should be assigned to a pointer. To create an unsigned short on the free store, you might write

```
unsigned short int * pPointer;
pPointer = new unsigned short int;
```

You can, of course, do this all on one line by initializing the pointer at the same time you declare it:

```
unsigned short int * pPointer = new unsigned short int;
```

In either case, pPointer now points to an unsigned short int on the free store. You can use this like any other pointer to a variable and assign a value into that area of memory by writing

```
*pPointer = 72;
```

This means "Put 72 at the value in pPointer," or "Assign the value 72 to the area on the free store to which pPointer points."

> **NOTE**
>
> If new cannot create memory on the free store (memory is, after all, a limited resource), it throws an exception (see Lesson 28, "Exception Handling").

Putting Memory Back: The delete Keyword

When you are finished with an area of memory, you must free it back to the system. You do this by calling delete on the pointer. delete returns the memory to the free store.

It is critical to remember that memory allocated with new is not freed automatically. If a pointer variable is pointing to memory on the free store and the pointer goes out of scope, the memory is not automatically returned to the free store. Rather, it is considered allocated and because the pointer is no longer available, you can no longer access the memory. This happens, for instance, if a pointer is a local variable. When the function in which that pointer is declared returns, that pointer goes out of scope and is lost. The memory allocated with new is not freed—instead, it becomes unavailable.

This situation is called a *memory leak*. It's called a memory leak because that memory can't be recovered until the program ends. It is as though the memory has leaked out of your computer.

To prevent memory leaks, you should restore any memory you allocate back to the free store. You do this by using the keyword delete. For example:

```
delete pPointer;
```

When you delete the pointer, you are really freeing up the memory whose address is stored in the pointer. You are saying, "Return to the free store the memory that this pointer points to." The pointer is still a pointer, and it can be reassigned. Listing 8.5 demonstrates allocating a variable on the heap, using that variable, and deleting it.

Most commonly, you will allocate items from the heap in a constructor, and deallocate them in the destructor. In other cases, you will initialize pointers in the constructor, allocate memory for those pointers as the object is used, and, in the destructor, test the pointers for null and deallocate them if they are not null.

CAUTION

> When you call `delete` on a pointer, the memory it points to is freed. Calling `delete` on that pointer again crashes your program! When you delete a pointer, set it to zero (null). Calling `delete` on a null pointer is guaranteed to be safe. For example:
>
> ```
> Animal *pDog = new Animal; // allocate memory
> delete pDog;    //frees the memory
>    pDog = 0;    //sets pointer to null
>    //...
> delete pDog;    //harmless
> ```

LISTING 8.5   Allocating, Using, and Deleting Pointers

```
 1:  // Listing 8.5
 2:  // Allocating and deleting a pointer
 3:  #include <iostream>
 4:  int main()
 5:  {
 6:     using namespace std;
 7:     int localVariable = 5;
 8:     int * pLocal= &localVariable;
 9:     int * pHeap = new int;
10:     *pHeap = 7;
11:     cout << "localVariable: " << localVariable << endl;
12:     cout << "*pLocal: " << *pLocal << endl;
13:     cout << "*pHeap: " << *pHeap << endl;
14:     delete pHeap;
15:     pHeap = new int;
16:     *pHeap = 9;
17:     cout << "*pHeap: " << *pHeap << endl;
18:     delete pHeap;
19:     return 0;
20:  }
```

Output ▼

```
localVariable: 5
*pLocal: 5
*pHeap: 7
*pHeap: 9
```

Analysis ▼

Line 7 declares and initializes a local variable ironically called `localVariable`. Line 8 declares a pointer called `pLocal` and initializes it with the address of the local variable. On line 9, a second pointer called `pHeap` is declared; however, it is initialized with the result obtained from calling `new int`. This allocates space on the free store for an `int`, which can be accessed using the `pHeap` pointer. This allocated memory is assigned the value 7 on line 10.

Lines 11–13 print a few values. Line 11 prints the value of the local variable (`localVariable`), line 12 prints the value pointed to by the `pLocal` pointer, and line 13 prints the value pointed to by the `pHeap` pointer. You should notice that, as expected, the values printed on lines 11 and 12 match. In addition, line 13 confirms that the value assigned on line 10 is, in fact, accessible.

On line 14, the memory allocated on line 9 is returned to the free store by a call to `delete`. This frees the memory and disassociates the pointer from that memory. `pHeap` is now free to be used to point to other memory. It is reassigned on lines 15 and 16, and line 17 prints the result. Line 18 restores that memory to the free store.

Although line 18 is redundant (the end of the program would have returned that memory), it is a good idea to free this memory explicitly. If the program changes or is extended, having already taken care of this step is beneficial.

Another Look at Memory Leaks

Memory leaks are one of the most serious issues and complaints about pointers. You have seen one way that memory leaks can occur. Another way you might inadvertently create a memory leak is by reassigning your pointer before deleting the memory to which it points. Consider this code fragment:

```
1:   unsigned short int * pPointer = new unsigned short int;
2:   *pPointer = 72;
3:   pPointer = new unsigned short int;
4:   *pPointer = 84;
```

Line 1 creates `pPointer` and assigns it the address of an area on the free store. Line 2 stores the value 72 in that area of memory. Line 3 reassigns `pPointer` to another area of memory. Line 4 places the value 84 in that area. The original area—in which the value 72 is now held—is unavailable because the pointer to that area of memory has been reassigned. No way exists to access that original area of memory, and there is no way to free it before the program ends. The code should have been written like this:

```
1: unsigned short int * pPointer = new unsigned short int;
2: *pPointer = 72;
3: delete pPointer;
4: pPointer = new unsigned short int;
5: *pPointer = 84;
```

Now the memory originally pointed to by `pPointer` is deleted, and thus freed, on line 3.

NOTE

> For every time in your program that you call new, there should be a call to delete. It is important to keep track of which pointer owns an area of memory and to ensure that the memory is returned to the free store when you are done with it.

Creating Objects on the Free Store

Just as you can create a pointer to an integer, you can create a pointer to any data type, including classes. If you have declared an object of type Cat, you can declare a pointer to that class and instantiate a Cat object on the free store, just as you can make one on the stack. The syntax is the same as for integers:

```
Cat *pCat = new Cat;
```

This calls the default constructor—the constructor that takes no parameters. The constructor is called whenever an object is created (on the stack or on the free store). Be aware, however, that you are not limited to using only the default constructor when creating an object with new—any constructor can be used.

Deleting Objects from the Free Store

When you call delete on a pointer to an object on the free store, that object's destructor is called before the memory is released. This gives your class a chance to clean up (generally deallocating heap-allocated memory), just as it does for objects destroyed on the stack. Listing 8.6 illustrates creating and deleting objects on the free store.

LISTING 8.6　Creating and Deleting Objects on the Free Store

```
 1:  // Listing 8.6 - Creating objects on the free store
 2:  // using new and delete
 3:
 4:  #include <iostream>
 5:
 6:  using namespace std;
 7:
 8:  class SimpleCat
 9:  {
10:  public:
11:      SimpleCat();
12:      ~SimpleCat();
13:  private:
```

LISTING 8.6   Continued

```
14:     int itsAge;
15:  };
16:
17:  SimpleCat::SimpleCat()
18:  {
19:      cout << "Constructor called. " << endl;
20:      itsAge = 1;
21:  }
22:
23:  SimpleCat::~SimpleCat()
24:  {
25:      cout << "Destructor called. " << endl;
26:  }
27:
28:  int main()
29:  {
30:      cout << "SimpleCat Frisky... " << endl;
31:      SimpleCat Frisky;
32:      cout << "SimpleCat *pRags = new SimpleCat..." << endl;
33:      SimpleCat * pRags = new SimpleCat;
34:      cout << "delete pRags... " << endl;
35:      delete pRags;
36:      cout << "Exiting, watch Frisky go... " << endl;
37:      return 0;
38:  }
```

Output ▼

```
SimpleCat Frisky...
Constructor called.
SimpleCat *pRags = new SimpleCat..
Constructor called.
delete pRags...
Destructor called.
Exiting, watch Frisky go...
Destructor called.
```

Analysis ▼

Lines 8–15 declare the stripped-down class SimpleCat. Line 11 declares SimpleCat's constructor, and lines 17–21 contain its definition. Line 12 declares SimpleCat's destructor, and lines 23–26 contain its definition. As you can see, both the constructor and destructor simply print a simple message to let you know they have been called.

On line 31, Frisky is created as a regular local variable, thus it is created on the stack. This creation causes the constructor to be called. On line 33, the SimpleCat pointed to by pRags is also created; however, because a pointer is being used, it is created on the heap. Once again, the constructor is called.

On line 35, delete is called on the pointer, pRags. This causes the destructor to be called and the memory that had been allocated to hold this SimpleCat object to be returned. When the function ends on line 38, Frisky goes out of scope and its destructor is called.

Stray, Wild, or Dangling Pointers

Yet again, issues with pointers are being brought up. This is because errors you create in your programs with pointers can be among the most difficult to find and among the most problematic. One source of bugs that are especially nasty and difficult to find in C++ is stray pointers. A stray pointer (also called a *wild* or *dangling pointer*) is created when you call delete on a pointer—thereby freeing the memory that it points to—and then you don't set it to null. If you try to use that pointer again without reassigning it, the result is unpredictable and, if you are lucky, your program will crash.

It is as though the Acme Mail Order company moved away, but you still pressed the programmed button on your phone. It is possible that nothing terrible happens—a telephone rings in a deserted warehouse. On the other hand, perhaps the telephone number has been reassigned to a munitions factory, and your call detonates an explosive and blows up your whole city!

In short, be careful not to use a pointer after you have called delete on it. The pointer still points to the old area of memory, but the compiler is free to put other data there; using the pointer without reallocating new memory for it can cause your program to crash. Worse, your program might proceed merrily on its way and crash several minutes later. This is called a *time bomb*, and it is no fun. To be safe, after you delete a pointer, set it to null (0). This disarms the pointer. Listing 8.7 illustrates creating a stray pointer.

CAUTION This program intentionally creates a stray pointer. Do NOT run this program—it will crash, if you are lucky.

LISTING 8.7   Creating a Stray Pointer

```
1:  // Listing 8.7 - Demonstrates a stray pointer
2:
3:  typedef unsigned short int USHORT;
4:  #include <iostream>
5:
```

LISTING 8.7 Continued

```
6:  int main()
7:  {
8:      USHORT * pInt = new USHORT;
9:      *pInt = 10;
10:     std::cout << "*pInt: " << *pInt << std::endl;
11:     delete pInt;
12:
13:     long * pLong = new long;
14:     *pLong = 90000;
15:     std::cout << "*pLong: " << *pLong << std::endl;
16:
17:     *pInt = 20;        // uh oh, this was deleted!
18:
19:     std::cout << "*pInt: " << *pInt  << std::endl;
20:     std::cout << "*pLong: " << *pLong  << std::endl;
21:     delete pLong;
22:     return 0;
23: }
```

Output ▼

```
*pInt:    10
*pLong:   90000
*pInt:    20
*pLong:   65556
```

Do not try to re-create this output. Yours will differ if you are lucky, or your computer will crash if you are not.

Analysis ▼

To repeat: This is a listing you should avoid running because it could lock up your machine. On line 8, pInt is declared to be a pointer to USHORT, and is pointed to newly allocated memory. On line 9, the value 10 is put into that memory allocated for pInt. The value pointed to is printed on line 10. After the value is printed, delete is called on the pointer. After line 11 executes, pInt is a stray, or dangling, pointer.

Line 13 declares a new pointer, pLong, which is pointed at the memory allocated by new. On line 14, the value 90000 is assigned to pLong, and on line 15, this value prints.

It is on line 17 that the troubles begin. On line 17, the value 20 is assigned to the memory that pInt points to, but pInt no longer points anywhere valid. The memory that pInt points to was freed by the call to delete on line 11. Assigning a value to that memory is certain disaster.

On line 19, the value at `pInt` is printed. Sure enough, it is `20`. Line 20 prints the value at `pLong`; it has suddenly been changed to `65556`. Two questions arise:

- How could `pLong`'s value change given that `pLong` wasn't touched?
- Where did the `20` go when `pInt` was used on line 17?

As you might guess, these are related questions. When a value was placed at `pInt` on line 17, the compiler happily placed the value `20` at the memory location that `pInt` previously pointed to. However, because that memory was freed on line 11, the compiler was free to reassign it. When `pLong` was created on line 13, it was given `pInt`'s old memory location. (On some computers, this might not happen, depending on where in memory these values are stored.) When the value `20` was assigned to the location that `pInt` previously pointed to, it wrote over the value pointed to by `pLong`. This is called *stomping on a pointer*. It is often the unfortunate outcome of using a stray pointer.

This is a particularly nasty bug because the value that changed wasn't associated with the stray pointer. The change to the value at `pLong` was a side effect of the misuse of `pInt`. In a large program, this would be very difficult to track down.

Just for Fun

Here are the details of how 65,556 got into the memory address of `pLong` in Listing 8.7:

1. `pInt` was pointed at a particular memory location, and the value `10` was assigned.

2. `delete` was called on `pInt`, which told the compiler that it could put something else at that location. Then `pLong` was assigned the same memory location.

3. The value `90000` was assigned to `*pLong`. The particular computer used in this example stored the four-byte value of 90,000 (`00 01 5F 90`) in byte-swapped order. Therefore, it was stored as `5F 90 00 01`.

4. `pInt` was assigned the value `20`—or `00 14` in hexadecimal notation. Because `pInt` still pointed to the same address, the first two bytes of `pLong` were overwritten, leaving `00 14 00 01`.

5. The value at `pLong` was printed, reversing the bytes back to their correct order of `00 01 00 14`, which was translated into the DOS value of `65556`.

FAQ

What is the difference between a null pointer and a stray pointer?

Answer: When you delete a pointer, you tell the compiler to free the memory, but the pointer itself continues to exist. It is now a stray pointer. When you then write `myPtr = 0;` you change it from being a stray pointer to being a null pointer.

Normally, if you delete a pointer and then delete it again, your program is undefined. That is, anything might happen—if you are lucky, the program will crash. If you delete a null pointer, nothing happens; it is safe.

Using a stray *or* a null pointer (for example, writing `myPtr = 5;`) is illegal, and it might crash your system. If the pointer is null, it *will* crash, another benefit of null over stray. Predictable crashes are preferred because they are easier to debug.

Using `const` **Pointers**

You can use the keyword `const` for pointers before the type, after the type, or in both places. For example, all the following declarations are legal:

```
const int * pOne;
int * const pTwo;
const int * const pThree;
```

Each of these, however, does something different:

- `pOne` is a pointer to a constant integer. The value that is pointed to can't be changed.
- `pTwo` is a constant pointer to an integer. The integer can be changed, but `pTwo` can't point to anything else.
- `pThree` is a constant pointer to a constant integer. The value that is pointed to can't be changed, and `pThree` can't be changed to point to anything else.

The trick to keeping this straight is to look to the right of the keyword `const` to find out what is being declared constant. If the type is to the right of the keyword, it is the value that is constant. If the variable is to the right of the keyword `const`, it is the pointer variable itself that is constant. The following helps to illustrate this:

```
const int * p1;  // the int pointed to is constant
int * const p2;  // p2 is constant, it can't point to anything else
```

DO	DON'T
DO protect objects passed by reference with `const` if they should not be changed.	**DON'T** use a pointer that has been deleted.
DO set pointers to null rather than leaving them uninitialized or dangling.	**DON'T** delete pointers more than once.

Summary

Pointers provide a powerful way to access data by indirection. Every variable has an address, which can be obtained using the address-of operator (&). The address can be stored in a pointer.

Pointers are declared by writing the type of object that they point to, followed by the indirection operator (*) and the name of the pointer. Pointers should be initialized to point to an object or to null (0). You access the value at the address stored in a pointer by using the indirection operator (*). You can declare `const` pointers, which can't be reassigned to point to other objects, and pointers to `const` objects, which can't be used to change the objects to which they point.

To create new objects on the free store, you use the `new` keyword and assign the address that is returned to a pointer. You free that memory by calling the `delete` keyword on the pointer. `delete` frees the memory, but it doesn't destroy the pointer. Therefore, you must reassign the pointer after its memory has been freed.

Q&A

Q Why are pointers so important?

A Pointers are important for a number of reasons. These include being able to use pointers to hold the address of objects and to use them to pass arguments by reference. In Lesson 12, "Polymorphism," you'll see how pointers are used in class polymorphism. In addition, many operating systems and class libraries create objects on your behalf and return pointers to them.

Q Why should I bother to declare anything on the free store?

A Objects on the free store persist after the return of a function. In addition, the ability to store objects on the free store enables you to decide at runtime how many objects you need, instead of having to declare this in advance.

Q Why should I declare an object `const` if it limits what I can do with it?

A As a programmer, you want to enlist the compiler in helping you find bugs. One serious bug that is difficult to find is a function that changes an object in ways that aren't obvious to the calling function. Declaring an object `const` prevents such changes.

8

Workshop

The Workshop provides quiz questions to help you solidify your understanding of the material covered and exercises to provide you with experience in using what you've learned. Try to answer the quiz and exercise questions before checking the answers in Appendix D, and be certain that you understand the answers before continuing to the next lesson.

Quiz

1. What operator is used to determine the address of a variable?
2. What operator is used to find the value stored at an address held in a pointer?
3. What is a pointer?
4. What is the difference between the address stored in a pointer and the value at that address?
5. What is the difference between the indirection operator and the address-of operator?
6. What is the difference between `const int * ptrOne` and `int * const ptrTwo`?

Exercises

1. What do these declarations do?

    A. `int * pOne;`

    B. `int vTwo;`

    C. `int * pThree = &vTwo;`

2. If you have an `unsigned short` variable named `yourAge`, how would you declare a pointer to manipulate `yourAge`?

3. Assign the value `50` to the variable `yourAge` by using the pointer that you declared in Exercise 2.

4. Write a small program that declares an integer and a pointer to integer. Assign the address of the integer to the pointer. Use the pointer to set a value in the integer variable.

5. **BUG BUSTERS:** What is wrong with this code?

```cpp
#include <iostream>
using namespace std;
int main()
{
    int *pInt;
    *pInt = 9;
    cout << "The value at pInt: " << *pInt;
    return 0;
}
```

6. **BUG BUSTERS:** What is wrong with this code?

```cpp
#include <iostream>
using namespace std;
int main()
{
    int SomeVariable = 5;
    cout << "SomeVariable: " << SomeVariable << endl;
    int *pVar = & SomeVariable;
    pVar = 9;
    cout << "SomeVariable: " << *pVar << endl;
    return 0;
}
```

LESSON 9
Exploiting References

In the previous lesson, you learned how to use pointers to manipulate objects on the free store and how to refer to those objects indirectly. References, the topic of this lesson, give you almost all the power of pointers but with a much easier syntax.

In this lesson, you will learn

- What references are

- How references differ from pointers

- How to create references and use them

- What the limitations of references are

- How to pass values and objects into and out of functions by reference

What Is a Reference?

A *reference* is an alias; when you create a reference, you initialize it with the name of another object, the target. From that moment on, the reference acts as an alternative name for the target, and anything you do to the reference is really done to the target.

You create a reference by writing the type of the target object, followed by the reference operator (&), followed by the name of the reference, followed by an equal sign, followed by the name of the target object.

References can have any legal variable name, but some programmers prefer to prefix reference names with the letter r. Thus, if you have an integer variable named someInt, you can make a reference to that variable by writing the following:

```
int &rSomeRef = someInt;
```

This statement is read as "rSomeRef is a reference to an integer. The reference is initialized to refer to someInt." References differ from other variables that you can declare in that they must be initialized when they are declared. If you try to create a reference variable without assigning, you receive a compiler error. Listing 9.1 shows how references are created and used.

> **NOTE** ___ | Note that the reference operator (&) is the same symbol as the one used for the address-of operator. These are not the same operators, however, although clearly they are related.
>
> The space before the reference operator is required; the space between the reference operator and the name of the reference variable is optional. Thus
>
> ```
> int &rSomeRef = someInt;  // ok
> int & rSomeRef = someInt; // ok
> ```

LISTING 9.1   Creating and Using References

```
1:  //Listing 9.1 - Demonstrating the use of references
2:
3:  #include <iostream>
4:
5:  int main()
6:  {
7:      using namespace std;
8:      int  intOne;
9:      int &rSomeRef = intOne;
10:
```

LISTING 9.1 Continued

```
11:        intOne = 5;
12:        cout << "intOne: " << intOne << endl;
13:        cout << "rSomeRef: " << rSomeRef << endl;
14:
15:        rSomeRef = 7;
16:        cout << "intOne: " << intOne << endl;
17:        cout << "rSomeRef: " << rSomeRef << endl;
18:
19:        return 0;
20:    }
```

9

Output ▼

```
intOne: 5
rSomeRef: 5
intOne: 7
rSomeRef: 7
```

Analysis ▼

On line 8, a local integer variable, intOne, is declared. On line 9, a reference to an integer (int), rSomeRef, is declared and initialized to refer to intOne. As already stated, if you declare a reference but don't initialize it, you receive a compile-time error. References must be initialized.

On line 11, intOne is assigned the value 5. On lines 12 and 13, the values in intOne and rSomeRef are printed, and are, of course, the same.

On line 15, 7 is assigned to rSomeRef. Because this is a reference, it is an alias for intOne, and thus the 7 is really assigned to intOne, as is shown by the printouts on lines 16 and 17.

Using the Address-Of Operator (&) on References

You have now seen that the & symbol is used for both the address of a variable and to declare a reference. But what if you take the address of a reference variable? If you ask a reference for its address, it returns the address of its target. That is the nature of references. They are aliases for the target. Listing 9.2 demonstrates taking the address of a reference variable called rSomeRef.

LISTING 9.2 Taking the Address of a Reference

```
 1:   //Listing 9.2 - Demonstrating the use of references
 2:
 3:   #include <iostream>
 4:
 5:   int main()
 6:   {
 7:      using namespace std;
 8:      int  intOne;
 9:      int &rSomeRef = intOne;
10:
11:      intOne = 5;
12:      cout << "intOne: " << intOne << endl;
13:      cout << "rSomeRef: " << rSomeRef << endl;
14:
15:      cout << "&intOne: "  << &intOne << endl;
16:      cout << "&rSomeRef: " << &rSomeRef << endl;
17:
18:      return 0;
19:   }
```

Output ▼

```
intOne: 5
rSomeRef: 5
&intOne:  0x3500
&rSomeRef: 0x3500
```

CAUTION	Because the final two lines print memory addresses that might be unique to your computer or to a specific run of the program, your output might differ.

Analysis ▼

rSomeRef is again initialized as a reference to intOne. This time, the addresses of the two variables are printed in lines 15 and 16, and they are identical.

C++ gives you no way to access the address of the reference itself because it is not meaningful as it would be if you were using a pointer or other variable. References are initialized when created, and they always act as a synonym for their target, even when the address-of operator is applied.

For example, if you have a class called `President`, you might declare an instance of that class as follows:

```
President George_Washington;
```

You might then declare a reference to `President` and initialize it with this object:

```
President &FatherOfOurCountry = George_Washington;
```

Only one `President` exists; both identifiers refer to the same object of the same class. Any action you take on `FatherOfOurCountry` is taken on `George_Washington` as well.

Be careful to distinguish between the & symbol on line 9 of Listing 9.2, which declares a reference to an integer named `rSomeRef`, and the & symbols on lines 15 and 16, which return the addresses of the integer variable `intOne` and the reference `rSomeRef`. The compiler knows how to distinguish between the two uses by the context in which they are being used.

9

NOTE
> Normally, when you use a reference, you do not use the address-of operator. You simply use the reference as you would use the target variable.

Attempting to Reassign References (Not!)

Reference variables cannot be reassigned. Even experienced C++ programmers can be confused by what happens when you try to reassign a reference. Reference variables are always aliases for their target. What appears to be a reassignment turns out to be the assignment of a new value to the target. Listing 9.3 illustrates this fact.

LISTING 9.3   Assigning to a Reference

```
 1:  //Listing 9.3 - //Reassigning a reference
 2:
 3:  #include <iostream>
 4:
 5:  int main()
 6:  {
 7:      using namespace std;
 8:      int  intOne;
 9:      int &rSomeRef = intOne;
10:
11:      intOne = 5;
12:      cout << "intOne:    " << intOne << endl;
13:      cout << "rSomeRef:  " << rSomeRef << endl;
```

LISTING 9.3 Continued

```
14:    cout << "&intOne:   " << &intOne << endl;
15:    cout << "&rSomeRef: " << &rSomeRef << endl;
16:
17:    int intTwo = 8;
18:    rSomeRef = intTwo;  // not what you think!
19:    cout << "\nintOne:    " << intOne << endl;
20:    cout << "intTwo:    " << intTwo << endl;
21:    cout << "rSomeRef:  " << rSomeRef << endl;
22:    cout << "&intOne:   " << &intOne << endl;
23:    cout << "&intTwo:   " << &intTwo << endl;
24:    cout << "&rSomeRef: " << &rSomeRef << endl;
25:    return 0;
26: }
```

Output ▼

```
intOne:    5
rSomeRef:  5
&intOne:    0012FEDC
&rSomeRef: 0012FEDC

intOne:    8
intTwo:    8
rSomeRef:  8
&intOne:    0012FEDC
&intTwo:    0012FEE0
&rSomeRef: 0012FEDC
```

Analysis ▼

On lines 8 and 9, an integer variable and a reference to an integer are declared. The integer is assigned the value 5 on line 11, and the values and their addresses are printed on lines 12–15.

On line 17, a new variable, intTwo, is created and initialized with the value 8. On line 18, the programmer tries to reassign rSomeRef to be an alias to the variable intTwo, but that is not what happens. What actually happens is that rSomeRef continues to act as an alias for intOne, so this assignment is equivalent to the following:

```
intOne = intTwo;
```

Sure enough, when the values of intOne and rSomeRef are printed (lines 19–21), they are the same as intTwo. In fact, when the addresses are printed on lines 22–24, you see that rSomeRef continues to refer to intOne and not intTwo.

DO	DON'T
DO use references to create an alias to an object.	**DON'T** try to reassign a reference.
DO initialize all references.	**DON'T** confuse the address-of operator with the reference operator.

Null Pointers and Null References

When pointers are not initialized or when they are deleted, they ought to be assigned to null (0). This is not true for references because they must be initialized to what they reference when they are declared.

However, because C++ needs to be usable for device drivers, embedded systems, and real-time systems that can reach directly into the hardware, the ability to reference specific addresses is valuable and required. For this reason, most compilers support a null or numeric initialization of a reference without much complaint, crashing only if you try to use the object in some way when that reference would be invalid.

Taking advantage of this in normal programming, however, is still not a good idea. When you move your program to another machine or compiler, mysterious bugs might develop if you have null references.

Passing Function Arguments by Reference

In Lesson 6, "Organizing Code with Functions," you learned that functions have two limitations: Arguments are passed by value, and the `return` statement can return only one value.

Passing values to a function by reference can overcome both of these limitations. In C++, passing a variable by reference is accomplished in two ways: using pointers and using references. Note the difference: You pass *by reference* using a pointer, or you pass *a reference* using a reference.

The syntax of using a pointer is different from that of using a reference, but the net effect is the same. Rather than a copy being created within the scope of the function, the actual original object is (effectively) made directly available to the function.

Passing an object by reference enables the function to change the object being referred to. In Lesson 6, you learned that functions are passed their parameters on the stack.

When a function is passed a value by reference (using either pointers or references), the address of the original object is put on the stack, not the entire object. In fact, on some computers, the address is actually held in a register and nothing is put on the stack. In either case, because an address is being passed, the compiler now knows how to get to the original object, and changes made by the function are made there and not in a local copy.

Recall that Listing 6.4 in Lesson 6 demonstrated that a call to the swap() function did not affect the values in the calling function. Listing 6.4 is reproduced here as Listing 9.4, for your convenience.

LISTING 9.4   Demonstrating Passing by Value

```
1:   //Listing 9.4 - Demonstrates passing by value
2:   #include <iostream>
3:
4:   using namespace std;
5:   void swap(int x, int y);
6:
7:   int main()
8:   {
9:      int x = 5, y = 10;
10:
11:     cout << "Main. Before swap, x: " << x << " y: " << y << endl;
12:     swap(x,y);
13:     cout << "Main. After swap, x: " << x << " y: " << y << endl;
14:     return 0;
15:   }
16:
17:   void swap (int x, int y)
18:   {
19:      int temp;
20:
21:      cout << "Swap. Before swap, x: " << x << " y: " << y << endl;
22:
23:      temp = x;
24:      x = y;
25:      y = temp;
26:
27:      cout << "Swap. After swap, x: " << x << " y: " << y << endl;
28:   }
```

Output ▼

```
Main. Before swap, x: 5 y: 10
Swap. Before swap, x: 5 y: 10
Swap. After swap, x: 10 y: 5
Main. After swap, x: 5 y: 10
```

Analysis ▼

This program initializes two variables in `main()` and then passes them to the `swap()` function, which appears to swap them. When they are examined again in `main()`, they are unchanged!

The problem here is that x and y are being passed to `swap()` by value. That is, local copies were made in the function. These local copies were changed and then thrown away when the function returned and its local storage was deallocated. What is preferable is to pass x and y by reference, which changes the source values of the variable rather than a local copy.

Two ways to solve this problem are possible in C++: You can make the parameters of `swap()` pointers to the original values or you can pass in references to the original values.

Making `swap()` Work with Pointers

When you pass in a pointer, you pass in the address of the object, and thus the function can manipulate the value at that address. To make `swap()` change the actual values of x and y by using pointers, the function, `swap()`, should be declared to accept two `int` pointers. By dereferencing the pointers, the values of x and y will actually be accessed and, in fact, be swapped. Listing 9.5 demonstrates this idea.

LISTING 9.5 Passing by Reference Using Pointers

```
1:   //Listing 9.5 Demonstrates passing by reference
2:   #include <iostream>
3:
4:   using namespace std;
5:   void swap(int *x, int *y);
6:
7:   int main()
8:   {
9:      int x = 5, y = 10;
10:
11:     cout << "Main. Before swap, x: " << x << " y: " << y << endl;
12:     swap(&x,&y);
13:     cout << "Main. After swap, x: " << x << " y: " << y << endl;
14:     return 0;
15:  }
16:
17:  void swap (int *px, int *py)
18:  {
19:     int temp;
20:
21:     cout << "Swap. Before swap, *px: " << *px <<
22:        " *py: " << *py << endl;
23:
```

9

LISTING 9.5   Continued

```
24:     temp = *px;
25:     *px = *py;
26:     *py = temp;
27:
28:     cout << "Swap. After swap, *px: " << *px <<
29:         " *py: " << *py << endl;
30:
31: }
```

Output ▼

```
Main. Before swap, x: 5 y: 10
Swap. Before swap, *px: 5 *py: 10
Swap. After swap, *px: 10 *py: 5
Main. After swap, x: 10 y: 5
```

Analysis ▼

Success! On line 5, the prototype of swap() is changed to indicate that its two parameters will be pointers to int rather than int variables. When swap() is called on line 12, the addresses of x and y are passed as the arguments. You can see that the addresses are passed because the address-of operator (&) is being used.

On line 19, a local variable, temp, is declared in the swap() function. temp need not be a pointer; it will just hold the value of *px (that is, the value of x in the calling function) for the life of the function. After the function returns, temp is no longer needed.

On line 24, temp is assigned the value at px. On line 25, the value at px is assigned to the value at py. On line 26, the value stashed in temp (that is, the original value at px) is put into py. The net effect of this is that the values in the calling function, whose address was passed to swap(), are, in fact, swapped.

Implementing swap() with References

The preceding program works, but the syntax of the swap() function is cumbersome in two ways. First, the repeated need to dereference the pointers within the swap() function makes it error-prone. For instance, if you fail to dereference the pointer, the compiler still lets you assign an integer to the pointer, and a subsequent user experiences an addressing error. This is also hard to read. Finally, the need to pass the address of the variables in the calling function makes the inner workings of swap() overly apparent to its users.

It is a goal of an object-oriented language such as C++ to prevent the user of a function from worrying about how it works. Passing by pointers puts the burden on the calling function rather than where it belongs—on the function being called. Listing 9.6 rewrites the swap() function using references.

LISTING 9.6 swap() Rewritten with References

```
1:  //Listing 9.6 Demonstrates passing by reference
2:  // using references!
3:  #include <iostream>
4:
5:  using namespace std;
6:  void swap(int &x, int &y);
7:
8:  int main()
9:  {
10:      int x = 5, y = 10;
11:
12:      cout << "Main. Before swap, x: " << x << " y: "
13:          << y << endl;
14:
15:      swap(x,y);
16:
17:      cout << "Main. After swap, x: " << x << " y: "
18:          << y << endl;
19:
20:      return 0;
21:  }
22:
23:  void swap (int &rx, int &ry)
24:  {
25:      int temp;
26:
27:      cout << "Swap. Before swap, rx: " << rx << " ry: "
28:          << ry << endl;
29:
30:      temp = rx;
31:      rx = ry;
32:      ry = temp;
33:
34:
35:      cout << "Swap. After swap, rx: " << rx << " ry: "
36:          << ry << endl;
37:
38:  }
```

9

Output ▼

```
Main. Before swap, x:5 y: 10
Swap. Before swap, rx:5 ry:10
Swap. After swap, rx:10 ry:5
Main. After swap, x:10, y:5
```

Analysis ▼

Just as in the example with pointers, two variables are declared on line 10, and their values are printed on line 12. On line 15, the function swap() is called, but note that x and y, not their addresses, are passed. The calling function simply passes the variables.

When swap() is called, program execution jumps to line 23, where the variables are identified as references. The values from the variables are printed on line 27, but note that no special operators are required. These variables are aliases for the original variables and can be used as such.

On lines 30–32, the values are swapped, and then they're printed on line 35. Program execution jumps back to the calling function, and on line 17, the values are printed in main(). Because the parameters to swap() are declared to be references, the variables from main() are passed by reference, and thus their changed values are what is seen in main() as well. As you can see from this listing, references provide the convenience and ease of use of normal variables, but with the power and pass-by-reference capability of pointers!

Returning Multiple Values

As discussed, functions can return only one value. What if you need to get two values back from a function? One way to solve this problem is to pass two objects into the function by reference. The function can then fill the objects with the correct values. Because passing by reference allows a function to change the original objects, this effectively enables the function to return two pieces of information. This approach bypasses the return value of the function, which can then be reserved for reporting errors.

Again, this can be done with references or pointers. Listing 9.7 demonstrates a function that returns three values: two as pointer parameters and one as the return value of the function.

LISTING 9.7 Returning Values with Pointers

```
 1:  //Listing 9.7 - Returning multiple values from a function
 2:
 3:  #include <iostream>
 4:
 5:  using namespace std;
 6:  short Factor(int n, int* pSquared, int* pCubed);
 7:
 8:  int main()
 9:  {
10:      int number, squared, cubed;
11:      short error;
12:
13:      cout << "Enter a number (0 - 20): ";
14:      cin >> number;
15:
16:      error = Factor(number, &squared, &cubed);
17:
18:      if (!error)
19:      {
20:         cout << "number: " << number << endl;
21:         cout << "square: " << squared << endl;
22:         cout << "cubed: "  << cubed   << endl;
23:      }
24:      else
25:         cout << "Error encountered!!" << endl;
26:      return 0;
27:  }
28:
29:  short Factor(int n, int *pSquared, int *pCubed)
30:  {
31:      short Value = 0;
32:      if (n > 20)
33:         Value = 1;
34:      else
35:      {
36:         *pSquared = n*n;
37:         *pCubed = n*n*n;
38:         Value = 0;
39:      }
40:      return Value;
41:  }
```

Output ▼

```
Enter a number (0-20): 3
number: 3
square: 9
cubed: 27
```

Analysis ▼

On line 10, `number`, `squared`, and `cubed` are defined as short integers. `number` is assigned a value based on user input on line 14. On line 16, this number and the addresses of `squared` and `cubed` are passed to the function `Factor()`.

On line 32, `Factor()` examines the first parameter, which is passed by value. If it is greater than 20 (the maximum value this function can handle), it sets the return value, `Value`, to a simple error value. Note that the return value from `Function()` is reserved for either this error value or the value `0`, indicating all went well, and note that the function returns this value on line 40.

The actual values needed, the square and cube of `number`, are not returned by using the return mechanism; rather, they are returned by changing the pointers that were passed into the function. On lines 36 and 37, the pointers are assigned their return values. These values are assigned to the original variables by the use of indirection. You know this by the use of the dereference operator (`*`) with the pointer names. On line 38, `Value` is assigned a success value, and on line 40, it is returned.

TIP	Because passing by reference or by pointer allows uncontrolled access to object attributes and methods, you should pass the minimum required for the function to do its job. This helps to ensure that the function is safer to use and more easily understandable.

Returning Values by Reference

Although Listing 9.7 works, it can be made easier to read and maintain by using references rather than pointers. Listing 9.8 shows the same program rewritten to use references.

Listing 9.8 also includes a second improvement. An enum has been added to make the return value easier to understand. Rather than returning `0` or `1`, using an enum, the program can return `SUCCESS` or `FAILURE`.

LISTING 9.8 Listing 9.7 Rewritten Using References

```
1:  //Listing 9.8
2:  // Returning multiple values from a function
3:  // using references
4:  #include <iostream>
5:
```

LISTING 9.8 Continued

```
 6:  using namespace std;
 7:
 8:  enum ERR_CODE { SUCCESS, ERROR };
 9:
10:  ERR_CODE Factor(int, int&, int&);
11:
12:  int main()
13:  {
14:     int number, squared, cubed;
15:     ERR_CODE result;
16:
17:     cout << "Enter a number (0 - 20): ";
18:     cin >> number;
19:
20:     result = Factor(number, squared, cubed);
21:
22:     if (result == SUCCESS)
23:     {
24:        cout << "number: " << number << endl;
25:        cout << "square: " << squared << endl;
26:        cout << "cubed: "  << cubed   << endl;
27:     }
28:     else
29:        cout << "Error encountered!!" << endl;
30:     return 0;
31:  }
32:
33:  ERR_CODE Factor(int n, int &rSquared, int &rCubed)
34:  {
35:     if (n > 20)
36:        return ERROR;   // simple error code
37:     else
38:     {
39:        rSquared = n*n;
40:        rCubed = n*n*n;
41:        return SUCCESS;
42:     }
43:  }
```

Output ▼

```
Enter a number (0 - 20): 3
number: 3
square: 9
cubed: 27
```

Analysis ▼

Listing 9.8 is identical to Listing 9.7, with two exceptions. The `ERR_CODE` enumeration makes the error reporting a bit more explicit on lines 36 and 41, as well as the error handling on line 22.

The larger change, however, is that `Factor()` is now declared to take references to `squared` and `cubed` rather than to pointers. This makes the manipulation of these parameters far simpler and easier to understand.

Passing by Reference for Efficiency

Each time you pass an object into a function by value, a copy of the object is made. Each time you return an object from a function by value, another copy is made. This copy-step results in zero to little loss in performance for small objects such as integers.

However, with larger, user-created objects such as `struct` or `class` objects, the cost of copying can be very high. The size of a user-created object on the stack is the sum of each of its member variables. These, in turn, can each be user-created objects, and passing such a massive structure by copying it onto the stack can be very expensive in performance and memory consumption.

Another cost occurs as well. With the classes you create, each of these temporary copies is created when the compiler calls a special constructor: the copy constructor. Later, you will learn how copy constructors work and how you can make your own, but for now it is enough to know that the copy constructor is called each time a temporary copy of the object is put on the stack.

When the temporary object is destroyed, which happens when the function returns, the object's destructor is called. If an object is returned by the function by value, a copy of that object must be made and destroyed as well.

With large objects, these constructor and destructor calls can be expensive in speed and use of memory. To illustrate this idea, Listing 9.9 creates a stripped-down, user-created object: `SimpleCat`. A real object would be larger and more expensive, but this is sufficient to show how often the copy constructor and destructor are called when the object is passed by value. Because you have not yet studied the concept of a `class`, don't focus your attention on the syntax; rather, understand how passing by reference reduces function calls by focusing on the outcome.

LISTING 9.9   Passing Objects by Reference

```
1:  //Listing 9.9 - Passing pointers to objects
2:
3:  #include <iostream>
4:
5:  using namespace std;
6:  class SimpleCat
7:  {
8:    public:
9:      SimpleCat ();                  // constructor
10:     SimpleCat(SimpleCat&);         // copy constructor
11:     ~SimpleCat();                  // destructor
12:  };
13:
14:  SimpleCat::SimpleCat()
15:  {
16:     cout << "Simple Cat Constructor..." << endl;
17:  }
18:
19:  SimpleCat::SimpleCat(SimpleCat&)
20:  {
21:     cout << "Simple Cat Copy Constructor..." << endl;
22:  }
23:
24:  SimpleCat::~SimpleCat()
25:  {
26:     cout << "Simple Cat Destructor..." << endl;
27:  }
28:
29:  SimpleCat FunctionOne (SimpleCat theCat);
30:  SimpleCat* FunctionTwo (SimpleCat *theCat);
31:
32:  int main()
33:  {
34:     cout << "Making a cat..." << endl;
35:     SimpleCat Frisky;
36:     cout << "Calling FunctionOne..." << endl;
37:     FunctionOne(Frisky);
38:     cout << "Calling FunctionTwo..." << endl;
39:     FunctionTwo(&Frisky);
40:     return 0;
41:  }
42:
43:  // FunctionOne, passes by value
44:  SimpleCat FunctionOne(SimpleCat theCat)
45:  {
46:     cout << "Function One. Returning... " << endl;
47:     return theCat;
48:  }
49:
```

LISTING 9.9 Continued

```
50:  // functionTwo, passes by reference
51:  SimpleCat* FunctionTwo (SimpleCat  *theCat)
52:  {
53:     cout << "Function Two. Returning... " << endl;
54:     return theCat;
55:  }
```

Output ▼

```
Making a cat...
Simple Cat Constructor...
Calling FunctionOne...
Simple Cat Copy Constructor...
Function One. Returning...
Simple Cat Copy Constructor...
Simple Cat Destructor...
Simple Cat Destructor...
Calling FunctionTwo...
Function Two. Returning...
Simple Cat Destructor...
```

Analysis ▼

Listing 9.9 creates the SimpleCat object and then calls two functions. The first function receives the Cat by value and then returns it by value. The second one receives a pointer to the object, rather than the object itself, and returns a pointer to the object.

The very simplified SimpleCat class is declared on lines 6–12. The constructor, copy constructor, and destructor all print an informative message so that you can tell when they've been called.

On line 34, main() prints out a message that is shown on the first line of the output. On line 35, a SimpleCat object is instantiated. This causes the constructor to be called, and the output from the constructor is seen on the second line of output.

On line 36, main() reports that it is calling FunctionOne, which creates the third line of output. Because FunctionOne() is called passing the SimpleCat object by value, a copy of the SimpleCat object is made on the stack as an object local to the called function. This causes the copy constructor to be called, which creates the fourth line of output.

Program execution jumps to line 46 in the called function, which prints an informative message, the fifth line of output. The function then returns, and returns the SimpleCat object by value. This creates yet another copy of the object, calling the copy constructor and producing the sixth line of output.

The return value from FunctionOne() is not assigned to any object, and so the temporary object created for the return is thrown away, calling the destructor, which produces the seventh line of output. Because FunctionOne() has ended, its local copy goes out of scope and is destroyed, calling the destructor and producing the eighth line of output.

Program execution returns to main(), and FunctionTwo() is called, but the parameter is passed by reference. No copy is produced, so there's no output. FunctionTwo() prints the message that appears as the tenth line of output and then returns the SimpleCat object, again by reference, and so again produces no calls to the constructor or destructor.

Finally, the program ends and Frisky goes out of scope, causing one final call to the destructor and printing the final line of output. The net effect of this is that the call to FunctionOne(), because it passed the Frisky by value, produced two calls to the copy constructor and two to the destructor, whereas the call to FunctionTwo() produced none.

Passing a const Pointer

Although passing a pointer to FunctionTwo() is more efficient, it is dangerous. FunctionTwo() is not meant to be allowed to change the SimpleCat object it is passed, yet it is given the address of the SimpleCat. This seriously exposes the original object to change and defeats the protection offered in passing by value.

Passing by value is like giving a museum a photograph of your masterpiece instead of the real thing. If vandals mark it up, there is no harm done to the original. Passing by reference is like sending your home address to the museum and inviting guests to come over and look at the real thing.

The solution is to pass a pointer to a constant SimpleCat. Doing so prevents calling any non-const method on SimpleCat, and thus protects the object from change.

Passing a constant reference allows your "guests" to see the original "painting," but not to alter it in any way. Listing 9.10 demonstrates this idea.

LISTING 9.10   Passing Pointer to a Constant Object

```
1:  //Listing 9.10 - Passing pointers to objects
2:
3:  #include <iostream>
4:
5:  using namespace std;
6:  class SimpleCat
7:  {
8:    public:
9:      SimpleCat();
10:      SimpleCat(SimpleCat&);
```

LISTING 9.10   Continued

```
11:       ~SimpleCat();
12:
13:       int GetAge() const { return itsAge; }
14:       void SetAge(int age) { itsAge = age; }
15:
16:    private:
17:       int itsAge;
18:   };
19:
20:   SimpleCat::SimpleCat()
21:   {
22:      cout << "Simple Cat Constructor..." << endl;
23:      itsAge = 1;
24:   }
25:
26:   SimpleCat::SimpleCat(SimpleCat&)
27:   {
28:      cout << "Simple Cat Copy Constructor..." << endl;
29:   }
30:
31:   SimpleCat::~SimpleCat()
32:   {
33:      cout << "Simple Cat Destructor..." << endl;
34:   }
35:
36:   const SimpleCat * const FunctionTwo
37:       (const SimpleCat * const theCat);
38:
39:   int main()
40:   {
41:      cout << "Making a cat..." << endl;
42:      SimpleCat Frisky;
43:      cout << "Frisky is " ;
44:      cout << Frisky.GetAge();
45:      cout << " years old" << endl;
46:      int age = 5;
47:      Frisky.SetAge(age);
48:      cout << "Frisky is " ;
49:      cout << Frisky.GetAge();
50:      cout << " years old" << endl;
51:      cout << "Calling FunctionTwo..." << endl;
52:      FunctionTwo(&Frisky);
53:      cout << "Frisky is " ;
54:      cout << Frisky.GetAge();
55:      cout << " years old" << endl;
56:      return 0;
57:   }
58:
```

LISTING 9.10   Continued

```
59:   // functionTwo, passes a const pointer
60:   const SimpleCat * const FunctionTwo
61:      (const SimpleCat * const theCat)
62:   {
63:      cout << "Function Two. Returning..." << endl;
64:      cout << "Frisky is now " << theCat->GetAge();
65:      cout << " years old " << endl;
66:      // theCat->SetAge(8);    const!
67:      return theCat;
68:   }
```

9

Output ▼

```
Making a cat...
Simple Cat constructor...
Frisky is 1 years old
Frisky is 5 years old
Calling FunctionTwo...
FunctionTwo. Returning...
Frisky is now 5 years old
Frisky is 5 years old
Simple Cat Destructor...
```

Analysis ▼

SimpleCat has added two accessor functions, GetAge() on line 13, which is a const function, and SetAge() on line 14, which is not a const function. It has also added the member variable, itsAge, on line 17.

The constructor, copy constructor, and destructor are still defined to print their messages. The copy constructor is never called, however, because the object is passed by reference and so no copies are made. On line 42, an object is created, and its default age is printed, starting on line 43.

On line 47, itsAge is set using the accessor SetAge, and the result is printed on line 48. FunctionOne is not used in this program, but FunctionTwo() is called. FunctionTwo() has changed slightly; the parameter and return value are now declared, on line 36, to take a constant pointer to a constant object and to return a constant pointer to a constant object.

Because the parameter and return value are still passed by reference, no copies are made and the copy constructor is not called. The object being pointed to in FunctionTwo(), however, is now constant, and thus cannot call the non-const method, SetAge(). If the call to SetAge() on line 66 was not commented out, the program would not compile.

Note that the object created in `main()` is not constant, and `Frisky` can call `SetAge()`. The address of this nonconstant object is passed to `FunctionTwo()`, but because `FunctionTwo()`'s declaration declares the pointer to be a constant pointer to a constant object, the object is treated as if it were constant!

References as an Alternative

Listing 9.10 solves the problem of making extra copies, and thus saves the calls to the copy constructor and destructor. It uses constant pointers to constant objects, and thereby solves the problem of the function changing the object. It is still somewhat cumbersome, however, because the objects passed to the function are pointers.

Because you know the object will never be null, it would be easier to work within the function if a reference were passed in, rather than a pointer. Listing 9.11 illustrates this approach.

LISTING 9.11   Passing References to Objects

```
 1:  //Listing 9.11 - Passing references to objects
 2:
 3:  #include <iostream>
 4:
 5:  using namespace std;
 6:  class SimpleCat
 7:  {
 8:    public:
 9:       SimpleCat();
10:       SimpleCat(SimpleCat&);
11:       ~SimpleCat();
12:
13:       int GetAge() const { return itsAge; }
14:       void SetAge(int age) { itsAge = age; }
15:
16:    private:
17:       int itsAge;
18:  };
19:
20:  SimpleCat::SimpleCat()
21:  {
22:     cout << "Simple Cat Constructor..." << endl;
23:     itsAge = 1;
24:  }
25:
26:  SimpleCat::SimpleCat(SimpleCat&)
27:  {
28:     cout << "Simple Cat Copy Constructor..." << endl;
29:  }
30:
```

LISTING 9.11   Continued

```
31:  SimpleCat::~SimpleCat()
32:  {
33:      cout << "Simple Cat Destructor..." << endl;
34:  }
35:
36:  const     SimpleCat & FunctionTwo (const SimpleCat & theCat);
37:
38:  int main()
39:  {
40:      cout << "Making a cat..." << endl;
41:      SimpleCat Frisky;
42:      cout << "Frisky is " << Frisky.GetAge() << " years old" << endl;
43:      int age = 5;
44:      Frisky.SetAge(age);
45:      cout << "Frisky is " << Frisky.GetAge() << " years old" << endl;
46:      cout << "Calling FunctionTwo..." << endl;
47:      FunctionTwo(Frisky);
48:      cout << "Frisky is " << Frisky.GetAge() << " years old" << endl;
49:      return 0;
50:  }
51:
52:  // functionTwo, passes a ref to a const object
53:  const SimpleCat & FunctionTwo (const SimpleCat & theCat)
54:  {
55:      cout << "Function Two. Returning..." << endl;
56:      cout << "Frisky is now " << theCat.GetAge();
57:      cout << " years old " << endl;
58:      // theCat.SetAge(8);    const!
59:      return theCat;
60:  }
```

Output ▼

```
Making a cat...
Simple Cat constructor...
Frisky is 1 years old
Frisky is 5 years old
Calling FunctionTwo...
FunctionTwo. Returning...
Frisky is now 5 years old
Frisky is 5 years old
Simple Cat Destructor...
```

9

Analysis ▼

The output is identical to that produced by Listing 9.10. The only significant change is that FunctionTwo() now takes and returns a reference to a constant object. Once again, working with references is somewhat simpler than working with pointers, and the same savings and efficiency are achieved, as well as the safety provided by using const.

---

const References

C++ programmers do not usually differentiate between "constant reference to a SimpleCat object" and "reference to a constant SimpleCat object." References themselves can never be reassigned to refer to another object, and so they are always constant. If the keyword const is applied to a reference, it is to make constant the object referred to.

Knowing When to Use References Versus Pointers

Experienced C++ programmers strongly prefer references to pointers. References are cleaner and easier to use, and they do a better job of hiding information, as you saw in the previous example.

References cannot be reassigned, however. If you need to point first to one object and then to another, you must use a pointer. References cannot be null, so if any chance exists that the object in question might be null, you must not use a reference. You must use a pointer.

An example of the latter concern is the operator new. If new cannot allocate memory on the free store, it returns a null pointer. Because a reference shouldn't be null, you must not initialize a reference to this memory until you've checked that it is not null. The following example shows how to handle this:

```
int *pInt = new int;
if (pInt != NULL)
int &rInt = *pInt;
```

In this example, a pointer to int, pInt, is declared and initialized with the memory returned by the operator new. The address in pInt is tested, and if it is not null, pInt is dereferenced. The result of dereferencing an int variable is an int object, and rInt is initialized to refer to that object. Thus, rInt becomes an alias to the int returned by the operator new.

DO	DON'T
DO pass parameters by reference whenever possible.	**DON'T** use pointers if references will work.
DO use const to protect references and pointers whenever possible.	**DON'T** try to reassign a reference to a different variable. You can't.

Mixing References and Pointers

9

It is perfectly legal to declare both pointers and references in the same function parameter list, along with objects passed by value. Here's an example:

```
Cat * SomeFunction (Person &theOwner, House *theHouse, int age);
```

This declaration says that SomeFunction takes three parameters. The first is a reference to a Person object, the second is a pointer to a House object, and the third is an integer. It returns a pointer to a Cat object.

The question of where to put the reference (&) or the indirection operator (*) when declaring these variables is a great controversy. When declaring a reference, you can legally write any of the following:

```
1:  Cat&  rFrisky;
2:  Cat & rFrisky;
3:  Cat  &rFrisky;
```

Whitespace is completely ignored, so anywhere you see a space here you can put as many spaces, tabs, and new lines as you want.

Setting aside freedom of expression issues, which is best? Here are the arguments for all three:

The argument for case 1 is that rFrisky is a variable whose name is rFrisky and whose type can be thought of as "reference to Cat object." Thus, this argument says that the & should be with the type.

The counterargument is that the type is Cat. The & is part of the "declarator," which includes the variable name and the ampersand. More important, having the & near the Cat can lead to the following bug:

```
Cat&  rFrisky, rBoots;
```

Casual examination of this line would lead you to think that both rFrisky and rBoots are references to Cat objects, but you'd be wrong. This really says that rFrisky is a reference to a `Cat`, and `rBoots` (despite its name) is not a reference but a plain old `Cat` variable. This should be rewritten as follows:

```
Cat    &rFrisky, rBoots;
```

The answer to this objection is that declarations of references and variables should never be combined like this. Here's the right way to declare the reference and nonreference variable:

```
Cat& rFrisky;
Cat  boots;
```

Finally, many programmers opt out of the argument and go with the middle position—that of putting the `&` in the middle of the two, as illustrated in case 2.

Of course, everything said so far about the reference operator (`&`) applies equally well to the indirection operator (`*`). The important thing is to recognize that reasonable people differ in their perceptions of the one true way. Choose a style that works for you, and be consistent within any one program; clarity is, and remains, the goal.

NOTE

> Many programmers like the following conventions for declaring references and pointers:
>
> - Put the ampersand and asterisk in the middle, with a space on either side.
>
> - Never declare references, pointers, and variables on the same line.

Returning Out-of-Scope Object References

After C++ programmers learn to pass by reference, they have a tendency to go hog-wild. It is possible, however, to overdo it. Remember that a reference is always an alias to some other object. If you pass a reference into or out of a function, be certain to ask yourself, "What is the object I'm aliasing, and will it still exist every time it's used?" Listing 9.12 illustrates the danger of returning a reference to an object that no longer exists.

LISTING 9.12   Returning a Reference to a Nonexistent Object

```
1: #include <iostream>
2:
3: int& GetInt ();
4:
5: int main()
6: {
7:     int & rInt = GetInt ();
8:     std::cout << "rInt = " << rInt << std::endl;
9:
10:    return 0;
11: }
12:
13: int & GetInt ()
14: {
15:     int nLocalInt = 25;
16:
17:     return nLocalInt;
18: }
```

Output ▼

```
Compile error: Attempting to return a reference to a local object!
```

CAUTION | This program won't compile on the Borland compiler. It will compile on Microsoft compilers, perhaps with warnings; however, it should be noted that it is a poor coding practice.

Analysis ▼

The body of GetInt() declares a local object of type int and initializes its value to 25. It then returns that local object by reference. Some compilers are smart enough to catch this error and don't let you run the program. Others let you run the program, with unpredictable results.

When GetInt() returns, the local object, nLocalInt, is destroyed (painlessly, I assure you). The reference returned by this function is an alias to a nonexistent object, and this is a bad thing.

9

The Problem with Returning a Reference to an Object on the Heap/Free Store

You might be tempted to solve the problem in Listing 9.12 by having `GetInt()` create `nLocalInt` on the heap. That way, when you return from `GetInt()`, the location that was called `nLocalInt` still exists.

The problem with this approach is this: What do you do with the memory allocated for `nLocalInt` when you are done with it? Listing 9.13 illustrates this problem.

LISTING 9.13   Memory Leaks

```
 1: #include <iostream>
 2:
 3: int& GetInt ();
 4:
 5: int main()
 6: {
 7:     int & rInt = GetInt ();
 8:     std::cout << "rInt = " << rInt << std::endl;
 9:
10:     return 0;
11: }
12:
13: int & GetInt ()
14: {
15:     // Instantiate an integer object on the free store / heap
16:     int* pInteger = new int (25);
17:
18:     return *pInteger;
19: }
```

Output ▼

```
rInt = 25
```

CAUTION | This compiles, links, and appears to work. But it is a time bomb waiting to go off.

Analysis ▼

`GetInt()` in lines 13 and 19 has been changed so that it no longer returns a reference to a local variable. Memory is allocated on the free store and assigned to a pointer on line 16. This pointer is dereferenced and the object pointed to by `pInteger` is returned by reference. On line 7, the return of `GetInt()` is assigned to a reference, and that object is used to obtain the integer value, which is printed on line 8.

So far, so good. But how will that memory be freed? You can't call `delete` on the reference. One solution is to create another pointer, initialize it with the address obtained from `rInt`, and then invoke `delete` on that pointer. This does delete the memory, and it plugs the memory leak. One small problem, though: What would `rInt` refer to after such an action? As stated earlier, a reference must always alias an actual object; if it references a null object (as this does now), the program is invalid. So, as far as possible, such constructs should be avoided because there are ways to do the same thing in a simpler, cleaner way.

9

> **NOTE**
>
> It cannot be overemphasized that a program with a reference to a null object might compile, but it is invalid and its performance is unpredictable.

In the case you just saw, the problem would be solved by one of the following that would help do the job better:

```
int GetInt ();

int* GetInt ();

void GetInt (int & nInt);
```

DO	DON'T
DO pass parameters by value when you must.	**DON'T** pass by reference if the item referred to might go out of scope.
DO return by value when you must.	**DON'T** lose track of when and where memory is allocated so that you can be certain it is also freed.

Summary

You learned what references are and how they compare to pointers. You saw that references must be initialized to refer to an existing object and cannot be reassigned to refer to anything else. Any action taken on a reference is in fact taken on the reference's target object. Proof of this is that taking the address of a reference returns the address of the target.

You saw that passing objects by reference can be more efficient than passing by value. Passing by reference also allows the called function to change the value in the arguments back in the calling function.

You saw that arguments to functions and values returned from functions can be passed by reference, and that this can be implemented with pointers or with references.

You saw how to use pointers to constant objects and constant references to pass values between functions safely while achieving the efficiency of passing by reference.

Q&A

Q Why have references if pointers can do everything references can?

A References are easier to use and to understand. The indirection is hidden, and no need exists to repeatedly dereference the variable.

Q Why have pointers if references are easier?

A References cannot be null, and they cannot be reassigned. Pointers offer greater flexibility but are slightly more difficult to use.

Q Why would you ever return by value from a function?

A If the object being returned is local, you must return by value or you will be returning a reference to a nonexistent object.

Q Given the danger in returning by reference, why not always return by value?

A Far greater efficiency is achieved in returning by reference. Memory is saved and the program runs faster.

Workshop

The Workshop provides quiz questions to help you solidify your understanding of the material covered and exercises to provide you with experience in using what you've learned. Try to answer the quiz and exercise questions before checking the answers in Appendix D, and be certain that you understand the answers before going to the next lesson.

Quiz

1. What is the difference between a reference and a pointer?
2. When must you use a pointer rather than a reference?
3. What does new return if there is insufficient memory to make your new object?
4. What is a constant reference?

5. What is the difference between passing by reference and passing a reference?

6. When declaring a reference, which is correct:

    A. `int& myRef = myInt;`

    B. `int & myRef = myInt;`

    C. `int  &myRef = myInt;`

Exercises

1. Write a program that declares an `int`, a reference to an `int`, and a pointer to an `int`. Use the pointer and the reference to manipulate the value in the `int`.

2. Write a program that declares a constant pointer to a constant integer. Initialize the pointer to an integer variable, `varOne`. Assign 6 to `varOne`. Use the pointer to assign 7 to `varOne`. Create a second integer variable, `varTwo`. Reassign the pointer to `varTwo`. Do not compile this exercise yet.

3. Now compile the program in Exercise 2. What produces errors? What produces warnings?

4. Write a program that produces a stray pointer.

5. Fix the program from Exercise 4.

6. Write a program that produces a memory leak.

7. Fix the program from Exercise 6.

8. **BUG BUSTERS:** What is wrong with this program?

```
1:     #include <iostream>
2:     using namespace std;
3:     class CAT
4:     {
5:        public:
6:           CAT(int age) { itsAge = age; }
7:           ~CAT(){}
8:           int GetAge() const { return itsAge;}
9:        private:
10:          int itsAge;
11:     };
12:
13:     CAT & MakeCat(int age);
14:     int main()
15:     {
16:        int age = 7;
17:        CAT Boots = MakeCat(age);
18:        cout << "Boots is " << Boots.GetAge()
19:             << " years old" << endl;
20:        return 0;
```

9

```
21:     }
22:
23:     CAT & MakeCat(int age)
24:     {
25:         CAT * pCat = new CAT(age);
26:         return *pCat;
27:     }
```

9. Fix the program from Exercise 8.

PART II:
Fundamentals of Object-Oriented Programming and C++

LESSON 10
Classes and Objects

Classes extend the built-in capabilities of C++ to assist you in representing and solving complex, real-world problems.

In this lesson, you will learn

- What classes and objects are

- How to define a new class and create objects of that class

- What member functions and member data are

- What constructors are and how to use them

Is C++ Object-Oriented?

At one point, C, the predecessor to C++, was the world's most popular programming language for commercial software development. It was used for creating operating systems (such as the UNIX operating system), for real-time programming (machine, device, and electronics control), and only later began to be used as a language for programming conventional languages. Its intent was to provide an easier and safer way to program down close to the hardware.

C was a middle ground between high-level business application languages such as COBOL and the pedal-to-the-metal, high-performance, but difficult-to-use Assembler language. C was to enforce "structured" programming, in which problems were "decomposed" into smaller units of repeatable activities called *procedures* and data was assembled into packages called *structures.*

But research languages such as Smalltalk and CLU had begun to pave a new direction— object-orientation—which combined the data locked away in assemblies like structures with the capabilities of procedures into a single unit: the object.

The world is filled with objects: cars, dogs, trees, clouds, flowers. Objects. Each *object* has characteristics (fast, friendly, brown, puffy, pretty). Most objects have behavior (move, bark, grow, rain, wilt). You don't generally think about a car's specifications and how those specifications might be manipulated. Rather, a car is thought of as an object that looks and acts a certain way. And the same should be true with any real-world object brought into the domain of the computer.

The programs written early in the twenty-first century are much more complex than those written at the end of the twentieth century. Programs created in procedural languages tend to be difficult to manage, hard to maintain, and expensive to extend. Graphical user interfaces, the Internet, digital and wireless telephony, and a host of new technologies have dramatically increased the complexity of our projects at the same time that consumer expectations for the quality of the user interface are rising.

Object-oriented software development offers a tool to help with the challenges of software development. Although there are no silver bullets for complex software development, object-oriented programming languages build a strong link between the data structures and the methods that manipulate that data and have a closer fit to the way humans (programmers and clients) think, improving communication and improving the quality of delivered software. In object-oriented programming, you no longer think about data structures and manipulating functions; you think instead about objects as if they were their real-world counterparts: as things that look and act a certain way.

C++ was a bridge between object-oriented programming and C. The goal was to provide object-oriented design to a fast, commercial software development platform, with a special focus on high performance. Next, you'll see more about how C++ meets its objectives.

Creating New Types

Programs are usually written to solve real-world problems, such as keeping track of employee records or simulating the workings of a heating system. Although it is possible to solve complex problems by using programs written with only numbers and characters, it is far easier to grapple with large, complex problems if you can create representations of the objects that you are talking about. In other words, simulating the workings of a heating system is easier if you can create variables that represent rooms, heat sensors, thermostats, and boilers. The closer these variables correspond to reality, the easier it is to write the program.

10

You've already learned about a number of variable types, including `unsigned` integers and characters. The type of a variable tells you quite a bit about it. For example, if you declare `Height` and `Width` to be `unsigned short` integers, you know that each one can hold a number between 0 and 65,535, assuming an `unsigned short` integer is two bytes. That is the meaning of saying they are `unsigned` integers; trying to hold anything else in these variables causes an error. You can't store your name in an `unsigned short` integer, and you shouldn't try.

Just by declaring these variables to be `unsigned short` integers, you know that it is possible to add `Height` to `Width` and to assign the result to another number.

The type of these variables tells you

- Their size in memory
- What information they can hold
- What actions can be performed on them

In traditional languages such as C, types were built in to the language. In C++, the programmer can extend the language by creating any type needed, and each new type can have all the functionality and power of the built-in types.

> **Downsides of Creating Types with** `struct`
>
> Some capabilities to extend the C language with new types were provided by the ability to combine related variables into `structs`, which could be made available as a new data type through the `typedef` statement. There were things lacking in this capability, however:
>
> - `Structs` and the functions that operate on them aren't cohesive wholes; functions can be found only by reading the header files for the libraries available and looking for those with the new type as a parameter.
>
> - Coordinating the activities of groups of related functions on the `struct` is harder because any piece of program logic can change anything in the `struct` at any time. There is no way to protect `struct` data from interference.
>
> - The built-in operators don't work on `structs`—it does not work to add two `structs` with a plus sign (+) even when that might be the most natural way to represent the solution to a problem (for instance, when each `struct` represents a complex piece of text to be joined together).

Introducing Classes and Members

You make a new type in C++ by declaring a class. A *class* is just a collection of variables—often of different types—combined with a set of related functions.

One way to think about a car is as a collection of wheels, doors, seats, windows, and so forth. Another way is to think about what a car can do: It can move, speed up, slow down, stop, park, and so on. A class enables you to encapsulate, or bundle, these various parts and various functions into one collection, which is called an object.

Encapsulating everything you know about a car into one class has a number of advantages for a programmer. Everything is in one place, which makes it easy to refer to, copy, and call on functions that manipulate the data. Likewise, clients of your class—that is, the parts of the program that use your class—can use your object without worrying about what is in it or how it works.

A class can consist of any combination of the variable types and other class types. Member variables, also known as *data members*, are the variables in your class. A `Car` class might have member variables representing the seats, radio type, tires, and so forth. Member variables are part of your class, just as the wheels and engine are part of your car.

A class can also contain functions called *member functions* or *methods*. Member functions are as much a part of your class as the member variables. They determine what your class can do.

The member functions in the class typically manipulate the member variables. For example, methods of the Car class might include Start() and Brake(). A Cat class might have data members that represent age and weight; its methods might include Sleep(), Meow(), and ChaseMice().

Declaring a Class

Declaring a class tells the compiler about the class. To declare a class, use the class keyword followed by the class name, an opening brace, and then a list of the data members and methods of that class. End the declaration with a closing brace and a semicolon. Here's the declaration of a class called Cat:

```
class Cat
{
    unsigned int  itsAge;
    unsigned int  itsWeight;
    void Meow();
};
```

10

Declaring this class doesn't allocate memory for a Cat. It just tells the compiler what a Cat is, what data members it contains (itsAge and itsWeight), and what it can do (Meow()). Although memory isn't allocated, it does let the compiler know how big a Cat is—that is, how much room the compiler must set aside for each Cat that you will create. In this example, if an integer is four bytes, a Cat is eight bytes big: itsAge is four bytes, and itsWeight is another four bytes. Meow() takes up only the room required for storing information on the location of Meow(). This is a pointer to a function that can take four bytes on a 32-bit platform.

A Word on Naming Conventions

As a programmer, you must name all your member variables, member functions, and classes. As you learned in Lesson 3, "Using Variables, Declaring Constants," these should be easily understood and meaningful names. Cat, Rectangle, and Employee are good class names. Meow(), ChaseMice(), and StopEngine() are good function names because they tell you what the functions do. Many programmers name the member variables with the prefix its, as in itsAge, itsWeight, and itsSpeed. This helps to distinguish member variables from nonmember variables.

Other programmers use different prefixes. Some prefer myAge, myWeight, and mySpeed. Still others simply use the letter m (for member), possibly with an underscore (_) such as mAge or m_age, mWeight or m_weight, or mSpeed or m_speed.

Some programmers like to prefix every class name with a particular letter—for example, cCat or cPerson—whereas others put the name in all uppercase or all lowercase. The convention that this book uses is to name all classes with initial capitalization, as in `Cat` and `Person`.

Similarly, many programmers begin all functions with capital letters and all variables with lowercase. Words are usually separated with an underscore—as in `Chase_Mice`—or by capitalizing each word—for example, `ChaseMice` or `DrawCircle`.

The important idea is that you should pick one style and stay with it through each program. Over time, your style will evolve to include not only naming conventions, but also indentation, alignment of braces, and commenting style.

NOTE

It's common for development companies to have house standards for many style issues. This ensures that all developers can easily read one another's code. Unfortunately, this extends to the companies that develop operating systems and libraries of reusable classes, which usually means that C++ programs must work with several different naming conventions at once.

CAUTION

As stated before, C++ is case sensitive, so all class, function, and variable names should follow the same pattern so that you never have to check how to spell them—was it `Rectangle`, `rectangle`, or `RECTANGLE`?

Defining an Object

After you declare a class, you can then use it as a new type to declare variables of that type. You declare an object of your new type the same as you declare an integer variable:

```
unsigned int GrossWeight;    // define an unsigned integer
Cat Frisky;                  // define a Cat
```

This code defines a variable called `GrossWeight`, whose type is an `unsigned` integer. It also defines `Frisky`, which is an object whose class (or type) is `Cat`.

Classes Versus Objects

You never pet the definition of a cat; you pet an individual cat. You draw a distinction between the idea of a cat and the particular cat that right now is shedding all over your living room. In the same way, C++ differentiates between the class `Cat`, which is the idea of a cat, and each individual `Cat` object. Thus, `Frisky` is an object of type `Cat` in the same way that `GrossWeight` is a variable of type `unsigned int`. An object is an individual instance of a class.

Accessing Class Members

After you define an actual `Cat` object—for example,

```
Cat Frisky;
```

you use the dot operator (`.`) to access the members of that object. Therefore, to assign `50` to `Frisky`'s `Weight` member variable, you would write

```
Frisky.itsWeight = 50;
```

In the same way, to call the `Meow()` function, you would write

```
Frisky.Meow();
```

When you use a class method, you call the method. In this example, you are calling `Meow()` on `Frisky`.

10

Assigning to Objects, Not to Classes

In C++, you don't assign values to types; you assign values to variables. For example, you would never write

```
int = 5;                // wrong
```

The compiler would flag this as an error because you can't assign `5` to an integer. Rather, you must define an integer variable and assign `5` to that variable. For example,

```
int  x;                 // define x to be an int
x = 5;                  // set x's value to 5
```

This is a shorthand way of saying, "Assign `5` to the variable x, which is of type `int`." In the same way, you wouldn't write

```
Cat.itsAge=5;           // wrong
```

The compiler would flag this as an error because you can't assign `5` to the age part of a class called `Cat`. Rather, you must define a specific `Cat` object and assign `5` to that object. For example,

```
Cat Frisky;             // just like  int x;
Frisky.itsAge = 5;      // just like  x = 5;
```

If You Don't Declare It, Your Class Won't Have It

Try this experiment: Walk up to a three-year-old and show her a cat. Then say, "This is Frisky. Frisky knows a trick. Frisky, bark." The child will giggle and say, "No, silly, cats can't bark."

If you wrote

```
Cat  Frisky;          // make a Cat named Frisky
Frisky.Bark()         // tell Frisky to bark
```

the compiler would say, "No, silly, Cats can't bark." (Your compiler's wording will probably look more like [531] Error: Member function Bark not found in class Cat.) The compiler knows that Frisky can't bark because the Cat class doesn't have a Bark() method. The compiler wouldn't even let Frisky meow if you didn't define a Meow() function.

DO	DON'T
DO use the keyword class to declare a class. **DO** use the dot operator (.) to access class members and functions.	**DON'T** confuse a declaration with a definition. A declaration says what a class is. A definition sets aside memory for an object. **DON'T** confuse a class with an object. **DON'T** assign values to a class. Assign values to the data members of an object.

Private Versus Public Access

Additional keywords are often used in the declaration of a class. Two of the most important are public and private.

The private and public keywords are used with members of a class—both data members and member methods. Private members can be accessed only within methods of the class itself. Public members can be accessed through any object of the class. This distinction is both important and confusing. All members of a class are private, by default. To make this a bit clearer, consider an example from earlier:

```
class Cat
{
  unsigned int   itsAge;
  unsigned int   itsWeight;
  void Meow();
};
```

In this declaration, `itsAge`, `itsWeight`, and `Meow()` are private because all members of a class are private by default. Unless you specify otherwise, they are private. If you create a program and try to write the following within `main` (for example):

```
int main()
{
  Cat  Boots;
  Boots.itsAge=5;        // error! can't access private data!
  ...
```

the compiler flags this as an error. In effect, by leaving these members as private, you've said to the compiler, "I'll access `itsAge`, `itsWeight`, and `Meow()` only from within member functions of the `Cat` class." Yet, here, you've accessed the `itsAge` member variable of the `Boots` object from outside a `Cat` method. Just because `Boots` is an object of class `Cat`, that doesn't mean that you can access the parts of `Boots` that are private (even though they are visible in the declaration).

This is a source of endless confusion to new C++ programmers. I can almost hear you yelling, "Hey! I just said `Boots` is a `Cat`. Why can't `Boots` access his own age?" The answer is that `Boots` can, but you can't. `Boots`, in his own methods, can access all his parts—public and private. Even though you've created a `Cat`, that doesn't mean that you can see or change the parts of it that are private.

The way to use `Cat` so that you can access the data members is to make some of the members public:

```
class Cat
{
  public:
    unsigned int  itsAge;
    unsigned int  itsWeight;
    void Meow();
};
```

In this declaration, `itsAge`, `itsWeight`, and `Meow()` are public. `Boots.itsAge=5` from the previous example will compile without problems.

NOTE

> The keyword `public` applies to all members in the declaration until the keyword `private` is encountered—and vice versa. This lets you easily declare sections of your class as public or private.

Listing 10.1 shows the declaration of a `Cat` class with public member variables.

LISTING 10.1   Accessing the Public Members of a Simple Class

```
 1:  // Demonstrates declaration of a class and
 2:  // definition of an object of the class
 3:
 4:  #include <iostream>
 5:
 6:  class Cat                 // declare the Cat class
 7:  {
 8:    public:                 // members that follow are public
 9:      int itsAge;           // member variable
10:      int itsWeight;        // member variable
11:  };              // note the semicolon
12:
13:  int main()
14:  {
15:      Cat Frisky;
16:      Frisky.itsAge = 5;     // assign to the member variable
17:      std::cout << "Frisky is a cat who is " ;
18:      std::cout << Frisky.itsAge << " years old.\n";
19:      return 0;
20:  }
```

Output ▼

Frisky is a cat who is 5 years old.

Analysis ▼

Line 6 contains the keyword class. This tells the compiler that what follows is a declaration. The name of the new class comes after the keyword class. In this case, the name is Cat.

The body of the declaration begins with the opening brace on line 7 and ends with a closing brace and a semicolon on line 11. Line 8 contains the keyword public followed by a colon, which indicates that everything that follows is public until the keyword private or the end of the class declaration. Lines 9 and 10 contain the declarations of the class members itsAge and itsWeight.

Line 13 begins the main() function of the program. Frisky is defined on line 15 as an instance of a Cat—that is, as a Cat object. On line 16, Frisky's age is set to 5. On lines 17 and 18, the itsAge member variable is used to print out a message about Frisky. You should notice on lines 16 and 18 how the member of the Frisky object is accessed. itsAge is accessed by using the object name (Frisky in this case) followed by a period and then the member name (itsAge in this case).

NOTE Try commenting out line 8 and then recompiling. You will receive an error on line 16 because itsAge will no longer have public access. Rather, itsAge and the other members go to the default access, which is private access.

Making Member Data Private

As a general rule of design, you should keep the data members of a class private. Of course, if you make all the data members private, you might wonder how you access information about the class. For example, if itsAge is private, how would you be able to set or get a Cat object's age?

To access private data in a class, you must create public functions known as *accessor methods*. Use these methods to set and get the private member variables. These accessor methods are the member functions that other parts of your program call to get and set your private member variables. A public accessor method is a class member function used either to read (get) the value of a private class member variable or to set its value.

Why bother with this extra level of indirect access? Why add extra functions when it is simpler and easier to use the data directly? Why work through accessor functions?

The answer to these questions is that accessor functions enable you to separate the details of how the data is *stored* from how it is *used*. By using accessor functions, you can later change how the data is stored without having to rewrite any of the other functions in your programs that use the data.

If a function that needs to know a Cat's age accesses itsAge directly, that function would need to be rewritten if you, as the author of the Cat class, decided to change how that data is stored. By having the function call GetAge(), your Cat class can easily return the right value no matter how you arrive at the age. The calling function doesn't need to know whether you are storing it as an unsigned integer or a long, or whether you are computing it as needed.

This technique makes your program easier to maintain. It gives your code a longer life because design changes don't make your program obsolete.

In addition, accessor functions can include additional logic—for instance, whether a Cat's age is unlikely to be more than 100 or its weight is unlikely to be 1000. These values should probably not be allowed. An accessor function can enforce these types of restrictions as well as do other tasks.

Listing 10.2 shows the `Cat` class modified to include private member data and public accessor methods. Note that this is not a listing that can be run if it is compiled.

LISTING 10.2   A Class with Accessor Methods

```
1:  // Cat class declaration
2:  // Data members are private, public accessor methods
3:  // mediate setting and getting the values of the private data
4:
4:  class Cat
5:  {
6:     public:
7:        // public accessors
8:        unsigned int GetAge();
9:        void SetAge(unsigned int Age);
10:
11:        unsigned int GetWeight();
12:        void SetWeight(unsigned int Weight);
13:
14:        // public member functions
15:        void Meow();
16:
17:        // private member data
18:     private:
19:        unsigned int  itsAge;
20:        unsigned int  itsWeight;
21:  };
```

Analysis ▼

This class has five public methods. Lines 8 and 9 contain the accessor methods for `itsAge`. You can see that on line 8 there is a method for getting the age and on line 9 there is one for setting it. Lines 11 and 12 contain similar accessor methods for `itsWeight`. These accessor functions set the member variables and return their values.

The public member function `Meow()` is declared on line 15. `Meow()` is not an accessor function. It doesn't get or set a member variable; it performs another service for the class, printing the word "Meow." The member variables themselves are declared on lines 19 and 20.

To set `Frisky`'s age, you would pass the value to the `SetAge()` method, as in

```
Cat  Frisky;
Frisky.SetAge(5);    // set Frisky's age using the public accessor
```

Later in this lesson, you'll see the specific code for making SetAge and the other methods work.

Declaring methods or data private enables the compiler to find programming mistakes before they become bugs. Any programmer worth his consulting fees can find a way around privacy if he wants to. Bjarne Stroustrup, the inventor of C++, said, "The C++ access control mechanisms provide protection against accident—not against fraud" (ARM, 1990).

The class Keyword

Syntax for the class keyword is as follows:

```
class class_name
{
    // access control keywords here
    // class variables and methods declared here
};
```

You use the class keyword to declare new types. A class is a collection of class member data, which are variables of various types, including other classes. The class also contains class functions—or methods—which are functions used to manipulate the data in the class and to perform other services for the class.

You define objects of the new type in much the same way in which you define any variable. State the type (class) and then the variable name (the object). You access the class members and functions by using the dot (.) operator.

You use access control keywords to declare sections of the class as public or private. The default for access control is private. Each keyword changes the access control from that point on to the end of the class or until the next access control keyword. Class declarations end with a closing brace and a semicolon.

Example 1

```
class Cat
{
            public:
                unsigned int Age;
                unsigned int Weight;
                void Meow();
};

Cat  Frisky;
Frisky.Age = 8;
Frisky.Weight = 18;
Frisky.Meow();
```

10

Example 2

```
class Car
{
  public:                            // the next five are public

            void Start();
            void Accelerate();
            void Brake();
            void SetYear(int year);
            int GetYear();

  private:                           // the rest is private

             int Year;
            Char Model [255];
  };                                 // end of class declaration

Car OldFaithful;                     // make an instance of car
int bought;                          // a local variable of type int
OldFaithful.SetYear(84) ;            // assign 84 to the year
bought = OldFaithful.GetYear();      // set bought to 84
OldFaithful.Start();                 // call the start method
```

DO	DON'T
DO use public accessor methods.	**DON'T** declare member variables public if you don't need to.
DO access private member variables from within class member functions.	**DON'T** try to use private member variables from outside the class.

Implementing Class Methods

As you've seen, an accessor function provides a public interface to the private member data of the class. Each accessor function, along with any other class methods that you declare, must have an implementation. The implementation is called the *function definition*.

A member function definition begins similarly to the definition of a regular function. First, you state the return type that will come from the function, or void if nothing will be returned. This is followed by the name of the class, two colons, the name of the function, and then the function's parameters. Listing 10.3 shows the complete declaration of a simple Cat class and the implementation of its accessor function and one general class member function.

LISTING 10.3 Implementing the Methods of a Simple Class

```
1:  // Demonstrates declaration of a class and
2:  // definition of class methods
3:  #include <iostream>          // for cout
4:
5:  class Cat                    // begin declaration of the class
6:  {
7:    public:                    // begin public section
8:      int GetAge();            // accessor function
9:      void SetAge (int age);   // accessor function
10:     void Meow();             // general function
11:   private:                   // begin private section
12:     int itsAge;              // member variable
13:  };
14:
15:  // GetAge, Public accessor function
16:  // returns value of itsAge member
17:  int Cat::GetAge()
18:  {
19:      return itsAge;
20:  }
21:
22:  // definition of SetAge, public
23:  // accessor function
24:  // sets itsAge member
25:  void Cat::SetAge(int age)
26:  {
27:      // set member variable itsAge to
28:      // value passed in by parameter age
29:      itsAge = age;
30:  }
31:
32:  // definition of Meow method
33:  // returns: void
34:  // parameters: None
35:  // action: Prints "meow" to screen
36:  void Cat::Meow()
37:  {
38:      std::cout << "Meow.\n";
39:  }
40:
41:  // create a cat, set its age, have it
42:  // meow, tell us its age, then meow again.
43:  int main()
44:  {
45:      Cat Frisky;
46:      Frisky.SetAge(5);
47:      Frisky.Meow();
48:      std::cout << "Frisky is a cat who is " ;
```

10

LISTING 10.3 Continued

```
49:     std::cout << Frisky.GetAge() << " years old.\n";
50:     Frisky.Meow();
51:     return 0;
52: }
```

Output ▼

```
Meow.
Frisky is a cat who is 5 years old.
Meow.
```

Analysis ▼

Lines 5–13 contain the definition of the Cat class. Line 7 contains the keyword public, which tells the compiler that what follows is a set of public members. Line 8 has the declaration of the public accessor method GetAge(). GetAge() provides access to the private member variable itsAge, which is declared on line 12. Line 9 has the public accessor function SetAge(). SetAge() takes an integer as an argument and sets itsAge to the value of that argument.

Line 10 has the declaration of the class method Meow(). Meow() is not an accessor function; it is a general method that prints the word "Meow" to the screen.

Line 11 begins the private section, which includes only the declaration on line 12 of the private member variable itsAge. The class declaration ends with a closing brace and semicolon on line 13.

Lines 17–20 contain the definition of the member function GetAge(). This method takes no parameters, and it returns an integer. Note on line 17 that class methods include the class name followed by two colons and the function name. This syntax tells the compiler that the GetAge() function you are defining here is the one that you declared in the Cat class. With the exception of this header line, the GetAge() function is created the same as any other function.

The GetAge() function takes only one line; it returns the value in itsAge. Note that the main() function cannot access itsAge because itsAge is private to the Cat class. The main() function has access to the public method GetAge().

Because GetAge() is a member function of the Cat class, it has full access to the itsAge variable. This access enables GetAge() to return the value of itsAge to main().

Line 25 contains the definition of the SetAge() member function. You can see that this function takes one integer value, called age, and doesn't return any values, as indicated by void. SetAge() takes the value of the age parameter and assigns it to itsAge on line 29. Because SetAge() is a member of the Cat class, it has direct access to the private member variable itsAge.

Line 36 begins the definition, or implementation, of the Meow() method of the Cat class. It is a one-line function that prints the word "Meow" to the screen, followed by a new line. Remember that the \n character prints a new line to the screen. You can see that Meow is set up just like the accessor functions in that it begins with the return type, the class name, the function name, and the parameters (none in this case).

Line 43 begins the body of the program with the familiar main() function. On line 45, main() declares an object called Frisky of type Cat. Read a different way, you could say that main() declares a Cat named Frisky.

On line 46, the value 5 is assigned to the itsAge member variable by way of the SetAge() accessor method. Note that the method is called by using the object name (Frisky) followed by the member operator (.) and the method name (SetAge()). In this same way, you can call any of the other methods in a class.

10

NOTE	The terms *member function* and *method* can be used interchangeably.

Line 47 calls the Meow() member function, and line 49 prints a message using the GetAge() accessor. Line 50 calls Meow() again. Although these methods are a part of a class (Cat) and are being used through an object (Frisky), they operate just like the functions you have seen before.

Adding Constructors and Destructors

Two ways exist to define an integer variable. You can define the variable and then assign a value to it later in the program. For example:

```
int Weight;          // define a variable
...                  // other code here
Weight = 7;          // assign it a value
```

Or you can define the integer and immediately initialize it. For example:

```
int Weight = 7;      // define and initialize to 7
```

Initialization combines the definition of the variable with its initial assignment. Nothing stops you from changing that value later. Initialization ensures that your variable is never without a meaningful, known value.

How do you initialize the member data of a class? You can initialize the member data of a class using a special member function called a *constructor*. The constructor can take parameters as needed, but it cannot have a return value—not even void. The constructor is a class method with the same name as the class itself.

Whenever you declare a constructor, you'll also want to declare a destructor. Just as constructors create and initialize objects of your class, destructors clean up after your object and free any resources or memory that you might have allocated (either in the constructor or throughout the lifespan of the object). A destructor always has the name of the class, preceded by a tilde (~). Destructors take no arguments and have no return value. If you were to declare a destructor for the Cat class, its declaration would look like the following:

```
~Cat();
```

Getting a Default Constructor and Destructor

Many types of constructors are available; some take arguments, others do not. The one that takes no arguments is called the *default* constructor. There is only one destructor. Like the default constructor, it takes no arguments.

It turns out that if you don't create a constructor or a destructor, the compiler provides one for you. The constructor provided by the compiler is the default constructor. The default constructor and destructor created by the compiler don't have arguments. In addition, they don't appear to do anything! If you want them to do something, you must create your own default constructor or destructor.

Using the Default Constructor

What good is a constructor that does nothing? In part, it is a matter of form. All objects must be "constructed" and "destructed," and these do-nothing functions are called as a part of the process of constructing and destructing.

To declare an object without passing in parameters, such as

```
Cat Rags;          // Rags gets no parameters
```

you must have a constructor in the form

```
Cat();
```

When you define an object of a class, the constructor is called. If the Cat constructor took two parameters, you might define a Cat object by writing

```
Cat Frisky (5,7);
```

In this example, the first parameter might be its age and the second might be its weight. If the constructor took one parameter, you would write

```
Cat Frisky (3);
```

In the event that the constructor takes no parameters at all (that is, that it is a *default* constructor), you leave off the parentheses and write

```
Cat Frisky;
```

This is an exception to the rule that states all functions require parentheses, even if they take no parameters. This is why you are able to write

```
Cat Frisky;
```

This is interpreted as a call to the default constructor. It provides no parameters, and it leaves off the parentheses.

Note that you don't have to use the compiler-provided default constructor. You are always free to write your own default constructor—that is, a constructor with no parameters. You are free to give your default constructor a function body in which you might initialize the object. As a matter of form, it is always recommended that you define a constructor, and set the member variables to appropriate defaults, to ensure that the object will always behave correctly.

Also as a matter of form, if you declare a constructor, be certain to declare a destructor, even if your destructor does nothing. Although it is true that the default destructor would work correctly, it doesn't hurt to declare your own. It makes your code clearer.

Listing 10.4 rewrites the Cat class to use a nondefault constructor to initialize the Cat object, setting its age to whatever initial age you provide, and it demonstrates where the destructor is called.

LISTING 10.4   Using Constructors and Destructors

```
1:  // Demonstrates declaration of  constructors and
2:  // destructor for the Cat class
3:  // Programmer created default constructor
4:  #include <iostream>        // for cout
5:
6:  class Cat               // begin declaration of the class
7:  {
8:    public:               // begin public section
```

LISTING 10.4   Continued

```
 9:        Cat(int initialAge);   // constructor
10:        ~Cat();                // destructor
11:        int GetAge();          // accessor function
12:        void SetAge(int age);  // accessor function
13:        void Meow();
14:     private:                  // begin private section
15:        int itsAge;            // member variable
16:    };
17:
18:    // constructor of Cat,
19:    Cat::Cat(int initialAge)
20:    {
21:       itsAge = initialAge;
22:    }
23:
24:    Cat::~Cat()                 // destructor, takes no action
25:    {
26:    }
27:
28:    // GetAge, Public accessor function
29:    // returns value of itsAge member
30:    int Cat::GetAge()
31:    {
32:       return itsAge;
33:    }
34:
35:    // Definition of SetAge, public
36:    // accessor function
37:    void Cat::SetAge(int age)
38:    {
39:       // set member variable itsAge to
40:       // value passed in by parameter age
41:       itsAge = age;
42:    }
43:
44:    // definition of Meow method
45:    // returns: void
46:    // parameters: None
47:    // action: Prints "meow" to screen
48:    void Cat::Meow()
49:    {
50:       std::cout << "Meow.\n";
51:    }
52:
53:    // create a cat, set its age, have it
54:    // meow, tell us its age, then meow again.
55:    int main()
56:    {
57:       Cat Frisky(5);
```

LISTING 10.4 Continued

```
58:      Frisky.Meow();
59:      std::cout << "Frisky is a cat who is " ;
60:      std::cout << Frisky.GetAge() << " years old.\n";
61:      Frisky.Meow();
62:      Frisky.SetAge(7);
63:      std::cout << "Now Frisky is " ;
64:      std::cout << Frisky.GetAge() << " years old.\n";
65:      return 0;
66:  }
```

Output ▼

```
Meow.
Frisky is a cat who is 5 years old.
Meow.
Now Frisky is 7 years old.
```

10

Analysis ▼

Listing 10.4 is similar to Listing 10.3, except that line 9 adds a constructor that takes an integer. Line 10 declares the destructor, which takes no parameters. Destructors never take parameters, and neither constructors nor destructors return a value—not even void.

Lines 19–22 show the implementation of the constructor. It is similar to the implementation of the SetAge() accessor function. As you can see, the class name precedes the constructor name. As mentioned earlier, this identifies the method, Cat() in this case, as a part of the Cat class. This is a constructor, so there is no return value—not even void. This constructor does, however, take an initial value that is assigned to the data member, itsAge, on line 21.

Lines 24–26 show the implementation of the destructor ~Cat(). For now, this function does nothing, but you must include the definition of the function if you declare it in the class declaration. Like the constructor and other methods, the destructor is preceded by the class name. Like the constructor, but differing from other methods, no return time or parameters are included. This is standard for a destructor.

Line 57 contains the definition of a Cat object, Frisky. The value 5 is passed in to Frisky's constructor. No need exists to call SetAge() because Frisky was created with the value 5 in its member variable itsAge, as shown on line 60. On line 62, Frisky's itsAge variable is reassigned to 7. Line 64 prints the new value.

DO	DON'T
DO use constructors to initialize your objects.	**DON'T** give constructors or destructors a return value.
DO add a destructor if you add a constructor.	**DON'T** give destructors parameters.

Including `const` **Member Functions**

You have used the `const` keyword to declare variables that would not change. You can also use the `const` keyword with member functions within a class. If you declare a class method `const`, you are promising that the method won't change the value of any of the members of the class.

To declare a class method constant, put the keyword `const` after the parentheses enclosing any parameters but before the semicolon ending the method declaration. For example:

```
void SomeFunction() const;
```

This declares a constant member method called `SomeFunction()` that takes no arguments and returns `void`. You know this will not change any of the data members within the same class because it has been declared `const`.

Accessor functions that only get values are often declared as constant functions by using the `const` modifier. Earlier, you saw that the `Cat` class has two accessor functions:

```
void SetAge(int anAge);
```

```
int GetAge();
```

`SetAge()` cannot be `const` because it changes the member variable `itsAge`. `GetAge()`, on the other hand, can and should be `const` because it doesn't change the class at all. `GetAge()` simply returns the current value of the member variable `itsAge`. Therefore, the declaration of these functions should be written like this:

```
void SetAge(int anAge);
```

```
int GetAge() const;
```

If you declare a function to be `const` and the implementation of that function changes the object by changing the value of any of its members, the compiler flags it as an error. For example, if you wrote `GetAge()` in such a way that it kept count of the number of times that the `Cat` was asked its age, it would generate a compiler error. This is because you would be changing the `Cat` object when the method was called.

It is good programming practice to declare as many methods to be const as possible. Each time you do, you enable the compiler to catch your errors instead of letting your errors become bugs that will show up when your program is running.

Why Use the Compiler to Catch Errors?

It would be wonderful to write entirely bug-free code, but few programmers have been able to do so. However, many programmers have developed a system to help minimize bugs by catching and fixing them early in the process.

Although compiler errors are infuriating and are the bane of a programmer's existence, they are far better than the alternative. A weakly typed language enables you to violate your contracts without a peep from the compiler, but your program crashes at runtime—when, for example, your boss is watching. Worse yet, testing is of comparatively little help in catching errors because there are too many paths through real programs to have any hope of testing them all.

Compile-time errors—that is, errors found while you are compiling—are far better than *runtime* errors—that is, errors found while you are executing the program. This is because compile-time errors can be found much more reliably. It is possible to run a program many times without going down every possible code path. Thus, a runtime error can hide for quite a while. Compile-time errors are found every time you compile. Thus, they are easier to identify and fix. It is the goal of quality programming to ensure that the code has no runtime bugs. One tried-and-true technique to accomplish this is to use the compiler to catch your mistakes early in the development process.

10

Where to Put Class Declarations and Method Definitions

Each function that you declare for your class must have a definition, also called the *function implementation*. Like other functions, the definition of a class method has a function header and a function body.

The definition must be in a file that the compiler can find. Most C++ compilers want that file to end with .cpp. Check your compiler to see what it prefers.

NOTE

Many compilers assume that files ending with .c are C programs, and that C++ program files end with .cpp. You can use any extension, but .cpp minimizes confusion.

You are free to put the declaration in this file as well, but that is not good programming practice. The convention that most programmers adopt is to put the declaration into what is called a header file, usually with the same name but ending in .h, .hp, or .hpp. This book names the header files with .h, but check your compiler to see what it prefers.

For example, you put the declaration of the Cat class into a file named Cat.hpp, and you put the definition of the class methods into a file called Cat.cpp. You then attach the header file to the .cpp file by putting the following code at the top of Cat.cpp:

```
#include "Cat.h"
```

This tells the compiler to read Cat.h into the file, the same as if you had typed in its contents at this point. Be aware that some compilers insist that the capitalization agree between your #include statement and your file system.

Why bother separating the contents of your .hpp file and your .cpp file if you're just going to read the .hpp file back into the .cpp file? Most of the time, clients of your class don't care about the implementation specifics. Reading the header file tells them everything they need to know; they can ignore the implementation files. In addition, you might very well end up including the .hpp file into more than one .cpp file.

> **NOTE**
>
> The declaration of a class tells the compiler what the class is, what data it holds, and what functions it has. The declaration of the class is called its *interface* because it tells the user how to interact with the class. The interface is usually stored in an .hpp file, which is referred to as a *header file*.
>
> The function definition tells the compiler how the function works. The function definition is called the implementation of the class method, and it is kept in a .cpp file. The implementation details of the class are of concern only to the author of the class. Clients of the class—that is, the parts of the program that use the class—don't need to know, and don't care, how the functions are implemented.

Inline Implementation

Just as you can ask the compiler to make a regular function inline, you can make class methods inline. The keyword inline appears before the return type. The inline implementation of the GetWeight() function, for example, looks like this:

```
inline int Cat::GetWeight()
{
    return itsWeight;     // return the Weight data member
}
```

You can also put the definition of a function into the declaration of the class, which automatically makes that function inline. For example:

```
class Cat
{
  public:
    int GetWeight() { return itsWeight; }  // inline
    void SetWeight(int aWeight);
};
```

Note the syntax of the `GetWeight()` definition. The body of the inline function begins
immediately after the declaration of the class method; no semicolon is used after the
parentheses. Like any function, the definition begins with an opening brace and ends
with a closing brace. As usual, whitespace doesn't matter; you could have written the
declaration as

```
class Cat
{
  public:
    int GetWeight() const
    {
       return itsWeight;
    }                        // inline
    void SetWeight(int aWeight);
};
```

Listings 10.5 and 10.6 re-create the `Cat` class, but they put the declaration in `Cat.h` and
the implementation of the functions in `Cat.cpp`. Listing 10.5 also changes the accessor
functions and the `Meow()` function to inline.

LISTING 10.5   Cat Class Declaration in `Cat.h`

```
 1:  #include <iostream>
 2:  class Cat
 3:  {
 4:    public:
 5:       Cat (int initialAge);
 6:       ~Cat();
 7:       int GetAge() const { return itsAge;}       // inline!
 8:       void SetAge (int age) { itsAge = age;}      // inline!
 9:       void Meow() const  { std::cout << "Meow.\n";}  // inline!
10:    private:
11:       int itsAge;
12:  };
```

LISTING 10.6   Cat Implementation in `Cat.cpp`

```
1:  // Demonstrates inline functions
2:  // and inclusion of header files
3:  // be sure to include the header files!
4:  #include "Cat.h"
5:
6:
7:  Cat::Cat(int initialAge)    //constructor
8:  {
9:      itsAge = initialAge;
10: }
11:
12: Cat::~Cat()               //destructor, takes no action
13: {
14: }
15:
16: // Create a cat, set its age, have it
17: // meow, tell us its age, then meow again.
18: int main()
19: {
20:     Cat Frisky(5);
21:     Frisky.Meow();
22:     std::cout << "Frisky is a cat who is " ;
23:     std::cout << Frisky.GetAge() << " years old.\n";
24:     Frisky.Meow();
25:     Frisky.SetAge(7);
26:     std::cout << "Now Frisky is " ;
27:     std::cout << Frisky.GetAge() << " years old.\n";
28:     return 0;
29: }
```

Output ▼

```
Meow.
Frisky is a cat who is 5 years old.
Meow.
Now Frisky is 7 years old.
```

Analysis ▼

The code presented in Listing 10.5 and Listing 10.6 is similar to the code in Listing 10.4, except that three of the methods are written inline in the declaration file and the declaration has been separated into `Cat.h` (Listing 10.5).

`GetAge()` is declared on line 6 of `Cat.h`, and its inline implementation is provided. Lines 7 and 8 provide more inline functions, but the functionality of these functions is unchanged from the previous "outline" implementations.

Line 4 of Cat.cpp (Listing 10.6) shows #include "Cat.h", which brings in the listings from Cat.h. By including Cat.h, you have told the precompiler to read Cat.h into the file as if it had been typed there, starting on line 5.

This technique enables you to put your declarations into a different file from your implementation, yet have that declaration available when the compiler needs it. This is a very common technique in C++ programming. Typically, class declarations are in an .hpp file that is then #included into the associated .cpp file.

Lines 18–29 repeat the main function from Listing 10.4. This shows that making these functions inline doesn't change their performance.

Classes with Other Classes as Member Data

10

It is common to build up a complex class by declaring simpler classes and including them in the declaration of the more complicated class. For example, you might declare a wheel class, a motor class, a transmission class, and so forth, and then combine them into a car class. This declares a has-a relationship. A car has a motor, it has wheels, and it has a transmission.

Consider a second example. A rectangle is composed of lines. A line is defined by two points. A point is defined by an x-coordinate and a y-coordinate. Listing 10.7 shows a complete declaration of a Rectangle class, as might appear in Rectangle.h. Because a rectangle is defined as four lines connecting four points, and each point refers to a coordinate on a graph, you first declare a Point class to hold the x-coordinate and y-coordinate of each point. Listing 10.8 provides the implementation for both classes.

LISTING 10.7   Declaring a Complete Class

```
1:  // Begin Rectangle.h
2:  #include <iostream>
3:  class Point      // holds x,y coordinates
4:  {
5:    // no constructor, use default
6:    public:
7:      void SetX(int x) { itsX = x; }
8:      void SetY(int y) { itsY = y; }
9:      int GetX()const { return itsX;}
10:     int GetY()const { return itsY;}
11:   private:
12:     int itsX;
13:     int itsY;
```

LISTING 10.7   Continued

```
14:  };    // end of Point class declaration
15:
16:
17:  class  Rectangle
18:  {
19:    public:
20:      Rectangle (int top, int left, int bottom, int right);
21:      ~Rectangle () {}
22:
23:      int GetTop() const { return itsTop; }
24:      int GetLeft() const { return itsLeft; }
25:      int GetBottom() const { return itsBottom; }
26:      int GetRight() const { return itsRight; }
27:
28:      Point  GetUpperLeft() const { return itsUpperLeft; }
29:      Point  GetLowerLeft() const { return itsLowerLeft; }
30:      Point  GetUpperRight() const { return itsUpperRight; }
31:      Point  GetLowerRight() const { return itsLowerRight; }
32:
33:      void SetUpperLeft(Point Location)   {itsUpperLeft = Location;}
34:      void SetLowerLeft(Point Location)   {itsLowerLeft = Location;}
35:      void SetUpperRight(Point Location)  {itsUpperRight = Location;}
36:      void SetLowerRight(Point Location)  {itsLowerRight = Location;}
37:
38:      void SetTop(int top) { itsTop = top; }
39:      void SetLeft (int left) { itsLeft = left; }
40:      void SetBottom (int bottom) { itsBottom = bottom; }
41:      void SetRight (int right) { itsRight = right; }
42:
43:      int GetArea() const;
44:
45:    private:
46:      Point  itsUpperLeft;
47:      Point  itsUpperRight;
48:      Point  itsLowerLeft;
49:      Point  itsLowerRight;
50:      int    itsTop;
51:      int    itsLeft;
52:      int    itsBottom;
53:      int    itsRight;
54:  };
55:  // end Rectangle.h
```

LISTING 10.8   Rect.cpp

```
1:  // Begin Rect.cpp
2:  #include "Rectangle.h"
3:  Rectangle::Rectangle(int top, int left, int bottom, int right)
```

LISTING 10.8 Continued

```
 4:  {
 5:      itsTop = top;
 6:      itsLeft = left;
 7:      itsBottom = bottom;
 8:      itsRight = right;
 9:
10:      itsUpperLeft.SetX(left);
11:      itsUpperLeft.SetY(top);
12:
13:      itsUpperRight.SetX(right);
14:      itsUpperRight.SetY(top);
15:
16:      itsLowerLeft.SetX(left);
17:      itsLowerLeft.SetY(bottom);
18:
19:      itsLowerRight.SetX(right);
20:      itsLowerRight.SetY(bottom);
21:  }
22:
23:
24:  // compute area of the rectangle by finding sides,
25:  // establish width and height and then multiply
26:  int Rectangle::GetArea() const
27:  {
28:      int Width = itsRight-itsLeft;
29:      int Height = itsTop - itsBottom;
30:      return (Width * Height);
31:  }
32:
33:  int main()
34:  {
35:      //initialize a local Rectangle variable
36:      Rectangle MyRectangle (100, 20, 50, 80 );
37:
38:      int Area = MyRectangle.GetArea();
39:
40:      std::cout << "Area: " << Area << "\n";
41:      std::cout << "Upper Left X Coordinate: ";
42:      std::cout << MyRectangle.GetUpperLeft().GetX();
43:      return 0;
44:  }
```

10

Output ▼

```
Area: 3000
Upper Left X Coordinate: 20
```

Analysis ▼

Lines 3–14 in `Rectangle.h` (Listing 10.7) declare the class `Point`, which is used to hold a specific x-coordinate and y-coordinate on a graph. As written, this program doesn't use `Point`s much; however, other drawing methods require `Point`s.

> **NOTE**
>
> Some compilers report an error if you declare a class named `Rectangle`. This is usually because of the existence of an internal class named `Rectangle`. If you have this problem, simply rename your class to `myRectangle`.

Within the declaration of the class `Point`, you declare two member variables (`itsX` and `itsY`) on lines 12 and 13. These variables hold the values of the coordinates. As the x-coordinate increases, you move to the right on the graph. As the y-coordinate increases, you move upward on the graph. Other graphs use different systems. Some windowing programs, for example, increase the y-coordinate as you move down in the window.

The `Point` class uses inline accessor functions declared on lines 7–10 to get and set the x and y points. The `Point`s class uses the default constructor and destructor. Therefore, you must set their coordinates explicitly.

Line 17 begins the declaration of a `Rectangle` class. A `Rectangle` consists of four points that represent the corners of the `Rectangle`. The constructor for the `Rectangle` (line 20) takes four integers, known as `top`, `left`, `bottom`, and `right`. The four parameters to the constructor are copied into four member variables (Listing 10.8), and then the four `Point`s are established.

In addition to the usual accessor functions, `Rectangle` has a function `GetArea()` declared on line 43. Instead of storing the area as a variable, the `GetArea()` function computes the area on lines 28 and 29 of Listing 10.8. To do this, it computes the width and the height of the rectangle, and then it multiplies these two values.

Getting the x-coordinate of the upper-left corner of the rectangle requires that you access the `UpperLeft` point and ask that point for its x value. Because `GetUpperLeft()` is a method of `Rectangle`, it can directly access the private data of `Rectangle`, including `itsUpperLeft`. Because `itsUpperLeft` is a `Point` and `Point`'s `itsX` value is private, `GetUpperLeft()` cannot directly access this data. Rather, it must use the public accessor function `GetX()` to obtain that value.

Line 33 of Listing 10.8 is the beginning of the body of the actual program. Until line 36, no memory has been allocated, and nothing has really happened. The only thing you've done is tell the compiler how to make a point and how to make a rectangle, in case one is ever needed. On line 36, you define a `Rectangle` by passing in values for `top`, `left`, `bottom`, and `right`.

On line 38, you make a local variable, `Area`, of type `int`. This variable holds the area of the `Rectangle` that you've created. You initialize `Area` with the value returned by `Rectangle`'s `GetArea()` function. A client of `Rectangle` could create a `Rectangle` object and get its area without ever looking at the implementation of `GetArea()`.

`Rectangle.h` is shown in Listing 10.7. Just by looking at the header file, which contains the declaration of the `Rectangle` class, the programmer knows that `GetArea()` returns an `int`. How `GetArea()` does its magic is not of concern to the user of class `Rectangle`. In fact, the author of `Rectangle` could change `GetArea()` without affecting the programs that use the `Rectangle` class as long as it still returned an integer.

Line 42 of Listing 10.8 might look a little strange, but if you think about what is happening, it should be clear. In this line of code, you are getting the x-coordinate from the upper-left point of your rectangle. In this line of code, you are calling the `GetUpperLeft()` method of your rectangle, which returns to you an object of type `Point`. From this `Point`, you want to get the x-coordinate. You saw that the accessor for an x-coordinate in the `Point` class is `GetX()`. Therefore, to get the x-coordinate of the upper-left corner of the rectangle, use the `GetX()` accessor on the `GetUpperLeft` accessor function of the `MyRectangle` object, as seen in Line 42:

```
MyRectangle.GetUpperLeft().GetX();
```

10

FAQ

What is the difference between declaring and defining?

Answer: A declaration introduces a name of something but does not allocate memory. A definition allocates memory.

With a few exceptions, all declarations are also definitions. The most important exceptions are the declaration of a global function (a prototype) and the declaration of a class (usually in a header file).

Exploring Structures

A very close cousin to the keyword `class` is the keyword `struct`, which is used to declare a structure. In C++, a `struct` is the same as a class, except that its members are public by default and that it inherits publicly, by default. You can declare a structure exactly as you declare a class, and you can give it the same data members and functions. In fact, if you follow the good programming practice of always explicitly declaring the private and public sections of your class, no difference will exist whatsoever. Try re-entering Listing 10.7 with these changes:

- On line 3, change `class Point` to `struct Point`.
- On line 17, change `class Rectangle` to `struct Rectangle`.

Now run the program again and compare the new output to that from the original version. No change should have occurred.

You're probably wondering why two keywords do the same thing. This is an accident of history. When C++ was developed, it was built as an extension of the C language. C has structures, although C structures don't have class methods. Bjarne Stroustrup, the creator of C++, built upon `structs`, but he changed the name to `class` to represent the new expanded functionality and the change in the default visibility of members. This also allowed the continued use of a vast library of C functions in C++ programs.

DO	DON'T
DO put your class declaration in an `.h` (header) file and your member functions in a `.cpp` file.	**DON'T** move on until you understand classes.
DO use `const` whenever you can.	

Summary

In this lesson, you learned how to create new data types using classes. You learned how to define variables of these new types, which are called *objects*.

A class can have data members, which are variables of various types, including other classes. A class can also include member functions—also known as *methods*. You use these member functions to manipulate the member data and to perform other services.

Class members, both data and functions, can be public or private. Public members are accessible to any part of your program. Private members are accessible only to the member functions of the class. Members of a class are private by default.

It is good programming practice to isolate the interface, or declaration, of the class in a header file. You usually do this in a file with an `.h` extension and then use it in your code files (`.cpp`) using an `include` statement. The implementation of the class methods is written in a file with a `.cpp` extension.

Class constructors can be used to initialize object data members. Class destructors are executed when an object is destroyed and are often used to free memory and other resources that might be allocated by methods of the class.

Q&A

Q How big is a class object?

A A class object's size in memory is determined by the sum of the sizes of its member variables. Class methods take up just a small amount of memory, which is used to store information on the location of the method (a pointer).

Some compilers align variables in memory in such a way that two-byte variables actually consume somewhat more than two bytes. Check your compiler manual to be certain, but at this point you do not need to be concerned with these details.

Q If I declare a class `Cat` with a private member `itsAge` and then define two `Cat` objects, `Frisky` and `Boots`, can `Boots` access `Frisky`'s `itsAge` member variable?

A No. Different instances of a class can access each other's nonpublic data. In other words, if `Frisky` and `Boots` are both instances of `Cat`, `Frisky`'s member functions can access `Frisky`'s data but not `Boots`'s data.

Q Why shouldn't I make all the member data public?

A Making member data private enables the client of the class to use the data without being dependent on how it is stored or computed. For example, if the `Cat` class has a method `GetAge()`, clients of the `Cat` class can ask for the `Cat`'s age without knowing or caring whether the `Cat` stores its age in a member variable or computes its age on-the-fly. This means the programmer of the `Cat` class can change the design of the `Cat` class in the future without requiring all the users of `Cat` to change their programs as well.

Q If using a `const` function to change the class causes a compiler error, why shouldn't I just leave out the word `const` and be certain to avoid errors?

A If your member function logically shouldn't change the class, using the keyword `const` is a good way to enlist the compiler in helping you find mistakes. For example, `GetAge()` might have no reason to change the `Cat` class, but your implementation has this line:

```
if (itsAge = 100) cout << "Hey! You're 100 years old\n";
```

Declaring `GetAge()` to be `const` causes this code to be flagged as an error. You meant to check whether `itsAge` is equal to 100, but instead you inadvertently assigned 100 to `itsAge`. Because this assignment changes the class—and you said this method would not change the class—the compiler is able to find the error.

10

This kind of mistake can be hard to find just by scanning the code. The eye often sees only what it expects to see. More importantly, the program might appear to run correctly, but `itsAge` has now been set to a bogus number. This causes problems sooner or later.

Q Is there ever a reason to use a structure in a C++ program?

A Many C++ programmers reserve the `struct` keyword for classes that have no functions. This is a throwback to the old C structures, which could not have functions. Frankly, it is confusing and poor programming practice. Today's methodless structure might need methods tomorrow. Then you'll be forced either to change the type to `class` or to break your rule and end up with a structure with methods. If you need to call a legacy C function that requires a particular struct, you would have the only good reason to use one.

Q Some people working with object-oriented programming use the term *instantiation*. What is it?

A *Instantiation* is simply a fancy word for the process of creating an object from a class. A specific object defined as being of the type of a class is a single *instance* of a class.

Workshop

The Workshop contains quiz questions to help you solidify your understanding of the material that was covered and exercises to provide you with experience in using what you've learned. Try to answer the quiz and exercise questions before checking the answers in Appendix D, and be certain you understand the answers before continuing to the next lesson.

Quiz

1. What is the dot operator and what is it used for?
2. Which sets aside memory—a declaration or a definition?
3. Is the declaration of a class its interface or its implementation?
4. What is the difference between public and private data members?
5. Can member functions be private?
6. Can member data be public?
7. If you declare two `Cat` objects, can they have different values in their `itsAge` member data?
8. Do class declarations end with a semicolon? Do class method definitions?

9. What would the header be for a `Cat` function, `Meow`, that takes no parameters and returns `void`?

10. What function is called to initialize a class?

Exercises

1. Write the code that declares a class called `Employee` with these data members: `itsAge`, `itsYearsOfService`, and `itsSalary`.

2. Rewrite the `Employee` class declaration to make the data members private, and provide public accessor methods to get and set each of the data members.

3. Write a program with the `Employee` class that makes two employees; sets their `itsAge`, `itsYearsOfService`, and `itsSalary`; and prints their values. You'll need to add the code for the accessor methods as well.

4. Continuing from Exercise 3, write the code for a method of `Employee` that reports how many thousands of dollars the employee earns, rounded to the nearest 1,000.

5. Change the `Employee` class so that you can initialize `itsAge`, `itsYearsOfService`, and `itsSalary` when you create the employee.

6. **BUG BUSTERS:** What is wrong with the following declaration?

```
class Square
{
  public:
    int Side;
}
```

7. **BUG BUSTERS:** Why isn't the following class declaration very useful?

```
class Cat
{
    int GetAge() const;
  private:
    int itsAge;
};
```

8. **BUG BUSTERS:** What three bugs in this code should the compiler find?

```
class  TV
{
  public:
    void SetStation(int Station);
    int GetStation() const;
  private:
    int itsStation;
};
```

10

```
main()
{
    TV myTV;
    myTV.itsStation = 9;
    TV.SetStation(10);
    TV myOtherTv(2);
}
```

LESSON 11
Implementing Inheritance

Inheritance is one of the most important aspects of an object oriented programming language that, when correctly used, results in well-programmed, maintainable, and scalable applications.

In this lesson, you will learn

- The nature of what inheritance is

- How to use inheritance to derive one class from another

- What protected access is and how to use it

- What virtual functions are

- What private inheritance is

What Is Inheritance?

What is a dog? When you look at your pet, what do you see? I see four legs in service to a mouth. A biologist sees a network of interacting organs, a physicist sees atoms and forces at work, and a taxonomist sees a representative of the species *canine domesticus*.

It is that last assessment that is of interest at the moment. A dog is a kind of canine, a canine is a kind of mammal, and so forth. Taxonomists divide the world of living things into the categories Kingdom, Phylum, Class, Order, Family, Genus, and Species.

This specialization/generalization hierarchy establishes an *is-a* relationship. A *Homo sapiens* (human) is a kind of primate. This relationship can be seen everywhere: A station wagon is a kind of car, which is a kind of vehicle. A sundae is a kind of dessert, which is a kind of food.

When something is said to be a kind of something else, it is implied that it is a specialization of that thing. That is, a car is a special kind of vehicle.

Inheritance and Derivation

The concept dog inherits—that is, it automatically gets—all the features of a mammal. Because it is a mammal, you know that it moves and that it breathes air. All mammals, by definition, move and breathe air. The concept of a dog adds the idea of barking, wagging its tail, eating my revisions to this chapter just when I was finally done, barking when I'm trying to sleep… Sorry. Where was I? Oh, yes: You can divide dogs into working dogs, sporting dogs, and terriers, and you can divide sporting dogs into retrievers, spaniels, and so forth. Finally, each of these can be specialized further; for example, retrievers can be subdivided into Labradors and Goldens.

A Golden is a kind of retriever, which is a sporting dog, which is a dog, and thus a kind of mammal, which is a kind of animal, and, therefore, a kind of living thing. This hierarchy is represented in Figure 11.1.

C++ attempts to represent these relationships by enabling you to define classes that derive from one another. *Derivation* is a way of expressing the is-a relationship. You derive a new class, Dog, from the class Mammal. You don't have to state explicitly that dogs move because they inherit that from Mammal.

A class that adds new functionality to an existing class is said to derive from that original class. The original class is said to be the new class's base class.

If the Dog class derives from the Mammal class, Mammal is a base class of Dog. Derived classes are supersets of their base classes. Just as dog adds certain features to the idea of mammal, the Dog class adds certain methods or data to the Mammal class.

FIGURE 11.1
Hierarchy of
animals.

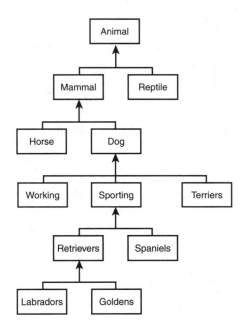

Typically, a base class has more than one derived class. Because dogs, cats, and horses are all types of mammals, their classes would all derive from the `Mammal` class.

11

The Animal Kingdom

To facilitate the discussion of derivation and inheritance, this chapter focuses on the relationships among a number of classes representing animals. You can imagine that you have been asked to design a children's game—a simulation of a farm.

In time, you will develop a whole set of farm animals, including horses, cows, dogs, cats, sheep, and so forth. You will create methods for these classes so that they can act in the ways the child might expect, but for now you'll stub-out each method with a simple print statement.

Stubbing-out a function means you'll write only enough to show that the function was called, leaving the details for later when you have more time. Please feel free to extend the minimal code provided in this lesson to enable the animals to act more realistically.

You should find that the examples using animals are easy to follow. You also find it easy to apply the concepts to other areas. For example, if you were building an ATM bank machine program, you might have a checking account, which is a type of bank account, which is a type of account. This parallels the idea of a dog being a mammal, which in turn is an animal.

The Syntax of Derivation

When you declare a class, you can indicate what class it derives from by writing a colon after the class name, the type of derivation (public or otherwise), and the class from which it derives. The format of this is

```
class derivedClass : accessType baseClass
```

As an example, if you create a new class called Dog that inherits from the existing class Mammal:

```
class Dog : public Mammal
```

The type of derivation (*accessType*) is discussed later in today's lesson. For now, always use public. The class from which you derive must have been declared earlier or you receive a compiler error. Listing 11.1 illustrates how to declare a Dog class that is derived from a Mammal class.

LISTING 11.1   Simple Inheritance

```
1:   //Listing 11.1 Simple inheritance
2:   #include <iostream>
3:   using namespace std;
4:
5:   enum BREED { GOLDEN, CAIRN, DANDIE, SHETLAND, DOBERMAN, LAB };
6:
7:   class Mammal
8:   {
9:     public:
10:       // constructors
11:       Mammal();
12:       ~Mammal();
13:
14:       //accessors
15:       int GetAge() const;
16:       void SetAge(int);
17:       int GetWeight() const;
18:       void SetWeight();
19:
20:       //Other methods
21:       void Speak() const;
22:       void Sleep() const;
23:
24:
25:     protected:
26:       int itsAge;
27:       int itsWeight;
28:   };
29:
```

LISTING 11.1   Continued

```
30:  class Dog : public Mammal
31:  {
32:    public:
33:
34:       // Constructors
35:       Dog();
36:       ~Dog();
37:
38:       // Accessors
39:       BREED GetBreed() const;
40:       void  SetBreed(BREED);
41:
42:       // Other methods
43:       WagTail();
44:       BegForFood();
45:
46:    protected:
47:       BREED itsBreed;
48:  };
```

This program has no output because it is only a set of class declarations without their implementations. Nonetheless, there is much to see here.

Analysis ▼

On lines 7–28, the Mammal class is declared. Note that, in this example, Mammal does not derive from any other class. In the real world, mammals do derive—that is, mammals are kinds of animals. In a C++ program, you can represent only a fraction of the information you have about any given object. Reality is far too complex to capture all of it, so every C++ hierarchy is a carefully limited representation of the data available. The trick of good design is to represent the areas that you care about in a way that maps back to reality in a reasonably faithful manner without adding unnecessary complication.

The hierarchy has to begin somewhere; this program begins with Mammal. Because of this decision, some member variables might properly belong in a higher base class than those now represented here. Certainly all animals have an age and weight, for example, so if Mammal is derived from Animal, you would expect to inherit those attributes. As it is, the attributes appear in the Mammal class.

In the future, if another animal sharing some of these features were added (for instance, Insect), the relevant attributes could be hoisted to a newly created Animal class that would become the base class of Mammal and Insect. This is how class hierarchies evolve over time.

To keep the program reasonably simple and manageable, only six methods have been put in the Mammal class—Speak(), Sleep(), and four accessor methods.

The Dog class inherits from Mammal, as indicated on line 30. You know Dog inherits from Mammal because of the colon following the class name (Dog), which is then followed by the base class name (Mammal).

Every Dog object will have three member variables: itsAge, itsWeight, and itsBreed. Note that the class declaration for Dog does not include the member variables itsAge and itsWeight. Dog objects inherit these variables from the Mammal class, along with all Mammal's methods except the copy operator and the constructors and destructor.

Private Versus Protected

You might have noticed that a new access keyword, protected, has been introduced on lines 25 and 46 of Listing 11.1. Previously, class data had been declared private. However, private members are not available outside of the existing class. This privacy even applies to prevent access from derived classes. You could make itsAge and itsWeight public, but that is not desirable. You don't want other classes accessing these data members directly.

NOTE

> There is an argument to be made that you ought to make all member data private and never protected. Bjarne Stroustrup (the creator of C++) makes this argument in *The Design and Evolution of C++*, (ISBN 0-201-543330-3, Addison Wesley, 1994). Protected methods, however, are not generally regarded as problematic, and can be very useful.

What you want is a designation that says, "Make these visible to this class and to classes that derive from this class." That designation is protected. Protected data members and functions are fully visible to derived classes, but are otherwise private.

In total, three access specifiers exist: public, protected, and private. If a function has an object of your class, it can access all the public member data and functions. The member functions, in turn, can access all private data members and functions of their own class and all protected data members and functions of any class from which they derive. Thus, the function Dog::WagTail() can access the private data itsBreed and can access the protected data of itsAge and itsWeight in the Mammal class.

Even if other classes are layered between Mammal and Dog (for example, DomesticAnimals), the Dog class will still be able to access the protected members of Mammal, assuming that these other classes all use public inheritance. Private inheritance is discussed later in this lesson.

Listing 11.2 demonstrates how to create objects of type Dog and then how to access the data and methods of that type.

LISTING 11.2   Using a Derived Object

```
1:  //Listing 11.2 Using a derived object
2:  #include <iostream>
3:  using std::cout;
4:  using std::endl;
5:
6:  enum BREED { GOLDEN, CAIRN, DANDIE, SHETLAND, DOBERMAN, LAB };
7:
8:  class Mammal
9:  {
10:   public:
11:      // constructors
12:      Mammal():itsAge(2), itsWeight(5){}
13:      ~Mammal(){}
14:
15:      //accessors
16:      int GetAge() const    { return itsAge; }
17:      void SetAge(int age) { itsAge = age; }
18:      int GetWeight() const { return itsWeight; }
19:      void SetWeight(int weight) { itsWeight = weight; }
20:
21:      //Other methods
22:      void Speak()const { cout << "Mammal sound!\n"; }
23:      void Sleep()const { cout << "shhh. I'm sleeping.\n"; }
24:
25:   protected:
26:      int itsAge;
27:      int itsWeight;
28:  };
29:
30:  class Dog : public Mammal
31:  {
32:   public:
33:
34:      // Constructors
35:      Dog():itsBreed(GOLDEN){}
36:      ~Dog(){}
37:
38:      // Accessors
39:      BREED GetBreed() const { return itsBreed; }
```

11

LISTING 11.2   Continued

```
40:        void SetBreed(BREED breed) { itsBreed = breed; }
41:
42:        // Other methods
43:        void WagTail() const { cout << "Tail wagging...\n"; }
44:        void BegForFood() const { cout << "Begging for food...\n"; }
45:
46:    private:
47:        BREED itsBreed;
48:    };
49:
50:    int main()
51:    {
52:        Dog Fido;
53:        Fido.Speak();
54:        Fido.WagTail();
55:        cout << "Fido is " << Fido.GetAge() << " years old" << endl;
56:        return 0;
57:    }
```

Output ▼

```
Mammal sound!
Tail wagging...
Fido is 2 years old
```

Analysis ▼

On lines 8–28, the Mammal class is declared (all its functions are inline to save space here). On lines 30–48, the Dog class is declared as a derived class of Mammal. Thus, by these declarations, all Dogs have an age, a weight, and a breed. As stated before, the age and weight come from the base class, Mammal.

On line 52, a Dog is declared: Fido. Fido inherits all the attributes of a Mammal, as well as all the attributes of a Dog. Thus, Fido knows how to WagTail(), but he also knows how to Speak() and Sleep(). On lines 53 and 54, Fido calls two of these methods from the Mammal base class. On line 55, the GetAge() accessor method from the base class is also called successfully.

Inheritance with Constructors and Destructors

Dog objects are Mammal objects. This is the essence of the is-a relationship.

When Fido is created, his base constructor is called first, creating a Mammal. Then the Dog constructor is called, completing the construction of the Dog object. Because Fido is given no parameters, the default constructor was called in each case. Fido doesn't exist until he is completely constructed, which means that both his Mammal part and his Dog part must be constructed. Thus, both constructors must be called.

When Fido is destroyed, first the Dog destructor is called and then the destructor for the Mammal part of Fido is called. Each destructor is given an opportunity to clean up after its own part of Fido. Remember to clean up after your Dog! Listing 11.3 demonstrates the calling of the constructors and destructors.

LISTING 11.3 Constructors and Destructors Called

```
1:  //Listing 11.3 Constructors and destructors called.
2:  #include <iostream>
3:  using namespace std;
4:  enum BREED { GOLDEN, CAIRN, DANDIE, SHETLAND, DOBERMAN, LAB };
5:
6:  class Mammal
7:  {
8:    public:
9:        // constructors
10:       Mammal();
11:       ~Mammal();
12:
13:       //accessors
14:       int GetAge() const { return itsAge; }
15:       void SetAge(int age) { itsAge = age; }
16:       int GetWeight() const { return itsWeight; }
17:       void SetWeight(int weight) { itsWeight = weight; }
18:
19:       //Other methods
20:       void Speak() const { cout << "Mammal sound!\n"; }
21:       void Sleep() const { cout << "shhh. I'm sleeping.\n"; }
22:
23:    protected:
24:       int itsAge;
25:       int itsWeight;
26:  };
27:
28:  class Dog : public Mammal
29:  {
```

11

LISTING 11.3 Continued

```
30:    public:
31:
32:       // Constructors
33:       Dog();
34:       ~Dog();
35:
36:       // Accessors
37:       BREED GetBreed() const { return itsBreed; }
38:       void SetBreed(BREED breed) { itsBreed = breed; }
39:
40:       // Other methods
41:       void WagTail() const { cout << "Tail wagging...\n"; }
42:       void BegForFood() const { cout << "Begging for food...\n"; }
43:
44:    private:
45:       BREED itsBreed;
46:  };
47:
48:  Mammal::Mammal():
49:  itsAge(3),
50:  itsWeight(5)
51:  {
52:     std::cout << "Mammal constructor... " << endl;
53:  }
54:
55:  Mammal::~Mammal()
56:  {
57:     std::cout << "Mammal destructor... " << endl;
58:  }
59:
60:  Dog::Dog():
61:  itsBreed(GOLDEN)
62:  {
63:     std::cout << "Dog constructor... " << endl;
64:  }
65:
66:  Dog::~Dog()
67:  {
68:     std::cout << "Dog destructor... " << endl;
69:  }
70:  int main()
71:  {
72:     Dog Fido;
73:     Fido.Speak();
74:     Fido.WagTail();
75:     std::cout << "Fido is " << Fido.GetAge() << " years old" << endl;
76:     return 0;
77:  }
```

Output ▼

```
Mammal constructor...
Dog constructor...
Mammal sound!
Tail wagging...
Fido is 3 years old
Dog destructor...
Mammal destructor...
```

Analysis ▼

Listing 11.3 is like Listing 11.2, except that on lines 48–69 the constructors and destructors now print to the screen when called. Mammal's constructor is called, and then Dog's. At that point, the Dog fully exists, and its methods can be called.

When Fido goes out of scope, Dog's destructor is called, followed by a call to Mammal's destructor. You see that this is confirmed in the output from the listing.

Passing Arguments to Base Constructors

It is possible that you will want to initialize values in a base constructor. For example, you might want to overload the constructor of Mammal to take a specific age and overload the Dog constructor to take a breed. How do you get the age and weight parameters passed up to the right constructor in Mammal? What if Dogs want to initialize weight but Mammals don't?

Base class initialization can be performed during class initialization by writing the base class name, followed by the parameters expected by the base class. Listing 11.4 demonstrates this.

LISTING 11.4   Overloading Constructors in Derived Classes

```
 1:  //Listing 11.4 Overloading constructors in derived classes
 2:  #include <iostream>
 3:  using namespace std;
 4:
 5:  enum BREED { GOLDEN, CAIRN, DANDIE, SHETLAND, DOBERMAN, LAB };
 6:
 7:  class Mammal
 8:  {
 9:    public:
10:      // constructors
11:      Mammal();
12:      Mammal(int age);
13:      ~Mammal();
14:
```

11

LISTING 11.4   Continued

```
15:        //accessors
16:        int GetAge() const { return itsAge; }
17:        void SetAge(int age) { itsAge = age; }
18:        int GetWeight() const { return itsWeight; }
19:        void SetWeight(int weight) { itsWeight = weight; }
20:
21:        //Other methods
22:        void Speak() const { cout << "Mammal sound!\n"; }
23:        void Sleep() const { cout << "shhh. I'm sleeping.\n"; }
24:
25:
26:    protected:
27:        int itsAge;
28:        int itsWeight;
29:    };
30:
31:    class Dog : public Mammal
32:    {
33:      public:
34:
35:        // Constructors
36:        Dog();
37:        Dog(int age);
38:        Dog(int age, int weight);
39:        Dog(int age, BREED breed);
40:        Dog(int age, int weight, BREED breed);
41:        ~Dog();
42:
43:        // Accessors
44:        BREED GetBreed() const { return itsBreed; }
45:        void SetBreed(BREED breed) { itsBreed = breed; }
46:
47:        // Other methods
48:        void WagTail() const { cout << "Tail wagging...\n"; }
49:        void BegForFood() const { cout << "Begging for food...\n"; }
50:
51:      private:
52:        BREED itsBreed;
53:    };
54:
55:    Mammal::Mammal():
56:    itsAge(1),
57:    itsWeight(5)
58:    {
59:        cout << "Mammal constructor..." << endl;
60:    }
61:
62:    Mammal::Mammal(int age):
63:    itsAge(age),
```

LISTING 11.4   Continued

```
 64:  itsWeight(5)
 65:  {
 66:     cout << "Mammal(int) constructor..." << endl;
 67:  }
 68:
 69:  Mammal::~Mammal()
 70:  {
 71:     cout << "Mammal destructor..." << endl;
 72:  }
 73:
 74:  Dog::Dog():
 75:  Mammal(),
 76:  itsBreed(GOLDEN)
 77:  {
 78:     cout << "Dog constructor..." << endl;
 79:  }
 80:
 81:  Dog::Dog(int age):
 82:  Mammal(age),
 83:  itsBreed(GOLDEN)
 84:  {
 85:     cout << "Dog(int) constructor..." << endl;
 86:  }
 87:
 88:  Dog::Dog(int age, int weight):
 89:  Mammal(age),
 90:  itsBreed(GOLDEN)
 91:  {
 92:     itsWeight = weight;
 93:     cout << "Dog(int, int) constructor..." << endl;
 94:  }
 95:
 96:  Dog::Dog(int age, int weight, BREED breed):
 97:  Mammal(age),
 98:  itsBreed(breed)
 99:  {
100:     itsWeight = weight;
101:     cout << "Dog(int, int, BREED) constructor..." << endl;
102:  }
103:
104:  Dog::Dog(int age, BREED breed):
105:  Mammal(age),
106:  itsBreed(breed)
107:  {
108:     cout << "Dog(int, BREED) constructor..." << endl;
109:  }
110:
111:  Dog::~Dog()
112:  {
```

11

LISTING 11.4   Continued

```
113:     cout << "Dog destructor..." << endl;
114:  }
115:  int main()
116:  {
117:      Dog Fido;
118:      Dog rover(5);
119:      Dog buster(6,8);
120:      Dog yorkie (3,GOLDEN);
121:      Dog dobbie (4,20,DOBERMAN);
122:      Fido.Speak();
123:      rover.WagTail();
124:      cout << "Yorkie is " << yorkie.GetAge()
125:           << " years old" << endl;
126:      cout << "Dobbie weighs ";
127:      cout << dobbie.GetWeight() << " pounds" << endl;
128:      return 0;
129:  }
```

NOTE   The output has been numbered here so that each line can be referred to in the analysis.

Output ▼

```
1:  Mammal constructor...
2:  Dog constructor...
3:  Mammal(int) constructor...
4:  Dog(int) constructor...
5:  Mammal(int) constructor...
6:  Dog(int, int) constructor...
7:  Mammal(int) constructor...
8:  Dog(int, BREED) constructor....
9:  Mammal(int) constructor...
10: Dog(int, int, BREED) constructor...
11: Mammal sound!
12: Tail wagging...
13: Yorkie is 3 years old.
14: Dobbie weighs 20 pounds.
15: Dog destructor. . .
16: Mammal destructor...
17: Dog destructor...
18: Mammal destructor...
19: Dog destructor...
20: Mammal destructor...
21: Dog destructor...
22: Mammal destructor...
23: Dog destructor...
24: Mammal destructor...
```

Analysis ▼

In Listing 11.4, Mammal's constructor has been overloaded on line 12 to take an integer, the Mammal's age. The implementation on lines 62–67 initializes itsAge with the value passed into the constructor and initializes itsWeight with the value 5.

Dog has overloaded five constructors on lines 36–40. The first is the default constructor. On line 37, the second constructor takes the age, which is the same parameter that the Mammal constructor takes. The third constructor takes both the age and the weight, the fourth takes the age and the breed, and the fifth takes the age, the weight, and the breed.

On line 74 is the code for Dog's default constructor. You can see that this has something new. When this constructor is called, it in turn calls Mammal's default constructor as you can see on line 75. Although it is not strictly necessary to do this, it serves as documentation that you intended to call the base constructor, which takes no parameters. The base constructor would be called in any case, but actually doing so makes your intentions explicit.

The implementation for the Dog constructor, which takes an integer, is on lines 81–86. In its initialization phase (lines 82 and 83), Dog initializes its base class, passing in the parameter, and then it initializes its breed.

Another Dog constructor is on lines 88–94. This constructor takes two parameters. It again initializes its base class by calling the appropriate constructor on line 89, but this time it also assigns weight to its base class's variable itsWeight. Note that you cannot assign to the base class variable in the initialization phase. Because Mammal does not have a constructor that takes this parameter, you must do this within the body of the Dog's constructor.

Walk through the remaining constructors to be certain you are comfortable with how they work. Note what is initialized and what must wait for the body of the constructor.

The output has been numbered so that each line can be referred to in this analysis. The first two lines of output represent the instantiation of Fido, using the default constructor.

In the output, lines 3 and 4 represent the creation of rover. Lines 5 and 6 represent buster. Note that the Mammal constructor that was called is the constructor that takes one integer, but the Dog constructor is the constructor that takes two integers.

After all the objects are created, they are used and then go out of scope. As each object is destroyed, first the Dog destructor and then the Mammal destructor is called, five of each in total.

11

Overriding Base Class Functions

A Dog object has access to all the data members and functions in class Mammal, as well as to any of its own data members and functions, such as WagTail(), that the declaration of the Dog class might add. A derived class can also override a base class function. *Overriding* a function means changing the implementation of a base class function in a derived class.

When a derived class creates a function with the same return type and signature as a member function in the base class, but with a new implementation, it is said to be overriding that function. When you make an object of the derived class, the correct function is called.

When you override a function, its signature must agree with the signature of the function in the base class. The signature is the function prototype other than the return type; that is, the name of the function, the parameter list, and the keyword const, if used. The return types might differ.

Listing 11.5 illustrates what happens if the Dog class overrides the Speak() method in Mammal. To save room, the accessor functions have been left out of these classes.

LISTING 11.5   Overriding a Base Class Method in a Derived Class

```
1:  //Listing 11.5 Overriding a base class method in a derived class
2:  #include <iostream>
3:  using std::cout;
4:
5:  enum BREED { GOLDEN, CAIRN, DANDIE, SHETLAND, DOBERMAN, LAB };
6:
7:  class Mammal
8:  {
9:    public:
10:      // constructors
11:      Mammal() { cout << "Mammal constructor...\n"; }
12:      ~Mammal() { cout << "Mammal destructor...\n"; }
13:
14:      //Other methods
15:      void Speak()const { cout << "Mammal sound!\n"; }
16:      void Sleep()const { cout << "shhh. I'm sleeping.\n"; }
17:
18:    protected:
19:      int itsAge;
20:      int itsWeight;
21:  };
22:
23:  class Dog : public Mammal
24:  {
```

LISTING 11.5   Continued

```
25:     public:
26        // Constructors
27:        Dog(){ cout << "Dog constructor...\n"; }
28:        ~Dog(){ cout << "Dog destructor...\n"; }
29:
30:        // Other methods
31:        void WagTail() const  { cout << "Tail wagging...\n"; }
32:        void BegForFood() const  { cout << "Begging for food...\n"; }
33:        void Speak() const { cout << "Woof!\n"; }
34:
35:     private:
36:        BREED itsBreed;
37: };
38:
39:  int main()
40:  {
41:     Mammal bigAnimal;
42:     Dog Fido;
43:     bigAnimal.Speak();
44:     Fido.Speak();
45:     return 0;
46:  }
```

11

Output ▼

```
Mammal constructor...
Mammal constructor...
Dog constructor...
Mammal sound!
Woof!
Dog destructor...
Mammal destructor...
Mammal destructor...
```

Analysis ▼

Looking at the Mammal class, you can see a method called Speak() defined on line 15.
The Dog class declared on lines 23–37 inherits from Mammal (line 23), and, therefore, has
access to this Speak() method. The Dog class, however, overrides this method on line 33,
causing Dog objects to say Woof! when the Speak() method is called.

In the main() function, a Mammal object, bigAnimal, is created on line 41, causing the
first line of output when the Mammal constructor is called. On line 42, a Dog object, Fido,
is created, causing the next two lines of output, where the Mammal constructor and then
the Dog constructor are called.

On line 43, the Mammal object calls its Speak() method; then on line 44, the Dog object calls its Speak() method. The output reflects that the correct methods were called. The bigAnimal made a mammal sound and Fido woofed. Finally, the two objects go out of scope and the destructors are called.

> **Overloading Versus Overriding**
>
> When you overload a method, you create more than one method with the same name but with a different signature. When you override a method, you create a method in a derived class with the same name as a method in the base class and the same signature.

Hiding the Base Class Method

In the previous listing, the Dog class's Speak() method hides the base class's method. This is what is wanted, but it can have unexpected results. If Mammal has a method, Move(), which is overloaded, and Dog overrides that method, the Dog method hides all the Mammal methods with that name.

If Mammal overloads Move() as three methods—one that takes no parameters, one that takes an integer, and one that takes an integer and a direction—and Dog overrides just the Move() method that takes no parameters, it will not be easy to access the other two methods using a Dog object. Listing 11.6 illustrates this problem.

LISTING 11.6   Hiding Methods

```
1:   //Listing 11.6 Hiding methods
2:   #include <iostream>
3:   using std::cout;
4:
5:   class Mammal
6:   {
7:     public:
8:        void Move() const { cout << "Mammal move one step.\n"; }
9:        void Move(int distance) const
10:      {
11:         cout << "Mammal move ";
12:         cout << distance <<" steps.\n";
13:      }
14:    protected:
15:       int itsAge;
16:       int itsWeight;
17:  };
18:
```

LISTING 11.6 Continued

```
19:  class Dog : public Mammal
20:  {
21:    public:
22:      // You might receive a warning that you are hiding a function!
23:      void Move() const { cout << "Dog move 5 steps.\n"; }
24:  };
25:
26:  int main()
27:  {
28:      Mammal bigAnimal;
29:      Dog Fido;
30:      bigAnimal.Move();
31:      bigAnimal.Move(2);
32:      Fido.Move();
33:      // Fido.Move(10);
34:      return 0;
35:  }
```

Output ▼

```
Mammal move one step.
Mammal move 2 steps.
Dog move 5 steps.
```

Analysis ▼

All the extra methods and data have been removed from these classes. On lines 8 and 9, the Mammal class declares the overloaded Move() methods. On line 23, Dog overrides the version of Move() with no parameters. These methods are invoked on lines 30–32, and the output reflects this as executed.

Line 33, however, is commented out because it causes a compile-time error. After you override one of the methods, you can no longer use any of the base methods of the same name. So, although the Dog class could have called the Move(int) method if it had not overridden the version of Move() without parameters, now that it has done so, it must override both if it wants to use both. Otherwise, it *hides* the method that it doesn't override. This is reminiscent of the rule that if you supply any constructor, the compiler no longer supplies a default constructor.

The rule is this: After you override any overloaded method, all the other overrides of that method are hidden. If you want them not to be hidden, you must override them all.

It is a common mistake to hide a base class method when you intend to override it by forgetting to include the keyword const. const is part of the signature; leaving it off changes the signature, and thus hides the method rather than overrides it.

NOTE

In the next section, virtual methods are described. Overriding a virtual method supports polymorphism—hiding it undermines polymorphism. You'll see more on this very soon.

Calling the Base Method

If you have overridden the base method, it is still possible to call it by fully qualifying the name of the method. You do this by writing the base name, followed by two colons and then the method name:

`baseClass::Method()`

You can call the `Move()` method of the `Mammal` class as follows:

`Mammal::Move()`.

You can use these qualified names just as you would any other method name. It would have been possible to rewrite line 33 in Listing 11.6 so that it would compile, by writing

`Fido.Mammal::Move(10);`

This calls the `Mammal` method explicitly. Listing 11.7 fully illustrates this idea.

LISTING 11.7   Calling a Base Method from a Overridden Method

```
1:  //Listing 11.7 Calling a base method from a overridden method.
2:  #include <iostream>
3:  using namespace std;
4:
5:  class Mammal
6:  {
7:    public:
8:       void Move() const { cout << "Mammal move one step\n"; }
9:       void Move(int distance) const
10:      {
11:        cout << "Mammal move " << distance;
12:        cout << " steps." << endl;
13:      }
14:
15:    protected:
16:       int itsAge;
17:       int itsWeight;
18:  };
19:
20:  class Dog : public Mammal
21:  {
22:    public:
```

LISTING 11.7 Continued

```
23:      void Move() const;
24:  };
25:
26:  void Dog::Move() const
27:  {
28:     cout << "In dog move...\n";
29:     Mammal::Move(3);
30:  }
31:
32:  int main()
33:  {
34:     Mammal bigAnimal;
35:     Dog Fido;
36:     bigAnimal.Move(2);
37:     Fido.Mammal::Move(6);
38:     return 0;
39:  }
```

Output ▼

```
Mammal move 2 steps.
Mammal move 6 steps.
```

Analysis ▼

On line 34, a `Mammal`, `bigAnimal`, is created, and on line 35, a `Dog`, `Fido`, is created. The method call on line 36 invokes the `Move()` method of `Mammal`, which takes an integer.

The programmer wanted to invoke `Move(int)` on the `Dog` object, but had a problem. `Dog` overrides the `Move()` method with no parameters, but does not overload the method that takes an integer—it does not provide a version that takes an integer. This is solved by the explicit call to the base class `Move(int)` method on line 37.

TIP

When calling overridden ancestor class functions using ":: ", keep in mind that if a new class is inserted in the inheritance hierarchy between the descendant and its ancestor, the descendant will be now making a call that skips past the intermediate class and, therefore, might miss invoking some key capability implemented by the intermediate ancestor.

DO	**DON'T**
DO extend the functionality of existing, tested classes by deriving.	**DON'T** hide a base class function by changing the function signature.
DO change the behavior of certain functions in the derived class by overriding the base class methods.	**DON'T** forget that const is a part of the signature.
	DON'T forget that the return type is not part of the signature.

Virtual Methods

This lesson has emphasized the fact that a Dog object is a Mammal object. So far that has meant only that the Dog object has inherited the attributes (data) and capabilities (methods) of its base class. In C++, the is-a relationship runs deeper than that, however.

C++ extends its polymorphism to allow pointers to base classes to be assigned to derived class objects. Thus, you can write

```
Mammal* pMammal = new Dog;
```

This creates a new Dog object on the heap and returns a pointer to that object, which it assigns to a pointer to Mammal. This is fine because a dog is a mammal.

NOTE

> This is the essence of polymorphism. For example, you could create many types of windows, including dialog boxes, scrollable windows, and list boxes, and give them each a virtual draw() method. By creating a pointer to a window and assigning dialog boxes and other derived types to that pointer, you can call draw() without regard to the actual runtime type of the object pointed to. The correct draw() function will be called.

You can then use this pointer to invoke any method on Mammal. What you would like is for those methods that are overridden in Dog() to call the correct function. Virtual functions enable you to do that. To create a virtual function, you add the keyword virtual in front of the function declaration. Listing 11.8 illustrates how this works and what happens with nonvirtual methods.

LISTING 11.8   Using Virtual Methods

```
1:   //Listing 11.8 Using virtual methods
2:   #include <iostream>
3:   using std::cout;
4:
5:   class Mammal
6:   {
7:     public:
8:         Mammal():itsAge(1) { cout << "Mammal constructor...\n"; }
9:         virtual ~Mammal() { cout << "Mammal destructor...\n"; }
10:        void Move() const { cout << "Mammal move one step\n"; }
11:        virtual void Speak() const { cout << "Mammal speak!\n"; }
12:
13:    protected:
14:        int itsAge;
15:  };
16:
17:  class Dog : public Mammal
18:  {
19:    public:
20:       Dog() { cout << "Dog Constructor...\n"; }
21:       virtual ~Dog() { cout << "Dog destructor...\n"; }
22:       void WagTail() { cout << "Wagging Tail...\n"; }
23:       void Speak()const { cout << "Woof!\n"; }
24:       void Move()const { cout << "Dog moves 5 steps...\n"; }
25:  };
26:
27:  int main()
28:  {
29:     Mammal *pDog = new Dog;
30:     pDog->Move();
31:     pDog->Speak();
32:
33:     return 0;
34:  }
```

11

Output ▼

```
Mammal constructor...
Dog Constructor...
Mammal move one step
Woof!
```

Analysis ▼

On line 11, `Mammal` is provided a virtual method: `Speak()`. The designer of this class thereby signals that she expects this class eventually to be another class's base type. The derived class will probably want to override this function.

On line 29, a pointer to Mammal is created, pDog, but it is assigned the address of a new Dog object. Because a dog is a mammal, this is a legal assignment. The pointer is then used on line 30 to call the Move() function. Because the compiler knows pDog only to be a Mammal, it looks to the Mammal object to find the Move() method. On line 10, you can see that this is a standard, nonvirtual method, so the Mammal's version is called.

On line 31, the pointer then calls the Speak() method. Because Speak() is virtual (see line 11), the Speak() method overridden in Dog is invoked.

This is almost magical. As far as the calling function knew, it had a Mammal pointer, but here a method on Dog was called. In fact, if you had an array of pointers to Mammal, each of which pointed to a different subclass of Mammal, you could call each in turn, and the correct function would be called. Listing 11.9 illustrates this idea.

LISTING 11.9   Multiple Virtual Functions Called in Turn

```
1:  //Listing 11.9 Multiple virtual functions called in turn
2:  #include <iostream>
3:  using namespace std;
4:
5:  class Mammal
6:  {
7:    public:
8:        Mammal():itsAge(1) {  }
9:        virtual ~Mammal() { }
10:       virtual void Speak() const { cout << "Mammal speak!\n"; }
11:
12:   protected:
13:       int itsAge;
14:  };
15:
16:  class Dog : public Mammal
17:  {
18:    public:
19:      void Speak()const { cout << "Woof!\n"; }
20:  };
21:
22:  class Cat : public Mammal
23:  {
24:    public:
25:      void Speak()const { cout << "Meow!\n"; }
26:  };
27:
28:
29:  class Horse : public Mammal
30:  {
31:    public:
32:      void Speak()const { cout << "Winnie!\n"; }
33:  };
34:
```

LISTING 11.9 Continued

```
35:   class Pig : public Mammal
36:   {
37:     public:
38:         void Speak()const { cout << "Oink!\n"; }
39:   };
40:
41:   int main()
42:   {
43:       Mammal* theArray[5];
44:       Mammal* ptr;
45:       int choice, i;
46:       for ( i = 0; i<5; i++)
47:       {
48:           cout << "(1)dog (2)cat (3)horse (4)pig: ";
49:           cin >> choice;
50:           switch (choice)
51:           {
52:             case 1: ptr = new Dog;
53:                     break;
54:             case 2: ptr = new Cat;
55:                     break;
56:             case 3: ptr = new Horse;
57:                     break;
58:             case 4: ptr = new Pig;
59:                     break;
60:             default: ptr = new Mammal;
61:                     break;
62:           }
63:           theArray[i] = ptr;
64:       }
65:       for (i=0;i<5;i++)
66:           theArray[i]->Speak();
67:       return 0;
68:   }
```

11

Output ▼

```
(1)dog (2)cat (3)horse (4)pig: 1
(1)dog (2)cat (3)horse (4)pig: 2
(1)dog (2)cat (3)horse (4)pig: 3
(1)dog (2)cat (3)horse (4)pig: 4
(1)dog (2)cat (3)horse (4)pig: 5
Woof!
Meow!
Whinny!
Oink!
Mammal speak!
```

Analysis ▼

This stripped-down program, which provides only the barest functionality to each class, illustrates virtual functions in their purest form. Four classes are declared: Dog, Cat, Horse, and Pig. All four are derived from Mammal.

On line 10, Mammal's Speak() function is declared to be virtual. On lines 19, 25, 32, and 38, the four derived classes override the implementation of Speak().

On lines 46–64, the program loops five times. Each time, the user is prompted to pick which object to create, and a new pointer to that object type is added to the array from within the switch statement on lines 50–62.

At the time this program is compiled, it is impossible to know which object types will be created, and thus which Speak() methods will be invoked. The pointer ptr is bound to its object at runtime. This is called *dynamic binding*, as opposed to static binding, *run-time binding*, or *compile-time binding*.

On lines 65 and 66, the program loops through the array again. This time, each object in the array has its Speak() method called. Because Speak() was virtual in the base class, the appropriate Speak() methods are called for each type. You can see in the output that if you choose each different type, that the corresponding method is indeed called.

FAQ

If I mark a member method as virtual in the base class, do I need to also mark it as virtual in derived classes?

Answer: No, after a method is virtual, if you override it in derived classes, it remains virtual. It is a good idea (although not required) to continue to mark it virtual—this makes the code easier to understand.

How Virtual Functions Work

When a derived object, such as a Dog object, is created, first the constructor for the base class is called and then the constructor for the derived class is called. Figure 11.2 shows what the Dog object looks like after it is created. Note that the Mammal part of the object is contiguous in memory with the Dog part.

When a virtual function is created in an object, the object must keep track of that function. Many compilers build a virtual function table, called a *v-table*. One of these is kept for each type, and each object of that type keeps a virtual table pointer (called a *vptr* or *v-pointer*) that points to that table.

FIGURE 11.2
The Dog object
after it is created.

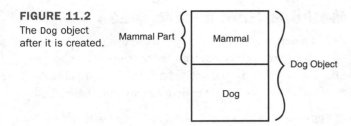

Although implementations vary, all compilers must accomplish the same thing. Each object's vptr points to the v-table that, in turn, has a pointer to each of the virtual functions. When the Mammal part of the Dog is created, the vptr is initialized to point to the correct part of the v-table, as shown in Figure 11.3.

FIGURE 11.3
The v-table of a
Mammal.

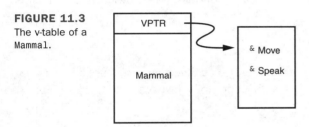

11

When the Dog constructor is called and the Dog part of this object is added, the vptr is adjusted to point to the virtual function overrides (if any) in the Dog object (see Figure 11.4).

FIGURE 11.4
The v-table of
a Dog.

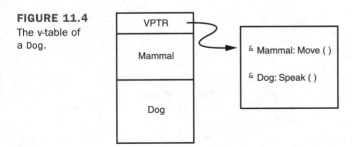

When a pointer to a Mammal is used, the vptr continues to point to the correct function, depending on the "real" type of the object. Thus, when Speak() is invoked, the correct function is invoked.

Trying to Access Methods from a Base Class

You have seen methods accessed in a derived class from a base class using virtual functions. What if there is a method in the derived class that isn't in the base class? Can you access it in the same way you have been using the base class to access the virtual methods? There shouldn't be a name conflict because only the derived class has the method.

If the Dog object had a method, WagTail(), which is not in Mammal, you could not use the pointer to Mammal to access that method. Because WagTail() is not a virtual function, and because it is not in a Mammal object, you can't get there without either a Dog object or a Dog pointer.

You could cast the Mammal to act as a Dog; however, this is not safe if the Mammal is not a Dog. Although this would transform the Mammal pointer into a Dog pointer, a much better and safer way exists to call the WagTail() method. Besides, C++ frowns on explicit casts because they are error-prone.

Slicing

Note that the virtual function magic operates only on pointers and references. Passing an object by value does not enable the virtual functions to be invoked. Listing 11.10 illustrates this problem.

LISTING 11.10   Data Slicing With Passing by Value

```
1:  //Listing 11.10 Data slicing with passing by value
2:  #include <iostream>
3:  using namespace std;
4:
5:  class Mammal
6:  {
7:    public:
8:        Mammal():itsAge(1) { }
9:        virtual ~Mammal() { }
10:       virtual void Speak() const { cout << "Mammal speak!\n"; }
11:
12:   protected:
13:       int itsAge;
14: };
15:
16: class Dog : public Mammal
17: {
18:   public:
19:      void Speak()const { cout << "Woof!\n"; }
20: };
21:
22: class Cat : public Mammal
23: {
```

LISTING 11.10 Continued

```
24:    public:
25:        void Speak()const { cout << "Meow!\n"; }
26:    };
27:
28:    void ValueFunction (Mammal);
29:    void PtrFunction (Mammal*);
30:    void RefFunction (Mammal&);
31:    int main()
32:    {
33:        Mammal* ptr=0;
34:        int choice;
35:        while (1)
36:        {
37:            bool fQuit = false;
38:            cout << "(1)dog (2)cat (0)Quit: ";
39:            cin >> choice;
40:            switch (choice)
41:            {
42:                case 0: fQuit = true;
43:                        break;
44:                case 1: ptr = new Dog;
45:                        break;
46:                case 2: ptr = new Cat;
47:                        break;
48:                default: ptr = new Mammal;
49:                         break;
50:            }
51:            if (fQuit == true)
52:                break;
53:            PtrFunction(ptr);
54:            RefFunction(*ptr);
55:            ValueFunction(*ptr);
56:        }
57:        return 0;
58:    }
59:
60:    void ValueFunction (Mammal MammalValue)
61:    {
62:        MammalValue.Speak();
63:    }
64:
65:    void PtrFunction (Mammal * pMammal)
66:    {
67:        pMammal->Speak();
68:    }
69:
70:    void RefFunction (Mammal & rMammal)
71:    {
72:        rMammal.Speak();
73:    }
```

11

Output ▼

```
(1)dog (2)cat (0)Quit: 1
Woof
Woof
Mammal Speak!
(1)dog (2)cat (0)Quit: 2
Meow!
Meow!
Mammal Speak!
(1)dog (2)cat (0)Quit: 0
```

Analysis ▼

On lines 5–26, stripped-down versions of the `Mammal`, `Dog`, and `Cat` classes are declared. Three functions are declared: `PtrFunction()`, `RefFunction()`, and `ValueFunction()`. They take a pointer to a `Mammal`, a `Mammal` reference, and a `Mammal` object, respectively. As you can see on lines 60–73, all three functions do the same thing—they call the `Speak()` method.

The user is prompted to choose a `Dog` or a `Cat`, and based on the choice that is made, a pointer to the correct type is created on lines 44 or 46. In the first line of the output, the user chooses `Dog`. The `Dog` object is created on the free store on line 44. The `Dog` is then passed to a function as a pointer on line 53, as a reference on line 54, and by value on line 55.

The pointer and reference calls invoke the virtual functions, and the `Dog->Speak()` member function is invoked. This is shown on the first two lines of output after the user's choice.

The dereferenced pointer, however, is passed by value on line 55 to the function on lines 60–63. The function expects a `Mammal` object, and so the compiler slices down the `Dog` object to just the `Mammal` part. When the `Mammal Speak()` method is called on line 72, only `Mammal` information is available. The `Dog` pieces are gone. This is reflected in the third line of output after the user's choice. This effect is called *slicing* because the `Dog` portions (your derived class portions) of your object were sliced off when converting to just a `Mammal` (the base class). This experiment is then repeated for the `Cat` object, with similar results.

Creating Virtual Destructors

It is legal and common to pass a pointer to a derived object when a pointer to a base object is expected. What happens when that pointer to a derived subject is deleted? If the destructor is virtual, as it should be, the right thing happens—the derived class's destructor is called. Because the derived class's destructor automatically invokes the base class's destructor, the entire object is properly destroyed.

The rule of thumb is this: If any function in your class is virtual, the destructor should be as well.

> **NOTE**
>
> You should have noticed that the listings in this lesson have been including virtual destructors. Now you know why! As a general practice, it is wise to always make destructors virtual.

Virtual Copy Constructors

Constructors cannot be virtual, and so, technically, no such thing exists as a virtual copy constructor. Nonetheless, at times, your program desperately needs to be able to pass in a pointer to a base object and have a copy of the correct derived object that is created. A common solution to this problem is to create a Clone() method in the base class and to make it virtual. The Clone() method creates a new object copy of the current class and returns that object.

Because each derived class overrides the Clone() method, a copy of the derived class is created. Listing 11.11 illustrates how the Clone() method is used.

LISTING 11.11   Virtual Copy Constructor

```
1:  //Listing 11.11 Virtual copy constructor
2:  #include <iostream>
3:  using namespace std;
4:
5:  class Mammal
6:  {
7:    public:
8:       Mammal():itsAge(1) { cout << "Mammal constructor...\n"; }
9:       virtual ~Mammal() { cout << "Mammal destructor...\n"; }
10:      Mammal (const Mammal & rhs);
11:      virtual void Speak() const { cout << "Mammal speak!\n"; }
12:      virtual Mammal* Clone() { return new Mammal(*this); }
13:      int GetAge()const { return itsAge; }
14:    protected:
15:       int itsAge;
16:  };
17:
18:  Mammal::Mammal (const Mammal & rhs):itsAge(rhs.GetAge())
19:  {
```

11

LISTING 11.11   Continued

```
20:        cout << "Mammal Copy Constructor...\n";
21:    }
22:
23:    class Dog : public Mammal
24:    {
25:      public:
26:        Dog() { cout << "Dog constructor...\n"; }
27:        virtual ~Dog() { cout << "Dog destructor...\n"; }
28:        Dog (const Dog & rhs);
29:        void Speak()const { cout << "Woof!\n"; }
30:        virtual Mammal* Clone() { return new Dog(*this); }
31:    };
32:
33:    Dog::Dog(const Dog & rhs):
34:    Mammal(rhs)
35:    {
36:        cout << "Dog copy constructor...\n";
37:    }
38:
39:    class Cat : public Mammal
40:    {
41:      public:
42:        Cat() { cout << "Cat constructor...\n"; }
43:        ~Cat() { cout << "Cat destructor...\n"; }
44:        Cat (const Cat &);
45:        void Speak()const { cout << "Meow!\n"; }
46:        virtual Mammal* Clone() { return new Cat(*this); }
47:    };
48:
49:    Cat::Cat(const Cat & rhs):
50:    Mammal(rhs)
51:    {
52:        cout << "Cat copy constructor...\n";
53:    }
54:
55:    enum ANIMALS { MAMMAL, DOG, CAT};
56:    const int NumAnimalTypes = 3;
57:    int main()
58:    {
59:        Mammal *theArray[NumAnimalTypes];
60:        Mammal* ptr;
61:        int choice, i;
62:        for ( i = 0; i<NumAnimalTypes; i++)
63:        {
64:            cout << "(1)dog (2)cat (3)Mammal: ";
65:            cin >> choice;
66:            switch (choice)
67:            {
```

LISTING 11.11 Continued

```
68:           case DOG:  ptr = new Dog;
69:                      break;
70:           case CAT:  ptr = new Cat;
71:                      break;
72:           default:   ptr = new Mammal;
73:                      break;
74:        }
75:        theArray[i] = ptr;
76:     }
77:     Mammal *OtherArray[NumAnimalTypes];
78:     for (i=0;i<NumAnimalTypes;i++)
79:     {
80:        theArray[i]->Speak();
81:        OtherArray[i] = theArray[i]->Clone();
82:     }
83:     for (i=0;i<NumAnimalTypes;i++)
84:        OtherArray[i]->Speak();
85:     return 0;
86: }
```

Output ▼

```
1:  (1)dog (2)cat (3)Mammal: 1
2:  Mammal constructor...
3:  Dog constructor...
4:  (1)dog (2)cat (3)Mammal: 2
5:  Mammal constructor...
6:  Cat constructor...
7:  (1)dog (2)cat (3)Mammal: 3
8:  Mammal constructor...
9:  Woof!
10: Mammal Copy Constructor...
11: Dog copy constructor...
12: Meow!
13: Mammal Copy Constructor...
14: Cat copy constructor...
15: Mammal speak!
16: Mammal Copy Constructor...
17: Woof!
18: Meow!
19: Mammal speak!
```

Analysis ▼

Listing 11.11 is very similar to the previous two listings, except that on line 12 a new virtual method has been added to the Mammal class: Clone(). This method returns a pointer to a new `Mammal` object by calling the copy constructor, passing in itself (`*this`) as a `const` reference.

`Dog` and `Cat` both override the `Clone()` method, initializing their data and passing in copies of themselves to their own copy constructors. Because `Clone()` is virtual, this effectively creates a virtual copy constructor. You see this when line 81 executes.

Similar to the last listing, the user is prompted to choose dogs, cats, or mammals, and these are created on lines 68–73. A pointer to each choice is stored in an array on line 75.

As the program iterates over the array on lines 78–82, each object has its `Speak()` and its `Clone()` methods called, in turn. The result of the `Clone()` call on line 81 is a pointer to a copy of the object, which is then stored in a second array.

On line 1 of the output, the user is prompted and responds with 1, choosing to create a dog. The `Mammal` and `Dog` constructors are invoked. This is repeated for `Cat` on line 4 and for `Mammal` on line 7 of the constructor.

Line 9 of the output represents the call to `Speak()` on the first object, the `Dog`. The virtual `Speak()` method is called and the correct version of `Speak()` is invoked. The `Clone()` function is then called, and because this is also virtual, `Dog`'s `Clone()` method is invoked, causing the `Mammal` constructor and the `Dog` copy constructor to be called.

The same is repeated for `Cat` on lines 12–14, and then for `Mammal` on lines 15–16. Finally, the new array is iterated on lines 83–84 of the listing, and each of the new objects has `Speak()` invoked, as can be seen by output lines 17–19.

The Cost of Virtual Methods

Because objects with virtual methods must maintain a v-table, some overhead occurs in having virtual methods. If you have a very small class from which you do not expect to derive other classes, there might not be a reason to have any virtual methods at all.

After you declare any methods virtual, you've paid most of the price of the v-table (although each entry does add a small memory overhead). At that point, you want the destructor to be virtual, and the assumption is that all other methods probably are virtual as well. Take a long, hard look at any nonvirtual methods, and be certain you understand why they are not virtual

DO	**DON'T**
DO use virtual methods when you expect to derive from a class.	**DON'T** mark the constructor as virtual.
DO use a virtual destructor if any methods are virtual.	**DON'T** try to access private data in a base class from a derived class.

Private Inheritance

In the preceding samples, the derived class Dog features a public derivation from the base class Mammal:

```
class Dog : public Mammal
```

This form of derivation results in an is-a relationship—one that emphasizes the behavioral need of a Dog to be akin to that of a Mammal. This helps class Dog to use the protected and public members of the class Mammal, and override virtual ones. However, there are cases in which programmers want to make use of an existing base class; that is, use existing functionality—something that derivation would bring them, but the is-a relationship would make no sense, if not also be poor programming practice. This is where private inheritance may play a role.

Using Private Inheritance

Imagine that a class ElectricMotor needs to be (re-)used in the creation of a class Fan. A Fan is not an ElectricMotor, rather it's an application thereof. Therefore, public inheritance would be way too awkward in this scenario. The programmer can, however, do this:

```
class Fan : private ElectricMotor
```

This form of derivation allows Fan to use all the underlying functionality of the ElectricMotor, and even override virtual functions. However, it does not let the users of Fan (such as those in possession of a Fan object) to access the base class ElectricMotor and its functions—all contents of the base class are private to the users of Fan, irrespective of their actual access modifiers. Listing 11.12 demonstrates these restrictions brought into force by private inheritance effectively.

LISTING 11.12   Private Inheritance

```
 1:  //Listing 11.12 Demonstration of Private Inheritance
 2:  #include <iostream>
 3:  using namespace std;
 4:
 5:  class ElectricMotor
 6:  {
 7:  public:
 8:      ElectricMotor () {};
 9:      virtual ~ElectricMotor () {};
10:
11:  public:
12:      void StartMotor ()
13:      {
```

11

LISTING 11.12 Continued

```
14:            Accelerate ();
15:            Cruise ();
16:        }
17:
18:        void StopMotor ()
19:        {
20:            cout << "Motor stopped" << endl;
21:        };
22:
23: private:
24:        void Accelerate ()
25:        {
26:            cout << "Motor started" << endl;
27:        }
28:
29:        void Cruise ()
30:        {
31:            cout << "Motor running at constant speed" << endl;
32:        }
33: };
34:
35: class Fan : private ElectricMotor
36: {
37: public:
38:        Fan () {};
39:        ~Fan () {}
40:
41:        void StartFan ()
42:        {
43:            StartMotor ();
44:        }
45:
46:        void StopFan ()
47:        {
48:            StopMotor ();
49:        }
50: };
51:
52: int main ()
53: {
54:     Fan mFan;
55:
56:     mFan.StartFan ();
57:     mFan.StopFan ();
58:
59:     /*
60:         Note: the next two lines access the base class ElectricMotor
61:         However, as Fan features 'private inheritance' from ElectricMotor,
62:         neither the base class instance nor its public methods are
```

LISTING 11.12   Continued

```
63:          accessible to the users of class Fan.
64:          Un-comment them to see a compile failure!
65:      */
66:      // mFan.Accelerate ();
67:      // ElectricMotor * pMotor = &mFan;
68:
69:      return 0;
70: }
```

Analysis ▼

The preceding code is quite simple, and it demonstrates how class Fan was able to use the public methods of ElectricMotor by deriving from it, yet intentionally makes them unavailable for use for those that use objects of Fan. Lines 66 and 67 attempt to access the instance of the base class ElectricMotor via mFan. However, they cannot access any public method of the base class ElectricMotor via an instance of the derived class Fan, as the inheritance relationship between them is private and therefore forbids such access. Those two lines, when uncommented, will result in a compile failure.

Private Inheritance Versus Aggregation (Composition)

11

Listing 11.12 could alternatively have featured ElectricMotor as a private member of Fan, instead of having the latter derive privately from it. This scenario is one that is called *aggregation* or *composition*. To understand the use of this word, imagine that the class Fan would have the option of containing an array of objects of type class ElectricMotor—in other words, aggregating the latter. Listing 11.13 demonstrates this in detail.

LISTING 11.13   Version of Class Fan Aggregating ElectricMotor

```
 1:  //Listing 11.13 Version of class Fan that aggregates ElectricMotor
 2: class Fan
 3: {
 4: public:
 5:     Fan () {};
 6:     ~Fan () {}
 7:
 8:    void StartFan ()
 9:    {
10:        m_ElectricMotor.StartMotor();
11:    }
12:    void StopFan ()
13:    {
```

LISTING 11.13 Continued

```
14:        m_ElectricMotor.StopMotor ();
15:    }
16: private:
17:    ElectricMotor m_ElectricMotor;
18: };
```

Analysis ▼

This is about as simple or complex as the version that featured private inheritance. However, as apparent, the programmer in this version has the option (or the flexibility) to upgrade his class Fan to use a collection of ElectricMotors; that is, change from having a member object of one motor to having an array thereof.

On a finer and more invisible level, there is another advantage in the use of aggregation over inheritance: The absence of an inheritance hierarchy avoids the presence of a v-table, as discussed in section, "The Cost of Virtual Methods," and therefore avoids unnecessary performance issues.

The advantages of private inheritance are as follows:

- It allows the derived class to access the protected member functions of the base class.
- It allows the derived class to override virtual functions of the base class.

For these advantages, the tradeoffs are the following:

- Code that becomes less flexible and error-prone in a multiple programmer scenario.
- Inheritance, and the performance issues that come with it.

Therefore, the use of private inheritance is best avoided when aggregation or composition is a viable option.

Summary

In this lesson, you learned how derived classes inherit from base classes. The class discussed public inheritance and virtual functions. Classes inherit all the public and protected data and functions from their base classes.

Protected access is public to derived classes and private to all other classes. Even derived classes cannot access private data or functions in their base classes.

Constructors can be initialized before the body of the constructor. At that time, the base constructors are invoked and parameters can be passed to the base class.

Functions in the base class can be overridden in the derived class. If the base class functions are virtual, and if the object is accessed by pointer or reference, the derived class's functions will be invoked based on the runtime type of the object pointed to.

Methods in the base class can be invoked by explicitly naming the function with the prefix of the base class name and two colons. For example, if Dog inherits from Mammal, Mammal's walk() method can be called with Mammal::walk().

In classes with virtual methods, the destructor should almost always be made virtual. A virtual destructor ensures that the derived part of the object will be freed when delete is called on the pointer. Constructors cannot be virtual. Virtual copy constructors can be effectively created by making a virtual member function that calls the copy constructor.

Q&A

Q **Are inherited members and functions passed along to subsequent generations? If Dog derives from Mammal, and Mammal derives from Animal, does Dog inherit Animal's functions and data?**

A Yes. As derivation continues, derived classes inherit the sum of all the functions and data in all their base classes, but can access only those that are public or protected.

Q **If, in the preceding example, Mammal overrides a function in Animal, which does Dog get, the original or the overridden function?**

A If Dog inherits from Mammal, it gets the overridden function.

Q **Can a derived class make a public base function private?**

A Yes, the derived class can override the method and make it private. It then remains private for all subsequent derivation. However, this should be avoided when possible because users of your class will expect it to contain the sum of the methods provided by its ancestors.

Q **Why not make all class functions virtual?**

A Overhead occurs with the first virtual function in the creation of a v-table. After that, the overhead is trivial. Many C++ programmers feel that if one function is virtual, all others should be. Other programmers disagree, feeling that there should always be a reason for what you do.

11

Q If a function (`SomeFunc()`) is virtual in a base class and is also overloaded so as to take either an integer or two integers, and the derived class overrides the form taking one integer, what is called when a pointer to a derived object calls the two-integer form?

A As you learned in this lesson, the overriding of the one-integer form hides the entire base class function, and thus you receive a compile error complaining that that function requires only one `int`.

Workshop

The Workshop contains quiz questions to help you solidify your understanding of the material that was covered and exercises to provide you with experience in using what you've learned. Try to answer the quiz and exercise questions before checking the answers in Appendix D, and be certain you understand the answers before continuing to the next lesson.

Quiz

1. What is a v-table?
2. What is a virtual destructor?
3. How do you show the declaration of a virtual constructor?
4. How can you create a virtual copy constructor?
5. How do you invoke a base member function from a derived class in which you've overridden that function?
6. How do you invoke a base member function from a derived class in which you have not overridden that function?
7. If a base class declares a function to be virtual and a derived class does not use the term `virtual` when overriding that class, is it still virtual when inherited by a third-generation class?
8. What is the `protected` keyword used for?

Exercises

1. Show the declaration of a virtual function that takes an integer parameter and returns void.
2. Show the declaration of a class `Square`, which derives from `Rectangle`, which in turn derives from `Shape`.

3. If, in Exercise 2, Shape takes no parameters, Rectangle takes two (length and width), but Square takes only one (length), show the constructor initialization for Square.

4. Write a virtual copy constructor for the class Square (in Exercise 3).

5. **BUG BUSTERS:** What is wrong with this code snippet?

```
void SomeFunction (Shape);
Shape * pRect = new Rectangle;
SomeFunction(*pRect);
```

6. **BUG BUSTERS:** What is wrong with this code snippet?

```
class Shape()
{
  public:
     Shape();
     virtual ~Shape();
     virtual Shape(const Shape&);
};
```

11

LESSON 12
Polymorphism

In Lesson 11, "Implementing Inheritance," you learned how to write virtual functions in derived classes. This is the fundamental building block of polymorphism: the capability to bind specific, derived class objects to base class pointers at runtime.

In this lesson, you will learn

- What multiple inheritance is and how to use it
- What virtual inheritance is and when to use it
- What abstract classes are and when to use them
- What pure virtual functions are

Problems with Single Inheritance

Suppose that you've been working with your animal classes for a while, and you've divided the class hierarchy into `Bird` and `Mammal`. The `Bird` class includes the member function `Fly()`. The `Mammal` class has been divided into a number of types of `Mammals`, including `Horse`. The `Horse` class includes the member functions `Whinny()` and `Gallop()`.

Suddenly, you realize you need a `Pegasus` object: a cross between a `Horse` and a `Bird`. A `Pegasus` can `Fly()`, it can `Whinny()`, and it can `Gallop()`. With single inheritance, you're in quite a jam.

With single inheritance, you can only pull from one of these existing classes. You can make `Pegasus` a `Bird`, but then it won't be able to `Whinny()` or `Gallop()`. You can make it a `Horse`, but then it won't be able to `Fly()`.

Your first solution is to copy the `Fly()` method into the `Pegasus` class and derive `Pegasus` from `Horse`. This works fine, at the cost of having the `Fly()` method in two places (`Bird` and `Pegasus`). If you change one, you must remember to change the other. Of course, a developer who comes along months or years later to maintain your code must also know to fix both places.

Soon, however, you have a new problem. You want to create a list of `Horse` objects and a list of `Bird` objects. You'd like to be able to add your `Pegasus` objects to either list, but if a `Pegasus` is a `Horse`, you can't add it to a list of `Birds`.

You have a couple of potential solutions. You can rename the `Horse` method `Gallop()` to `Move()`, and then override `Move()` in your `Pegasus` object to do the work of `Fly()`. You would then override `Move()` in your other horses to do the work of `Gallop()`. Perhaps `Pegasus` could be clever enough to gallop short distances and fly longer distances, as seen in the following sample:

```
Pegasus::Move(long distance)
{
    if (distance > veryFar)
        fly(distance);
    else
        gallop(distance);
}
```

This is a bit limiting. Perhaps one day `Pegasus` will want to fly a short distance or gallop a long distance. Your next solution might be to move `Fly()` up into `Horse`, as illustrated in Listing 12.1. The problem is that most horses can't fly, so you have to make this method do nothing unless it is a `Pegasus`.

LISTING 12.1   Getting Horses to Fly with Single Inheritance

```
0:   // Listing 12.1. If horses could fly...
1:   // Percolating Fly() up into Horse
2:
3:   #include <iostream>
4:   using namespace std;
5:
6:   class Horse
7:   {
8:     public:
9:        void Gallop(){ cout << "Galloping...\n"; }
10:       virtual void Fly() { cout << "Horses can't fly.\n" ; }
11:    private:
12:       int itsAge;
13:   };
14:
15:   class Pegasus : public Horse
16:   {
17:     public:
18:        void Fly()
19:           {cout<<"I can fly! I can fly! I can fly!\n";}
20:   };
21:
22:   const int NumberHorses = 5;
23:   int main()
24:   {
25:      Horse* Ranch[NumberHorses];
26:      Horse* pHorse;
27:      int choice,i;
28:      for (i=0; i<NumberHorses; i++)
29:      {
30:         cout << "(1)Horse (2)Pegasus: ";
31:         cin >> choice;
32:         if (choice == 2)
33:            pHorse = new Pegasus;
34:         else
35:            pHorse = new Horse;
36:         Ranch[i] = pHorse;
37:      }
38:      cout << endl;
39:      for (i=0; i<NumberHorses; i++)
40:      {
41:         Ranch[i]->Fly();
42:         delete Ranch[i];
43:      }
44:      return 0;
45:   }
```

12

Output ▼

```
(1)Horse (2)Pegasus: 1
(1)Horse (2)Pegasus: 2
(1)Horse (2)Pegasus: 1
(1)Horse (2)Pegasus: 2
(1)Horse (2)Pegasus: 1

Horses can't fly.
I can fly! I can fly! I can fly!
Horses can't fly.
I can fly! I can fly! I can fly!
Horses can't fly.
```

Analysis ▼

This program certainly works, although at the expense of the Horse class having a Fly() method. On line 10, the method Fly() is provided to Horse. In a real-world class, you might have it issue an error or fail quietly. On line 18, the Pegasus class overrides the Fly() method to "do the right thing," represented here by printing a happy message.

The array of Horse pointers called Ranch on line 25 is used to demonstrate that the correct Fly() method is called, based on the runtime binding of the Horse or Pegasus object.

In lines 28–37, the user is prompted to select a Horse or a Pegasus. An object of the corresponding type is then created and placed into the Ranch array.

In lines 38–43, the program loops again through the Ranch array. This time, each object in the array has its Fly() method called. Depending on whether the object is a Horse or a Pegasus, the correct Fly() method is called. You can see this in the output. Because this program will no longer use the objects in Ranch, in line 42, a call to delete is made to free the memory used by each object.

> **NOTE**
>
> These examples have been stripped down to their bare essentials to illustrate the points under consideration. Constructors, virtual destructors, and so on have been removed to keep the code simple. This is not recommended for your programs.

Percolating Upward

Putting the required function higher in the class hierarchy is a common solution to this problem and results in many functions "percolating up" into the base class. The base class is then in grave danger of becoming a global namespace for all the functions that might be used by any of the derived classes. This can seriously undermine the class typing of C++, and can create a large and cumbersome base class.

In general, you want to percolate shared functionality up the hierarchy without migrating the interface of each class. This means that if two classes that share a common base class (for example, Horse and Bird both share Animal) and have a function in common (both birds and horses eat, for example), you'll want to move that functionality up into the base class and create a virtual function.

What you'll want to avoid, however, is percolating up a function (such as Fly) where it doesn't belong just so that you can call it only on some derived classes, when it doesn't fit the meaning of that base class.

Casting Down

An alternative to this approach, still within single inheritance, is to keep the Fly() method within Pegasus and call only it if the pointer is actually pointing to a Pegasus object. To make this work, you need to be able to ask your pointer what type it is really pointing to. This is known as runtime type identification (RTTI).

CAUTION Beware of using RTTI in your programs. Needing to use it might be an indication of poor inheritance hierarchy design. Consider using virtual functions, templates, or multiple inheritance instead.

12

In the previous example, you declared both Horse and Pegasus objects and placed them in an array of Horse objects. Everything was placed as a Horse. With RTTI, you would check each of these Horses to see whether it was just a horse or if indeed a Pegasus had actually been created.

To call Fly(), however, you must cast the pointer, telling it that the object it is pointing to is a Pegasus object, not a Horse. This is called *casting down* because you are casting down the Horse object to a more derived type. C++ supports casting down (RTTI) using the dynamic_cast operator. Here's how it works.

If you have a pointer to a base class such as `Horse`, and you assign to it a pointer to a derived class, such as `Pegasus`, you can use the `Horse` pointer polymorphically. If you then need to get at the `Pegasus` object, you create a `Pegasus` pointer and use the `dynamic_cast` operator to make the conversion.

At runtime, the base pointer is examined. If the conversion is proper, your new `Pegasus` pointer is fine. If the conversion is improper, if you didn't really have a `Pegasus` object after all, your new pointer is null. Listing 12.2 illustrates this point.

LISTING 12.2   Casting Down Using RTTI

```
0:    // Listing 12.2 Using dynamic_cast.
1:    // Using rtti
2:
3:    #include <iostream>
4:    using namespace std;
5:
6:    enum TYPE { HORSE, PEGASUS };
7:
8:    class Horse
9:    {
10:      public:
11:        virtual void Gallop(){ cout << "Galloping...\n"; }
12:
13:      private:
14:        int itsAge;
15:    };
16:
17:    class Pegasus : public Horse
18:    {
19:      public:
20:        virtual void Fly()
21:            {cout<<"I can fly! I can fly! I can fly!\n";}
22:    };
23:
24:    const int NumberHorses = 5;
25:    int main()
26:    {
27:       Horse* Ranch[NumberHorses];
28:       Horse* pHorse;
29:       int choice,i;
30:       for (i=0; i<NumberHorses; i++)
31:       {
32:          cout << "(1)Horse (2)Pegasus: ";
33:          cin >> choice;
34:          if (choice == 2)
35:             pHorse = new Pegasus;
36:          else
37:             pHorse = new Horse;
```

LISTING 12.2 Continued

```
38:        Ranch[i] = pHorse;
39:     }
40:     cout << endl;
41:     for (i=0; i<NumberHorses; i++)
42:     {
43:        Pegasus *pPeg = dynamic_cast< Pegasus *> (Ranch[i]);
44:        if (pPeg != NULL)
45:           pPeg->Fly();
46:        else
47:           cout << "Just a horse\n";
48:
49:        delete Ranch[i];
50:     }
51:     return 0;
52:  }
```

Output ▼

```
(1)Horse (2)Pegasus: 1
(1)Horse (2)Pegasus: 2
(1)Horse (2)Pegasus: 1
(1)Horse (2)Pegasus: 2
(1)Horse (2)Pegasus: 1

Just a horse
I can fly! I can fly! I can fly!
Just a horse
I can fly! I can fly! I can fly!
Just a horse
```

FAQ

When compiling, I got a warning from Microsoft Visual C++:

```
warning C4541: 'dynamic_cast' used on polymorphic type 'class
Horse' with /GR-; unpredictable behavior may result.
```

What should I do? When running this program, I get a message:

```
This application has requested the Runtime to terminate it in an
unusual way. Please contact the application's support team for
more information.
```

Answer: These are some of this compiler's most confusing error messages. To fix these, do the following:

1. In your project, choose Project, Settings.

2. Go to the C++ tab.

3. Change the drop-down to C++ Language.

4. Click Enable Runtime Type Information (RTTI).

5. Rebuild your entire project.

Alternatively, if you are using the command-line compiler for Visual C++, add the /GR flag:

```
cl /GR List1402.cpp
```

Analysis ▼

This solution also works; however, it is not recommended.

The desired results are achieved. Fly() is kept out of Horse and it is not called on Horse objects. When it is called on Pegasus objects (line 45), however, the objects must be explicitly cast (line 43); Horse objects don't have the method Fly(), so the pointer must be told it is pointing to a Pegasus object before being used.

The need for you to cast the Pegasus object is a warning that something might be wrong with your design. This program effectively undermines the virtual function polymorphism because it depends on casting the object to its real runtime type.

Adding to Two Lists

The other problem with these solutions is that you've declared Pegasus to be a type of Horse, so you cannot add a Pegasus object to a list of Birds. You've paid the price of either moving Fly() up into Horse or casting down the pointer, and yet you still don't have the full functionality you need.

One final, single inheritance solution presents itself. You can push Fly(), Whinny(), and Gallop() up into a common base class of both Bird and Horse: Animal. Now, instead of having a list of Birds and a list of Horses, you can have one unified list of Animals. This works, but eventually leads to a base class that has all the characteristics of all of its descendant classes. So, who needs descendant classes?

Alternatively, you can leave the methods where they are and cast down Horses and Birds and Pegasus objects, but that is even worse!

DO	DON'T
DO move functionality up the inheritance hierarchy when it is conceptually cohesive with the meaning of the ancestor class.	**DON'T** clutter ancestor classes with capabilities that are only added to support a need for polymorphism in descendant classes.
DO avoid performing actions based on the runtime type of the object—use virtual methods, templates, and multiple inheritance.	**DON'T** cast pointers to base objects down to derived objects.

Multiple Inheritance

It is possible to derive a new class from more than one base class. This is called *multiple inheritance*. To derive from more than the base class, you separate each base class by commas in the class designation, as shown here:

```
class DerivedClass : public BaseClass1, public BaseClass2 {}
```

This is exactly like declaring single inheritance with an additional base class, `BaseClass2`, added.

Listing 12.3 illustrates how to declare `Pegasus` so that it derives from both `Horses` and `Birds`. The program then adds `Pegasus` objects to both types of lists.

LISTING 12.3 Multiple Inheritance

```
0:  // Listing 12.3. Multiple inheritance.
1:
2:  #include <iostream>
3:  using std::cout;
4:  using std::cin;
5:  using std::endl;
6:
7:  class Horse
8:  {
9:    public:
10:      Horse() { cout << "Horse constructor... "; }
11:      virtual ~Horse() { cout << "Horse destructor... "; }
12:      virtual void Whinny() const { cout << "Whinny!... "; }
13:    private:
14:      int itsAge;
15:  };
16:
```

LISTING 12.3   Continued

```
17:   class Bird
18:   {
19:     public:
20:       Bird() { cout << "Bird constructor... "; }
21:       virtual ~Bird() { cout << "Bird destructor... "; }
22:       virtual void Chirp() const { cout << "Chirp... ";  }
23:       virtual void Fly() const
24:       {
25:           cout << "I can fly! I can fly! I can fly! ";
26:       }
27:     private:
28:       int itsWeight;
29:   };
30:
31:   class Pegasus : public Horse, public Bird
32:   {
33:     public:
34:       void Chirp() const { Whinny(); }
35:       Pegasus() { cout << "Pegasus constructor... "; }
36:       ~Pegasus() { cout << "Pegasus destructor...  "; }
37:   };
38:
39:   const int MagicNumber = 2;
40:   int main()
41:   {
42:       Horse* Ranch[MagicNumber];
43:       Bird* Aviary[MagicNumber];
44:       Horse * pHorse;
45:       Bird * pBird;
46:       int choice,i;
47:       for (i=0; i<MagicNumber; i++)
48:       {
49:           cout << "\n(1)Horse (2)Pegasus: ";
50:           cin >> choice;
51:           if (choice == 2)
52:               pHorse = new Pegasus;
53:           else
54:               pHorse = new Horse;
55:           Ranch[i] = pHorse;
56:       }
57:       for (i=0; i<MagicNumber; i++)
58:       {
59:           cout << "\n(1)Bird (2)Pegasus: ";
60:           cin >> choice;
61:           if (choice == 2)
62:               pBird = new Pegasus;
63:           else
64:               pBird = new Bird;
```

LISTING 12.3 Continued

```
65:        Aviary[i] = pBird;
66:      }
67:
68:      cout << endl;
69:      for (i=0; i<MagicNumber; i++)
70:      {
71:          cout << "\nRanch[" << i << "]: " ;
72:          Ranch[i]->Whinny();
73:          delete Ranch[i];
74:      }
75:
76:      for (i=0; i<MagicNumber; i++)
77:      {
78:          cout << "\nAviary[" << i << "]: " ;
79:          Aviary[i]->Chirp();
80:          Aviary[i]->Fly();
81:          delete Aviary[i];
82:      }
83:      return 0;
84:  }
```

Output ▼

```
(1)Horse (2)Pegasus: 1
Horse constructor...
(1)Horse (2)Pegasus: 2
Horse constructor... Bird constructor... Pegasus constructor...
(1)Bird (2)Pegasus: 1
Bird constructor...
(1)Bird (2)Pegasus: 2
Horse constructor... Bird constructor... Pegasus constructor...

Ranch[0]: Whinny!... Horse destructor...
Ranch[1]: Whinny!... Pegasus destructor...  Bird destructor...
Horse destructor...
Aviary[0]: Chirp... I can fly! I can fly! I can fly! Bird destructor...
Aviary[1]: Whinny!... I can fly! I can fly! I can fly!
Pegasus destructor... Bird destructor... Horse destructor...
```

Analysis ▼

On lines 7–15, a Horse class is declared. The constructor and destructor print out a message, and the Whinny() method prints **Whinny!...**.

On lines 17–29, a Bird class is declared. In addition to its constructor and destructor, this class has two methods: Chirp() and Fly(), both of which print identifying messages. In a real program, these might, for example, activate the speaker or generate animated images.

Finally, on lines 31–37, you see the new code—using multiple inheritance, the class Pegasus is declared. In line 31, you can see that this class is derived from both Horse and Bird. The Pegasus class overrides the Chirp() method in line 34. The Pegasus' Chirp() method simply does a call to the Whinny() method, which it inherits from Horse.

In the main section of this program, two lists are created: a Ranch with pointers to Horse objects on line 42, and an Aviary with pointers to Bird objects on line 43. On lines 47–56, Horse and Pegasus objects are added to the Ranch. On lines 57–66, Bird and Pegasus objects are added to the Aviary.

Invocations of the virtual methods on both the Bird pointers and the Horse pointers do the right things for Pegasus objects. For example, on line 79, the members of the Aviary array are used to call Chirp() on the objects to which they point. The Bird class declares this to be a virtual method, so the right function is called for each object.

Note that each time a Pegasus object is created, the output reflects that both the Bird part and the Horse part of the Pegasus object are also created. When a Pegasus object is destroyed, the Bird and Horse parts are destroyed as well, thanks to the destructors being made virtual.

Declaring Multiple Inheritance

Declare an object to inherit from more than one class by listing the base classes following the colon after the class name. Separate the base classes by commas.

Example 1

```
class Pegasus : public Horse, public Bird
```

Example 2

```
class Schnoodle : public Schnauzer, public Poodle
```

The Parts of a Multiply Inherited Object

When the Pegasus object is created in memory, both base classes form part of the Pegasus object, as illustrated in Figure 12.1. This figure represents an entire Pegasus object. This includes the new features added in the Pegasus class and the features picked up from the base classes.

FIGURE 12.1
Multiply inherited
objects.

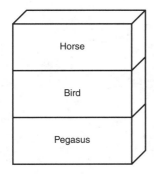

Several issues arise with objects with multiple base classes. For example, what happens if two base classes that happen to have the same name have virtual functions or data? How are multiple base class constructors initialized? What happens if multiple base classes both derive from the same class? The next sections answer these questions and explore how multiple inheritance can be put to work.

Constructors in Multiply Inherited Objects

If Pegasus derives from both Horse and Bird, and each of the base classes has constructors that take parameters, the Pegasus class initializes these constructors in turn. Listing 12.4 illustrates how this is done.

LISTING 12.4 Using Overloaded Base Class Constructors

```
0:  // Listing 12.4
1:  // Calling multiple constructors
2:
3:  #include <iostream>
4:  using namespace std;
5:
6:  typedef int HANDS;
7:  enum COLOR { Red, Green, Blue, Yellow, White, Black, Brown } ;
8:
9:  class Horse
10: {
11:    public:
12:      Horse(COLOR color, HANDS height);
13:      virtual ~Horse() { cout << "Horse destructor...\n"; }
14:      virtual void Whinny()const { cout << "Whinny!... "; }
15:      virtual HANDS GetHeight() const { return itsHeight; }
16:      virtual COLOR GetColor() const { return itsColor; }
17:    private:
18:      HANDS itsHeight;
```

12

LISTING 12.4   Continued

```
19:       COLOR itsColor;
20:    };
21:
22:    Horse::Horse(COLOR color, HANDS height):
23:    itsColor(color),itsHeight(height)
24:    {
25:        cout << "Horse constructor...\n";
26:    }
27:
28:    class Bird
29:    {
30:      public:
31:        Bird(COLOR color, bool migrates);
32:        virtual ~Bird() {cout << "Bird destructor...\n";  }
33:        virtual void Chirp()const { cout << "Chirp... ";  }
34:        virtual void Fly()const
35:        {
36:          cout << "I can fly! I can fly! I can fly! ";
37:        }
38:        virtual COLOR GetColor()const { return itsColor; }
39:        virtual bool GetMigration() const { return itsMigration; }
40:
41:      private:
42:        COLOR itsColor;
43:        bool itsMigration;
44:    };
45:
46:    Bird::Bird(COLOR color, bool migrates):
47:    itsColor(color), itsMigration(migrates)
48:    {
49:        cout << "Bird constructor...\n";
50:    }
51:
52:    class Pegasus : public Horse, public Bird
53:    {
54:      public:
55:        void Chirp()const { Whinny(); }
56:        Pegasus(COLOR, HANDS, bool,long);
57:        ~Pegasus() {cout << "Pegasus destructor...\n";}
58:        virtual long GetNumberBelievers() const
59:        {
60:          return  itsNumberBelievers;
61:        }
62:
63:      private:
64:        long itsNumberBelievers;
65:    };
66:
67:    Pegasus::Pegasus(
68:       COLOR aColor,
```

LISTING 12.4 Continued

```
69:     HANDS height,
70:     bool migrates,
71:     long NumBelieve):
72:     Horse(aColor, height),
73:     Bird(aColor, migrates),
74:     itsNumberBelievers(NumBelieve)
75: {
76:     cout << "Pegasus constructor...\n";
77: }
78:
79: int main()
80: {
81:     Pegasus *pPeg = new Pegasus(Red, 5, true, 10);
82:     pPeg->Fly();
83:     pPeg->Whinny();
84:     cout << "\nYour Pegasus is " << pPeg->GetHeight();
85:     cout << " hands tall and ";
86:     if (pPeg->GetMigration())
87:         cout << "it does migrate.";
88:     else
89:         cout << "it does not migrate.";
90:     cout << "\nA total of " << pPeg->GetNumberBelievers();
91:     cout << " people believe it exists." << endl;
92:     delete pPeg;
93:     return 0;
94: }
```

Output ▼

```
Horse constructor...
Bird constructor...
Pegasus constructor...
I can fly! I can fly! I can fly! Whinny!...
Your Pegasus is 5 hands tall and it does migrate.
A total of 10 people believe it exists.
Pegasus destructor...
Bird destructor...
Horse destructor...
```

Analysis ▼

On lines 9–20, the Horse class is declared. The constructor takes two parameters: One is an enumeration for colors, which is declared on line 7, and the other is a typedef declared on line 6. The implementation of the constructor on lines 22–26 simply initializes the member variables and prints a message.

On lines 28–44, the `Bird` class is declared, and the implementation of its constructor is on lines 46–50. Again, the `Bird` class takes two parameters. Interestingly, the `Horse` constructor takes color (so that you can detect horses of different colors), and the `Bird` constructor takes the color of the feathers (so that those of one feather can stick together). This leads to a problem when you want to ask the `Pegasus` for its color (which you'll see in Listing 12.5).

The `Pegasus` class itself is declared on lines 52–65, and its constructor is on lines 67–77. The initialization of the `Pegasus` object includes three statements. First, the `Horse` constructor is initialized with color and height (line 72). The `Bird` constructor is then initialized with color and the Boolean indicating whether it migrates (line 73). Finally, the `Pegasus` member variable `itsNumberBelievers` is initialized. After all that is accomplished, the body of the `Pegasus` constructor is called.

In the `main()` function, a `Pegasus` pointer is created in line 81. This object is then used to access the member functions that were derived from the base classes. The access of these methods is straightforward.

Ambiguity Resolution

In Listing 12.4, both the `Horse` class and the `Bird` class have the method `GetColor()`. You'll notice that these methods were not called in Listing 12.4! You might need to ask the `Pegasus` object to return its color, but you have a problem—the `Pegasus` class inherits from both `Bird` and `Horse`. Both have a color, and their methods for getting that color have the same name and signature. This creates an ambiguity for the compiler, which you must resolve.

If you simply write

```
COLOR currentColor = pPeg->GetColor();
```

you receive a compiler error:

```
Member is ambiguous: 'Horse::GetColor' and 'Bird::GetColor'
```

You can resolve the ambiguity with an explicit call to the function you want to invoke:

```
COLOR currentColor = pPeg->Horse::GetColor();
```

Anytime you need to resolve which class a member function or member data inherits from, you can fully qualify the call by prepending the class name to the base class data or function.

Note that if `Pegasus` were to override this function, the problem would be moved, as it should be, into the `Pegasus` member function:

```
virtual COLOR GetColor()const { return Horse::GetColor(); }
```

This hides the problem from clients of the Pegasus class and encapsulates within Pegasus the knowledge of which base class from which it wants to inherit its color. A client is still free to force the issue by writing

```
COLOR currentColor = pPeg->Bird::GetColor();
```

Inheriting from Shared Base Class

What happens if both Bird and Horse inherit from a common base class, such as Animal? Figure 12.2 illustrates what this looks like.

FIGURE 12.2
Common base classes.

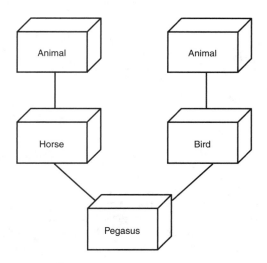

As you can see in Figure 12.2, two base class objects exist. When a function or data member is called in the shared base class, another ambiguity exists. For example, if Animal declares itsAge as a member variable and GetAge() as a member function, and you call pPeg->GetAge(), did you mean to call the GetAge() function you inherit from Animal by way of Horse, or by way of Bird? You must resolve this ambiguity as well, as illustrated in Listing 12.5.

LISTING 12.5 Resolving Ambiguity in Case of Multiple Inheritance Involving Common Base Classes

```
0:   // Listing 12.5
1:   // Common base classes
2:
3:   #include <iostream>
4:   using namespace std;
5:
6:   typedef int HANDS;
```

12

LISTING 12.5 Continued

```
 7:  enum COLOR { Red, Green, Blue, Yellow, White, Black, Brown } ;
 8:
 9:  class Animal          // common base to both horse and bird
10:  {
11:    public:
12:      Animal(int);
13:      virtual ~Animal() { cout << "Animal destructor...\n"; }
14:      virtual int GetAge() const { return itsAge; }
15:      virtual void SetAge(int age) { itsAge = age; }
16:    private:
17:      int itsAge;
18:  };
19:
20:  Animal::Animal(int age):
21:  itsAge(age)
22:  {
23:     cout << "Animal constructor...\n";
24:  }
25:
26:  class Horse : public Animal
27:  {
28:    public:
29:      Horse(COLOR color, HANDS height, int age);
30:      virtual ~Horse() { cout << "Horse destructor...\n"; }
31:      virtual void Whinny()const { cout << "Whinny!... "; }
32:      virtual HANDS GetHeight() const { return itsHeight; }
33:      virtual COLOR GetColor() const { return itsColor; }
34:    protected:
35:      HANDS itsHeight;
36:      COLOR itsColor;
37:  };
38:
39:  Horse::Horse(COLOR color, HANDS height, int age):
40:  Animal(age),
41:  itsColor(color),itsHeight(height)
42:  {
43:     cout << "Horse constructor...\n";
44:  }
45:
46:  class Bird : public Animal
47:  {
48:    public:
49:      Bird(COLOR color, bool migrates, int age);
50:      virtual ~Bird() {cout << "Bird destructor...\n";  }
51:      virtual void Chirp()const { cout << "Chirp... ";  }
52:      virtual void Fly()const
53:              { cout << "I can fly! I can fly! I can fly! "; }
54:      virtual COLOR GetColor()const { return itsColor; }
55:      virtual bool GetMigration() const { return itsMigration; }
```

LISTING 12.5 Continued

```
56:    protected:
57:       COLOR itsColor;
58:       bool itsMigration;
59:    };
60:
61:    Bird::Bird(COLOR color, bool migrates, int age):
62:    Animal(age),
63:    itsColor(color), itsMigration(migrates)
64:    {
65:       cout << "Bird constructor...\n";
66:    }
67:
68:    class Pegasus : public Horse, public Bird
69:    {
70:      public:
71:         void Chirp()const { Whinny(); }
72:         Pegasus(COLOR, HANDS, bool, long, int);
73:         virtual ~Pegasus() {cout << "Pegasus destructor...\n";}
74:         virtual long GetNumberBelievers() const
75:         { return  itsNumberBelievers; }
76:         virtual COLOR GetColor()const { return Horse::itsColor; }
77:         virtual int GetAge() const { return Horse::GetAge(); }
78:      private:
79:         long itsNumberBelievers;
80:    };
81:
82:    Pegasus::Pegasus(
83:       COLOR aColor,
84:       HANDS height,
85:       bool migrates,
86:       long NumBelieve,
87:       int age):
88:       Horse(aColor, height,age),
89:       Bird(aColor, migrates,age),
90:       itsNumberBelievers(NumBelieve)
91:    {
92:       cout << "Pegasus constructor...\n";
93:    }
94:
95:    int main()
96:    {
97:       Pegasus *pPeg = new Pegasus(Red, 5, true, 10, 2);
98:       int age = pPeg->GetAge();
99:       cout << "This pegasus is " << age << " years old.\n";
100:      delete pPeg;
101:      return 0;
102:   }
```

12

Output ▼

```
Animal constructor...
Horse constructor...
Animal constructor...
Bird constructor...
Pegasus constructor...
This pegasus is 2 years old.
Pegasus destructor...
Bird destructor...
Animal destructor...
Horse destructor...
Animal destructor...
```

Analysis ▼

Several interesting features are in this listing. The Animal class is declared on lines 9–18. Animal adds one member variable, itsAge, and two accessors: GetAge() and SetAge().

On line 26, the Horse class is declared to derive from Animal. The Horse constructor now has a third parameter, age, which it passes to its base class, Animal (see line 40). Note that the Horse class does not override GetAge(), it simply inherits it.

On line 46, the Bird class is declared to derive from Animal. Its constructor also takes an age and uses it to initialize its base class, Animal (see line 62). It also inherits GetAge() without overriding it.

Pegasus inherits from both Bird and Horse in line 68, and so has two Animal classes in its inheritance chain. If you were to call GetAge() on a Pegasus object, you would have to disambiguate or fully qualify the method you want if Pegasus did not override the method. This is solved on line 77 when the Pegasus object overrides GetAge() to do nothing more than to chain up—that is, to call the same method in a base class.

Chaining up is done for one of two reasons: either to disambiguate which base class to call, as in this case, or to do some work and then let the function in the base class do some more work. At times, you might want to do work and then chain up, or chain up and then do the work when the base class function returns.

The Pegasus constructor, which starts on line 82, takes five parameters: the creature's color, its height (in HANDS), whether it migrates, how many believe in it, and its age. The constructor initializes the Horse part of the Pegasus with the color, height, and age on line 88. It initializes the Bird part with color, whether it migrates, and age on line 89. Finally, it initializes itsNumberBelievers on line 90.

The call to the Horse constructor on line 88 invokes the implementation shown on line 39. The Horse constructor uses the age parameter to initialize the Animal part of the

Horse part of the Pegasus. It then goes on to initialize the two member variables of Horse: itsColor and itsHeight.

The call to the Bird constructor on line 89 invokes the implementation shown on line 61. Here, too, the age parameter is used to initialize the Animal part of the Bird.

Note that the color parameter to the Pegasus is used to initialize member variables in each of Bird and Horse. Note also that the age is used to initialize itsAge in the Horse's base Animal and in the Bird's base Animal.

CAUTION   Keep in mind that whenever you explicitly disambiguate an ancestor class, you create a risk that a new class inserted between your class and its ancestor will cause this class to inadvertently call "past" the new ancestor into the old ancestor, which can have unexpected effects.

Virtual Inheritance

In Listing 12.5, the Pegasus class went to some lengths to disambiguate which of its Animal base classes it meant to invoke. Most of the time, the decision as to which one to use is arbitrary—after all, the Horse and the Bird have the same base class.

It is possible to tell C++ that you do not want two copies of the shared base class, as shown in Figure 12.2, but rather to have a single shared base class, as shown in Figure 12.3.

FIGURE 12.3
A diamond inheritance.

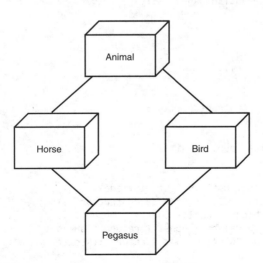

12

You accomplish this by making `Animal` a virtual base class of both `Horse` and `Bird`. The `Animal` class does not change at all. The `Horse` and `Bird` classes change only in their use of the term `virtual` in their declarations. `Pegasus`, however, changes substantially.

Normally, a class's constructor initializes only its own variables and its base class. Virtually inherited base classes are an exception, however. They are initialized by their most derived class. Thus, `Animal` is initialized not by `Horse` and `Bird`, but by `Pegasus`. `Horse` and `Bird` have to initialize `Animal` in their constructors, but these initializations will be ignored when a `Pegasus` object is created. Listing 12.6 rewrites Listing 12.5 to take advantage of virtual derivation.

LISTING 12.6   Illustration of the Use of Virtual Inheritance

```
0:  // Listing 12.6
1:  // Virtual inheritance
2:  #include <iostream>
3:  using namespace std;
4:
5:  typedef int HANDS;
6:  enum COLOR { Red, Green, Blue, Yellow, White, Black, Brown } ;
7:
8:  class Animal          // common base to both horse and bird
9:  {
10:    public:
11:      Animal(int);
12:      virtual ~Animal() { cout << "Animal destructor...\n"; }
13:      virtual int GetAge() const { return itsAge; }
14:      virtual void SetAge(int age) { itsAge = age; }
15:    private:
16:      int itsAge;
17:  };
18:
19:  Animal::Animal(int age):
20:  itsAge(age)
21:  {
22:     cout << "Animal constructor...\n";
23:  }
24:
25:  class Horse : virtual public Animal
26:  {
27:    public:
28:      Horse(COLOR color, HANDS height, int age);
29:      virtual ~Horse() { cout << "Horse destructor...\n"; }
30:      virtual void Whinny()const { cout << "Whinny!... "; }
31:      virtual HANDS GetHeight() const { return itsHeight; }
32:      virtual COLOR GetColor() const { return itsColor; }
33:    protected:
34:      HANDS itsHeight;
```

LISTING 12.6 Continued

```
35:      COLOR itsColor;
36:  };
37:
38:  Horse::Horse(COLOR color, HANDS height, int age):
39:  Animal(age),
40:  itsColor(color),itsHeight(height)
41:  {
42:      cout << "Horse constructor...\n";
43:  }
44:
45:  class Bird : virtual public Animal
46:  {
47:    public:
48:      Bird(COLOR color, bool migrates, int age);
49:      virtual ~Bird() {cout << "Bird destructor...\n";  }
50:      virtual void Chirp()const { cout << "Chirp... ";  }
51:      virtual void Fly()const
52:              { cout << "I can fly! I can fly! I can fly! "; }
53:      virtual COLOR GetColor()const { return itsColor; }
54:      virtual bool GetMigration() const { return itsMigration; }
55:    protected:
56:      COLOR itsColor;
57:      bool itsMigration;
58:  };
59:
60:  Bird::Bird(COLOR color, bool migrates, int age):
61:  Animal(age),
62:  itsColor(color), itsMigration(migrates)
63:  {
64:      cout << "Bird constructor...\n";
65:  }
66:
67:  class Pegasus : public Horse, public Bird
68:  {
69:    public:
70:      void Chirp()const { Whinny(); }
71:      Pegasus(COLOR, HANDS, bool, long, int);
72:      virtual ~Pegasus() {cout << "Pegasus destructor...\n";}
73:      virtual long GetNumberBelievers() const
74:            { return  itsNumberBelievers; }
75:      virtual COLOR GetColor()const { return Horse::itsColor; }
76:    private:
77:      long itsNumberBelievers;
78:  };
79:
80:  Pegasus::Pegasus(
81:      COLOR aColor,
82:      HANDS height,
83:      bool migrates,
```

LISTING 12.6   Continued

```
84:      long NumBelieve,
85:      int age):
86:      Horse(aColor, height,age),
87:      Bird(aColor, migrates,age),
88:      Animal(age*2),
89:      itsNumberBelievers(NumBelieve)
90:  {
91:      cout << "Pegasus constructor...\n";
92:  }
93:
94:  int main()
95:  {
96:      Pegasus *pPeg = new Pegasus(Red, 5, true, 10, 2);
97:      int age = pPeg->GetAge();
98:      cout << "This pegasus is " << age << " years old.\n";
99:      delete pPeg;
100:     return 0;
101: }
```

Output ▼

```
Animal constructor...
Horse constructor...
Bird constructor...
Pegasus constructor...
This pegasus is 4 years old.
Pegasus destructor...
Bird destructor...
Horse destructor...
Animal destructor...
```

Analysis ▼

On line 25, Horse declares that it inherits virtually from Animal, and on line 45, Bird makes the same declaration. Note that the constructors for both Bird and Animal still initialize the Animal object.

Pegasus inherits from both Bird and Animal, and as the most derived object of Animal, it also initializes Animal. It is Pegasus's initialization which is called, however, and the calls to Animal's constructor in Bird and Horse are ignored. You can see this because the value 2 is passed in, and Horse and Bird pass it along to Animal, but Pegasus doubles it. The result, 4, is reflected in the output generated from line 98.

Pegasus no longer has to disambiguate the call to GetAge(), and so is free to simply inherit this function from Animal. Note that Pegasus must still disambiguate the call to GetColor() because this function is in both of its base classes and not in Animal.

> **Declaring Classes for Virtual Inheritance**
>
> To ensure that derived classes have only one instance of common base classes, declare the intermediate classes to inherit virtually from the base class.
>
> **Example 1**
>
> ```
> class Horse : virtual public Animal
> class Bird : virtual public Animal
> class Pegasus : public Horse, public Bird
> ```
>
> **Example 2**
>
> ```
> class Schnauzer : virtual public Dog
> class Poodle : virtual public Dog
> class Schnoodle : public Schnauzer, public Poodle
> ```

Problems with Multiple Inheritance

Although multiple inheritance offers several advantages over single inheritance, many C++ programmers are reluctant to use it. The problems they cite are that it makes debugging harder, that evolving multiple inheritance class hierarchies is harder and more risky than evolving single inheritance class hierarchies, and that nearly everything that can be done with multiple inheritance can be done without it. Other languages, such as Java and C#, don't support multiple inheritance of classes for some of these same reasons.

These are valid concerns, and you will want to be on your guard against installing needless complexity into your programs. Some debuggers have a hard time with multiple inheritance, and some designs are needlessly made complex by using multiple inheritance when it is not needed.

12

DO	DON'T
DO use multiple inheritance when a new class needs functions and features from more than one base class.	**DON'T** use multiple inheritance when single inheritance will do.
DO use virtual inheritance when more than one derived classes have only one instance of the shared base class.	
DO initialize the shared base class from the most derived class when using virtual base classes.	

Mixins and Capabilities Classes

One way to strike a middle ground between multiple inheritance and single inheritance is to use what are called *mixins*. Thus, you might have your Horse class derive from Animal and from Displayable. Displayable would just add a few methods for displaying any object onscreen.

A *mixin*, or capability class, is a class that adds specialized functionality without adding many additional methods or much data.

Capability classes are mixed into a derived class the same as any other class might be, by declaring the derived class to inherit publicly from them. The only difference between a capability class and any other class is that the capability class has little or no data. This is an arbitrary distinction, of course, and is just a shorthand way of noting that at times all you want to do is mix in some additional capabilities without complicating the derived class.

This will, for some debuggers, make it easier to work with mixins than with more complex multiply inherited objects. In addition, less likelihood exists of ambiguity in accessing the data in the other principal base class.

For example, if Horse derives from Animal and from Displayable, Displayable would have no data. Animal would be just as it always was, so all the data in Horse would derive from Animal, but the functions in Horse would derive from both.

NOTE	The term *mixin* comes from an ice cream store in Sommerville, Massachusetts, where candies and cakes were mixed into the basic ice cream flavors. This seemed like a good metaphor to some of the object-oriented programmers who used to take a summer break there, especially while working with the object-oriented programming language SCOOPS.

Abstract Data Types

Often, you will create a hierarchy of classes together. For example, you might create a Shape class and from it derive Rectangle and Circle. From Rectangle, you might derive Square as a special case of Rectangle.

Each of the derived classes will override the Draw() method, the GetArea() method, and so forth. Listing 12.7 illustrates a bare-bones implementation of the Shape class and its derived Circle and Rectangle classes.

LISTING 12.7   Shape Classes

```
0:   //Listing 12.7. Shape classes.
1:
2:   #include <iostream>
3:   using std::cout;
4:   using std::cin;
5:   using std::endl;
6:
7:   class Shape
8:   {
9:     public:
10:      Shape(){}
11:      virtual ~Shape(){}
12:      virtual double GetArea() { return -1; } // error value returned
13:      virtual double GetPerim() { return -1; }
14:      virtual void Draw() {}
15:    private:
16:   };
17:
18:   class Circle : public Shape
19:   {
20:     public:
21:      Circle(int radius):itsRadius(radius){}
22:      ~Circle(){}
23:      double GetArea() { return 3 * itsRadius * itsRadius; }
24:      double GetPerim() { return 6 * itsRadius; }
25:      void Draw();
26:    private:
27:      int itsRadius;
28:      int itsCircumference;
29:   };
30:
31:   void Circle::Draw()
32:   {
33:      cout << "Circle drawing routine here!\n";
34:   }
35:
36:
37:   class Rectangle : public Shape
38:   {
39:     public:
40:      Rectangle(int len, int width):
41:      itsLength(len), itsWidth(width){}
42:      virtual ~Rectangle(){}
43:      virtual double GetArea() { return itsLength * itsWidth; }
44:      virtual double GetPerim() {return 2*itsLength + 2*itsWidth; }
45:      virtual int GetLength() { return itsLength; }
46:      virtual int GetWidth() { return itsWidth; }
47:      virtual void Draw();
48:    private:
```

12

LISTING 12.7   Continued

```
49:      int itsWidth;
50:      int itsLength;
51:  };
52:
53:  void Rectangle::Draw()
54:  {
55:     for (int i = 0; i<itsLength; i++)
56:     {
57:        for (int j = 0; j<itsWidth; j++)
58:           cout << "x ";
59:
60:     cout << "\n";
61:     }
62:  }
63:
64:  class Square : public Rectangle
65:  {
66:    public:
67:      Square(int len);
68:      Square(int len, int width);
69:      ~Square(){}
70:      double GetPerim() {return 4 * GetLength();}
71:  };
72:
73:  Square::Square(int len):
74:  Rectangle(len,len)
75:  {}
76:
77:  Square::Square(int len, int width):
78:  Rectangle(len,width)
79:  {
80:     if (GetLength() != GetWidth())
81:     cout << "Error, not a square... a Rectangle??\n";
82:  }
83:
84:  int main()
85:  {
86:     int choice;
87:     bool fQuit = false;
88:     Shape * sp;
89:
90:     while ( !fQuit )
91:     {
92:        cout << "(1)Circle (2)Rectangle (3)Square (0)Quit: ";
93:        cin >> choice;
94:
95:        switch (choice)
96:        {
97:          case 0:   fQuit = true;
98:             break;
```

LISTING 12.7 Continued

```
99:          case 1: sp = new Circle(5);
100:             break;
101:          case 2: sp = new Rectangle(4,6);
102:             break;
103:          case 3: sp = new Square(5);
104:             break;
105:          default:
106:             cout <<"Please enter a number between 0 and 3"<<endl;
107:             continue;
108:             break;
109:          }
110:          if( !fQuit )
111:             sp->Draw();
112:          delete sp;
113:          sp = 0;
114:          cout << endl;
115:       }
116:    return 0;
117: }
```

Output ▼

```
(1)Circle (2)Rectangle (3)Square (0)Quit: 2
x x x x x x
x x x x x x
x x x x x x
x x x x x x

(1)Circle (2)Rectangle (3)Square (0)Quit:3
x x x x x
x x x x x
x x x x x
x x x x x
x x x x x

(1)Circle (2)Rectangle (3)Square (0)Quit:0
```

Analysis ▼

On lines 7–16, the Shape class is declared. The GetArea() and GetPerim() methods
return an error value, and Draw() takes no action. After all, what does it mean to draw a
Shape? Only types of shapes (circles, rectangles, and so on) can be drawn; Shapes as an
abstraction cannot be drawn.

Circle derives from Shape in lines 18–29 and overrides the three virtual methods. Note
that no reason exists to add the word virtual because that is part of their inheritance.

12

But there is no harm in doing so either, as shown in the Rectangle class on lines 43, 44, and 47. It is a good idea to include the term virtual as a reminder, a form of documentation.

Square derives from Rectangle in lines 64–71, and it, too, overrides the GetPerim() method, inheriting the rest of the methods defined in Rectangle. It is troubling, though, that a client might try to instantiate a Shape, and it might be desirable to make that impossible. After all, the Shape class exists only to provide an interface for the classes derived from it; as such, it is an abstract data type, or ADT.

In an *abstract* class, the interface represents a concept (such as shape) rather than a specific object (such as circle). In C++, an abstract class is always the base class to other classes, and it is not valid to make an instance of an abstract class.

Pure Virtual Functions

C++ supports the creation of abstract classes by providing the pure virtual function. A virtual function is made pure by initializing it with zero, as in

```
virtual void Draw() = 0;
```

In this example, the class has a Draw() function, but it has a null implementation and cannot be called. It can, however, be overwritten within descendant classes.

Any class with one or more pure virtual functions is an abstract class, and it becomes illegal to instantiate. In fact, it is illegal to instantiate an object of any class that is an abstract class or any class that inherits from an abstract class and doesn't implement all of the pure virtual functions. Trying to do so causes a compile-time error. Putting a pure virtual function in your class signals two things to clients of your class:

- Don't make an object of this class; derive from it.
- Be certain to override the pure virtual functions your class inherits.

Any class that derives from an abstract class inherits the pure virtual function as pure, and so must override every pure virtual function if it wants to instantiate objects. Thus, if Rectangle inherits from Shape, and Shape has three pure virtual functions, Rectangle must override all three or it, too, will be an abstract class. Listing 12.8 rewrites the Shape class to be an abstract data type. To save space, the rest of Listing 12.7 is not reproduced here. Replace the declaration of Shape in Listing 12.7, lines 7–16, with the declaration of Shape in Listing 12.8 and run the program again.

LISTING 12.8   Shape As an Abstract Base Class

```
0:   //Listing 12.8 Abstract Classes
1:
2:   class Shape
3:   {
4:     public:
5:         Shape(){}
6:         ~Shape(){}
7:         virtual double GetArea() = 0;
8:         virtual double GetPerim()= 0;
9:         virtual void Draw() = 0;
10:  };
```

Output ▼

```
(1)Circle (2)Rectangle (3)Square (0)Quit: 2
x x x x x x
x x x x x x
x x x x x x
x x x x x x

(1)Circle (2)Rectangle (3)Square (0)Quit: 3
x x x x x
x x x x x
x x x x x
x x x x x
x x x x x

(1)Circle (2)Rectangle (3)Square (0)Quit: 0
```

12

Analysis ▼

As you can see, the workings of the program are totally unaffected. The only difference is that it would now be impossible to make an object of class Shape.

Abstract Data Types

Declare a class to be an abstract class (also called an *abstract data type*) by including one or more pure virtual functions in the class declaration. Declare a pure virtual function by writing = 0 after the function declaration.

Example

```
class Shape
{
    virtual void Draw() = 0;    // pure virtual
};
```

Implementing Pure Virtual Functions

Typically, the pure virtual functions in an abstract base class are never implemented. Because no objects of that type are ever created, no reason exists to provide implementations, and the abstract class works purely as the definition of an interface to objects that derive from it.

It is possible, however, to provide an implementation to a pure virtual function. The function can then be called by objects derived from the abstract class, perhaps to provide common functionality to all the overridden functions. Listing 12.9 reproduces Listing 12.7, this time with Shape as an abstract class and with an implementation for the pure virtual function Draw(). The Circle class overrides Draw(), as it must, but it then chains up to the base class function for additional functionality.

In this example, the additional functionality is simply an additional message printed, but you can imagine that the base class provides a shared drawing mechanism, perhaps setting up a window that all derived classes will use.

LISTING 12.9   Implementing Pure Virtual Functions

```
0:  //Listing 12.9 Implementing pure virtual functions
1:
2:  #include <iostream>
3:  using namespace std;
4:
5:  class Shape
6:  {
7:    public:
8:      Shape(){}
9:      virtual ~Shape(){}
10:      virtual double GetArea() = 0;
11:      virtual double GetPerim()= 0;
12:      virtual void Draw() = 0;
13:    private:
14:  };
15:
16:  void Shape::Draw()
17:  {
18:      cout << "Abstract drawing mechanism!\n";
19:  }
20:
21:  class Circle : public Shape
22:  {
23:    public:
24:      Circle(int radius):itsRadius(radius){}
25:      virtual ~Circle(){}
26:      double GetArea() { return 3.14 * itsRadius * itsRadius; }
```

LISTING 12.9   Continued

```
27:        double GetPerim() { return 2 * 3.14 * itsRadius; }
28:        void Draw();
29:     private:
30:        int itsRadius;
31:        int itsCircumference;
32:    };
33:
34:    void Circle::Draw()
35:    {
36:       cout << "Circle drawing routine here!\n";
37:       Shape::Draw();
38:    }
39:
40:
41:    class Rectangle : public Shape
42:    {
43:     public:
44:        Rectangle(int len, int width):
45:        itsLength(len), itsWidth(width){}
46:        virtual ~Rectangle(){}
47:        double GetArea() { return itsLength * itsWidth; }
48:        double GetPerim() {return 2*itsLength + 2*itsWidth; }
49:        virtual int GetLength() { return itsLength; }
50:        virtual int GetWidth() { return itsWidth; }
51:        void Draw();
52:     private:
53:        int itsWidth;
54:        int itsLength;
55:    };
56:
57:    void Rectangle::Draw()
58:    {
59:       for (int i = 0; i<itsLength; i++)
60:       {
61:          for (int j = 0; j<itsWidth; j++)
62:             cout << "x ";
63:
64:       cout << "\n";
65:       }
66:       Shape::Draw();
67:    }
68:
69:
70:    class Square : public Rectangle
71:    {
72:     public:
73:        Square(int len);
74:        Square(int len, int width);
75:        virtual ~Square(){}
```

12

LISTING 12.9   Continued

```
76:       double GetPerim() {return 4 * GetLength();}
77: };
78:
79: Square::Square(int len):
80: Rectangle(len,len)
81: {}
82:
83: Square::Square(int len, int width):
84: Rectangle(len,width)
85:
86: {
87:    if (GetLength() != GetWidth())
88:    cout << "Error, not a square... a Rectangle??\n";
89: }
90:
91: int main()
92: {
93:    int choice;
94:    bool fQuit = false;
95:    Shape * sp;
96:
97:    while (fQuit == false)
98:    {
99:       cout << "(1)Circle (2)Rectangle (3)Square (0)Quit: ";
100:      cin >> choice;
101:
102:      switch (choice)
103:      {
104:       case 1: sp = new Circle(5);
105:             break;
106:       case 2: sp = new Rectangle(4,6);
107:             break;
108:       case 3: sp = new Square (5);
109:             break;
110:       default: fQuit = true;
111:             break;
112:      }
113:      if (fQuit == false)
114:      {
115:         sp->Draw();
116:         delete sp;
117:         cout << endl;
118:      }
119:    }
120:    return 0;
121: }
```

Output ▼

```
(1)Circle (2)Rectangle (3)Square (0)Quit: 2
x x x x x x
x x x x x x
x x x x x x
x x x x x x
Abstract drawing mechanism!

(1)Circle (2)Rectangle (3)Square (0)Quit: 3
x x x x x
x x x x x
x x x x x
x x x x x
x x x x x
Abstract drawing mechanism!

(1)Circle (2)Rectangle (3)Square (0)Quit: 0
```

Analysis ▼

On lines 5–14, the abstract class Shape is declared, with all three of its accessor methods declared to be pure virtual. Note that this is not necessary, but is still a good practice. If any one were declared pure virtual, the class would have been an abstract class.

The GetArea() and GetPerim() methods are not implemented, but Draw() is implemented in lines 16–19. Circle and Rectangle both override Draw(), and both chain up to the base method, taking advantage of shared functionality in the base class.

Complex Hierarchies of Abstraction

At times, you will derive abstract classes from other abstract classes. It might be that you will want to make some of the derived pure virtual functions nonpure, and leave others pure.

If you create the Animal class, you can make Eat(), Sleep(), Move(), and Reproduce() all pure virtual functions. Perhaps from Animal you derive Mammal and Fish.

On examination, you decide that every Mammal will reproduce in the same way, and so you make Mammal::Reproduce() nonpure, but you leave Eat(), Sleep(), and Move() as pure virtual functions.

From Mammal, you derive Dog, and Dog must override and implement the three remaining pure virtual functions so that you can make objects of type Dog. What you've said, as class designer, is that no Animals or Mammals can be instantiated, but that all Mammals can inherit the provided Reproduce() method without overriding it. Listing 12.10 illustrates this technique with a bare-bones implementation of these classes.

LISTING 12.10   Deriving Abstract Classes from Other Abstract Classes

```
0:   // Listing 12.10
1:   // Deriving Abstract Classes from other Abstract Classes
2:   #include <iostream>
3:   using namespace std;
4:
5:   enum COLOR { Red, Green, Blue, Yellow, White, Black, Brown } ;
6:
7:   class Animal       // common base to both Mammal and Fish
8:   {
9:     public:
10:       Animal(int);
11:       virtual ~Animal() { cout << "Animal destructor...\n"; }
12:       virtual int GetAge() const { return itsAge; }
13:       virtual void SetAge(int age) { itsAge = age; }
14:       virtual void Sleep() const = 0;
15:       virtual void Eat() const = 0;
16:       virtual void Reproduce() const = 0;
17:       virtual void Move() const = 0;
18:       virtual void Speak() const = 0;
19:     private:
20:       int itsAge;
21:   };
22:
23:   Animal::Animal(int age):
24:   itsAge(age)
25:   {
26:      cout << "Animal constructor...\n";
27:   }
28:
29:   class Mammal : public Animal
30:   {
31:     public:
32:       Mammal(int age):Animal(age)
33:         { cout << "Mammal constructor...\n";}
34:       virtual ~Mammal() { cout << "Mammal destructor...\n";}
35:       virtual void Reproduce() const
36:         { cout << "Mammal reproduction depicted...\n"; }
37:   };
38:
39:   class Fish : public Animal
40:   {
41:     public:
42:       Fish(int age):Animal(age)
43:         { cout << "Fish constructor...\n";}
44:       virtual ~Fish() {cout << "Fish destructor...\n";  }
45:       virtual void Sleep() const { cout << "fish snoring...\n"; }
46:       virtual void Eat() const { cout << "fish feeding...\n"; }
47:       virtual void Reproduce() const
48:         { cout << "fish laying eggs...\n"; }
```

LISTING 12.10 Continued

```
49:        virtual void Move() const
50:          { cout << "fish swimming...\n";    }
51:        virtual void Speak() const { }
52:    };
53:
54:    class Horse : public Mammal
55:    {
56:      public:
57:        Horse(int age, COLOR color ):
58:        Mammal(age), itsColor(color)
59:          { cout << "Horse constructor...\n"; }
60:        virtual ~Horse() { cout << "Horse destructor...\n"; }
61:        virtual void Speak()const { cout << "Whinny!... \n"; }
62:        virtual COLOR GetItsColor() const { return itsColor; }
63:        virtual void Sleep() const
64:          { cout << "Horse snoring...\n"; }
65:        virtual void Eat() const { cout << "Horse feeding...\n"; }
66:        virtual void Move() const { cout << "Horse running...\n";}
67:
68:      protected:
69:        COLOR itsColor;
70:    };
71:
72:    class Dog : public Mammal
73:    {
74:      public:
75:        Dog(int age, COLOR color ):
76:        Mammal(age), itsColor(color)
77:           { cout << "Dog constructor...\n"; }
78:        virtual ~Dog() { cout << "Dog destructor...\n"; }
79:        virtual void Speak()const { cout << "Whoof!... \n"; }
80:        virtual void Sleep() const { cout << "Dog snoring...\n"; }
81:        virtual void Eat() const { cout << "Dog eating...\n"; }
82:        virtual void Move() const { cout << "Dog running...\n"; }
83:        virtual void Reproduce() const
84:          { cout << "Dogs reproducing...\n"; }
85:
86:      protected:
87:        COLOR itsColor;
88:    };
89:
90:    int main()
91:    {
92:       Animal *pAnimal=0;
93:       int choice;
94:       bool fQuit = false;
95:
96:       while (fQuit == false)
97:       {
```

12

LISTING 12.10   Continued

```
98:        cout << "(1)Dog (2)Horse (3)Fish (0)Quit: ";
99:        cin >> choice;
100:
101:       switch (choice)
102:       {
103:         case 1: pAnimal = new Dog(5,Brown);
104:                 break;
105:         case 2: pAnimal = new Horse(4,Black);
106:                 break;
107:         case 3: pAnimal = new Fish (5);
108:                 break;
109:        default: fQuit = true;
110:                 break;
111:       }
112:       if (fQuit == false)
113:       {
114:          pAnimal->Speak();
115:          pAnimal->Eat();
116:          pAnimal->Reproduce();
117:          pAnimal->Move();
118:          pAnimal->Sleep();
119:          delete pAnimal;
120:          cout << endl;
121:       }
122:     }
123:     return 0;
124: }
```

Output ▼

```
(1)Dog (2)Horse (3)Bird (0)Quit: 1
Animal constructor...
Mammal constructor...
Dog constructor...
Whoof!...
Dog eating...
Dog reproducing....
Dog running...
Dog snoring...
Dog destructor...
Mammal destructor...
Animal destructor...

(1)Dog (2)Horse (3)Bird (0)Quit: 0
```

Analysis ▼

On lines 7–21, the abstract class `Animal` is declared. `Animal` has nonpure virtual accessors for `itsAge`, which are shared by all `Animal` objects. It has five pure virtual functions, `Sleep()`, `Eat()`, `Reproduce()`, `Move()`, and `Speak()`.

`Mammal` is derived from `Animal` on lines 29–37 and adds no data. It overrides `Reproduce()`, however, providing a common form of reproduction for all mammals. `Fish` must override `Reproduce()` because `Fish` derives directly from `Animal` and cannot take advantage of mammalian reproduction (and a good thing, too!). `Fish` does this in lines 47–48.

`Mammal` classes no longer have to override the `Reproduce()` function, but they are free to do so if they choose, as `Dog` does on line 83. `Fish`, `Horse`, and `Dog` override the remaining pure virtual functions so that objects of their type can be instantiated.

In the body of the main program, an `Animal` pointer is used to point to the various derived objects in turn. The virtual methods are invoked, and based on the runtime binding of the pointer, the correct method is called in the derived class. It would be a compile-time error to try to instantiate an `Animal` or a `Mammal` because both are abstract classes.

Which Classes Are Abstract?

In one program, the class `Animal` is abstract; in another, it is not. What determines whether to make a class abstract?

The answer to this question is decided not by any real-world intrinsic factor, but by what makes sense in your program. If you are writing a program that depicts a farm or a zoo, you might want `Animal` to be an abstract class, but `Dog` to be a class from which you can instantiate objects.

On the other hand, if you are making an animated kennel, you might want to keep `Dog` as an abstract class and instantiate only types of dogs: retrievers, terriers, and so forth. The level of abstraction is a function of how finely you need to distinguish your types.

12

DO	DON'T
DO use abstract classes to provide common description of capabilities provided in a number of related classes. **DO** make pure virtual any function that must be overridden.	**DON'T** try to instantiate an object of abstract classes.

Summary

In this lesson, you learned how to overcome some of the limitations in single inheritance. You learned about the danger of percolating functions up the inheritance hierarchy and the risks in casting down the inheritance hierarchy. You also learned how to use multiple inheritance, what problems multiple inheritance can create, and how to solve them using virtual inheritance.

You also learned what abstract classes are and how to create abstract classes using pure virtual functions. You learned how to implement pure virtual functions and when and why you might do so.

Q&A

Q **Why is making a decision on the runtime type of an object bad?**

A Because this is an indication that the inheritance hierarchy for the class has not been properly constructed, and it is better to go back and fix the design than to use this workaround.

Q **Why is casting bad?**

A Casting isn't bad if it is done in a way that is type safe. Casting can, however, be used to undermine the strong type checking in C++, and that is what you want to avoid. If you are switching on the runtime type of the object and then casting a pointer, that might be a warning sign that something is wrong with your design.

Q **Why not make all functions virtual?**

A Virtual functions are supported by a virtual function table, which incurs runtime overhead, both in the size of the program and in the performance of the program. If you have very small classes that you don't expect to subclass, you might not want to make any of the functions virtual. However, when this assumption changes, you need to be careful to go back and make the ancestor class functions virtual, or unexpected problems can result.

Q **When should the destructor be made virtual?**

A The destructor should be made virtual anytime you think the class will be subclassed and a pointer to the base class will be used to access an object of the subclass. As a general rule of thumb, if you've made any functions in your class virtual, be certain to make the destructor virtual as well.

Q What is an interface?

A An interface is a mechanism of enforcing methods and their signatures on classes that implement them. If IAnimal is an interface and CDog is a class that implements IAnimal, CDog has to implement methods that the IAnimal interface declares. Therefore, an interface works as a contract and classes that implement this interface guarantee compliance by adhering to that contract (otherwise they cannot implement only a part or none of an interface).

Q How do I implement an interface in C++?

A The C++ equivalent of an interface is an abstract base class that contains only pure virtual functions. Any class that inherits from this abstract base class needs to necessarily implement (pure) virtual functions declared by it and be compliant with their signature.

Workshop

The Workshop contains quiz questions to help you solidify your understanding of the material that was covered and exercises to provide you with experience in using what you've learned. Try to answer the quiz and exercise questions before checking the answers in Appendix D, and be certain you understand the answers before continuing to the next lesson.

Quiz

1. What is a down cast?
2. What does "percolating functionality upward" mean?
3. If a round rectangle has straight edges and rounded corners, and your RoundRect class inherits both from Rectangle and from Circle, and they in turn both inherit from Shape, how many Shapes are created when you create a RoundRect?
4. If Horse and Bird inherit from Animal using public virtual inheritance, do their constructors initialize the Animal constructor? If Pegasus inherits from both Horse and Bird, how does it initialize Animal's constructor?
5. Declare a class called Vehicle and make it an abstract class.
6. If a base class is an abstract class, and it has three pure virtual functions, how many of these must be overridden in its derived classes?

12

Exercises

1. Show the declaration for a class JetPlane, which inherits from Rocket and Airplane.

2. Show the declaration for Seven47, which inherits from the JetPlane class described in Exercise 1.

3. Write the code that derives Car and Bus from the class Vehicle. Make Vehicle be an abstract class with two pure virtual functions. Make Car and Bus not be abstract classes.

4. Modify the code in Exercise 3 so that Car is an abstract class, and derive SportsCar and Coupe from Car. In the Car class, provide an implementation for one of the pure virtual functions in Vehicle and make it nonpure.

LESSON 13
Operator Types and Operator Overloading

Although operators exist in C programming, they take on new meaning in C++ because they can be programmed to function on user-defined types such as classes, and they can also be overloaded.

In this lesson, you will learn

- Using the operator keyword
- Unary and binary operators
- Conversion operators
- Operators that cannot be redefined

What Are Operators in C++?

On a syntactical level, there is very little that differentiates an operator from a function, save for the usage of the keyword operator. An operator declaration looks quite like a function declaration:

```
return_type operator operator_symbol (...parameter list...);
```

The operator_symbol in this case could be any of the several operator-types that the programmer can define. It could be + (addition), or && (logical AND), and so on. The operands help the compiler distinguish one operator from another. So, why does C++ provide operators when functions are also supported?

Imagine that you are using a string class called CUsefulString. Now, you have two string objects to this class:

```
CUsefulString string1 ("Hello ");

CUsefulString string2 ("World!");
```

Now, if you wanted to concatenate the two, what would be more convenient if not also intuitive?

Option 1:

```
CUsefulString stringSum;
stringSum = string1 + string2;    // Hello World!
```

Or Option 2:

```
CUsefulString stringSum;
stringSum = string1.Concatenate (string2); // Hello World!
```

Clearly, the member operator + implemented by CUsefulString scores over the member function Concatenate. Both supply the same result, however, the operator-based mechanism uses of an intuitive and an easy to understand (hence, maintain) implementation.

So, the bottom line is clear: Don't use operators with the intention to simplify the implementation of the class that contains it. Use operators to make it easy and intuitive for others to use your class.

On a very broad level, operators in C++ can be classified into two types: unary operators and binary operators.

Unary Operators

As the name suggests, operators that function on a single operand are called *unary operators*. The typical definition of a unary operator implemented as a global function or a static member function is

```
return_type operator operator_type (parameter_type)
{
    // ... implementation
}
```

A unary operator that is the member of a class is defined as

```
return_type operator operator_type ()
{
    // ... implementation
}
```

Types of Unary Operators

The unary operators that can be overloaded (or redefined) are shown in Table 13.1.

TABLE 13.1 Unary Operators

Operator	Name
++	Increment
--	Decrement
*	Pointer dereference
->	Member selection
!	Logical NOT
&	Address-of
~	One's complement
+	Unary plus
–	Unary negation
Conversion operators	Conversion operators

Programming a Unary Increment/Decrement Operator

Let's start our exploration of unary operators by programming the unary increment and decrement operator. Consider a calendar class `CDate` that contains three integer members representing the day, month and year respectively. Wouldn't it be useful if one could

13

simply increment or decrement CDate values by using the very ++ and -- operators that work so well with integers? To make this possible, we need to supply this class with the unary increment and decrement operators, as seen in Listing 13.1.

LISTING 13.1 A Calendar Class That Handles Day, Month and Year, and Allows Increments in Days

```
 1: #include <iostream>
 2:
 3: class CDate
 4: {
 5: private:
 6:     int m_nDay;      // Range: 1 - 30 (lets assume all months have 30 days!
 7:     int m_nMonth;    // Range: 1 - 12
 8:     int m_nYear;
 9:
10:     void AddDays (int nDaysToAdd)
11:     {
12:         m_nDay += nDaysToAdd;
13:
14:         if (m_nDay > 30)
15:         {
16:             AddMonths (m_nDay / 30);
17:
18:             m_nDay %= 30;    // rollover 30th -> 1st
19:         }
20:     }
21:
22:     void AddMonths (int nMonthsToAdd)
23:     {
24:         m_nMonth += nMonthsToAdd;
25:
26:         if (m_nMonth > 12)
27:         {
28:             AddYears (m_nMonth / 12);
29:
30:             m_nMonth %= 12;    // rollover dec -> jan
31:         }
32:     }
33:
34:     void AddYears (int m_nYearsToAdd)
35:     {
36:         m_nYear += m_nYearsToAdd;
37:     }
38:
39: public:
40:
41:     // Constructor that initializes the object to a day, month and year
42:     CDate (int nDay, int nMonth, int nYear)
```

LISTING 13.1 Continued

```
43:            : m_nDay (nDay), m_nMonth (nMonth), m_nYear (nYear) {};
44:
45:     // Unary increment operator (prefix)
46:     CDate& operator ++ ()
47:     {
48:         AddDays (1);
49:         return *this;
50:     }
51:
52:     // postfix operator: differs from prefix in return-type and parameters
53:     CDate operator ++ (int)
54:     {
55:         // Create a copy of the current object, before incrementing day
56:         CDate mReturnDate (m_nDay, m_nMonth, m_nYear);
57:
58:         AddDays (1);
59:
60:         // Return the state before increment was performed
61:         return mReturnDate;
62:     }
63:
64:     void DisplayDate ()
65:     {
66:         std::cout << m_nDay << " / " << m_nMonth << " / " << m_nYear;
67:     }
68: };
69:
70: int main ()
71: {
72:     // Instantiate and initialize a date object to 25 May 2008
73:     CDate mDate (25, 6, 2008);
74:
75:     std::cout << "The date object is initialized to: ";
76:
77:     // Display initial date
78:     mDate.DisplayDate ();
79:     std::cout << std::endl;
80:
81:     // Applying the prefix increment operator
82:     ++ mDate;
83:
84:     std::cout << "Date after prefix-increment is: ";
85:
86:     // Display date after incrementing
87:     mDate.DisplayDate ();
88:     std::cout << std::endl;
89:
90:     return 0;
91: }
```

13

Output ▼

```
The date object is initialized to: 25 / 5 / 2008
Date after prefix-increment is: 26 / 5 / 2008
```

Analysis ▼

The code of interest lies in lines 45–50. This is the implementation of the unary prefix operator (++) that allows us to simply increment the date held in the object by a day using a syntax such as ++mDate, as shown in line 82 inside main().

Essentially, ++mDate is implemented by the compiler as a call to operator ++ that would look like this when explicitly invoked:

```
mDate.operator++ ();
```

Note that the implementation of the postfix increment operator as seen in lines 52–62 differs from the prefix by the presence of a redundant input parameter and the return of a copy of the object by value. Listing 13.2 displays the same, for further discussion.

LISTING 13.2 Postfix Increment Operator

```
 1: // postfix operator: differs from prefix in return-type and input param
 2: CDate operator ++ (int)
 3: {
 4:    // Store a copy of the current state, before incrementing day
 5:    CDate mReturnDate (m_nDay, m_nMonth, m_nYear);
 6:
 7:    IncrementDay ();
 8:
 9:    // Return the state before increment was performed
10:    return mReturnDate;
11: }
```

Analysis ▼

The postfix increment operator is different in function from the prefix increment operator in that y = x++; would result in y containing the old value of x, whereas y = ++x; would result in y containing the incremented value of x. It is for this reason that the postfix operator ++ does not return the current object by reference, but returns a copy of the object at pre-increment stage by value.

This postfix operator can therefore also be used like so:

```
// mDate initially contains 25 / 5 / 2008

// Use postfix increment
CDate mOldDate (mDate++);

// mDate now contains 26 / 5 / 2008
// mOldDate contains 25 / 5 / 2008
```

NOTE

The prefix and postfix decrement operators (that is, operator-) are similar in syntax to the increment operators, but would typically differ in functionality because they would reduce the value of the object they are performed on.

Programming Dereference Operator * and Member Selection Operator ->

These two operators probably find their most often used application in the programming of smart pointer classes. Smart pointers are classes that wrap regular pointers and aim to make memory management easy by taking care of ownership and copy issues. In some cases, they can even help improve the performance of the application. Smart pointers are discussed in detail in Lesson 26, "Understanding Smart Pointers."

For now, let's just look at a usage of the std::auto_ptr in Listing 13.3, and understand how it uses the dereference operator * to make the smart-pointer class behave like any normal pointer.

LISTING 13.3 Usage of the std::auto_ptr

```
1: // Listing 13.3: How smart pointers that simulate normal pointer semantics
2: #include <memory>
3: #include <iostream>
4: using namespace std;
5:
6: class Dog
7: {
8: public:
9:     Dog () {};      // Constructor
10:    ~Dog () {};     // Destructor
11:
12:    void Bark ()
13:    {
14:        cout << "Bark! Bark!" << endl;
15:    }
```

13

LISTING 13.3 Continued

```
16: };
17:
18: int main ()
19: {
20:     // a smart pointer equivalent of an int*
21:     auto_ptr <int> pSmartIntPtr (new int);
22:
23:     // Use this smart pointer like any normal pointer...
24:     *pSmartIntPtr = 25;
25:     cout << "*pSmartIntPtr = " << *pSmartIntPtr << endl;
26:
27:     // a smart pointer equivalent of a Dog*
28:     auto_ptr <Dog> pSmartDog (new Dog);
29:
30:     // Use this smart pointer like any ordinary pointer
31:     pSmartDog->Bark ();
32:
33:     return 0;
34: }
```

Analysis ▼

Note the usage of the smart pointer instances pSmartIntPtr in lines 24, 25, and that of pSmartDog in line 31. If you had not noted the definition of these two smart pointers, you could be forgiven for assuming that pSmartIntPtr is a regular pointer of the type:

```
int* pSmartIntPtr = new int;
```

Or that pSmartDog is a pointer of type:

```
Dog* pSmartDog = new Dog;
```

However, both pSmartIntPtr and pSmartDog are not raw pointers, rather instances of smart pointer class auto_ptr supplied by the standard library and present in the std namespace. The reason why an object of class auto_ptr can be used as a normal pointer is that this class implements operator * and operator ->. Note that we intentionally did not de-allocate the integer using delete, as auto_ptr does it for us (and hence called a smart pointer).

A simple smart-pointer class that implements a dereference and a member selection operator can be seen in Listing 13.4.

LISTING 13.4 Illustration of a Simple Smart Pointer Class

```
1: #template <typename T>
2: #class smart_pointer
3: {
4: private:
```

LISTING 13.4 Continued

```
 5:      T* m_pRawPointer;
 6: public:
 7:      // constructor
 8:      smart_pointer (T* pData) : m_pRawPointer (pData) {}
 9:
10:      // destructor
11:      ~smart_pointer () {delete m_pRawPointer ;}
12:
13:      // copy constructor
14:      smart_pointer (const smart_pointer & anotherSP);
15:
16:      // assignment operator
17:      smart_pointer& operator= (const smart_pointer& anotherSP);
18:
19:      // dereferencing operator
20:      T& operator* () const
21:      {
22:          return *(m_pRawPointer);
23:      }
24:
25:      // member selection operator
26:      T* operator-> () const
27:      {
28:          return m_pRawPointer;
29:      }
30: };
```

Analysis ▼

The simple implementation of the dereference operator in lines 20–23 and the member selection operator in lines 26–29 is the punch behind the usage of the smart pointer as seen in the previous sample, Listing 13.3. Note how the constructor saves an instance of the supplied pointer in a local variable that is then used by the two operators mentioned previously. The user of the smart pointer class never gets the impression that he is using a class and not a raw pointer.

13

> **NOTE**
>
> Smart pointer classes can do a lot more than just parade around as normal pointers, or de-allocate allocate memory when they go out of scope. This topic has been dealt with in detail in Lesson 26.
>
> If the usage of auto_ptr in Listing 13.3 makes you curious, look up the implementation of auto_ptr in the header file <memory> as supplied by your compiler or IDE to understand what it does behind the scenes to make its objects function like normal raw pointers.

Programming Conversion Operators

What if you wanted int nSomeNumber = Date (25, 5, 2008); to be a meaningful construct? That is, what if you wanted every date object be convertible into an integer that would make it easy for you to convey the date as a number to other modules that accepted only integers as input parameters? How would you achieve that?

C++ allows you to achieve this by defining custom unary operators. These typically follow the syntax:

```
operator conversion_type();
```

So, if we were to write a conversion operator that converted all dates into integers, we would define it as follows:

```
operator int()
{
    // implementation
    return intValue;
}
```

Very convenient, isn't it? Let's look at it in action (see Listing 13.5).

LISTING 13.5   Using Conversion Operators to Convert a CDate into an Integer

```
 1: #include <iostream>
 2:
 3: class CDate
 4: {
 5: private:
 6:     int m_nDay; // Range: 1 - 30 (lets assume all months have 30 days!)
 7:     int m_nMonth;     // Range: 1 - 12
 8:     int m_nYear;
 9:
10: public:
11:
12:     // Constructor that initializes the object to a day, month and year
13:     CDate (int nDay, int nMonth, int nYear)
14:          : m_nDay (nDay), m_nMonth (nMonth), m_nYear (nYear) {};
15:
16:     // Convert date object into an integer.
17:     operator int()
18:     {
19:         return ((m_nYear * 10000) + (m_nMonth * 100) + m_nDay);
20:     }
21:
22:     void DisplayDate ()
23:     {
```

LISTING 13.5 Continued

```
24:            std::cout << m_nDay << " / " << m_nMonth << " / " << m_nYear;
25:        }
26: };
27:
28: int main ()
29: {
30:     // Instantiate and initialize a date object to 25 May 2008
31:     CDate mDate (25, 6, 2008);
32:
33:     std::cout << "The date object is initialized to: ";
34:
35:     // Display initial date
36:     mDate.DisplayDate ();
37:     std::cout << std::endl;
38:
39:     // Get the integer equivalent of the date
40:     int nDate = mDate;
41:
42:     std::cout << "The integer equivalent of the date is: " << nDate;
43:
44:     return 0;
45: }
```

Output ▼

```
The date object is initialized to: 25 / 6 / 2008
The integer equivalent of the date is: 20080625
```

Analysis ▼

The conversion operator int() defined in lines 17–20 simply returns (what it considers to be) the integer equivalent of the existing state of the date object. Now, as a programmer you can use this powerful feature to convert your CDate object into any other type that you might find useful.

Another conversion operator that would be suitable here could be a string type that would display the string equivalent of the date held in the object:

```
operator std::string()
{
    // return a std::string containing the string equivalent of the date
}
```

13

Binary Operators

Operators that function on two operands are called *binary operators*. The definition of a binary operator implemented as a global function or a static member function is as follows:

```
return_type operator_type (parameter1, parameter2);
```

The definition of a binary operator implemented as a class member is

```
return_type operator_type (parameter);
```

The reason the class member version of a binary operator accepts only one parameter is that the second parameter is usually derived from the attributes of the class itself.

Types of Binary Operators

Table 13.2 contains binary operators that can be overloaded or redefined in your C++ application.

TABLE 13.2   Overloadable Binary Operators

Operator	Name
,	Comma
!=	Inequality
%	Modulus
%=	Modulus/assignment
&	Bitwise AND
&&	Logical AND
&=	Bitwise AND/assignment
*	Multiplication
*=	Multiplication/assignment
+	Addition
+=	Addition/assignment
–	Subtraction
–=	Subtraction/assignment
–>*	Pointer-to-member selection
/	Division
/=	Division/assignment
<	Less than
<<	Left shift
<<=	Left shift/assignment

TABLE 13.2 Continued

Operator	Name
<=	Less than or equal to
=	Assignment
==	Equality
>	Greater than
>=	Greater than or equal to
>>	Right shift
>>=	Right shift/assignment
^	Exclusive OR
^=	Exclusive OR/assignment
|	Bitwise inclusive OR
|=	Bitwise inclusive OR/assignment
||	Logical OR
[]	Subscript operator

Programming Binary Addition (a+b) and Subtraction (a–b) Operators

Similar to the increment/decrement operators, the binary plus and minus, when defined, allow you to add or subtract the value of a supported data type from an object of the class that implements these operators. Let's take a look at our calendar class CDate again. Although we have already implemented the capability to increment CDate so that it moves the calendar one day forward, we still do not support the capability to move it, say, 5 days ahead. To do this, we need to implement the binary plus operator, as the following code in Listing 13.6 demonstrates.

LISTING 13.6 Calendar Class Featuring the Binary Addition Operator

```
1: #include <iostream>
2:
3: class CDate
4: {
5: private:
6:     int m_nDay;      // Range: 1 - 30 (lets assume all months have 30 days!)
7:     int m_nMonth;    // Range: 1 - 12
8:     int m_nYear;
9:
10:    void AddDays (int nDaysToAdd)
11:    {
```

13

LISTING 13.6 Continued

```
12:          m_nDay += nDaysToAdd;
13:
14:          if (m_nDay > 30)
15:          {
16:              AddMonths (m_nDay / 30);
17:
18:              m_nDay %= 30;    // rollover 30th -> 1st
19:          }
20:      }
21:
22:      void AddMonths (int nMonthsToAdd)
23:      {
24:          m_nMonth += nMonthsToAdd;
25:
26:          if (m_nMonth > 12)
27:          {
28:              AddYears (m_nMonth / 12);
29:
30:              m_nMonth %= 12;    // rollover dec -> jan
31:          }
32:      }
33:
34:      void AddYears (int m_nYearsToAdd)
35:      {
36:          m_nYear += m_nYearsToAdd;
37:      }
38:
39: public:
40:
41:      // Constructor that initializes the object to a day, month and year
42:      CDate (int nDay, int nMonth, int nYear)
43:            : m_nDay (nDay), m_nMonth (nMonth), m_nYear (nYear) {};
44:
45:      CDate operator + (int nDaysToAdd)
46:      {
47:          CDate newDate (m_nDay, m_nMonth, m_nYear);
48:          newDate.AddDays (nDaysToAdd);
49:
50:          return newDate;
51:      }
52:
53:      void DisplayDate ()
54:      {
55:          std::cout << m_nDay << " / " << m_nMonth << " / " << m_nYear;
56:      }
57: };
58:
59: int main ()
60: {
```

LISTING 13.6 Continued

```
61:     // Instantiate and initialize a date object to 25 May 2008
62:     CDate mDate (25, 6, 2008);
63:
64:     std::cout << "The date object is initialized to: ";
65:
66:     // Display initial date
67:     mDate.DisplayDate ();
68:     std::cout << std::endl;
69:
70:     std::cout << "Date after adding 10 days is: ";
71:
72:     // Adding 10 (days)...
73:     CDate datePlus10 (mDate + 10);
74:
75:     datePlus10.DisplayDate ();
76:
77:     return 0;
78: }
```

Output ▼

```
The date object is initialized to: 25 / 6 / 2008
Date after adding 10 days is: 5 / 7 / 2008
```

Analysis ▼

Lines 45–51 contain the implementation of the binary + operator that permits the syntax used in line 73. This code adds the integer value 10 to an existing CDate object; mDate is equivalent to invoking the binary + operator in the following style:

```
CDate datePlus10 (mDate.operator+ (10));
```

Note that the preceding sample does not implement the binary subtraction operator (the operator -). This has exactly the same call syntax and differs only in implementation because you would typically make a subtraction instead of an addition of values.

Programming Addition-Assignment and Subtraction-Assignment Operators

The addition assignment operators allow syntax such as "a += b"; that allows the programmer to increment the value of an object a by an amount b. In doing this, the utility of the addition-assignment operator is that it can be overloaded to accept different types of parameter b. In the sample shown in Listing 13.7, this is an integer, but it could as well be a CDay object that defines the number of days by which the calendar is supposed to be set forward.

13

CAUTION

The following sample is incomplete. It contains only the code of relevance—that is, the addition assignment operator. The rest of the code can be taken from the previous sample shown in Listing 13.6.

LISTING 13.7 Using the Addition Assignment Operator to Increment Days in the Calendar Given an Integer Input

```
1: #class CDate
2: {
3: private:
4:     int m_nDay; // Range: 1 - 30 (lets assume all months have 30 days!)
5:     int m_nMonth; // Range: 1 - 12
6:     int m_nYear;
7:
8:     void AddDays (int nDaysToAdd);
9:     void AddMonths (int nMonthsToAdd);
10:    void AddYears (int m_nYearsToAdd);
11:
12: public:
13:
14:    // Constructor that initializes the object to a day, month and year
15:    CDate (int nDay, int nMonth, int nYear)
16:         : m_nDay (nDay), m_nMonth (nMonth), m_nYear (nYear) {};
17:
18:    // The addition-assignment operator    void operator += (int nDaysToAdd)
19:    {
20:        AddDays (nDaysToAdd);
21:    }
22:
23:    void DisplayDate ();
24: };
```

Analysis ▼

This operator now allows us to increment an existing date via syntax such as the following:

```
// Instantiate and initialize a date object to 25 May 2008
CDate mDate (25, 6, 2008);

// Adding 10 (days)...
mDate += 10;
```

Just as the addition-assignment operator above was programmed for integer input, we can also `overload` these to take other input parameter types. For instance, an addition-assignment operator that works with instances of a class `CDays` would be programmed like this:

```
// The addition-assignment operator that add a CDays to an existing date
void operator += (const CDays& mDaysToAdd)
{
    AddDays (mDaysToAdd.GetDays ());
}
```

NOTE

The multiplication assignment *=, division assignment /=, modulus assignment %=, subtraction assignment -=, left-shift assignment <<=, right-shift assignment >>=, XOR assignment ^=, bitwise inclusive OR assignment |=, and bitwise AND assignment &= operators have a similar syntax to the addition assignment operator shown in the Listing 13.7.

Note that although the ultimate objective of overloading operators is making the class easy and intuitive to use, there are many situations where implementing an operator might not make sense. For example, our calendar class `CDate` has absolutely no use for a bitwise AND assignment &= operator. No user of this class should ever expect (or even think of) getting useful results from an operation such as `mDate &= 20;`.

Overloading Comparison Operators

What do we expect when the user of our date class compares one class to another, as in the following:

```
if (mDate1 == mDate2)
{
    // Do something
}
else
{
    // Do something else
}
```

13

Because we have not defined an equality operator (yet), the compiler will simply perform a binary comparison of the two objects and return true if they are exactly identical. This might work in some case (including with the `CDate` class as of now). But it will probably not work to our expectations if the `CDate` class has a nonstatic string member that contains a string value (char*). In such a case, a binary comparison of the member attributes would actually compare the string pointers that would not be equal (even if the strings pointed to are identical in content) and would return false consistently.

So, it is a good practice to define the comparison operator. The inequality operator can be the inverse (logical NOT) of the result of the equality operator. Listing 13.8 demonstrates comparison operators defined by our calendar class CDate.

LISTING 13.8 Overloading Equality and Inequality Operators

```
 1: #include <iostream>
 2: using namespace std;
 3: class CDate
 4: {
 5: private:
 6:     int m_nDay;      // Range: 1 - 30 (lets assume all months have 30 days!)
 7:     int m_nMonth;    // Range: 1 - 12
 8:     int m_nYear;
 9:
10:     void AddDays (int nDaysToAdd);
11:     void AddMonths (int nMonthsToAdd);
12:     void AddYears (int m_nYearsToAdd);
13:
14: public:
15:
16:     // Constructor that initializes the object to a day, month and year
17:     CDate (int nDay, int nMonth, int nYear)
18:         : m_nDay (nDay), m_nMonth (nMonth), m_nYear (nYear) {};
19:
20:     void DisplayDate ()
21:     {
22:         cout << m_nDay << " / " << m_nMonth << " / " << m_nYear;
23:     }
24:
25:     // integer conversion operator
26:     operator int();
27:
28:     // equality operator that helps with: if (mDate1 == mDate2)...
29:     bool operator == (const CDate& mDateObj);
30:
31:     // overloaded equality operator that helps with: if (mDate == nInteger)
32:     bool operator == (int nDateNumber);
33:
34:     // inequality operator
35:     bool operator != (const CDate& mDateObj);
36:
37:     // overloaded inequality operator for integer types
```

LISTING 13.8 Continued

```
38:     bool operator != (int nDateNumber);
39: };
40:
41: CDate::operator int()
42: {
43:     return ((m_nYear * 10000) + (m_nMonth * 100) + m_nDay);
44: }
45:
46: // equality operator that helps with if (mDate1 == mDate2)...
47: bool CDate::operator == (const CDate& mDateObj)
48: {
49:     return ( (mDateObj.m_nYear == m_nYear)
50:             && (mDateObj.m_nMonth == m_nMonth)
51:             && (mDateObj.m_nDay == m_nDay) );
52: }
53:
54: bool CDate::operator == (int nDateNumber)
55: {
56:     return nDateNumber == (int)*this;
57: }
58:
59: // inequality operator
60: bool CDate::operator != (const CDate& mDateObj)
61: {
62:     return !(this->operator== (mDateObj));
63: }
64:
65: bool CDate::operator != (int nDateNumber)
66: {
67:     return !(this->operator == (nDateNumber));
68: }
69:
70: void CDate::AddDays (int nDaysToAdd)
71: {
72:     m_nDay += nDaysToAdd;
73:
74:     if (m_nDay > 30)
75:     {
76:         AddMonths (m_nDay / 30);
77:
78:         m_nDay %= 30;     // rollover 30th -> 1st
79:     }
80: }
81: void CDate::AddMonths (int nMonthsToAdd)
82: {
83:     m_nMonth += nMonthsToAdd;
84:
85:     if (m_nMonth > 12)
86:     {
```

13

LISTING 13.8   Continued

```
87:          AddYears (m_nMonth / 12);
88:
89:          m_nMonth %= 12;    // rollover dec -> jan
90:       }
91: }
92: void CDate::AddYears (int m_nYearsToAdd)
93: {
94:    m_nYear += m_nYearsToAdd;
95: }
96:
97: int main ()
98: {
99:    // Instantiate and initialize a date object to 25 May 2008
100:    CDate mDate1 (25, 6, 2008);
101:
102:    cout << "mDate1 contains: ";
103:
104:    // Display initial date
105:    mDate1.DisplayDate ();
106:    cout << endl;
107:
108:    CDate mDate2 (23, 5, 2009);
109:    cout << "mDate2 contains: ";
110:    mDate2.DisplayDate ();
111:    cout << endl;
112:
113:    // Use the inequality operator
114:    if (mDate2 != mDate1)
115:       cout << "The two dates are not equal... As expected!" << endl;
116:
117:    CDate mDate3 (23, 5, 2009);
118:    cout << "mDate3 contains: ";
119:    mDate3.DisplayDate ();
120:    cout << endl;
121:
122:    // Use the inequality operator
123:    if (mDate3 == mDate2)
124:       cout << "mDate3 and mDate2 are evaluated as equals" << endl;
125:
126:    // Get the integer equivalent of mDate3 using operator int()
127:    int nIntegerDate3 = mDate3;
128:
129:    cout<< "The integer equivalent of mDate3 is:"<< nIntegerDate3<< endl;
130:
131:    // Use overloaded operator== (for int comparison)
132:    if (mDate3 == nIntegerDate3)
133:       cout << "The integer  and mDate3 are equivalent" << endl;
134:
```

LISTING 13.8 Continued

```
135:     // Use overloaded operator != that accepts integers
136:     if (mDate1 != nIntegerDate3)
137:         cout << "The mDate1 is inequal to mDate3";
138:
139:     return 0;
140: }
```

Output ▼

```
mDate1 contains: 25 / 6 / 2008
mDate2 contains: 23 / 5 / 2009
The two dates are not equal... As expected!
mDate3 contains: 23 / 5 / 2009
mDate3 and mDate2 are evaluated as equals using the equality operator
The integer equivalent of mDate3 is: 20090523
The integer and mDate3 are equivalent
The mDate1 is inequal to mDate3
```

Analysis ▼

The implementation of the equality operator for types CDate and the overloaded version for type int is shown in lines 47–57. The operator takes an input operand and functions by comparing it against data held inside the object. This comparison is up to the user to implement on the basis of criteria that are relevant and important to his application. The inequality operators implemented in lines 60–68 are simply the logically inverted equivalents of the equality operators.

Overloading <, >, <=, and >= Operators

The code in Listing 13.8 made the CDate class intelligent enough to be able to tell whether two CDate objects are equal, or whether an integer contains the integral equivalent of the date contained in a CDate object.

However, what if the user of the class is required to perform a conditional check akin to this:

```
if (mDate1 < mDate2) {// do something}
```

or

```
if (mDate1 <= mDate2) {// do something}
```

or

```
if (mDate1 > mDate2) {// do something}
```

or

```
if (mDate >= mDate2) {// do something}
```

13

The user of our calendar class would definitely find it very useful if he could simply compare two dates to know whether one precedes or follows another. The programmer of the class needs to implement this comparison to make using his class as user friendly and intuitive as possible, as demonstrated by the code shown in Listing 13.9.

LISTING 13.9   Implementing <, <=, >, and >= Operators

```
 1: #include <iostream>
 2:
 3: class CDate
 4: {
 5: private:
 6:     int m_nDay;     // Range: 1 - 30 (lets assume all months have 30 days!)
 7:     int m_nMonth;   // Range: 1 - 12
 8:     int m_nYear;
 9:
10:     void AddDays (int nDaysToAdd);
11:     void AddMonths (int nMonthsToAdd);
12:     void AddYears (int m_nYearsToAdd);
13:
14: public:
15:
16:     // Constructor that initializes the object to a day, month and year
17:     CDate (int nDay, int nMonth, int nYear)
18:           : m_nDay (nDay), m_nMonth (nMonth), m_nYear (nYear) {};
19:
20:     void DisplayDate ()
21:     {
22:         cout << m_nDay << " / " << m_nMonth << " / " << m_nYear;
23:     }
24:
25:     bool operator < (const CDate& mDateObj) const;
26:     bool operator <= (const CDate& mDateObj) const;
27:
28:     bool operator > (const CDate& mDateObj) const;
29:     bool operator >= (const CDate& mDateObj) const;
30: };
31:
32: CDate::operator int() const
33: {
34:     return ((m_nYear * 10000) + (m_nMonth * 100) + m_nDay);
35: }
36:
37: bool CDate::operator < (const CDate& mDateObj) const
38: {
39:     return (this->operator int () < mDateObj.operator int ());
40: }
41:
```

LISTING 13.9 Continued

```
42: bool CDate::operator > (const CDate& mDateObj) const
43: {
44:     return (this->operator int () > mDateObj.operator int ());
45: }
46:
47: bool CDate::operator <= (const CDate& mDateObj) const
48: {
49:     return (this->operator int () <= mDateObj.operator int ());
50: }
51:
52: bool CDate::operator >= (const CDate& mDateObj) const
53: {
54:     return (this->operator int () >= mDateObj.operator int ());
55: }
56:
57: // Pick the definition of other functions from listing 13.8
58:
59: int main ()
60: {
61:     // Instantiate and initialize a date object to 25 May 2008
62:     CDate mDate1 (25, 6, 2008);
63:     CDate mDate2 (23, 5, 2009);
64:     CDate mDate3 (23, 5, 2009);
65:
66:     cout << "mDate1 contains: ";
67:     mDate1.DisplayDate ();
68:     cout << endl;
69:
70:     cout << "mDate2 contains: ";
71:     mDate2.DisplayDate ();
72:     cout << endl;
73:
74:     cout << "mDate3 contains: ";
75:     mDate3.DisplayDate ();
76:     cout << endl;
77:
78:     // Use the operator <
79:     cout << "mDate3 < mDate2 is: ";
80:     cout << ((mDate3 < mDate2) ? "true" : "false") << endl;
81:
82:     // Use the operator <=
83:     cout << "mDate3 <= mDate2 is: ";
84:     cout << ((mDate3 <= mDate2) ? "true" : "false") << endl;
85:
86:     // Use operator >=
87:     cout << "mDate3 >= mDate1 is: ";
88:     cout << ((mDate3 >= mDate1) ? "true" : "false") << endl;
89:
```

13

LISTING 13.9 Continued

```
90:     // Use operator >
91:     cout << "mDate1 > mDate3 is: ";
92:     cout << ((mDate1 > mDate3) ? "true" : "false") << endl;
93:
94:     return 0;
95: }
```

Output ▼

```
mDate1 contains: 25 / 6 / 2008
mDate2 contains: 23 / 5 / 2009
mDate3 contains: 23 / 5 / 2009
mDate3 < mDate2 is: false
mDate3 <= mDate2 is: true
mDate3 >= mDate1 is: true
mDate1 > mDate3 is: false
```

Analysis ▼

The operators of interest are implemented in lines 37–55. Note how these operators have been implemented: Rather than have to compare individual elements of the date such as year, month, and day, in that order, the operators simply make use of the conversion operator int() and reduce their job to comparing two integers appropriately.

The usage of the operators inside the main() function between lines 78–92 indicates how the implementation of these operators make using the CDate class easy and intuitive.

NOTE

There are other binary operators as seen in Table 13.2 that can be redefined or overloaded but that have not been discussed further in this lesson. Their implementation however is similar to those that have already been discussed.

Other operators, such as the logical operators and the bitwise operators, need to be programmed if the purpose of the class would be enhanced by having them. Clearly, a calendar class such as CDate does not necessarily need to implement logical operators, whereas a class that performs string and numeric functions might need them all the time.

Keep the objective of your class and its usage in perspective when overloading operators or writing new ones.

Subscript Operators

Operators that allow array-style [ ] access to a class are called *subscript* operators. The typical syntax of a subscript operator is

```
return_type& operator [] (subscript_type& subscript);
```

So, when writing a dynamic array class (CMyArray) for integers, which should allow array-like access to internal elements, you would typically program the subscript operator like this:

```
class CMyArray
{
    // ... other class members
public:
    int& operator [] (int nIndex)

{
        // return the integer at position nIndex
}
};
```

The following sample contained in Listing 13.10 displays the implementation of a rudimentary dynamic array class, and demonstrates how the subscript operator [] helps the user in iterating through the elements contained in this dynamic array class using normal array semantics.

LISTING 13.10   Using the Subscript Operator in Programming a Dynamic Array

```
 1: #include <iostream>
 2:
 3: class CMyArray
 4: {
 5: private:
 6:     int* m_pnInternalArray;
 7:     int m_nNumElements;
 8: public:
 9:     CMyArray (int nNumElements);
10:     ~CMyArray ();
11:
12:     // declare a subscript operator
13:     int& operator [] (int nIndex);
14: };
15:
16: // subscript operator: allows direct access to an element given an index
17: int& CMyArray::operator [] (int nIndex)
18: {
```

13

LISTING 13.10   Continued

```
19:      return m_pnInternalArray [nIndex];
20: }
21:
22: CMyArray::CMyArray (int nNumElements)
23: {
24:     m_pnInternalArray = new int [nNumElements];
25:    m_nNumElements = nNumElements;
26: }
27: CMyArray::~CMyArray ()
28: {
29:    delete [] m_pnInternalArray;
30: }
31:
32: int main ()
33: {
34:    // instantiate a dynamic array with 5 elements
35:    CMyArray mArray (5);
36:
37:    // write into the array using the subscript operator []
38:    mArray [0] = 25;
39:    mArray [1] = 20;
40:    mArray [2] = 15;
41:    mArray [3] = 10;
42:    mArray [4] = 5;
43:
44:    cout << "The contents of the array are: "  << std::endl << "{";
45:
46:    // read from the dynamic array using the same subscript operator
47:    for (int nIndex = 0; nIndex < 5; ++ nIndex)
48:        std::cout << mArray [nIndex] << " ";
49:
50:    std::cout << "}";
51:
52:    return 0;
53: }
```

Output ▼

```
The contents of the array are:
{25 20 15 10 5 }
```

Analysis ▼

This very basic version of a dynamic array class has no real-world value other than in demonstrating to you how the subscript operator enables you to write contents and read them using an array-like syntax. The subscript operator is defined in lines 17–20, and it is what implements the functionality called in the main() function between lines 38–48.

NOTE

When implementing subscript operators, you can improve on the version seen in Listing 13.10. That one is an implementation of a single subscript operator that works for both reading from and writing to the slots in the dynamic array.

You can, however, implement two subscript operators, one as a const function and the other as a non-const one:

```
int& operator [] (int nIndex);
int& operator [] (int nIndex) const;
```

The compiler is smart enough to invoke the const function for read operations and the non-const version for operations that write into the CMyArray object. Thus, you can (if you want to) have separate functionalities in the two subscript functions. For example, one function can log writes into the container while the other can log reads from it.

Function operator()

These are operators that make objects work like functions. They find application in STL (standard template library) and are typically used in STL algorithms. Their usage can include making decisions (such function objects are typically called *unary* or *binary predicate*, depending on the number of operands they work on). Let's analyze a really simple function object as seen in Listing 13.11 to first understand what gives them such an intriguing name!

LISTING 13.11   A Function Object Implemented Using operator()

```
1: #include <string>
2: #include <iostream>
3:
4: class CDisplay
5: {
6: public:
7:     void operator () (std::string strIn) const
8:     {
9:         std::cout << strIn << std::endl;
10:    }
11: };
12:
13: int main ()
14: {
```

13

LISTING 13.11 Continued

```
15:    CDisplay mDisplayFuncObject;
16:
17:    // equivalent to mDisplayFuncObject.operator () ("Display this string!");
18:    mDisplayFuncObject ("Display this string!");
19:
20:    return 0;
21: }
```

Output ▼

```
Display this string!
```

Analysis ▼

Lines 7–10 implement `operator()` that is then used inside the function `main()` at line 18. Note how the compiler allows the use of `object mDisplayFuncObject` as a `function` in line 18 by implicitly converting what looks like a function call to a call to `operator()`.

Hence, this operator is also called the function `operator()` and the object of `CDisplay` is also called a `function object` or *functor*.

Operators That Cannot Be Redefined

With all the flexibility that C++ gives you, the programmer, in customizing the behavior of the operators and making your classes as easy to use, it still keeps some cards to itself by not allowing you to change or alter the behavior of some operators that are expected to perform consistently. The operators that cannot be redefined are shown in Table 13.3.

TABLE 13.3 Operators That CANNOT Be Overloaded or Redefined

Operator	Name
.	Member selection
.*	Pointer-to-member selection
::	Scope resolution
? :	Conditional ternary operator
sizeof	Gets the size of an object/class type

DO	DON'T
DO remember to use the `const` keyword when defining member operators that don't need to be changing the object's attributes.	**DON'T** add more operators than necessary. Doing so is a waste of time if no one uses them.
DO remember that programming operators might take effort for the person programming the class, but makes it easy for the person using it.	
DO make it a practice to write `const` and non-`const` versions for subscript operators that allow bidirectional access—one for reading and the other for writing.	

Summary

You learned the different kinds of operators and how overloading them appropriately makes using your class intuitive and easy. You also now know to write operators that can help in conversion, and others that help your object to be used as a function. Last but not least, you learned that operators such as ., .*, ::, ?: and `sizeof` cannot be redefined.

Q&A

Q When should I mark my operator as a `const` function?

A It is a good practice to mark operators that are not intended to change the member variables of a class as `const` functions. Not only does this help the compiler optimize the application, but it also points out errors that happen when someone at a later stage modifies the class's member attributes in a operator meant to be `const`.

Q Do I need to overload all operators that can be overloaded whenever I program a new class?

A No, definitely not. The object of defining operators is to make using your class easy and intuitive. That does not mean, however, that you go into overdrive and redefine every operator possible. Keep the application in perspective when overriding operators. Some classes, such as those that work in a mathematical context, might be aided by overloading logical and arithmetic operators, whereas other

13

classes that deal with strings might be aided by operators that convert types. Finally, there are also classes that might be accessible only via an interface (by design) and overloading operators does not make sense for them.

Q **What operators need to be defined when writing a smart pointer class?**

A The operators * and -> need to be necessarily defined by a smart pointer class.

Workshop

The Workshop contains quiz questions to help solidify your understanding of the material covered and exercises to provide you with experience in using what you've learned. Try to answer the quiz and exercise questions before checking the answers in Appendix D, and be certain you understand the answers before going to the next lesson.

Quiz

1. Can I have two versions of the same subscript operator[], one as a const version and other as non-const? How does that help anyone?

2. You have to write a string class for char-string types. What operators would you definitely define?

3. You have been assigned the task of writing a class that manipulates a date in bits. Would you define bitwise operators for this class?

Exercises

1. Write the declaration of the unary decrement operator for the class CDate.

2. Write a dynamic integer array class (you can use CMyArray as a starting point) that implements the following requirement:

   - Condition (mArray1 == mArray2) should be satisfied if both arrays are of the same length and contents are equal.

   - Condition (mArray1 < mArray2) should be satisfied if array 1 has fewer elements than array 2 or, if they are the same size, if the sum of the contents of array 1 is less than that of array 2.

LESSON 14
Casting Operators

Operators that change the interpretation of an object are called *casting operators*.

In this lesson, you will learn:

- The need for casting operators

- Why traditional C-style casts are not popular with some C++ programmers

- The four C++ casting operators

- Why C++ casting operators are not all-time favorites

What Is Casting?

Casting is a mechanism by which the programmer can temporarily or permanently change the interpretation of an object by the compiler. Note that this does not imply that the programmer changes the object itself—no, he simply changes the interpretation thereof.

The Need for Casting

In a perfectly type-safe and type-strong world comprising well-written C++ applications, there should be no need for casting and for casting-operators. However, we live in a real world where modules programmed by a lot of different people and vendors often using different environments have to work together. To make this happen, compilers very often need to be instructed to interpret data in ways that will make them compile and the application function correctly.

Let's take a real world example: Although some C++ compilers might support `bool` as a native type, a lot of libraries are still in use that were programmed years back and in C. These libraries made for C compilers had to rely on the use of an integral type to hold Boolean data. So, a `bool` on these compilers is something akin to

```
typedef unsigned short BOOL;
```

A function that returns Boolean data would be declared as

```
BOOL IsX ();
```

Now, if such a library is to be used with a new application programmed in the latest version of the C++ compiler, the programmer has to find a way to make the `bool` data-type as understood by his C++ compiler function with the `BOOL` data-type as understood by the library. The way to make this happen is by using casts:

```
bool bCPPResult = (bool)IsX ();    // C-Style cast
```

The evolution of C++ saw the emergence of new C++ casting operators and that created a split in the C++ programming community: a group that continued using C-style casts in their C++ applications, and another that religiously converted to casting keywords introduced by C++ compilers. The argument of the former group is that the C++ casts are cumbersome to use, and sometimes differ in functionality to such a small extent that they are of only theoretical value. The latter group, which evidently comprises C++ syntax purists, points out at the flaws in the C-style casts to make their case.

Because the real world contains both kinds of code in operation, it would be good to simply read through this lesson, know the advantages and disadvantages of each style, and formulate your own opinion.

Why C-Style Casts Are Not Popular with Some C++ Programmers

Type safety is one of the mantras that C++ programmers swear by when singing praises to the qualities of this programming language. In fact, most C++ compilers won't even let you get away with this:

```
char* pszString = "Hello World!";
int* pBuf = pszString;    // error: cannot convert char* to unsigned char*
```

...and quite rightfully so!

Now, C++ compilers still do see the need to be backward compliant to keep old and legacy code building, and therefore automatically allow syntax such as

```
int* pBuf = (int*)pszString;    // Cast one problem away to create a bigger one!
```

However, C-style casts actually force the compiler to interpret the destination as a type that is very conveniently of the programmer's choice—a programmer who in this case did not bother thinking that the compiler reported an error in the first place for good reason, and simply muzzled the compiler and forced it to obey. This, of course, does not go well down the throats of C++ programmers who see their type safety being compromised by casts that force anything through.

The C++ Casting Operators

Despite the disadvantages of casting, the concept of casting itself cannot be discarded. In many situations, casts are legitimate requirements to solve important compatibility issues. C++ additionally supplies a new casting operator specific to inheritance-based scenarios that did not exist with C programming.

The four C++ casting operators are

- static_cast
- dynamic_cast
- reinterpret_cast
- const_cast

14

The usage syntax of the casting operators is consistent:

```
destination_type result = cast_type <destination_type> (object_to_be_casted);
```

Using `static_cast`

`static_cast` is a mechanism that can be used to convert pointers between related types, and perform explicit type conversions for standard data types that would otherwise happen automatically or implicitly. As far as pointers go, `static_cast` implements a basic compile-time check to ensure that the pointer is being cast to a related type. This is an improvement over a C-style cast that allows a pointer to one object to be cast to an absolutely unrelated type without any complaint. Using `static_cast`, a pointer can be up-casted to the base-type, or can be down-casted to the derived type, as the following code-sample indicates.

```
CBase* pBase = new CDerived ();    // construct a CDerived object
CDerived* pDerived = static_cast<CDerived*>(pBase);    // ok!

// CUnrelated is not related to CBase via any inheritance hierarchy
CUnrelated* pUnrelated = static_cast<CUnrelated*>(pBase); // Error

//The cast above is not permitted as types are unrelated
```

However, note that `static_cast` verifies only that the pointer types are related. It does *not* perform any runtime checks. So, with `static_cast`, a programmer could still get away with this bug:

```
CBase* pBase = new CBase ();
CDerived* pDerived = static_cast<CDerived*>(pBase); // Still no errors!
```

Here, pDerived actually points to a partial CDerived object because the object being pointed to is actually a CBase() type. Because `static_cast` performs only a compile-time check of verifying that the types in question are related and does not perform a runtime check, a call to pDerived->SomeDerivedClassFunction() would get compiled, but probably result in unexpected behavior during runtime.

Apart from helping in up-casting or down-casting, `static_cast` can in many cases help make implicit casts explicit and bring them to the attention of the programmer or reader:

```
double dPi = 3.14159265;
int nNum = static_cast<int>(dPi); // Making an otherwise implicit cast, explicit
```

In the preceding code, nNum = dPi would have worked as well and to the same effect. However, using a `static_cast` brings the nature of conversion to the attention of the reader and indicates (to someone who knows `static_cast`) that the compiler has performed the necessary adjustments based on the information available at compile-time to perform the required type-conversion.

Using `dynamic_cast` and Runtime Type Identification

Dynamic casting, as the name suggests, is the opposite of static casting and actually executes the cast at runtime—that is, at application execution time. The result of a `dynamic_cast` operation can be checked to see whether the attempt at casting succeeded. The typical usage syntax of the `dynamic_cast` operator is

```
destination_type* pDest = dynamic_cast <class_type*> (pSource);

if (pDest)      // Check for success of the casting operation
    pDest->CallFunc ();
```

For example:

```
CBase* pBase = new CDerived();

// Perform a downcast
CDerived* pDerived = dynamic_cast <CDerived*> (pBase);

if (pDerived)     // Check for success of the cast
    pDerived->CallDerivedClassFunction ();
```

As shown in the preceding tiny example, given a pointer to a base-class object, the programmer can resort to `dynamic_cast` to verify the type of the destination object being pointed to before proceeding to use the pointer as such. Note that in the code sample it is apparent that the destination object *is* a `CDerived`-type. So, the sample is of demonstrative value only. However, this might not always be the case. Given a base-class object, the programmer might not be certain of the derived-class type it actually belongs to. This is where `dynamic_cast` helps determine the type at runtime and use a casted pointer when it is safe to do so. Therefore, this mechanism of identifying the type of the object at runtime is called *runtime type identification* or *RTTI* (see Listing 14.1).

LISTING 14.1   Dynamic Casting That Helps Tell Whether an Animal Object Is a Cat or a Dog

```
 1: #include <iostream>
 2: using namespace std;
 3: class CAnimal
 4: {
 5: public:
 6:     virtual void Speak () = 0;
 7: };
 8:
 9: class CDog : public CAnimal
10: {
11: public:
```

14

LISTING 14.1 Continued

```
12:     void WagTail () {cout << "Dog: I wagged my tail!" << endl;}
13:
14:     void Speak () {cout << "Dog: Bow-Wow!" << endl;}
15: };
16:
17: class CCat : public CAnimal
18: {
19: public:
20:     void CatchMice () {cout << "Cat: I caught a mouse!" << endl;}
21:
22:     void Speak () {cout << "Cat: Meow!" << endl;}
23: };
24:
25: void DetermineType (CAnimal* pAnimal);
26:
27: int main ()
28: {
29:     // pAnimal1 points to a Dog object
30:     CAnimal* pAnimal1 = new CDog ();
31:
32:     // pAnimal2 points to a Cat object
33:     CAnimal* pAnimal2 = new CCat ();
34:
35:     cout << "Using dynamic_cast to determine type of Animal 1" << endl;
36:     DetermineType (pAnimal1);
37:
38:     cout << "Using dynamic_cast to determine type of Animal 2" << endl;
39:     DetermineType (pAnimal2);
40:
41:     // Use the virtual function overridden by the subclasses to prove type
42:     cout << "Verifying type: Asking Animal 1 to speak!" << endl;
43:     pAnimal1->Speak ();
44:
45:     cout << "Verifying type: Asking pAnimal 2 to speak!" << endl;
46:     pAnimal2->Speak ();
47:
48:     return 0;
49: }
50:
51: void DetermineType (CAnimal* pAnimal)
52: {
53:     CDog* pDog = dynamic_cast <CDog*>(pAnimal);
54:     if (pDog)
55:     {
56:         cout << "The animal is a dog!" << endl;
57:
58:         // Call the derived class' function
59:         pDog->WagTail ();
60:     }
61:
```

LISTING 14.1 Continued

```
62:     CCat* pCat = dynamic_cast <CCat*>(pAnimal);
63:     if (pCat)
64:     {
65:         cout << "The animal is a cat!" << endl;
66:
67:         pCat->CatchMice ();
68:     }
69: }
```

Output ▼

```
Using dynamic_cast to determine type of Animal 1
The animal is a dog!
Dog: I wagged my tail!
Using dynamic_cast to determine type of Animal 2
The animal is a cat!
Cat: I caught a mouse!
Verifying type: Asking Animal 1 to speak!
Dog: Bow-Wow!
Verifying type: Asking pAnimal 2 to speak!
Cat: Meow!
```

Analysis ▼

The abstract base class CAnimal here is specialized by two derived classes: CDog and CCat. In doing so, these classes have to define the pure virtual function Speak() that the Dog uses to bark and the Cat uses to meow! The function that uses dynamic_cast to tell a Dog from a Cat, given a pointer to CAnimal, is the function DetermineType, which is implemented in lines 51–69. After determining the animal type, this function also uses the pointer to call a function that is peculiar to each of the derived classes—that is, it invokes the function WagTail() using a valid pointer to a CDog object and the function CatchMice() using a valid pointer to a CCat object. The main() function helps verify the runtime type identification done by DetermineType by invoking the virtual function Speak() using the respective CAnimal* pointers.

Using reinterpret_cast

reinterpret_cast is the closest a C++ casting operator gets to the C-style cast. It really does allow the programmer to cast one object type to another, regardless of whether or not the types are related; that is, it forces a reinterpretation of type using a syntax as seen in the following sample:

```
CBase * pBase = new CBase ();
CUnrelated * pUnrelated = reinterpret_cast<CUnrelated*>(pBase);

// The code above is not good programming, even if it compiles!
```

This cast actually forces the compiler to accept situations that static_cast would normally not permit. It finds usage in certain low-level applications (such as drivers, for example) where data needs to be converted to a simple type that the API can accept (for example, some APIs work only with BYTE streams; that is, unsigned char*):

```
CSomeClass* pObject = new CSomeClass ();
// Need to send the object as a byte-stream...
unsigned char* pBytes = reinterpret_cast <unsigned char*>(pObject);
```

The cast used in the preceding code has not changed the binary representation of the source object, and has effectively cheated the compiler into allowing the programmer to peek into individual bytes contained by an object of type CSomeClass. Because no other C++ casting operator would allow such a conversion, reinterpret_cast explicitly warns the user that a potentially unsafe (and nonportable) conversion is occurring.

TIP	As far as possible, you should refrain from using reinterpret_cast in your applications.

Using const_cast

const_cast allows you to turn off the const access modifier to an object. If you are wondering why this cast is necessary at all, you are probably right in doing so. In an ideal situation where programmers write their classes correctly, they remember to use the const keyword frequently and in the right places. The practical world unfortunately is far from ideal. Missing const qualifiers as seen in the following code are quite prevalent:

```
CSomeClass
{
public:
    // ...
    void DisplayMembers ();     // ought to be a const member
};
```

So, when you program a function such as

```
void DisplayAllData (const CSomeClass& mData)
{
    mData.DisplayMembers ();  // Compile failure
    // reason for failure: call to a non-const member using a const reference
}
```

you are evidently correct in passing the mData object as a const reference. After all, a display function should be read-only, should not be allowed to call non-const member functions; that is, should not be allowed to call a function that can change the state of the object. However, the implementation of DisplayMembers(), which also ought to be const, unfortunately is not. Now, so long as CSomeClass belongs to you and the source code is in your control, you can make corrective changes to DisplayMembers(). In many cases, however, it might belong to a third-party library and making changes to it is not possible. In situations such as these, const_cast is your savior.

The syntax for invoking DisplayMembers() in such a scenario is

```
void DisplayAllData (const CSomeClass& mData)
{
    CSomeClass& refData = const_cast <CSomeClass&>(mData);
    refData.DisplayMembers();    // Allowed!
}
```

NOTE

Note that using const_cast to invoke non-const functions should be a last resort. In general, keep in mind that using const_cast to modify a const object can result in undefined behavior.

Note also that const_cast can be used with pointers:

```
void DisplayAllData (const CSomeClass* pData)
{
    // pData->DisplayMembers(); Error: attempt to invoke a non-const function!
    CSomeClass* pCastedData = const_cast <CSomeClass*>(pData);
    pCastedData->DisplayMembers();    // Allowed!
}
```

14

Problems with the C++ Casting Operators

Not everyone is happy with all C++ casting operators–not even those who swear by C++. Their reasons range from the syntax being cumbersome and nonintuitive to being redundant.

Let's simply compare this code:

```
double dPi = 3.14159265;

// C++ style cast: static_cast
int nNum = static_cast <int>(dPi);     // result: nNum is 3

// C-style cast
int nNum2 = (int)dPi;                  // result: nNum is 3

// leave casting to the compiler
int nNum3 = dPi;           // result: nNum is 3. No errors!
```

In all the three cases, the programmer achieved the same result. In practical scenarios, the second option is probably the most prevalent, followed by the third. Few people might use the first option. In any case, the compiler is intelligent enough to convert such types correctly. This gives the cast syntax an impression that it makes the code more difficult to read.

Similarly, other uses of static_cast are also handled well by C-style casts that are admittedly simpler looking:

```
// using static_cast
CDerived* pDerived = static_cast <CDerived*>(pBase);

// But, this works just as well...
CDerived* pDerivedSimple = (CDerived*)pBase;
```

Thus, the advantage of using static_cast is often overshadowed by the clumsiness of its syntax. Bjarne Stroustrup's own words express the situation accurately: "Maybe, because static_cast is so ugly and so relatively hard to type, you're more likely to think twice before using one? That would be good, because casts really are mostly avoidable in modern C++." (See Stroustrup's C++ Style and Technique FAQ at http://www.research.att.com/~bs/bs_faq2.html.)

Looking at other operators, reinterpret_cast is for forcing your way through when static_cast does not work; ditto for const_cast with respect to modifying the const access modifiers. Thus, C++ casting operators other than dynamic_cast are avoidable in modern C++ applications. Only when addressing the needs of legacy applications might other casting operators become relevant. In such cases, preferring C-style casts to C++ casting operators is often a matter of taste. What's important is that you avoid casting as far as possible, and when you do use it, you know what happens behind the scenes.

Summary

In this lesson, you learned the different C++ casting operators, the arguments for and against using them. You also learned that in general you should avoid the usage of casts.

Q&A

Q **Is it okay to modify the contents of a const-object by casting a pointer / reference to it using `const_cast`?**

A Most definitely not. The result of such an operation is not defined, and definitely not desired.

Q **I need a `CBird*`, but have a `CDog*` at hand. The compiler does not allow me to use the pointer to the `CDog` object as a `CBird*`. However, when I use `reinterpret_cast` to cast the `CDog*` to `CBird*`, the compiler does not complain and it seems I can use this pointer to call `Bird`'s member function, `Fly()`. Is this okay?**

A Again, definitely not. `reinterpret_cast` changed only the interpretation of the pointer, and did not change the object being pointed to (that is still a `Dog`). Calling a `Fly()` function on a `CDog` object will not give the results you are looking for, and could possibly cause an application failure.

Q **I have a `CDerived` object being pointed to by a `pBase` that is a `CBase*`. I am sure that `pBase` points to a `CDerived` object, so do I really need to use `dynamic_cast`?**

A Because you are sure that the object being pointed to is a `CDerived` type, you can save on runtime performance by using `static_cast`.

Q **C++ provides casting operators, and yet I am advised to not use them as far as possible. Why is that?**

A You keep aspirin at home, but you don't make it your staple diet just because it's available, right? Use casts only when you need them.

Workshop

The workshop provides quiz questions to help solidify your understanding of the material covered and exercises to provide you with experience in using what you've learned. Try to answer the quiz and exercise questions before checking the answers in Appendix D, and be certain you understand the answers before going to the next lesson.

Quiz

1. You have a base class object pointer pBase. What cast would you use to determine whether it is a CDerived1 type or a CDerived2 type?

2. You have a const reference to an object and tried calling a public member function, written by you. The compiler does not allow this because the function in question is not a const member. Would you correct the function or would you use const_cast?

3. reinterpret_cast should be used only when static_cast does not work, and the cast is known to be required and safe. True or false?

4. Is it true that many instances of static_cast-based conversions, especially between simple data-types, would be performed automatically by a good C++ compiler?

LESSON 15

An Introduction to Macros and Templates

By now, you should have a solid understanding of basic C++ syntax. Programs written in C++ should be understandable and you are poised to learn language features that help you write applications efficiently.

In this lesson, you will learn

- An introduction to the preprocessor

- The #define keyword and macros

- An introduction to templates

- Writing templates for functions and classes

- The difference between macros and templates

The Preprocessor and the Compiler

Every time you compile a C++ file, the compiler first preprocesses it. This unit of the compiler that processes your code before it is actually compiled is called the *preprocessor*.

C++ features syntax elements by which the programmer can control the compile-time behavior of the application using preprocessor instructions, each of which begins with a pound symbol (#). These instructions influence the text of the source code which is modified precompilation, and the compiler then proceeds to compile this modified output.

You've seen the effect of the preprocessor already with the `#include` directive that effectively places the content of the included file into the source code.

The `#define` Preprocessor Directive

You can create substitutions using the `#define` command. For example, if you write

```
#define BIG 512
```

you have instructed the precompiler to substitute the string 512 wherever it sees the string BIG. This is not a string in the C++ sense. The characters "512" are substituted in your source code wherever the word "BIG" is seen. Thus, if you write

```
#define BIG 512
int myArray[BIG];
```

The code, after being worked on by the preprocessor, would look like this when submitted for compilation:

```
int myArray[512];
```

As you can see, the preprocessor has performed a text replacement of BIG by 512.

TIP

It is important to note that the preprocessor has made a purely text-based replacement, exchanging BIG used in the array declaration with 512 as defined previously. It did not perform a context-sensitive check to verify whether the value being substituted for BIG makes for an appropriate insertion at the code that defines the array.

BIG might as well have been defined as the string "Tiny" instead and the preprocessor would supply the array declaration to the compiler as

```
int myarray ["Tiny"]
```

This would, of course, result in a compilation error. There is no type safety when using the preprocessor and we see some more serious implications of this problem later.

Macro Functions

The #define directive can also be used to create macro functions. A *macro function* is a symbol created using #define that takes an argument, much like a function does. The preprocessor substitutes the substitution string for whatever argument it is given. For example, you can define the macro TWICE as

```
#define TWICE(x) ( (x) * 2 )
```

and then in your code you write

```
TWICE(4)
```

The entire string TWICE(4) is removed and the value ((4) * 2) is substituted. When the precompiler sees the 4, it substitutes ((4) * 2), which then evaluates to 4×2, or 8.

A macro can have more than one parameter, and each parameter can be used repeatedly in the replacement text. Two common macros are MAX and MIN:

```
#define MAX(x,y) ( (x) > (y) ? (x) : (y) )
#define MIN(x,y) ( (x) < (y) ? (x) : (y) )
```

Note that, in a macro function definition, the opening parenthesis for the parameter list must immediately follow the macro name with no spaces. The preprocessor is not as forgiving of whitespace as is the compiler. If there is a space, a standard substitution is used, such as you saw earlier in this lesson.

For example, if you write

```
#define MAX (x,y) ( (x) > (y) ? (x) : (y) )
```

and then try to use MAX like this:

```
int x = 5, y = 7, z;
z = MAX(x,y);
```

the intermediate code is

```
int x = 5, y = 7, z;
z = (x,y) ( (x) > (y) ? (x) : (y) )(x,y)
```

A simple text substitution is done, rather than the macro function being invoked. Thus, the token MAX has substituted for it (x,y) ((x) > (y) ? (x) : (y)), and that is followed by the (x,y), which follows MAX.

By removing the space between MAX and (x,y), however, the intermediate code becomes

```
int x = 5, y = 7, z;
a = ( (5) > (7) ? (5) : (7) );
```

This, of course, evaluates to 7.

Why All the Parentheses?

You might be wondering why so many parentheses are in many of the macros presented so far. The preprocessor does not demand that parentheses be placed around the arguments in the substitution string, but the parentheses help you to avoid unwanted side effects when you pass complicated values to a macro. For example, if you define MAX as

```
#define MAX(x,y) x > y ? x : y
```

and pass in the values 5 and 7, the macro works as intended. But, if you pass in a more complicated expression, you receive unintended results, as shown in Listing 15.1.

LISTING 15.1   Using Parentheses in Macros

```
0:  // Listing 15.1 Macro Expansion
1:  #include <iostream>
2:  using namespace std;
3:
4:  #define CUBE(a) ( (a) * (a) * (a) )
5:  #define THREE(a) a * a * a
6:
7:  int main()
8:  {
9:     long x = 5;
10:    long y = CUBE(x);
11:    long z = THREE(x);
12:
13:    cout << "y: " << y << endl;
14:    cout << "z: " << z << endl;
15:
16:    long a = 5, b = 7;
17:    y = CUBE(a+b);
18:    z = THREE(a+b);
19:
20:    cout << "y: " << y << endl;
21:    cout << "z: " << z << endl;
22:    return 0;
23: }
```

Output ▼

```
y: 125
z: 125
y: 1728
z: 82
```

Analysis ▼

On line 4, the macro CUBE is defined, with the argument x put into parentheses each time it is used. On line 5, the macro THREE is defined, without using parentheses.

In the first use of these macros on lines 10 and 11, the value 5 is given as the parameter, and both macros work fine. CUBE(5) expands to ((5) * (5) * (5)), which evaluates to 125, and THREE(5) expands to 5 * 5 * 5, which also evaluates to 125.

In the second use, on lines 16–18, the parameter is 5 + 7. In this case, CUBE(5+7) evaluates to

```
( (5+7) * (5+7) * (5+7) )
```

which evaluates to

```
( (12) * (12) * (12) )
```

which, in turn, evaluates to 1728. THREE(5+7), however, evaluates to

```
5 + 7 * 5 + 7 * 5 + 7
```

Because multiplication has a higher precedence than addition, this becomes

```
5 + (7 * 5) + (7 * 5) + 7
```

which evaluates to

```
5 + (35) + (35) + 7
```

which finally evaluates to 82. As you can see, without the parenthesis, an error occurs—three of 5+7 is really 36!

How Macros and Poor Type Safety Go Hand-in-Hand

Let's get back to our previous simple macro function:

```
#define MAX(x,y) ( (x) > (y) ? (x) : (y) )
```

Evidently, this macro is designed to compare like types.

But because macros are only a text-replacement feature supplied by the preprocessor, there is no level of type safety or type checks performed on the nature of text (or variables) being processed by the macro.

In an ideal scenario, we would have liked to restrict a generic function in ways that it compares only like objects. In the pages to come, you'll see how templates help you do exactly that.

Macros Versus Functions and Templates

Macros suffer from four problems in C++. The first is that they can be confusing if they get large because all macros must be defined on one line. You can extend that line by using the backslash character (\), but larger macros quickly become difficult to manage.

The second problem is that macros are expanded inline each time they are used. This means that if a macro is used a dozen times, the substitution appears a dozen times in your program, rather than appearing once, as a function call does. On the other hand, they are usually quicker than a function call because the overhead of a function call is avoided.

The fact that they are expanded inline leads to the third problem, which is that the macro does not appear in the intermediate source code used by the compiler; therefore, it is unavailable in most debuggers. This makes debugging macros tricky.

The final problem, however, is the biggest: Macros are not type safe. Although it is convenient that absolutely any argument can be used with a macro, this completely undermines the strong typing of C++ and so is anathema to C++ programmers.

Inline Functions

It is often possible to declare an inline function rather than a macro. For example, Listing 15.2 creates an inline Cube() function, which accomplishes the same thing as the CUBE macro in the previous Listing 15.1, but it does so in a type-safe way.

LISTING 15.2 Using an Inline Function Instead of a Macro

```
0:  #include <iostream>
1:  using namespace std;
2:
3:  inline unsigned long Square(unsigned long a) { return a * a; }
4:  inline unsigned long Cube(unsigned long a)
5:     { return a * a * a; }
6:  int main()
7:  {
8:     unsigned long x=1 ;
9:     for (;;)
10:    {
11:       cout << "Enter a number (0 to quit): ";
12:       cin >> x;
13:       if (x == 0)
14:          break;
```

LISTING 15.2 Continued

```
15:        cout << "You entered: " << x;
16:        cout << ".  Square(" << x << "): ";
17:        cout  << Square(x);
18:        cout<< ".  Cube(" << x << "): ";
19:        cout << Cube(x) << "." << endl;
20:     }
21:     return 0;
22: }
```

Output ▼

```
Enter a number (0 to quit): 1
You entered: 1.  Square(1): 1. Cube(1): 1.
Enter a number (0 to quit): 2
You entered: 2.  Square(2): 4. Cube(2): 8.
Enter a number (0 to quit): 3
You entered: 3.  Square(3): 9. Cube(3): 27.
Enter a number (0 to quit): 4
You entered: 4.  Square(4): 16. Cube(4): 64.
Enter a number (0 to quit): 5
You entered: 5.  Square(5): 25. Cube(5): 125.
Enter a number (0 to quit): 6
You entered: 6.  Square(6): 36. Cube(6): 216.
Enter a number (0 to quit): 0
```

Analysis ▼

On lines 3 and 4, two inline functions are defined: `Square()` and `Cube()`. Each is declared to be inline, so like a macro function, these are expanded in place for each call and no function call overhead occurs.

As a reminder, expanded inline means that the content of the function is placed into the code wherever the function call is made (for example, on line 17). Because the function call is never made, there is no overhead of putting the return address and the parameters on the stack.

On line 17, the function `Square` is called, as is the function `Cube` on line 19. Again, because these are inline functions, it is exactly as if this line had been written like this:

```
16:        cout << ".  Square(" << x << "): "  ;
17:        cout << x * x ;
18:        cout << ".  Cube(" << x << "): " ;
19:        cout << x * x * x << "." << endl;
```

DO	DON'T
DO use CAPITALS for your macro names. This is a pervasive convention, and other programmers will be confused if you don't.	**DON'T** allow your macros to have side effects. Don't increment variables or assign values from within a macro.
DO surround all arguments with parentheses in macro functions.	**DON'T** use #define values when a constant variable will work.

An Introduction to Templates

Templates are probably one of the most powerful features of the C++ language that often are the least approached, or understood. Before we tackle with this matter, let's first look at the definition of a template as supplied by Webster's Dictionary:

Pronunciation: \'tem-plət\

Function: noun

Etymology: Probably from French templet, diminutive of temple, part of a loom, probably from Latin templum

Date: 1677

1: a short piece or block placed horizontally in a wall under a beam to distribute its weight or pressure (as over a door)

2 a (1): a gauge, pattern, or mold (as a thin plate or board) used as a guide to the form of a piece being made (2): a molecule (as of DNA) that serves as a pattern for the generation of another macromolecule (as messenger RNA) b: overlay

3: something that establishes or serves as a pattern

The last definition probably comes closest to the interpretation of the word *template* as used in the C++ parlance. Templates in C++ allow you to define a behavior that you can apply to objects of varying types. This sounds ominously close to what macros let you do (refer to the simple macro MAX that determined the greater of two numbers), save for the fact that macros are type unsafe and templates are type safe.

Template Declaration Syntax

You begin the declaration of a template using the `template` keyword followed by a type parameter list. The format of this declaration is

```
template <parameter list>
...template declaration..
```

Let's analyze a sample template declaration that is the equivalent of the previously discussed macro MAX:

```
template <typename objectType>
objectType & GetMax (const objectType & value1, const objectType & value2)
{
    if (value1 > value2)
        return value1;
    else
        return value2;
};
```

The keyword template marks the start of a template declaration and is followed by the template parameter list. This parameter list contains the typename keyword that defines the template parameter objectType, making it a placeholder for the type of the object that the template is being instantiated for. The template declaration is what contains the pattern that you want to implement.

Sample usage:

```
int nInteger1 = 25;
int nInteger2 = 40;
int nMaxValue = GetMax <int> (nInteger1, nInteger2);
double dDouble1  = 1.1;
double dDouble2 = 1.001;
double dMaxValue = GetMax <double> (nDouble1, nDouble2);
```

Note the detail <int> used in the call to GetMax. It effectively defines the template parameter objectType as int. The preceding code would lead to the compiler generating two versions of the template function GetMax that can be visualized as the following:

```
const int & GetMax (const int& value1, const int& value2)
{
    //...
}
const double & GetMax (const double& value1, const double& value2)
{
    // ...
}
```

In reality, however, template functions don't necessarily need an accompanying type specifier. So, the following function call would work perfectly well:

```
int nMaxValue = GetMax (nInteger1, nInteger2);
```

Compilers in this case are intelligent enough to understand that the template function is being invoked for the integer type. However, this is true only for template functions and not for classes.

The Different Types of Template Declarations

A template declaration can be

- A declaration or definition of a function (as you saw earlier)
- A declaration or definition of a class
- A definition of a member function or a member class of a class template
- A definition of a static data member of a class template
- A definition of a static data member of a class nested within a class template
- A definition of a member template of a class or class template

Template Classes

Template classes are the templatized versions of C++ classes that you've learned since Lesson 10, "Classes and Objects."

A simple template class that features a single template parameter T can be written as:

```
template <typename T>
class CMyFirstTemplateClass
{
public:
    void SetVariable (T& newValue) { m_Value = newValue; };

    T& GetValue () {return m_Value;};

private:
    T m_Value;
};
```

The class `CMyFirstTemplate` class has been designed to hold a variable of type `T`—the type of which is assigned at the time the template is used. So, let's look at a sample usage of this template class:

```
CMyFirstTemplate <int> mHoldInteger;  // Template instantiation
mHoldInteger.SetValue (5);
std::cout << "The value stored is: " << mHoldInteger.GetValue ();
```

We have used this template class to hold and retrieve an object of type `int`; that is, the `Template` class is instantiated for a template parameter of type `int`. Similarly, the same class can be used to deal with character strings, in a similar manner:

```
CMyFirstTemplate <char*> mHoldString;
mHoldInteger.SetValue ("Sample string");
std::cout << "The value stored is: " << mHoldInteger.GetValue ();
```

Thus, the class defines a pattern and gets reused for applying that same pattern it implements on different data types.

Template Instantiation and Specialization

15

The terminology changes a bit when it comes to templates. The word *instantiation,* when used in the context of classes, normally refers to *objects* as instances of *classes*.

In case of templates, however, *instantiation* is the act or *process* of creating a specific type from a template declaration and one or more template arguments.

So, if we look at a template declaration:

```
template <typename T>
class CTemplateClass
{
    T m_member;
};
```

When we use this template, we would write the code as

```
CTemplateClass <int> mIntTemplate;
```

The specific type created as a result of this instantiation is called a *specialization*.

Template and Type Safety

The template version of the MAX macro is type safe and a meaningless call to GetMax like this one

```
int nMaxValue = GetMax (nInteger, "Some string");
```

would immediately result in a compile failure, whereas the macro implementation MAX would compile it, probably even without a warning.

Declaring Templates with Multiple Parameters

The template parameter list can be expanded to declare multiple parameters separated by a comma. So, if you want to declare a generic class that holds a pair of objects that can be of differing types, you can do so using the construct as shown in the following sample (that displays a template class with two template parameters):

```
template <typename T1, typename T2>
class CHoldsPair
{
private:
    T1 m_Value1;
    T2 m_Value2;
```

```
public:
    // Constructor that initializes member variables
    CHoldsPair (const T1& value1, const T2& value2)
    {
        m_Value1 = value1;
        m_Value2 = value2;
    };
    // ... Other function declarations
};
```

In here, the class CHoldsPair accepts two template parameters named T1 and T2. We can use this class to hold two objects of the same type or of different types as you can see here:

```
// A template instantiation that pairs an int with a double
CHoldsPair <int, double> pairIntDouble (6, 1.99);

// A template instantiation that pairs an int with an int
CHoldsPair <int, int> pairIntDouble (6, 500);
```

Declaring Templates with Default Parameters

We could modify the previous version of CHoldsPair <...> to declare int as the default template parameter type.

```
template <typename T1=int, typename T2=int>
class CHoldsPair
{
    // ... Function declarations
};
```

This is quite similar in construction to functions that define default input parameter values except for the fact that, in this case, we define default *types*.

The second usage of CHoldsPair can thus be compacted to

```
// A template instantiation that pairs an int with an int (default type)
CHoldsPair <> pairIntDouble (6, 500);
```

A Template Sample

It's time to develop further on the template version of CHoldsPair that we've discussed so far, as Listing 15.3 demonstrates.

LISTING 15.3   Sample Usage of Template Class Defined in Listing 15.3

```
1:     // Template class with default template parameters
2: template <typename T1=int, typename T2=double>
3: class CHoldsPair
4: {
5: private:
6:     T1 m_Value1;
7:     T2 m_Value2;
8: public:
9:     // Constructor that initializes member variables
10:     CHoldsPair (const T1& value1, const T2& value2)
11:     {
12:         m_Value1 = value1;
13:         m_Value2 = value2;
14:     };
15:
16:     // Accessor functions
17:     const T1 & GetFirstValue ()
18:     {
19:         return m_Value1;
20:     };
21:
22:     const T2& GetSecondValue ()
23:     {
24:         return m_Value2;
25:     };
26: };
```

Analysis ▼

As you can see, we have a template parameter list in line 2 that defines two parameters with default types as int and double. Additionally, we also have accessor functions, GetFirstValue () and GetSecondValue(), that can be used to query the values held by the object. Doesn't this class already look like a framework that can be specialized to handle data of a type as decided by its user?

The following code in Listing 15.4 demonstrates exactly that.

LISTING 15.4   Sample Usage of the Template Class

```
1: // LISTING 15.4 - Sample Usage of the Template Class CHoldsPair
2: int main ()
3: {
4:     using namespace std;
5:
```

LISTING 15.4   Continued

```
 6:     // Two instantiations of template CHoldsPair -
 7:     CHoldsPair <> mIntFloatPair (300, 10.09);
 8:     CHoldsPair<short,char*>mShortStringPair(25,"Learn templates, love C++");
 9:
10:     // Output values contained in the first object...
11:     cout << "The first object contains -" << endl;
12:     cout << "Value 1: " << mIntFloatPair.GetFirstValue () << endl;
13:     cout << "Value 2: " << mIntFloatPair.GetSecondValue () << endl;
14:
15:     // Output values contained in the second object...
16:     cout << "The second object contains -" << endl;
17:     cout << "Value 1: " << mShortStringPair.GetFirstValue () << endl;
18:     cout << "Value 2: " << mShortStringPair.GetSecondValue ();
19:
20:     return 0;
21: }
```

Output ▼

```
The first object contains -
Value 1: 300
Value 2: 10.09
The second object contains -
Value 1: 25
Value 2: Learn templates, love C++
```

Analysis ▼

This simple program illustrates how to declare the template class CHoldsPair to hold a pair of values of types that are dependent on the template's parameter list. Note how accessor functions GetFirstValue and GetSecondValue get adapted on the basis of the template instantiation syntax to return the appropriate object types.

You have managed to define a pattern in CHoldsPair that can be reused to deliver the same logic for different variable types. Thus, templates increase code reusability.

Using Templates in Practical C++ Programming

The most important and powerful application of templates are in the standard template library (STL). STL comprises a collection of template classes and functions containing generic utility classes and algorithms. These STL template classes enable you to implement dynamic arrays, lists, and key-value pair containers, while algorithms such as sort work on those containers and process the data they contain.

The knowledge of template syntax you gained earlier will greatly assist you in using STL containers and functions that are presented in great detail in the following lessons of this book. A better understanding of STL containers and algorithms will in turn help you write efficient C++ applications that use STL's tested and reliable implementation, and help you avoid spending time in boilerplate details.

15

DO	DON'T
DO use templates whenever you have a concept that can operate across objects of different classes or across different primitive data types.	**DON'T** stop learning about templates. This lesson covered only some of what you can do with templates. Detailed coverage of templates is beyond the scope of this book.
DO use the parameters to template functions to narrow their instances to be type safe.	**DON'T** fret if you don't yet fully understand how to create your own templates. It is more immediately important to know how to use them.
DO specialize template behavior by overriding template functions by type.	

Summary

In this lesson, you learned more details about working with the preprocessor. Each time you run the compiler, the preprocessor runs first and translates directives such as `#define`.

The preprocessor does text substitution, although with the use of macros these can be somewhat complex. Macro functions provide complex text substitution based on arguments passed at compile time to the macro. It is important to put parentheses around every argument in the macro to ensure that the correct substitution takes place.

Templates help you write reusable code that supplies the developer with a pattern that can be used for a variety of data types. They also make for a type-safe replacement of macros. With the knowledge of templates gained in this lesson, you are now poised to learn to use the standard template library!

Q&A

Q **If C++ offers better alternatives than the preprocessor, why is this option still available?**

A First, C++ is backward-compatible with C and all significant parts of C must be supported in C++. Second, some uses of the preprocessor are still used frequently in C++, such as inclusion guards.

Q **Why use macro functions when I can use a regular function?**

A Macro functions are expanded inline and are used as a substitute for repeatedly typing the same commands with minor variations. Again, however, templates usually offer a better alternative.

Q **How do I know when to use a macro versus an inline function?**

A Use inline functions whenever possible. Although macros offer character substitution, "stringizing," and concatenation, they are not type safe and can make code that is more difficult to maintain.

Q **What is the alternative to using the preprocessor to print interim values during debugging?**

A The best alternative is to use watch (sometimes called *trace*) statements within a debugger. For information on watch statements, consult your compiler or debugger documentation.

Q **Why use templates when macros will do?**

A Templates are type safe and built in to the language, so they are checked by the compiler—at least when you instantiate the class to create a particular variable.

Q **What is the difference between the parameterized type of a template function and the parameters to a normal function?**

A A regular function (nontemplate) takes parameters on which it can take action. A template function enables you to parameterize the type of a particular parameter to the function. That is, you can pass an `Array` of `Type` to a function and then have the `Type` determined by the definition of the variable that is an instance of the class for a specific type.

Workshop

The Workshop provides quiz questions to help you solidify your understanding of the material covered and exercises to provide you with experience in using what you've learned. Try to answer the quiz and exercise questions before checking the answers in Appendix D, and be certain you understand the answers before going to the next lesson.

Quiz

1. What is an inclusion guard?
2. What is the difference between `#define debug 0` and `#undef debug`?

3. Consider the following macro:

```
#define HALVE(x) x / 2
```

What is the result if this is called with 4?

4. What is the result if the HALVE macro in Question 3 is called with 10+10?

5. How would you modify the HALVE macro to avoid erroneous results?

6. What is the difference between a template and a macro?

7. What is the difference between the parameter in a template and the parameter in a (nontemplate) function?

8. What does STL stand for and why is the STL important?

Exercises

1. Write a macro that adds two numbers.

2. Write a template version of the macro in Exercise 1.

3. Implement a template function for swap that exchanges two variables.

4. **BUG BUSTERS**: How would you improve the following macro that computes the quarter of an input value?

```
#define QUARTER(x) (x / 4)
```

5. Write a simple template class that holds two arrays of types that are defined via the class's template parameter list. The size of the array is 10, and the template class should have accessor functions that allow for the manipulation of array elements.

PART III:

Learning the Standard Template Library (STL)

LESSON 16
An Introduction to the Standard Template Library

Put in simple terms, the standard template library (STL) is a set of template classes and functions that supply the programmer with

- Containers for storing information
- Iterators for accessing the information stored
- Algorithms for manipulating the content of the containers

In this lesson, you will gain an overview on these three pillars of STL.

STL Containers

`Containers` are STL classes that are used to store data. STL supplies two types of container classes:

- Sequential containers
- Associative containers

Sequential Containers

As the name suggests, these are containers used to hold data in a sequential fashion, such as arrays and lists. Sequential containers are characterized by a fast insertion time, but are relatively slow in `find` operations.

The STL sequential containers are

- **`std::vector`**—Operates like a dynamic array and grows at the end
- **`std::deque`**—Similar to `std::vector` except that it allows for new elements to be inserted at the beginning, too
- **`std::list`**—Operates like a linked list

The STL `vector` class is akin to an array and allows for random access of an element; that is, you can directly access or manipulate an element in the `vector` given its position (index) using the `subscript operator []`. In addition to this, the STL `vector` is a dynamic array and therefore can resize itself to suit the application's runtime requirements. To keep the property of being able to randomly access an element in the array when given a position, most implementations of the STL `vector` keep all elements in contiguous locations. Therefore, a `vector` that needs to resize itself often can reduces the performance of the application, depending on the type of the object it contains.

The STL `list` can be thought of as STL's implementation of a regular linked list. Although elements in a `list` cannot be randomly accessed, as they can be in the STL `vector`, a `list` can organize elements in noncontiguous sections of memory. Therefore it does not have the performance issues that come up with a `vector` when the `vector` needs to reallocate its internal array.

Associative Containers

Associative containers are those that store data in a sorted fashion—akin to a dictionary. This results in slower insertion times, but presents significant advantages when it comes to searching.

The associative containers supplied by STL are

- **std::set**—A sorted list of unique values.

- **std::map**—Stores key-value pairs sorted by their unique keys.

- **std::multiset**—Akin to a set. Additionally, supports the ability to store multiple items having the same value; that is, the value doesn't need to be unique.

- **std::multimap**—Akin to a map. Additionally, supports the ability to store key-value pairs where keys don't need to be unique.

The sort criteria of STL containers can be customized by programming predicate functions.

16

TIP

Some implementations of STL also feature associative containers such as hash_set, hash_multiset, hash_map, and hash_multimap. These containers claim to be even better at searching for an element in the sense that many offer constant time access independent of the size of the container, in comparison to the standard-compliant versions that feature an increase in time to access elements proportional to the logarithm of the number of elements in the container. Typically, these containers also present public functions that are identical to those supplied by their standard counterparts and hence are as easy to use.

Note that using standard-compliant containers results in code that is easier to port across platforms and compilers. It is also possible that the logarithmic reduction in performance of a standard-compliant container might not significantly affect your application.

Choosing the Right Container

Clearly, your application might have requirements that can be satisfied by more than one STL container. There is a selection to be made, and this selection is important because a wrong choice could result in a functional application that under-performs.

Therefore, it is important to evaluate the advantages and disadvantages of the containers before selecting one. See Table 16.1 for more details.

TABLE 16.1 Properties of STL's Container Classes

Container	Container Type	Advantages	Disadvantages
std::vector	Sequential	Quick (constant time) insertion at the end.	Resizing can result in performance loss.
		Array-like access.	Search time is proportional to the number of elements in the container.
			Insertion only at the end.
std::deque	Sequential	All advantages of the vector, in addition to allowing for constant-time insertion at the beginning of the container.	All disadvantages of the vector are also applicable to the deque.
			Unlike the vector, the deque by specification does not need to feature the reserve() function that allows the programmer to reserve memory space to be used as a vector—a feature that avoids frequent resizing to improve performance.
std::list	Sequential	Constant time insertion at the front, middle, or end of the list.	Elements cannot be accessed randomly given an index as in an array.
		Removal of elements from a list is a constant-time activity regardless of the position of the element.	Search can be slower than the vector because elements are not stored in adjacent memory locations.
		Insertion or removal of elements does not invalidate iterators that point to other elements in the list.	Search time is proportional to the number of elements in the container.
std::set	Associative	Search is not directly proportional to the number of elements in the container and hence is often significantly faster than sequential containers.	Insertion of elements is slower than in sequential counterparts.

TABLE 16.1 Continued

Container	Container Type	Advantages	Disadvantages
`std::multiset`	Associative	Advantages similar to that of the `std::set`.	Disadvantages similar to that of a `std::set`.
		To be used when requirements necessitate storage of nonunique elements in a sorted container.	
`std::map`	Associative	Key-value pair's container that sorts on the basis of the key.	
		Search is not directly proportional to the number of elements in the container and hence often significantly faster than sequential containers.	
`std::multimap`	Associative	Advantages similar to that of the `std::map`.	Disadvantages similar to that of `std::map`.
		To be selected over `std::map` when requirements necessitate the need of a key-value pairs container that holds elements with nonunique keys.	

16

STL Iterators

The simplest example of an iterator is a pointer. Given a pointer to the first element in an array, you can increment it and point to the next element or, in many cases, manipulate the element at that location.

Iterators in STL are template classes that in some ways are generalization of pointers. These are template classes that give the programmer a handle by which he can work with and manipulate STL containers and perform operations on them. Note that operations could as well be STL algorithms that are template functions, Iterators are the bridge that allows these template functions to work with containers, which are template classes, in a consistent and seamless manner.

Iterators supplied by STL can be broadly classified into the following:

- **Input iterator**—One that can be dereferenced to reference an object. The object can be in a collection, for instance. Input iterators of the purest kinds guarantee read access only.

- **Output iterator**—One that allows the programmer to write to the collection. Output iterators of the strictest types guarantee write access only.

The basic iterator types mentioned in the preceding list are further refined into the following:

- **Forward iterator**—A refinement of the input and output iterators allowing both input and output. Forward iterators may be constant, allowing for read-only access to the object the iterator points to, and otherwise allow for both read and write operations, making it mutable. A forward iterator would typically find use in a singly linked list.

- **Bidirectional iterator**—A refinement of the forward iterator in that it can be decremented to move backward as well. A bidirectional iterator would typically find use in a doubly linked list.

- **Random access iterators**—In general, a refinement over the concept of bidirectional iterators that allow addition and subtraction of offsets or allow one iterator to be subtracted from another to find the relative separation or distance between the two objects in a collection. A random iterator would typically find use in an array.

NOTE	At an implementation level, a `refinement` can be thought of as an `inheritance` or a `specialization`.

STL Algorithms

Finding, sorting, reversing, and the like are standard programming requirements that should not require the programmer to reinvent implementation to support. This is precisely why STL supplies these functions in the form of STL algorithms that work well with containers using iterators to help the programmer with some of the most common requirements.

Some of the most used STL algorithms are

- `std::find`—Helps find a value in a collection
- `std::find_if`—Helps find a value in a collection on the basis of a specific user-defined predicate

- **std::reverse**—Reverses a collection
- **std::remove_if**—Helps remove an item from a collection on the basis of a user-defined predicate
- **std::transform**—Helps apply a user-defined transformation function to elements in a container

These algorithms are template functions in the std namespace and require that the standard header <algorithm> be included.

16

The Interaction Between Containers and Algorithms Using Iterators

Let's examine how iterators seamlessly connect containers and the STL algorithms using an example. The program shown in Listing 16.1 uses the STL sequential container std::vector, which is akin to a dynamic array. This array is used to store integer values, and the program finds one in the collection using the algorithm std::find. Note how iterators form the bridge connecting algorithms to the containers they operate on.

LISTING 16.1   Find an Element and Its Position in a Vector

```
1: #include <iostream>
2: #include <vector>
3: #include <algorithm>
4: using namespace std;
5:
6: int main ()
7: {
8:     // A dynamic array of integers
9:     vector <int> vecIntegerArray;
10:
11:     // Insert sample integers into the array
12:     vecIntegerArray.push_back (50);
13:     vecIntegerArray.push_back (2991);
14:     vecIntegerArray.push_back (23);
15:     vecIntegerArray.push_back (9999);
16:
17:     cout << "The contents of the vector are: " << endl;
18:
19:     // Walk the vector and read values using an iterator
20:     vector <int>::iterator iArrayWalker = vecIntegerArray.begin ();
21:
22:     while (iArrayWalker != vecIntegerArray.end ())
23:     {
```

LISTING 16.1   Continued

```
24:        // Write the value to the screen
25:        cout << *iArrayWalker << endl;
26:
27:        // Increment the iterator to access the next element
28:        ++ iArrayWalker;
29:    }
30:
31:    // Find an element (say 2991) in the array using the 'find' algorithm...
32:    vector <int>::iterator iElement = find (vecIntegerArray.begin ()
33:                        ,vecIntegerArray.end (), 2991);
34:
35:    // Check if value was found
36:    if (iElement != vecIntegerArray.end ())
37:    {
38:        // Value was found... Determine position in the array:
39:        int nPosition = distance (vecIntegerArray.begin (), iElement);
40:        cout << "Value "<< *iElement;
41:        cout << " found in the vector at position: " << nPosition << endl;
42:    }
43:
44:    return 0;
45: }
```

Output ▼

```
The contents of the vector are:
50
2991
23
9999
Value 2991 found in the vector at position: 1
```

Analysis ▼

Listing 16.1 displays the use of iterators in walking through the vector and as interfaces that help connect algorithms such as find to containers like vector that contains the data on which the algorithm is meant to operate. The iterator object iArrayWalker is declared in line 20 and is initialized to the beginning of the container; that is, the vector using the return value of the member function begin(). Lines 22–29 demonstrate how this iterator is used in a loop to locate and display the elements contained in the vector, in a manner that is quite similar to how one can display the contents of a static array. The usage of the iterator is quite consistent across all STL containers. They all feature a function begin() that points to the first element, and a function end() that points to the end of the container after the last element. This also explains why the while loop in line 22 stops at the element before `end()` and not with `end()`. Line 32 demonstrates how `find` is used to locate a value in the `vector`. The result of the `find` operation is an iterator as well, and the success of the `find` is tested by comparing the iterator against the end of the container, as seen in line 36. If an element is found, it can be displayed by dereferencing that iterator (such as how one would dereference a pointer). The algorithm `distance` is applied by computing the offset position of the element found.

NOTE

You will learn the `std::vector` in detail in Lesson 18, "STL Dynamic Array Classes," and STL algorithms in Lesson 23, "STL Algorithms."

16

Summary

In this lesson, you learned the concepts on which STL containers, iterators, and algorithms are based. These three elements are probably the most important of STL, and a thorough understanding of the concepts behind them will help you in the efficient use of STL in your application. Lessons 17 through 25 explain the implementation of these concepts and their application in greater detail.

Q&A

Q I need to use an array. I don't know the number of elements it needs to contain. What STL container should I use?

A A `std::vector` or a `std::deque` is perfectly suited to this requirement. Both manage memory and can dynamically scale themselves to an application's increasing requirements.

Q My application has a requirement that involves frequent searches. What kind of container should I choose?

A An associative container is most suited to requirements that involve frequent searches.

Q I need to store key-value pairs for quick lookup. However, the situation can result in multiple keys that are not unique. What container should I choose?

A An associative container of type `std::multimap` is suited to this requirement. A `multimap` can hold nonunique key-value pairs, and can offer a quick lookup that is characteristic of associative containers.

Q **An application needs to be ported across platforms and compilers. There is a requirement for a container that helps in a quick lookup based on a key. Should I use `std::map` or `std::hash_map`?**

A Portability is an important constraint and using standard-compliant containers is necessary. `std::map` is the container to choose.

Workshop

The Workshop contains quiz questions to help solidify your understanding of the material covered and exercises to provide you with experience in using what you've learned. Try to answer the quiz and exercise questions before checking the answers in Appendix D, and be certain you understand the answers before going to the next lesson.

Quiz

1. What would be your choice of a container that has to contain an array of objects with insertion possible at the top and at the bottom?

2. You need to store elements for quick lookup. What container would you choose?

3. You need to store elements in a `std::set` but still have the storage and lookup criteria altered, based on conditions that are not necessarily the value of the elements. Is this possible?

4. What part of STL helps connect algorithms to containers so that algorithms can work on those elements?

5. Would you choose to use container `hash_set` in an application that needs to be ported to different platforms and built using different C++ compilers?

LESSON 17
The STL string Class

The standard template library (STL) supplies the programmer with a container class that aids in string operations and manipulations. The `string` class not only dynamically resizes itself to cater to the application's requirement but also supplies useful helper functions/methods that help manipulate the string and work using it. Thus, it helps programmers make use of standard, portable, and tested functionality in their applications and focus time on developing features that are critical to it.

In this lesson, you will learn

- The need for string manipulation classes
- Working with the STL `string` class
- The template-based implementation of the STL `string`

The Need for String Manipulation Classes

In C++, a `string` is an array of characters. As you saw in Lesson 3, "Using Variables, Declaring Constants," the simplest character array can be defined as following:

```
char pszName [20];
```

This is the declaration of a character array (or `string`) of 20 elements. As you see, this buffer can hold a `string` of limited length and would soon be overrun if you tried to hold a greater number of characters in it. Resizing this statically allocated array is not possible. To overcome this constraint, C++ supplies dynamic allocation of data. Therefore, a more dynamic representation of a `string` array is

```
char* pszName = new char [nArrayLength];
```

You now have a dynamically allocated character array that can be instantiated to the length as stored in the value `nArrayLength`, determinable at runtime, and hence can be allocated to hold a data of variable length. However, should you want to change the length of the array at runtime, you would first have to deallocate the allocated memory earlier and then reallocate to hold the required data.

Things will get more complicated if these strings implemented as character arrays are present as member attributes of a class. In situations where an object of this class is to be copied into another, in the absence of a well-programmed copy constructor and assignment operator, you would probably end up in a scenario where objects of the class, when copied, will result in pointer addresses of the member strings getting copies. With two string pointers in two objects pointing to the same location in memory, the destruction of the source object would result in the pointer in the destination object being invalid.

Using string classes instead of plain character arrays or pointers solves these issues for you. The STL `string` class `std::string` thus helps you in the following ways:

- Reduces the effort of creation and manipulating strings
- Increases the stability of the application being programmed by internally managing memory allocation details
- Supplies copy constructor and assignment operators that automatically ensure that member strings get correctly copied
- Supplies useful utility functions that help in copying, truncating, finding, and erasing to name a few

- Provides operators that help in comparisons
- Focuses efforts on your application's primary requirements rather than on string manipulation details

You will soon learn of some useful helper functions that the string class supplies.

Working with the STL string Class

The most commonly used string functions are

- Copying.
- Concatenating.
- Finding characters and substrings.
- Truncating.
- String reversal and case conversions are achieved using algorithms provided by the standard library.

To use the STL string class, you must include the header <string>.

Instantiating the STL string and Making Copies

The string class features many overloaded constructors and therefore can be instantiated and initialized in many different ways. For example, simply initialize and assign a constant character string to a regular STL string object:

```
const char* pszConstString = "Hello String!";
std::string strFromConst (pszConstString);
```

or

```
std::string strFromConst = pszConstString;
```

The preceding is quite similar to

```
std::string str2 ("Hello String!");
```

As is apparent, instantiating a string object and initializing it to a value did not require supplying the length of the string or the memory allocation details—the constructor of the STL string class automatically did this.

Similarly, it is possible to use one string object to initialize another:

```
std::string str2Copy (str2);
```

17

You can also instruct the `string` constructor to accept only the first *n* characters of the supplied input string:

```
// Initialize a string to the first 5 characters of another
std::string strPartialCopy (pszConstString, 5);
```

You can also initialize a `string` to contain a specific number of instances of a particular character:

```
// Initialize a string object to contain 10 'a's
std::string strRepeatChars (10, 'a');
```

LISTING 17.1   STL string Instantiation and Copy Techniques

```
 1: #include <string>
 2: #include <iostream>
 3:
 4: int main ()
 5: {
 6:    using namespace std;
 7:    const char* pszConstString = "Hello String!";
 8:    cout << "Constant string is: " << pszConstString << endl;
 9:
10:    std::string strFromConst (pszConstString);
11:    cout << "strFromConst is: " << strFromConst << endl;
12:
13:     std::string str2 ("Hello String!");
14:    std::string str2Copy (str2);
15:    cout << "str2Copy is: " << str2Copy << endl;
16:
17:    // Initialize a string to the first 5 characters of another
18:    std::string strPartialCopy (pszConstString, 5);
19:    cout << "strPartialCopy is: " << strPartialCopy << endl;
20:
21:    // Initialize a string object to contain 10 'a's
22:    std::string strRepeatChars (10, 'a');
23:    cout << "strRepeatChars is: " << strRepeatChars << endl;
24:
25:    return 0;
26: }
```

Output ▼

```
Constant string is: Hello String!
strFromConst is: Hello String!
str2Copy is: Hello String!
strPartialCopy is: Hello
strRepeatChars is: aaaaaaaaaa
```

Analysis ▼

The preceding code sample displays how you can instantiate a STL string object and initialize it to another string; that is, copy a part of another string and create a partial copy or initialize it to a set of recurring characters. pszConstString is a C-style character string that contains a sample value, initialized in line 7. Line 10 displays how easy it is with std::string to create a copy using the constructor. Line 13 copies another constant string into a std::string object str2, and line 14 demonstrates how std::string has another overloaded constructor that allows you to copy a std::string object, to get str2Copy. Line 18 demonstrates how partial copies can be achieved and line 22 how a std::string can be instantiated and initialized to contain repeating occurrences of the same character. This code sample was just a small demonstration of how std::string and its numerous copy constructors make it easy for a programmer to create strings, copy them, and display them.

Note that if you were to use C-style strings to copy another of the same kind, the equivalent of line 10 would be this:

17

```
const char* pszConstString = "Hello World!"; // To be copied

// To create a copy, first allocate memory for one...
char * pszCopy = new char [strlen (pszConstString) + 1];
strcpy (pszCopy, pszConstString);  // The copy step

// deallocate memory after using pszCopy
delete [] pszCopy;
```

As you can see, this needs many more lines of code, increases the probability of introducing errors, and also needs you to worry about memory management and deallocations. The STL string does all this for you, and more!

Accessing a string and Its Contents

The character contents of an STL string can be accessed via iterators or via an array-like syntax where the offset is supplied, using the subscript operator []. A C-style representation of the string can be obtained via member function c_str (). See Listing 17.2.

LISTING 17.2   Accessing Character Elements of an STL String

```
1: #include <string>
2: #include <iostream>
3:
4: int main ()
5: {
```

LISTING 17.2 Continued

```
 6:    using namespace std;
 7:
 8:     // The sample string
 9:    string strSTLString ("Hello String");
10:
11:     // Access the contents of the string using array syntax
12:    cout << "Displaying characters using array-syntax: " << endl;
13:    for ( size_t nCharCounter = 0
14:        ; nCharCounter < strSTLString.length ()
15:        ; ++ nCharCounter )
16:    {
17:       cout << "Character [" << nCharCounter << "] is: ";
18:       cout << strSTLString [nCharCounter] << endl;
19:    }
20:    cout << endl;
21:
22:     // Access the contents of a string using iterators
23:    cout << "Displaying characters using iterators: " << endl;
24:    int nCharOffset = 0;
25:    string::const_iterator iCharacterLocator;
26:    for ( iCharacterLocator = strSTLString.begin ()
27:        ; iCharacterLocator != strSTLString.end ()
28:        ; ++ iCharacterLocator )
29:    {
30:       cout << "Character [" << nCharOffset ++ << "] is: ";
31:        cout << *iCharacterLocator << endl;
32:    }
33:    cout << endl;
34:
35:     // Access the contents of a string as a C-style string
36:    cout << "The char* representation of the string is: ";
37:    cout << strSTLString.c_str () << endl;
38:
39:    return 0;
40: }
```

Output ▼

```
Displaying the elements in the string using array-syntax:
Character [0] is: H
Character [1] is: e
Character [2] is: l
Character [3] is: l
Character [4] is: o
Character [5] is:
Character [6] is: S
Character [7] is: t
```

```
Character [8] is: r
Character [9] is: i
Character [10] is: n
Character [11] is: g

Displaying the contents of the string using iterators:
Character [0] is: H
Character [1] is: e
Character [2] is: l
Character [3] is: l
Character [4] is: o
Character [5] is:
Character [6] is: S
Character [7] is: t
Character [8] is: r
Character [9] is: i
Character [10] is: n
Character [11] is: g

The char* representation of the string is: Hello String
```

17

Analysis ▼

The code displays the multiple ways of accessing the contents of a string. Iterators are important in the sense that many of the string's member function return their results in the form of iterators. Lines 12–19 display the characters in the string using array-like semantics via the subscript operator [], implemented by the std::string class. Note that this operator needs you to supply the offset as seen in line 18. Therefore, it is very important that you do not cross the bounds of the string; that is, you do not read a character at an offset beyond the length of the string. Lines 26–32 also print the content of the string character-by-character, but they use iterators.

String Concatenation

String concatenation can be achieved by using either the += operator or the append member function. See Listing 17.3.

LISTING 17.3   Concatenate Using STL string

```
1: #include <string>
2: #include <iostream>
3:
4: int main ()
5: {
```

LISTING 17.3   Continued

```
 6:    using namespace std;
 7:
 8:    string strSample1 ("Hello");
 9:    string strSample2 (" String!");
10:
11:    // Concatenate
12:    strSample1 += strSample2;
13:    cout << strSample1 << endl << endl;
14:
15:    string strSample3 (" Fun is not needing to use pointers!");
16:    strSample1.append (strSample3);
17:    cout << strSample1 << endl << endl;
18:
19:    const char* pszConstString = "You however still can!";
20:    strSample1.append (pszConstString);
21:    cout << strSample1 << endl;
22:
23:    return 0;
24: }
```

Output ▼

```
Hello String!
Hello String! Fun is not needing to use pointers!

Hello String! Fun is not needing to use pointers when working with strings. You
however still can!
```

Analysis ▼

Lines 12, 16, and 20 display different methods of concatenating to an STL string. Note the use of the += operator and the capability of the append function, which has many overloads, to accept another string object (as shown in line 11) and to accept a C-style character string.

Finding a Character or Substring in a string

The STL string supplies a find member function with a few overloaded versions that help find a character or a substring in a given string object. Listing 17.4 demonstrates the utility of this member function.

LISTING 17.4   Using the string::find Function

```
 1: #include <string>
 2: #include <iostream>
 3:
 4: int main ()
 5: {
 6:     using namespace std;
 7:
 8:     string strSample ("Good day String! Today is beautiful!");
 9:     cout << "The sample string is: " << endl;
10:     cout << strSample << endl << endl;
11:
12:     // Find substring "day" in it...
13:     size_t nOffset = strSample.find ("day", 0);
14:
15:     // Check if the substring was found...
16:     if (nOffset != string::npos)
17:         cout << "First instance of \"day\" was found at offset " << nOffset;
18:     else
19:         cout << "Substring not found." << endl;
20:
21:     cout << endl << endl;
22:
23:     cout << "Locating all instances of substring \"day\"" << endl;
24:     size_t nSubstringOffset = strSample.find ("day", 0);
25:
26:     while (nSubstringOffset != string::npos)
27:     {
28:         cout << "\"day\" found at offset " << nSubstringOffset << endl;
29:
30:     // Make the 'find' function search the next character onwards
31:         size_t nSearchOffset = nSubstringOffset + 1;
32:
33:         nSubstringOffset = strSample.find ("day", nSearchOffset);
34:     }
35:
36:     cout << endl;
37:
38:     cout << "Locating all instances of character 'a'" << endl;
39:     const char chCharToSearch = 'a';
40:     size_t nCharacterOffset = strSample.find (chCharToSearch, 0);
41:
42:     while (nCharacterOffset != string::npos)
43:     {
44:         cout << "'" << chCharToSearch << "' found";
45:         cout << " at position: " << nCharacterOffset << endl;
46:
47:     // Make the 'find' function search forward from the next character
onwards
```

17

LISTING 17.4   Continued

```
48:           size_t nCharSearchOffset = nCharacterOffset + 1;
49:
50:    nCharacterOffset = strSample.find(chCharToSearch,nCharSearchOffset);
51:    }
52:
53:    return 0;
54: }
```

Output ▼

```
The sample string is:
Good day String! Today is beautiful!

First instance of "day" was found at offset 5

Locating all instances of substring "day"
"day" found at offset 5
"day" found at offset 19

Locating all instances of character 'a'
'a' found at position: 6
'a' found at position: 20
'a' found at position: 28
```

Analysis ▼

Lines 13–19 display the simplest usage of the find function where it ascertains whether a particular substring is found in a string. This is done by comparing the result of the find operation against std::string::npos (that is actually −1) and indicates that the element searched for has not been found. When the find function does not return npos, it returns the offset that indicates the position of the substring or character in the string.

The code thereafter indicates how find can be used in a while loop to locate all instances of a character or a substring in an STL string. The overloaded version of the find function used here accepts two parameters: the substring or character to search for and the search offset that indicates the point from which find should search.

NOTE

The STL string also features functions akin to find, such as find_first_of, find_first_not_of, find_last_of, and find_last_not_of, which assist the programmer further in his programming requirements.

Truncating an STL `string`

The STL `string` features a function called `erase` that can erase:

- A number of characters when given an offset position and count
- A character when supplied with an iterator pointing to it
- A number of characters given a range supplied by two iterators that bind the same

The sample that follows in Listing 17.5 demonstrates different applications of the overloaded versions of `string::erase()` function.

LISTING 17.5   Using the `erase` Member Function to Truncate a String

```
 1: #include <string>
 2: #include <algorithm>
 3: #include <iostream>
 4:
 5: int main ()
 6: {
 7:     using namespace std;
 8:
 9:     string strSample ("Hello String! Wake up to a beautiful day!");
10:     cout << "The original sample string is: " << endl;
11:     cout << strSample << endl << endl;
12:
13:     // Delete characters from the string given position and count
14:     cout << "Truncating the second sentence: " << endl;
15:     strSample.erase (13, 28);
16:     cout << strSample << endl << endl;
17:
18:     // Find a character 'S' in the string using STL find algorithm
19:     string::iterator iCharS = find ( strSample.begin ()
20:                               , strSample.end (), 'S');
21:
22:     // If character found, 'erase' to deletes a character
23:     cout << "Erasing character 'S' from the sample string:" << endl;
24:     if (iCharS != strSample.end ())
25:         strSample.erase (iCharS);
26:
27:     cout << strSample << endl << endl;
28:
29:     // Erase a range of characters using an overloaded version of erase()
30:     cout << "Erasing a range between begin() and end(): " << endl;
31:     strSample.erase (strSample.begin (), strSample.end ());
32:
33:     // Verify the length after the erase() operation above
34:     if (strSample.length () == 0)
```

17

LISTING 17.5 Continued

```
35:        cout << "The string is empty" << endl;
36:
37:    return 0;
38: }
```

Output ▼

```
The original sample string is:
Hello String! Wake up to a beautiful day!

Truncating the second sentence:
Hello String!

Erasing character 'S' from the sample string:
Hello tring!

Erasing a range between begin() and end():
The string is empty
```

Analysis ▼

The listing indicates the three versions of the `erase` function. One version erases a set of characters when supplied a staring offset and count, as shown in line 15. Another version erases a specific character given an iterator that points to it, as shown in line 25. The final version erases a range of characters given a couple of iterators that supply the bounds of this range, as shown in line 31. As the bounds of this range are supplied by `begin()` and `end ()` member functions of the `string` that effectively include all the contents of the string, calling an `erase()` on this range clears the string object of its contents. Note that the `string` class also supplies a `clear ()` function that effectively clears the internal buffer and resets the `string` object.

String Reversal

Sometimes it is important to reverse the contents of a string. Say you want to determine whether the string input by the user is a palindrome. STL strings can be reversed easily using the `std::reverse` algorithm, as seen in Listing 17.6.

LISTING 17.6 Reversing an STL String

```
1: #include <string>
2: #include <iostream>
3: #include <algorithm>
4:
```

LISTING 17.6 Continued

```
 5: int main ()
 6: {
 7:     using namespace std;
 8:
 9:     string strSample ("Hello String! We will reverse you!");
10:     cout << "The original sample string is: " << endl;
11:     cout << strSample << endl << endl;
12:
13:     reverse (strSample.begin (), strSample.end ());
14:
15:     cout << "After applying the std::reverse algorithm: " << endl;
16:      cout << strSample;
17:
18:     return 0;
19:
20: }
```

Output ▼

```
The original sample string is:
Hello String! We will reverse you!

After applying the std::reverse algorithm:
!uoy esrever lliw eW !gnirtS olleH
```

Analysis ▼

The `std::reverse` algorithm used in line 13 works on the bounds of the container that are supplied to it using the two input parameters. In this case, these bounds are the starting and the ending bounds of the `string` object, and therefore reverse the contents of the entire string. It would also be possible to reverse a string in parts by supplying the appropriate bounds as input. Note that the bounds should never exceed `end()`.

String Case Conversion

String case conversion can be effected using the algorithm `std::transform`, which applies a user-specified function to every element of a collection. In this case, the collection is the `string` object itself. The sample in Listing 17.7 shows how to switch the case of characters in a `string`.

LISTING 17.7   Performing Case Conversions on an STL String Using `std::transform`

```
1: #include <string>
2: #include <iostream>
3: #include <algorithm>
4:
5: int main ()
6: {
7:    using namespace std;
8:
9:    cout << "Please enter a string for case-conversion:" << endl;
10:    cout << "> ";
11:
12:    string strInput;
13:    getline (cin, strInput);
14:    cout << endl;
15:
16:    transform (strInput.begin(),strInput.end(),strInput.begin(),toupper);
17:    cout << "The string converted to upper case is: " << endl;
18:    cout << strInput << endl << endl;
19:
20:    transform (strInput.begin(),strInput.end(),strInput.begin(),tolower);
21:    cout << "The string converted to lower case is: " << endl;
22:    cout << strInput << endl << endl;
23:
24:    return 0;
25: }
```

Output ▼

```
Please enter a string for case-conversion:
> ConverT thIS StrINg!

The string converted to upper case is:
CONVERT THIS STRING!

The string converted to lower case is:
convert this string!
```

Analysis ▼

Lines 12 and 15 demonstrate how efficiently `std::transform` can be used to change the case of the contents of an STL string.

Template-Based Implementation of an STL `string`

The `std::string` class, as you have learned, is actually a specialization of the STL template class `std::basic_string <T>`. The template declaration of container class `basic_string` is as follows:

```
template<class _Elem,
    class _Traits,
    class _Ax>
    class basic_string
```

In this template definition, the parameter of utmost importance is the first one: `_Elem`. This is the type collected by the `basic_string` object. The `std::string` is therefore the template specialization of `basic_string` for `_Elem=char`, whereas the `wstring` is the template specialization of `basic_string` for `_Elem=wchar_t`.

17

In other words, the STL `string` class is defined as

```
typedef basic_string<char, char_traits<char>, allocator<char> >
    string;
```

and the STL `wstring` class is defined as

```
typedef basic_string<wchar_t, char_traits<wchar_t>, allocator<wchar_t> >
    string;
```

So, all string features and functions studied so far are actually those supplied by `basic_string`, and are therefore also applicable to the STL `wstring` class.

Summary

In this lesson, you learned that the STL `string` class is a container supplied by the standard template library that helps the programmer with many string manipulation requirements. The advantage of using this class is apparent in that the need for the programmer to implement memory management, string comparison, and string manipulation functions is taken care of by a container class supplied by the STL framework.

Q&A

Q **I need to reverse a string using `std::reverse`. What header has to be included for me to be able to use this function?**

A `<algorithm>` is the header that needs to be included for `std::reverse` to be available.

Q **What role does `std::transform` play in converting a string to lowercase using `tolower ()` function?**

A `std::transform` invokes `tolower ()` for the characters in the `string` object that are within the bounds supplied to the transform function.

Q **Why do `std::wstring` and `std::string` feature exactly the same behavior and member functions?**

A They do so because they are both template specializations of the template class `std::basic_string`.

Q **Does the comparison operator `<` of the STL `string` class produce results that are case sensitive or not case sensitive?**

A The results are based on a case-sensitive comparison.

Workshop

The Workshop contains quiz questions to help solidify your understanding of the material covered and exercises to provide you with experience in using what you've learned. Try to answer the quiz and exercise questions before checking the answers in Appendix D, and be certain you understand the answers before going to the next lesson.

Quiz

1. What STL template class does the `std::string` specialize?
2. If you were to perform a case-insensitive comparison of two strings, how would you do it?
3. Are the STL string and a C-style string similar?

Exercises

1. Write a program to verify whether the word input by the user is a palindrome. For example: ATOYOTA is a palindrome, as the word does not change when reversed.
2. Write a program that tells the user the number of vowels in a sentence.
3. Convert every alternate character of a string into uppercase.
4. Your program should have four string objects that are initialized to "I", "Love", "STL", "String." Append them with a space in between and display the sentence.

LESSON 18
STL Dynamic Array Classes

Dynamic arrays supply the programmer with the flexibility of storing data without needing to know the exact volume thereof at the time of programming the application, the way static arrays do. Naturally, this is a frequently needed requirement and the standard template library (STL) supplies a ready-to-use solution in the form of the `std::vector` class.

In this lesson, you will learn

- The characteristics of `std::vector`

- Typical `vector` operations

- Understanding the concept of size and capacity

- The STL deque class

The Characteristics of `std::vector`

`vector` is a template class that supplies generic functionality of a dynamic array and features the following characteristics:

- Addition of elements to the end of the array in constant time; that is, the time needed to insert at the end is not dependent on the size of the array. Ditto for removal of an element at the end.

- The time required for the insertion or removal of elements at the middle is directly proportional to the number of elements behind the element being removed.

- The number of elements held is dynamic and the `vector` class manages the memory usage.

A *vector* is a dynamic array that can be visualized as seen in Figure 18.1.

FIGURE 18.1
The internals of a vector.

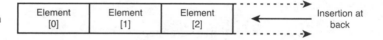

To use the `std::vector` class, you need to include the following header:

```
#include <vector>
```

Typical Vector Operations

The behavioral specifications and public members of the `std::vector` class are defined by the C++ standard. Consequently, operations on the `vector` that you will learn in this lesson are supported by a variety of C++ programming platforms that are standard compliant.

Instantiating a `vector`

A `vector` is a template class that needs to be instantiated in accordance with template instantiation techniques that we studied in Lesson 15, "An Introduction to Macros and Templates." The template instantiation of `vector` needs to specify the type of object that you want to `collect` in this dynamic array. This complicated-sounding procedure is actually quite simple as seen in Listing 18.1.

LISTING 18.1   Instantiating a std::vector

```
1: #include <vector>
2:
3: int main ()
4: {
5:     std::vector <int> vecDynamicIntegerArray;
6:
7:     // Instantiate a vector with 10 elements (it can grow larger)
8:     std::vector <int> vecArrayWithTenElements (10);
9:
10:    // Instantiate a vector with 10 elements, each initialized to 90
11:    std::vector <int> vecArrayWithTenInitializedElements (10, 90);
12:
13:    // Instantiate one vector and initialize it to the contents of another
14:    std::vector <int> vecArrayCopy (vecArrayWithTenInitializedElements);
15:
16:    // Instantiate a vector to 5 elements taken from another
17:    std::vector<int> vecSomeElementsCopied(vecArrayWithTenElements.begin()
18:                                  , vecArrayWithTenElements.begin () + 5);
19:
20:    return 0;
21: }
```

Analysis ▼

The preceding code features a template specialization of the vector class for type integer, or in other words, it instantiates a vector of integers. This vector, named vecDynamicIntegerArray, uses the default constructor that is quite useful when you do not know the minimal size requirements of the container; that is, when you do not know how many integers you wish to hold in it. The second and third forms of vector instantiation as seen in lines 11 and 14 are ones in which the programmer knows that he needs a vector that contains at least 10 elements. Note that this does not limit the ultimate size of the container, rather just sets the initializing size. The fourth form in lines 17 and 18 is the one in which a vector can be used to instantiate the contents of another; that is, to create one vector object that is the copy of another, or a part thereof. This is also a construct that works for all STL containers. The last form is the one that uses iterators. vecSomeElementsCopied contains the first five elements from vecArrayWithTenElements.

18

> **NOTE**
>
> The fourth construct can work only with objects of like types. So, you could instantiate a vecArrayCopy—a vector of integer objects using another vector of integer objects. If one of them were to be a vector of, say, type float, the code would not compile.

Inserting Elements in a vector

Having instantiated a vector of integers, the next task that beckons is to insert elements (integers) into it. Insertion in a vector happens at the end of the array and elements are "pushed" into its back using the member method push_back, as seen in the following code sample in Listing 18.2.

LISTING 18.2   Inserting Elements in a vector Using the push_back Method

```
 1: #include <iostream>
 2: #include <vector>
 3:
 4: int main ()
 5: {
 6:     std::vector <int> vecDynamicIntegerArray;
 7:
 8:     // Insert sample integers into the vector:
 9:     vecDynamicIntegerArray.push_back (50);
10:     vecDynamicIntegerArray.push_back (1);
11:     vecDynamicIntegerArray.push_back (987);
12:     vecDynamicIntegerArray.push_back (1001);
13:
14:     std::cout << "The vector contains ";
15:     std::cout << vecDynamicIntegerArray.size () << " Elements";
16:
17:     return 0;
18: }
```

Output ▼

```
The vector contains 4 Elements
```

Analysis ▼

push_back, as seen in lines 9–12 is the vector class's public member method that inserts objects at the end of the dynamic array. Note the usage of function size (), which returns the number of elements held in the vector.

A different way of inserting the values than the way shown earlier would be by specifying the number of elements to be kept in the vector and then copying values into individual locations as in an array.

LISTING 18.3 Set Element Values in a vector Using Array Semantics

```
1: #include <vector>
2: #include <iostream>
3:
4: int main ()
5: {
6:     std::vector <int> vecDynamicIntegerArray (4);
7:
8:     // Copy integer values into individual element locations
9:     vecDynamicIntegerArray [0] = 50;
10:    vecDynamicIntegerArray [1] = 1;
11:    vecDynamicIntegerArray [2] = 987;
12:    vecDynamicIntegerArray [3] = 1001;
13:
14:    std::cout << "The vector contains ";
15:    std::cout << vecDynamicIntegerArray.size () << " Elements";
16:
17:    return 0;
18: }
```

Output ▼

```
The vector contains 4 Elements
```

Analysis ▼

This code instantiates the vector of integers and specifies the initial/starting number of elements the vector contains. Line 6 constructs the vector object with four integers. The next lines use array semantics to copy values of interest in those four locations in the vector. Use of this subscript operator [] can be done safely only for offset positions within the bounds of the vector. Finally, the code outputs the number of elements the vector contains to the screen. You should observe output identical to that of Listing 18.1, which inserted elements into a noninitialized vector using push_back.

Note that initializing the vector as one that contains four elements does not restrict it to containing that many elements only. The programmer is free to push_back more elements into the vector depending on his application's requirements.

In addition to featuring push_back and allowing the subscript operator to write values directly into a vector initialized to contain those elements, like many STL containers the std::vector features an insert function where you can specify the position at which elements can be inserted into the sequence, as seen in the following sample in Listing 18.4.

LISTING 18.4 Using vector::insert to Insert Elements in the Middle

```
1: #include <vector>
2: #include <iostream>
3:
4: int main ()
5: {
6:     using namespace std;
7:
8:     // Instantiate a vector with 4 elements, each initialized to 90
9:     vector <int> vecIntegers (4, 90);
10:
11:     cout << "The initial contents of the vector are: ";
12:
13:     vector <int>::iterator iElement;
14:     for ( iElement = vecIntegers.begin ()
15:         ; iElement != vecIntegers.end ()
16:         ; ++ iElement )
17:     {
18:         cout << *iElement << ' ';
19:     }
20:
21:     cout << endl;
22:
23:     // Insert 25 at the beginning
24:     vecIntegers.insert (vecIntegers.begin (), 25);
25:
26:     cout << "The vector after inserting an element at the beginning: ";
27:     for ( iElement = vecIntegers.begin ()
28:         ; iElement != vecIntegers.end ()
29:         ; ++ iElement )
30:     {
31:         cout << *iElement << ' ';
32:     }
33:
34:     cout << endl;
35:
36:     // Insert 2 numbers of value 45 at the end
37:     vecIntegers.insert (vecIntegers.end (), 2, 45);
38:
39:     cout << "The vector after inserting two elements at the end: ";
40:     for ( iElement = vecIntegers.begin ()
41:         ; iElement != vecIntegers.end ()
42:         ; ++ iElement )
43:     {
```

LISTING 18.4 Continued

```
44:          cout << *iElement << ' ';
45:       }
46:       cout << endl;
47:
48:       // Another vector containing 2 elements of value 30
49:       vector <int> vecAnother (2, 30);
50:
51:       // Insert two elements from another container in position [1]
52:       vecIntegers.insert (vecIntegers.begin () + 1,
53:                          vecAnother.begin (), vecAnother.end ());
54:
55:       cout << "The vector after inserting contents from another ";
56:       cout << "in the middle:" << endl;
57:       for ( iElement = vecIntegers.begin ()
58:          ; iElement != vecIntegers.end ()
59:          ; ++ iElement )
60:       {
61:          cout << *iElement << ' ';
62:       }
63:
64:       return 0;
65: }
```

18

Output ▼

```
The initial contents of the vector are: 90 90 90 90
The vector after inserting an element at the beginning: 25 90 90 90 90
The vector after inserting two elements at the end: 25 90 90 90 90 45 45
The vector after inserting contents from another container in the middle:

25 30 30 90 90 90 90 45 45
```

Analysis ▼

This code effectively demonstrates the power of the insert function by allowing you to put values in the middle of the container. It starts with a vector in line 9 that contains four elements, all initialized to 90, and proceeds with inserting elements by using various overloads of vector::insert member function as seen in lines 24, 37, and 52 that demonstrate how elements can be inserted at the beginning, end, and in the middle of the vector, respectively.

<table>
<tr>
<td><u>NOTE</u></td>
<td>Note that this is possibly the most inefficient way to add elements to the <code>vector</code> (when adding in a position that is not the end of the sequence) because adding elements in the beginning or the middle makes the <code>vector</code> class shift all subsequent elements backward (after making space for the last ones at the end). Thus, depending on the type of the objects contained in the sequence, the cost of this shift operation can be significant in terms of the copy constructor or assignment operator invoked. In our little sample, the <code>vector</code> contains object of type int that are relatively inexpensive to move around. This might not be the case in many other uses of the <code>vector</code> class.</td>
</tr>
</table>

Accessing Elements in a vector

Elements in a `vector` can be accessed using the following methods: via array semantics using the subscript operator `[]`, or the member function `at()`, or using iterators.

Listing 18.5 demonstrates how elements in a `vector` can be accessed using the subscript operator [], that incidentally was used to set values in the `vector` in Listing 18.3.

LISTING 18.5 Accessing Elements in a Vector Using Array Semantics

```
 1: #include <iostream>
 2: #include <vector>
 3:
 4: int main ()
 5: {
 6:     using namespace std;
 7:
 8:     vector <int> vecDynamicIntegerArray;
 9:
10:     // Insert sample integers into the vector:
11:     vecDynamicIntegerArray.push_back (50);
12:     vecDynamicIntegerArray.push_back (1);
13:     vecDynamicIntegerArray.push_back (987);
14:     vecDynamicIntegerArray.push_back (1001);
15:
16:     unsigned int nElementIndex = 0;
17:     while (nElementIndex < vecDynamicIntegerArray.size ())
18:     {
19:         cout << "Element at position " << nElementIndex;
20:         cout << " is: " << vecDynamicIntegerArray [nElementIndex] << endl;
21:
22:         ++ nElementIndex;
23:     }
24:
25:     return 0;
26: }
```

Output ▼

```
Element at position 0 is: 50
Element at position 1 is: 1
Element at position 2 is: 987
Element at position 3 is: 1001
```

Analysis ▼

At line 20, the sample code shows that the vector can be used the same way you might use a static array to access values using vector's subscript operator []. The subscript operator accepts an element-index that is zero-based just as in a static array.

CAUTION

> Accessing elements in a vector using [] is fraught with the same dangers as accessing elements in an array; that is, you should not cross the bounds of the container. If you use the subscript operator[] to access elements in a <u>vector</u> at a position that is beyond its bounds, the result of the operation will be undefined (anything could happen, possibly an access violation).
>
> A safer alternative is to use the at() member function:
>
> ```
> // gets element at position 2
> cout << vecDynamicIntegerArray.at (2);
> // the vector::at() version of the code above in Listing
> ➥18.5, line 20:
> cout << vecDynamicIntegerArray.at (nElementIndex);
> ```
>
> at() performs a runtime check against the size of the container and throws an exception if you cross the boundaries.
>
> Note that the subscript operator[] is safe to use when done in a manner that ensures bound integrity, as in the sample above.

18

Elements in a vector can also be accessed using pointer-like semantics by the use of iterators, as seen in Listing 18.6.

LISTING 18.6 Accessing Elements in a Vector Using Pointer Semantics (Iterators)

```
1: #include <iostream>
2: #include <vector>
3:
4: int main ()
5: {
6:     using namespace std;
7:
```

LISTING 18.6   Continued

```
 8:     vector <int> vecDynamicIntegerArray;
 9:
10:     // Insert sample integers into the vector:
11:     vecDynamicIntegerArray.push_back (50);
12:     vecDynamicIntegerArray.push_back (1);
13:     vecDynamicIntegerArray.push_back (987);
14:     vecDynamicIntegerArray.push_back (1001);
15:
16:     // Access objects in a vector using iterators:
"17:    vector<int>::iterator iElementLocator = vecDynamicIntegerArray.begin();"
18:
19:     while (iElementLocator != vecDynamicIntegerArray.end ())
20:     {
21:         size_t nElementIndex = distance (vecDynamicIntegerArray.begin (),
22:                         iElementLocator);
23:
24:         cout << "Element at position ";
25:         cout << nElementIndex << " is: " << *iElementLocator << endl;
26:
27:         // move to the next element
28:         ++ iElementLocator;
29:     }
30:
31:     return 0;
32: }
```

Output ▼

```
Element at position 0 is: 50
Element at position 1 is: 1
Element at position 2 is: 987
Element at position 3 is: 1001
```

Analysis ▼

The iterator in this example behaves more or less like a pointer and the nature of its usage in the preceding application is quite like pointer arithmetic, as seen in lines 28 and 29. Notice how we used `std::distance` in line 21 to evaluate the offset of the element. The iterator that points to the element is sent as the second parameter, and the first being the beginning of the `vector` as returned by the iterator from `begin()`.

Removing Elements from a `vector`

Just the same way as the `vector` features insertion at the end via the `push_back` method, it also features the removal of an element at the end via the `pop_back` function. Removal of an element from the vector using pop_back takes constant time—that is, the time required is independent of the number of elements stored in the vector. The code that follows in Listing 18.7 demonstrates the usage of function pop_back to erase elements from the back of the vector.

LISTING 18.7 Using pop_back to Erase the Last Element

```
1: #include <iostream>
2: #include <vector>
3:
4: int main ()
5: {
6:     using namespace std;
7:
8:     vector <int> vecDynamicIntegerArray;
9:
10:     // Insert sample integers into the vector:
11:     vecDynamicIntegerArray.push_back (50);
12:     vecDynamicIntegerArray.push_back (1);
13:     vecDynamicIntegerArray.push_back (987);
14:     vecDynamicIntegerArray.push_back (1001);
15:
16:     cout << "The vector contains ";
17:     cout << vecDynamicIntegerArray.size ();
18:     cout << " elements before calling pop_back" << endl;
19:
20:     // Erase one element at the end
21:     vecDynamicIntegerArray.pop_back ();
22:
23:     cout << "The vector contains ";
24:     cout << vecDynamicIntegerArray.size ();
25:     cout << " elements after calling pop_back" << endl;
26:
27:     cout << "Enumerating items in the vector... " << endl;
28:
29:     unsigned int nElementIndex = 0;
30:     while (nElementIndex < vecDynamicIntegerArray.size ())
31:     {
32:         cout << "Element at position " << nElementIndex << " is: ";
33:         cout << vecDynamicIntegerArray [nElementIndex] << endl;

34:         // move to the next element
35:         ++ nElementIndex;
36:     }
37:
38:     return 0;
39: }
```

18

Output ▼

```
The vector contains 4 elements before calling pop_back
The vector contains 3 elements after calling pop_back
Enumerating items in the vector...
Element at position 0 is: 50
Element at position 1 is: 1
Element at position 2 is: 987
```

Analysis ▼

The output indicates that the pop_back function used at line 20 has reduced the elements in the vector by erasing the last element inserted into it. Line 24 calls size() again to demonstrate that the number of elements in the vector has reduced by one, as indicated in the output.

Understanding size() and capacity()

The *size* of a vector is the actual number of elements stored in a vector. The *capacity* of a vector is the total number of elements that can potentially be stored in the vector before it reallocates memory to accommodate more elements. Therefore, a vector's size is less than or equal to its capacity.

A vector can cause some amount of performance problems when it needs to frequently re-allocate the memory of the internal dynamic array. To a great extent, this problem can be addressed by using the member function reserve (*number*). What reserve essentially does is increase the amount of memory allocated for the vector's internal array so as to accommodate that number of elements without needing to re-allocate. Depending on the type of the objects stored in the vector, reducing the number of re-allocations also reduces the number of times the objects are copied and saves on performance. The code sample that follows in Listing 18.8 demonstrates the difference between size and capacity.

LISTING 18.8 Demonstration of size() and capacity()

```
1: #include <iostream>
2: #include <vector>
3:
4: int main ()
5: {
6:     using namespace std;
7:
```

LISTING 18.8   Continued

```
 8:    // Instantiate a vector object that holds 5 integers of default value
 9:    vector <int> vecDynamicIntegerArray (5);
10:
11:    cout << "Vector of integers was instantiated with " << endl;
12:    cout << "Size: " << vecDynamicIntegerArray.size ();
13:    cout << ", Capacity: " <<  vecDynamicIntegerArray.capacity () << endl;
14:
15:    // Inserting a 6th element in to the vector
16:    vecDynamicIntegerArray.push_back (666);
17:
18:    cout << "After inserting an additional element... " << endl;
19:    cout << "Size: " << vecDynamicIntegerArray.size ();
20:    cout << ", Capacity: " <<  vecDynamicIntegerArray.capacity () << endl;
21:
22:    // Inserting another element
23:    vecDynamicIntegerArray.push_back (777);
24:
25:    cout << "After inserting yet another element... " << endl;
26:    cout << "Size: " << vecDynamicIntegerArray.size ();
27:    cout << ", Capacity: " <<  vecDynamicIntegerArray.capacity () << endl;
28:
29:    return 0;
30: }
```

18

Output ▼

```
Vector of integers was instantiated with
Size: 5, Capacity: 5
After inserting an additional element...
Size: 6, Capacity: 7
After inserting yet another element...
Size: 7, Capacity: 7
```

Analysis ▼

Line 8 shows the instantiation of a vector of integers containing five integers at default value (0). Lines 12 and 13, which prints the size and the capacity of the vector, respectively, display that both are equal at instantiation time. Line 9 inserts a sixth element in the vector. Given that the capacity of the vector was five prior to the insertion, there isn't adequate memory in the internal buffer of the vector to support this new sixth element. In other words, for the vector class to scale itself and store six elements, it needs to re-allocate the internal buffer. The implementation of the re-allocation logic is smart—in order avoid another re-allocation on insertion of another element, it preemptively allocates a capacity greater than the requirements of the immediate scenario.

The output shows that on insertion of a sixth element in a vector that has the capacity for 5, the re-allocation involved increases the capacity to 7 elements. size() always reflects the number of elements in the vector and has a value of 6 at this stage. The addition of a seventh element in line 23 results in no increase in capacity—the existing allocated memory meets the demand sufficiently. Both size and capacity display an equal value at this stage, indicating that the vector is used to its full capacity, and insertion of the next element will cause the vector to re-allocate its internal buffer, copying existing values before it inserts the new value.

NOTE The preemptive increase in the capacity of the vector when the internal buffer is re-allocated is not regulated by any clause in the standard. This is independent of the flavor of STL being used.

The STL deque Class

deque (pronunciation rhymes with *deck*) is an STL dynamic array class quite similar in properties to that of the vector except that it allows for the insertion and removal of elements at the front and back of the array. A deque can be visualized as seen in Figure 18.2.

FIGURE 18.2
Internals of a deque.

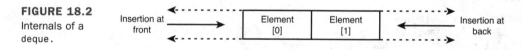

The header to be included for using the deque class is <deque>. And, as Listing 18.9 displays, it bears a remarkable similarity to using std::vector.

LISTING 18.9 Using the STL deque Class

```
 1: #include <deque>
 2: #include <iostream>
 3: #include <algorithm>
 4:
 5: int main ()
 6: {
 7:     using namespace std;
 8:
 9:     // Define a deque of integers
10:     deque <int> dqIntegers;
11:
```

LISTING 18.9   Continued

```
12:     // Insert integers at the bottom of the array
13:     dqIntegers.push_back (3);
14:     dqIntegers.push_back (4);
15:     dqIntegers.push_back (5);
16:
17:     // Insert integers at the top of the array
18:     dqIntegers.push_front (2);
19:     dqIntegers.push_front (1);
20:     dqIntegers.push_front (0);
21:
22:     cout << "The contents of the deque after inserting elements ";
23:     cout << "at the top and bottom are:" << endl;
24:
25:     // Display contents on the screen
26:     for ( size_t nCount = 0
27:         ; nCount < dqIntegers.size ()
28:         ; ++ nCount )
29:     {
30:         cout << "Element [" << nCount << "] = ";
31:         cout << dqIntegers [nCount] << endl;
32:     }
33:
34:     cout << endl;
35:
36:     // Erase an element at the top
37:     dqIntegers.pop_front ();
38:
39:     // Erase an element at the bottom
40:     dqIntegers.pop_back ();
41:
42:     cout << "The contents of the deque after erasing an element ";
43:     cout << "from the top and bottom are:" << endl;
44:
45:     // Display contents again: this time using iterators
46:     deque <int>::iterator iElementLocator;
47:     for ( iElementLocator = dqIntegers.begin ()
48:         ; iElementLocator != dqIntegers.end ()
49:         ; ++ iElementLocator )
50:     {
51:         size_t nOffset = distance (dqIntegers.begin (), iElementLocator);
52:     cout<<"Element [" << nOffset << "] = " << *iElementLocator<<endl;"
53:     }
54:
55:     return 0;
56: }
```

18

Output ▼

```
The contents of the deque after inserting elements at the top and bottom are:
Element [0] = 0
Element [1] = 1
Element [2] = 2
Element [3] = 3
Element [4] = 4
Element [5] = 5

The contents of the deque after erasing an element from the top and bottom are:
Element [0] = 1
Element [1] = 2
Element [2] = 3
Element [3] = 4
```

Analysis ▼

Line 10 is where we instantiate a deque of integers. Note how similar this syntax is to the instantiation of a vector of integers. Lines 13–16 display the usage of the deque member function push_back followed by push_front in lines 18–20. The latter makes the deque unique in comparison to the vector. Ditto for the usage of pop_front, as shown in line 37. The first mechanism of displaying the contents of deque uses the array-like syntax to access elements, whereas the latter uses iterators. In case of the latter, as shown in lines 47–53, the algorithm std::distance is used to evaluate the offset position of the element in the deque in the same manner that we have already seen work with the vector in Listing 18.6.

Summary

In this lesson, you learned the basics on using the vector and the deque as a dynamic array. The concepts of size and capacity were explained, and you saw how the usage of the vector can be optimized to reduce the number of re-allocations of its internal buffer, which copies the objects contained and potentially reduces performance. The vector is the simplest of the STL's containers, yet the most used and, arguably, efficient one.

Q&A

Q Does the vector change the order of the elements stored in it?

A The vector is a sequential container and elements are stored and accessed in the very order that they are inserted.

Q **What function is used to insert items in a vector and where is the object inserted?**

A The member function `push_back` inserts elements at the end of the `vector`.

Q **What function gets the number of elements stored in a vector?**

A The member function `size ()` returns the number of elements stored in a `vector`. Incidentally, this is true for all STL containers.

Q **Does the insertion or removal of elements at the end of the vector take more time if the vector contains more elements?**

A No. Insertion and removal of elements at the end of a `vector` are constant time activities.

Q **What is the advantage of using the reserve member function?**

A `reserve (...)` allocates space in the internal buffer of the `vector`, and insertion of elements does not need the `vector` to re-allocate the buffer and copy existing contents. Depending on the nature of the objects stored in the `vector`, reserving space in a `vector` can result in performance improvements.

Q **Are the properties of the deque any different than the vector when it comes to insertion of elements?**

A No, the properties of the deque are similar to that of the vector when it comes to insertion, which is a constant time activity for elements added at the end of sequence and a linear time activity for elements inserted in the middle. However, the vector allows insertion at only one end (the bottom), whereas the deque allows for insertion at both (the top and the bottom).

18

Workshop

The Workshop contains quiz questions to help solidify your understanding of the material covered and exercises to provide you with experience in using what you've learned. Try to answer the quiz and exercise questions before checking the answers in Appendix D, and be certain you understand the answers before going to the next lesson.

Quiz

1. Can elements be inserted at the middle or the beginning of a `vector` in constant time?

2. My `vector` returns `size ()` as `10` and `capacity ()` as `20`. How many more elements can I insert in it without needing the `vector` class to trigger a buffer re-allocation?

3. What does the `pop_back` function do?

4. If `vector <int>` is a dynamic array of integers, a `vector <CMammal>` is a dynamic array of what type?

5. Can elements in a `vector` be randomly accessed? If so, how?

6. What iterator type allows random access of elements in a `vector`?

Exercises

1. Write an interactive program that accepts integer input from the user and saves it in the `vector`. The user should be able to query a value stored in the `vector` at any time, given an index.

2. Extend the program from Exercise 1 to be able to tell the user whether a value he queries for already exists in the `vector`.

3. Jack sells jars on eBay. To help him with packaging and shipment, write a program in which he can enter the dimensions of each of these articles, store them in a `vector`, and have them printed on the screen.

LESSON 19
STL `list`

The standard template library (STL) supplies the programmer with a doubly linked list in the form of template class `std::list`.

In this lesson, you will learn

- The characteristics of a `std::list`
- Basic `list` operations

The Characteristics of a `std::list`

A *linked list* is a collection of nodes in which each node, in addition to containing a value or object of interest, also points to the next node; that is, each node links to the next one as the following visual representation in Figure 19.1 indicates.

FIGURE 19.1
Visual representation of a singly linked list.

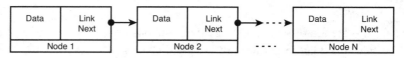

In addition, in a doubly linked list as provided by STL, each node also points to the previous one. A doubly linked list can therefore be visualized as a linked list where one can traverse nodes in both directions, as seen in Figure 19.2.

FIGURE 19.2
Visual representation of a doubly linked list.

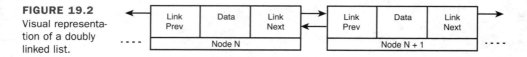

STL's `list` class allows for constant time insertions at the front, back, or middle of the sequence.

Basic `list` Operations

Standard compliant implementations of STL's `list` class need the header file `<list>`, which the programmer must include before using this class. The template class `list` that exists in the `std` namespace is a generic implementation that needs to be template-instantiated before you can use any of its member functions.

Instantiating a `std::list` Object

Instantiating a list of integers requires a specialization of template class `std::list` for type `int`, as shown in Listing 19.1.

LISTING 19.1   Instantiating an STL List of Integers

```
1: #include <list>
2: int main ()
3: {
4:     using namespace std;
5:
6:     list <int> listIntegers;
7:     return 0;
8: }
```

Analysis ▼

Line 6 shows a template instantiation of an STL `list` class for type `int`; that is, it defines a `list` of integers called `listIntegers`. A `list` of any other type would be instantiated using the syntax:

```
list <MyFavoriteType> listMyFavoriteObjects;
```

Inserting Elements at the Front of the `list`

Insertion of an element at the front (that is, at a position before existing elements in the sequence) is effected using the `list` member method `push_front`, which accepts a single parameter—the value to be inserted, as seen in Listing 19.2.

LISTING 19.2   Inserting Elements in the List Using push_front

```cpp
1: #include <list>
2: #include <iostream>
3:
4: int main ()
5: {
6:     std::list <int> listIntegers;
7:
8:     listIntegers.push_front (10);
9:     listIntegers.push_front (2001);
10:     listIntegers.push_front (-1);
11:     listIntegers.push_front (9999);
12:
13:     std::list <int> ::iterator iElementLocator;
14:
15:     for ( iElementLocator = listIntegers.begin ()
16:         ; iElementLocator != listIntegers.end ()
17:         ; ++ iElementLocator )
18:         std::cout << *iElementLocator << std::endl;
19:
20:     return 0;
21: }
```

19

Output ▼

```
9999
-1
2001
10
```

Analysis ▼

The numbers displayed in the output: 10, 2001, −1, and 9999 were inserted at the front of the list and in that order, as seen in the usage of push::front in lines 8–11. Thus, when the contents of the list are accessed as seen in lines 15–18, you see that every number inserted at the front appears before its predecessor—effectively putting the newest element at the front of the list and the oldest at the back.

Inserting Elements at the Back of the list

Insertion of elements at the back (that is, at a position behind existing elements in the sequence) is effected using the list member method push_back, which accepts a single parameter—the value to be inserted, as seen in Listing 19.3.

LISTING 19.3   Inserting Elements in the List Using push_back

```
 1: #include <list>
 2: #include <iostream>
 3:
 4: int main ()
 5: {
 6:     std::list <int> listIntegers;
 7:
 8:     listIntegers.push_back (10);
 9:     listIntegers.push_back (2001);
10:     listIntegers.push_back (-1);
11:     listIntegers.push_back (9999);
12:
13:     std::list <int> ::iterator iElementLocator;
14:
15:     for ( iElementLocator = listIntegers.begin ()
16:         ; iElementLocator != listIntegers.end ()
17:         ; ++ iElementLocator )
18:         std::cout << *iElementLocator << std::endl;
19:
20:     return 0;
21: }
```

Output ▼

```
10
2001
-1
9999
```

Analysis ▼

Numbers inserted in the list in lines 8–11 using push_back are placed after the previously inserted element. When the contents of the list are printed on the screen, as shown in lines 15–18, they are found to be in the very order in which they were inserted as insertion using push_back happens at the end of the sequence.

Inserting at the Middle of the list

std::list is characterized by its capability to insert elements at the middle of the collection in constant time. This is done using the member function insert.

The list::insert member function is available in three forms:

Form 1

```
iterator insert(iterator pos, const T& x)
```

Here the insert function accepts the position of insertion as the first parameter and the value to insert as the second. This function returns an iterator pointing to the recently inserted element in the list.

Form 2

```
void insert(iterator pos, size_type n, const T& x)
```

This function accepts the position of insertion as the first parameter, the value to insert as the last parameter, and the number of elements in variable n.

Form 3

```
template <class InputIterator>
void insert(iterator pos, InputIterator f, InputIterator l)
```

This overloaded variant is a template function that accepts, in addition to the position, two input iterators that mark the bounds of the collection to insert into the list. Note that the input type InputIterator is a template-parameterized type and therefore can point to the bounds of any collection—be it an array, a vector, or just another list.

Listing 19.4 demonstrates the usage of these overloaded variants of the list::insert function.

LISTING 19.4   The Various Methods of Inserting Elements in a list

```
1: #include <list>
2: #include <iostream>
3:
4: using namespace std;
5:
```

LISTING 19.4 Continued

```
 6: void PrintListContents (const list <int>& listInput);
 7:
 8: int main ()
 9: {
10:     list <int> listIntegers1;
11:
12:     // Inserting elements at the beginning...
13:     listIntegers1.insert (listIntegers1.begin (), 4);
14:     listIntegers1.insert (listIntegers1.begin (), 3);
15:     listIntegers1.insert (listIntegers1.begin (), 2);
16:     listIntegers1.insert (listIntegers1.begin (), 1);
17:
18:     // Inserting an element at the end...
19:     listIntegers1.insert (listIntegers1.end (), 5);
20:
21:     cout << "The contents of list 1 after inserting elements:" << endl;
22:     PrintListContents (listIntegers1);
23:
24:     list <int> listIntegers2;
25:
26:     // Inserting 4 elements of the same value 0...
27:     listIntegers2.insert (listIntegers2.begin (), 4, 0);
28:
29:     cout << "The contents of list 2 after inserting '";
30:     cout << listIntegers2.size () << "' elements of a value:" << endl;
31:     PrintListContents (listIntegers2);
32:
33:     list <int> listIntegers3;
34:
35:     // Inserting elements from another list at the beginning...
36:     listIntegers3.insert (listIntegers3.begin (),
37:                           listIntegers1.begin (), listIntegers1.end ());
38:
39:     cout << "The contents of list 3 after inserting the contents of ";
40:     cout << "list 1 at the beginning:" << endl;
41:     PrintListContents (listIntegers3);
42:
43:     // Inserting elements from another list at the end...
44:     listIntegers3.insert (listIntegers3.end (),
45:                           listIntegers2.begin (), listIntegers2.end ());
46:
47:     cout << "The contents of list 3 after inserting ";
48:     cout << "the contents of list 2 at the beginning:" << endl;
49:     PrintListContents (listIntegers3);
50:
51:     return 0;
52: }
53:
54: void PrintListContents (const list <int>& listInput)
55: {
```

LISTING 19.4   Continued

```
56:    // Write values to the screen...
57:    cout << "{ ";
58:
59:    std::list <int>::const_iterator iElementLocator;
60:    for ( iElementLocator = listInput.begin ()
61:        ; iElementLocator != listInput.end ()
62:        ; ++ iElementLocator )
63:        cout << *iElementLocator << " ";
64:
65:    cout << "}" << endl << endl;
66: }
```

Output ▼

```
The contents of list 1 after inserting elements:
{ 1 2 3 4 5 }

The contents of list 2 after inserting '4' elements of a value:
{ 0 0 0 0 }

The contents of list 3 after inserting the contents of list 1 at the beginning:
{ 1 2 3 4 5 }

The contents of list 3 after inserting the contents of list 2 at the beginning:
{ 1 2 3 4 5 0 0 0 0 }
```

Analysis ▼

In Listing 19.4, begin() and end() are member functions that return iterators pointing to the beginning and the end of the list. The list::insert function accepts an iterator that marks the position before which items are to be inserted. The iterator returned by the end() function, as used in line 12, points to after the last element in the list. Therefore, that line inserts integer value 5 before the end.

Lines 20 and 23 display how the contents of one list can be inserted into another. Note that the version of the insert function used here accepts parameters of type input iterator. Although this example inserts a list of integers into another list, the range inserted could as well have been the limits of a vector or a regular static array.

Erasing Elements in a list

The list member function erase comes in two overloaded forms: One that erases one element given an iterator that points to it and another that accepts a range and therefore erases a range of elements from the list. The list::erase function can be seen in

19

action in Listing 19.5 and demonstrates how you erase an element or a range of elements from a list.

LISTING 19.5   Erasing Elements in a list

```
1: #include <list>
2: #include <iostream>
3:
4: using namespace std;
5:
6: void PrintListContents (const list <int>& listInput);
7:
8: int main ()
9: {
10:     std::list <int> listIntegers;
11:
12:     // Insert elements at the beginning...
13:     listIntegers.push_front (4);
14:     listIntegers.push_front (3);
15:
16:     // Store an iterator obtained in using the 'insert' function
17:     list <int>::iterator iElementValueTwo;
18:     iElementValueTwo = listIntegers.insert (listIntegers.begin (), 2);
19:
20:     listIntegers.push_front (1);
21:     listIntegers.push_front (0);
22:
23:     // Insert an element at the end...
24:     listIntegers.push_back (5);
25:
26:     cout << "Initial contents of the list:" << endl;
27:     PrintListContents (listIntegers);
28:
29:     listIntegers.erase (listIntegers.begin (), iElementValueTwo);
30:     cout << "Contents after erasing a range of elements:" << endl;
31:     PrintListContents (listIntegers);
32:
33:     cout<<"Contents after erasing element
'"<<*iElementValueTwo<<"':"<<endl;"
34:     listIntegers.erase (iElementValueTwo);
35:     PrintListContents (listIntegers);
36:
37:     listIntegers.erase (listIntegers.begin (), listIntegers.end ());
38:     cout << "Contents after erasing a range:" << endl;
39:     PrintListContents (listIntegers);
40:
41:     return 0;
42: }
43:
44: void PrintListContents (const list <int>& listInput)
45: {
```

LISTING 19.5 Continued

```
46:    if (listInput.size () > 0)
47:    {
48:        // Write values to the screen...
49:        cout << "{ ";
50:
51:        std::list <int>::const_iterator iElementLocator;
52:        for ( iElementLocator = listInput.begin ()
53:            ; iElementLocator != listInput.end ()
54:            ; ++ iElementLocator )
55:            cout << *iElementLocator << " ";
56:
57:        cout << "}" << endl << endl;
58:    }
59:    else
60:        cout << "List is empty!" << endl;
61: }
```

Output ▼

```
Initial contents of the list:
{ 0 1 2 3 4 5 }

Contents after erasing a range of elements:
{ 2 3 4 5 }

Contents after erasing element '2':
{ 3 4 5 }

Contents after erasing a range:
List is empty!
```

Analysis ▼

Line 18 uses the list function insert to insert an element at the top of the list instead of using push_front as at other places. This is because the insert function returns an iterator that points to the element inserted, as stored in iElementValueTwo. As shown in line 29, this iterator is later used to define the range of the elements to be erased from the list, starting at the beginning of the list and going until the element pointed to by iElementValueTwo, but not including it. Line 34 displays the usage of the other variants of list's erase member function that erases the element pointed to by the iterator iElementValueTwo supplied. Note how we printed the value pointed by iElementValueTwo in line 33 before using it in the call to the erase function. This was intentional because the iterator after the call to erase is invalid.

The erase member function used in line 37 is supplied with a range that encompasses all the elements held in the list itself via begin(), and end() empties the list. However, list does also supply clear()—a function that effectively does exactly what the erase function did when used in this way: It empties the collection.

Reversing and Sorting Elements in a list

list has a special property that iterators pointing to the elements in a list remain valid in spite of rearrangement of the elements or insertion of new elements and so on. To keep this important property intact, the list function features sort and reverse as member methods even though the standard template library supplies these as algorithms that will and do work on the list class. The member versions of these algorithms ensure that iterators pointing to elements in the list are not invalidated when the relative position of the elements is disturbed.

Reversing Elements

list features a member function reverse() that takes no parameters and reverses the order of contents in a list for the programmer, as seen in Listing 19.6.

LISTING 19.6   Reversing Elements in a list

```
1: #include <list>
2: #include <iostream>
3:
4: using namespace std;
5:
6: void PrintListContents (const list <int>& listInput);
7:
8: int main ()
9: {
10:     std::list <int> listIntegers;
11:
12:     // Insert elements at the beginning...
13:     listIntegers.push_front (4);
14:     listIntegers.push_front (3);
15:     listIntegers.push_front (2);
16:
17:     listIntegers.push_front (1);
18:     listIntegers.push_front (0);
19:
20:     // Insert an element at the end...
21:     listIntegers.push_back (5);
22:
23:     cout << "Initial contents of the list:" << endl;
```

LISTING 19.6 Continued

```
24:     PrintListContents (listIntegers);
25:
26:     listIntegers.reverse ();
27:
28:     cout << "Contents of the list after using reverse ():" << endl;
29:     PrintListContents (listIntegers);
30:
31:     return 0;
32: }
33:
34: void PrintListContents (const list <int>& listInput)
35: {
36:     if (listInput.size () > 0)
37:     {
38:         // Write values to the screen...
39:         cout << "{ ";
40:
41:         std::list <int>::const_iterator iElementLocator;
42:         for ( iElementLocator = listInput.begin ()
43:             ; iElementLocator != listInput.end ()
44:             ; ++ iElementLocator )
45:             cout << *iElementLocator << " ";
46:
47:         cout << "}" << endl << endl;
48:     }
49:     else
50:         cout << "List is empty!" << endl;
51: }
```

Output ▼

```
Initial contents of the list:
{ 0 1 2 3 4 5 }

Contents of the list after using reverse ():
{ 5 4 3 2 1 0 }
```

Analysis ▼

As shown in line 26, reverse() simply reverses the order of elements in the list. It is a simple call without parameters that ensures that iterators pointing to elements in the list, if kept by the programmer, remain valid even after the reversal.

19

Sorting Elements

The list member function sort() is available in one version that takes no parameters and another that accepts a binary predicate function as a parameter and can sort on the criteria specified in this predicate.

The former needs the programmer to program operator < of the class-type that the list contains for the list's sort function to work according to his expectations. In the absence of a sort predicate, std::list invokes operator < via std::less to compare elements before rearranging them in a sorted fashion. Alternatively, the programmer supplies list::sort a second parameter—a binary predicate, which is a function that takes two values as input and returns a Boolean value indicating whether the first value is smaller than the second. These techniques are demonstrated in Listing 19.7.

LISTING 19.7 Sorting a List of Integers in Ascending and Descending Order

```
 1: #include <list>
 2: #include <iostream>
 3:
 4: using namespace std;
 5:
 6: void PrintListContents (const list <int>& listInput);
 7: bool SortPredicate_Descending (const int& lsh, const int& rsh);
 8:
 9: int main ()
10: {
11:     std::list <int> listIntegers;
12:
13:     // Insert elements at the beginning...
14:     listIntegers.push_front (444);
15:     listIntegers.push_front (300);
16:     listIntegers.push_front (21111);
17:
18:     listIntegers.push_front (-1);
19:     listIntegers.push_front (0);
20:
21:     // Insert an element at the end...
22:     listIntegers.push_back (-5);
23:
24:     cout << "Initial contents of the list are - " << endl;
25:     PrintListContents (listIntegers);
26:
27:     listIntegers.sort ();
28:
29:     cout << "Order of elements after sort():" << endl;
30:     PrintListContents (listIntegers);
31:
32:     listIntegers.sort (SortPredicate_Descending);
33:     cout << "Order of elements after sort() with a predicate:" << endl;
34:
```

LISTING 19.7   Continued

```
35:      PrintListContents (listIntegers);
36:
37:      return 0;
38: }
39:
40: void PrintListContents (const list <int>& listInput)
41: {
42:      if (listInput.size () > 0)
43:      {
44:          // Write the output...
45:          cout << "{ ";
46:
47:          std::list <int>::const_iterator iElementLocator;
48:          for ( iElementLocator = listInput.begin ()
49:              ; iElementLocator != listInput.end ()
50:              ; ++ iElementLocator )
51:              cout << *iElementLocator << " ";
52:
53:          cout << "}" << endl << endl;
54:      }
55:      else
56:          cout << "List is empty!" << endl;
57: }
58:
59: bool SortPredicate_Descending (const int& lsh, const int& rsh)
60: {
61:      return (rsh < lsh);
62: }
```

19

Output ▼

```
Initial contents of the list are -
{ 0 -1 21111 300 444 -5 }

Order of elements after sort():
{ -5 -1 0 300 444 21111 }

Order of elements after sort() with a predicate:
{ 21111 444 300 0 -1 -5 }
```

Analysis ▼

This sample displays the sort functionality on a `list` of integers. The first few lines of code create the `list` object and insert sample values in it. Line 27 displays the usage of a `sort()` function without parameters that sorts elements in ascending order by default, comparing integers using `operator <`. However, if the programmer wants to override this default behavior, he must supply the sort function with a binary predicate. The function SortPredicate_Descending, defined in lines 59–62, is a binary predicate that helps the list's sort function decide whether one element is less than the other. If not, it swaps their positions. This function is passed as a parameter to the variant of the sort() function as seen in line 32. Essentially, the binary predicate defines the relationship < between two elements on the basis of the requirements of the application. Because our requirement was to sort in descending order, the predicate returns true only if the first value is greater than the second. That is, the first value (lsh) is considered logically less than the second (rsh) only if the numeric value of the former is greater than that of the latter.

NOTE Predicates are discussed in detail in Lesson 22, "Understanding Function Objects," and STL's std::sort algorithm, in addition to many others, is discussed in Lesson 23, "STL Algorithms."

Most practical applications involving STL containers rarely collect integers, rather user-defined types such as classes or structs. Listing 19.8 demonstrates one using the example of a contacts list.

LISTING 19.8 A list of struct Objects: Creating a Contacts List

```
 1: #include <list>
 2: #include <string>
 3: #include <iostream>
 4:
 5: using namespace std;
 6:
 7: enum MenuOptionSelection
 8: {
 9:     InsertContactListEntry = 0,
10:     SortOnName = 1,
11:     SortOnNumber = 2,
12:     DisplayEntries = 3,
13:     EraseEntry = 4,
14:     QuitContactList = 5
15: };
16:
17: struct ContactListItem
18: {
19:     string strContactsName;
20:     string strPhoneNumber;
21:
22:     // Constructor and destructor
23:     ContactListItem (const string& strName, const string & strNumber)
24:     {
25:         strContactsName = strName;
```

LISTING 19.8 Continued

```
26:            strPhoneNumber = strNumber;
27:        }
28:
29:        bool operator == (const ContactListItem& itemToCompare) const
30:        {
31:            return (itemToCompare.strContactsName == this->strContactsName);
32:        }
33:
34:        bool operator < (const ContactListItem& itemToCompare) const
35:        {
36:            return (this->strContactsName < itemToCompare.strContactsName);
37:        }
38: };
39:
40:
41: int ShowMenu ();
42: ContactListItem GetContactInfo ();
43: void DisplayContactList (const list <ContactListItem>& listContacts);
44: void EraseEntryFromList (list <ContactListItem>& listContacts);
45: bool Predicate_CheckItemsOnNumber (const ContactListItem& item1,
46:                                    const ContactListItem& item2);
47:
48: int main ()
49: {
50:     list <ContactListItem> listContacts;
51:     int nUserSelection = 0;
52:
53:     while ((nUserSelection = ShowMenu ()) != (int) QuitContactList)
54:     {
55:         switch (nUserSelection)
56:         {
57:         case InsertContactListEntry:
58:             listContacts.push_back (GetContactInfo ());
59:             cout << "Contacts list updated!" << endl << endl;
60:             break;
61:
62:         case SortOnName:
63:             listContacts.sort ();
64:             DisplayContactList (listContacts);
65:             break;
66:
67:         case SortOnNumber:
68:             listContacts.sort (Predicate_CheckItemsOnNumber);
69:             DisplayContactList (listContacts);
70:             break;
71:
72:         case DisplayEntries:
73:             DisplayContactList (listContacts);
74:             break;
75:
```

19

LISTING 19.8   Continued

```
76:        case EraseEntry:
77:            EraseEntryFromList (listContacts);
78:            DisplayContactList (listContacts);
79:            break;
80:
81:        case QuitContactList:
82:            cout << "Ending application, bye!" << endl;
83:            break;
84:
85:        default:
86:            cout << "Invalid input '" << nUserSelection << ".'";
87:            cout << "Choose an option between 0 and 4" << endl << endl;
88:            break;
89:        }
90:    }
91:
92:    cout << "Quitting! Bye!" << endl;
93:
94:    return 0;
95: }
96:
97: int ShowMenu ()
98: {
99:     cout << "*** What would you like to do next? ***" << endl << endl;
100:    cout << "Enter 0 to feed a name and phone number" << endl;
101:    cout << "Enter 1 to sort the list by name" << endl;
102:    cout << "Enter 2 to sort the list by number" << endl;
103:    cout << "Enter 3 to Display all entries" << endl;
104:    cout << "Enter 4 to erase an entry" << endl;
105:    cout << "Enter 5 to quit this application" << endl << endl;
106:    cout << "> ";
107:
108:    int nOptionSelected = 0;
109:
110:    // Accept user input
111:    cin >> nOptionSelected ;
112:
113:    cout << endl;
114:    return nOptionSelected;
115: }
116:
117: bool Predicate_CheckItemsOnNumber (const ContactListItem& item1,
118:                                    const ContactListItem& item2)
119: {
120:    return (item1.strPhoneNumber < item2.strPhoneNumber);
121: }
122:
123: ContactListItem GetContactInfo ()
124: {
125:    cout << "*** Feed contact information ***" << endl;
```

LISTING 19.8   Continued

```
126:     string strName;
127:     cout << "Please enter the person's name" << endl;;
128:     cout << "> ";
129:     cin >> strName;
130:
131:     string strPhoneNumber;
132:     cout << "Please enter "<< strName << "'s phone number" << endl;
133:     cout << "> ";
134:     cin >> strPhoneNumber;
135:
136:     return ContactListItem (strName, strPhoneNumber);
137: }
138:
139: void DisplayContactList (const list <ContactListItem>& listContacts)
140: {
141:     cout << "*** Displaying contact information ***" << endl;
142:     cout << "There are " << listContacts.size ();
143:     cout << " entries in the contact-list" << endl;
144:
145:     list <ContactListItem>::const_iterator iContact;
146:     for ( iContact = listContacts.begin ()
147:         ; iContact != listContacts.end ()
148:         ; ++ iContact )
149:     {
150:         cout << "Name: '" << iContact->strContactsName;
151:         cout << "' Number: '" << iContact->strPhoneNumber << "'" << endl;
152:     }
153:
154:     cout << endl;
155: }
156:
157: void EraseEntryFromList (list <ContactListItem>& listContacts)
158: {
159:     cout << "*** Erase an entry ***" << endl;
160:     cout << "Enter the name of the contact you wish to delete" << endl;
161:     cout << "> ";
162:     string strNameToErase;
163:     cin >> strNameToErase;
164:
165:     listContacts.remove (ContactListItem (strNameToErase, ""));
166: }
```

19

Output ▼

```
*** What would you like to do next? ***

Enter 0 to feed a name and phone number
Enter 1 to sort the list by name
Enter 2 to sort the list by number
Enter 3 to Display all entries
```

```
Enter 4 to erase an entry
Enter 5 to quit this application

> 0

*** Feed contact information ***
Please enter the person's name
> John
Please enter John's phone number
> 989812132
Contacts list updated!

*** What would you like to do next? ***

Enter 0 to feed a name and phone number
Enter 1 to sort the list by name
Enter 2 to sort the list by number
Enter 3 to Display all entries
Enter 4 to erase an entry
Enter 5 to quit this application

> 0

*** Feed contact information ***
Please enter the person's name
> Alanis
Please enter Alanis's phone number
> 78451245
Contacts list updated!

*** What would you like to do next? ***

Enter 0 to feed a name and phone number
Enter 1 to sort the list by name
Enter 2 to sort the list by number
Enter 3 to Display all entries
Enter 4 to erase an entry
Enter 5 to quit this application

> 0

*** Feed contact information ***
Please enter the person's name
> Tim
Please enter Tim's phone number
> 45121655
Contacts list updated!

*** What would you like to do next? ***

Enter 0 to feed a name and phone number
Enter 1 to sort the list by name
```

```
Enter 2 to sort the list by number
Enter 3 to Display all entries
Enter 4 to erase an entry
Enter 5 to quit this application

> 0

*** Feed contact information ***
Please enter the person's name
> Ronald
Please enter Ronald's phone number
> 123456987
Contacts list updated!

*** What would you like to do next? ***

Enter 0 to feed a name and phone number
Enter 1 to sort the list by name
Enter 2 to sort the list by number
Enter 3 to Display all entries
Enter 4 to erase an entry
Enter 5 to quit this application

> 3

*** Displaying contact information ***
There are 4 entries in the contact-list
Name: 'John' Number: '989812132'
Name: 'Alanis' Number: '78451245'
Name: 'Tim' Number: '45121655'
Name: 'Ronald' Number: '123456987'

*** What would you like to do next? ***

Enter 0 to feed a name and phone number
Enter 1 to sort the list by name
Enter 2 to sort the list by number
Enter 3 to Display all entries
Enter 4 to erase an entry
Enter 5 to quit this application

> 1

*** Displaying contact information ***
There are 4 entries in the contact-list
Name: 'Alanis' Number: '78451245'
Name: 'John' Number: '989812132'
Name: 'Ronald' Number: '123456987'
Name: 'Tim' Number: '45121655'

*** What would you like to do next? ***
```

19

```
Enter 0 to feed a name and phone number
Enter 1 to sort the list by name
Enter 2 to sort the list by number
Enter 3 to Display all entries
Enter 4 to erase an entry
Enter 5 to quit this application

> 2

*** Displaying contact information ***
There are 4 entries in the contact-list
Name: 'Ronald' Number: '123456987'
Name: 'Tim' Number: '45121655'
Name: 'Alanis' Number: '78451245'
Name: 'John' Number: '989812132'

*** What would you like to do next? ***

Enter 0 to feed a name and phone number
Enter 1 to sort the list by name
Enter 2 to sort the list by number
Enter 3 to Display all entries
Enter 4 to erase an entry
Enter 5 to quit this application

> 4

*** Erase an entry ***
Enter the name of the contact you wish to delete
> Tim
*** Displaying contact information ***
There are 3 entries in the contact-list
Name: 'Ronald' Number: '123456987'
Name: 'Alanis' Number: '78451245'
Name: 'John' Number: '989812132'

*** What would you like to do next? ***

Enter 0 to feed a name and phone number
Enter 1 to sort the list by name
Enter 2 to sort the list by number
Enter 3 to Display all entries
Enter 4 to erase an entry
Enter 5 to quit this application

> 5

Quitting! Bye!
```

Analysis ▼

This sample uses all the previous learning that you've gained in this lesson, and adapts it to a list of objects of type ContactListItem. Lines 17–38 define the structure ContactListItem that contains two member variables: one that holds the name of the person and another that keeps the phone number. Note the presence of the operators == and <. The former helps STL algorithms and list member functions, such as remove, to be able to remove an element from a list (as seen in line 165). The latter helps algorithms and list members, such as sort, to sort a list of ContactListItem objects as shown in line 63. The operator < thus provides the default sort criterion (the person's name in alphabetical order) for the objects in the list. However, if the list needs to be sorted to another criterion (say, the phone number), the version of the sort function that accepts a binary predicate is to be used as seen in line 68. This binary predicate is a simple function that accepts two values and returns a bool to indicate whether the first value is less than the other. The sort function uses this binary predicate to compare different values and swaps items (thus sorting them) according to the return value of the predicate function. In Listing 19.8, the function Predicate_CheckItemsOnNumber declared in line 35 and defined in lines 92–95 helps sort a list on the basis of the phone number attribute of struct ContactListItem.

This sample therefore demonstrated not only how STL's template version of the linked list can be used to create a list of any object type, but also the importance of operators and predicates.

Summary

19

This lesson taught you the properties of the list and the different list operations. You now know some of the most useful list functions and can create a list of any object type.

Q&A

Q **Why does the list provide member functions such as sort and remove?**

A The STL list class is bound to respect the property that iterators pointing to elements in the list should remain valid irrespective of the position of the elements in the list itself. Although STL algorithms work on list too, the list's member functions ensure that the abovementioned property of the list is withheld and iterators pointing to elements in the list before the sort was done continue to point to the same elements even after the sort.

Q You are using a `list` of type `CAnimal`, which is a class. What operators should `CAnimal` define for `list` member functions to be able to work on it accurately?

A You must provide the default comparison operator `==` and the default `<` operator to any class that can be used in STL containers.

Q You are using a `list` of type `CAnimal`, which is a class. What operators should `CAnimal` define for `list` member functions to be able to work on it accurately?

A You must provide the default comparison operator `==` and the `<` operator. Note that `std::list` functions such as `sort` can also be provided with a sort predicate that can override the default behavior.

Workshop

The Workshop contains quiz questions to help solidify your understanding of the material covered and exercises to provide you with experience in using what you've learned. Try to answer the quiz and exercise questions before checking the answers in Appendix D, and be certain you understand the answers before going to the next lesson.

Quiz

1. Is there any loss in performance when inserting items in the middle of the STL `list` as compared to the beginning or the end?

2. Two iterators are pointing to two elements in an STL `list` object and then an element is inserted between them. Are these iterators invalidated by the insert action?

3. How can the contents of a `std::list` be cleared?

4. Is it possible to insert multiple elements in a `list`?

Exercises

1. Write a short program that accepts numbers from the user and inserts them at the top of the `list`.

2. Using a short program, demonstrate that an iterator pointing to an element in a `list` continues to remain valid even after another element has been inserted before it, thus changing the relative position of the former element.

3. Write a program that inserts the contents of a vector into an STL `list` using the `list`'s insert function.

4. Write a program that sorts and reverses a `list` of strings.

LESSON 20
STL set **and** multiset

The standard template library (STL) supplies the programmer with container classes that help with applications requiring frequent and quick searches.

In this lesson, you will learn

- An introduction to the STL set and multiset
- Basic STL set and multiset operations
- Advantages and disadvantages in using these containers

An Introduction

The set and multiset are containers that facilitate a quick lookup of keys in a container that stores them; that is, the keys are the values stored in the one-dimensional container. The difference between the set and the multiset is that the latter allows for duplicates whereas the former can store only unique values.

FIGURE 20.1
Visual representa-
tion of a set and
a multiset of
names.

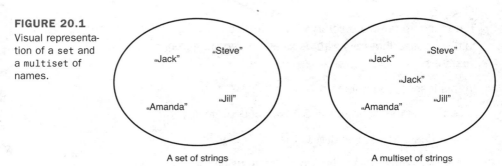

A set of strings   A multiset of strings

Figure 20.1 is only demonstrative and indicates that a set of names contains unique names, whereas a multiset permits duplicates. STL containers, being template classes are generic, and can therefore contain strings the way they can contain integers, structures, or class objects—depending on the template instantiation.

To facilitate quick searching, STL implementations of the set and multiset internally look like a binary tree. This means that elements inserted in a set or a multiset are sorted on insertion for quicker lookups. It also means that, unlike in a vector where elements at a position can be replaced by another, an element at a given position in a set cannot be replaced by a new element of a different value. This is true because the set would ideally like to have it placed in a possible different location in accordance with its value relative to those in the internal tree.

Basic STL set and multiset Operations

STL set and multiset are template classes that need to be instantiated before you can use any of their member functions. To use the STL set or multiset class, the programmer needs to include <set>.

Instantiating a std::set Object

Instantiating a set or multiset of integers requires a specialization of the template class std::set or std::multiset for type int, as shown in Listing 20.1.

LISTING 20.1 Instantiating STL set and multiset of Integers

```
 1: #include <set>
 2:
 3: int main ()
 4: {
 5:     using namespace std;
 6:
 7:     set <int> setIntegers;
 8:     multiset <int> msetIntegers;
 9:
10:     return 0;
11: }
```

Analysis ▼

Line 1 tells the standard header to be included for using the STL classes set and multiset, which are in the std namespace. Lines 7 and 8 demonstrate the template instantiation of these classes for the type int.

TIP

> This form of creating a set is one that relies on sorting using std::less <T>. This is the default sort predicate that works by invoking the < operator. There might be applications in which you want to override the sort mechanism, and you would do so by instantiating the set with a sort predicate (binary predicate) that is the optional second template parameter, like this:
>
> ```
> set <ObjectType, OptionalBinaryPredicate>
> setWithCustomSortPredicate;
> ```

Inserting Elements in an STL set or multiset

Most functions in a set and multiset work in a similar fashion. They accept similar parameters and return similar value types. For instance, inserting elements in both kinds of containers can be done using the member insert, which accepts the value to be inserted. There are other variations of the insert function, too, one of which you can see in Listing 20.2.

LISTING 20.2 Inserting Elements in an STL set and multiset

```
 1: #include <set>
 2: #include <iostream>
 3: using namespace std;
 4:
```

20

LISTING 20.2   Continued

```
 5: template <typename Container>
 6: void PrintContents (const Container & stlContainer);
 7:
 8: int main ()
 9: {
10:     set <int> setIntegers;
11:     multiset <int> msetIntegers;
12:
13:     setIntegers.insert (60);
14:     setIntegers.insert (-1);
15:     setIntegers.insert (3000);
16:     cout << "Writing the contents of the set to the screen" << endl;
17:     PrintContents (setIntegers);
18:
19:     msetIntegers.insert (setIntegers.begin (), setIntegers.end ());
20:     msetIntegers.insert (3000);
21:
22:     cout << "Writing the contents of the multiset to the screen" << endl;
23:     PrintContents (msetIntegers);
24:
25:     cout << "Number of instances of '3000' in the multiset are: '";
26:     cout << msetIntegers.count (3000) << "'" << endl;
27:
28:     return 0;
29: }
30:
31: template <typename Container>
32: void PrintContents (const Container & stlContainer)
33: {
34:     Container::const_iterator iElementLocator = stlContainer.begin ();
35:
36:     while (iElementLocator != stlContainer.end ())
37:     {
38:         cout << *iElementLocator << endl;
39:         ++ iElementLocator;
40:     }
41:
42:     cout << endl;
43: }
```

Output ▼

```
Writing the contents of the set to the screen
-1
60
3000
```

```
Writing the contents of the multiset to the screen
-1
60
3000
3000

Number of instances of '3000' in the multiset are: '2'
```

Analysis ▼

Lines 5 and 6 contain the declaration of the template function PrintContents, which is defined later in lines 31–43 and writes the contents of an STL container to the console or screen. Lines 10 and 11, as you already know, define a set and a multiset object. Lines 13–15 insert values into the set using the insert member function. Line 19 displays how the insert function can be used to insert the contents of one container into another, inserting in this case the contents of setIntegers into the multiset, msetIntegers. After inserting the contents of the set into the multiset, as in line 19, the code inserts an element with value 3000 that already exists in the multiset in line 15. The output demonstrates that the multiset is able to hold multiple values. Lines 25 and 26 demonstrate the utility of the multiset::count() member function, which returns the number of elements in the multiset that hold that particular value.

Finding Elements in an STL set or multiset

Associative containers like set and multiset, map, and multimap feature find()—a member function that allows you to find a value given a key, as demonstrated in Listing 20.3. In case of a multiset this function will find the first value that matches the supplied key.

LISTING 20.3 Using the find Member Function

```
1: #include <set>
2: #include <iostream>
3:
4: using namespace std;
5: typedef set <int> SETINT;
6:
7: int main ()
8: {
9:     SETINT setIntegers;
10:
11:     // Insert some random values
12:     setIntegers.insert (43);
13:     setIntegers.insert (78);
```

20

LISTING 20.3   Continued

```
14:    setIntegers.insert (-1);
15:    setIntegers.insert (124);
16:
17:    SETINT::const_iterator iElement;
18:
19:    // Write contents of the set to the screen
20:    for ( iElement = setIntegers.begin ()
21:         ; iElement != setIntegers.end ()
22:         ; ++ iElement )
23:        cout << *iElement << endl;
24:
25:    // Try finding an element
26:    SETINT::iterator iElementFound = setIntegers.find (-1);
27:
28:    // Check if found...
29:    if (iElementFound != setIntegers.end ())
30:        cout << "Element " << *iElementFound << " found!" << endl;
31:    else
32:        cout << "Element not found in set!" << endl;
33:
34:    // Try finding another element
35:    SETINT::iterator iAnotherFind = setIntegers.find (12345);
36:
37:    // Check if found...
38:    if (iAnotherFind != setIntegers.end ())
39:        cout << "Element " << *iAnotherFind << " found!" << endl;
40:    else
41:        cout << "Element 12345 not found in set!" << endl;
42:
43:    return 0;
44: }
```

Output ▼

```
-1
43
78
124
Element -1 found!
Element 12345 not found in set!
```

Analysis ▼

At line 5, the code typedefs the set of integers to make using the set syntax a little easier and probably more readable. Lines 26–32 display the usage of the find member function. find() returns an iterator that needs to be compared against end() as seen in line 29 to verify whether an element was found.

NOTE

> The example in Listing 20.3 would work correctly for a multiset, too; that is, if line 5 typedef-ed a multiset instead of a set, it would not change the way the application works:
>
> ```
> typedef multiset <int> MSETINT;
> ```

Erasing Elements in an STL set or multiset

Associative containers like set and multiset, map, and multimap feature erase(), which is a member function that allows you to delete a value given a key:

```
setObject.erase (key);
```

Another form of the erase function allows the deletion of a particular element given an iterator that points to it:

```
setObject.erase (iElement);
```

You can erase a range of elements from a set or a multiset using iterators that supply the bounds:

```
setObject.erase (iLowerBound, iUpperBound);
```

The sample in Listing 20.4 demonstrates the use of the erase() in removing elements from the set or multiset.

LISTING 20.4   Using the erase Member Function on a Multiset

```
 1: #include <set>
 2: #include <iostream>
 3:
 4: using namespace std;
 5: typedef multiset <int> MSETINT;
 6:
 7: int main ()
 8: {
 9:     MSETINT msetIntegers;
10:
11:     // Insert some random values
12:     msetIntegers.insert (43);
13:     msetIntegers.insert (78);
14:     msetIntegers.insert (78);     // Duplicate
15:     msetIntegers.insert (-1);
16:     msetIntegers.insert (124);
17:
18:     MSETINT::const_iterator iElement;
19:
```

20

LISTING 20.4 Continued

```
20:     cout << "multiset contains " << msetIntegers.size () << " elements.";
21:     cout << " These are: " << endl;
22:
23:     // Write contents of the multiset to the screen
24:     for ( iElement = msetIntegers.begin ()
25:         ; iElement != msetIntegers.end ()
26:         ; ++ iElement )
27:         cout << *iElement << endl;
28:
29:     cout << "Please enter a number to be erased from the set" << endl;
30:     int nNumberToErase = 0;
31:     cin >> nNumberToErase;
32:
33:     cout << "Erasing " << msetIntegers.count (nNumberToErase);
34:     cout << " instances of value " << nNumberToErase << endl;
35:
36:     // Try finding an element
37:     msetIntegers.erase (nNumberToErase);
38:
39:     cout << "multiset contains " << msetIntegers.size () << " elements.";
40:     cout << " These are: " << endl;
41:     for ( iElement = msetIntegers.begin ()
42:         ; iElement != msetIntegers.end ()
43:         ; ++ iElement )
44:         cout << *iElement << endl;
45:
46:     return 0;
47: }
```

Output ▼

```
multiset contains 5 elements. These are:
-1
43
78
78
124
Please enter a number to be erased from the set
78
Erasing 2 instances of value 78
multiset contains 3 elements. These are:
-1
43
124
```

Analysis ▼

This sample calls the erase function on a multiset, and not on a set (even though the syntax would have been no different) to demonstrate the effect of erase() on a value that belongs to multiple elements in the container—something that can only be possible in a multiset. Lines 12–16 insert sample values in the multiset, one of which is a duplicate. The program asks the user to enter the value to erase() from the multiset as seen in lines 29–31. The output indicates that the user feeds value 78, the value present in duplicate, and the erase operation in line 37 gets going. A display of the contents of the multiset after the erase() operation indicates that the multiset deleted all elements of value 78.

Note that erase() is overloaded. You can call erase() on an iterator, say one returned by a find operation to delete one element of the value found, as seen here:

```
MSETINT::iterator iElementFound = msetIntegers.find (nNumberToErase);
if (iElementFound != msetIntegers.end ())
    msetIntegers.erase (iElementFound);
else
    cout << "Element not found!" << endl;
```

Similarly, erase() can be used to remove a range of values from the multiset:

```
MSETINT::iterator iElementFound = msetIntegers.find (nValue);

if (iElementFound != msetIntegers.end ())
    msetIntegers.erase (msetIntegers.begin (), iElementFound);
```

The preceding snippet would remove all elements from the start to the element of value nValue, not including the latter. Both set and multiset can be emptied of their contents using member function clear().

Now that you have an overview of the basic set and multiset functions, it's time to review a sample that features a practical application made using this container class. The sample in Listing 20.5 is a simple implementation of a menu-based telephone directory that allows the user to insert names and telephone numbers, find them, erase them, and display them all.

20

LISTING 20.5 A Telephone Directory Featuring STL set, find, and erase

```
1: #include <set>
2: #include <iostream>
3: #include <string>
4:
5: using namespace std;
6:
```

LISTING 20.5   Continued

```
 7: enum MenuOptionSelection
 8: {
 9:     InsertContactsetEntry = 0,
10:     DisplayEntries = 1,
11:     FindNumber = 2,
12:     EraseEntry = 3,
13:     QuitApplication = 4
14: };
15:
16: struct ContactItem
17: {
18:     string strContactsName;
19:     string strPhoneNumber;
20:
21:     // Constructor
22:     ContactItem (const string& strName, const string & strNumber)
23:     {
24:         strContactsName = strName;
25:         strPhoneNumber = strNumber;
26:     }
27:
28:     bool operator == (const ContactItem& itemToCompare) const
29:     {
30:         return (itemToCompare.strContactsName == this->strContactsName);
31:     }
32:
33:     bool operator < (const ContactItem& itemToCompare) const
34:     {
35:         return (this->strContactsName < itemToCompare.strContactsName);
36:     }
37: };
38:
39: int ShowMenu ();
40: ContactItem GetContactInfo ();
41: void DisplayContactset (const set <ContactItem>& setContacts);
42: void FindContact (const set <ContactItem>& setContacts);
43: void EraseContact (set <ContactItem>& setContacts);
44:
45: int main ()
46: {
47:     set <ContactItem> setContacts;
48:     int nUserSelection = InsertContactsetEntry;
49:
50:     while ((nUserSelection = ShowMenu ()) != (int) QuitApplication)
51:     {
52:         switch (nUserSelection)
53:         {
54:         case InsertContactsetEntry:
55:             setContacts.insert (GetContactInfo ());
```

LISTING 20.5 Continued

```
56:                    cout << "Contacts set updated!" << endl << endl;
57:                    break;
58:
59:          case DisplayEntries:
60:                    DisplayContactset (setContacts);
61:                    break;
62:
63:          case FindNumber:
64:                    FindContact (setContacts);
65:                    break;
66:
67:          case EraseEntry:
68:                    EraseContact (setContacts);
69:                    DisplayContactset (setContacts);
70:                    break;
71:
72:          default:
73:                    cout << "Invalid input '" << nUserSelection;
74:                    cout << ".' Please choose an option between 0 and 4" << endl;
75:                    break;
76:          }
77:     }
78:
79:     cout << "Quitting! Bye!" << endl;
80:     return 0;
81: }
82:
83: void DisplayContactset (const set <ContactItem>& setContacts)
84: {
85:     cout << "*** Displaying contact information ***" << endl;
86:     cout << "There are " << setContacts.size () << " entries:" << endl;
87:
88:     set <ContactItem>::const_iterator iContact;
89:     for ( iContact = setContacts.begin ()
90:            ; iContact != setContacts.end ()
91:            ; ++ iContact )
92:          cout << "Name: '" << iContact->strContactsName << "' Number: '"
93:               << iContact->strPhoneNumber << "'" << endl;
94:
95:     cout << endl;
96: }
97:
98: ContactItem GetContactInfo ()
99: {
100:     cout << "*** Feed contact information ***" << endl;
101:     string strName;
102:     cout << "Please enter the person's name" << endl;;
103:     cout << "> ";
104:     cin >> strName;
105:
```

20

LISTING 20.5   Continued

```
106:        string strPhoneNumber;
107:        cout << "Please enter "<< strName << "'s phone number" << endl;
108:        cout << "> ";
109:        cin >> strPhoneNumber;
110:
111:        return ContactItem (strName, strPhoneNumber);
112: }
113:
114: int ShowMenu ()
115: {
116:        cout << "*** What would you like to do next? ***" << endl << endl;
117:        cout << "Enter 0 to feed a name and phone number" << endl;
118:        cout << "Enter 1 to Display all entries" << endl;
119:        cout << "Enter 2 to find an entry" << endl;
120:        cout << "Enter 3 to erase an entry" << endl;
121:        cout << "Enter 4 to quit this application" << endl << endl;
122:        cout << "> ";
123:
124:        int nOptionSelected = 0;
125:
126:        // Accept user input
127:        cin >> nOptionSelected ;
128:        cout << endl;
129:        return nOptionSelected;
130: }
131:
132: void FindContact (const set <ContactItem>& setContacts)
133: {
134:        cout << "*** Find a contact ***" << endl;
135:        cout << "Whose number do you wish to find?" << endl;
136:        cout << "> ";
137:        string strName;
138:        cin >> strName;
139:
140:        set <ContactItem>::const_iterator iContactFound
141:            = setContacts.find (ContactItem (strName, ""));
142:
143:        if (iContactFound != setContacts.end ())
144:        {
145:            cout << strName << " is reachable at number: ";
146:            cout << iContactFound->strPhoneNumber << endl;
147:        }
148:        else
149:            cout << strName << " was not found in the contacts list" << endl;
150:
151:        cout << endl;
152:
153:        return;
154: }
155:
```

LISTING 20.5 Continued

```cpp
156: void EraseContact (set <ContactItem>& setContacts)
157: {
158:     cout << "*** Erase a contact ***" << endl;
159:     cout << "Whose number do you wish to erase?" << endl;
160:     cout << "> ";
161:     string strName;
162:     cin >> strName;
163:
164:     size_t nErased = setContacts.erase (ContactItem (strName, ""));
165:     if (nErased > 0)
166:         cout << strName << "'s contact information erased." << endl;
167:     else
168:         cout << strName << " was not found!" << endl;
169:
170:     cout << endl;
171: }
```

Output ▼

```
*** What would you like to do next? ***

Enter 0 to feed a name and phone number
Enter 1 to Display all entries
Enter 2 to find an entry
Enter 3 to erase an entry
Enter 4 to quit this application

> 0

*** Feed contact information ***
Please enter the person's name
> Tina
Please enter Tina's phone number
> 78966413
Contacts set updated!

*** What would you like to do next? ***

Enter 0 to feed a name and phone number
Enter 1 to Display all entries
Enter 2 to find an entry
Enter 3 to erase an entry
Enter 4 to quit this application

> 0
```

20

```
*** Feed contact information ***
Please enter the person's name
> Jack
Please enter Jack's phone number
> 456654213
Contacts set updated!

*** What would you like to do next? ***

Enter 0 to feed a name and phone number
Enter 1 to Display all entries
Enter 2 to find an entry
Enter 3 to erase an entry
Enter 4 to quit this application

> 0

*** Feed contact information ***
Please enter the person's name
> Shawn
Please enter Shawn's phone number
> 77746123
Contacts set updated!

*** What would you like to do next? ***

Enter 0 to feed a name and phone number
Enter 1 to Display all entries
Enter 2 to find an entry
Enter 3 to erase an entry
Enter 4 to quit this application

> 0

*** Feed contact information ***
Please enter the person's name
> Fritz
Please enter Fritz's phone number
> 654666123
Contacts set updated!

*** What would you like to do next? ***

Enter 0 to feed a name and phone number
Enter 1 to Display all entries
Enter 2 to find an entry
Enter 3 to erase an entry
Enter 4 to quit this application

> 1
```

```
*** Displaying contact information ***
There are 4 entries:
Name: 'Fritz' Number: '654666123'
Name: 'Jack' Number: '456654213'
Name: 'Shawn' Number: '77746123'
Name: 'Tina' Number: '78966413'

*** What would you like to do next? ***

Enter 0 to feed a name and phone number
Enter 1 to Display all entries
Enter 2 to find an entry
Enter 3 to erase an entry
Enter 4 to quit this application

> 2

*** Find a contact ***
Whose number do you wish to find?
> Shawn
Shawn is reachable at number: 77746123

*** What would you like to do next? ***

Enter 0 to feed a name and phone number
Enter 1 to Display all entries
Enter 2 to find an entry
Enter 3 to erase an entry
Enter 4 to quit this application

> 3

*** Erase a contact ***
Whose number do you wish to erase?
> Steve
Steve was not found!

*** Displaying contact information ***
There are 4 entries:
Name: 'Fritz' Number: '654666123'
Name: 'Jack' Number: '456654213'
Name: 'Shawn' Number: '77746123'
Name: 'Tina' Number: '78966413'

*** What would you like to do next? ***

Enter 0 to feed a name and phone number
Enter 1 to Display all entries
Enter 2 to find an entry
```

20

```
Enter 3 to erase an entry
Enter 4 to quit this application

> 3

*** Erase a contact ***
Whose number do you wish to erase?
> Jack
Jack's contact information erased.

*** Displaying contact information ***
There are 3 entries:
Name: 'Fritz' Number: '654666123'
Name: 'Shawn' Number: '77746123'
Name: 'Tina' Number: '78966413'

*** What would you like to do next? ***

Enter 0 to feed a name and phone number
Enter 1 to Display all entries
Enter 2 to find an entry
Enter 3 to erase an entry
Enter 4 to quit this application

> 4

Quitting! Bye!
```

Analysis ▼

This simple implementation of a telephone directory is based on an STL set that contains objects of type ContactItem—a structure containing two attributes: a name and a telephone number that is defined in lines 16–37. operator < as defined in the structure supplies the default sort paradigm that is necessary for the set to store objects of this structure within it, sorted by name. Accordingly, when items stored in the set are displayed, the output indicates that the items are displayed in alphabetical order of the names of the contacts. The function FindContact, as shown in lines 132–154, demonstrates the application of the set::find() member function. Note that the result of a find operation is an iterator, as shown in line 140. This iterator is first compared against the end of the collection, as in line 112, to determine whether the find operation was successful in finding the value in the set. If so, the iterator returns points to the member in the set (a ContactItem) and is used accordingly to display the phone number, as shown in line 146. Else, a message indicating that the item not found is displayed by line 149. Note that the find syntax is applicable to all STL containers and gets intuitive to use. Similarly, lines 156–171 define EraseContact that demonstrates the usage of the erase member function to remove an element from the STL set.

TIP

This implementation of the telephone directory is based on the STL set and therefore does not allow for multiple entries containing the same value. If you need your implementation of the directory to allow two people with the same name (say, Tom) to be stored, you would choose the STL multiset. The preceding code would still work correctly if setContacts were to be a multiset. To make further use of the multiset's capability to store multiple entries of the same value, you would use the count() member function to know the number of items that hold a particular value, as seen in Listing 20.4. This is demonstrated in the previous code sample. Similar items are placed adjacently in a multiset, and the find function returns an iterator to the first found value. This iterator can be incremented the number of times as returned by count() (less one) to reach the next items.

Pros and Cons of Using STL set and multiset

The STL set and multiset provide significant advantages in applications that need frequent lookups because their contents are sorted and therefore quicker to locate. However, to present this advantage, the container needs to sort elements at insertion-time. Thus, there is an overhead in inserting elements because elements are sorted—an overhead that might be a worthwhile compromise if you need to use features and functions like find() that make use of the internal binary tree structure. This sorted binary tree structure results in another implicit disadvantage over sequential containers such as the vector. In a vector, the element pointed to by an iterator (say, one returned by a std::find() operation) can be overwritten by a new value. In case of a set however, elements are sorted by the set class according to their respective values, and therefore overwriting an element using an iterator should never be done, even if that were programmatically possible.

20

Summary

In this lesson, you learned about using the STL set and multiset, their significant member functions, and their characteristics. You also saw their application in the programming of a simple menu-based telephone directory that also features search and erase functions.

Q&A

Q **How would I declare a set of integers to be sorted and stored in order of descending magnitude?**

A `set <int>` defines a set of integers. This takes the default sort predicate `std::less <T>` to sort items in order of ascending magnitude, and can also be expressed as `set <int, less <int> >`. To sort in order of descending magnitude, define the set as `set <int, greater <int> >`.

Q **What would happen if, in a set of strings, I inserted the string `"Jack"` twice?**

A A set is not meant to be used to insert nonunique values. So, the implementation of the `std::set` class would not allow insertion of the second value.

Q **In the preceding example, if I wanted to have two instances of `"Jack"`, what would I change?**

A By design, a set holds only unique values. You would need to change your selection of container to a `multiset`.

Q **What `multiset` member function returns the count of items of a particular value in the container?**

A `count (value)` is the function of interest.

Q **I have found an element in the set using the `find` function and have an iterator pointing to it. Would I use this iterator to change the value being pointed to?**

A No. Some STL implementations might allow the user to change the value of an element inside a set via an iterator returned by, for example, `find`. However, this is not the correct thing to do. An iterator to an element in the set should be used as a `const` iterator—even when the STL implementation has not enforced it as such.

Workshop

The Workshop contains quiz questions to help solidify your understanding of the material covered and exercises to provide you with experience in using what you've learned. Try to answer the quiz and exercise questions before checking the answers in Appendix D, and be certain you understand the answers before going to the next lesson.

Quiz

1. You declare a set of integers as `set <int>`. What function supplies the sort criteria?

2. Where would you find duplicate elements in a `multiset`?

3. What set or `multiset` function supplies the number of elements in the container?

Exercises

1. Extend the telephone directory example in this lesson to find a person's name given a phone number, without changing structure `ContactItem`. (Hint: Define the `set` with a binary predicate that sorts items in accordance with the number, thus overriding the default sort based on the < operator.)

2. Define a `multiset` to store words and their meanings; that is, make a `multiset` work as a dictionary. (Hint: The `multiset` should be one of a structure that contains two strings: the word and its meaning.)

3. Demonstrate via a simple program that a `set` cannot accept duplicate entries, whereas a `multiset` can.

LESSON 21
STL map **and** multimap

The standard template library (STL) supplies the programmer with container classes that help with applications that require frequent and quick searches.

In this lesson, you will learn

- An introduction to the STL map and `multimap`

- Basic STL map and `multimap` operations

- Customizing behavior using a sort predicate

A Brief Introduction

The map and multimap are key-value pair containers that allow for a lookup on the basis of a key. The difference between the map and the multimap is that only the latter allows for duplicates, whereas the former can store only unique keys.

To facilitate quick searching, STL implementations of the map and multimap internally look like a binary tree. This means that elements inserted in a map or a multimap are sorted on insertion. It also means that, unlike in a vector where elements at a position can be replaced by another, elements in a map at a given position cannot be replaced by a new element of a different value. This is because the map would ideally like to have it placed in a possible different location in accordance with its value relative to those in the internal tree.

To use the STL map or multimap class, the programmer needs to include <map>.

Basic STL map and multimap Operations

STL map and multimap are template classes that need to be instantiated before you can use any of their member functions. To use the STL map or multimap class, the programmer needs to include <map>.

Instantiating a std::map Object

Instantiating a map or multimap requires a specialization of the respective template classes available in the std namespace. The template instantiation of the map class needs the programmer to specify the key type, the value type, and optionally a predicate that helps the map class to sort the elements on insertion. Therefore, typical map instantiation syntax looks like this:

```
#include <map>
using namespace std;
...
map <keyType, valueType, Predicate=std::less <keyType> > mapObject;
multimap <keyType, valueType, Predicate=std::less <keyType> > mmapObject;
```

Listing 21.1 illustrates this in greater detail.

LISTING 21.1   Instantiating an STL map and multimap (Key Type: integer, Value Type: string)

```
1: #include <map>
2: #include <string>
3:
```

LISTING 21.1   Continued

```
 4: int main ()
 5: {
 6:     using namespace std;
 7:
 8:     map <int, string> mapIntegersToString;
 9:     multimap <int, string> mmapIntegersToString;
10:
11:     return 0;
12: }
```

Analysis ▼

Line 1 indicates that the standard header map is included for using the STL classes map and multimap, which are in the std namespace. Lines 8 and 9 demonstrate the template instantiation of these classes, for key-type int, and value-type string.

TIP

> The template instantiation of a map also requires a third parameter that supplies the sorting criterion. In the preceding example, the absence of the third parameter results in the use of the default sort criterion. It is based on the STL function less <>, which compares two objects using operator <. To override the default sort mechanism, you would supply the map template instantiation syntax with a third parameter, a binary predicate, like this:
>
> ```
> map <KeyType, ValueType, BinaryPredicate>
> mapWithCustomSortPredicate;
> ```

Inserting Elements in an STL map or multimap

Most functions in a map and multimap work in a similar fashion. They accept similar parameters and return similar value types. For instance, you can insert elements in both kinds of containers by using the insert member function, as demonstrated in Listing 21.2.

LISTING 21.2   Inserting Elements in an STL map and multimap

21

```
1: #include <map>
2: #include <iostream>
3:
4: using namespace std;
5:
```

LISTING 21.2 Continued

```
 6: // Type-define the map and multimap definition for easy readability
 7: typedef map <int, string> MAP_INT_STRING;
 8: typedef multimap <int, string> MMAP_INT_STRING;
 9:
10: int main ()
11: {
12:     MAP_INT_STRING mapIntToString;
13:
14:     // Insert key-value pairs into the map using value_type
15:     mapIntToString.insert (MAP_INT_STRING::value_type (3, "Three"));
16:
17:     // Insert a pair using function make_pair
18:     mapIntToString.insert (make_pair (-1, "Minus One"));
19:
20:     // Insert a pair object directly
21:     mapIntToString.insert (pair <int, string> (1000, "One Thousand"));
22:
23:     // Insert using an array-like syntax for inserting key-value pairs
24:     mapIntToString [1000000] = "One Million";
25:
26:     cout << "The map contains " << mapIntToString.size ();
27:     cout << " key-value pairs. " << endl;
28:     cout << "The elements in the map are: " << endl;
29:
30:     // Print the contents of the map to the screen
31:     MAP_INT_STRING::const_iterator iMapPairLocator;
32:
33:     for ( iMapPairLocator = mapIntToString.begin ()
34:         ; iMapPairLocator != mapIntToString.end ()
35:         ; ++ iMapPairLocator )
36:     {
37:         cout << "Key: " << iMapPairLocator->first;
38:         cout << " Value: " << iMapPairLocator->second.c_str ();
39:
40:         cout << endl;
41:     }
42:
43:     MMAP_INT_STRING mmapIntToString;
44:
45:     // The insert function works the same way for multimap too
46:     mmapIntToString.insert (MMAP_INT_STRING::value_type (3, "Three"));
47:     mmapIntToString.insert (MMAP_INT_STRING::value_type (45, "Forty Five"));
48:     mmapIntToString.insert (make_pair (-1, "Minus One"));
49:     mmapIntToString.insert (pair <int, string> (1000, "One Thousand"));
50:
51:     // A multimap can store duplicates - insert one
52:     mmapIntToString.insert (MMAP_INT_STRING::value_type (1000, "Thousand"));
53:
54:     cout << endl << "The multimap contains " << mmapIntToString.size ();
```

LISTING 21.2 Continued

```
55:        cout << " key-value pairs." << endl;
56:        cout << "The elements in the multimap are: " << endl;
57:
58:        // Print the contents of the map to the screen
59:        MMAP_INT_STRING::const_iterator iMultiMapPairLocator;
60:
61:        for ( iMultiMapPairLocator = mmapIntToString.begin ()
62:            ; iMultiMapPairLocator != mmapIntToString.end ()
63:            ; ++ iMultiMapPairLocator )
64:        {
65:            cout << "Key: " << iMultiMapPairLocator->first;
66:            cout << " Value: " << iMultiMapPairLocator->second.c_str ();
67:
68:            cout << endl;
69:        }
70:
71:        cout << endl;
72:
73:        // The multimap can also return the number of pairs with the same key
74:        cout << "The number of pairs in the multimap with 1000 as their key: "
75:            << mmapIntToString.count (1000) << endl;
76:
77:        return 0;
78: }
```

Output ▼

```
The map contains 4 key-value pairs.
The elements in the map are:
Key: -1 Value: Minus One
Key: 3 Value: Three
Key: 1000 Value: One Thousand
Key: 1000000 Value: One Million

The multimap contains 5 key-value pairs.
The elements in the multimap are:
Key: -1 Value: Minus One
Key: 3 Value: Three
Key: 45 Value: Forty Five
Key: 1000 Value: One Thousand
Key: 1000 Value: One Thousand

The number of pairs in the multimap with 1000 as their key are: 2
```

21

Analysis ▼

The sample `typedef`s the template instantiation of the `map` and `multimap` in lines 7 and 8. Lines 14–24 display the different ways to insert elements in a `map`. Of these four methods illustrated in the sample, only the last one, which features element insertion using an array-like syntax via subscript `operator[]`, is peculiar to the `map`. All the other methods can be used with a `multimap` also. Also note how the elements in a `map` or a `multimap` can be accessed using iterators, as seen in lines 29–37. An iterator points to an element in a container. If the container is a `map` or a `multimap`, this element is a `pair`, and therefore the iterator points to a `pair`. The contents of the `pair` can be accessed using member elements `first` and `second`, as seen in lines 37 and 38. The former is the key, and the latter is the value, as the output also demonstrates.

Finding Elements in an STL `map` or `multimap`

Associative containers such as `map` and `multimap` feature a member function called `find` that allows you to find a value given a key. The sample in Listing 21.3 demonstrates the usage of `multimap::find`.

LISTING 21.3   Usage of the `find` Member Function in a `multimap`

```
 1: #include <map>
 2: #include <iostream>
 3: #include <string>
 4:
 5: using namespace std;
 6:
 7: // Typedef the multimap definition for easy readability
 8: typedef multimap <int, string> MMAP_INT_STRING;
 9:
10: int main ()
11: {
12:     MMAP_INT_STRING mmapIntToString;
13:
14:     // The insert function works the same way for multimap too
15:     mmapIntToString.insert (MMAP_INT_STRING::value_type (3, "Three"));
16:     mmapIntToString.insert (MMAP_INT_STRING::value_type (45, "Forty Five"));
17:     mmapIntToString.insert (MMAP_INT_STRING::value_type (-1, "Minus One"));
18:     mmapIntToString.insert (MMAP_INT_STRING::value_type (1000, "Thousand"));
19:
20:     // A multimap can store duplicates - insert one
21:     mmapIntToString.insert (MMAP_INT_STRING::value_type
22:                             (1000, "Thousand (duplicate)"));
23:
24:     cout << "The multimap contains " << mmapIntToString.size ();
25:     cout << " key-value pairs." << endl;
```

LISTING 21.3 Continued

```
26:     cout << "The elements in the multimap are: " << endl;
27:
28:     // Print the contents of the map to the screen
29:     MMAP_INT_STRING::const_iterator iMultiMapPairLocator;
30:
31:     for ( iMultiMapPairLocator = mmapIntToString.begin ()
32:         ; iMultiMapPairLocator != mmapIntToString.end ()
33:         ; ++ iMultiMapPairLocator )
34:     {
35:         cout << "Key: " << iMultiMapPairLocator->first;
36:         cout << ", Value: " << iMultiMapPairLocator->second << endl;
37:     }
38:
39:     cout << endl;
40:
41:     cout << "Finding all key-value pairs with 1000 as their key: " << endl;
42:
43:     // Find an element in the multimap using the 'find' function
44:     MMAP_INT_STRING::const_iterator iElementFound;
45:
46:     iElementFound = mmapIntToString.find (1000);
47:
48:     // Check if "find" succeeded
49:     if (iElementFound != mmapIntToString.end ())
50:     {
51:         // Find the number of pairs that have the same supplied key
52:         size_t nNumPairsInMap = mmapIntToString.count (1000);
53:         cout << "The number of pairs in the multimap with 1000 as key: ";
54:         cout << nNumPairsInMap << endl;
55:
56:         // Output those values to the screen
57:         cout << "The values corresponding to the key 1000 are: " << endl;
58:         for ( size_t nValuesCounter = 0
59:             ; nValuesCounter < nNumPairsInMap
60:             ; ++ nValuesCounter )
61:         {
62:             cout << "Key: " << iElementFound->first;
63:             cout << ", Value [" << nValuesCounter << "] = ";
64:             cout << iElementFound->second << endl;
65:
66:             ++ iElementFound;
67:         }
68:     }
69:     else
70:         cout << "Element not found in the multimap";
71:
72:     return 0;
73: }
```

21

Output ▼

```
The multimap contains 5 key-value pairs.
The elements in the multimap are:
Key: -1, Value: Minus One
Key: 3, Value: Three
Key: 45, Value: Forty Five
Key: 1000, Value: Thousand
Key: 1000, Value: Thousand (duplicate)

Finding all pairs with 1000 as their key...
The number of pairs in the multimap with 1000 as key: 2
The values corresponding to the key 1000 are:
Key: 1000, Value [0] = Thousand
Key: 1000, Value [1] = Thousand (duplicate)
```

Analysis ▼

The syntax of instantiating a `multimap` and inserting elements as seen in lines 1–21 was studied in Listings 21.1 and 21.2. Line 46 displays the usage of the `find` member function. In STL, `find` always returns an iterator that potentially points to the element found, an element which in this case would be a key-value `pair`. To determine the success of the `find` operation, that iterator should first be compared against another as returned by member `end()` as seen in line 49. Lines 52–67 indicate how the elements with similar keys in the `multimap` can be accessed and displayed. Note how `count()` was used in line 52 to determine the number of pairs in the `map` that have the same key. As the iterator returned by `find` points to the first element, and as a `multimap` arranges all elements of a value in sequential positions, we simply move the iterator that many elements forward to access other pairs containing the same key.

Erasing Elements from an STL `map` or `multimap`

The `map` and `multimap` feature a member function, `erase`, which deletes an element from the container. The `erase` function is invoked with the key as the parameter to delete all pairs with a certain key:

```
mapObject.erase (key);
```

Another form of the `erase` function allows the deletion of a particular element given an iterator that points to it:

```
mapObject.erase (iElement);
```

You can erase a range of elements from a `map` or a `multimap` using iterators that supply the bounds:

```
mapObject.erase (iLowerBound, iUpperBound);
```

Listing 21.4 illustrates the usage of the `erase` functions.

LISTING 21.4 Erasing Elements from a multimap

```
 1: #include <map>
 2: #include <iostream>
 3: #include <string>
 4:
 5: using namespace std;
 6:
 7: // typedef the multimap definition for easy readability
 8: typedef multimap <int, string> MULTIMAP_INT_STRING;
 9:
10: int main ()
11: {
12:     MULTIMAP_INT_STRING mmapIntToString;
13:
14:     // Insert key-value pairs into the multimap
15:     mmapIntToString.insert (MULTIMAP_INT_STRING::value_type (3, "Three"));
16:     mmapIntToString.insert (MULTIMAP_INT_STRING::value_type(45, "Forty
Five"));
17:     mmapIntToString.insert (MULTIMAP_INT_STRING::value_type (-1, "Minus
One"));
18:     mmapIntToString.insert (MULTIMAP_INT_STRING::value_type (1000,
"Thousand"));
19:
20:     // Insert duplicates into the multimap
21:     mmapIntToString.insert (MULTIMAP_INT_STRING::value_type (-1, "Minus
One"));
22:     mmapIntToString.insert (MULTIMAP_INT_STRING::value_type (1000,
"Thousand"));
23:
24:     cout << "The multimap contains " << mmapIntToString.size ();
25:     cout << " key-value pairs. " << "They are: " << endl;
26:
27:     // Print the contents of the multimap to the screen
28:     MULTIMAP_INT_STRING::const_iterator iPairLocator;
29:
30:     for ( iPairLocator = mmapIntToString.begin ()
31:         ; iPairLocator != mmapIntToString.end ()
32:         ; ++ iPairLocator )
33:     {
34:         cout << "Key: " << iPairLocator->first;
35:         cout << ", Value: " << iPairLocator->second.c_str () << endl;
36:     }
37:
38:     cout << endl;
39:
40:     // Eraseing an element with key as -1 from the multimap
41:     if (mmapIntToString.erase (-1) > 0)
42:         cout << "Erased all pairs with -1 as key." << endl;
43:
```

21

LISTING 21.4   Continued

```
44:    // Erase an element given an iterator from the multimap
45:    MULTIMAP_INT_STRING::iterator iElementLocator =
mmapIntToString.find(45);
46:    if (iElementLocator != mmapIntToString.end ())
47:    {
48:        mmapIntToString.erase (iElementLocator);
49:        cout << "Erased a pair with 45 as key using an iterator" << endl;
50:    }
51:
52:    // Erase a range from the multimap...
53:    cout << "Erasing the range of pairs with 1000 as key." << endl;
54:    mmapIntToString.erase ( mmapIntToString.lower_bound (1000)
55:        , mmapIntToString.upper_bound (1000) );
56:
57:    cout << endl;
58:    cout << "The multimap now contains " << mmapIntToString.size ();
59:    cout << " key-value pair(s)." << "They are: " << endl;
60:
61:    // Print the contents of the multimap to the screen
62:    for ( iPairLocator = mmapIntToString.begin ()
63:        ; iPairLocator != mmapIntToString.end ()
64:        ; ++ iPairLocator )
65:    {
66:        cout << "Key: " << iPairLocator->first;
67:        cout << ", Value: " << iPairLocator->second.c_str () << endl;
68:    }
69:
70:    return 0;
71: }
```

Output ▼

```
The multimap contains 6 key-value pairs. They are:
Key: -1, Value: Minus One
Key: -1, Value: Minus One
Key: 3, Value: Three
Key: 45, Value: Forty Five
Key: 1000, Value: Thousand
Key: 1000, Value: Thousand

Erased all pairs with -1 as key.
Erased a pair with 45 as key using an iterator
Erasing the range of pairs with 1000 as key.

The multimap now contains 1 key-value pair(s).They are:
Key: 3, Value: Three
```

Analysis ▼

Lines 15–22 insert sample values into the multimap, some of them being duplicates (because a multimap, unlike a map, does support the insertion of duplicate items). After pairs have been inserted into the multimap, the code erases items by using the version of the erase function that accepts a key and erases all items with that key (–1) as seen in line 41. In line 45, the multimap::find function is used to locate the pair with key 45 in the map. In line 48, this pair is erased from the multimap using the very iterator that was returned by the find operation. Finally the code erases a range of elements with the key 1000, as shown in line 54. The bounds of the range are supplied by functions lower_bound and upper_bound, and as the output indicates, the erase operation on these bounds results in the map being devoid of pairs with 1000 as the key.

TIP

In Listing 21.3, note that the iterator iPairLocator used to enumerate the elements in the map is of type const_iterator, but the iterator iElementFound that was returned by the find operation and used in erase isn't one. This is by intention. Iterators that need to enumerate a container and need to display elements don't need to change the container and therefore should be of the type const_iterator. Iterators that are used in operations such as erase that need to modify the contents of the container cannot be of type const_iterator.

Supplying a Custom Sort Predicate

The map and multimap template definition includes a third parameter that accepts the sort predicate for the map to function correctly. This third parameter, when not mentioned (as in the preceding examples), is substituted with the default sort criterion provided by std::less <>, which essentially compares two objects using the < operator.

There are, however, cases in which a map might need to be sorted, and therefore searched, according to a different criterion. A map that holds a std::string type as the key will have a default sort criterion based on the < operator defined by the std::string class, and therefore will be case sensitive. For many applications, such as a telephone directory, it is important to feature an insertion and search operation that is not case sensitive. One way of solving this requirement is to supply the map with a sort predicate that returns either true or false on the basis of a comparison that is not case sensitive:

```
map <keyType, valueType, Predicate> mapObject;
```

Listing 21.5 explains this in detail.

LISTING 21.5   Using a std::map with a Custom sort Predicate to Program a Telephone
Directory

```
 1: #include <map>
 2: #include <algorithm>
 3: #include <string>
 4: #include <iostream>
 5:
 6: using namespace std;
 7:
 8: /*
 9: This is the binary predicate that helps the map sort
10: string-keys irrespective of their case
11: */
12: struct CCaseInsensitive
13: {
14:     bool operator () (const string& str1, const string& str2) const
15:     {
16:         string str1NoCase (str1), str2NoCase (str2);
17:         transform (str1.begin(), str1.end(), str1NoCase.begin(), tolower);
18:         transform (str2.begin(), str2.end(), str2NoCase.begin(), tolower);
19:
20:         return (str1NoCase < str2NoCase);
21:     };
22: };
23:
24:
25: // Typedef map definitions for easy readability...
26: // A directory that sorts keys using string::operator < (case sensitive)
27: typedef map <string, string> DIRECTORY_WITHCASE;
28:
29: // A case-insensitive directory definition
30: typedef map <string, string, CCaseInsensitive> DIRECTORY_NOCASE;
31:
32: int main ()
33: {
34:     // Case-insensitive directory: case of the string-key plays no role
35:     DIRECTORY_NOCASE dirNoCase;
36:
37:     dirNoCase.insert (DIRECTORY_NOCASE::value_type ("John", "2345764"));
38:     dirNoCase.insert (DIRECTORY_NOCASE::value_type ("JOHN", "2345764"));
39:     dirNoCase.insert (DIRECTORY_NOCASE::value_type ("Sara", "42367236"));
40:     dirNoCase.insert (DIRECTORY_NOCASE::value_type ("Jack", "32435348"));
41:
42:     cout << "Displaying contents of the case-insensitive map:" << endl;
43:
44:     // Print the contents of the map to the screen
```

LISTING 21.5 Continued

```
45:        DIRECTORY_NOCASE::const_iterator iPairLocator1;
46:        for ( iPairLocator1 = dirNoCase.begin()
47:             ; iPairLocator1 != dirNoCase.end()
48:             ; ++ iPairLocator1 )
49:        {
50:            cout << "Name: " << iPairLocator1->first;
51:            cout << ", Phone number: " << iPairLocator1->second << endl;
52:        }
53:
54:        cout << endl;
55:
56:        // Case-sensitive directory: case of the string-key affects
57:        // insertion & search
58:        DIRECTORY_WITHCASE dirWithCase;
59:
60:        // Take sample values from previous map...
61:        dirWithCase.insert ( dirNoCase.begin(), dirNoCase.end() );
62:
63:        cout << "Displaying contents of the case-sensitive map:" << endl;
64:
65:        // Print the contents of the map to the screen
66:        DIRECTORY_WITHCASE::const_iterator iPairLocator2;
67:        for ( iPairLocator2 = dirWithCase.begin()
68:             ; iPairLocator2 != dirWithCase.end()
69:             ; ++ iPairLocator2 )
70:        {
71:            cout << "Name: " << iPairLocator2->first;
72:            cout << ", Phone number: " << iPairLocator2->second << endl;
73:        }
74:
75:        cout << endl;
76:
77:        // Search for a name in the two maps and display result
78:        cout << "Please enter a name to search: " << endl << "> ";
79:        string strNameInput;
80:        cin >> strNameInput;
81:
82:        DIRECTORY_NOCASE::const_iterator iSearchResult1;
83:
84:        // find in the map...
85:        iSearchResult1 = dirNoCase.find (strNameInput);
86:        if (iSearchResult1 != dirNoCase.end())
87:        {
88:            cout<<iSearchResult1->first<< "'s number in the case-insensitive";
89:            cout << " directory is: " << iSearchResult1->second << endl;
90:        }
91:        else
92:        {
```

21

LISTING 21.5   Continued

```
93:            cout << strNameInput << "'s number not found ";
94:            cout << "in the case-insensitive directory" << endl;
95:        }
96:
97:        DIRECTORY_WITHCASE::const_iterator iSearchResult2;
98:
99:        // find in the case-sensitive map...
100:       iSearchResult2 = dirWithCase.find (strNameInput);
101:       if (iSearchResult2 != dirWithCase.end())
102:       {
103:           cout<< iSearchResult2->first<< "'s number in the case-sensitive";
104:           cout << " directory is: " << iSearchResult2->second << endl;
105:       }
106:       else
107:       {
108:           cout << strNameInput << "'s number was not found ";
109:           cout << "in the case-sensitive directory" << endl;
110:       }
111:
112:       return 0;
113: }
```

Output ▼

```
Displaying the contents of the case-insensitive map on the screen...
Name: Jack, Phone number: 32435348
Name: John, Phone number: 2345764
Name: Sara, Phone number: 42367236

Displaying the contents of the case-sensitive map on the screen...
Name: Jack, Phone number: 32435348
Name: John, Phone number: 2345764
Name: Sara, Phone number: 42367236

Please enter a name to search in the directories:
> JOHN
John's number from the case-insensitive directory is: 2345764
JOHN's number was not found in the case-sensitive directory
```

Analysis ▼

Listing 21.5 features two directories based on a map of a string as a key to a string as the value. One is a case-sensitive directory that does not feature any predicate, as shown in line 27, and therefore uses the default predicate (that is, std::less <>) that invokes operator < of the key, that is, std::string class, which is case sensitive. The other is a map that features the predicate CCaseInsensitive that compares two strings irrespective of the case of the characters they contain, and returns true when the first is evaluated as less than the second. Lines 14–21 demonstrate the binary predicate that essentially accepts the two strings as input, reduces them both to lowercase before comparing them, and returns a Boolean value. When supplied to a map, this predicate helps it insert and, therefore, search elements irrespective of their case. The output demonstrates that the two directory objects contain exactly the same elements. Yet, when the user inserts a name (that is, a key to search) that is present in both the directories but in a different case, the version that is not case sensitive is able to locate the item, thanks to the predicate function object, whereas the case-sensitive directory fails.

This sample demonstrated how you can use predicates to customize the behavior of a map. It also implies that the key could potentially be of any type, and that the programmer can supply a predicate that defines the behavior of the map for that type. Note that the predicate was a struct that implemented operator(). It could have also been a class. Such objects that double as functions are called Function Objects or Functors. This topic is addressed in further detail in Lesson 22, "Understanding Function Objects."

Summary

In this lesson, you learned about using the STL map and multimap, their significant member functions, and their characteristics. You also learned the importance of being able to customize the sort criterion using a predicate, as demonstrated in the Directory application of Listing 21.5.

Q&A

Q How would I declare a map of integers to be sorted / stored in order of descending magnitude?

A map <int> defines a map of integers. This takes the default sort predicate std::less <T> to sort items in order of ascending magnitude, and can also be expressed as map <int, less <int> >. To sort in order of descending magnitude, define the map as map <int, greater <int> >.

Q What would happen if in a map of strings I inserted the string Jack twice?

A A map is not meant to be used to insert nonunique values. So, the implementation of the std::map class will not allow insertion of the second value.

21

Q In the above example, if I wished to have two instances of `Jack`, what would you change?

A A `map` by design holds only unique values. You would need to change your selection of container to a `multimap`.

Q What multimap member function returns the count of items of a particular value in the container?

A `count (value)` is the function of interest.

Q I have found an element in the map using the 'find' function and have an iterator pointing to it. Would I use this iterator to change the value being pointed to?

A No. Some STL implementations may allow the user to change the value of an element inside a `map` via an iterator returned by say 'find'. This however is not the correct thing to do. An iterator to an element in the `map` should be used as a 'const' iterator—even when the STL implementation has not enforced it as such.

Workshop

The Workshop contains quiz questions to help solidify your understanding of the material covered and exercises to provide you with experience in using what you've learned. Try to answer the quiz and exercise questions before checking the answers in Appendix D, and be certain you understand the answers before going to the next lesson.

Quiz

1. If you declare a `map` of integers as map `<int>`, what function supplies the sort criteria?

2. Where would you find duplicate elements in a `multimap`?

3. What `map` or `multimap` function supplies the number of elements in the container?

4. Where would you find duplicate elements in a `map`?

Exercises

1. You need to write an application that works as a telephone directory where the name of the people need not be unique. What container would you choose? Write a definition of the container.

2. The following is a map template definition in your dictionary application:

```
map <wordProperty, string, fPredicate> mapWordDefinition;
```

where word is the structure

```
struct wordProperty
{
string strWord;
bool bIsFromLatin;
};
```

Define the binary predicate fPredicate that will help the map sort a key of type wordProperty according to the string attribute it contains.

3. Demonstrate via a simple program that a map cannot accept duplicate entries, whereas a multimap can.

PART IV:
More STL

LESSON 22
Understanding Function Objects

Function objects or *functors* might sound exotic or intimidating, but they are entities of C++ that you have probably seen if not also used, without having realized it. In this lesson, you will learn

- The concept of function objects

- The usage of function objects as predicates

- How unary and binary predicates are implemented using function objects

The Concept of Function Objects and Predicates

On a conceptual level, function objects are objects that work as functions. On an implementation level, however, function objects are objects of a class that implements `operator()`. Although functions and function-pointers can also be classified as function objects, it is the capability of an object of a class that implements `operator()` to carry `state` (that is, values in member attributes of the class) that makes it useful with standard template library (STL) algorithms.

Function objects as typically used by a C++ programmer working with STL are classifiable into the following types:

- **Unary function**—A function called with one argument; for example, `f(x)`. When a unary function returns a `bool`, it is called a *predicate*.

- **Binary function**—A function called with two arguments; for example, `f(x, y)`. A binary function that returns a `bool` is called a *binary predicate*.

Function objects that return a `boolean` type naturally find use in algorithms that need decision-making. A function object that combines two function objects is called an *adaptive function object*.

Typical Applications of Function Objects

It is possible to explain function objects over pages and pages of theoretical explanations. It is also possible to understand how they look and work via tiny sample applications. Let's take the practical approach and dive straight into the world of C++ programming with function objects or functors!

Unary Functions

Functions that operate on a single parameter are unary functions. A unary function can do something very simple, for example displays an element on the screen. This can be programmed as

```
// A unary function
template <typename elementType>
void FuncDisplayElement (const elementType & element)
{
    cout << element << ' ';
};
```

The function `FuncDisplayElement` accepts one parameter of templatized type `elementType` that it displays using console output statement `std::cout`. The same function can also have another representation in which the implementation of the function is actually contained by the `operator()` of a `class` or a `struct`:

```
// Struct that can behave as a unary function
template <typename elementType>
struct DisplayElement
{
    void operator () (const elementType& element) const
    {
        cout << element << ' ';
    }
};
```

22

TIP

Note that `DisplayElement` is a `struct`. If it were a `class`, `operator()` would need to be given a `public` access modifier. A `struct` is akin to a `class` where members are `public` by default.

Either of these implementations can be used with the STL algorithm `for_each` to print the contents of a collection to the screen, an element at a time, as seen in Listing 22.1.

LISTING 22.1   Displaying the Contents of a Collection on the Screen Using a Unary Function

```
 1: #include <algorithm>
 2: #include <iostream>
 3: #include <vector>
 4: #include <list>
 5:
 6: using namespace std;
 7:
 8: // struct that behaves as a unary function
 9: template <typename elementType>
10: struct DisplayElement
11: {
12:     void operator () (const elementType& element) const
13:     {
14:         cout << element << ' ';
15:     }
16: };
17:
18: int main ()
19: {
20:     vector <int> vecIntegers;
21:
```

LISTING 22.1 Continued

```
22:     for (int nCount = 0; nCount < 10; ++ nCount)
23:         vecIntegers.push_back (nCount);
24:
25:     list <char> listChars;
26:
27:     for (char nChar = 'a'; nChar < 'k'; ++nChar)
28:         listChars.push_back (nChar);
29:
30:     cout << "Displaying the vector of integers: " << endl;
31:
32:     // Display the array of integers
33:     for_each ( vecIntegers.begin ()      // Start of range
34:             , vecIntegers.end ()         // End of range
35:             , DisplayElement <int> () ); // Unary function object
36:
37:     cout << endl << endl;
38:     cout << "Displaying the list of characters: " << endl;
39:
40:     // Display the list of characters
41:     for_each ( listChars.begin ()        // Start of range
42:             , listChars.end ()           // End of range
43:             , DisplayElement <char> () );// Unary function object
44:
45:     return 0;
46: }
```

Output ▼

```
Displaying the vector of integers:
0 1 2 3 4 5 6 7 8 9

Displaying the list of characters:
a b c d e f g h i j
```

Analysis ▼

Lines 9–16 contain the function object DisplayElement, which implements operator(). The usage of this function object is seen with STL algorithm std::for_each, in lines 33–35. for_each accepts three parameters: First the starting point of the range, second being the end of the range, and the third parameter is the function that is called for every element in the specified range. In other words, that code invokes DisplayElement::operator() for every element in the vector vecIntegers. Note that instead of using the struct DisplayElement, we could have also used FuncDisplayElement to the same effect. Lines 40–43 demonstrate the same functionality with a list of characters.

The real advantage of using a function object implemented in a `struct` becomes apparent when you are able to use the object of the `struct` to store information. This is something `FuncDisplayElement` cannot do the way a `struct` can because a struct can have member attributes, other than the `operator()`. A slightly modified version that makes use of member attributes would be:

22

```
template <typename elementType>
struct DisplayElementKeepCount
{
    int m_nCount;

    DisplayElementKeepCount ()   // constructor
    {
        m_nCount = 0;
    }

    void operator () (const elementType& element)
    {
        ++ m_nCount;
        cout << element << ' ';
    }
};
```

In the snippet above, `DisplayElementKeepCount` is a slight modification over the previous version. `operator()` is not a `const` member function anymore as it increments (hence, changes) member m_nCount, to keep a count of the number of times it was called to display data. This count is made available via the public member attribute m_nCount. The advantage of using such function objects that can also store `state` is seen in Listing 22.2.

LISTING 22.2   Use a Function Object to Hold `state`

```
1: #include <algorithm>
2: #include <iostream>
3: #include <vector>
4: #include <list>
5:
6: using namespace std;
7:
8: template <typename elementType>
9: struct DisplayElementKeepCount
10: {
11:     // Hold the count in a member variable
12:     int m_nCount;
13:
14:     // Constructor
15:     DisplayElementKeepCount ()
16:     {
```

LISTING 22.2   Continued

```
17:            m_nCount = 0;
18:        }
19:
20:        // Display the element, hold count!
21:        void operator () (const elementType& element)
22:        {
23:            ++ m_nCount;
24:            cout << element << ' ';
25:        }
26: };
27:
28: int main ()
29: {
30:     vector <int> vecIntegers;
31:
32:     for (int nCount = 0; nCount < 10; ++ nCount)
33:         vecIntegers.push_back (nCount);
34:
35:     cout << "Displaying the vector of integers: " << endl;
36:
37:     // Display the array of integers
38:     DisplayElementKeepCount <int> mResult;
39:     mResult = for_each ( vecIntegers.begin ()    // Start of range
40:                        , vecIntegers.end ()       // End of range
41:                        , DisplayElementKeepCount <int> () );// function object
42:
43:     cout << endl << endl;
44:
45:     // Use the state stores in the return value of for_each!
46:     cout << "'" << mResult.m_nCount << "' elements were displayed!" << endl;
47:
48:     return 0;
49: }
```

Output ▼

```
Displaying the vector of integers:
0 1 2 3 4 5 6 7 8 9

'10' elements were displayed!
```

Analysis ▼

The biggest difference between this sample and the previous one seen in Listing 22.1 is the usage of DisplayElementKeepCount as the return value of for_each. operator() that displays the element and increments the internal counter when called on a per-element basis stores the number of times the object was used in m_nCount. After for_each is done, we use the object in line 46 to display the number of times elements were displayed. Note that a regular function used in this scenario instead of the function implemented in a struct would not be able to supply this feature in such a direct way.

Unary Predicate

A unary function that returns a bool is a predicate. Such functions help make decisions for STL algorithms. Listing 22.3 is a sample predicate that determines whether an input element is a multiple of an initial value.

LISTING 22.3 A Unary Predicate That Determines Whether a Number Is a Multiple of Another

```
1: // A structure as a unary predicate
2: template <typename numberType>
3: struct IsMultiple
4: {
5:     numberType m_Divisor;
6:
7:     // divisorialize the divisor
8:     IsMultiple (const numberType& divisor)
9:     {
10:         m_Divisor = divisor;
11:     }
12:
13:     // The comparator of type: bool f(x)
14:     bool operator () (const numberType& element) const
15:     {
16:         // Check if the dividend is a multiple of the divisor
17:         return ((element % m_Divisor) == 0);
18:     }
19: };
```

Analysis ▼

Here the operator() returns bool and works as a unary predicate. The structure has a constructor and is initialized to the value of the divisor. This value stored in the object is then used to determine whether the elements sent for comparison are divisible by it, as you can see in the implementation of operator(), using the math operation modulus % that return the remainder of a division operation. The predicate compares that remainder to zero to determine whether the number is a multiple.

In Listing 22.4, we make use of the predicate as seen previously in Listing 22.3 to determine whether numbers in a collection are multiples of 4.

LISTING 22.4   Using the Unary Predicate `IsMultiple`

```
1: #include <algorithm>
2: #include <vector>
3: #include <iostream>
4:
5: using namespace std;
6:
7: // Insert definition of struct IsMultiple from Listing 22.3 here
8:
9: int main ()
10: {
11:     vector <int> vecIntegers;
12:
13:     cout << "The vector contains the following sample values: ";
14:
15:     // Insert sample values: 25 - 31
16:     for (int nCount = 25; nCount < 32; ++ nCount)
17:     {
18:         vecIntegers.push_back (nCount);
19:         cout << nCount << ' ';
20:     }
21:
22:     cout << endl;
23:
24:     // Find the first element that is a multiple of 4 in the collection
25:     vector <int>::iterator iElement;
26:     iElement = find_if ( vecIntegers.begin ()
27:         , vecIntegers.end ()
28:         , IsMultiple <int> (4) );   // Unary predicate initialized to 4
29:
30:     if (iElement != vecIntegers.end ())
31:     {
32:         cout << "The first element in the vector divisible by 4 is: ";
33:         cout << *iElement << endl;
34:     }
35:
36:     return 0;
37: }
```

Output ▼

```
The vector contains the following sample values: 25 26 27 28 29 30 31
The first element in the vector that is divisible by 4 is: 28
```

Analysis ▼

The sample starts with a sample container that is a vector of integers. In lines 16–20, it inserts sample numbers into this container. The usage of the unary predicate is in find_if as seen in lines 26–28. In here, the function object IsMultiple is initialized to a divisor value of 4. find_if works by invoking the unary predicate IsMultiple::operator() for every element in the specified range. When the operator() returns true for an element (which happens when that element when divided by 4 does not produce a remainder), find_if returns an iterator iElement to that element. The result of the find_if operation is compared against the end() of the container to verify that an element was found, as seen in line 30, and the iterator iElement is then used to display the value, as seen in line 33.

Unary predicates find application in a lot of STL algorithms such as std::partition that can partition a range using the predicate, or stable_partition that does the same while keeping relative order of the elements partitioned, or in find functions such as std::find_if, and functions that help erase elements such as std::remove_if that erases elements in a range that satisfy the predicate.

Binary Functions

Functions of type f(x, y) are particularly useful when they return a value based on the input supplied. Such binary functions can be used for a host of arithmetic activity that involves two operands, such as addition, multiplication, subtraction, and so on. A sample binary function that returns the multiple of input arguments can be written as:

```
template <typename elementType>
class CMultiply
{
public:
    elementType operator () (const elementType& elem1,
                             const elementType& elem2)
    {
        return (elem1 * elem2);
    }
};
```

The implementation of interest is again in operator() that accepts two arguments and returns their multiple. Such binary functions are used in algorithms such as std::transform where you can use it to multiply the contents of two containers. Listing 22.5 demonstrates the usage of such binary functions in std::transform.

LISTING 22.5   Using a Binary Function to Multiply Two Ranges

```
1: #include <vector>
2: #include <iostream>
3: #include <algorithm>
4:
```

LISTING 22.5 Continued

```
 5: template <typename elementType>
 6: class CMultiply
 7: {
 8: public:
 9:     elementType operator () (const elementType& elem1,
10:         const elementType& elem2)
11:     {
12:         return (elem1 * elem2);
13:     }
14: };
15:
16: int main ()
17: {
18:     using namespace std;
19:
20:     // Create two sample vector of integers with 10 elements each
21:     vector <int> vecMultiplicand, vecMultiplier;
22:
23:     // Insert sample values 0 to 9
24:     for (int nCount1 = 0; nCount1 < 10; ++ nCount1)
25:         vecMultiplicand.push_back (nCount1);
26:
27:     // Insert sample values 100 to 109
28:     for (int nCount2 = 100; nCount2 < 110; ++ nCount2)
29:         vecMultiplier.push_back (nCount2);
30:
31:     // A third container that holds the result of multiplication
32:     vector <int> vecResult;
33:
34:     // Make space for the result of the multiplication
35:     vecResult.resize (10);
36:
37:     transform (    vecMultiplicand.begin (), // range of multiplicands
38:                    vecMultiplicand.end (), // end of range
39:                    vecMultiplier.begin (),  // multiplier values
40:                    vecResult.begin (), // range that holds result
41:                    CMultiply <int> () );    // the function that multiplies
42:
43:     cout << "The contents of the first vector are: " << endl;
44:     for (size_t nIndex1 = 0; nIndex1 < vecMultiplicand.size (); ++ nIndex1)
45:         cout << vecMultiplicand [nIndex1] << ' ';
46:     cout << endl;
47:
48:     cout << "The contents of the second vector are: " << endl;
49:     for (size_t nIndex2 = 0; nIndex2 < vecMultiplier.size (); ++nIndex2)
50:         cout << vecMultiplier [nIndex2] << ' ';
51:     cout << endl << endl;
52:
53:     cout << "The result of the multiplication is: " << endl;
```

LISTING 22.5 Continued

```
54:     for (size_t nIndex = 0; nIndex < vecResult.size (); ++ nIndex)
55:         cout << vecResult [nIndex] << ' ';
56:
57:     return 0;
58: }
```

22

Output ▼

```
The contents of the first vector are:
0 1 2 3 4 5 6 7 8 9
The contents of the second vector are:
100 101 102 103 104 105 106 107 108 109

The result of the multiplication held in the third vector is:
0 101 204 309 416 525 636 749 864 981
```

Analysis ▼

Lines 5–14 contain the class CMultiply, as seen in the preceeding code snippet. In this sample, we use the algorithm std::transform to multiple the content of two ranges and store in a third. In our case, the ranges in question are held in std::vector as vecMultiplicand, vecMultiplier, and vecResult. In other words, we use std::transform in lines 37–41 to multiply every element in vecMultiplicand by its corresponding element in vecMultiplier and store the result of the multiplication in vecResult. The multiplication itself is done by the binary function CMultiple::operator () that is invoked for every element in the vectors that make the source and destination ranges. The return value of the operator() is held in vecResult.

This sample thus demonstrates the application of binary functions in performing arithmetic operations on elements in STL containers.

Binary Predicate

A function that accepts two arguments and returns a bool is a binary predicate. Such functions find application in STL functions such as std::sort. Listing 22.6 demonstrates the usage of a binary predicate in doing a case-insensitive sort on a container that holds std::string values.

LISTING 22.6 A Binary Predicate for Case-Insensitive String Sort

```
1: #include <algorithm>
2: #include <string>
3: using namespace std;
4:
```

LISTING 22.6 Continued

```
 5: class CCompareStringNoCase
 6: {
 7: public:
 8:     bool operator () (const string& str1, const string& str2) const
 9:     {
10:         string str1LowerCase;
11:         // Assign space
12:         str1LowerCase.resize (str1.size ());
13:         // Convert every character to the lower case
14:         transform ( str1.begin (), str1.end ()
15:                     , str1LowerCase.begin (), tolower );
16:
17:         string str2LowerCase;
18:         str2LowerCase.resize (str2.size ());
19:
20:         transform ( str2.begin (), str2.end ()
21:                     , str2LowerCase.begin (), tolower);
22:
23:         return (str1LowerCase < str2LowerCase);
24:     }
25: };
```

Analysis ▼

The binary predicate implemented in operator() first brings the input strings down to
lowercase using std::transform in lines 14 and 20 before using the string's comparison
operator, operator <, to do its job. Although this binary-predicate can be used with
algorithm std::sort, it can also be supplied as the predicate parameter of associative
containers such as std::set, as Listing 22.7 will show.

LISTING 22.7 Using a Binary Predicate in a std::set to Store a Set of Names

```
 1: #include <set>
 2: #include <iostream>
 3:
 4: // Insert CCompareStringNoCase from listing 22.6 here
 5:
 6: int main ()
 7: {
 8:     typedef set <string, CCompareStringNoCase> SET_NAMES;
 9:
10:     // Define a set of string to hold names
11:     SET_NAMES setNames;
12:
```

LISTING 22.7 Continued

```
13:        // Insert some sample names in to the set
14:        setNames.insert ("Tina");
15:        setNames.insert ("jim");
16:        setNames.insert ("Jack");
17:        setNames.insert ("Sam");
18:
19:        cout << "The sample names in the set are: " << endl;
20:
21:        // Display the names in the set
22:        SET_NAMES::const_iterator iNameLocator;
23:        for ( iNameLocator = setNames.begin ()
24:             ; iNameLocator != setNames.end ()
25:             ; ++ iNameLocator )
26:            cout << *iNameLocator << endl;
27:
28:        cout << "Enter a name you wish to search the set for: ";
29:        string strUserInput;
30:        cin >> strUserInput;
31:
32:        SET_NAMES::iterator iNameFound = setNames.find (strUserInput);
33:
34:        if (iNameFound != setNames.end ())
35:            cout << "'" << *iNameFound << "' was found in the set" << endl;
36:        else
37:            cout << "Name '" << strUserInput << "' was not found in the set";
38:
39:        return 0;
40: }
```

Output ▼

```
The sample names in the set are:
Jack
jim
Sam
Tina
Enter a name you wish to search the set for: JiM
'jim' was found in the set
```

Analysis ▼

The typedef declaration in line 8 to simplify the code features the all-important usage of the binary predicate CCompareStringNoCase, which helps the std::set sort its contents on a case-insensitive basis. Lines 14–17 insert sample values into setNames. In line 30, the user supplies a name to search for in setNames. Line 32 does a find using this string input from the user "JiM", which is in a case-inconsistent format to the name existing in the set, "jim." Thanks to the predicate CCompareStringNoCase, the set's find function is nevertheless able to find the entry. In the absence of the predicate (you can try it out!), std::set would have invoked operator < implemented by std::string, and that would have resulted in a case-sensitive sort, which in return would not find names in setNames when the user input would not be an exact match, also in case.

Binary predicates are required in a variety of STL algorithms. For example, std::unique that erases duplicate neighboring elements, std::sort that sorts, std::stable_sort that sorts while maintaining relative order, and std::transform that can perform an operation on two ranges are some of the STL algorithms that need a binary predicate.

Summary

In this lesson, you gained an insight into the world of functors or function objects. You learned how function objects are more useful when implemented in a structure or a class than those that are simple functions because the former can also be used to hold state-related information. You got an insight into predicates, which are a special class of function objects, and saw some practical examples that display their utility.

Q&A

Q **A predicate is a special category of a function object. What makes it special?**

A Predicates always return boolean.

Q **What kind of a function object should I use in a call to a function such as remove_if?**

A You should use a unary predicate that would take the value to be processed as the initial state via the constructor.

Q **What kind of a function object should I use for a map?**

A You should use a binary predicate.

Q **Is it possible that a simple function with no return value can be used as a predicate?**

A Yes. A function with no return values can still do something useful. For example, it can display input data.

Workshop

The Workshop provides quiz questions to help you solidify your understanding of the material covered and exercises to provide you with experience in using what you've learned. Try to answer the quiz and exercise questions before checking the answers in Appendix D.

Quiz

1. What is the term used for a unary function that returns a `bool` result?

2. What would be the utility of a function object that neither modifies data nor returns `bool`? Can you can explain using an example?

3. What is the definition of the term *function objects*?

Exercises

1. Write a unary function that can be used with `std::for_each` to display the double of the input parameter.

2. Extend this predicate to indicate the number of times it was used.

3. Write a binary predicate that helps sort in ascending order.

LESSON 23
STL Algorithms

One important part of the standard template library (STL) is a set of generic functions, supplied by the header <algorithm>, that help manipulate or work with the contents of a container. In this lesson, you will learn about using different STL algorithms and customizing them to your needs.

What Are STL Algorithms?

Finding, searching, removing, and counting are some generic algorithmic activities that find application in a broad range of programs. STL solves these and many other requirements in the form of generic template functions that work on containers via iterators. To use STL algorithms, the programmer first has to include the header, <algorithm>.

NOTE	Although most algorithms work via iterators on containers, not all algorithms necessarily work on containers and hence not all algorithms need iterators. Some, such as swap, simply accept a pair of values to swap them. Similarly, min and max work directly on values, too.

Classification of STL Algorithms

STL algorithms can be broadly classified into two types: nonmutating and mutating algorithms.

Nonmutating Algorithms

Algorithms that change neither the order nor the contents of a container are called nonmutating algorithms. Some of the prominent nonmutating algorithms are shown in Table 23.1.

TABLE 23.1   Nonmutating Algorithms

Algorithm	Description
Counting Algorithms	
count	Finds all elements in a range whose values match a supplied value
count_if	Finds all elements in a range whose values satisfy a supplied condition
Search Algorithms	
search	Searches for the first occurrence of a given sequence within a target range either on the basis of element equality (that is, the operator ==) or using a specified binary predicate
search_n	Searches a specified target range for the first occurrence of *n* number of elements of a given value or those that satisfy a given predicate

TABLE 23.1 Continued

Algorithm	Description
Search Algorithms	
find	Searches for the first element in the range that matches the specified value
find_if	Searches for the first element in a range that satisfies the specified condition
find_end	Searches for the last occurrence of a particular subrange in a supplied range
find_first_of	Searches for the first occurrence of any element supplied in one range within a target range; or, in an overloaded version, searches for the first occurrence of an element that satisfies a supplied find criterion
adjacent_find	Searches for two elements in a collection that are either equal or satisfy a supplied condition
Comparison Algorithms	
equal	Compares two elements for equality or uses a specified binary predicate to determine the same
mismatch	Locates the first difference position in two ranges of elements using a specified binary predicate
lexicographical_compare	Compares the elements between two sequences to determine which is the lesser of the two

Mutating Algorithms

Mutating algorithm are those that change the contents or the order of the sequence they are operating on. Some of the most useful mutating algorithms supplied by STL are as shown in Table 23.2.

TABLE 23.2 Mutating Algorithms

Algorithm	Description
Initialization Algorithms	
fill	Assigns the specified value to every element in the specified range.
fill_n	Assigns the specified value to the first *n* elements in the specified range.
generate	Assigns the return value of a specified function object to each element in the supplied range.
generate_n	Assigns the value generated by a function to a specified count of values in a specified range.

TABLE 23.2   Continued

Algorithm	Description
Modifying Algorithms	
for_each	Performs an operation on every element in a range. When the specified argument modifies the range, for_each becomes a mutating algorithm.
transform	Applies a specified unary function on every element in the specified range.
Copy Algorithms	
copy	Copies one range into another.
copy_backward	Copies one range into another, arranging elements in the destination range in the reverse order.
Removal Algorithms	
remove	Removes an element of a specified value from a specified range.
remove_if	Removes an element that satisfies a specified unary predicate from a specified range.
remove_copy	Copies all elements from a source range to a destination range, except those of a specified value.
remove_copy_if	Copies all elements from a source range to a destination range except those that satisfy a specified unary predicate.
unique	Compares adjacent elements in a range and removes the following duplicates. An overloaded version works using a binary predicate.
unique_copy	Copies all but adjacent duplicate elements from a specified source range to a specified destination range.
Replacement Algorithms	
replace	Replaces every element in a specified range that matches a specified value by a replacement value.
replace_if	Replaces every element in a specified range that matches a specified value by a replacement value.
Sort Algorithms	
sort	Sorts elements in a range using a specified sort criterion: a binary predicate that needs supply a strict-weak-ordering. sort might change relative positions of equivalent elements.
stable_sort	Stable sort is similar to sort, but preserves order, too.
partial_sort	Sorts a specified number of elements in a range.
partial_sort_copy	Copies elements from a specified source range to a destination range that holds them in a sort order.

TABLE 23.2   Continued

Algorithm	Description
Partitioning Algorithms	
partition	Given a specified range, splits elements into two sets within it: those that satisfy a unary predicate come first and the rest after. Might not maintain the relative order of elements in a set.
stable_partition	Partitions an input range into two sets as in partition, but maintains relative ordering.
Algorithms That Work on Sorted Containers	
binary_search	Used to determine whether an element exists in a sorted collection.
lower_bound	Returns an iterator pointing to the first position where an element can potentially be inserted in a sorted collection based on its value or on a supplied binary predicate.
upper_bound	Returns an iterator pointing to the last position where an element can potentially be inserted into a sorted collection based on its value or on a supplied binary predicate.

23

Usage of STL Algorithms

The usage of the STL algorithms mentioned in Tables 23.1 and 23.2 is best learned directly by a hands-on coding session. To that end, learn the details of using the algorithms from the code examples that follow and start applying them to your application.

Counting and Finding Elements

std::count, count_if, find, and find_if are algorithms that help in counting and finding elements in a range. The following code in Listing 23.1 demonstrates the usage of these functions.

LISTING 23.1   Sample That Demonstrates the Usage of std::count, count_if, find, and find_if on a Sample Collection

```
1: #include <algorithm>
2: #include <vector>
3: #include <iostream>
4:
5: // A unary predicate for the *_if functions
6: template <typename elementType>
7: bool IsEven (const elementType& number)
8: {
9:     // return true if the number is even
```

LISTING 23.1   Continued

```
10:     return ((number % 2) == 0);
11: }
12:
13: int main ()
14: {
15:     using namespace std;
16:
17:     // A sample container - vector of integers
18:     vector <int> vecIntegers;
19:
20:     // Inserting sample values
21:     for (int nNum = -9; nNum < 10; ++ nNum)
22:         vecIntegers.push_back (nNum);
23:
24:     // Display all elements in the collection
25:     cout << "Elements in our sample collection are: " << endl;
26:     vector <int>::const_iterator iElementLocator;
27:     for ( iElementLocator = vecIntegers.begin ()
28:         ; iElementLocator != vecIntegers.end ()
29:         ; ++ iElementLocator )
30:         cout << *iElementLocator << ' ';
31:
32:     cout << endl << endl;
33:
34:     // Determine the total number of elements
35:     cout << "The collection contains '";
36:     cout << vecIntegers.size () << "' elements" << endl;
37:
38:     // Use the count_if algorithm with the unary predicate IsEven:
39:     size_t nNumEvenElements = count_if (vecIntegers.begin (),
40:                                 vecIntegers.end (), IsEven <int> );
41:
42:     cout << "Number of even elements: " << nNumEvenElements << endl;
43:     cout << "Number of odd elements: ";
44:     cout << vecIntegers.size () - nNumEvenElements << endl;
45:
46:     // Use count to determine the number of '0's in the vector
47:     size_t nNumZeroes = count (vecIntegers.begin (),vecIntegers.end (),0);
48:     cout << "Number of instances of '0': " << nNumZeroes << endl << endl;
49:
50:     cout << "Searching for an element of value 3 using find: " << endl;
51:
52:     // Find a sample integer '3' in the vector using the 'find' algorithm
53:     vector <int>::iterator iElementFound;
54:     iElementFound = find ( vecIntegers.begin ()    // Start of range
55:                         , vecIntegers.end ()     // End of range
56:                         , 3 );                   // Element to find
57:
58:     // Check if find succeeded
59:     if ( iElementFound != vecIntegers.end ())
```

LISTING 23.1 Continued

```
60:            cout << "Result: Element found!" << endl << endl;
61:     else
62:            cout << "Result: Element was not found in the collection." << endl;
63:
64:     cout << "Finding the first even number using find_if: " << endl;
65:
66:     // Find the first even number in the collection
67:     vector <int>::iterator iEvenNumber;
68:     iEvenNumber = find_if ( vecIntegers.begin ()// Start of range
69:                           , vecIntegers.end ()   // End of range
70:                           , IsEven <int> );       // Unary Predicate
71:
72:     if (iEvenNumber != vecIntegers.end ())
73:     {
74:            cout << "Number '" << *iEvenNumber << "' found at position [";
75:            cout << distance (vecIntegers.begin (), iEvenNumber);
76:            cout << "]" << endl;
77:     }
78:
79:     return 0;
80: }
```

Output ▼

```
Elements in our sample collection are:
-9 -8 -7 -6 -5 -4 -3 -2 -1 0 1 2 3 4 5 6 7 8 9

The collection contains '19' elements
Number of even elements: 9
Number of odd elements: 10
Number of instances of '0': 1

Searching the collection for an element of value 3 using find:
Result: Element found!

Finding the first even number in the collection using find_if:
Number '-8' found at position [1]
```

Analysis ▼

The functions count and find do not require a predicate, but count_if and find_if do. This predicate is implemented by template function IsEven that returns true if the input number is even, as seen in lines 7–11. The sample demonstrates the usage of these STL algorithms on a sample container, which is a vector vecIntegers that collects integer objects. count_if is used in line 39 to determine the number of even-valued integers in the vector. count is used in line 47 to determine the number of zeroes vecIntegers contains. Algorithm `find` is used in line 54 to find the first instance of element 3 in the vector, while `find_if` uses predicate `IsEven` to find the first even number in the same.

As you can see, a single predicate `IsEven` helped us perform two very different operations on a range: one was to count the number of elements that satisfied the condition implemented by the predicate, and another was to find elements that satisfied the predicate. Thus, this sample also demonstrated that predicates and STL algorithms increase reusability and help make the code efficient, yet simpler to maintain.

Searching for an Element or a Range in a Collection

The previous sample demonstrated how you could find an element in a container. Sometimes however, you need to find a range of values. In such situations, rather than depend on a find algorithm that works on an element-by-element basis, you should use `search` or `search_n`, which are designed to work with ranges, as seen in Listing 23.2.

LISTING 23.2   Finding a Range in a Collection Using `search` and `search_n`

```
1: #include <algorithm>
2: #include <vector>
3: #include <list>
4: #include <iostream>
5:
6: int main ()
7: {
8:     using namespace std;
9:
10:     // A sample container - vector of integers
11:     vector <int> vecIntegers;
12:
13:     for (int nNum = -9; nNum < 10; ++ nNum)
14:         vecIntegers.push_back (nNum);
15:
16:     // Insert some more sample values into the vector
17:     vecIntegers.push_back (9);
18:     vecIntegers.push_back (9);
19:
20:     // Another sample container - a list of integers
21:     list <int> listIntegers;
22:
23:     for (int nNum = -4; nNum < 5; ++ nNum)
24:         listIntegers.push_back (nNum);
25:
26:     // Display the contents of the collections...
27:     cout << "The contents of the sample vector are: " << endl;
28:     vector <int>::const_iterator iVecElementLocator;
29:     for ( iVecElementLocator = vecIntegers.begin ()
30:         ; iVecElementLocator != vecIntegers.end ()
31:         ; ++ iVecElementLocator )
```

LISTING 23.2   Continued

```
32:              cout << *iVecElementLocator << ' ';
33:
34:      cout << endl << "The contents of the sample list are: " << endl;
35:      list <int>::const_iterator ilistElementLocator;
36:      for ( ilistElementLocator = listIntegers.begin ()
37:           ; ilistElementLocator != listIntegers.end ()
38:           ; ++ ilistElementLocator )
39:          cout << *ilistElementLocator << ' ';
40:
41:      cout << endl << endl;
42:      cout << "'search' the contents of the list in the vector: " << endl;
43:
44:      // Search the vector for the elements present in the list
45:      vector <int>::iterator iRangeLocated;
46:      iRangeLocated = search ( vecIntegers.begin () // Start of range
47:                         , vecIntegers.end ()       // End of range to search in
48:                         , listIntegers.begin ()    // Start of range to search for
49:                         , listIntegers.end () );   // End of range to search for
50:
51:      // Check if search found a match
52:      if (iRangeLocated != vecIntegers.end ())
53:      {
54:          cout << "The sequence in the list found a match in the vector at ";
55:          cout << "position: ";
56:          cout << distance (vecIntegers.begin (), iRangeLocated);
57:
58:          cout << endl << endl;
59:      }
60:
61:      cout << "Searching for {9, 9, 9} in the vector using 'search_n': ";
62:      cout << endl;
63:
64:      // Now search the vector for the occurrence of pattern {9, 9, 9}
65:      vector <int>::iterator iPartialRangeLocated;
66:      iPartialRangeLocated = search_n ( vecIntegers.begin () // Start range
67:                         , vecIntegers.end ()    // End range
68:                         , 3            // Count of item to be searched for
69:                         , 9 );        // Item to search for
70:
71:      if (iPartialRangeLocated != vecIntegers.end ())
72:      {
73:          cout << "The sequence {9, 9, 9} found a match in the vector at ";
74:          cout << "offset-position: ";
75:          cout << distance (vecIntegers.begin (), iPartialRangeLocated);
76:
77:          cout << endl;
78:      }
79:
80:      return 0;
81: }
```

Output ▼

```
The contents of the sample vector are:
-9 -8 -7 -6 -5 -4 -3 -2 -1 0 1 2 3 4 5 6 7 8 9 9 9
The contents of the sample list are:
-4 -3 -2 -1 0 1 2 3 4

'search' the contents of the list in the vector:
The sequence in the list found a match in the vector at position: 5

Searching for {9, 9, 9} in the vector using 'search_n':
The sequence {9, 9, 9} found a match in the vector at offset-position: 18
```

Analysis ▼

The sample starts with two sample containers, a vector and a list that are initially populated with sample integer values. search is used to find the presence of the list in the vector, as seen in line 46. The parameters supplied to search are the beginning and the end of the range to search in, and the beginning and the end of the range to be searched for. As we want to search in the entire vector for the contents of the entire list, we supply a range as returned by their corresponding begin() and end() member methods. This actually demonstrates how well iterators connect the algorithms to the containers. The physical characteristics of the containers that supply those iterators are of no significance to algorithms. search_n is used in line 66 to find the first occurrence of series {9, 9, 9} in the vector.

Initializing Elements in a Container to a Specific Value

fill and fill_n are the STL algorithms that help set the contents of a given to a specified value. fill is used to overwrite the elements in a range given the bounds of the range and the value to be inserted. fill_n needs a starting position, a count n, and the value to fill, as Listing 23.3 demonstrates.

LISTING 23.3   Using fill and fill_n to Set Initial Values in a Container

```
1: #include <algorithm>
2: #include <vector>
3: #include <iostream>
4:
5: int main ()
6: {
7:     using namespace std;
8:
```

LISTING 23.3   Continued

```
 9:      // Initialize a sample vector with 3 elements
10:      vector <int> vecIntegers (3);
11:
12:      // fill all elements in the container with value 9
13:      fill (vecIntegers.begin (), vecIntegers.end (), 9);
14:
15:      // Increase the size of the vector to hold 6 elements
16:      vecIntegers.resize (6);
17:
18:      // Fill the three elements starting at offset position 3 with value -9
19:      fill_n (vecIntegers.begin () + 3, 3, -9);
20:
21:      cout << "Contents of the vector are: " << endl;
22:      for (size_t nIndex = 0; nIndex < vecIntegers.size (); ++ nIndex)
23:      {
24:          cout << "Element [" << nIndex << "] = ";
25:          cout << vecIntegers [nIndex] << endl;
26:      }
27:
28:      return 0;
29: }
```

23

Output ▼

```
Contents of the vector are:
Element [0] = 9
Element [1] = 9
Element [2] = 9
Element [3] = -9
Element [4] = -9
Element [5] = -9
```

Analysis ▼

Listing 23.3 uses the `fill` and `fill_n` functions to initialize the contents of the container to two separate sets of values, as seen in lines 13 and 19. Note the usage of the `resize()` function before we filled values into the range, essentially creating elements that were later `filled` with values. The `fill` algorithm works on a complete range, whereas `fill_n` has the potential to work on a partial range.

Just as the `fill` functions fill the collection with a programmer-determined value, STL algorithms such as `generate` and `generate_n` can be used to initialize collections to the contents of a file, for example, or simply to random values, as seen in Listing 23.4.

LISTING 23.4   Using generate and generate_n to Initialize Collections to Random Values

```
1: #include <algorithm>
2: #include <vector>
3: #include <list>
4: #include <iostream>
5:
6: int main ()
7: {
8:     using namespace std;
9:
10:     vector <int> vecIntegers (10);
11:     generate ( vecIntegers.begin (), vecIntegers.end ()    // range
12:                , rand );    // generator function to be called
13:
14:     cout << "Elements in the vector of size " << vecIntegers.size ();
15:     cout << " assigned by 'generate' are: " << endl << "{";
16:     for (size_t nCount = 0; nCount < vecIntegers.size (); ++ nCount)
17:         cout << vecIntegers [nCount] << " ";
18:
19:     cout << "}" << endl << endl;
20:
21:     list <int> listIntegers (10);
22:     generate_n (listIntegers.begin (), 5, rand);
23:
24:     cout << "Elements in the list of size: " << listIntegers.size ();
25:     cout << " assigned by 'generate_n' are: " << endl << "{";
26:     list <int>::const_iterator iElementLocator;
27:     for ( iElementLocator = listIntegers.begin ()
28:         ; iElementLocator != listIntegers.end ()
29:         ; ++ iElementLocator )
30:         cout << *iElementLocator << ' ';
31:
32:     cout << "}" << endl;
33:
34:     return 0;
35: }
```

Output ▼

```
Elements in the vector of size 10 assigned by 'generate' are:
{41 18467 6334 26500 19169 15724 11478 29358 26962 24464 }

Elements in the list of size: 10 assigned by 'generate_n' are:
{5705 28145 23281 16827 9961 0 0 0 0 0 }
```

Analysis ▼

Listing 23.4 uses the generate function to populate all elements in the vector with a random value supplied by the rand function. Note that the generate function accepts a range as an input and consequently calls the specified function object rand for every element in the range. generate_n, in comparison, accepts only the starting position. It then invokes the specified function object, rand, the number of times specified by the count parameter to overwrite the contents of that many elements. The elements in the container that are beyond the specified offset go untouched.

Processing Elements in a Range Using for_each

The for_each algorithm applies a specified unary function object to every element in the supplied range. The usage of for_each is

```
unaryFunctionObjectType mReturn = for_each ( start_of_range
                                           , end_of_range
                                           , unaryFunctionObject );
```

The return value indicates that for_each returns the function object (also called functor) used to process every element in the supplied range. The implication of this specification is that the usage of a struct or a class as a function object can help in storing state information, that can later be queried once for_each is done. This is demonstrated by Listing 23.5, which uses the function object to display elements in a range, and also uses it to count the number of elements displayed.

LISTING 23.5   Using for_each to Display the Contents of a Collection

```
1: #include <algorithm>
2: #include <iostream>
3: #include <vector>
4: #include <string>
5:
6: using namespace std;
7:
8: // Unary function object type invoked by for_each
9: template <typename elementType>
10: class DisplayElementKeepCount
11: {
12: private:
13:     int m_nCount;
14:
15: public:
16:     DisplayElementKeepCount ()
17:     {
```

LISTING 23.5   Continued

```
18:            m_nCount = 0;
19:        }
20:
21:        void operator () (const elementType& element)
22:        {
23:            ++ m_nCount;
24:            cout << element << ' ';
25:        }
26:
27:        int GetCount ()
28:        {
29:            return m_nCount;
30:        }
31: };
32:
33: int main ()
34: {
35:     vector <int> vecIntegers;
36:
37:     for (int nCount = 0; nCount < 10; ++ nCount)
38:         vecIntegers.push_back (nCount);
39:
40:     cout << "Displaying the vector of integers: " << endl;
41:
42:     // Display the array of integers
43:     DisplayElementKeepCount<int> mIntResult =
44:         for_each ( vecIntegers.begin ()    // Start of range
45:                  , vecIntegers.end ()         // End of range
46:                  , DisplayElementKeepCount<int> () );// Functor
47:
48:     cout << endl;
49:
50:     // Use the state stored in the return value of for_each!
51:     cout << "'" << mIntResult.GetCount () << "' elements ";
52:     cout << " in the vector were displayed!" << endl << endl;
53:
54:     string strSample ("for_each and strings!");
55:     cout << "String sample is: " << strSample << endl << endl;
56:
57:     cout << "String displayed using DisplayElementKeepCount:" << endl;
58:     DisplayElementKeepCount<char> mCharResult = for_each (strSample.begin()
59:                       , strSample.end ()
60:                       , DisplayElementKeepCount<char> () );
61:     cout << endl;
62:
63:     cout << "'" << mCharResult.GetCount () << "' characters were displayed";
64:
65:     return 0;
66: }
```

Output ▼

```
Displaying the vector of integers:
0 1 2 3 4 5 6 7 8 9
'10' elements in the vector were displayed!

String sample is: for_each and strings!

String displayed using DisplayElementKeepCount:"
f o r _ e a c h   a n d   s t r i n g s !
'21' characters were displayed
```

23

Analysis ▼

The code sample demonstrates the utility of not only for_each but also of its characteristic to return the function object that is programmed to hold information such as the count of the number of times it was invoked. The code features two sample ranges, one contained in a vector of integers, vecIntegers and the other being a std::string object strSample. The sample invokes for_each on these ranges in lines 44 and 58 respectively, with DisplayElementKeepCount as the Functor. for_each invokes the operator() for every element in the supplied range, which in turn prints the element on the screen and increments an internal counter. The function object is returned once for_each is done, and the member function GetCount() tells the number of times the object was used.

This facility of storing information (or state) in the object that is returned by the algorithm can be quite useful in practical programming situations.

Performing Transformations on a Range Using std::transform

for_each and std::transform are quite similar in that they both invoke a function object for every element in a source range. However, std::transform has two versions: one that accepts a unary function and another that accepts a binary function. So, the transform algorithm can also process a pair of elements taken from two different ranges. Both versions of the transform function always assign the result of the specified transformation function to a supplied destination range, unlike for_each, which works on only a single range. The usage of std::transform is demonstrated in Listing 23.6.

LISTING 23.6 Using std::transform with Unary and Binary Functions

```
1: #include <algorithm>
2: #include <string>
3: #include <vector>
4: #include <deque>
```

LISTING 23.6   Continued

```cpp
5: #include <iostream>
6: #include <functional>
7:
8: int main ()
9: {
10:     using namespace std;
11:
12:     string strSample ("THIS is a TEst string!");
13:     cout << "The sample string is: " << strSample << endl;
14:
15:     string strLowerCaseCopy;
16:     strLowerCaseCopy.resize (strSample.size ());
17:
18:     transform ( strSample.begin ()            // start of source range
19:               , strSample.end ()             // end of source range
20:               , strLowerCaseCopy.begin ())// start of destination range
21:               , tolower );          // unary function
22:
23:     cout << "Result of 'transform' on the string with 'tolower':" << endl;
24:     cout << "\"" << strLowerCaseCopy << "\"" << endl << endl;
25:
26:     // Two sample vectors of integers...
27:     vector <int> vecIntegers1, vecIntegers2;
28:     for (int nNum = 0; nNum < 10; ++ nNum)
29:     {
30:         vecIntegers1.push_back (nNum);
31:         vecIntegers2.push_back (10 - nNum);
32:     }
33:
34:     // A destination range for holding the result of addition
35:     deque <int> dqResultAddition (vecIntegers1.size ());
36:
37:     transform ( vecIntegers1.begin ()     // start of source range 1
38:               , vecIntegers1.end ()       // end of source range 1
39:               , vecIntegers2.begin ()     // start of source range 2
40:               , dqResultAddition.begin ())// start of destination range
41:               , plus <int> () );          // binary function
42:
43:     cout << "Result of 'transform' using binary function 'plus': " << endl;
44:     cout <<endl << "Index    Vector1 + Vector2 = Result (in Deque)" << endl;
45:     for (size_t nIndex = 0; nIndex < vecIntegers1.size (); ++ nIndex)
46:     {
47:         cout << nIndex << "    \t " << vecIntegers1 [nIndex] << "\t+   ";
48:         cout << vecIntegers2 [nIndex] << " \t =    ";
49:
50:         cout << dqResultAddition [nIndex] << endl;
51:     }
52:
53:     return 0;
54: }
```

Output ▼

```
The sample string is: THIS is a TEst string!
Result of using 'transform' with unary function 'tolower' on the string:
"this is a test string!"

Result of 'transform' using binary function 'plus':

Index   Vector1 + Vector2 = Result (in Deque)
0       0       +  10     =  10
1       1       +  9      =  10
2       2       +  8      =  10
3       3       +  7      =  10
4       4       +  6      =  10
5       5       +  5      =  10
6       6       +  4      =  10
7       7       +  3      =  10
8       8       +  2      =  10
9       9       +  1      =  10
```

23

Analysis ▼

The sample demonstrates both versions of `std::transform`, one that works on a single range using a unary function `tolower` and another that works on two ranges and uses a binary function `plus`. The first as seen in lines 18–21 changes the case of a string, character-by-character to lower-case. If you use `toupper` here instead of `tolower`, you would effect a case conversion to upper case. The other version of `std::transform` is seen in lines 37–41 and acts on elements taken from two input ranges (two vectors in this case) and uses a binary predicate in the form of the STL function `plus` (supplied by the header `<functional>`) to add them. `std::transform` takes one pair at a time, supplies it to the binary function `plus`, and assigns the result to an element in the destination range—one that happens to belong to an `std::deque`. Note that the change in container used to hold the result is purely for demonstration purposes. It only displays how well iterators are used to abstract containers and their implementation from STL algorithms; `transform`, being an algorithm deals with ranges and really does not need to know details on the containers that implement these ranges. So, the input ranges happened to be a vector, and the output ranges happened to be a deque, and it all works fine—so long as the bounds that define the range (supplied as input parameters to `transform`) are valid.

Copy and Remove Operations

STL supplies two prominent copy functions: `copy` and `copy_backward`. `copy` can assign the contents of a source range into a destination range in the forward direction, whereas `copy_backward` assigns the contents to the destination range in the backward direction.

remove, on the other hand, deletes elements in a container that matches a specified value. remove_if uses a unary predicate and removes from the container those elements for which the predicate evaluates to true.

Listing 23.7 demonstrates the usage of these copy and removal functions.

LISTING 23.7   Demonstration of copy, copy_backward, remove, and remove_if

```
 1: #include <algorithm>
 2: #include <vector>
 3: #include <list>
 4: #include <iostream>
 5:
 6: // A unary predicate for the remove_if function
 7: template <typename elementType>
 8: bool IsOdd (const elementType& number)
 9: {
10:     // returns true if the number is odd
11:     return ((number % 2) == 1);
12: }
13:
14: int main ()
15: {
16:     using namespace std;
17:
18:     // A list with sample values
19:     list <int> listIntegers;
20:
21:     for (int nCount = 0; nCount < 10; ++ nCount)
22:         listIntegers.push_back (nCount);
23:
24:     cout << "Elements in the source (list) are: " << endl;
25:
26:     // Display all elements in the collection
27:     list <int>::const_iterator iElementLocator;
28:     for ( iElementLocator = listIntegers.begin ()
29:         ; iElementLocator != listIntegers.end ()
30:         ; ++ iElementLocator )
31:         cout << *iElementLocator << ' ';
32:
33:     cout << endl << endl;
34:
35:     // Initialize the vector to hold twice as many elements as the list
36:     vector <int> vecIntegers (listIntegers.size () * 2);
37:
38:     vector <int>::iterator iLastPos;
39:     iLastPos = copy ( listIntegers.begin ()  // start of source range
```

LISTING 23.7   Continued

```
40:                      , listIntegers.end ()      // end of source range
41:                      , vecIntegers.begin () );// start of destination range
42:
43:      // Now, use copy_backward to copy the same list into the vector
44:      copy_backward ( listIntegers.begin ()
45:                          , listIntegers.end ()
46:                          , vecIntegers.end () );
47:
48:      cout << "Elements in the destination (vector) after copy: " << endl;
49:
50:      // Display all elements in the collection
51:      vector <int>::const_iterator iDestElementLocator;
52:      for ( iDestElementLocator = vecIntegers.begin ()
53:          ; iDestElementLocator != vecIntegers.end ()
54:          ; ++ iDestElementLocator )
55:          cout << *iDestElementLocator << ' ';
56:
57:      cout << endl << endl;
58:
59:      /*
60:          Remove all instances of '0':
61:          std::remove does not change the size of the container,
62:          it simply moves elements forward to fill gaps created
63:          and returns the new 'end' position.
64:      */
65:      vector <int>::iterator iNewEnd;
66:      iNewEnd = remove (vecIntegers.begin (), vecIntegers.end (), 0);
67:
68:      // Use this new 'end position' to resize vector
69:      vecIntegers.erase (iNewEnd, vecIntegers.end ());
70:
71:      // Remove all odd numbers from the vector using remove_if
72:      iNewEnd = remove_if (vecIntegers.begin (), vecIntegers.end (),
73:                           IsOdd <int>);    // The predicate
74:
75:      vecIntegers.erase (iNewEnd , vecIntegers.end ());
76:
77:      cout << "Elements in the destination (vector) after remove: " << endl;
78:
79:      // Display all elements in the collection
80:      for ( iDestElementLocator = vecIntegers.begin ()
81:          ; iDestElementLocator != vecIntegers.end ()
82:          ; ++ iDestElementLocator )
83:          cout << *iDestElementLocator << ' ';
84:
85:      return 0;
86: }
```

23

Output ▼

```
Elements in the source (list) are:
0 1 2 3 4 5 6 7 8 9

Elements in the destination (vector) after copy:
0 1 2 3 4 5 6 7 8 9 0 1 2 3 4 5 6 7 8 9

Elements in the destination (vector) after remove:
2 4 6 8 2 4 6 8
```

Analysis ▼

The sample starts with the definition of function IsOdd that returns true when the input number, as its name suggests, is odd. This predicate is used by the STL algorithm remove_if, as seen in line 72. The copy and remove functions both return the end position iterators. The iterator returned, in the case of copy, can be used to copy more elements from that point onward. In the case of remove or remove_if, the iterator returned can be used to correct the size of the container in a subsequent erase operation, as the code demonstrated. It is true that remove or remove_if will delete the element in question by moving the elements behind it one position forward; that is, overwrite the element to be removed. It will not, however, resize the container or reduce the number of elements reported until the programmer chooses to perform an erase using the iterator (iNewEnd in the code) returned by it. remove is used in line 66 to remove all instances of zero in the collection, and it is immediately followed by a vector::erase operation to correct the dimensions of the container. Line 39 demonstrates how copy is used to transfer the contents of a list of integers to a vector. Note that the copy function accepts only the beginning of the destination range. It assumes that the destination range is wide enough to hold the result of the copy operation. This is why vecIntegers was initialized to hold at least as many elements as contained by the source list, listIntegers. copy_backward as seen in line 44 does the copy, but in the reverse direction. Note that the third parameter of this function is the end of the destination range.

The result of using copy_backward, given the end position of the destination container, is the same as the result you would obtain by using copy in this format:

```
copy ( listIntegers.begin () // start of source range
     , listIntegers.end ()    // end of source range
     , iLastPos );            // returned by previous 'copy'
```

Replacing Values and Replacing Element Given a Condition

replace and replace_if are the STL algorithms that can replace elements in a collection that are equivalent to a supplied value or satisfy a given condition, respectively. Whereas the former replaces elements based on the return value of the comparison operator ==, the latter needs a user-specified unary predicate that returns true for every value that needs to be replaced. The usage of these functions is demonstrated by Listing 23.8.

LISTING 23.8 Using replace and replace_if to Replace Values in a Specified Range

```
 1: #include <iostream>
 2: #include <algorithm>
 3: #include <vector>
 4:
 5: // The unary predicate used by replace_if to replace even numbers
 6: bool IsEven (const int & nNum)
 7: {
 8:     return ((nNum % 2) == 0);
 9: }
10:
11: int main ()
12: {
13:     using namespace std;
14:
15:     // Initialize a sample vector with 6 elements
16:     vector <int> vecIntegers (6);
17:
18:     // fill first 3 elements with value 8
19:     fill (vecIntegers.begin (), vecIntegers.begin () + 3, 8);
20:
21:     // fill last 3 elements with value 5
22:     fill_n (vecIntegers.begin () + 3, 3, 5);
23:
24:     // shuffle the container
25:     random_shuffle (vecIntegers.begin (), vecIntegers.end ());
26:
27:     cout << "The initial contents of the vector are: " << endl;
28:     for (size_t nIndex = 0; nIndex < vecIntegers.size (); ++ nIndex)
29:     {
30:         cout << "Element [" << nIndex << "] = ";
31:         cout << vecIntegers [nIndex] << endl;
32:     }
33:
34:     cout << endl << "Using 'std::replace' to replace value 5 by 8" << endl;
35:     replace (vecIntegers.begin (), vecIntegers.end (), 5, 8);
36:
```

LISTING 23.8   Continued

```
37:     cout << "Using 'std::replace_if' to replace even values by -1" << endl;
38:     replace_if (vecIntegers.begin (), vecIntegers.end (), IsEven, -1);
39:
40:     cout << endl << "Contents of the vector after replacements:" << endl;
41:     for (size_t nIndex = 0; nIndex < vecIntegers.size (); ++ nIndex)
42:     {
43:         cout << "Element [" << nIndex << "] = ";
44:         cout << vecIntegers [nIndex] << endl;
45:     }
46:
47:     return 0;
48: }
```

Output ▼

```
The initial contents of the vector are:
Element [0] = 5
Element [1] = 8
Element [2] = 5
Element [3] = 8
Element [4] = 8
Element [5] = 5

Using 'std::replace' to replace value 5 by 8
Using 'std::replace_if' to replace even values by -1

Contents of the vector after replacements:
Element [0] = -1
Element [1] = -1
Element [2] = -1
Element [3] = -1
Element [4] = -1
Element [5] = -1
```

Analysis ▼

The sample fills a vector of integers vecIntegers with sample values and then shuffles it using the STL algorithm std::random_shuffle as seen in line 25. Line 35 demonstrates the usage of replace to replace all 5s by 8s. Hence, when replace_if, in line 38, replaces all even numbers with –1, the end result is that the collection has six elements, all containing an identical value of –1, as seen in the output.

Sorting and Searching in a Sorted Collection, and Erasing Duplicates

Sorting and searching a sorted range (for sake of performance) are requirements that come up in practical applications way too often. Very often you have an array of information that needs to be sorted—say, for presentation's sake. Sometimes this sorted information needs to be filtered on user request. Similarly, duplicates need to be deleted before the collection is displayed. The following example in Listing 23.9 explains a solution to this familiar problem by using STL algorithms `std::sort` that can sort a range, `std::binary_search` that can search a sorted range, and `std::unique` that eliminates duplicate neighboring elements (that become neighbors after a `sort`).

23

LISTING 23.9 Using `std::sort`, `binary_search`, and `unique`

```
1: #include <algorithm>
2: #include <vector>
3: #include <string>
4: #include <iostream>
5:
6: int main ()
7: {
8:     using namespace std;
9:     typedef vector <string> VECTOR_STRINGS;
10:
11:     // A vector of strings
12:     VECTOR_STRINGS vecNames;
13:
14:     // Insert sample values
15:     vecNames.push_back ("John Doe");
16:     vecNames.push_back ("Jack Nicholson");
17:     vecNames.push_back ("Sean Penn");
18:     vecNames.push_back ("Anna Hoover");
19:
20:     // insert a duplicate into the vector
21:     vecNames.push_back ("Jack Nicholson");
22:
23:     cout << "The initial contents of the vector are:" << endl;
24:     for (size_t nItem = 0; nItem < vecNames.size (); ++ nItem)
25:     {
26:         cout << "Name [" << nItem << "] = \"";
27:         cout << vecNames [nItem] << "\"" << endl;
28:     }
29:
30:     cout << endl;
31:
32:     // sort the names using std::sort
33:     sort (vecNames.begin (), vecNames.end ());
34:
```

LISTING 23.9   Continued

```
35:     cout << "The sorted vector contains names in the order:" << endl;
36:     for (size_t nItem = 0; nItem < vecNames.size (); ++ nItem)
37:     {
38:         cout << "Name [" << nItem << "] = \"";
39:         cout << vecNames [nItem] << "\"" << endl;
40:     }
41:
42:     cout << endl;
43:
44:     cout << "Searching for \"John Doe\" using 'binary_search':" << endl;
45:     bool bElementFound = binary_search (vecNames.begin (), vecNames.end (),
46:                                         "John Doe");
47:
48:     // Check if search found a match
49:     if (bElementFound)
50:         cout << "Result: \"John Doe\" was found in the vector!" << endl;
51:     else
52:         cout << "Element not found " << endl;
53:
54:     cout << endl;
55:
56:     VECTOR_STRINGS::iterator iNewEnd;
57:
58:     // Erase adjacent duplicates
59:     iNewEnd = unique (vecNames.begin (), vecNames.end ());
60:     vecNames.erase (iNewEnd, vecNames.end ());
61:
62:     cout << "The contents of the vector after using 'unique':" << endl;
63:     for (size_t nItem = 0; nItem < vecNames.size (); ++ nItem)
64:     {
65:         cout << "Name [" << nItem << "] = \"";
66:         cout << vecNames [nItem] << "\"" << endl;
67:     }
68:
69:     return 0;
70: }
```

Output ▼

```
The initial contents of the vector are:
Name [0] = "John Doe"
Name [1] = "Jack Nicholson"
Name [2] = "Sean Penn"
Name [3] = "Anna Hoover"
Name [4] = "Jack Nicholson"
```

```
The sorted vector contains names in the order:
Name [0] = "Anna Hoover"
Name [1] = "Jack Nicholson"
Name [2] = "Jack Nicholson"
Name [3] = "John Doe"
Name [4] = "Sean Penn"

Searching for "John Doe" using 'binary_search':
Result: "John Doe" was found in the vector!

The contents of the vector after using 'unique':
Name [0] = "Anna Hoover"
Name [1] = "Jack Nicholson"
Name [2] = "John Doe"
Name [3] = "Sean Penn"
```

23

Analysis ▼

Search algorithms such as `binary_search` are applicable only to sorted containers; use of this algorithm on an unsorted vector could have undesirable consequences. Hence, the code above first sorts the sample vector, `vecNames` in line 33, before using `binary_search` to find "John Doe" in it. Similarly, `std::unique` is used to delete the second occurrence of an adjacent duplicate in lines 59 and 60. In most scenarios, this algorithm is also most effective only after the collection has been sorted.

> **NOTE**
>
> The usage of `stable_sort` is the same as that of `sort`, which you saw earlier. `stable_sort` ensures that the relative order of the sorted elements is maintained. Maintaining relative order comes at the cost of performance—a factor that needs to be kept in mind, especially if the relative ordering of elements is not essential.

Partitioning a Range

`std::partition` helps partition an input range into two sections: one that satisfies a unary predicate and another that doesn't. `std::partition`, however, does not guarantee the relative order of elements within each partition. To maintain relative order, `std::stable_partition` should be used. Listing 23.10 demonstrates the usage of these algorithms.

LISTING 23.10 Using partition and stable_partition to Partition a Range of Integers into Even and Odd Values

```
 1: #include <algorithm>
 2: #include <vector>
 3: #include <iostream>
 4:
 5: bool IsEven (const int& nNumber)
 6: {
 7:     return ((nNumber % 2) == 0);
 8: }
 9:
10: int main ()
11: {
12:     using namespace std;
13:
14:     // a sample collection...
15:     vector <int> vecIntegers;
16:
17:     // fill sample values 0 - 9, in that order
18:     for (int nNum = 0; nNum < 10; ++ nNum)
19:         vecIntegers.push_back (nNum);
20:
21:     // a copy of the sample vector
22:     vector <int> vecCopy (vecIntegers);
23:
24:     // separate even values from the odd ones - even comes first.
25:     partition (vecIntegers.begin (), vecIntegers.end (), IsEven);
26:
27:     // display contents
28:     cout << "The contents of the vector after using 'partition' are:";
29:     cout << endl << "{";
30:
31:     for (size_t nItem = 0;  nItem < vecIntegers.size (); ++ nItem)
32:         cout << vecIntegers [nItem] << ' ';
33:
34:     cout << "}" << endl << endl;
35:
36:     // now use stable_partition on the vecCopy - maintains relative order
37:     stable_partition (vecCopy.begin (), vecCopy.end (), IsEven);
38:
39:     // display contents of vecCopy
40:     cout << "The effect of using 'stable_partition' is: " << endl << "{";
41:
42:     for (size_t nItem = 0; nItem < vecCopy.size (); ++ nItem)
43:         cout << vecCopy [nItem] << ' ';
44:
45:     cout << "}" << endl << endl;
46:
47:     return 0;
48: }
```

Output ▼

```
The contents of the vector after using 'partition' are:
{0 8 2 6 4 5 3 7 1 9 }

The effect of using 'stable_partition' is:
{0 2 4 6 8 1 3 5 7 9 }
```

Analysis ▼

The code partitions a range of integers, as contained inside vector, `vecIntegers` into even and odd values. This partitioning is first done using `std::partition` as seen in line 25, and done using `stable_partition` in line 37. For sake of being able to compare, we copy the sample range `vecIntegers` into `vecCopy`, the former partitioned using `std::partition` and the latter using `std::stable_partition`. The effect of using `stable_partition` rather than partition is apparent in the output. `stable_partition` maintains the relative order of elements in each partition. Note that this order comes at a price, which may be small as in this case or significant, depending on the type of object contained in the range. `stable_partition` is slower than `partition` and therefore should be used only when the relative order of the container is important.

23

Inserting Elements in a Sorted Collection

It is often necessary, if not important, that elements inserted in a sorted collection be inserted at the correct positions. STL supplies functions such as `lower_bound` and `upper_bound` to assist in meeting that need.

`lower_bound` and `upper_bound` hence return the minimal and the maximal positions in a sorted range where an element can be inserted without breaking the order of the sort. Listing 23.11 demonstrates the usage of `lower_bound` in inserting an element at the minimal position in a sorted `list` of names.

LISTING 23.11   Using `lower_bound` and `upper_bound` on a Sorted Range

```
1: #include <algorithm>
2: #include <list>
3: #include <string>
4: #include <iostream>
5:
6: int main ()
7: {
8:     using namespace std;
9:
10:     typedef list <string> LIST_STRINGS;
11:
```

LISTING 23.11   Continued

```
12:    // A sample list of strings
13:    LIST_STRINGS listNames;
14:
15:    // Insert sample values
16:    listNames.push_back ("John Doe");
17:    listNames.push_back ("Brad Pitt");
18:    listNames.push_back ("Jack Nicholson");
19:    listNames.push_back ("Sean Penn");
20:    listNames.push_back ("Anna Hoover");
21:
22:    // Sort all the names in the list
23:    listNames.sort ();
24:
25:    cout << "The sorted contents of the list are: " << endl;
26:    LIST_STRINGS::iterator iNameLocator;
27:    for ( iNameLocator = listNames.begin ()
28:        ; iNameLocator != listNames.end ()
29:        ; ++ iNameLocator )
30:    {
31:        cout << "Name [" << distance (listNames.begin (), iNameLocator);
32:        cout << "] = \"" << *iNameLocator << "\"" << endl;
33:    }
34:
35:    cout << endl;
36:
37:    LIST_STRINGS::iterator iMinInsertPosition;
38:
39:    // The closest / lowest position where the element can be inserted
40:    iMinInsertPosition = lower_bound ( listNames.begin (), listNames.end ()
41:                                    , "Brad Pitt" );
42:
43:    LIST_STRINGS::iterator iMaxInsertPosition;
44:
45:    // The farthest / highest position where an element may be inserted
46:    iMaxInsertPosition = upper_bound ( listNames.begin (), listNames.end ()
47:                                    , "Brad Pitt" );
48:
49:    cout << "The lowest index where \"Brad Pitt\" can be inserted is: ";
50:    cout << distance (listNames.begin (), iMinInsertPosition) << endl;
51:
52:    cout << "The highest index where \"Brad Pitt\" can be inserted is: ";
53:    cout << distance (listNames.begin (), iMaxInsertPosition) << endl;
54:
55:    cout << endl;
56:
57:    cout << "Inserting \"Brad Pitt\" in the sorted list:" << endl;
58:    listNames.insert (iMinInsertPosition, "Brad Pitt");
59:
60:    cout << "The contents of the list now are: " << endl;
```

LISTING 23.11 Continued

```
61:    for ( iNameLocator = listNames.begin ()
62:        ; iNameLocator != listNames.end ()
63:        ; ++ iNameLocator )
64:    {
65:        cout << "Name [" << distance (listNames.begin (), iNameLocator);
66:        cout << "] = \"" << *iNameLocator << "\"" << endl;
67:    }
68:
69:    return 0;
70: }
```

23

Output ▼

```
The sorted contents of the list are:
Name [0] = "Anna Hoover"
Name [1] = "Brad Pitt"
Name [2] = "Jack Nicholson"
Name [3] = "John Doe"
Name [4] = "Sean Penn"

The lowest index where "Brad Pitt" can be inserted is: 1
The highest index where "Brad Pitt" can be inserted is: 2

Inserting "Brad Pitt" in the sorted list:
The contents of the list now are:
Name [0] = "Anna Hoover"
Name [1] = "Brad Pitt"
Name [2] = "Brad Pitt"
Name [3] = "Jack Nicholson"
Name [4] = "John Doe"
Name [5] = "Sean Penn"
```

Analysis ▼

An element can be inserted into a sorted collection at two potential positions: one as returned by lower_bound and is the lowest (closest to the beginning of the collection) and another being the iterator returned by upper_bound that is the highest (farthest away from the beginning of the collection). In the case of Listing 23.11, where the string, "Brad Pitt," being inserted into the sorted collection exists in it, the lower and upper bounds are different (else, they would've been identical). The usage of these functions is seen in lines 40 and 46, respectively. As the output demonstrates, the iterator returned by lower_bound when used in inserting the string into the list, as seen in line 58 resulted in the list keeping its sorted state. That is, you were able to make an insertion at a point in the collection that did not break the sorted nature of the contents of the collection. Using the iterator returned by upper_bound would have been just as fine.

Summary

In this lesson, you learned one of the most important and powerful aspects of STL: algorithms. You gained an insight into the different types of algorithms and via samples have a clearer understanding of their application.

Q&A

Q Would I use a mutating algorithm like `std::transform` on an associative container such as `std::set`?

A Even if it were possible, this should not be done. The contents of an associative container should be treated as constants. This is because associative containers sort their elements on insertion, and the relative position of the elements hence plays an important role not only in functions such as `find`, but also in the efficiency of the container. For this reason, mutating algorithms such as `std::transform` should not be used on STL sets.

Q I need to set the content of every element of a sequential container to a particular value. Would I use `std::transform` for this activity?

A Although `std::transform` could be used for this activity, `fill` or `fill_n` is more suited to the task.

Q Does `copy_backward` reverse the contents of the elements in the destination container?

A No, it doesn't. The STL algorithm `copy_backward` reverses the order in which elements are copied but not the order in which elements are stored; that is, it starts with the end of the range and reaches the top. To reverse the contents of a collection, `std::reverse` should be used.

Q Should I use `std::sort` on a list?

A `std::sort` can be used on a list in the same way it can be used on any sequential container. However, the list needs to maintain a special property that an operation on the list does not invalidate existing iterators—a property that `std::sort` cannot guarantee to upkeep. So, for this reason, STL `list` supplies the `sort` algorithm in the form of the member function `list::sort`, which should be used because it guarantees that iterators to elements in the list are not invalidated even if their relative position in the list has changed.

Q Why is it important to use functions such as `lower_bound` or `upper_bound` while inserting into a sorted range?

A These functions supply the first and the last positions, respectively, where an element can be inserted into a sorted collection without disturbing the sort.

Workshop

The Workshop contains quiz questions to help solidify your understanding of the material covered and exercises to provide you with experience in using what you've learned. Try to answer the quiz and exercise questions before checking the answers in Appendix D, and be certain you understand the answers before going to the next lesson.

Quiz

1. You need to remove items that meet a specific condition from a list. Would you use `std::remove_if` or `list::remove_if`?

2. You have a list of a class type `CContactItem`. How does the `list::sort` function sort items of this type in the absence of an explicitly specified binary predicate?

3. How often does the `generate` STL algorithm invoke the `generator` function?

4. What differentiates `std::transform` from `std::for_each`?

Exercises

1. Write a binary predicate that accepts strings as input arguments and returns a value based on case-insensitive comparison.

2. Demonstrate how STL algorithms such as `copy` use iterators to do their function without needing to know the nature of the destination collections by copying between two sequences held in two dissimilar containers.

3. You are writing an application that records the characteristics of stars that come up on the horizon in the order in which they rise. In astronomy, the size of the star is important as well as information on their relative rise and set sequences. If sorting this collection of stars on the basis of their size, would you use `std::sort` or `std::stable_sort`?

LESSON 24
Adaptive Containers: stack and queue

The standard template library (STL) features containers that adapt others to simulate stack and queue behavior. Such containers that internally use another and present a distinct behavior are called *adaptive containers*.

In this lesson, you will learn

- The behavioral characteristics of stacks and queues
- Using the STL stack
- Using the STL queue
- Using the STL priority_queue

The Behavioral Characteristics of Stacks and Queues

Stacks and queues are quite like arrays or lists, but present a restriction on how elements are inserted, accessed, and removed. Their behavioral characteristics are decided exactly by the placement of elements on insertion or the position of the element that can be erased from the container.

Stacks

Stacks are LIFO (last-in-first-out) systems where elements can be inserted or removed at the top of the container. A stack can be visualized as a stack of plates. The last plate added to the stack is going to be the first one taken off. Plates in the middle and at the bottom cannot be inspected.

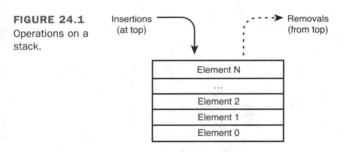

FIGURE 24.1
Operations on a stack.

This behavior of a stack of plates is simulated in the generic STL container std::stack that can be utilized after including the header <stack>.

Queues

Queues are FIFO (first-in-first-out) systems where elements can be inserted behind the previous one, and the one inserted first gets removed first. A queue can be visualized as a queue of people waiting for stamps at the post office—those who join the queue earlier, leave earlier.

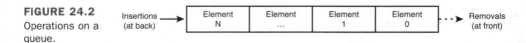

FIGURE 24.2
Operations on a queue.

This behavior of a queue is simulated in the generic STL container std::queue that can be utilized after including the header <queue>.

Using the STL stack Class

The STL stack is a template class that needs the inclusion of header <stack>. It is a generic class that allows insertions and removal of elements at the top, and does not permit any access or inspection of elements at the middle. In that sense, the std::stack is quite similar in behavior to a stack of plates.

Instantiating the Stack

std::stack is defined by some implementations of STL as

```
template <
    class elementType,
    class Container=deque<Type>
> class stack;
```

The parameter *elementType* is the type of object that is collected by the stack. The second template parameter Container is the stack's default underlying container implementation class. std::deque is the default for the stack's internal data storage, and can be replaced by the vector and the list respectively, when the user explicitly instantiates the stack template class with the appropriate second template parameter. Listing 24.1 demonstrates the template instantiation of the std::stack.

24

LISTING 24.1   Instantiation of an STL Stack

```
1: #include <stack>
2: #include <vector>
3:
4: int main ()
5: {
6:     using namespace std;
7:
8:     // A stack of integers
9:     stack <int> stackIntegers;
10:
11:    // A stack of doubles
12:    stack <double> stackDoubles;
13:
14:    // A stack of doubles contained in a vector
15:    stack <double, vector <double> > stackDoublesInVector;
16:
17:    return 0;
18: }
```

Analysis ▼

The sample produces no output, but demonstrates the template instantiation of the STL stack. Lines 9 and 11 instantiate two stack objects to hold elements of type int and double, respectively. Line 15 also instantiates a stack of doubles, but specifies a second template parameter—the type of collection class that the stack should use internally, a vector. If the second template parameter is not supplied, the stack automatically defaults to using a std::deque instead.

Stack Member Functions

The stack, which adapts another container such as the deque, list, or vector, implements its functionality by restricting the manner in which elements can be inserted or removed, to supply a behavior that is expected strictly from a stack-like mechanism. Table 24.1 explains the public member functions of the stack class and demonstrates their usage for a stack of integers.

TABLE 24.1   Member Function of a std::stack

Function	Description
push	Inserts an element at the top of the stack
	stackIntegers.push (25);
pop	Removes the element at the top of the stack
	stackIntegers.pop ();
empty	Tests whether the stack is empty; returns bool
	if (stackIntegers.empty ())
	DoSomething ();
size	Returns the number of elements in the stack
	size_t nNumElements = stackIntegers.size ();
top	Gets a reference to the topmost element in the stack
	cout << "Element at the top = " << stackIntegers.top ();

As the table indicates, the public member functions of the stack expose only those methods that will allow insertion and removal at positions that are compliant with a stack's behavior. That is, even though the underlying container might be a deque, a vector, or a list, the functionality of that container has been suppressed to enforce the behavioral characteristics of a stack.

Listing 24.2 demonstrates inserting elements in a stack and removing elements from one.

LISTING 24.2 Working with a stack of Integers

```cpp
1: #include <stack>
2: #include <iostream>
3:
4: int main ()
5: {
6:     using namespace std;
7:
8:     // A stack of integers
9:     stack <int> stackIntegers;
10:
11:     // Push sample values to the top of the stack
12:     cout << "Pushing numbers {25, 10, -1, 5} into the stack:" << endl;
13:
14:     // push = insert at top of the container
15:     stackIntegers.push (25);
16:     stackIntegers.push (10);
17:     stackIntegers.push (-1);
18:     stackIntegers.push (5);
19:     // So, 25 is at the bottom and 5 is at the top!
20:
21:     cout << "The stack contains " << stackIntegers.size () << " elements";
22:     cout << endl;
23:
24:     // pop = remove the topmost element
25:     cout << endl << "Popping them one after another..." << endl;
26:
27:     while (stackIntegers.size () != 0)
28:     {
29:         cout << "The element at the top is: " << stackIntegers.top();
30:         cout << endl <<  "Removing it from the stack!" << endl;
31:
32:         // Remove the topmost element
33:         stackIntegers.pop ();
34:     }
35:
36:     if (stackIntegers.empty ())
37:         cout << endl << "The stack is now empty!";
38:
39:     return 0;
40: }
```

24

Output ▼

```
Pushing numbers {25, 10, -1, 5} into the stack:
The stack contains 4 elements

Popping them one after another...
The element at the top is: 5
```

```
Removing it from the stack!
The element at the top is: -1
Removing it from the stack!
The element at the top is: 10
Removing it from the stack!
The element at the top is: 25
Removing it from the stack!

The stack is now empty!
```

Analysis ▼

The preceding sample first inserts sample numbers into a stack of integers, stackIntegers, using the stack::push function. The sample then proceeds to delete elements from the stack. As stack permits access to only the topmost element, an element at the top can be accessed using member stack::pop() as seen in line 29. Elements can be deleted from the stack one at a time using stack::pop(), as seen in line 33. The while-loop around it ensures that the pop() operation is repeated till the stack is empty. As is visible from the order of the elements that were popped, the element inserted last was popped first, demonstrating the typical LIFO (last-in-first-out) behavior of a stack.

Listing 24.2 demonstrated all five member functions of the stack. Note that push_back and insert, which are available with all STL sequential containers, used as underlying containers by the stack class, are not available as public member functions of the stack. Ditto for iterators that help you peek at elements that are not at the top of the container. All that the stack exposes is the element at the top, nothing else.

Using the STL queue Class

The STL queue is a template class that requires the inclusion of the header <queue>. It is a generic class that allows insertion only at the end and removal of elements only at the front. A queue does not permit any access or inspection of elements at the middle; however, elements at the beginning and the end can be accessed. In a sense, the std::queue is quite similar in behavior to a queue of people at the cashier in a supermarket!

Instantiating the Queue

std::queue is defined as

```
template <
   class elementType,
   class Container = deque<Type>
> class queue;
```

Here, *elementType* is the type of elements collected by the queue object. *Container* is the type of collection that the std::queue class uses to maintain its data. The std::list, vector, and deque are possible candidates for this template parameter, and the deque is the default.

Listing 24.3 demonstrates the template instantiation of std::queue.

LISTING 24.3   Instantiating an STL Queue

```
 1: #include <queue>
 2: #include <list>
 3:
 4: int main ()
 5: {
 6:     using namespace std;
 7:
 8:     // A queue of integers
 9:     queue <int> qIntegers;
10:
11:     // A queue of doubles
12:     queue <double> qDoubles;
13:
14:     // A queue of doubles stored internally in a list
15:     queue <double, list <double> > qDoublesInList;
16:
17:     return 0;
18: }
```

24

Analysis ▼

The sample demonstrates how the generic STL class queue can be instantiated to create a queue of integers, as seen in line 9, or a queue for objects of type double, as seen in line 12. qDoublesInList, as instantiated in line 15, is a queue in which we have explicitly specified that the underlying container adapted by the queue to manage its internals be a std::list, as specified by the second template parameter. In the absence of the second template parameter, as in the first two queues, the std::deque will be used as default underlying container for the contents of the queue.

Member Functions of a queue

As is the case with the std::stack, the std::queue also bases its implementation on an STL container such as the vector, list, or deque. The queue exposes a few member functions that implement the behavioral characteristics of a queue. Table 24.2 explains the member functions using qIntegers, which as Listing 24.3 demonstrates, is a queue of integers.

TABLE 24.2   Member Functions of a std::queue

Function	Description
push	Inserts an element at the back of the queue; that is, at the last position `qIntegers.push (10);`
pop	Removes the element at the front of the queue; that is, at the first position `qIntegers.pop ();`
front	Returns a reference to the element at the front of the queue `cout << "Element at front: " << qIntegers.front ();`
back	Returns a reference to the element at the back of the queue; that is, the last inserted element `cout << "Element at back: " << qIntegers.back ();`

empty	Tests whether the queue is empty; returns a boolean value
	`if (qIntegers.empty ())`
	`cout << "The queue is empty!";`

size	Returns the number of elements in the queue `size_t nNumElements = qIntegers.size ();`

STL queue does not feature functions such as begin() and end(), which are supplied by most STL containers, including the underlying deque, vector or list, as used by the queue class. This is by intention so that the only permissible operations on the queue are those in compliance with the queue's behavioral characteristics. Note that unlike the stack, the queue allows elements at both ends; that is, front and back, of the container to be inspected. Insertion is permitted at the end and removal at the beginning, a behavior also demonstrated by Listing 24.4.

LISTING 24.4   Working with a Queue of Integers

```
1: #include <queue>
2: #include <iostream>
3:
4: int main ()
5: {
6:     using namespace std;
7:
8:     // A queue of integers
9:     queue <int> qIntegers;
10:
11:     cout << "Inserting {10, 5, -1, 20} into the queue" << endl;
12:
13:     // elements pushed into the queue are inserted at the end
14:     qIntegers.push (10);
```

LISTING 24.4 Continued

```
15:     qIntegers.push (5);
16:     qIntegers.push (-1);
17:     qIntegers.push (20);
18:     // the elements in the queue now are {20, -1, 5, 10} in that order
19:
20:     cout << "The queue contains " << qIntegers.size ();
21:     cout << " elements" << endl;
22:     cout << "Element at the front: " << qIntegers.front() << endl;
23:     cout << "Element at the back: " << qIntegers.back ();
24:     cout << endl << endl;
25:
26:     cout << "Removing them one after another..." << endl;
27:     while (qIntegers.size () != 0)
28:     {
29:         cout << "Deleting element " << qIntegers.front () << endl;
30:
31:         // Remove the element at the front of the queue
32:         qIntegers.pop ();
33:     }
34:
35:     cout << endl;
36:
37:     // Test if the queue is empty
38:     if (qIntegers.empty ())
39:         cout << "The queue is now empty!";
40:
41:     return 0;
42: }
```

24

Output ▼

```
Inserting {10, 5, -1, 20} into the queue
The queue contains 4 elements
Element at the front: 10
Element at the back: 20

Removing them one after another...
Deleting element 10
Deleting element 5
Deleting element -1
Deleting element 20

The queue is now empty!
```

Analysis ▼

Elements were added to the queue `qIntegers` using `push` that inserts them at the end (or back) of the queue in lines 14–17. Functions `front()` and `back()` are used to reference elements at the beginning and the end positions of the queue, as seen in lines 22 and 23. The `while loop` in lines 27–33 displays the element at the beginning of the queue, before removing it using a `pop()` operation. It continues doing this until the `queue` is empty. The output demonstrates that elements were erased from the queue in the same order in which they were inserted.

Using the STL Priority Queue

The STL `priority_queue` is a template class that also requires the inclusion of the header `<queue>`. The `priority_queue` is different from the `queue` in that the element of the highest value (or the value deemed as highest by a binary predicate) is available at the front of the queue, and queue operations are restricted to the front.

Instantiating the `priority_queue` Class

`std::priority_queue` class is defined as

```
template <
   class elementType,
   class Container=vector<Type>,
      class Compare=less<typename Container::value_type>
>
class priority_queue
```

Here, *elementType* is the template parameter that conveys the type of elements to be collected in the priority queue. The second template parameter tells the collection class to be internally used by `priority_queue` for holding data, whereas the third parameter allows the programmer to specify a binary predicate that helps the queue determine the element that is at the top. In the absence of a specified binary predicate, the `priority_queue` class uses the default in `std::less`, which compares two objects using `operator <`.

The instantiation of a `priority_queue` object is demonstrated by Listing 24.5.

LISTING 24.5   Instantiating an STL `priority_queue`

```
1: #include <queue>
2:
3: int main ()
4: {
```

LISTING 24.5   Continued

```
 5:      using namespace std;
 6:
 7:      // A priority queue of integers sorted using std::less <> (default)
 8:      priority_queue <int> pqIntegers;
 9:
10:      // A priority queue of doubles
11:      priority_queue <double> pqDoubles;
12:
13:      // A priority queue of integers sorted using std::greater <>
14:      priority_queue <int, deque <int>, greater <int> > pqIntegers_Inverse;
15:
16:      return 0;
17: }
```

24

Analysis ▼

Lines 8 and 11 instantiate two `priority_queues`. The former is for objects of type `int` and the latter for `double`. The absence of any other template parameter results in the usage of `std::vector` as the internal container of data, and the default comparison criterion is provided by `std::less`. These queues are therefore so prioritized that the integer of the highest value is available at the `front` of the priority queue. `pqIntegers_Inverse`, however, supplies a `deque` for the second parameter as the internal container, and `std::greater` as the predicate. This predicate results in a queue where the smallest number is available at the front. (The effect of using this predicate will be clear in Listing 24.7.)

Member Functions of `priority_queue`

The member functions `front()` and `back()`, available in the `queue`, are not available in the `priority_queue`. Table 24.3 introduces the member functions of a `priority_queue`.

TABLE 24.3   Member Functions of a `std::priority_queue`

Function	Description
push	Inserts an element into the priority queue
	`pqIntegers.push (10);`
pop	Removes the element at the top of the queue; that is, the largest element in the queue
	`pqIntegers.pop ();`
top	Returns a reference to the largest element in the queue (which also holds the topmost position)
	`cout << "The largest element in the priority  queue is: " << pqIntegers.top ();`

TABLE 24.3 Continued

Function	Description

empty	Tests whether the priority queue is empty; returns a boolean value
	
	`if (pqIntegers.empty ())`
	    `cout << "The queue is empty!";`

size	Returns the number of elements in the priority queue: `size_t nNumElements = pqIntegers.size ();`

As the table indicates, queue members can only be accessed using top(), which returns the element of the highest value, evaluated using the user-defined predicate or by std::less in the absence of one. The usage of priority_queue members is demonstrated by Listing 24.6.

LISTING 24.6 Working with a priority_queue

```
1: #include <queue>
2: #include <iostream>
3:
4: int main ()
5: {
6:     using namespace std;
7:
8:     priority_queue <int> pqIntegers;
9:     cout << "Inserting {10, 5, -1, 20} into the priority_queue" << endl;
10:
11:     // elements get push-ed into the p-queue
12:     pqIntegers.push (10);
13:     pqIntegers.push (5);
14:     pqIntegers.push (-1);
15:     pqIntegers.push (20);
16:
17:     cout << "The queue contains " << pqIntegers.size () << " elements";
18:     cout << endl;
19:     cout << "Element at the top: " << pqIntegers.top () << endl << endl;
20:
21:     while (!pqIntegers.empty ())
22:     {
23:         cout << "Deleting the topmost element: " << pqIntegers.top ();
24:         cout << endl;
25:
26:         pqIntegers.pop ();
27:     }
28:
29:     return 0;
30: }
```

Output ▼

```
Inserting {10, 5, -1, 20} into the priority_queue
The queue contains 4 elements
Element at the top: 20

Deleting the topmost element: 20
Deleting the topmost element: 10
Deleting the topmost element: 5
Deleting the topmost element: -1
```

Analysis ▼

As in the previous sample that used a `std::queue` (Listing 24.4), the preceding one inserts sample integers into a `priority_queue` and then erases the element on the top / front using pop, as seen in line 26. The output indicates that the element of greatest value is available at the top of the queue. Usage of `priority_queue::pop` therefore effectively deletes the element that evaluates to having the greatest value among all elements in the container.

The next sample, in Listing 24.7, demonstrates the instantiation of a `priority_queue` with `std::greater <int>` as the `predicate`. This predicate results in the queue evaluating the smallest number as the element with greatest value, which is then available at the front of the priority queue.

24

LISTING 24.7   A `priority_queue` with the Smallest Value at the Front Using a Predicate

```
1: #include <queue>
2: #include <iostream>
3:
4: int main ()
5: {
6:     using namespace std;
7:
8:     // Define a priority_queue object with greater <int> as predicate
9:     // So, numbers of smaller magnitudes are evaluated as greater in value
10:     priority_queue <int, vector <int>, greater <int> > pqIntegers;
11:
12:     cout << "Inserting {10, 5, -1, 20} into the priority queue" << endl;
13:
14:     // elements get push-ed into the p-queue
15:     pqIntegers.push (10);
16:     pqIntegers.push (5);
17:     pqIntegers.push (-1);
18:     pqIntegers.push (20);
19:
```

LISTING 24.7   Continued

```
20:     cout << "The queue contains " << pqIntegers.size () << " elements";
21:     cout << endl;
22:     cout << "Element at the top: " << pqIntegers.top () << endl << endl;
23:
24:     while (!pqIntegers.empty ())
25:     {
26:         cout << "Deleting the topmost element " << pqIntegers.top ();
27:         cout << endl;
28:
29:         // delete the number at the 'top'
30:         pqIntegers.pop ();
31:     }
32:
33:     return 0;
34: }
```

Output ▼

```
Inserting {10, 5, -1, 20} into the priority queue
The queue contains 4 elements
Element at the top: -1

Deleting the topmost element -1
Deleting the topmost element 5
Deleting the topmost element 10
Deleting the topmost element 20
```

Analysis ▼

Most of the code and all the values supplied to the priority_queue in this sample are intentionally the same as those in the previous sample, Listing 24.6. Yet the output displays how the two queues behave differently. This priority_queue compares the elements in it using the predicate greater <int> as seen in line 10. As a result of this predicate, the integer with the lowest magnitude is evaluated as greater than others, and is therefore placed at the top position. So, function top() used in line 26 always displays the smallest integer number in the priority_queue, one that is deleted soon after using a pop() operation in line 30.

Thus, when elements are popped, this priority_queue pops the integers in order of increasing magnitude.

Summary

This lesson explained the usage of the three key adaptive containers — the STL `stack`, `queue`, and the `priority_queue`. These adapt sequential containers for their internal storage requirements, yet via their member functions, they present the behavioral characteristics that make stacks and queues so unique.

Q&A

Q Can an element in the middle of a stack be modified?

A No, this would be against the behavior of a stack.

Q Can I iterate through all the elements of a queue?

A The queue does not feature iterators and elements in a queue can be accessed only at its ends.

Q Can STL algorithms work with adaptive containers?

A STL algorithms work using iterators. Because neither the `stack` nor the `queue` class supplies iterators that mark the end of the ranges, the use of STL algorithms with these containers would not be possible.

Workshop

The Workshop contains quiz questions to help solidify your understanding of the material covered and exercises to provide you with experience in using what you've learned. Try to answer the quiz and exercise questions before checking the answers in Appendix D, and be certain you understand the answers before going to the next lesson.

Quiz

1. Can you change the behavior of the `priority_queue` for a certain element, such that the one with the greatest value is popped last?

2. You have a `priority_queue` of class `CCoins`. What member operator do you need to define for the `priority_queue` class to present the coin with the greater value at the top position?

3. You have a stack of class `CCoins` and have pushed six objects into it. Can you access or delete the first coin inserted?

Exercises

1. A queue of people (class `CPerson`) are lining up at the post office. `CPerson` contains a member attributes that holds age and gender and is defined as

   ```
   class CPerson
   {
       public:
           int m_nAge;
           bool m_bIsFemale;
   };
   ```

   Write a binary predicate for the `priority_queue` that helps service older people and women (in that order) on a priority.

2. Write a program that reverses the user's string input using the `stack` class.

LESSON 25
Working with Bit Flags Using STL

Bits can be a very efficient way of storing settings and flags. STL supplies classes that help organize and manipulate bitwise information. This lesson will introduce you to

- The `bitset` class
- The `vector<bool>`

The bitset Class

std::bitset is an STL class designed for handling information in bits and bit flags. The std::bitset is not classified as an STL container class because it cannot resize itself and does not exhibit other characteristics of containers, such as access via iterators. This is a utility class that is optimized for working with a sequence of bits whose length is known at compile-time.

Instantiating the std::bitset

This template class requires the inclusion of the header <bitset> and needs one template parameter that supplies the number of bits the instance of the class has to manage. Listing 25.1 demonstrates the template instantiation of the bitset class.

LISTING 25.1   Instantiating a std::bitset

```
 1: #include <bitset>
 2: #include <iostream>
 3: #include <string>
 4:
 5: int main ()
 6: {
 7:     using namespace std;
 8:
 9:     // instantiate a bitset object for holding 4 bits
10:     // all initialized to '0000'
11:     bitset <4> fourBits;
12:     cout << "The initial contents of fourBits: " << fourBits << endl;
13:
14:     // instantiate a bitset object for holding 5 bits
15:     // initialize it to a bit sequence supplied by a string
16:     bitset <5> fiveBits (string ("10101"));
17:     cout << "The initial contents of fiveBits: " << fiveBits << endl;
18:
19:     // instantiate a bitset object for 8 bits
20:     // given an unsigned long init value
21:     bitset <8> eightbits (255);
22:     cout << "The initial contents of eightBits: " << eightbits << endl;
23:
24:     return 0;
25: }
```

Output ▼

```
The initial contents of fourBits: 0000
The initial contents of fiveBits: 10101
The initial contents of eightBits: 11111111
```

Analysis ▼

The sample demonstrates three different ways of constructing a `bitset` object: via the default constructor that initializes the bit sequence to 0 as seen in line 11, via an STL string that contains the string representation of the desired bit sequence as seen in line 16, and via an `unsigned long` that holds the decimal value of the binary sequence as seen in line 21. Note that in each of these instances, we had to supply the number of bits that the `bitset` is supposed to contain, as a template parameter. This number is fixed at compile-time, it isn't dynamic. You can't insert more bits into a `bitset` than what you specified in your code the way you can insert more elements in a vector than the `size` planned at compile-time.

Using `std::bitset` and Its Members

The `bitset` class supplies member functions that help perform insertions into the `bitset`, set or reset contents, read them or write them into a stream. It also supplies operators that help display the contents of a `bitset`, and perform bitwise logical operations among others.

std:bitset Operators

25

You learned operators in Lesson 13, "Operator Types and Operator Overloading," and you also learned that the most important role played by operators is in increasing the usability of a class. `std::bitset` provides some very useful operators as shown in Table 25.1 that make using it really easy. The operators are explained using the sample `bitset` you learned in Listing 25.1, `fourBits`.

TABLE 25.1 Operators Supported by `std::bitset`

Operator	Description
operator <<	Inserts a text representation of the bit sequence into the output stream
	cout << fourBits;
operator >>	Inserts a string into the bitset object
	"0101" >> fourBits;
operator &	Performs a bitwise AND operation
	bitset <4> result (fourBits1 & fourBits2);
operator |	Performs a bitwise OR operation
	bitwise <4> result (fourBits1 | fourBits2);

TABLE 25.1   Continued

Operator	Description
operator ^	Performs a bitwise XOR operation
	`bitwise <4> result (fourBits1 ^ fourBits2);`
operator ~	Performs a bitwise NOT operation
	`bitwise <4> result (~fourBits1);`
operator >>=	Performs a bitwise right shift
	`fourBits >>= (2); // Shift two bits to the right`
operator <<=	Performs a bitwise left shift
	`fourBits <<= (2); // Shift two bits to the left`
operator [N]	Returns a reference to the (N+1) bit in the sequence
	`fourBits [2] = 0;  // sets the 3^{rd} bit to 0`
	`bool bNum = fourBits [2]; // reads the third bit`

In addition to these `std::bitset` also features operators such as `|=`, `&=`, `^=`, and `~=` that help perform bitwise operations on a bitset object.

`std::bitset` Member Methods

Bits can hold two states—they are either set (1) or reset (0). To help manipulate the contents of a `bitset`, you can use the member functions as listed in Table 25.2 that can help you work with a `bit`, or with all the `bits` in a `bitset`.

TABLE 25.2   Member Methods of a `std::bitset`

Function	Description
set	Sets all bits in the sequence to 1
	`fourBits.set (); // sequence now contains: '1111'`
set (N, val=1)	Sets the (N+1) bit with the value as specified by val (default 1)
	`fourBits.set (2, 0); // sets the third bit to 0`
reset	Resets all bits in the sequence to 0
	`fourBits.reset (); // sequence now contains: '0000'`
reset (N)	Clears the bit at offset position (N+1)
	`fourBits.reset (2); // the third bit is now 0`
flip	Toggles all bits in the sequence
	`fourBits.flip (); // 0101 changes to → 1010`

TABLE 25.2 Continued

Function	Description
size	Returns the number of bits in the sequence
	`size_t nNumBits = fourBits.size (); // returns 4`
count	Returns the number of bits that are set
	`size_t nNumBitsSet = fourBits.count ();`
	`size_t nNumBitsReset = fourBits.size () -` `fourBits.count ();`

The usage of these member methods and operators is demonstrated in Listing 25.2.

LISTING 25.2 Performing Logical Operations Using a Bitset

```
1: #include <bitset>
2: #include <string>
3: #include <iostream>
4:
5: int main ()
6: {
7:     using namespace std;
8:
9:     // A bitset to hold 8-bits
10:    bitset <8> eightBits;
11:    cout << "Enter a 8-bit sequence: ";
12:
13:    // Store user-supplied sequence into the bitset
14:    cin >> eightBits;
15:    cout << endl;
16:
17:    // Supply info on number of 1s and 0s in it:
18:    cout << "The number of 1s in the input sequence: ";
19:    cout << eightBits.count () << endl;
20:    cout << "The number of 0s in the input sequence: ";
21:    cout << eightBits.size () - eightBits.count () << endl;
22:
23:    // create a copy
24:    bitset <8> flipInput (eightBits);
25:
26:    // flip the bits
27:    flipInput.flip ();
28:    cout << "The flipped version of the input sequence is: "
29:         << flipInput << endl << endl;
30:
31:    // another 8-bit sequence to perform bitwise-ops against the first
32:    bitset <8> eightMoreBits;
33:    cout << "Enter another 8-bit sequence: ";
```

25

LISTING 25.2 Continued

```
34:       cin >> eightMoreBits;
35:       cout << endl;
36:
37:       cout << "Result of AND, OR and XOR between the two sequences:" << endl;
38:       cout << eightBits << " & " << eightMoreBits << " = "
39:                        << (eightBits & eightMoreBits)    // bitwise AND
40:                        << endl;
41:
42:       cout << eightBits << " | " << eightMoreBits << " = "
43:                        << (eightBits | eightMoreBits)    // bitwise OR
44:                        << endl;
45:
46:       cout << eightBits << " ^ " << eightMoreBits << " = "
47:                        << (eightBits ^ eightMoreBits)    // bitwise XOR
48:                        << endl;
49:
50:       return 0;
51: }
```

Output ▼

```
Enter a 8-bit sequence: 11100101

The number of 1s in the input sequence: 5
The number of 0s in the input sequence: 3
The flipped version of the input sequence is: 00011010

Enter another 8-bit sequence: 10010111

Result of AND, OR and XOR between the two sequences:
11100101 & 10010111 = 10000101
11100101 | 10010111 = 11110111
11100101 ^ 10010111 = 01110010
```

Analysis ▼

The sample is an interactive program that demonstrates not only how easy and hassle-free performing bitwise operations between two bit-sequences using std::bitset is, but also the utility of its stream operators. Operators >> and << are the ones that made writing a bit sequence to the screen and reading a bit sequence from the user in string format a simple task. eightBits contains a user-supplied sequence that is fed into it in line 14. count() used in line 19 tells the number of ones in the sequence, and the number of zeroes is evaluated as the difference between size() that returns the number of bits in the bitset and count(), as seen in line 21. flipInput is at the beginning a copy of eightBits, and then flipped using flip(), as seen in line 27. It now contains the sequence with individual bits inverted. The rest of the sample indicates the result of bit-wise AND, OR, and XOR operations between two bitsets.

Note here that one relative disadvantage of this STL class is its inability to resize itself dynamically; that is, the bitset can be used only when the number of bits to be stored in the sequence is known at compile-time. STL supplies the programer with a class vector<bool> (also called bit_vector in some implementations of STL) that overcomes this shortcoming.

The vector<bool>

The vector<bool> is a partial specialization of the std::vector and is intended for storing boolean data. This class is able to dynamically size itself and hence the programmer does not need to know the number of boolean-flags to be stored at compile-time.

Instantiating a vector<bool>

To use a vector<bool>, you need to include the header <vector>. The following sample in Listing 25.3 demonstrates the instantiation of a vector<bool>.

LISTING 25.3   The Instantiation of vector<bool>

```
 1: #include <vector>
 2:
 3: int main ()
 4: {
 5:     using namespace std;
 6:
 7:     // Instantiate an object using the default constructor
 8:     vector <bool> vecBool1;
 9:
10:     // A vector of 10 elements with value true (default: false)
11:     vector <bool> vecBool2 (10, true);
12:
13:     // Instantiate one object as a copy of another
14:     vector <bool> vecBool2Copy (vecBool2);
15:
16:     return 0;
17: }
```

25

Analysis ▼

This sample presents some of the ways in which a vector<bool> object can be constructed. Line 8 is one that uses the default constructor. Line 11 demonstrates the creation of an object that is initialized to contain 10 boolean flags, each holding the value true. Line 14 demonstrates how one vector<bool> can be constructed as a copy of another.

Using the vector<bool>

The vector<bool> features the function flip() that toggles the state of the boolean values in the sequence. Otherwise, this class is quite similar to the std::vector in the sense that you can, for example, even push_back flags into the sequence. The following sample in Listing 25.4 demonstrates the usage of this class, in further detail.

LISTING 25.4   Using the vector<bool>

```
1: #include <vector>
2: #include <iostream>
3:
4: int main ()·
5: {
6:     using namespace std;
7:
8:     // Instantiate a vector<bool> to hold 3 elements
9:     vector <bool> vecBool (3);
10:
11:     // Assign 3 elements using the array operator []
12:     vecBool [0] = true;
13:     vecBool [1] = true;
14:     vecBool [2] = false;
15:
16:     // Insert a 4th element using push_back:
17:     // this will cause the vector to resize the buffer
18:     vecBool.push_back (true);
19:
20:     cout << "The contents of the vector are: " << endl << "{";
21:     for (size_t nIndex = 0; nIndex < vecBool.size (); ++ nIndex)
22:         cout << vecBool [nIndex] << ' ';
23:     cout << "}" << endl << endl;
24:
25:     vecBool.flip ();
26:
27:     cout << "The flipped contents of the vector are: " << endl << "{";
28:     for (size_t nIndex = 0; nIndex < vecBool.size (); ++ nIndex)
29:         cout << vecBool [nIndex] << ' ';
30:     cout << "}";
31:
32:     return 0;
33: }
```

Output ▼

```
The contents of the vector are:
{1 1 0 1 }

The flipped contents of the vector are:
0 0 1 0 }
```

Analysis ▼

In this sample, the Boolean flags in the vector have been accessed using the `operator[]`, as seen in line 22, quite like in a regular vector. The function `flip()` used in line 25 toggles the contents of the bit lags, essentially converting all 0s to 1s and vice versa.

Summary

In this lesson, you learned about the most effective tool in handling bit sequences and bit flags: the `std::bitset` class. You also gained knowledge on the `vector<bool>` class that allows you to store Boolean flags—the number of which does not need to be known at compile time.

Q&A

Q Given a situation where `std::bitset` and `vector<bool>` can both be used, which of the two classes would you prefer to hold your binary flags?

A The bitset as it is most suited to this requirement.

Q I have a `std::bitset` object called `myBitSeq` that contains a certain number of stored bits. How would I determine the number of bits that are at value 0 (or false)?

A `bitset::count()` supplies the number of bits at value 1. This number, when subtracted from `bitset::size()` (which indicates the total number of bits stored), would give you the number of 0s in the sequence.

Q Can I use iterators to access the individual elements in a `vector<bool>`?

A Yes. Because the `vector<bool>` is a partial specialization of the `std::vector`, iterators are supported.

Q Can I specify the number of elements to be held in a `vector<bool>` at compile time?

A Yes, by either specifying the number in the overloaded constructor, or by using `vector<bool>::resize` function at a later instance.

25

Workshop

The Workshop contains quiz questions to help solidify your understanding of the material covered and exercises to provide you with experience in using what you've learned. Try to answer the quiz and exercise questions before checking the answers in Appendix D, and be certain you understand the answers before going to the next lesson.

Quiz

1. Can the `bitset` expand its internal buffer to hold a variable number of elements?

2. Why is the `bitset` not classified as an STL container class?

3. Would you use the `std::vector` to hold a number of bits that is fixed and known at compile time?

Exercises

1. Write a `bitset` class that contains four bits. Initialize it to a number, display the result, and add it to another bitset object. (The catch: Bitsets don't allow bitsetA = bitsetX + bitsetY.)

2. Demonstrate how you would toggle (that is, switch) the bits in a bitset.

PART V:
Advanced C++ Concepts

LESSON 26
Understanding Smart Pointers

C++ programmers do not necessarily need to use plain pointer types when managing memory on the heap (or the free store); they can make use of a smarter option.

In this lesson, you will learn

- What smart pointers are and why you need them

- How smart pointers are implemented

- Different smart pointer types

- The C++ standard library–supplied smart pointer class `auto_ptr`

- Popular smart pointer libraries

What Are Smart Pointers?

Very simply said, a *smart pointer* in C++ is a class, with overloaded operators, which behaves like a conventional pointer yet supplies additional value by ensuring proper and timely destruction of dynamically allocated data and/or implementation of a well-defined object life-cycle management strategy.

What Is the Problem with Using Conventional (Raw) Pointers?

Unlike other modern programming languages, C++ supplies full flexibility to the programmer in memory allocation, deallocation, and management. Unfortunately, this flexibility is a double-edged sword. On one side it makes C++ a powerful language, but on the other it allows the programmer to create memory-related problems, such as memory leaks, when dynamically allocated objects are not correctly released.

For example:

```
CData *pData = mObject.GetData ();
/*
   Questions: Is the object pointed to by pData dynamically allocated?
   Who will perform the deallocation: caller or the called, if necessary?
   Answer: No idea!
*/
pData->Display ();
```

In the preceding line of code, there is no obvious way to tell whether the memory pointed to by `pData`

- Was allocated on the `heap`, and therefore eventually needs to be `deallocated`
- Is the responsibility of the caller to `deallocate`
- Will automatically be destroyed by the object's `destructor`

Although such ambiguities can be partially solved by inserting comments and enforcing coding practices, these mechanisms are much too loose to efficiently avoid all errors caused by abuse of dynamically allocated data and pointers.

How Do Smart Pointers Help?

Given the problems with using conventional pointer and conventional memory management techniques, it should be noted that the C++ programmer is not forced to use them when he needs to manage data on the heap/free store. The programmer can choose a smarter way to allocate and manage dynamic data by adopting the use of smart pointers in his programs:

```
smart_pointer<CData> spData = mObject.GetData ();

// Use a smart pointer like a conventional pointer!
spData->Display ();
(*spData).Display ();

// Don't have to worry about de-allocation
// (the smart pointer's destructor does it for you)
```

Thus, smart pointers behave like conventional pointers (let's call those raw pointers now) but supply useful features via their overloaded operators and destructors to ensure that dynamically allocated data is destroyed in a timely manner.

How Are Smart Pointers Implemented?

This question can for the moment be simplified to "How did the smart pointer spData function like a conventional pointer?" The answer is this: Smart pointer classes overload operator* (dereferencing operator) and operator-> (member selection operator) to make you, the programmer, use them as conventional pointers. Operator overloading was discussed previously in Lesson 13, "Operator Types and Operator Overloading."

Additionally, to allow you to manage a type of your choice on the heap, almost all good smart pointer classes are template classes that contain a generic implementation of their functionality. Being templates, they are versatile and can be specialized to manage an object of a type of your choice.

26

A sample implementation of a simple smart pointer class can be seen in Listing 26.1.

LISTING 26.1   The Minimal Essential Components of a Smart Pointer Class

```
 1: template <typename T>
 2: class smart_pointer
 3: {
 4: private:
 5:     T* m_pRawPointer;
 6: public:
 7:     smart_pointer (T* pData) : m_pRawPointer (pData) {}    // constructor
 8:     ~smart_pointer () {delete pData;};                    // destructor
 9:
10:     // copy constructor
11:     smart_pointer (const smart_pointer & anotherSP);
12:     // assignment operator
13:     smart_pointer& operator= (const smart_pointer& anotherSP);
14:
```

LISTING 26.1   Continued

```
15:     T& operator* () const          // dereferencing operator
16:     {
17:         return *(m_pRawPointer);
18:     }
19:
20:     T* operator-> () const         // member selection operator
21:     {
22:         return m_pRawPointer;
23:     }
24: };
```

Analysis ▼

The preceding smart pointer class displays the implementation of the two operators * and
->, as declared in lines 15–18 and 20–24 that help this class to function as a "pointer," in
the conventional sense. For example, if you have a class CDog, you would be able to use
the smart pointer on an object of type CDog like this:

```
smart_pointer <CDog> pSmartDog (new CDog);
pSmartDog->Bark ();
int nAge = (*pSmartDog).GetAge ();
```

This class smart_pointer still doesn't display or implement any functionality that would
make this pointer class very smart, and make using it an advantage over using a conventional pointer. The constructor, as seen in line 7, accepts a pointer that is saved as the
internal pointer object in the smart pointer class. The destructor frees this pointer,
allowing for automatic memory release.

The implementation that makes a smart pointer really "smart" is the implementation of the
copy constructor, the assignment operator, and the destructor. They determine the
behavior of the smart pointer object when it is passed across functions, assigned, or goes
out of scope (that is, gets destructed like any other class-object). So, before looking at a
complete smart pointer implementation, you should understand some smart pointer types.

Types of Smart Pointers

The management of the memory resource (that is, the ownership model implemented) is
what sets smart pointer classes apart. Smart pointers decide what they do with the
resource when they are copied and assigned to. The simplest implementations often
result in performance issues, whereas the fastest ones might not suit all applications. In
the end, it is for the programmer to understand how a smart pointer functions before he
decides to use it in his application.

Classification of smart pointers is actually a classification of their memory resource management strategies. These are

- Deep Copy
- Copy on Write (COW)
- Reference counted
- Reference linked
- Destructive copy

Let's take a brief look into each of these strategies before studying the smart pointer supplied by the C++ standard library, the std::auto_ptr.

Deep Copy

In a smart pointer that implements *deep copy*, every smart pointer instance holds a complete copy of the object that is being *managed*. Whenever the smart pointer is copied, the object pointed to is also copied (thus, deep copy). When the smart pointer goes out of scope, it releases the memory it points to (via the destructor).

Although the deep-copy-based smart pointer does not seem to render any value over passing objects by value, its advantage becomes apparent in the treatment of polymorphic objects, as seen in the following, where it can avoid *slicing*:

```
// Example of Slicing When Passing Polymorphic Objects by Value
// CAnimal is a base class for CDog and CCat.
void MakeAnimalTalk (CAnimal mAnimal)    // note parameter type
{
    mAnimal.Talk (); // virtual function
}

// ... Some function
CCat mCat;
MakeAnimalTalk (mCat);
// Slicing: only the CAnimal part of mCat is sent to MakeAnimalTalk

CDog mDog;
MakeAnimalTalk (mDog);      // Slicing again
```

Slicing issues are resolved when the programmer chooses a deep-copy smart pointer, as seen in Listing 26.2.

26

LISTING 26.2   Using a Deep-Copy-Based Smart Pointer to Pass Polymorphic Objects by Their Base Type

```
1: template <typename T>
2: class deepcopy_smart_pointer
3: {
4: private:
5:     T* m_pObject;
6: public:
7:     //... other functions
8:
9:     // copy constructor of the deepcopy pointer
10:     deepcopy_smart_pointer (const deepcopy_smart_pointer& source)
11:     {
12:         // Use a virtual clone function defined in the derived class
13:         // to get a complete copy of the object
14:         m_pObject = source->Clone ();
15:     }
16: };
17:
18: void MakeAnimalTalk (deepcopy_smart_pointer<CAnimal> mAnimal)
19: {
20:     mAnimal.Talk ();
21: }
```

Analysis ▼

As you can see, deepcopy_smart_pointer implements a copy constructor in lines 10–15 that allows a deep copy of the polymorphic object via a Clone function that the object needs to implement. For the sake of simplicity, it is taken for granted in this example that the virtual function implemented by the base class CAnimal is called Clone. Typically, smart pointers that implement deep-copy models will have this function supplied as either a template parameter or a function object.

A sample usage of the deepcopy_smart_pointer is as follows:

```
deepcopy_smart_pointer <CAnimal> pDog (new CDog());
MakeAnimalTalk (pDog);     // No slicing issues as pDog is deep-copied

deepcopy_smart_pointer <CAnimal> pAnimal (new CCat());
MakeAnimalTalk (pCat);     // No slicing
```

Thus, when the smart pointer itself is passed as a pointer to base class type CAnimal, the deep-copy implemented in the smart pointer's constructor kicks in to ensure that the object being passed is not sliced, even though syntactically only the base part of it is required by the destination function MakeAnimalTalk().

The disadvantage of the deep-copy-based mechanism is performance. This might not be a factor for some applications, but for many others it might inhibit the programmer from using a smart pointer for his application altogether, and simply pass a base type pointer (conventional pointer, CAnimal*) to functions such as MakeAnimalTalk(). Other pointers types try to address this performance issue in various ways.

Copy on Write Mechanism

Copy on Write (*COW* as it is popularly called) attempts to optimize the performance of deep-copy smart pointers by sharing pointers until the first attempt at writing to the object is made. On the first attempt at invoking a non-const function, a COW pointer typically creates a copy of the object on which the non-const function is invoked, whereas other instances of the pointer continue sharing the source object.

COW has its fair share of fans. For those that swear by COW, implementing operators * and -> in their const and non-const versions is key to the functionality of the COW pointer. The latter creates a copy.

The point is that when you chose a pointer implementation that follows the COW philosophy, be sure that you understand the implementation details before you proceed to use such an implementation. Otherwise, you might land in situations where you have a copy too few or a copy too many.

Reference Counted Smart Pointers

Reference counting in general is a mechanism that keeps a count of the number of users of an object. When the count reduces to zero, the object is released. So, reference counting makes a very good mechanism for sharing objects without having to copy them. If you have ever worked with a Microsoft technology called COM, the concept of reference counting would have definitely crossed your path on at least one occasion.

26

Such smart pointers, when copied, need to have the reference count of the object in question incremented; there are at least two popular ways to keep this count:

- Reference count maintained in the object
- Reference count maintained by the pointer class in a shared object

The former is called *intrusive reference counting* because the object needs to be modified such that it maintains, increments, and supplies the reference count to any smart pointer class that manages it. This incidentally is the approach chosen by COM. The latter is a mechanism where the smart pointer class can keep the reference count on the free store (a dynamically allocated integer, for example) and when copied, the copy constructor will increment this value.

The reference-counting mechanism hence makes it pertinent that the programmer works with the smart pointers only when using the object. A smart pointer managing the object and a raw pointer pointing to it is a bad idea because the smart pointer will (smartly) release the object when the count maintained by it goes down to zero, but the raw pointer will continue pointing to the part of the memory that no longer belongs to your application. Similarly, reference counting can cause issues peculiar to their situation: Two objects that hold a pointer to each other will never be released because their cyclic dependency will hold their reference counts at a minimum of 1.

Reference-Linked Smart Pointers

Reference-linked smart pointers are ones that don't proactively count the number of references using the object; rather, they just need to know when the number comes down to zero so that the object can be released.

They are called reference-linked because their implementation is based on a double-linked list. When a new smart pointer is created by copying an existing one, it is appended to the list. When a smart pointer goes out of scope, is destroyed, the destructor de-indexes the smart pointer from this list. Reference linking also suffers from the problem caused by cyclic dependency, as applicable to reference-counted pointers.

Destructive Copy

Destructive copy is a mechanism where a smart pointer, when copied, transfers complete ownership of the object being handled to the destination, and resets itself.

```
destructive_copy_smartptr <CSomeClass> pSmartPtr (new CSomeClass ());

SomeFunc (pSmartPtr);     // Ownership transferred to SomeFunc
// Don't use pSmartPtr in the caller any more!
```

Although this mechanism is obviously not intuitive to use, the advantage supplied by destructive copy smart pointers is that they ensure that at any point in time, only one active pointer points to an object. So, they make good mechanisms for returning pointers from functions, and are of use in scenarios where you can use their "destructive" properties to your advantage.

`std::auto_ptr` is by far the most popular (or most notorious, depending on how you look at it) pointer that follows the principles of destructive copy. The disadvantage of using such a pointer is highlighted by the preceding code snippet. It demonstrates that such a smart pointer is useless once it has been passed to a function or copied into another. The implementation of destructive copy pointers deviates from standard, recommended C++ programming techniques, as seen in Listing 26.3.

LISTING 26.3 A Sample Destructive-Copy Type Smart Pointer

```
1: template <typename T>
2: class destructivecopy_pointer
3: {
4: private:
5:     T* m_pObject;
6: public:
7:     // other members, constructors, destructors, operators* and ->, etc...
8:
9:     // copy constructor
10:     destructivecopy_pointer(destructivecopy_pointer& source)
11:     {
12:         // Take ownership on copy
13:         m_pObject = source.m_pObject;
14:
15:         // destroy source
16:         source.m_pObject = 0;
17:     }
18:
19:     // assignment operator
20:     destructivecopy_pointer& operator= (destructivecopy_pointer& rhs)
21:     {
22:         if (m_pObject != source.m_pObject)
23:         {
24:             delete m_pObject;
25:             m_pObject = source.m_pObject;
26:             source.m_pObject = 0;
27:         }
28:     }
29: };
```

26

Analysis ▼

Listing 26.3 describes the most important part of the implementation of a destructive–copy-based smart pointer. Lines 10–17 and lines 20–28 contain the copy constructor and the assignment operator. Here you see that these functions actually invalidate the source when making a copy; that is, the copy constructor sets the pointer by the source to zero, after copying it, therefore justifying the name destructive copy. The assignment operator does the same thing.

These lines of code that are critical to the implementation of destructive copy smart pointers also attract the maximum amount of criticism. You will note that unlike most C++ implementations, this smart pointer class cannot have the copy constructor and assignment operator that accepts a const reference, and for obvious reasons—it invalidates the input after copying it. This is a deviation from traditional copy-constructor and assignment-operator semantics, and C++ puritans dislike this smart pointer class for that reason.

The fact that such smart pointers destroy the source also makes them unsuitable for use in STL containers, such as the `std::vector`, or any other dynamic collection class that you might use. These containers need to copy your content internally and end up invalidating the pointers.

So, for reasons more than one, there are a lot of programmers who avoid destructive copy smart pointers like the plague. However, one of the most popular smart pointer implementations, the `std::auto_ptr`, is of this type, and that it is a part of the standard template library makes it important that you at least understand how it works.

Using the `std::auto_ptr`

The `auto_ptr` is a destructive copy-based smart pointer that transfers the ownership of the object on copy, and releases/destructs the object it owns when it goes out of scope.

To use `std:auto_ptr`, you should first include the header:

```
#include <memory>
```

To study the effects of using the `std::auto_ptr`, let's create a sample class `CSomeClass` that does little other than indicate its lifetime by printing some lines in its constructor and destructor:

```
#include <iostream>

class CSomeClass
{
public:
    // Constructor
    CSomeClass() {std::cout << "CSomeClass: Constructed!" << std::endl;}

    ~CSomeClass() {std::cout << "CSomeClass: Destructed!" << std::endl;}

    void SaySomething () {std::cout << "CSomeClass: Hello!" << std::endl;}
};
```

Now, let's use an `auto_ptr` object on it as shown in Listing 26.4.

LISTING 26.4   Using the `std::auto_ptr`

```
1: #include <memory>
2: void UsePointer (std::auto_ptr <CSomeClass> spObj);
3:
4: int main ()
5: {
6:     using namespace std;
7:     cout << "main() started" << endl;
8:
```

LISTING 26.4 Continued

```
 9:     auto_ptr <CSomeClass> spObject (new CSomeClass ());
10:
11:     cout << "main: Calling UsePointer()" << endl;
12:
13:     // Call a function, transfer ownership
14:     UsePointer (spObject);
15:
16:     cout << "main: UsePointer() returned, back in main()" << endl;
17:
18:     // spObject->SaySomthing ();    // invalid pointer!
19:
20:     cout << "main() ends" << endl;
21:
22:     return 0;
23: }
24:
25: void UsePointer (auto_ptr <CSomeClass> spObj)
26: {
27:     cout << "UsePointer: started, will use input pointer now" << endl;
28:
29:     // Use the input pointer
30:     spObj->SaySomething ();
31:
32:     cout << "UsePointer: will return now" << endl;
33: }
```

Output ▼

```
main() started
CSomeClass: Constructed!
main: Calling UsePointer()
UsePointer: started, will use input pointer now
CSomeClass: Hello!
UsePointer: will return now
CSomeClass: Destructed!
main: UsePointer() returned, back in main()
main() ends
```

26

Analysis ▼

Follow the construction and destruction sequence, as visible in the output. You will see that even though the object pointed to by spObject was constructed in main(), as expected, it was destroyed (and automatically so) even without you having to need to call the delete operator. Another point to be noted is that the object was destroyed somewhere between the point where the function UsePointer said, "UsePointer: will return now" and main() said, "main: UsePointer() returned, back in main()". In other words, the object was destroyed when `UsePointer()` returned, because variable `spObj` went out of scope, hence destroyed. This is the behavior of `auto_ptr` where the pointer that goes out of scope (in this case `spObj` supplied to `UsePointer`) also releases the object it owns. `spObject` inside `main()` had nothing to release as it lost the ownership during the copy step in line 13.

Note that line number 18 has been commented—using an `auto_ptr` object after it has been copied into another or passed into a function is dangerous as the copy step invalidated it. Don't do it!

To sum up, Listing 26.4 illustrates the advantage of using smart pointers (so long as you also know their behavior). They manage your object's lifetimes for you. In some cases, more sophisticated smart pointers can even help multithreaded applications have synchronized access to your dynamically allocated data.

Popular Smart Pointer Libraries

It's pretty apparent that the version of the smart pointer shipped with the C++ standard library is not going to meet every programmer's requirements. This is precisely why there are many smart pointer libraries out there.

Boost (www.boost.org) supplies you with some well-tested and well-documented smart pointer classes, among many other useful utility classes. You will find further information on Boost smart pointers and their downloads at

http://www.boost.org/libs/smart_ptr/smart_ptr.htm

Similarly, those programming COM applications on Windows platforms should start using the ATL framework's effective smart pointer classes such as `CComPtr` and `CComQIPtr` to manage their COM objects, rather than using raw interface pointers.

Summary

In this lesson, you learned how using the right smart pointers can help write code that uses pointers, yet does not pursue the programmer with memory allocation and object ownership related nuances. You also learned of the different smart pointer types and that it is important to know the behavior of a smart pointer class before adopting it in your application. Last but not least, you know of the most popular (or notorious) smart pointer, `std::auto_ptr`, and its drawbacks.

Q&A

Q **I need a vector of pointers. Should I choose `auto_ptr` as the object type to be held in the vector?**

A No, you shouldn't. A single copy or assignment operation from the element in the vector would render the object unusable.

Q **What two operators does a class always need to load to be called a smart pointer class?**

A The following: *operator** and *operator ->*. They help use objects of the class with regular pointer semantics.

Q **I have an application where `CClass1` and `CClass2` hold member attributes that point to objects of the other's type. Should I use a reference counted pointer in this scenario?**

A Probably you wouldn't because of the cyclic dependency that will keep the reference count from going down to zero, and consequently keep objects of the two classes permanently in the heap.

Q **How many smart pointers are there in the world?**

A Thousands. No, maybe millions. You should use only smart pointers that have a well-documented functionality and come from a trusted source, for example Boost.

Q **A string class also dynamically manages character arrays on the heap. Is a string class therefore a smart pointer too?**

A No, it isn't. These typically don't implement both *operator** and *operator ->*, and are therefore not classifiable as smart pointers.

26

Workshop

The Workshop contains quiz questions to help solidify your understanding of the material covered and exercises to provide you with experience in using what you've learned. Try to answer the quiz and exercise questions before checking the answers in Appendix D, and be certain you understand the answers before going to the next lesson.

Quiz

1. Where would you look before writing your own smart pointer for your application?
2. Would a smart pointer slow down your application significantly?
3. Where can reference counted smart pointers hold the reference count data?
4. Should the linked list mechanism used by reference linked pointers be singly or doubly linked?

Exercises

1. **BUG BUSTER:** Point out the bug in this code:

```
std::auto_ptr<CSomeClass> pObject (new CSomeClass ());
std::auto_ptr<CSomeClass> pAnotherObject (pObject);
pObject->DoSomething ();
pAnotherObject->DoSomething();
```

2. Use the auto_ptr class to instantiate a CDog that inherits from CAnimal. Pass the object as a CAnimal-pointer and comment on slicing, if any.

LESSON 27
Working with Streams

Until now, you've been using `cout` to write to the screen and `cin` to read from the keyboard, without a full understanding of how they work. In this lesson, you will learn all about both of these.

You will also learn

- What streams are and how they are used

- How to manage input and output using streams

- How to write to and read from files using streams

Overview of Streams

C++ defines neither how data is written to the screen or to a file, nor how data is read into a program. These are clearly essential parts of working with C++, however, and the standard C++ library includes the `iostream` library, which facilitates input and output (I/O).

The advantage of having the input and output kept apart from the language and handled in libraries is that it is easier to make the language platform-independent. That is, you can write C++ programs on a PC and then recompile them and run them on a Sun Workstation, or you can take code created using a Windows C++ compiler, recompile, and run it on Linux. The compiler manufacturer supplies the right library, and everything works. At least that's the theory.

NOTE

> A library is a collection of object (`.obj` or `.o`) files that can be linked to your program to provide additional functionality. This is the most basic form of code reuse and has been around since ancient programmers chiseled 1s and 0s into the walls of caves.

Today, streams are generally less important for C++ programming—except, perhaps, for file input. C++ programs have evolved to use operating system or compiler vendor-provided graphical user interface (GUI) libraries for working with the screen, files, and the user. This includes Windows libraries, X Window System libraries, Microsoft Foundation Classes, and Borland's Kylix abstraction of both the Windows and X Window System user interfaces. Because these libraries are specialized to the operating system and are not part of the C++ standard, this book will not discuss them.

This lesson discusses streams, however, because they are a part of the C++ standard. In addition, it is good to understand streams in order to comprehend the inner workings of input and output. You should, however, quickly move to learning your operating system or vendor-supplied GUI library as well.

Encapsulation of Data Flow

You can use the `iostream` classes to achieve text input and output. The `iostream` classes view the flow of data as a *stream* of data, one byte following another. If the destination of the stream is a file or the console screen, the source of the data that will be flowing is usually some part of your program. If you reverse the stream, you can "pour" data into your data variables from the keyboard or a disk file.

One principal goal of streams is to encapsulate the problems of getting the data to and from the disk or the console screen. After you create a stream, your program works with it and the stream takes care of the details. Figure 27.1 illustrates this fundamental idea.

FIGURE 27.1
Encapsulation through streams.

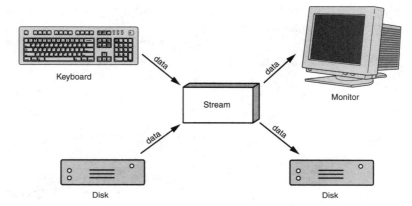

Understanding Buffering

Writing to the disk (and to a lesser extent the console screen) is very "expensive." It takes a long time (relatively speaking) to write data to the disk or to read data from the disk, and execution of a program can be blocked by disk writes and reads. To solve this problem, streams provide buffering. When buffering is in use, data is written into the stream, but is not written back out to the disk immediately. Instead, the stream's buffer fills and fills, and when it is full, it writes to the disk all at once.

NOTE   Although data is technically a plural noun, we treat it as singular, as do nearly all native speakers of English.

Imagine water trickling into the top of a tank and the tank filling and filling, but no water running out of the bottom. Figure 27.2 illustrates this idea.

FIGURE 27.2
Filling the buffer.

27

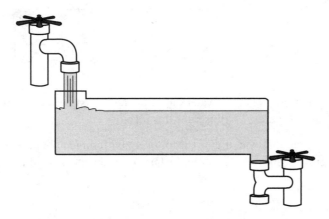

When the water (data) reaches the top, the valve opens and all the water flows out in a rush. Figure 27.3 illustrates this.

FIGURE 27.3
Emptying the buffer.

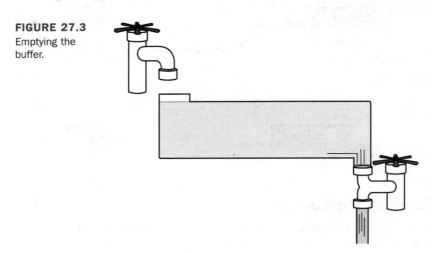

After the buffer is empty, the bottom valve closes, the top valve opens, and more water flows into the buffer tank. Figure 27.4 illustrates this.

FIGURE 27.4
Refilling the buffer.

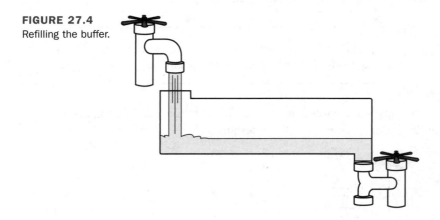

Occasionally, you need to get the water out of the tank even before it is full. This is *flushing the buffer*. Figure 27.5 illustrates this idea.

You should be aware that one of the risks of using buffering is the possibility that the program will crash while data is still in the buffers. If this occurs, you might lose that data.

FIGURE 27.5
Flushing the
buffer.

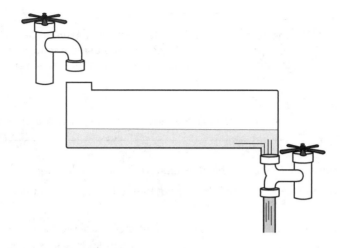

Streams and Buffers

As you might expect, C++ takes an object-oriented view toward implementing streams and buffers. It does this with the use of a number of classes and objects:

- The `streambuf` class manages the buffer, and its member functions provide the capability to fill, empty, flush, and otherwise manipulate the buffer.

- The `ios` class is the base class to the input and output stream classes. The `ios` class has a `streambuf` object as a member variable.

- The `istream` and `ostream` classes derive from the `ios` class; they specialize input and output stream behavior, respectively.

- The `iostream` class derives from both the `istream` and the `ostream` classes. It provides input and output methods for writing to the screen.

- The `fstream` classes provide input and output from files.

You'll learn more about these classes throughout the rest of this lesson.

27

Standard I/O Objects

When a C++ program that includes the `iostream` classes starts, four objects are created and initialized.

> **NOTE**
>
> The compiler automatically adds the `iostream` class library to your program. All you need to do to use these functions is to put the appropriate `include` statement at the top of your program listing:
>
> `#include <iostream>`
>
> This is something you have been doing in your programs already.

- `cin` (pronounced "see-in") handles input from the standard input, the keyboard.
- `cout` (pronounced "see-out") handles output to the standard output, the console screen.
- `cerr` (pronounced "see-err") handles unbuffered output to the standard error device, the console screen. Because this is unbuffered, everything sent to `cerr` is written to the standard error device immediately, without waiting for the buffer to fill or for a flush command to be received.
- `clog` (pronounced "see-log") handles buffered error messages that are output to the standard error device, the console screen. It is common for this to be redirected to a log file, as described in the following section.

Redirection of the Standard Streams

Each of the standard devices, input, output, and error, can be redirected to other devices. Programmers often redirect the standard error stream (`cerr`) to a file, and can use operating system commands to pipe standard input (`cin`) and output (`cout`) to files.

> **NOTE**
>
> *Redirecting* refers to sending output or input to a place different from the default. *Piping* refers to using the output of one program as the input of another.

Redirection is more a function of the operating system than of the `iostream` libraries. C++ just provides access to the four standard devices; it is up to the user to redirect the devices to whatever alternatives are needed.

The redirection operators for DOS, the Windows command prompt, and UNIX are (<) redirect input and (>) redirect output. UNIX provides more advanced redirection capabilities than DOS or the standard Windows command prompt. However, the general idea is the same: Take the output intended for the console screen and write it to a file or pipe it into another program. Alternatively, the input for a program can be extracted from a file rather than from the keyboard.

Input Using cin

The global object cin is responsible for input and is available to your program when you include iostream. In previous examples, you used the overloaded extraction operator (>>) to put data into your program's variables. How does this work? The syntax, as you might remember, is as follows:

```
int someVariable;
cout << "Enter a number: ";
cin >> someVariable;
```

This lesson discusses the global object cout later; for now, focus on the third line: cin >> someVariable;. What can you guess about cin?

Clearly, it must be a global object because you didn't define it in your own code. You know from previous operator experience that cin has overloaded the extraction operator (>>) and that the effect is to write whatever data cin has in its buffer into your local variable, someVariable.

What might not be immediately obvious is that cin has overloaded the extraction operator for a great variety of parameters, among them int&, short&, long&, double&, float&, char&, char*, and so forth. When you write cin >> someVariable;, the type of someVariable is assessed. In the preceding example, someVariable is an integer, so the following function is called:

```
istream & operator>> (int &)
```

Note that because the parameter is passed by reference, the extraction operator is able to act on the original variable. Listing 27.1 illustrates the use of cin.

27

LISTING 27.1   cin Handles Different Data Types

```
1:  //Listing 27.1 - character strings and cin
2:  #include <iostream>
3:  using namespace std;
4:
5:  int main()
6:  {
7:      int myInt;
```

LISTING 27.1   Continued

```
 8:    long myLong;
 9:    double myDouble;
10:    float myFloat;
11:    unsigned int myUnsigned;
12:
13:    cout << "Int: ";
14:    cin >> myInt;
15:    cout << "Long: ";
16:    cin >> myLong;
17:    cout << "Double: ";
18:    cin >> myDouble;
19:    cout << "Float: ";
20:    cin >> myFloat;
21:    cout << "Unsigned: ";
22:    cin >> myUnsigned;
23:
24:    cout << "\n\nInt:\t" << myInt << endl;
25:    cout << "Long:\t" << myLong << endl;
26:    cout << "Double:\t" << myDouble << endl;
27:    cout << "Float:\t" << myFloat << endl;
28:    cout << "Unsigned:\t" << myUnsigned << endl;
29:    return 0;
30: }
```

Output ▼

```
int: 2
Long: 70000
Double: 987654321
Float: 3.33
Unsigned: 25

Int:    2
Long:    70000
Double: 9.87654e+008
Float:  3.33
Unsigned:        25
```

Analysis ▼

Lines 7–11 declare variables of various types. On lines 13–22, the user is prompted to enter values for these variables, and the results are printed (using cout) on lines 24–28. The output reflects that the variables were put into the right "kinds" of variables, and the program works as you might expect.

Inputting Strings

cin can also handle character pointer (`char*`) arguments; thus, you can create a character buffer and use cin to fill it. For example, you can write the following:

```
char YourName[50]
cout << "Enter your name: ";
cin >> YourName;
```

If you enter Jesse, the variable YourName is filled with the characters J, e, s, s, e, \0. The last character is a null; cin automatically ends the string with a null character, and you must have enough room in the buffer to allow for the entire string plus the null. The null signals the "end of string" to the cin object.

String Problems

After all this success with cin, you might be surprised when you try to enter a full name into a string. cin has trouble getting the full name because it believes that any white-space is a separator. When it sees a space or a new line, it assumes that the input for the parameter is complete. In the case of strings, it adds a null character right then and there. Listing 27.2 illustrates this problem.

LISTING 27.2   Trying to Write More Than One Word to cin

```
 1:  //Listing 27.2 - character strings and cin
 2:  #include <iostream>
 3:
 4:  int main()
 5:  {
 6:      char YourName[50];
 7:      std::cout << "Your first name: ";
 8:      std::cin >> YourName;
 9:      std::cout << "Here it is: " << YourName << std::endl;
10:      std::cout << "Your entire name: ";
11:      std::cin >> YourName;
12:      std::cout << "Here it is: " << YourName << std::endl;
13:      return 0;
14:  }
```

Output ▼

```
Your first name: Jesse
Here it is: Jesse
Your entire name: Jesse Liberty
Here it is: Jesse
```

27

Analysis ▼

On line 6, a character array called YourName is created to hold the user's input. On line 7, the user is prompted to enter one name, and that name is stored properly, as shown in the output. On line 10, the user is prompted again, this time for a full name. cin reads the input and when it sees the space between the names, it puts a null character after the first word and terminates input. This is not exactly what was intended. To understand why this works this way, examine Listing 27.3, which shows input for several fields.

LISTING 27.3 Multiple Input

```
1:   //Listing 27.3 - character strings and cin
2:   #include <iostream>
3:   using namespace std;
4:
5:   int main()
6:   {
7:       int myInt;
8:       long myLong;
9:       double myDouble;
10:      float myFloat;
11:      unsigned int myUnsigned;
12:      char myWord[50];
13:
14:      cout << "int: ";
15:      cin >> myInt;
16:      cout << "Long: ";
17:      cin >> myLong;
18:      cout << "Double: ";
19:      cin >> myDouble;
20:      cout << "Float: ";
21:      cin >> myFloat;
22:      cout << "Word: ";
23:      cin >> myWord;
24:      cout << "Unsigned: ";
25:      cin >> myUnsigned;
26:
27:      cout << "\n\nInt:\t" << myInt << endl;
28:      cout << "Long:\t" << myLong << endl;
29:      cout << "Double:\t" << myDouble << endl;
30:      cout << "Float:\t" << myFloat << endl;
31:      cout << "Word: \t" << myWord << endl;
32:      cout << "Unsigned:\t" << myUnsigned << endl;
33:
34:      cout << "\n\nInt, Long, Double, Float, Word, Unsigned: ";
35:      cin >> myInt >> myLong >> myDouble;
36:      cin >> myFloat >> myWord >> myUnsigned;
```

LISTING 27.3   Continued

```
37:     cout << "\n\nInt:\t" << myInt << endl;
38:     cout << "Long:\t" << myLong << endl;
39:     cout << "Double:\t" << myDouble << endl;
40:     cout << "Float:\t" << myFloat << endl;
41:     cout << "Word: \t" << myWord << endl;
42:     cout << "Unsigned:\t" << myUnsigned << endl;
43:
44:     return 0;
45:  }
```

Output ▼

```
Int: 2
Long: 30303
Double: 393939397834
Float: 3.33
Word: Hello
Unsigned: 85

Int:    2
Long:   30303
Double: 3.93939e+011
Float:  3.33
Word:   Hello
Unsigned:       85

Int, Long, Double, Float, Word, Unsigned: 3 304938 393847473 6.66 bye -2

Int:    3
Long:   304938
Double: 3.93847e+008
Float:  6.66
Word:   bye
Unsigned: 4294967294
```

Analysis ▼

Again, several variables are created, this time including a char array. The user is prompted for input and the output is faithfully printed.

On line 34, the user is prompted for all the input at once, and then each "word" of input is assigned to the appropriate variable. It is to facilitate this kind of multiple assignment that cin must consider each word in the input to be the full input for each variable. If cin were to consider the entire input to be part of one variable's input, this kind of concatenated input would be impossible.

27

Note that on line 42, the last object requested was an unsigned integer, but the user entered -2. Because cin believes it is writing to an unsigned integer, the bit pattern of -2 was evaluated as an unsigned integer, and when written out by cout, the value 4294967294 was displayed. The unsigned value 4294967294 has the exact bit pattern of the signed value -2.

Later in this lesson, you will see how to enter an entire string into a buffer, including multiple words. For now, the question arises, "How does the extraction operator manage this trick of concatenation?"

The cin **Return Value**

The return value of cin is a reference to an istream object. Because cin itself is an istream object, the return value of one extraction operation can be the input to the next extraction.

```
int varOne, varTwo, varThree;
cout << "Enter three numbers: "
cin >> varOne >> varTwo >> varThree;
```

When you write cin >> varOne >> varTwo >> varThree;, the first extraction is evaluated (cin >> varOne). The return value from this is another istream object, and that object's extraction operator gets the variable varTwo. It is as if you had written this:

```
((cin >> varOne) >> varTwo) >> varThree;
```

You'll see this technique repeated later when cout is discussed.

Other Member Functions of cin

In addition to overloading operator>>, cin has a number of other member functions. These are used when finer control over the input is required. These functions allow you to do the following:

- Get a single character
- Get strings
- Ignore input
- Look at the next character in the buffer
- Put data back into the buffer

Single Character Input

operator>>, taking a character reference, can be used to get a single character from the standard input. The member function get() can also be used to obtain a single character, and can do so in two ways: get() can be used with no parameters, in which case the return value is used, or it can be used with a reference to a character.

Using get() with No Parameters

The first form of get() is without parameters. This returns the value of the character found and returns EOF (end of file) if the end of the file is reached. get() with no parameters is not often used.

Unlike using cin to get multiple values, it is not possible to concatenate this use of get() for multiple input because the return value is not an iostream object. Thus, the following doesn't work:

```
cin.get() >>myVarOne >> myVarTwo; //    illegal
```

The return value of cin.get() >> myVarOne is actually an integer, not an iostream object.

A common use of get() with no parameters is illustrated in Listing 27.4.

LISTING 27.4   Using get() with No Parameters

```
1:
2:  #include <iostream>
3:
4:  int main()
5:  {
6:      char ch;
7:      while ( (ch = std::cin.get()) != EOF)
8:      {
9:         std::cout << "ch: " << ch << std::endl;
10:      }
11:      std::cout << "\nDone!\n";
12:      return 0;
13:  }
```

27

NOTE

To exit this program, you must send end of file from the keyboard. On DOS computers, use Ctrl+Z; on UNIX workstations, use Ctrl+D.

Output ▼

```
Hello
ch: H
ch: e
ch: l
ch: l
ch: o
ch:

World
ch: W
ch: o
ch: r
ch: l
ch: d
ch:

^Z (ctrl-z)

Done!
```

Analysis ▼

On line 6, a local character variable, ch, is declared. The while loop assigns the input received from cin.get() to ch, and if it is not EOF, the string is printed out. This output is buffered until an end of line is read, however. When EOF is encountered (by pressing Ctrl+Z on a DOS machine, or Ctrl+D on a UNIX machine), the loop exits. Note that not every implementation of istream supports this version of get(), although it is now part of the ANSI/ISO standard.

Using get() with a Character Reference Parameter

When a character variable is passed as input to get(), that character variable is filled with the next character in the input stream. The return value is an iostream object, so this form of get() can be concatenated, as illustrated in Listing 27.5.

LISTING 27.5 Using get() with Parameters

```
1:
2:  #include <iostream>
3:
4:  int main()
5:  {
6:     char a, b, c;
7:
8:     std::cout << "Enter three letters: ";
9:
```

LISTING 27.5 Continued

```
10:     std::cin.get(a).get(b).get(c);
11:
12:     std::cout << "a: " << a << "\nb: ";
13:     std::cout << b << "\nc: " << c << std::endl;
14:     return 0;
15: }
```

Output ▼

```
Enter three letters: one
a: o
b: n
c: e
```

Analysis ▼

On line 6, three character variables, a, b, and c, are created. On line 10, cin.get() is called three times, concatenated. First, cin.get(a) is called. This puts the first letter into a and returns cin so that when it is done, cin.get(b) is called, putting the next letter into b. Finally, cin.get(c) is called and the third letter is put in c.

Because cin.get(a) evaluates to cin, you could have written this:

```
cin.get(a) >> b;
```

In this form, cin.get(a) evaluates to cin, so the second phrase is cin >> b;.

DO	DON'T
DO use the extraction operator (>>) when you need to skip over whitespace. **DO** use get() with a character parameter when you need to examine every character, including whitespace.	**DON'T** stack cin statements to get multiple input if it isn't clear what you are doing. It is better to use multiple commands that are easier to understand than to use one long command.

27

Getting Strings from Standard Input

The extraction operator (>>) can be used to fill a character array, as can the third version of the member functions get() and the member function getline().

This form of get() takes three parameters:

```
get( pCharArray, StreamSize, TermChar );
```

The first parameter (*pCharArray*) is a pointer to a character array, the second parameter (*StreamSize*) is the maximum number of characters to read plus one, and the third parameter (*TermChar*) is the termination character. If you enter **20** as the second parameter, get() reads 19 characters and then null-terminates the string, which it stores in the first parameter. The third parameter, the termination character, defaults to newline ('\n'). If a termination character is reached before the maximum number of characters is read, a null is written and the termination character is left in the buffer. Listing 27.6 illustrates the use of this form of get().

LISTING 27.6 Using get() with a Character Array

```
1:
2:  #include <iostream>
3:  using namespace std;
4:
5:  int main()
6:  {
7:      char stringOne[256];
8:      char stringTwo[256];
9:
10:     cout << "Enter string one: ";
11:     cin.get(stringOne,256);
12:     cout << "stringOne: " << stringOne << endl;
13:
14:     cout << "Enter string two: ";
15:     cin >> stringTwo;
16:     cout << "StringTwo: " << stringTwo << endl;
17:     return 0;
18: }
```

Output ▼

```
Enter string one: Now is the time
stringOne: Now is the time
Enter string two: For all good
StringTwo: For
```

Analysis ▼

On lines 7 and 8, two character arrays are created. On line 10, the user is prompted to enter a string. cin.get() is called on line 11. The first parameter is the buffer to fill, and the second is one more than the maximum number for get() to accept (the extra position being given to the null character, ['\0']). There is not a third parameter shown; however, this is defaulted. The defaulted third parameter is a newline.

The user enters **Now is the time**. Because the user ends the phrase with a newline, that phrase is put into `stringOne`, followed by a terminating null.

The user is prompted for another string on line 14, and this time the extraction operator is used. Because the extraction operator takes everything up to the first whitespace, only the string `For`, with a terminating null character, is stored in the second string, which, of course, is not what was intended.

Using `get()` with the three parameters is perfectly valid for obtaining strings; however, it is not the only solution. Another way to solve this problem is to use `getline()`, as illustrated in Listing 27.7.

LISTING 27.7   Using `getline()`

```
1:
2:    #include <iostream>
3:    using namespace std;
4:
5:    int main()
6:    {
7:        char stringOne[256];
8:        char stringTwo[256];
9:        char stringThree[256];
10:
11:       cout << "Enter string one: ";
12:       cin.getline(stringOne,256);
13:       cout << "stringOne: " << stringOne << endl;
14:
15:       cout << "Enter string two: ";
16:       cin >> stringTwo;
17:       cout << "stringTwo: " << stringTwo << endl;
18:
19:       cout << "Enter string three: ";
20:       cin.getline(stringThree,256);
21:       cout << "stringThree: " << stringThree << endl;
22:       return 0;
23:   }
```

27

Output ▼

```
Enter string one: one two three
stringOne: one two three
Enter string two: four five six
stringTwo: four
Enter string three: stringThree: five six
```

Analysis ▼

This example warrants careful examination; some potential surprises exist. On lines 7–9, three character arrays are declared this time.

On line 11, the user is prompted to enter a string, and that string is read by using `getline()`. Like `get()`, `getline()` takes a buffer and a maximum number of characters. Unlike `get()`, however, the terminating newline is read and thrown away. With `get()`, the terminating newline is not thrown away. It is left in the input buffer.

On line 15, the user is prompted for the second time, and this time the extraction operator is used. In the sample output, you can see that the user enters `four five six`; however, only the first word, `four`, is put in `stringTwo`. The string for the third prompt, `Enter string three`, is then displayed, and `getline()` is called again. Because `five six` is still in the input buffer, it is immediately read up to the newline; `getline()` terminates and the string in `stringThree` is printed on line 21.

The user has no chance to enter the third string because the input buffer contained data that fulfilled the request this prompt was making. The call to `cin` on line 16 does not use everything in the input buffer. The extraction operator (>>) on line 16 reads up to the first whitespace and puts the word into the character array.

> `get()` **and** `getline()`
>
> The member function `get()` is overloaded. In one version, it takes no parameters and returns the value of the character it receives. In the second version, it takes a single character reference and returns the `istream` object by reference.
>
> In the third and final version, `get()` takes a character array, the number of characters to get, and a termination character (which defaults to newline). This version of `get()` reads characters into the array until it gets to one fewer than its maximum number of characters or it encounters the termination character, whichever comes first. If `get()` encounters the termination character, it leaves that character in the input buffer and stops reading characters.
>
> The member function `getline()` also takes three parameters: the buffer to fill, one more than the maximum number of characters to get, and the termination character. `getline()` functions the same as `get()` does with these parameters, except that `getline()` throws away the terminating character.

Using `cin.ignore()`

At times, you want to ignore the remaining characters on a line until you hit either end of line (EOL) or EOF. The member function `ignore()` serves this purpose. `ignore()` takes two parameters: the maximum number of characters to ignore and the termination character. If you write ignore(80,'\n'), up to 80 characters will be thrown away until a newline character is found. The newline is then thrown away and the ignore() statement ends. Listing 27.8 illustrates the use of ignore().

LISTING 27.8 Using ignore()

```
1:   #include <iostream>
2:   using namespace std;
3:
4:   int main()
5:   {
6:       char stringOne[255];
7:       char stringTwo[255];
8:
9:       cout << "Enter string one:";
10:      cin.get(stringOne,255);
11:      cout << "String one: " << stringOne << endl;
12:
13:      cout << "Enter string two: ";
14:      cin.getline(stringTwo,255);
15:      cout << "String two: " << stringTwo << endl;
16:
17:      cout << "\n\nNow try again...\n";
18:
19:      cout << "Enter string one: ";
20:      cin.get(stringOne,255);
21:      cout << "String one: " << stringOne<< endl;
22:
23:      cin.ignore(255,'\n');
24:
25:      cout << "Enter string two: ";
26:      cin.getline(stringTwo,255);
27:      cout << "String Two: " << stringTwo<< endl;
28:      return 0;
29:  }
```

Output ▼

```
Enter string one:once upon a time
String one: once upon a time
Enter string two: String two:

Now try again...
Enter string one: once upon a time
String one: once upon a time
Enter string two: there was a
String Two: there was a
```

27

Analysis ▼

On lines 6 and 7, two character arrays are created. On line 9, the user is prompted for input; in response, the user types **once upon a time** and then presses the Enter key. On line 10, get() is used to read this string. get() fills stringOne and terminates on the newline, but leaves the newline character in the input buffer.

On line 13, the user is prompted again, but the getline() on line 14 reads the input buffer up to the newline. Because a newline was left in the buffer by the call to get(), line 14 terminates immediately, before the user can enter any new input.

On line 19, the user is prompted again and puts in the same first line of input. This time, however, on line 23, ignore() is used to empty the input stream by "eating" the newline character. Thus, when the getline() call on line 26 is reached, the input buffer is empty, and the user can input the next line of the story.

Peeking At and Returning Characters: peek() and putback()

The input object cin has two additional methods that can come in rather handy: peek(), which looks at but does not extract the next character, and putback(), which inserts a character into the input stream. Listing 27.9 illustrates how these might be used.

LISTING 27.9   Using peek() and putback()

```
1:  #include <iostream>
2:  using namespace std;
3:
4:  int main()
5:  {
6:      char ch;
7:      cout << "enter a phrase: ";
8:      while ( cin.get(ch) != 0 )
9:      {
10:         if (ch == '!')
11:             cin.putback('$');
12:         else
13:             cout << ch;
14:         while (cin.peek() == '#')
15:             cin.ignore(1,'#');
16:     }
17:     return 0;
18: }
```

Output ▼

```
enter a phrase: Now!is#the!time#for!fun#!
Now$isthe$timefor$fun$
```

Analysis ▼

On line 6, a character variable, ch, is declared, and on line 7, the user is prompted to enter a phrase. The purpose of this program is to turn any exclamation marks (!) into dollar signs ($) and to remove any pound symbols (#).

The program loops on lines 8–16 as long as it is getting characters other than the end of file (Ctrl+C on Windows machines, Ctrl+Z or Ctrl+D on other operating systems). Remember that cin.get() returns 0 for end of file.

If the current character is an exclamation point, it is thrown away and the $ symbol is put back into the input buffer. This $ symbol is then read the next time through the loop. If the current item is not an exclamation point, it is printed on line 13. On line 14, the next character is "peeked" at, and when pound symbols are found, they are removed using the ignore() method, as shown on line 15. This is not the most efficient way to do either of these things (and it won't find a pound symbol if it is the first character), but it illustrates how these methods work.

TIP	peek() and putback() are typically used for parsing strings and other data, such as when writing a compiler.

Outputting with cout

You have used cout along with the overloaded insertion operator (<<) to write strings, integers, and other numeric data to the screen. It is also possible to format the data, aligning columns and writing numeric data in decimal and hexadecimal. This section shows you how.

27

Flushing the Output

You've already seen that using endl writes a newline and then flushes the output buffer. endl calls cout's member function flush(), which writes all the data it is buffering. You can also call the flush() method directly, either by calling the flush() member method or by writing the following:

```
cout << flush();
```

This can be convenient when you need to ensure that the output buffer is emptied and that the contents are written to the screen.

Functions for Doing Output

Just as the extraction operator can be supplemented with `get()` and `getline()`, the insertion operator can be supplemented with `put()` and `write()`.

Writing Characters with `put()`

The function `put()` is used to write a single character to the output device. Because `put()` returns an `ostream` reference and because `cout` is an `ostream` object, you can concatenate `put()` the same as you can stack the insertion operator. Listing 27.10 illustrates this idea.

LISTING 27.10 Using put()

```
1:
2:  #include <iostream>
3:
4:  int main()
5:  {
6:      std::cout.put('H').put('e').put('l').put('l').put('o').put('\n');
7:      return 0;
8:  }
```

Output ▼

```
Hello
```

> **NOTE**
> Some nonstandard compilers have trouble printing using this code. If your compiler does not print the word `Hello`, you might want to skip this listing.

Analysis ▼

Line 6 is evaluated like this: `std::cout.put('H')` writes the letter H to the screen and returns a `cout` object. This leaves the following:

```
cout.put('e').put('l').put('l').put('o').put('\n');
```

The letter e is written. Again, a `cout` object is returned, leaving

```
cout.put('l').put('l').put('o').put('\n');
```

This process repeats, each letter being written and the cout object being returned, until the final character (`'\n'`) is written and the function returns.

Writing More with `write()`

The function `write()` works the same as the insertion operator (`<<`), except that it takes a parameter that tells the function the maximum number of characters to write:

```
cout.write(Text, Size)
```

As you can see, the first parameter for `write()` is the text that will be printed. The second parameter, *Size*, is the number of characters that will be printed from *Text*. Note that this number might be smaller or larger than the actual size of the *Text*. If it is larger, you will output the values that reside in memory after the *Text* value. Listing 27.11 illustrates its use.

LISTING 27.11   Using `write()`

```
1:  #include <iostream>
2:  #include <string.h>
3:  using namespace std;
4:
5:  int main()
6:  {
7:      char One[] = "One if by land";
8:
9:      int fullLength = strlen(One);
10:     int tooShort = fullLength -4;
11:     int tooLong = fullLength + 6;
12:
13:     cout.write(One,fullLength) << endl;
14:     cout.write(One,tooShort) << endl;
15:     cout.write(One,tooLong) << endl;
16:     return 0;
17: }
```

Output ▼

```
One if by land
One if by
One if by land i?!
```

NOTE   The final line of output might look different on your computer because the code accesses memory that is not part of an initialized variable.

27

Analysis ▼

This listing prints from a phrase. Each time it prints a different amount of the phrase. On line 7, one phrase is created. On line 9, the integer `fullLength` is set to the length of the phrase using a global `strlen()` method that was included with the string directive on line 2. Also set are two other length values that will be used: `tooShort` is set to the length of the phrase (`fullLength`) minus four, and `tooLong` is set to the length of the phrase plus six.

On line 13, the complete phrase is printed using `write()`. The length is set to the actual length of the phrase, and the correct phrase is printed.

On line 14, the phrase is printed again, but it is four characters shorter than the full phrase, and that is reflected in the output.

On line 15, the phrase is printed again, but this time `write()` is instructed to write an extra six characters. After the phrase is written, the next six bytes of contiguous memory are written. Anything could be in this memory, so your output might vary from what is shown in this example.

Manipulators, Flags, and Formatting Instructions

The output stream maintains a number of state flags, determining which base (decimal or hexadecimal) to use, how wide to make the fields, and what character to use to fill in fields. A *state flag* is a byte in which each individual bit is assigned a special meaning. Manipulating bits is discussed in Lesson 25, "Working with Bit Flags Using STL," and in Lesson 29, "Tapping Further into the Preprocessor." Each of `ostream`'s flags can be set using member functions and manipulators.

Using `cout.width()`

The default width of your output will be just enough space to print the number, character, or string in the output buffer. You can change this by using `width()`.

Because `width()` is a member function, it must be invoked with a `cout` object. It changes the width of only the very next output field and then immediately reverts to the default. Listing 27.12 illustrates its use.

LISTING 27.12 Adjusting the Width of Output

```
1:  #include <iostream>
2:  using namespace std;
3:
4:  int main()
5:  {
```

LISTING 27.12   Continued

```
 6:      cout << "Start >";
 7:      cout.width(25);
 8:      cout << 123 << "< End\n";
 9:
10:      cout << "Start >";
11:      cout.width(25);
12:      cout << 123<< "< Next >";
13:      cout << 456 << "< End\n";
14:
15:      cout << "Start >";
16:      cout.width(4);
17:      cout << 123456 << "< End\n";
18:
19:      return 0;
20:   }
```

Output ▼

```
Start >                 123< End
Start >                 123< Next >456< End
Start >123456< End
```

Analysis ▼

The first output, on lines 6–8, prints the number 123 within a field whose width is set to 25 on line 7. This is reflected in the first line of output.

The second line of output first prints the value 123 in the same field whose width is set to 25, and then prints the value 456. Note that 456 is printed in a field whose width is reset to just large enough; as stated, the effect of width() lasts only as long as the very next output. The final output reflects that setting a width that is smaller than the output is the same as setting a width that is just large enough. A width that is too small will not truncate what is being displayed.

Setting the Fill Characters

Normally, cout fills the empty field created by a call to width() with spaces, as shown previously. At times, you might want to fill the area with other characters, such as asterisks. To do this, you call fill() and pass in as a parameter the character you want used as a fill character. Listing 27.13 illustrates this.

27

LISTING 27.13   Using `fill()`

```
 1:
 2:  #include <iostream>
 3:  using namespace std;
 4:
 5:  int main()
 6:  {
 7:     cout << "Start >";
 8:     cout.width(25);
 9:     cout << 123 << "< End\n";
10:
11:     cout << "Start >";
12:     cout.width(25);
13:     cout.fill('*');
14:     cout << 123 << "< End\n";
15:
16:     cout << "Start >";
17:     cout.width(25);
18:     cout << 456 << "< End\n";
19:
20:     return 0;
21:  }
```

Output ▼

```
Start >                      123< End
Start >******************123< End
Start >*****************456< End
```

Analysis ▼

Lines 7–9 repeat the functionality from the previous example by printing the value 123 in a width area of 25. Lines 11–14 repeat this again, but this time, on line 13, the fill character is set to an asterisk, as reflected in the output. You should notice that unlike the `width()` function, which applies to only the next output, the new `fill()` character remains until you change it. You see this verified with the output from lines 16–18.

Managing the State of Output: Set Flags

Objects are said to *have state* when some or all of their data represents a condition that can change during the course of the program. For example, you can set whether to show trailing zeros (so that 20.00 is not truncated to 20).

`iostream` objects keep track of their state by using flags. You can set these flags by calling `setf()` and passing in one of the predefined enumerated constants. For example, to turn trailing zeros on, you call `setf(ios::showpoint)`.

The enumerated constants are scoped to the `iostream` class (`ios`) and thus when used with `setf()`, they are called with the full qualification `ios::`*`flagname`*, such as `ios::showpoint`. Table 27.1 shows some of the flags you can use. When using these flags, you need to include `iostream` in your listing. In addition, for those flags that require parameters, you need to include `iomanip`.

TABLE 27.1 Some of the `iostream` Set Flags

Flag	Purpose
showpoint	Displays a decimal point and trailing zeros as required by precision
showpos	Turns on the plus sign (+) before positive numbers
left	Aligns output to the left
right	Aligns output to the right
internal	Aligns the sign for a number to the left and aligns the value to the right
showpoint	Adds trailing zeros as required by the precision
scientific	Shows floating-point values in scientific notation
fixed	Shows floating-point numbers in decimal notation
showbase	Adds 0x in front of a hexadecimal number to indicate that it is a hexadecimal value
Uppercase	Shows hexadecimal and scientific numbers in uppercase
dec	Sets the base of the numbers for display to decimal
oct	Sets the base of the numbers for display to octal—base 8
hex	Sets the base of the numbers for display to hexadecimal—base 16

The flags in Table 27.1 can also be concatenated into the insertion operator. Listing 27.14 illustrates these settings. As a bonus, Listing 27.14 also introduces the `setw` manipulator, which sets the width but can also be concatenated with the insertion operator.

LISTING 27.14 Using `setf`

```
 1:  #include <iostream>
 2:  #include <iomanip>
 3:  using namespace std;
 4:
 5:  int main()
 6:  {
 7:     const int number = 185;
 8:     cout << "The number is " << number << endl;
 9:
10:     cout << "The number is " << hex <<  number << endl;
11:
```

27

LISTING 27.14   Continued

```
12:      cout.setf(ios::showbase);
13:      cout << "The number is " << hex <<  number << endl;
14:
15:      cout << "The number is " ;
16:      cout.width(10);
17:      cout << hex << number << endl;
18:
19:      cout << "The number is " ;
20:      cout.width(10);
21:      cout.setf(ios::left);
22:      cout << hex << number << endl;
23:
24:      cout << "The number is " ;
25:      cout.width(10);
26:      cout.setf(ios::internal);
27:      cout << hex << number << endl;
28:
29:      cout << "The number is " << setw(10) << hex << number << endl;
30:      return 0;
31:   }
```

Output ▼

```
The number is 185
The number is b9
The number is 0xb9
The number is         0xb9
The number is 0xb9
The number is 0x      b9
The number is:0x      b9
```

Analysis ▼

On line 7, the constant int number is initialized to the value 185. This is displayed normally on line 8.

The value is displayed again on line 10, but this time the manipulator hex is concatenated, causing the value to be displayed in hexadecimal as b9.

NOTE	The value b in hexadecimal represents 11. Eleven times 16 equals 176; add the 9 for a total of 185.

On line 12, the flag `showbase` is set. This causes the prefix `0x` to be added to all hexadecimal numbers, as reflected in the output.

On line 16, the width is set to 10. By default, the value is pushed to the extreme right. On line 20, the width is again set to 10, but this time the alignment is set to the left, and the number is printed flush left.

On line 25, the width is again set to 10, but this time the alignment is internal. Thus, the `0x` is printed flush left but the value, `b9`, is printed flush right.

Finally, on line 29, the concatenation operator `setw()` is used to set the width to 10, and the value is printed again.

You should notice in this listing that if the flags are used within the `cout` list, they do not need to be qualified; `hex` can be passed as `hex`. When you use the `setf()` function, you need to qualify the flags to the class; `hex` is passed as `ios::hex`. You see this difference on line 17 versus 21.

Streams Versus the `printf()` Function

Most C++ implementations also provide the standard C I/O libraries, including the `printf()` statement. Although `printf()` is in some ways easier to use than `cout`, it is much less desirable.

`printf()` does not provide type safety, so it is easy to inadvertently tell it to display an integer as if it were a character and vice versa. `printf()` also does not support classes, and so it is not possible to teach it how to print your class data; you must feed each class member to `printf()` one by one.

Because there is a lot of legacy code using `printf()`, this section briefly reviews how `printf()` is used. It is not, however, recommended that you use this function in your C++ programs.

To use `printf()`, be certain to include the `stdio.h` header file. In its simplest form, `printf()` takes a formatting string as its first parameter and then a series of values as its remaining parameters.

27

The formatting string is a quoted string of text and conversion specifiers. All conversion specifiers must begin with the percent symbol (`%`). The common conversion specifiers are presented in Table 27.2.

TABLE 27.2   The Common Conversion Specifiers

Specifier	Used For
%s	string
%d	integer
%l	long integer
%ld	double
%f	float

Each of the conversion specifiers can also provide a width statement and a precision statement, expressed as a float, where the digits to the left of the decimal are used for the total width and the digits to the right of the decimal provide the precision for floats. Thus, %5d is the specifier for a 5-digit-wide integer, and %15.5f is the specifier for a 15-digit-wide float, of which the final five digits are dedicated to the decimal portion. Listing 27.15 illustrates various uses of printf().

LISTING 27.15   Printing with printf()

```
 1:  #include <stdio.h>
 2:
 3:  int main()
 4:  {
 5:     printf("%s","hello world\n");
 6:
 7:     char *phrase = "Hello again!\n";
 8:     printf("%s",phrase);
 9:
10:     int x = 5;
11:     printf("%d\n",x);
12:
13:     char *phraseTwo = "Here's some values: ";
14:     char *phraseThree = " and also these: ";
15:     int y = 7, z = 35;
16:     long longVar = 98456;
17:     float floatVar =  8.8f;
18:
19:     printf("%s %d %d", phraseTwo, y, z);
20:     printf("%s %ld %f\n",phraseThree,longVar,floatVar);
21:
22:     char *phraseFour = "Formatted: ";
23:     printf("%s %5d %10d  %10.5f\n",phraseFour,y,z,floatVar);
24:
25:     return 0;
26:  }
```

Output ▼

```
hello world
Hello again!
5
Here's some values: 7 35  and also these: 98456 8.800000
Formatted:     7        35     8.800000
```

Analysis ▼

The first `printf()` statement, on line 5, uses the standard form: the term `printf`, followed by a quoted string with a conversion specifier (in this case `%s`), followed by a value to insert into the conversion specifier. The `%s` indicates that this is a string, and the value for the string is, in this case, the quoted string `"hello world"`.

The second `printf()` statement on line 8 is the same as the first, but this time a `char` pointer is used, rather than quoting the string right in place in the `printf()` statement. The result, however, is the same.

The third `printf()`, on line 11, uses the integer conversion specifier (`%d`), and for its value the integer variable x is used. The fourth `printf()` statement, on line 19, is more complex. Here, three values are concatenated. Each conversion specifier is supplied, and then the values are provided, separated by commas. Line 20 is similar to line 19; however, different specifiers and values are used.

Finally, on line 23, format specifications are used to set the width and precision. As you can see, all this is somewhat easier than using manipulators.

As stated previously, however, the limitation here is that no type checking occurs and `printf()` cannot be declared a friend or member function of a class. So, if you want to print the various member data of a class, you must call each accessor method in the argument list sent to the `printf()` statement.

27

FAQ

Can you summarize how to manipulate output?

Answer: (with special thanks to Robert Francis) To format output in C++, you use a combination of special characters, output manipulators, and flags.

The following special characters are included in an output string being sent to cout using the insertion operator:

\n—Newline

\r—Carriage return

\t—Tab

\\—Backslash

\ddd (octal number)—ASCII character

\a—Alarm (ring bell)

For example,

```
cout << "\aAn error occured\t"
```

rings the bell, prints an error message, and moves to the next tab stop. Manipulators are used with the `cout` operator. Those manipulators that take arguments require that you include `iomanip` in your file.

The following is a list of manipulators that do *not* require `iomanip`:

`flush`—Flushes the output buffer

`endl`—Inserts newline and flushes the output buffer

`oct`—Sets output base to octal

`dec`—Sets output base to decimal

`hex`—Sets output base to hexadecimal

The following is a list of manipulators that *do* require `iomanip`:

`setbase (base)`—Sets output base (0 = decimal, 8 = octal, 10 = decimal, 16 = hex)

`setw (width)`—Sets minimum output field width

`setfill (ch)`—Fills character to be used when width is defined

`setprecision (p)`—Sets precision for floating-point numbers

`setiosflags (f)`—Sets one or more ios flags

`resetiosflags (f)`—Resets one or more ios flags

For example,

```
cout << setw(12) << setfill('#') << hex << x << endl;
```

sets the field width to 12, sets the fill character to '#', specifies hex output, prints the value of 'x', puts a newline in the buffer, and flushes the buffer. All the manipulators except `flush`, `endl`, and `setw` remain in effect until changed or until the end of the program. `setw` returns to the default after the current `cout`.

A number of flags can be used with the `setiosflags` and `resetiosflags` manipulators. These were listed in Table 27.1 earlier. Additional information can be obtained from file ios and from your compiler's documentation.

File Input and Output

Streams provide a uniform way of dealing with data coming from the keyboard or the hard disk and going out to the console screen or hard disk. In either case, you can use the insertion and extraction operators or the other related functions and manipulators. To open and close files, you create `ifstream` and `ofstream` objects as described in the next few sections.

Using the `ofstream`

The particular objects used to read from or write to files are called `ofstream` *objects*. These are derived from the `iostream` objects you've been using so far.

To get started with writing to a file, you must first create an `ofstream` object, and then associate that object with a particular file on your disk. To use `ofstream` objects, you must be certain to include `fstream` in your program.

> **NOTE**
>
> Because `fstream` includes `iostream`, you do not need to include `iostream` explicitly.

Condition States

The `iostream` objects maintain flags that report on the state of your input and output. You can check each of these flags using the Boolean functions `eof()`, `bad()`, `fail()`, and `good()`. The function `eof()` returns `true` if the `iostream` object has encountered EOF. The function `bad()` returns `true` if you attempt an invalid operation. The function `fail()` returns `true` anytime `bad()` is true or an operation fails. Finally, the function `good()` returns `true` anytime all three of the other functions are `false`.

Opening Files for Input and Output

27

To use a file, you must first open it. To open the file `myfile.cpp` with an `ofstream` object, declare an instance of an `ofstream` object and pass in the filename as a parameter:

```
ofstream fout("myfile.cpp");
```

This attempts to open the file, `myfile.cpp`, for output. Opening this file for input works the same way, except that it uses an `ifstream` object:

```
ifstream fin("myfile.cpp");
```

Note that fout and fin are names you define; here, fout has been used to reflect its similarity to cout, and fin has been used to reflect its similarity to cin. These could also be given names that reflect what is in the file they are accessing.

One important file stream function that you will need right away is close(). Every file stream object you create opens a file for reading (input), writing (output), or both. It is important to close() the file after you finish reading or writing; this ensures that the file won't be corrupted and that the data you've written is flushed to the disk.

After the stream objects are associated with files, they can be used the same as any other stream objects. Listing 27.16 illustrates this.

LISTING 27.16   Opening Files for Read and Write

```
 1:   #include <fstream>
 2:   #include <iostream>
 3:   using namespace std;
 4:
 5:   int main()
 6:   {
 7:       char fileName[80];
 8:       char buffer[255];     // for user input
 9:       cout << "File name: ";
10:       cin >> fileName;
11:
12:       ofstream fout(fileName);  // open for writing
13:       fout << "This line written directly to the file...\n";
14:       cout << "Enter text for the file: ";
15:       cin.ignore(1,'\n');  // eat the newline after the file name
16:       cin.getline(buffer,255);  // get the user's input
17:       fout << buffer << "\n";   // and write it to the file
18:       fout.close();             // close the file, ready for reopen
19:
20:       ifstream fin(fileName);    // reopen for reading
21:       cout << "Here's the contents of the file:\n";
22:       char ch;
23:       while (fin.get(ch))
24:           cout << ch;
25:
26:       cout << "\n***End of file contents.***\n";
27:
28:       fin.close();              // always pays to be tidy
29:       return 0;
30:   }
```

Output ▼

```
File name: test1
Enter text for the file: This text is written to the file!
Here's the contents of the file:
This line written directly to the file...
This text is written to the file!

***End of file contents.***
```

Analysis ▼

On line 7, a buffer is created for the filename, and on line 8, another buffer is set aside for user input. The user is prompted to enter a filename on line 9, and this response is written to the `fileName` buffer. On line 12, an `ofstream` object is created, `fout`, which is associated with the new filename. This opens the file; if the file already exists, its contents are thrown away.

On line 13, a string of text is written directly to the file. On line 14, the user is prompted for input. The newline character left over from the user's input of the filename is eaten on line 15 by using the `ignore()` function you learned about earlier. The user's input for the file is stored into `buffer` on line 16. That input is written to the file along with a newline character on line 17, and then the file is closed on line 18.

On line 20, the file is reopened, this time in input mode by using the `ifstream`. The contents are then read one character at a time on lines 23 and 24.

Changing the Default Behavior of `ofstream` on Open

The default behavior upon opening a file is to create the file if it doesn't yet exist and to truncate the file (that is, delete all its contents) if it does exist. If you don't want this default behavior, you can explicitly provide a second argument to the constructor of your `ofstream` object.

Valid values for the second argument include

27

- **`ios::app`**—Appends to the end of existing files rather than truncating them.
- **`ios::ate`**—Places you at the end of the file, but you can write data anywhere in the file.
- **`ios::trunc`**—Causes existing files to be truncated; the default.
- **`ios::nocreate`**—If the file does not exist, the open fails.
- **`ios::noreplace`**—If the file does already exist, the open fails.

Note that app is short for *append*, ate is short for *at end*, and trunc is short for *truncate*. Listing 27.17 illustrates using app by reopening the file from Listing 27.16 and appending to it.

LISTING 27.17   Appending to the End of a File

```
 1:  #include <fstream>
 2:  #include <iostream>
 3:  using namespace std;
 4:
 5:  int main()    // returns 1 on error
 6:  {
 7:      char fileName[80];
 8:      char buffer[255];
 9:      cout << "Please reenter the file name: ";
10:      cin >> fileName;
11:
12:      ifstream fin(fileName);
13:      if (fin)                   // already exists?
14:      {
15:          cout << "Current file contents:\n";
16:          char ch;
17:          while (fin.get(ch))
18:              cout << ch;
19:          cout << "\n***End of file contents.***\n";
20:      }
21:      fin.close();
22:
23:      cout << "\nOpening " << fileName << " in append mode...\n";
24:
25:      ofstream fout(fileName,ios::app);
26:      if (!fout)
27:      {
28:          cout << "Unable to open " << fileName << " for appending.\n";
29:          return(1);
30:      }
31:
32:      cout << "\nEnter text for the file: ";
33:      cin.ignore(1,'\n');
34:      cin.getline(buffer,255);
35:      fout << buffer << "\n";
36:      fout.close();
37:
38:      fin.open(fileName);  // reassign existing fin object!
39:      if (!fin)
40:      {
41:          cout << "Unable to open " << fileName << " for reading.\n";
42:          return(1);
43:      }
```

LISTING 27.17 Continued

```
44:     cout << "\nHere's the contents of the file:\n";
45:     char ch;
46:     while (fin.get(ch))
47:         cout << ch;
48:     cout << "\n***End of file contents.***\n";
49:     fin.close();
50:     return 0;
51: }
```

Output ▼

```
Please reenter the file name: test1
Current file contents:
This line written directly to the file...
This text is written to the file!

***End of file contents.***

Opening test1 in append mode...

Enter text for the file: More text for the file!

Here's the contents of the file:
This line written directly to the file...
This text is written to the file!
More text for the file!

***End of file contents.***
```

Analysis ▼

As in the preceding listing, the user is prompted to enter the filename on lines 9 and 10. This time, an input file stream object is created on line 12. That open is tested on line 13, and if the file already exists, its contents are printed on lines 15–19. Note that `if(fin)` is synonymous with `if (fin.good())`.

The input file is then closed, and the same file is reopened, this time in append mode, on line 25. After this open (and every open), the file is tested to ensure that the file was opened properly. Note that `if(!fout)` is the same as testing `if (fout.fail())`. If the file didn't open, an error message is printed on line 28 and the program ends with the `return` statement. If the open is successful, the user is then prompted to enter text, and the file is closed again on line 36.

27

Finally, as in Listing 27.16, the file is reopened in read mode; however, this time `fin` does not need to be redeclared. It is just reassigned to the same filename. The open is tested again, on line 39, and if all is well, the contents of the file are printed to the screen and the file is closed for the final time.

DO	**DON'T**
DO test each open of a file to ensure that it opened successfully.	**DON'T** try to close or reassign `cin` or `cout`.
DO reuse existing `ifstream` and `ofstream` objects.	**DON'T** use `printf()` in your C++ programs if you don't need to.
DO close all `fstream` objects when you are done using them.	

Binary Versus Text Files

Some operating systems distinguish between text files and binary files. Text files store everything as text (as you might have guessed), so large numbers such as 54,325 are stored as a string of numerals ('5', '4', ',', '3', '2', '5'). This can be inefficient, but has the advantage that the text can be read using simple programs such as the DOS and Windows command-line program `type`.

To help the file system distinguish between text and binary files, C++ provides the `ios::binary` flag. On many systems, this flag is ignored because all data is stored in binary format. On some rather prudish systems, the `ios::binary` flag is illegal and doesn't even compile!

Binary files can store not only integers and strings, but also entire data structures. You can write all the data at one time by using the `write()` method of `fstream`.

If you use `write()`, you can recover the data using `read()`. Each of these functions expects a pointer to character, however, so you must cast the address of your class to be a pointer to character.

The second argument to these functions is the number of characters expected to be read or written, which you can determine using `sizeof()`. Note that what is being written is the data, not the methods. What is recovered is only data. Listing 27.18 illustrates writing the contents of an object to a file.

LISTING 27.18   Writing a Class to a File

```
1:   #include <fstream>
2:   #include <iostream>
3:   using namespace std;
4:
5:   class Animal
6:   {
7:     public:
8:         Animal(int weight,long days):itsWeight(weight),DaysAlive(days){}
9:         ~Animal(){}
10:
11:        int GetWeight()const { return itsWeight; }
12:        void SetWeight(int weight) { itsWeight = weight; }
13:
14:        long GetDaysAlive()const { return DaysAlive; }
15:        void SetDaysAlive(long days) { DaysAlive = days; }
16:
17:    private:
18:        int itsWeight;
19:        long DaysAlive;
20:  };
21:
22:  int main()   // returns 1 on error
23:  {
24:      char fileName[80];
25:
26:
27:      cout << "Please enter the file name: ";
28:      cin >> fileName;
29:      ofstream fout(fileName,ios::binary);
30:      if (!fout)
31:      {
32:         cout << "Unable to open " << fileName << " for writing.\n";
33:         return(1);
34:      }
35:
36:      Animal Bear(50,100);
37:      fout.write((char*) &Bear,sizeof Bear);
38:
39:      fout.close();
40:
41:      ifstream fin(fileName,ios::binary);
42:      if (!fin)
43:      {
44:         cout << "Unable to open " << fileName << " for reading.\n";
45:         return(1);
46:      }
47:
48:      Animal BearTwo(1,1);
49:
```

27

LISTING 27.18   Continued

```
50:     cout << "BearTwo weight: " << BearTwo.GetWeight() << endl;
51:     cout << "BearTwo days: " << BearTwo.GetDaysAlive() << endl;
52:
53:     fin.read((char*) &BearTwo, sizeof BearTwo);
54:
55:     cout << "BearTwo weight: " << BearTwo.GetWeight() << endl;
56:     cout << "BearTwo days: " << BearTwo.GetDaysAlive() << endl;
57:     fin.close();
58:     return 0;
59: }
```

Output ▼

```
Please enter the file name: Animals
BearTwo weight: 1
BearTwo days: 1
BearTwo weight: 50
BearTwo days: 100
```

Analysis ▼

On lines 5–20, a stripped-down `Animal` class is declared. On lines 24–34, a file is created and opened for output in binary mode. An animal whose weight is 50 and who is 100 days old is created on line 36, and its data is written to the file on line 37.

The file is closed on line 39 and reopened for reading in binary mode on line 41. A second animal is created, on line 48, whose weight is 1 and who is only one day old. The data from the file is read into the new animal object on line 53, wiping out the existing data and replacing it with the data from the file. The output confirms this.

Command-Line Processing

Many operating systems, such as DOS and UNIX, enable the user to pass parameters to your program when the program starts. These are called *command-line options* and are typically separated by spaces on the command line. For example:

```
SomeProgram Param1 Param2 Param3
```

These parameters are not passed to `main()` directly. Instead, every program's `main()` function is passed two parameters. The first is an integer count of the number of arguments on the command line. The program name itself is counted, so every program has at least one parameter. The sample command line shown previously has four. (The name `SomeProgram` plus the three parameters make a total of four command-line arguments.)

The second parameter passed to `main()` is an array of pointers to character strings. Because an array name is a constant pointer to the first element of the array, you can declare this argument to be a pointer to a pointer to `char`, a pointer to an array of `char`, or an array of arrays of `char`.

Typically, the first argument is called `argc` (argument count), but you can call it anything you like. The second argument is often called `argv` (argument vector), but again this is just a convention.

It is common to test `argc` to ensure that you've received the expected number of arguments and to use `argv` to access the strings themselves. Note that `argv[0]` is the name of the program, and `argv[1]` is the first parameter to the program, represented as a string. If your program takes two numbers as arguments, you need to translate these numbers to strings. Listing 27.19 illustrates how to use the command-line arguments.

LISTING 27.19   Using Command-Line Arguments

```
1:  #include <iostream>
2:  int main(int argc, char **argv)
3:  {
4:      std::cout << "Received " << argc << " arguments...\n";
5:      for (int i=0; i<argc; i++)
6:          std::cout << "argument " << i << ": " << argv[i] << std::endl;
7:      return 0;
8:  }
```

Output ▼

```
TestProgram  Teach Yourself C++ In 21 Days
Received 7 arguments...
argumnet 0: TestProgram
argument 1: Teach
argument 2: Yourself
argument 3: C++
argument 4: In
argument 5: 21
argument 6: Days
```

27

NOTE _____   You must either run this code from the command line (that is, from a DOS box) or you must set the command-line parameters in your compiler (see your compiler documentation).

Analysis ▼

The function `main()` declares two arguments: `argc` is an integer that contains the count of command-line arguments, and `argv` is a pointer to the array of strings. Each string in the array pointed to by `argv` is a command-line argument. Note that `argv` could just as easily have been declared as `char *argv[]` or `char argv[][]`. It is a matter of programming style how you declare `argv`; even though this program declared it as a pointer to a pointer, array offsets were still used to access the individual strings.

On line 4, `argc` is used to print the number of command-line arguments: seven in all, counting the program name itself. On lines 5 and 6, each of the command-line arguments is printed, passing the null-terminated strings to `cout` by indexing into the array of strings. A more common use of command-line arguments is illustrated by modifying Listing 27.18 to take the filename as a command-line argument, as shown in Listing 27.20.

LISTING 27.20   Using Command-Line Arguments to Get a Filename

```
1:  #include <fstream>
2:  #include <iostream>
3:  using namespace std;
4:
5:  class Animal
6:  {
7:    public:
8:        Animal(int weight,long days):itsWeight(weight),DaysAlive(days){}
9:        ~Animal(){}
10:
11:       int GetWeight()const { return itsWeight; }
12:       void SetWeight(int weight) { itsWeight = weight; }
13:
14:       long GetDaysAlive()const { return  DaysAlive; }
15:       void SetDaysAlive(long days) { DaysAlive = days; }
16:
17:   private:
18:       int itsWeight;
19:       long DaysAlive;
20: };
21:
22: int main(int argc, char *argv[])    // returns 1 on error
23: {
24:    if (argc != 2)
25:    {
26:        cout << "Usage: " << argv[0] << " <filename>" << endl;
27:        return(1);
28:    }
29:
```

LISTING 27.20 Continued

```
30:      ofstream fout(argv[1],ios::binary);
31:      if (!fout)
32:      {
33:         cout << "Unable to open " << argv[1] << " for writing.\n";
34:         return(1);
35:      }
36:
37:      Animal Bear(50,100);
38:      fout.write((char*) &Bear,sizeof Bear);
39:
40:      fout.close();
41:
42:      ifstream fin(argv[1],ios::binary);
43:      if (!fin)
44:      {
45:         cout << "Unable to open " << argv[1] << " for reading.\n";
46:         return(1);
47:      }
48:
49:      Animal BearTwo(1,1);
50:
51:      cout << "BearTwo weight: " << BearTwo.GetWeight() << endl;
52:      cout << "BearTwo days: " << BearTwo.GetDaysAlive() << endl;
53:
54:      fin.read((char*) &BearTwo, sizeof BearTwo);
55:
56:      cout << "BearTwo weight: " << BearTwo.GetWeight() << endl;
57:      cout << "BearTwo days: " << BearTwo.GetDaysAlive() << endl;
58:      fin.close();
59:      return 0;
60:  }
```

Output ▼

```
BearTwo weight: 1
BearTwo days: 1
BearTwo weight: 50
BearTwo days: 100
```

27

Analysis ▼

The declaration of the Animal class is the same as in Listing 27.18. This time, however, rather than prompting the user for the filename, command-line arguments are used. On line 22, main() is declared to take two parameters: the count of the command-line arguments and a pointer to the array of command-line argument strings.

On lines 24–28 the program ensures that the expected number of arguments (exactly two) is received. If the user fails to supply a single filename, an error message is printed:

```
Usage TestProgram <filename>
```

Then the program exits. Note that by using argv[0] rather than hard-coding a program name, you can compile this program to have any name, and this usage statement works automatically. You can even rename the executable after it was compiled and the usage statement will still be correct!

On line 30, the program attempts to open the supplied filename for binary output. No reason exists to copy the filename into a local temporary buffer. It can be used directly by accessing argv[1].

This technique is repeated on line 42 when the same file is reopened for input, and it is used in the error condition statements when the files cannot be opened, on lines 33 and 45.

Summary

In this lesson, streams were introduced, and the global objects cout and cin were described. The goal of the istream and ostream objects is to encapsulate the work of writing to device drivers and buffering input and output.

Four standard stream objects are created in every program: cout, cin, cerr, and clog. Each of these can be redirected by many operating systems.

The istream object cin is used for input, and its most common use is with the over-loaded extraction operator (>>). The ostream object cout is used for output, and its most common use is with the overloaded insertion operator (<<).

Each of these objects has a number of other member functions, such as get() and put(). Because the common forms of each of these methods returns a reference to a stream object, it is easy to concatenate each of these operators and functions.

The state of the stream objects can be changed by using manipulators. These can set the formatting and display characteristics and various other attributes of the stream objects.

File I/O can be accomplished by using the fstream classes, which derive from the stream classes. In addition to supporting the normal insertion and extraction operators, these objects also support read() and write() for storing and retrieving large binary objects.

Q&A

Q How do I know when to use the insertion and extraction operators and when to use the other member functions of the stream classes?

A In general, it is easier to use the insertion and extraction operators, and they are preferred when their behavior is what is needed. In those unusual circumstances when these operators don't do the job (such as reading in a string of words), the other functions can be used.

Q What is the difference between `cerr` and `clog`?

A `cerr` is not buffered. Everything written to `cerr` is immediately written out. This is fine for errors to be written to the console screen, but might have too high a performance cost for writing logs to disk. `clog` buffers its output, and thus can be more efficient, at the risk of losing part of the log if the program crashes.

Q Why were streams created if `printf()` works well?

A `printf()` does not support the strong type system of C++, and it does not support user-defined classes. Support for `printf()` is really just a carryover from the C programming language.

Q When would I ever use `putback()`?

A When one read operation is used to determine whether a character is valid, but a different read operation (perhaps by a different object) needs the character to be in the buffer. This is most often used when parsing a file; for example, the C++ compiler might use `putback()`.

Q My friends use `printf()` in their C++ programs. Can I?

A No. At this point, `printf()` should properly be considered obsolete.

Workshop

The Workshop contains quiz questions to help solidify your understanding of the material covered and exercises to provide you with experience in using what you've learned. Try to answer the quiz and exercise questions before checking the answers in Appendix D, and be certain you understand the answers before going to the next lesson.

27

Quiz

1. What is the insertion operator, and what does it do?
2. What is the extraction operator, and what does it do?
3. What are the three forms of `cin.get()`, and what are their differences?

4. What is the difference between `cin.read()` and `cin.getline()`?

5. What is the default width for outputting a `long` integer using the insertion operator?

6. What is the return value of the insertion operator?

7. What parameter does the constructor to an `ofstream` object take?

8. What does the `ios::ate` argument do?

Exercises

1. Write a program that writes to the four standard `iostream` objects: `cin`, `cout`, `cerr`, and `clog`.

2. Write a program that prompts the user to enter her full name and then displays it on the screen.

3. Rewrite Listing 27.9 to do the same thing, but without using `putback()` or `ignore()`.

4. Write a program that takes a filename as a parameter and opens the file for reading. Read every character of the file and display only the letters and punctuation to the screen. (Ignore all nonprinting characters.) Then close the file and exit.

5. Write a program that displays its command-line arguments in reverse order and does not display the program name.

LESSON 28
Exception Handling

The code you've seen in this book has been created for illustration purposes. It has not dealt with errors so that you would not be distracted from the central issues being presented. Real-world programs must take error conditions into consideration.

In this lesson, you will learn

- What exceptions are

- How exceptions are used and what issues they raise

- How to build exception hierarchies

- How exceptions fit into an overall error-handling approach

- What a debugger is

Bugs, Errors, Mistakes, and Code Rot

It is rare for a real-world-sized program not to have some sort of error, or bug. The bigger the program, the more likely there will be bugs. In fact, in larger programs, it is often the case that many bugs actually get out the door and into final, released software. That this is true does not make it okay. Making robust, bug-free programs should be the number-one priority of anyone serious about programming.

The single biggest problem in the software industry is buggy, unstable code. One of the biggest expenses in many major programming efforts is testing and fixing. The person who solves the problem of producing good, solid, bulletproof programs at low cost and on time will revolutionize the software industry.

A number of discrete kinds of errors can trouble a program. The first is poor logic: The program does just what you asked, but you haven't thought through the algorithms properly. The second is syntactic: You used the wrong idiom, function, or structure. These two are the most common, and they are the ones most programmers are on the lookout for.

Research and real-world experience have shown that the later in the development process you find a logic problem, the more it costs to fix. The least expensive problems or bugs to fix are the ones you manage to avoid creating. The next cheapest are those spotted by the compiler. The C++ standards force compilers to put a lot of energy into making more and more bugs show up at compile time.

Errors that get compiled in your program, but are caught at the first test—those that crash every time—are less expensive to find and fix than those that are flaky and only crash once in a while.

A more common runtime problem than logic or syntactic bugs is fragility: Your program works just fine if the user enters a number when you ask for one, but it crashes if the user enters letters. Other programs crash if they run out of memory, if the floppy disk is left out of the drive, or if an Internet connection is lost.

To combat this kind of fragility, programmers strive to make their programs bulletproof. A *bulletproof* program is one that can handle anything that comes up at runtime, from bizarre user input to running out of memory.

It is important to distinguish among bugs, which arise because the programmer made a mistake; logic errors, which arise because the programmer misunderstood the problem or how to solve it; and exceptions, which arise because of unusual but predictable problems such as running out of resources (memory or disk space).

Exceptional Circumstances

You can't eliminate exceptional circumstances, you can only prepare for them. What happens if your program requests memory to dynamically allocate an object, and there isn't any available? How will your program respond? Or what will your program do if you cause one of the most common math errors by dividing by zero? Your choices include

- Crash.
- Inform the user and exit gracefully.
- Inform the user and allow the user to try to recover and continue.
- Take corrective action and continue without disturbing the user.

Consider Listing 28.1, which is extremely simple and ready to crash; however, it illustrates a problem that makes it into many programs and that is extremely serious!

LISTING 28.1   Creating an Exceptional Situation

```
0:   // This program will crash
1:   #include <iostream>
2:   using namespace std;
3:
4:   const int DefaultSize = 10;
5:
6:   int main()
7:   {
8:       int top = 90;
9:       int bottom = 0;
10:
11:      cout << "top / 2 = " << (top/ 2) << endl;
12:
13:      cout << "top divided by bottom = ";
14:      cout << (top / bottom) << endl;
15:
16:      cout << "top / 3 = " << (top/ 3) << endl;
17:
18:      cout << "Done." << endl;
19:      return 0;
20: }
```

28

Output ▼

```
top / 2 = 45
top divided by bottom =
```

> **CAUTION** This program might display the preceding output to the console; however, it will most likely immediately crash afterward.

Analysis ▼

Listing 28.1 was actually designed to crash; however, if you had asked the user to enter two numbers, he could have encountered the same results. In lines 8 and 9, two integer variables are declared and given values. You could just as easily have prompted the user for these two numbers or read them from a file. In lines 11, 14, and 16, these numbers are used in math operations. Specifically, they are used for division. In lines 11 and 16, there are no issues; however, line 14 has a serious problem. Division by zero causes an exceptional problem to occur: a crash. The program ends and most likely an exception is displayed by the operating system.

Although it is not always necessary (or even desirable) to automatically and silently recover from all exceptional circumstances, it is clear that you must do better than this program. You can't simply let your program crash. C++ exception handling provides a type-safe, integrated method for coping with the predictable but unusual conditions that arise while running a program.

The Idea Behind Exceptions

The basic idea behind exceptions is fairly straightforward:

- The computer tries to run a piece of code. This code might try to allocate resources such as memory, might try to lock a file, or any of a variety of tasks.

- Logic (code) is included to be prepared in case the code you are trying to execute fails for some exceptional reason. For example, you would include code to catch any issues, such as memory not being allocated, a file being unable to be locked, or any of a variety of other issues.

- In case your code is being used by other code (for instance, one function calling another), you also need a mechanism to pass information about any problems (exceptions) from your level, up to the next. There should be a path from the code where an issue occurs to the code that can handle the error condition. If intervening layers of functions exist, they should be given an opportunity to clean the issue but should not be required to include code whose only purpose is to pass along the error condition.

Exception handling makes all three of these points come together and they do it in a relatively straightforward manner.

The Parts of Exception Handling

To handle exceptions, you have to first identify that you want a particular piece of code to be watched for any exceptions. This is accomplished by using a `try` block.

You should create a `try` block around any area of code that you believe has the potential to cause a problem. The basic format of the `try` block is

```
try
{
    SomeDangerousFunction();
}
catch (...)
{
}
```

In this case, when `SomeDangerousFunction()` executes, if any exception occurs, it is noted and caught. Adding the keyword `try` and the braces is all that is required to have your program start watching for exceptions. Of course, if an exception occurs, you need to act on it.

When the code within a `try` block is executed, if an exception occurs, the exception is said to be *thrown*. Thrown exceptions can then be caught, and as shown previously, you *catch* an exception with a `catch` block! When an exception is thrown, control transfers to the appropriate `catch` block following the current `try` block. In the previous example, the ellipsis (. . .) refers to any exception. But you can also catch specific types of exceptions. To do this, you use one or more `catch` blocks following your `try` block. For example,

```
try
{
    SomeDangerousFunction();
}
catch(OutOfMemory)
{
    // take some actions
}
catch(FileNotFound)
{
    // take other action
}
catch (...)
{
}
```

28

In this example, when `SomeDangerousFunction()` is executed, there will be handling in case there is an exception. If an exception is thrown, it is sent to the first `catch` block immediately following the `try` block. If that `catch` block has a type parameter, like those in the previous example, the exception is checked to see whether it matches the indicated type. If not, the next `catch` statement is checked, and so on, until either a match is found or something other than a `catch` block is found. When the first match is found, that `catch` block is executed. Unless you really intended to let other types of exceptions through, it is always a good idea to have the last `catch` use the ellipsis parameter.

NOTE	A `catch` block is also called a *handler* because it can handle an exception.

NOTE	You can look at the `catch` blocks as being like overloaded functions. When the matching signature is found, that function is executed.

The basic steps in handling exceptions are

1. Identify those areas of the program in which you begin an operation that might raise an exception, and put them in `try` blocks.

2. Create `catch` blocks to catch the exceptions if they are thrown. You can either create a `catch` for a specific type of exception (by specifying a typed parameter for the `catch` block) or all exceptions (by using an ellipsis (. . .) as the parameter).

Listing 28.2 adds basic exception handling to Listing 28.1. You can see this with the use of both a `try` block and a `catch` block.

NOTE	Some very old compilers do not support exceptions. Exceptions are part of the ANSI C++ standard, however, and every compiler vendor's latest edition fully supports exceptions. If you have an older compiler, you won't be able to compile and run the exercises in this lesson. It's still a good idea to read through the entire chapter, however, and return to this material when you upgrade your compiler.

LISTING 28.2   Catching an Exception

```
0:   // trying and catching
1:   #include <iostream>
2:   using namespace std;
3:
4:   const int DefaultSize = 10;
5:
6:   int main()
7:   {
8:       int top = 90;
9:       int bottom = 0;
10:
11:      try
12:      {
13:         cout << "top / 2 = " << (top/ 2) << endl;
14:
15:         cout << "top divided by bottom = ";
16:         cout << (top / bottom) << endl;
17:
18:         cout << "top / 3 = " << (top/ 3) << endl;
19:      }
20:      catch(...)
21:      {
22:         cout << "something has gone wrong!" << endl;
23:      }
24:
25:      cout << "Done." << endl;
26:      return 0;
27:   }
```

Output ▼

```
top / 2 = 45
top divided by bottom = something has gone wrong!
Done.
```

Analysis ▼

Unlike the prior listing, executing Listing 28.2 doesn't cause a crash. Rather, the program is able to report an issue and exit gracefully.

This time, a `try` block was added around the code where a potential issue could occur. In this case, it is around the division operations (lines 11–19). In case an exception does occur, a `catch` block is included in lines 20–23 after the `try` block.

The `catch` on line 20 contains three dots, or an ellipsis. As mentioned previously, this is a special case for `catch`, and indicates that all exceptions that occur in the preceding

28

try's code should be handled by this `catch` statement unless a prior `catch` block handled the exception. In this listing, that will most likely only be a division by zero error. As you will see later, it is often better to look for more specific types of exceptions so that you can customize the handling of each.

You should notice that this listing does not crash when it is run. In addition, you can see from the output that the program continued to line 25 right after the `catch` statement. This is confirmed by the fact that the word `Done` was printed to the console.

---

try Blocks

A `try` block is a series of statements that begins with the keyword `try`; it is followed by an opening brace and ends with a closing brace.

Example

```
try
{
    Function();
}
```

---

catch Blocks

A `catch` block is a piece of code that begins with the keyword `catch`, followed by an exception type in parentheses, followed by an opening brace, and ending with a closing brace. `catch` blocks are only allowed to follow a `try` block.

Example

```
try
{
    Function();
}
catch (OutOfMemory)
{
    // take action
}
```

Causing Your Own Exceptions

Listing 28.2 illustrated two of the aspects of exception handling: marking the code to be watched and specifying how the exception is to be handled. However, only predefined exceptions were handled. The third part of exception handling is the ability for you to create your own types of exceptions to be handled. By creating your own exceptions, you gain the ability to have customized handlers (`catch` blocks) for exceptions that are meaningful to your application.

To create an exception that causes the `try` statement to react, the keyword `throw` is used. In essence, you *throw* the exception and, hopefully, a handler (`catch` block) catches it. The basic format of the `throw` statement is

```
throw exception;
```

With this statement, *exception* is thrown. This causes control to pass to a handler. If a handler can't be found, the program terminates.

The value that you throw in the exception can be of virtually any type. As mentioned earlier, you can set up corresponding handlers for each different type of object your program might throw. Listing 28.3 illustrates how to throw a basic exception by modifying Listing 28.2.

LISTING 28.3   Throwing an Exception

```
0:  //Throwing
1:  #include <iostream>
2:
3:  using namespace std;
4:
5:  const int DefaultSize = 10;
6:
7:  int main()
8:  {
9:      int top = 90;
10:     int bottom = 0;
11:
12:     try
13:     {
14:       cout << "top / 2 = " << (top/ 2) << endl;
15:
16:        cout << "top divided by bottom = ";
17:        if ( bottom == 0 )
18:           throw "Division by zero!";
19:
20:        cout << (top / bottom) << endl;
21:
22:        cout << "top / 3 = " << (top/ 3) << endl;
23:     }
24:     catch( const char * ex )
25:     {
26:        cout << "\n*** " << ex << " ***" << endl;
27:     }
28:
29:     cout << "Done." << endl;
30:     return 0;
31: }
```

Output ▼

```
top / 2 = 45
top divided by bottom = *** Division by zero! ***
Done.
```

Analysis ▼

Unlike the prior listing, this listing takes more control of its exceptions. Although this isn't the best use of exceptions, it clearly illustrates using the throw statement.

In line 17, a check is done to see whether the value of bottom is equal to zero. If it is, an exception is thrown. In this case, the exception is a string value.

On line 24, a catch statement starts a handler. This handler is looking for a constant character pointer. With exceptions, strings are matched to a constant character pointer, so the handler starting in line 24 catches the throw in line 18. In line 26, the string that was passed is displayed between asterisks. Line 27 is the closing brace, which indicates the end of the handler, so control goes to the first line following the catch statements and the program continues to the end.

If your exception had been a more serious problem, you could have exited the application after printing the message in line 26. If you throw your exception in a function that was called by another function, you could have passed the exception up. To pass on an exception, you can simply call the throw command without any parameter. This causes the existing exception to be rethrown from the current location.

Creating an Exception Class

You can create much more complex classes for throwing an exception. Listing 28.4 presents a somewhat stripped-down Array class, which is a very primitive implementation of a dynamic array.

LISTING 28.4　Throwing an Exception

```
0:   #include <iostream>
1:   using namespace std;
2:
3:   const int DefaultSize = 10;
4:
5:   class Array
6:   {
7:     public:
8:       // constructors
9:       Array(int itsSize = DefaultSize);
```

LISTING 28.4 Continued

```
10:        Array(const Array &rhs);
11:        ~Array() { delete [] pType;}
12:
13:        // operators
14:        Array& operator=(const Array&);
15:        int& operator[](int offSet);
16:        const int& operator[](int offSet) const;
17:
18:        // accessors
19:        int GetitsSize() const { return itsSize; }
20:
21:        // friend function
22:        friend ostream& operator<< (ostream&, const Array&);
23:
24:        class xBoundary {};   // define the exception class
25:
26:     private:
27:        int *pType;
28:        int  itsSize;
29:  };
30:
31:  Array::Array(int size):
32:     itsSize(size)
33:  {
34:     pType = new int[size];
35:     for (int i = 0; i < size; i++)
36:        pType[i] = 0;
37:  }
38:
39:  Array& Array::operator=(const Array &rhs)
40:  {
41:     if (this == &rhs)
42:        return *this;
43:     delete [] pType;
44:     itsSize = rhs.GetitsSize();
45:     pType = new int[itsSize];
46:     for (int i = 0; i < itsSize; i++)
47:     {
48:        pType[i] = rhs[i];
49:     }
50:     return *this;
51:  }
52:
53:  Array::Array(const Array &rhs)
54:  {
55:     itsSize = rhs.GetitsSize();
56:     pType = new int[itsSize];
57:     for (int i = 0; i < itsSize; i++)
58:     {
```

28

LISTING 28.4   Continued

```
59:            pType[i] = rhs[i];
60:        }
61:    }
62:
63:    int& Array::operator[](int offSet)
64:    {
65:        int size = GetitsSize();
66:        if (offSet >= 0 && offSet < GetitsSize())
67:            return pType[offSet];
68:        throw xBoundary();
69:        return pType[0]; // appease MSC
70:    }
71:
72:    const int& Array::operator[](int offSet) const
73:    {
74:        int mysize = GetitsSize();
75:        if (offSet >= 0 && offSet < GetitsSize())
76:            return pType[offSet];
77:        throw xBoundary();
78:        return pType[0]; // appease MSC
79:    }
80:
81:    ostream& operator<< (ostream& output, const Array& theArray)
82:    {
83:        for (int i = 0; i<theArray.GetitsSize(); i++)
84:            output << "[" << i << "] " << theArray[i] << endl;
85:        return output;
86:    }
87:
88:    int main()
89:    {
90:        Array intArray(20);
91:        try
92:        {
93:            for (int j = 0; j< 100; j++)
94:            {
95:                intArray[j] = j;
96:                cout << "intArray[" << j << "] okay..." << endl;
97:            }
98:        }
99:        catch (Array::xBoundary)
100:       {
101:           cout << "Unable to process your input!" << endl;
102:       }
103:       cout << "Done." << endl;
104:       return 0;
105: }
```

Output ▼

```
intArray[0] okay...
intArray[1] okay...
intArray[2] okay...
intArray[3] okay...
intArray[4] okay...
intArray[5] okay...
intArray[6] okay...
intArray[7] okay...
intArray[8] okay...
intArray[9] okay...
intArray[10] okay...
intArray[11] okay...
intArray[12] okay...
intArray[13] okay...
intArray[14] okay...
intArray[15] okay...
intArray[16] okay...
intArray[17] okay...
intArray[18] okay...
intArray[19] okay...
Unable to process your input!
Done.
```

Analysis ▼

Listing 28.4 presents a somewhat stripped-down Array class; however, this time exception handling is added in case the array goes out of bounds. On line 24, a new class, xBoundary, is declared within the declaration of the outer class Array. This new class is not in any way distinguished as an exception class. It is just a class, the same as any other. This particular class is incredibly simple; it has no data and no methods. Nonetheless, it is a valid class in every way. In fact, it is incorrect to say it has no methods because the compiler automatically assigns it a default constructor, destructor, copy constructor, and the assignment operator (operator equals); so, it actually has four class functions, but no data. Note that declaring it from within Array serves only to couple the two classes together. Class Array has no special access to xBoundary, nor does xBoundary have preferential access to the members of Array.

On lines 63–70 and 72–79, the offset operators are modified to examine the offset requested, and if it is out of range, to throw the xBoundary class as an exception. The parentheses are required to distinguish between this call to the xBoundary constructor and the use of an enumerated constant.

28

In line 90, the main part of the program starts by declaring an `Array` object that can hold 20 values. On line 91, the keyword `try` begins a `try` block that ends on line 98. Within that `try` block, 101 integers are added to the array that was declared on line 90.

On line 99, the `handler` has been declared to catch any `xBoundary` exceptions.

In the driver program on lines 88–105, a `try` block is created in which each member of the array is initialized. When j (line 93) is incremented to 20, the member at offset 20 is accessed. This causes the test on line 66 to fail, and `operator[]` raises an `xBoundary` exception on line 67.

Program control switches to the `catch` block on line 99, and the exception is caught or handled by the `catch` on the same line, which prints an error message. Program flow drops through to the end of the `catch` block on line 102.

Placing `try` Blocks and `catch` Blocks

Figuring out where to put your `try` blocks can be hard: It is not always obvious which actions might raise an exception. The next question is where to catch the exception. It might be that you'll want to throw all memory exceptions where the memory is allocated, but you'll want to catch the exceptions high in the program where you deal with the user interface.

When trying to determine `try` block locations, look to where you allocate memory or use resources. Other things to look for are out-of-bounds errors, illegal input, and so forth. At the very least, put a `try/catch` around all the code in `main()`. `try/catch` usually belongs in high-level functions, particularly those that know about the program's user interface. For instance, a utility class should not generally catch exceptions that need to be reported to the user because it might be used in windowed programs or console programs, or even in programs that communicate with users via the Web or messaging.

How Catching Exceptions Work

Here's how it works: When an exception is thrown, the call stack is examined. The call stack is the list of function calls created when one part of the program invokes another function.

The call stack tracks the execution path. If `main()` calls the function `Animal::GetFavoriteFood()`, and `GetFavoriteFood()` calls `Animal::LookupPreferences()`, which, in turn, calls `fstream::operator>>()`, all these are on the call stack. A recursive function might be on the call stack many times.

The exception is passed up the call stack to each enclosing block. This is called *unwinding the stack*. As the stack is unwound, the destructors for local objects on the stack are invoked and the objects are destroyed.

One or more `catch` statements follow each `try` block. If the exception matches one of the `catch` statements, it is considered to be handled by having that statement execute. If it doesn't match any, the unwinding of the stack continues. If the exception reaches all the way to the beginning of the program (`main()`) and is still not caught, a built-in handler is called that terminates the program.

It is important to note that the exception unwinding of the stack is a one-way street. As it progresses, the stack is unwound and objects on the stack are destroyed. There is no going back: After the exception is handled, the program continues after the `try` block of the `catch` statement that handled the exception.

Thus, in Listing 28.4, execution continues on line 101, the first line after the `try` block of the `catch` statement that handled the xBoundary exception. Remember that when an exception is raised, program flow continues after the `catch` block, not after the point where the exception was thrown.

Using More Than One `catch` Specification

It is possible for more than one condition to cause an exception. In this case, the `catch` statements can be lined up one after another, much like the conditions in a switch statement. The equivalent to the default statement is the "catch everything" statement, indicated by `catch(...)`. Listing 28.5 illustrates multiple exception conditions.

LISTING 28.5 Multiple Exceptions

```
0:   #include <iostream>
1:   using namespace std;
2:
3:   const int DefaultSize = 10;
4:
5:   class Array
6:   {
7:     public:
8:       // constructors
9:       Array(int itsSize = DefaultSize);
10:      Array(const Array &rhs);
11:      ~Array() { delete [] pType;}
12:
13:      // operators
14:      Array& operator=(const Array&);
15:      int& operator[](int offSet);
16:      const int& operator[](int offSet) const;
17:
```

28

LISTING 28.5   Continued

```
18:        // accessors
19:        int GetitsSize() const { return itsSize; }
20:
21:        // friend function
22:        friend ostream& operator<< (ostream&, const Array&);
23:
24:        // define the exception classes
25:        class xBoundary {};
26:        class xTooBig {};
27:        class xTooSmall{};
28:        class xZero {};
29:        class xNegative {};
30:    private:
31:        int *pType;
32:        int  itsSize;
33:   };
34:
35:   int& Array::operator[](int offSet)
36:   {
37:      int size = GetitsSize();
38:      if (offSet >= 0 && offSet < GetitsSize())
39:         return pType[offSet];
40:      throw xBoundary();
41:      return pType[0];   // appease MFC
42:   }
43:
44:
45:   const int& Array::operator[](int offSet) const
46:   {
47:      int mysize = GetitsSize();
48:      if (offSet >= 0 && offSet < GetitsSize())
49:         return pType[offSet];
50:      throw xBoundary();
51:
52:      return pType[0];   // appease MFC
53:   }
54:
55:
56:   Array::Array(int size):
57:      itsSize(size)
58:   {
59:      if (size == 0)
60:         throw xZero();
61:      if (size < 10)
62:         throw xTooSmall();
63:      if (size > 30000)
64:         throw xTooBig();
65:      if (size < 1)
66:         throw xNegative();
67:
```

LISTING 28.5 Continued

```
68:      pType = new int[size];
69:      for (int i = 0; i < size; i++)
70:         pType[i] = 0;
71:  }
72:
73:  int main()
74:  {
75:      try
76:      {
77:         Array intArray(0);
78:         for (int j = 0; j < 100; j++)
79:         {
80:             intArray[j] = j;
81:             cout << "intArray[" << j << "] okay..." << endl;
82:         }
83:      }
84:      catch (Array::xBoundary)
85:      {
86:         cout << "Unable to process your input!" << endl;
87:      }
88:      catch (Array::xTooBig)
89:      {
90:         cout << "This array is too big..." << endl;
91:      }
92:      catch (Array::xTooSmall)
93:      {
94:         cout << "This array is too small..." << endl;
95:      }
96:      catch (Array::xZero)
97:      {
98:         cout << "You asked for an array";
99:         cout << " of zero objects!" << endl;
100:     }
101:     catch (...)
102:     {
103:        cout << "Something went wrong!" << endl;
104:     }
105:     cout << "Done." << endl;
106:     return 0;
107: }
```

Output ▼

```
You asked for an array of zero objects!
Done.
```

Analysis ▼

Four new classes are created in lines 25–29: xTooBig, xTooSmall, xZero, and xNegative. In the constructor, on lines 56–71, the size passed to the constructor is examined. If it's too big, too small, negative, or zero, an exception is thrown.

The try block is changed to include catch statements for each condition other than negative, which is caught by the "catch everything" statement catch(...), shown on line 101.

Try this with a number of values for the size of the array. Then try putting in –5. You might have expected xNegative to be called, but the order of the tests in the constructor prevented this: size < 10 was evaluated before size < 1. To fix this, swap lines 61 and 62 with lines 65 and 66 and recompile.

TIP	After the constructor has been invoked, memory has been allocated for the object. Therefore, throwing any exception from the constructor can leave the object allocated but unusable. Generally, you should wrap the constructor in a try/catch, and if an exception occurs, mark the object (internally) as unusable. Each member function should check this validity flag to be certain additional errors won't occur when someone uses an object whose initialization was interrupted.

Exception Hierarchies

Exceptions are classes, and as such, they can be derived from. It might be advantageous to create a class xSize, and to derive from it xZero, xTooSmall, xTooBig, and xNegative. Thus, some functions might just catch xSize errors, and other functions might catch the specific type of xSize error. Listing 28.6 illustrates this idea.

LISTING 28.6 Class Hierarchies and Exceptions

```
0:   #include <iostream>
1:   using namespace std;
2:
3:   const int DefaultSize = 10;
4:
5:   class Array
6:   {
7:     public:
8:       // constructors
9:       Array(int itsSize = DefaultSize);
```

LISTING 28.6 Continued

```
10:        Array(const Array &rhs);
11:        ~Array() { delete [] pType;}
12:
13:        // operators
14:        Array& operator=(const Array&);
15:        int& operator[](int offSet);
16:        const int& operator[](int offSet) const;
17:
18:        // accessors
19:        int GetitsSize() const { return itsSize; }
20:
21:        // friend function
22:        friend ostream& operator<< (ostream&, const Array&);
23:
24:        // define the exception classes
25:        class xBoundary {};
26:        class xSize {};
27:        class xTooBig : public xSize {};
28:        class xTooSmall : public xSize {};
29:        class xZero  : public xTooSmall {};
30:        class xNegative  : public xSize {};
31:     private:
32:        int *pType;
33:        int  itsSize;
34:  };
35:
36:
37:  Array::Array(int size):
38:     itsSize(size)
39:  {
40:     if (size == 0)
41:        throw xZero();
42:     if (size > 30000)
43:        throw xTooBig();
44:     if (size <1)
45:        throw xNegative();
46:     if (size < 10)
47:        throw xTooSmall();
48:
49:     pType = new int[size];
50:     for (int i = 0; i < size; i++)
51:        pType[i] = 0;
52:  }
53:
54:  int& Array::operator[](int offSet)
55:  {
56:     int size = GetitsSize();
57:     if (offSet >= 0 && offSet < GetitsSize())
58:        return pType[offSet];
59:     throw xBoundary();
```

28

LISTING 28.6   Continued

```
60:     return pType[0];  // appease MFC
61: }
62:
63: const int& Array::operator[](int offSet) const
64: {
65:     int mysize = GetitsSize();
66:
67:     if (offSet >= 0 && offSet < GetitsSize())
68:         return pType[offSet];
69:     throw xBoundary();
70:
71:     return pType[0];  // appease MFC
72: }
73:
74: int main()
75: {
76:     try
77:     {
78:         Array intArray(0);
79:         for (int j = 0; j < 100; j++)
80:         {
81:             intArray[j] = j;
82:             cout << "intArray[" << j << "] okay..." << endl;
83:         }
84:     }
85:     catch (Array::xBoundary)
86:     {
87:         cout << "Unable to process your input!" << endl;
88:     }
89:     catch (Array::xTooBig)
90:     {
91:         cout << "This array is too big..." << endl;
92:     }
93:
94:     catch (Array::xTooSmall)
95:     {
96:         cout << "This array is too small..." << endl;
97:     }
98:     catch (Array::xZero)
99:     {
100:         cout << "You asked for an array";
101:         cout << " of zero objects!" << endl;
102:     }
103:     catch (...)
104:     {
105:         cout << "Something went wrong!" << endl;
106:     }
107:     cout << "Done." << endl;
108:     return 0;
109: }
```

Output ▼

```
This array is too small...
Done.
```

Analysis ▼

The significant change is on lines 27–30, where the class hierarchy is established. Classes xTooBig, xTooSmall, and xNegative are derived from xSize, and xZero is derived from xTooSmall.

The Array is created with size zero, but what's this? The wrong exception appears to be caught! Examine the catch block carefully, however, and you will find that it looks for an exception of type xTooSmall before it looks for an exception of type xZero. Because an xZero object is thrown and an xZero object is an xTooSmall object, it is caught by the handler for xTooSmall. After being handled, the exception is not passed on to the other handlers, so the handler for xZero is never called.

The solution to this problem is to order the handlers carefully so that the most specific handlers come first and the less specific handlers come later. In this particular example, switching the placement of the two handlers xZero and xTooSmall fixes the problem.

Data in Exceptions and Naming Exception Objects

Often, you will want to know more than just what type of exception was thrown so that you can respond properly to the error. Exception classes are the same as any other class. You are free to provide data, initialize that data in the constructor, and read that data at any time. Listing 28.7 illustrates how to do this.

LISTING 28.7   Getting Data Out of an Exception Object

```
 0:   #include <iostream>
 1:   using namespace std;
 2:
 3:   const int DefaultSize = 10;
 4:
 5:   class Array
 6:   {
 7:     public:
 8:       // constructors
 9:       Array(int itsSize = DefaultSize);
10:       Array(const Array &rhs);
11:       ~Array() { delete [] pType;}
12:
```

28

LISTING 28.7 Continued

```
13:        // operators
14:        Array& operator=(const Array&);
15:        int& operator[](int offSet);
16:        const int& operator[](int offSet) const;
17:
18:        // accessors
19:        int GetitsSize() const { return itsSize; }
20:
21:        // friend function
22:        friend ostream& operator<< (ostream&, const Array&);
23:
24:        // define the exception classes
25:        class xBoundary {};
26:        class xSize
27:        {
28:          public:
29:            xSize(int size):itsSize(size) {}
30:            ~xSize(){}
31:            int GetSize() { return itsSize; }
32:          private:
33:            int itsSize;
34:        };
35:
36:        class xTooBig : public xSize
37:        {
38:          public:
39:            xTooBig(int size):xSize(size){}
40:        };
41:
42:        class xTooSmall : public xSize
43:        {
44:          public:
45:            xTooSmall(int size):xSize(size){}
46:        };
47:
48:        class xZero  : public xTooSmall
49:        {
50:          public:
51:            xZero(int size):xTooSmall(size){}
52:        };
53:
54:        class xNegative : public xSize
55:        {
56:          public:
57:            xNegative(int size):xSize(size){}
58:        };
59:
60:    private:
61:      int *pType;
```

LISTING 28.7 Continued

```
62:         int  itsSize;
63:    };
64:
65:
66:    Array::Array(int size):
67:    itsSize(size)
68:    {
69:       if (size == 0)
70:          throw xZero(size);
71:       if (size > 30000)
72:          throw xTooBig(size);
73:       if (size < 1)
74:          throw xNegative(size);
75:       if (size < 10)
76:          throw xTooSmall(size);
77:
78:       pType = new int[size];
79:       for (int i = 0; i < size; i++)
80:          pType[i] = 0;
81:    }
82:
83:
84:    int& Array::operator[] (int offSet)
85:    {
86:       int size = GetitsSize();
87:       if (offSet >= 0 && offSet < size)
88:          return pType[offSet];
89:       throw xBoundary();
90:       return pType[0];
91:    }
92:
93:     const int& Array::operator[] (int offSet) const
94:     {
95:       int size = GetitsSize();
96:       if (offSet >= 0 && offSet < size)
97:          return pType[offSet];
98:       throw xBoundary();
99:       return pType[0];
100:   }
101:
102:   int main()
103:   {
104:      try
105:      {
106:         Array intArray(9);
107:         for (int j = 0; j < 100; j++)
108:         {
109:            intArray[j] = j;
```

LISTING 28.7   Continued

```
110:            cout << "intArray[" << j << "] okay..." << endl;
111:          }
112:        }
113:        catch (Array::xBoundary)
114:        {
115:          cout << "Unable to process your input!" << endl;
116:        }
117:        catch (Array::xZero theException)
118:        {
119:          cout << "You asked for an Array of zero objects!" << endl;
120:          cout << "Received " << theException.GetSize() << endl;
121:        }
122:        catch (Array::xTooBig theException)
123:        {
124:          cout << "This Array is too big..." << endl;
125:          cout << "Received " << theException.GetSize() << endl;
126:        }
127:        catch (Array::xTooSmall theException)
128:        {
129:          cout << "This Array is too small..." << endl;
130:          cout << "Received " << theException.GetSize() << endl;
131:        }
132:        catch (...)
133:        {
134:          cout << "Something went wrong, but I've no idea what!\n";
135:        }
136:        cout << "Done." << endl;
137:        return 0;
138:  }
```

Output ▼

```
This array is too small...
Received 9
Done.
```

Analysis ▼

The declaration of xSize has been modified to include a member variable, itsSize, on line 33 and a member function, GetSize(), on line 31. In addition, a constructor has been added that takes an integer and initializes the member variable, as shown on line 29.

The derived classes declare a constructor that does nothing but initialize the base class. No other functions were declared, in part to save space in the listing.

The catch statements on lines 113–135 are modified to name the exception they catch, theException, and to use this object to access the data stored in itsSize.

NOTE

Keep in mind that if you are constructing an exception, it is because an exception has been raised: Something has gone wrong, and your exception should be careful not to kick off the same problem. Therefore, if you are creating an `OutOfMemory` exception, you probably don't want to allocate memory in its constructor.

It is tedious and error-prone to have each of these `catch` statements individually print the appropriate message. This job belongs to the object, which knows what type of object it is and what value it received. Listing 28.8 takes a more object-oriented approach to this problem, using virtual functions so that each exception "does the right thing."

LISTING 28.8 Passing by Reference and Using Virtual Functions in Exceptions

```
0:   #include <iostream>
1:   using namespace std;
2:
3:   const int DefaultSize = 10;
4:
5:   class Array
6:   {
7:     public:
8:     // constructors
9:       Array(int itsSize = DefaultSize);
10:      Array(const Array &rhs);
11:      ~Array() { delete [] pType;}
12:
13:      // operators
14:      Array& operator=(const Array&);
15:      int& operator[](int offSet);
16:      const int& operator[](int offSet) const;
17:
18:      // accessors
19:      int GetitsSize() const { return itsSize; }
20:
21:      // friend function
22:      friend ostream& operator<<
23:      (ostream&, const Array&);
24:
25:      // define the exception classes
26:      class xBoundary {};
27:      class xSize
28:      {
29:        public:
30:          xSize(int size):itsSize(size) {}
31:          ~xSize(){}
```

28

LISTING 28.8 Continued

```
32:        virtual int GetSize() { return itsSize; }
33:        virtual void PrintError()
34:        {
35:            cout << "Size error. Received: ";
36:            cout << itsSize << endl;
37:        }
38:     protected:
39:        int itsSize;
40:     };
41:
42:     class xTooBig : public xSize
43:     {
44:       public:
45:         xTooBig(int size):xSize(size){}
46:         virtual void PrintError()
47:         {
48:             cout << "Too big! Received: ";
49:             cout << xSize::itsSize << endl;
50:         }
51:     };
52:
53:     class xTooSmall : public xSize
54:     {
55:       public:
56:         xTooSmall(int size):xSize(size){}
57:         virtual void PrintError()
58:         {
59:             cout << "Too small! Received: ";
60:             cout << xSize::itsSize << endl;
61:         }
62:     };
63:
64:     class xZero   : public xTooSmall
65:     {
66:       public:
67:         xZero(int size):xTooSmall(size){}
68:         virtual void PrintError()
69:         {
70:             cout << "Zero!!. Received: " ;
71:             cout << xSize::itsSize << endl;
72:         }
73:     };
74:
75:     class xNegative : public xSize
76:     {
77:       public:
78:         xNegative(int size):xSize(size){}
79:         virtual void PrintError()
80:         {
```

LISTING 28.8 Continued

```
81:                    cout << "Negative! Received: ";
82:                    cout << xSize::itsSize << endl;
83:                }
84:        };
85:
86:    private:
87:        int *pType;
88:        int  itsSize;
89:    };
90:
91:    Array::Array(int size):
92:        itsSize(size)
93:    {
94:        if (size == 0)
95:            throw xZero(size);
96:        if (size > 30000)
97:            throw xTooBig(size);
98:        if (size < 0)
99:            throw xNegative(size);
100:        if (size < 10)
101:            throw xTooSmall(size);
102:
103:        pType = new int[size];
104:        for (int i = 0; i < size; i++)
105:            pType[i] = 0;
106:    }
107:
108:    int& Array::operator[] (int offSet)
109:    {
110:        int size = GetitsSize();
111:        if (offSet >= 0 && offSet < GetitsSize())
112:            return pType[offSet];
113:        throw xBoundary();
114:        return pType[0];
115:    }
116:
117:    const int& Array::operator[] (int offSet) const
118:    {
119:        int size = GetitsSize();
120:        if (offSet >= 0 && offSet < GetitsSize())
121:            return pType[offSet];
122:        throw xBoundary();
123:        return pType[0];
124:    }
125:
126:    int main()
127:    {
128:        try
129:        {
```

LISTING 28.8 Continued

```
130:        Array intArray(9);
131:        for (int j = 0; j < 100; j++)
132:        {
133:            intArray[j] = j;
134:            cout << "intArray[" << j << "] okay..." << endl;
135:        }
136:    }
137:    catch (Array::xBoundary)
138:    {
139:        cout << "Unable to process your input!" << endl;
140:    }
141:    catch (Array::xSize& theException)
142:    {
143:        theException.PrintError();
144:    }
145:    catch (...)
146:    {
147:        cout << "Something went wrong!" << endl;
148:    }
149:    cout << "Done." << endl;
150:    return 0;
151: }
```

Output ▼

```
Too small! Received: 9
Done.
```

Analysis ▼

Listing 28.8 declares a virtual method on lines 33–37 in the xSize class, PrintError(), that prints an error message and the actual size of the class. This is overridden in each of the derived classes.

On line 141 in the exception handler, the exception object is declared to be a reference. When PrintError() is called with a reference to an object, polymorphism causes the correct version of PrintError() to be invoked. The code is cleaner, easier to understand, and easier to maintain.

Exceptions and Templates

When creating exceptions to work with templates, you have a choice: You can create an exception for each instance of the template or you can use exception classes declared outside the template declaration. Listing 28.9 illustrates both approaches.

LISTING 28.9   Using Exceptions with Templates

```
0:   #include <iostream>
1:   using namespace std;
2:
3:   const int DefaultSize = 10;
4:   class xBoundary {};
5:
6:   template <class T>
7:   class Array
8:   {
9:     public:
10:       // constructors
11:       Array(int itsSize = DefaultSize);
12:       Array(const Array &rhs);
13:       ~Array() { delete [] pType;}
14:
15:       // operators
16:       Array& operator=(const Array<T>&);
17:       T& operator[](int offSet);
18:       const T& operator[](int offSet) const;
19:
20:       // accessors
21:       int GetitsSize() const { return itsSize; }
22:
23:       // friend function
24:       friend ostream& operator<< (ostream&, const Array<T>&);
25:
26:       // define the exception classes
27:
28:       class xSize {};
29:
30:     private:
31:       int *pType;
32:       int  itsSize;
33:   };
34:
35:   template <class T>
36:   Array<T>::Array(int size):
37:      itsSize(size)
38:   {
39:     if (size <10 || size > 30000)
40:        throw xSize();
41:     pType = new T[size];
42:     for (int i = 0; i<size; i++)
43:        pType[i] = 0;
44:   }
45:
46:   template <class T>
47:   Array<T>& Array<T>::operator=(const Array<T> &rhs)
48:   {
```

28

LISTING 28.9   Continued

```
49:        if (this == &rhs)
50:            return *this;
51:        delete [] pType;
52:        itsSize = rhs.GetitsSize();
53:        pType = new T[itsSize];
54:        for (int i = 0; i < itsSize; i++)
55:            pType[i] = rhs[i];
56:    }
57:    template <class T>
58:    Array<T>::Array(const Array<T> &rhs)
59:    {
60:        itsSize = rhs.GetitsSize();
61:        pType = new T[itsSize];
62:        for (int i = 0; i < itsSize; i++)
63:            pType[i] = rhs[i];
64:    }
65:
66:    template <class T>
67:    T& Array<T>::operator[](int offSet)
68:    {
69:        int size = GetitsSize();
70:        if (offSet >= 0 && offSet < GetitsSize())
71:            return pType[offSet];
72:        throw xBoundary();
73:        return pType[0];
74:    }
75:
76:    template <class T>
77:    const T& Array<T>::operator[](int offSet) const
78:    {
79:        int mysize = GetitsSize();
80:        if (offSet >= 0 && offSet < GetitsSize())
81:            return pType[offSet];
82:        throw xBoundary();
83:    }
84:
85:    template <class T>
86:    ostream& operator<< (ostream& output, const Array<T>& theArray)
87:    {
88:        for (int i = 0; i < theArray.GetitsSize(); i++)
89:            output << "[" << i << "] " << theArray[i] << endl;
90:        return output;
91:    }
92:
93:
94:    int main()
95:    {
96:        try
97:        {
```

LISTING 28.9 Continued

```
98:        Array<int> intArray(9);
99:        for (int j = 0; j < 100; j++)
100:       {
101:           intArray[j] = j;
102:           cout << "intArray[" << j << "] okay..." << endl;
103:       }
104:    }
105:    catch (xBoundary)
106:    {
107:       cout << "Unable to process your input!" << endl;
108:    }
109:    catch (Array<int>::xSize)
110:    {
111:       cout << "Bad Size!" << endl;
112:    }
113:
114:    cout << "Done." << endl;
115:    return 0;
116: }
```

Output ▼

```
Bad Size!
Done.
```

Analysis ▼

The first exception, xBoundary, is declared outside the template definition on line 4. The second exception, xSize, is declared from within the definition of the template on line 28.

The exception xBoundary is not tied to the template class, but it can be used the same as any other class. xSize is tied to the template and must be called based on the instantiated Array. You can see the difference in the syntax for the two catch statements. Line 105 shows catch (xBoundary), but line 109 shows catch (Array<int>::xSize). The latter is tied to the instantiation of an integer Array.

Exceptions Without Errors

When C++ programmers get together for a virtual beer in the cyberspace bar after work, talk often turns to whether exceptions should be used for routine conditions. Some maintain that by their nature, exceptions should be reserved for those predictable but exceptional circumstances (hence the name!) that a programmer must anticipate, but that are not part of the routine processing of the code.

28

Others point out that exceptions offer a powerful and clean way to return through many layers of function calls without danger of memory leaks. A frequent example is this: The user requests an action in a graphical user interface (GUI) environment. The part of the code that catches the request must call a member function on a dialog manager, which, in turn, calls code that processes the request, which calls code that decides which dialog box to use, which, in turn, calls code to put up the dialog box, which finally calls code that processes the user's input. If the user clicks Cancel, the code must return to the very first calling method where the original request was handled.

One approach to this problem is to put a `try` block around the original call and catch `CancelDialog` as an exception, which can be raised by the handler for the Cancel button. This is safe and effective, but clicking Cancel is a routine circumstance, not an exceptional one.

This frequently becomes something of a religious argument, but a reasonable way to decide the question is to ask the following: Does use of exceptions in this way make the code easier or harder to understand? Are there fewer risks of errors and memory leaks, or more? Will it be harder or easier to maintain this code? These decisions, like so many others, require an analysis of the trade-offs; no single, obvious right answer exists.

A Word About Code Rot

Code rot is a well-known phenomenon in which software deteriorates due to being neglected. A perfectly well-written, fully debugged program will turn bad on your customer's shelf just weeks after you deliver it. After a few months, your customer will notice that a green mold has covered your logic, and many of your objects have begun to flake apart.

Besides shipping your source code in airtight containers, your only protection is to write your programs so that when you go back to fix the spoilage, you can quickly and easily identify where the problems are.

Code rot is a programmer's joke that teaches an important lesson. Programs are enormously complex, and bugs, errors, and mistakes can hide for a long time before turning up. Protect yourself by writing easy-to-maintain code.

This means that your code must be written to be understood, and commented where tricky. Six months after you deliver your code, you will read it with the eyes of a total stranger, bewildered by how anyone could ever have written such convoluted and twisty logic.

Bugs and Debugging

Nearly all modern development environments include one or more high-powered debuggers. The essential idea of using a debugger is this: You run the debugger, which loads your source code, and then you run your program from within the debugger. This enables you to see each instruction in your program as it executes and to examine your variables as they change during the life of your program.

All compilers let you compile with or without symbols. Compiling with symbols tells the compiler to create the necessary mapping between your source code and the generated program; the debugger uses this to point to the line of source code that corresponds to the next action in the program.

Full-screen symbolic debuggers make this chore a delight. When you load your debugger, it reads through all your source code and shows the code in a window. You can step over function calls or direct the debugger to step into the function, line by line.

With most debuggers, you can switch between the source code and the output to see the results of each executed statement. More powerfully, you can examine the current state of each variable, look at complex data structures, examine the value of member data within classes, and look at the actual values in memory of various pointers and other memory locations. You can execute several types of control within a debugger that include setting breakpoints, setting watch points, examining memory, and looking at the assembler code.

Breakpoints

Breakpoints are instructions to the debugger that when a particular line of code is ready to be executed, the program should stop. This allows you to run your program unimpeded until the line in question is reached. Breakpoints help you analyze the current condition of variables just before and after a critical line of code.

Watch Points

It is possible to tell the debugger to show you the value of a particular variable or to break when a particular variable is read or written to. Watch points enable you to set these conditions, and, at times, even to modify the value of a variable while the program is running.

28

Examining Memory

At times, it is important to see the actual values held in memory. Modern debuggers can show values in the form of the actual variable; that is, strings can be shown as characters, longs as numbers rather than as four bytes, and so forth. Sophisticated C++ debuggers can even show complete classes and provide the current value of all the member variables, including the this pointer.

Assembler

Although reading through the source can be all that is required to find a bug, when all else fails, it is possible to instruct the debugger to show you the actual assembly code generated for each line of your source code. You can examine the memory registers and flags, and generally delve as deep into the inner workings of your program as required.

Learn to use your debugger. It can be the most powerful weapon in your holy war against bugs. Runtime bugs are the hardest to find and squash, and a powerful debugger can make it possible, if not easy, to find nearly all of them.

Summary

You learned the basics for creating and using exceptions. *Exceptions* are objects that can be created and thrown at points in the program where the executing code cannot handle the error or other exceptional condition that has arisen. Other parts of the program, higher in the call stack, implement catch blocks that catch the exception and take appropriate action.

Exceptions are normal, user-created objects, and as such can be passed by value or by reference. They can contain data and methods, and the catch block can use that data to decide how to deal with the exception.

It is possible to create multiple catch blocks, but after an exception matches a catch block's signature, it is considered to be handled and is not given to the subsequent catch blocks. It is important to order the catch blocks appropriately so that more specific catch blocks have first chance, and more general catch blocks handle those not otherwise handled.

This lesson also mentioned the fundamentals of symbolic debuggers, including using watch points, breakpoints, and so forth. These tools can help you zero in on the part of your program that is causing the error and let you see the value of variables as they change during the course of the execution of the program.

Q&A

Q **Why bother with raising exceptions? Why not handle the error right where it happens?**

A Often, the same error can be generated in different parts of the code. Exceptions let you centralize the handling of errors. In addition, the part of the code that generates the error might not be the best place to determine how to handle the error.

Q **Why generate an object? Why not just pass an error code?**

A Objects are more flexible and powerful than error codes. They can convey more information, and the constructor/destructor mechanisms can be used for the creation and removal of resources that might be required to properly handle the exceptional condition.

Q **Why not use exceptions for nonerror conditions? Isn't it convenient to be able to express-train back to previous areas of the code, even when nonexceptional conditions exist?**

A Yes, some C++ programmers use exceptions for just that purpose. The danger is that exceptions might create memory leaks as the stack is unwound and some objects are inadvertently left in the free store. With careful programming techniques and a good compiler, this can usually be avoided. Otherwise, it is a matter of personal aesthetic; some programmers feel that, by their nature, exceptions should not be used for routine conditions.

Q **Does an exception have to be caught in the same place where the try block created the exception?**

A No, it is possible to catch an exception anywhere in the call stack. As the stack is unwound, the exception is passed up the stack until it is handled.

Q **Why use a debugger when I can use cout and other such statements?**

A The debugger provides a much more powerful mechanism for stepping through your code and watching values change without having to clutter your code with thousands of debugging statements. In addition, there is a significant risk each time you add or remove lines from your code. If you have just removed problems by debugging, and you accidentally delete a real code line when deleting your use of cout, you haven't helped the situation.

28

Workshop

The Workshop contains quiz questions to help solidify your understanding of the material covered and exercises to provide you with experience in using what you've learned. Try to answer the quiz and exercise questions before checking the answers in Appendix D, and be certain you understand the answers before going to the following lesson.

Quiz

1. What is an exception?
2. What is a `try` block?
3. What is a `catch` statement?
4. What information can an exception contain?
5. When are exception objects created?
6. Should you pass exceptions by value or by reference?
7. Will a `catch` statement catch a derived exception if it is looking for the base class?
8. If two `catch` statements are used, one for base and one for derived, which should come first?
9. What does `catch(...)` mean?
10. What is a breakpoint?

Exercises

1. Create a `try` block, a `catch` statement, and a simple exception.
2. Modify the answer from Exercise 1, put data into the exception along with an accessor function, and use it in the `catch` block.
3. Modify the class from Exercise 2 to be a hierarchy of exceptions. Modify the `catch` block to use the derived objects and the base objects.
4. Modify the program from Exercise 3 to have three levels of function calls.
5. **BUG BUSTERS:** What is wrong with the following code?

```
#include "stringc.h"          // our string class

class xOutOfMemory
{
  public:
     xOutOfMemory( const String& where ) : location( where ){}
     ~xOutOfMemory(){}
     virtual String where(){ return location };
```

```
  private:
    String location;
}

int main()
{
    try
    {
        char *var = new char;
        if ( var == 0 )
            throw xOutOfMemory();
    }
    catch( xOutOfMemory& theException )
    {
        cout << "Out of memory at " << theException.location() << endl;
    }
    return 0;
}
```

This listing shows exception handling for handling an out-of-memory error.

28

LESSON 29

Tapping Further into the Preprocessor

Congratulations! You are nearly done with an intensive introduction to C++. By now, you should have a solid understanding of C++, but in modern programming there is always more to learn. This final lesson fills in some missing details and then sets the course for continued study.

Most of what you write in your source code files is C++. This is interpreted by the compiler and turned into your program. Before the compiler runs, however, the preprocessor runs, and this provides an opportunity for conditional compilation.

In this lesson, you will learn

- What conditional compilation is and how to manage it

- How to use the preprocessor in finding bugs

- How to manipulate individual bits and use them as flags

- What the next steps are in learning to use C++ effectively

The Preprocessor and the Compiler

Every time you run your compiler, your preprocessor runs first. The preprocessor looks for preprocessor instructions, each of which begins with a pound symbol (#). The effect of each of these instructions is a change to the text of the source code. The result is a new source code file—a temporary file that you normally don't see, but that you can instruct the compiler to save so you can examine it if you want to.

The compiler does not read your original source code file; it reads the output of the preprocessor and compiles that file. You've seen the effect of this already with the `#include` directive. This instructs the preprocessor to find the file whose name follows the `#include` directive and to write it into the intermediate file at that location. It is as if you had typed that entire file right into your source code, and by the time the compiler sees the source code, the included file is there.

> **TIP**   Nearly every compiler has a switch that you can set either in the Integrated Development Environment (IDE) or at the command line, which instructs the compiler to save the intermediate file. Check your compiler manual for the right switches to set for your compiler if you want to examine this file.

The #define Preprocessor Directive

You can create string substitutions using the `#define` command. For example, if you write

```
#define BIG 512
```

you have instructed the precompiler to substitute the string 512 wherever it sees the string BIG. This is not a string in the C++ sense. The characters "512" are substituted in your source code wherever the word "BIG" is seen. Thus, if you write

```
#define BIG 512
int myArray[BIG];
```

the intermediate file produced by the precompiler looks like this:

```
int myArray[512];
```

Note that the `#define` statement is gone. Precompiler statements are all removed from the intermediate file; they do not appear in the final source code at all.

Using #define **for Constants**

One way to use #define is as a substitute for constants. This is almost never a good idea, however, because #define merely makes a string substitution and does no type checking. As explained in the section on constants, tremendous advantages exist in using the const keyword rather than #define.

29

Using #define **for Tests**

A second way to use #define is simply to declare that a particular character string is defined. Therefore, you could write

```
#define DEBUG
```

Later in your listing, you can test to determine whether BIG has been defined and take action accordingly. To check whether it is defined, you can use the preprocessor #if command followed by the defined command:

```
#if defined DEBUG
cout << Debug defined";
#endif
```

The defined expression evaluates to true if the name it tests, DEBUG in this case, has been defined already. Keep in mind that this happens in the preprocessor, not in the compiler or in the executing program.

When the preprocessor reads the #if defined, it checks a table it has built to see whether you've defined the value that follows. If you have, defined evaluates to true and everything between the #if defined DEBUG and its #endif is written into the intermediate file for compiling. If it evaluates to false, nothing between #if defined DEBUG and #endif is written into the intermediate file; it is as if it were never in the source code in the first place.

A shortcut directive also exists for checking defined values. This is the #ifdef directive:

```
#ifdef DEBUG
cout << "Debug defined";
#endif
```

You can also test to see whether a value is not defined. This is done by using the not operator with the defined directive:

```
#if !defined DEBUG
cout << "Debug is not defined";
#endif
```

There is also a shortcut version for this as well, `#ifndef`:

```
#ifndef DEBUG
cout << "Debug is not defined.";
#endif
```

Note that `#ifndef` is the logical reverse of `#ifdef`. `#ifndef` evaluates to true if the string has not been defined up to that point in the file.

You should notice that all of these checks required that `#endif` also be included to indicate the end of the code impacted by the check.

The `#else` **Precompiler Command**

As you might imagine, the term `#else` can be inserted between either `#ifdef` or `#ifndef` and the closing `#endif`. Listing 29.1 illustrates how these terms are used.

LISTING 29.1   Using #define

```
 0:  #define DemoVersion
 1:  #define SW_VERSION 5
 2:  #include <iostream>
 3:
 4:  using std::endl;
 5:  using std::cout;
 6:
 7:  int main()
 8:  {
 9:      cout << "Checking on the definitions of DemoVersion,";
10:      cout << "SW_VERSION, and WINDOWS_VERSION..." << endl;
11:
12:      #ifdef DemoVersion
13:         cout << "DemoVersion defined." << endl;
14:      #else
15:         cout << "DemoVersion not defined." << endl;
16:      #endif
17:
18:      #ifndef SW_VERSION
19:         cout << "SW_VERSION not defined!" << endl;
20:      #else
21:         cout << "SW_VERSION defined as: "
22:                    << SW_VERSION << endl;
23:      #endif
24:
25:      #ifdef WINDOWS_VERSION
26:         cout << "WINDOWS_VERSION defined!" << endl;
27:      #else
28:         cout << "WINDOWS_VERSION was not defined." << endl;
```

LISTING 29.1 Continued

```
29:     #endif
30:
31:     cout << "Done."  << endl;
32:     return 0;
33: }
```

29

Output ▼

```
Checking on the definitions of DemoVersion, NT_VERSION,_and WINDOWS_VERSION...
DemoVersion defined.
NT_VERSION defined as: 5
WINDOWS_VERSION was not defined.
Done.
```

Analysis ▼

On lines 0 and 1, DemoVersion and NT_VERSION are defined, with SW_VERSION defined with the string 5. On line 12, the definition of DemoVersion is tested, and because DemoVersion is defined (albeit with no value), the test is true and the string on line 13 is printed.

On line 18 is the test that SW_VERSION is not defined. Because SW_VERSION is defined, this test fails and execution jumps to line 21. Here the string 5 is substituted for the word SW_VERSION; this is seen by the compiler as

```
cout << "SW_VERSION defined as: " << 5 << endl;
```

Note that the first word SW_VERSION is not substituted because it is in a quoted string. The second SW_VERSION is substituted, however, and thus the compiler sees 5 as if you had typed 5 there.

Finally, on line 25, the program tests for WINDOWS_VERSION. Because you did not define WINDOWS_VERSION, the test fails and the message on line 28 is printed.

Inclusion and Inclusion Guards

You will create projects with many different files. You will probably organize your directories so that each class has its own header file (for example, .hpp) with the class declaration and its own implementation file (for example, .cpp) with the source code for the class methods.

Your main() function will be in its own .cpp file, and all the .cpp files will be compiled into .obj files, which will then be linked into a single program by the linker.

Because your programs will use methods from many classes, many header files will be included in each file. Also, header files often need to include one another. For example, the header file for a derived class's declaration must include the header file for its base class.

Imagine that the Animal class is declared in the file ANIMAL.hpp. The Dog class (which derives from Animal) must include the file ANIMAL.hpp in DOG.hpp, or Dog will not be able to derive from Animal. The Cat header also includes ANIMAL.hpp for the same reason.

If you create a program that uses both a Cat and a Dog, you will be in danger of including ANIMAL.hpp twice. This generates a compile-time error because it is not legal to declare a class (Animal) twice, even though the declarations are identical.

You can solve this problem with inclusion guards. At the top of your ANIMAL header file, you write these lines:

```
#ifndef ANIMAL_HPP
#define ANIMAL_HPP
...                        // the whole file goes here
#endif
```

This says that if you haven't defined the term ANIMAL_HPP, go ahead and define it now. Between the #define statement and the closing #endif are the entire contents of the file.

The first time your program includes this file, it reads the first line and the test evaluates to true; that is, you have not yet defined ANIMAL_HPP. So, it defines it and then includes the entire file.

The second time your program includes the ANIMAL.hpp file, it reads the first line and the test evaluates to false because you have already included ANIMAL.hpp. The preprocessor, therefore, doesn't process any lines until it reaches the next #else (in this case, there isn't one) or the next #endif (at the end of the file). Thus, it skips the entire contents of the file, and the class is not declared twice.

The actual name of the defined symbol (ANIMAL_HPP) is not important, although it is customary to use the filename in all uppercase with the dot (.) changed to an underscore. This is purely convention, but because you won't be able to give two files the same name, this convention works.

NOTE It never hurts to use inclusion guards. Often, they will save you hours of debugging time.

String Manipulation

The preprocessor provides two special operators for manipulating strings in macros. The stringizing operator (#) substitutes a quoted string for whatever follows the stringizing operator. The concatenation operator bonds two strings into one.

Stringizing

The stringizing operator puts quotes around any characters following the operator, up to the next whitespace. Thus, if you write

```
#define WRITESTRING(x) cout << #x
```

and then call

```
WRITESTRING(This is a string);
```

the precompiler turns it into

```
cout << "This is a string";
```

Note that the string `This is a string` is put into quotes, as required by `cout`.

Concatenation

The concatenation operator allows you to bond more than one term into a new word. The new word is actually a token that can be used as a class name, a variable name, an offset into an array, or anywhere else a series of letters might appear.

Assume for a moment that you have five functions named `fOnePrint`, `fTwoPrint`, `fThreePrint`, `fFourPrint`, and `fFivePrint`. You can then declare

```
#define fPRINT(x) f ## x ## Print
```

and then use it with `fPRINT(Two)` to generate `fTwoPrint` and with `fPRINT(Three)` to generate `fThreePrint`.

Predefined Macros

Many compilers predefine a number of useful macros, including `__DATE__`, `__TIME__`, `__LINE__`, and `__FILE__`. Each of these names is surrounded by two underscore characters to reduce the likelihood that the names will conflict with names you've used in your program.

When the precompiler sees one of these macros, it makes the appropriate substitutes. For `__DATE__`, the current date is substituted. For `__TIME__`, the current time is substituted. `__LINE__` and `__FILE__` are replaced with the source code line number and filename, respectively. You should note that this substitution is made when the source is precompiled, not when the program is run. If you ask the program to print __DATE__, you do not get the current date; instead, you receive the date the program was compiled. These predefined macros are very useful in logging and in analyzing problem code paths.

The assert() Macro

Many compilers offer an assert() macro. The assert() macro returns true if its parameter evaluates to true and takes some kind of action if it evaluates false. Many compilers abort the program on an assert() that fails; others throw an exception.

The assert() macro is used for debugging your program before you release it. In fact, if DEBUG is not defined, the preprocessor collapses the assert() so that no code from it is included in the generated source for the compiler. This is a great help during development, and when the final product ships, there is no performance penalty or increase in the size of the executable version of the program.

Rather than depending on the compiler-provided assert(), you are free to write your own assert() macro. Listing 29.2 provides a simple custom assert() macro and shows its use.

LISTING 29.2 A Simple assert() Macro

```
0:  // Listing 29.2 ASSERTS
1:  #define DEBUG
2:  #include <iostream>
3:  using namespace std;
4:
5:  #ifndef DEBUG
6:      #define ASSERT(x)
7:  #else
8:      #define ASSERT(x) \
9:              if (! (x)) \
10:             { \
11:                cout << "ERROR!! Assert " << #x << " failed << endl; \
12:                cout << " on line " << __LINE__ << endl; \
13:                cout << " in file " << __FILE__ << endl;  \
14:             }
15:  #endif
16:
17:  int main()
18:  {
19:     int x = 5;
20:     cout << "First assert: " << endl;
21:     ASSERT(x==5);
```

LISTING 29.2   Continued

```
22:     cout << "\nSecond assert: " << endl;
23:     ASSERT(x != 5);
24:     cout << "\nDone. << endl";
25:     return 0;
26:  }
```

Output ▼

```
First assert:

Second assert:
ERROR!! Assert x !=5 failed
 on line 24
 in file List2104.cpp

Done.
```

Analysis ▼

On line 1, the term DEBUG is defined. Typically, this is done from the command line (or the IDE) at compile time, so you can turn this on and off at will. On lines 8–14, the ASSERT() macro is defined. Typically, this is done in a header file, and that header (assert.hpp) is included in all your implementation files.

On line 5, the term DEBUG is tested. If it is not defined, ASSERT() is defined to create no code at all. If DEBUG is defined, the functionality defined on lines 8–14 is applied.

The ASSERT() itself is one long statement split across seven source code lines as far as the precompiler is concerned. On line 9, the value passed in as a parameter is tested; if it evaluates false, the statements on lines 11–13 are invoked, printing an error message. If the value passed in evaluates to true, no action is taken.

Debugging with assert()

When writing your program, you will often know deep down in your soul that something is true: A function has a certain value, a pointer is valid, and so forth. It is the nature of bugs that what you know to be true might not be so under some conditions. For example, you know that a pointer is valid, yet the program crashes. assert() can help you find this type of bug, but only if you make it a regular practice to use assert() liberally in your code. Every time you assign or are passed a pointer as a parameter or function return value, be certain to assert that the pointer is valid. Anytime your code depends on a particular value being in a variable, assert() that that is true.

No penalty is assessed for frequent use of `assert()`; it is removed from the code when you undefine debugging. It also provides good internal documentation, reminding the reader of what you believe is true at any given moment in the flow of the code.

Using `assert()` Versus Exceptions

Yesterday, you saw how to work with exceptions to handle error conditions. It is important to note that `assert()` is not intended to handle runtime error conditions such as bad data, out-of-memory conditions, unable to open file, and so forth. `assert()` is created to catch programming errors only. That is, if `assert()` "fires," you know you have a bug in your code.

This is critical because when you ship your code to your customers, instances of `assert()` are removed. You can't depend on `assert()` to handle a runtime problem because the `assert()` won't be there.

It is a common mistake to use `assert()` to test the return value from a memory assignment:

```
Animal *pCat = new Cat;
Assert(pCat);   // bad use of assert
pCat->SomeFunction();
```

This is a classic programming error; every time the programmer runs the program, enough memory is available and `assert()` never fires. After all, the programmer is running with lots of extra RAM to speed up the compiler, debugger, and so forth. The programmer then ships the executable, and the poor user, who has less memory, reaches this part of the program and the call to `new` fails and returns NULL. `assert()`, however, is no longer in the code and nothing indicates that the pointer points to NULL. As soon as the statement `pCat->SomeFunction()` is reached, the program crashes.

Getting NULL back from a memory assignment is not a programming error, although it is an exceptional situation. Your program must be able to recover from this condition, if only by throwing an exception. Remember: The entire `assert()` statement is gone when DEBUG is undefined. Exceptions are covered in detail in Lesson 28, "Exception Handling."

Side Effects

It is not uncommon to find that a bug appears only after the instances of `assert()` are removed. This is almost always due to the program unintentionally depending on side effects of things done in `assert()` and other debug-only code. For example, if you write

```
ASSERT (x = 5)
```

when you mean to test whether x `==` 5, you create a particularly nasty bug.

Suppose that just prior to this assert(), you called a function that set x equal to 0. With this assert(), you think you are testing whether x is equal to 5; in fact, you are setting x equal to 5. The test returns true because x = 5 not only sets x to 5, but returns the value 5, and because 5 is nonzero, it evaluates as true.

When you pass the assert() statement, x really is equal to 5 (you just set it!). Your program runs just fine. You're ready to ship it, so you turn off debugging. Now, the assert() disappears, and you are no longer setting x to 5. Because x was set to 0 just before this, it remains at 0 and your program breaks.

In frustration, you turn debugging back on, but hey! Presto! The bug is gone. Again, this is rather funny to watch, but not to live through, so be very careful about side effects in debugging code. If you see a bug that appears only when debugging is turned off, look at your debugging code with an eye out for nasty side effects.

Class Invariants

Most classes have some conditions that should always be true whenever you are finished with a class member function. These class invariants are the sine qua non of your class. For example, it might be true that your CIRCLE object should never have a radius of zero or that your ANIMAL should always have an age greater than zero and less than 100.

It can be very helpful to declare an Invariants() method that returns true only if each of these conditions is still true. You can then ASSERT(Invariants()) at the start and at the completion of every class method. The exception would be that your Invariants() would not expect to return true before your constructor runs or after your destructor ends. Listing 29.3 demonstrates the use of the Invariants() method in a trivial class.

LISTING 29.3   Using Invariants()

```
0:  #define DEBUG
1:  #define SHOW_INVARIANTS
2:  #include <iostream>
3:  #include <string.h>
4:  using namespace std;
5:
6:  #ifndef DEBUG
7:     #define ASSERT(x)
8:  #else
9:     #define ASSERT(x) \
10:            if (! (x)) \
11:            { \
12:               cout << "ERROR!! Assert " << #x << " failed" << endl; \
13:               cout << " on line " << __LINE__  << endl; \
14:               cout << " in file " << __FILE__ << endl;  \
```

LISTING 29.3   Continued

```
15:              }
16:  #endif
17:
18:
19:  const int FALSE = 0;
20:  const int TRUE = 1;
21:  typedef int BOOL;
22:
23:
24:  class String
25:  {
26:    public:
27:      // constructors
28:      String();
29:      String(const char *const);
30:      String(const String &);
31:      ~String();
32:
33:      char & operator[](int offset);
34:      char operator[](int offset) const;
35:
36:      String & operator= (const String &);
37:      int GetLen()const { return itsLen; }
38:      const char * GetString() const { return itsString; }
39:      BOOL Invariants() const;
40:
41:    private:
42:      String (int);          // private constructor
43:      char * itsString;
44:      // unsigned short itsLen;
45:      int itsLen;
46:  };
47:
48:  // default constructor creates string of 0 bytes
49:  String::String()
50:  {
51:      itsString = new char[1];
52:      itsString[0] = '\0';
53:      itsLen=0;
54:      ASSERT(Invariants());
55:  }
56:
57:  // private (helper) constructor, used only by
58:  // class methods for creating a new string of
59:  // required size.  Null filled.
60:  String::String(int len)
61:  {
62:      itsString = new char[len+1];
63:      for (int i = 0; i <= len; i++)
```

29

LISTING 29.3   Continued

```
64:             itsString[i] = '\0';
65:         itsLen=len;
66:         ASSERT(Invariants());
67:     }
68:
69:     // Converts a character array to a String
70:     String::String(const char * const cString)
71:     {
72:         itsLen = strlen(cString);
73:         itsString = new char[itsLen+1];
74:         for (int i = 0; i < itsLen; i++)
75:             itsString[i] = cString[i];
76:         itsString[itsLen]='\0';
77:         ASSERT(Invariants());
78:     }
79:
80:     // copy constructor
81:     String::String (const String & rhs)
82:     {
83:         itsLen=rhs.GetLen();
84:         itsString = new char[itsLen+1];
85:         for (int i = 0; i < itsLen;i++)
86:             itsString[i] = rhs[i];
87:         itsString[itsLen] = '\0';
88:         ASSERT(Invariants());
89:     }
90:
91:     // destructor, frees allocated memory
92:     String::~String ()
93:     {
94:         ASSERT(Invariants());
95:         delete [] itsString;
96:         itsLen = 0;
97:     }
98:
99:     // operator equals, frees existing memory
100:    // then copies string and size
101:    String& String::operator=(const String & rhs)
102:    {
103:        ASSERT(Invariants());
104:        if (this == &rhs)
105:            return *this;
106:        delete [] itsString;
107:        itsLen=rhs.GetLen();
108:        itsString = new char[itsLen+1];
109:        for (int i = 0; i < itsLen;i++)
110:            itsString[i] = rhs[i];
111:        itsString[itsLen] = '\0';
112:        ASSERT(Invariants());
```

LISTING 29.3 Continued

```
113:      return *this;
114:    }
115:
116:    //non constant offset operator
117:    char & String::operator[](int offset)
118:    {
119:       ASSERT(Invariants());
120:       if (offset > itsLen)
121:       {
122:          ASSERT(Invariants());
123:          return itsString[itsLen-1];
124:       }
125:       else
126:       {
127:          ASSERT(Invariants());
128:          return itsString[offset];
129:       }
130:    }
131:
132:    // constant offset operator
133:    char String::operator[](int offset) const
134:    {
135:       ASSERT(Invariants());
136:       char retVal;
137:       if (offset > itsLen)
138:          retVal = itsString[itsLen-1];
139:       else
140:          retVal = itsString[offset];
141:       ASSERT(Invariants());
142:       return retVal;
143:    }
144:
145:    BOOL String::Invariants() const
146:    {
147:       #ifdef SHOW_INVARIANTS
148:          cout << "String Tested OK ";
149:       #endif
150:       return ( (itsLen && itsString) || (!itsLen && !itsString) );
151:    }
152:
153:    class Animal
154:    {
155:      public:
156:        Animal():itsAge(1),itsName("John Q. Animal")
157:           {ASSERT(Invariants());}
158:        Animal(int, const String&);
159:        ~Animal(){}
160:        int GetAge() { ASSERT(Invariants()); return itsAge;}
161:        void SetAge(int Age)
162:        {
```

LISTING 29.3 Continued

```
163:        ASSERT(Invariants());
164:        itsAge = Age;
165:        ASSERT(Invariants());
166:      }
167:      String& GetName()
168:      {
169:        ASSERT(Invariants());
170:        return itsName;
171:      }
172:      void SetName(const String& name)
173:      {
174:        ASSERT(Invariants());
175:        itsName = name;
176:        ASSERT(Invariants());
177:      }
178:      BOOL Invariants();
179:   private:
180:      int itsAge;
181:      String itsName;
182: };
183:
184: Animal::Animal(int age, const String& name):
185:      itsAge(age),
186:      itsName(name)
187: {
188:      ASSERT(Invariants());
189: }
190:
191: BOOL Animal::Invariants()
192: {
193:      #ifdef SHOW_INVARIANTS
194:         cout << "Animal Tested OK";
195:      #endif
196:         return (itsAge > 0 && itsName.GetLen());
197: }
198:
199: int main()
200: {
201:      Animal sparky(5,"Sparky");
202:      cout << endl << sparky.GetName().GetString() << " is ";
203:      cout << sparky.GetAge() << " years old.";
204:      sparky.SetAge(8);
205:      cout << endl << sparky.GetName().GetString() << " is ";
206:      cout << sparky.GetAge() << " years old.";
207:      return 0;
208: }
```

29

Output ▼

```
String Tested OK String Tested OK String Tested OK String Tested OK String Teste
d OK String Tested OK String Tested OK String Tested OK String Tested OK String
Tested OK String Tested OK String Tested OK String Tested OK String Tested OK An
imal Tested OK String Tested OK Animal Tested OK
Sparky is Animal Tested OK 5 years old.Animal Tested OK Animal Tested OK Animal
Tested OK
Sparky is Animal Tested OK 8 years old.String Tested OK
```

Analysis ▼

On lines 9–15, the `ASSERT()` macro is defined. If `DEBUG` is defined, this writes out an error message when the `ASSERT()` macro evaluates `false`.

On line 39, the `String` class member function `Invariants()` is declared; it is defined on lines 143–150. The constructor is declared on lines 49–55; on line 54, after the object is fully constructed, `Invariants()` is called to confirm proper construction.

This pattern is repeated for the other constructors, and the destructor calls `Invariants()` only before it sets out to destroy the object. The remaining class functions call `Invariants()` before taking any action and then again before returning. This both affirms and validates a fundamental principle of C++: Member functions other than constructors and destructors should work on valid objects and should leave them in a valid state.

On line 176, class `Animal` declares its own `Invariants()` method, implemented on lines 189–195. Note on lines 155, 158, 161, and 163 that inline functions can call the `Invariants()` method.

Printing Interim Values

In addition to asserting that something is true using the `ASSERT()` macro, you might want to print the current value of pointers, variables, and strings. This can be very helpful in checking your assumptions about the progress of your program and in locating off-by-one bugs in loops. Listing 29.4 illustrates this idea.

LISTING 29.4   Printing Values in DEBUG Mode

```
0:  // Listing 29.4 - Printing values in DEBUG mode
1:  #include <iostream>
2:  using namespace std;
3:  #define DEBUG
4:
5:  #ifndef DEBUG
```

LISTING 29.4   Continued

```
 6:     #define PRINT(x)
 7:  #else
 8:     #define PRINT(x) \
 9:         cout << #x << ":\t" << x << endl;
10:  #endif
11:
12:  enum BOOL { FALSE, TRUE } ;
13:
14:  int main()
15:  {
16:     int x = 5;
17:     long y = 738981;
18:     PRINT(x);
19:     for (int i = 0; i < x; i++)
20:     {
21:        PRINT(i);
22:     }
23:
24:     PRINT (y);
25:     PRINT("Hi.");
26:     int *px = &x;
27:     PRINT(px);
28:     PRINT (*px);
29:     return 0;
30:  }
```

Output ▼

```
x:      5
i:      0
i:      1
i:      2
i:      3
i:      4
y:      73898
"Hi.":  Hi.
px:        0012FEDC
*px:    5
```

Analysis ▼

The PRINT() macro on lines 6 and 8–9 provides printing of the current value of the supplied parameter. Note that the first thing fed to cout on line 9 is the stringized version of the parameter; that is, if you pass in x, cout receives "x".

Next, `cout` receives the quoted string `":\t"`, which prints a colon and then a tab. Third, `cout` receives the value of the parameter (x), and then finally, `endl`, which writes a new line and flushes the buffer. Note that you might receive a value other than `0012FEDC`.

Bit Twiddling

Often, you will want to set flags in your objects to keep track of the state of your object. (Is it in `AlarmState`? Has this been initialized yet? Are you coming or going?)

You can do this with user-defined Booleans but some applications, particularly those with low-level drivers and hardware devices, require you to be able to use the individual bits of a variable as flags. Each byte has eight bits, so in a four-byte `long` you can hold 32 separate flags. A bit is said to be *set* if its value is 1 and clear if its value is 0. When you set a bit, you make its value 1, and when you clear it, you make its value 0. (*Set* and *clear* are both adjectives and verbs.) You can set and clear bits by changing the value of the `long`, but that can be tedious and confusing.

NOTE Appendix A, "Working with Numbers: Binary and Hexadecimal," provides valuable additional information about binary and hexadecimal manipulation.

C++ provides bitwise operators that act upon the individual bits of a variable. These look like, but are different from, the logical operators, so many novice programmers confuse them. The bitwise operators are presented in Table 29.1.

TABLE 29.1 The Bitwise Operators

Symbol	Operator
&	AND
|	OR
^	Exclusive OR
~	Complement

Operator AND

The AND operator (`&`) is a single ampersand, in contrast to the logical AND, which is two ampersands. When you AND two bits, the result is 1 if both bits are 1, but 0 if either or both bits are 0. The way to think of this is the following: The result is 1 if bit 1 is set and if bit 2 is set; otherwise, the result is 0.

Operator OR

The second bitwise operator is OR (|). Again, this is a single vertical bar, in contrast to the logical OR, which is two vertical bars. When you OR two bits, the result is 1 if either bit is set or if both are. If neither bit is set, the value is 0.

Operator Exclusive OR

The third bitwise operator is exclusive OR (^). When you exclusive OR two bits, the result is 1 if the two bits are different. The result is 0 if both bits are the same—if both bits are set or neither bit is set.

The Complement Operator

The complement operator (~) clears every bit in a number that is set and sets every bit that is clear. If the current value of the number is 1010 0011, the complement of that number is 0101 1100.

Setting Bits

When you want to set or clear a particular bit, you use masking operations. If you have a four-byte flag and you want to set bit 8 so that it is true (on), you need to OR the flag with the value 128.

Why? 128 is 1000 0000 in binary; thus, the value of the eighth bit is 128. Whatever the current value of that bit (set or clear), if you OR it with the value 128, you will set that bit and not change any of the other bits. Assume that the current value of the eight bits is 1010 0110 0010 0110. OR-ing 128 to it looks like this:

```
        9 8765 4321
  1010 0110 0010 0110    // bit 8 is clear
| 0000 0000 1000 0000    // 128
  _ _ _ _ _ _ _ _ _ _ _
  1010 0110 1010 0110    // bit 8 is set
```

You should note a few more things. First, as usual, bits are counted from right to left. Second, the value 128 is all zeros except for bit 8, the bit you want to set. Third, the starting number 1010 0110 0010 0110 is left unchanged by the OR operation, except that bit 8 was set. Had bit 8 already been set, it would have remained set, which is what you want.

Clearing Bits

If you want to clear bit 8, you can AND the bit with the complement of 128. The complement of 128 is the number you get when you take the bit pattern of 128 (1000 0000), set every bit that is clear, and clear every bit that is set (0111 1111). When you AND these numbers, the original number is unchanged, except for the eighth bit, which is forced to zero.

```
  1010 0110 1010 0110   // bit 8 is set
& 1111 1111 0111 1111   // ~128
  _ _ _ _ _ _ _ _ _
  1010 0110 0010 0110   // bit 8 cleared
```

To fully understand this solution, do the math yourself. Each time both bits are 1, write 1 in the answer. If either bit is 0, write 0 in the answer. Compare the answer with the original number. It should be the same except that bit 8 was cleared.

Flipping Bits

Finally, if you want to flip bit 8, no matter what its state, you exclusive OR the number with 128. If you do this twice, you end up back with the original setting. Thus,

```
  1010 0110 1010 0110   // number
^ 0000 0000 1000 0000   // 128
  _ _ _ _ _ _ _ _ _
  1010 0110 0010 0110   // bit flipped
^ 0000 0000 1000 0000   // 128
  _ _ _ _ _ _ _ _ _
  1010 0110 1010 0110   // flipped back
```

DO	DON'T
DO set bits by using masks and the OR operator.	**DON'T** confuse the different bit operators.
DO clear bits by using masks and the AND operator.	**DON'T** forget to consider bits to the left of the bit(s) you are flipping. One byte is eight bits; you need to know how many bytes are in the variable you are using.
DO flip bits using masks and the exclusive OR operator.	

Bit Fields

Under some circumstances, every byte counts, and saving six or eight bytes in a class can make all the difference. If your class or structure has a series of Boolean variables or variables that can have only a very small number of possible values, you might save some room using bit fields.

Using the standard C++ data types, the smallest type you can use in your class is a type char, which might be just one byte. You will usually end up using an int, which is most often four bytes on a machine with a 32-bit processor. By using bit fields, you can store eight binary values in a char and 32 such values in a four-byte integer.

Here's how bit fields work: Bit fields are named and accessed the same as any class member. Their type is always declared to be unsigned int. After the bit field name, write a colon followed by a number.

The number is an instruction to the compiler as to how many bits to assign to this variable. If you write 1, the bit represents either the value 0 or 1. If you write 2, two bits are used to represent numbers; thus, the field would be able to represent 0, 1, 2, or 3, a total of four values. A three-bit field can represent eight values, and so forth. Appendix A reviews binary numbers. Listing 29.5 illustrates the use of bit fields.

LISTING 29.5   Using Bit Fields

```
0:  #include <iostream>
1:  using namespace std;
2:  #include <string.h>
3:
4:  enum STATUS { FullTime, PartTime } ;
5:  enum GRADLEVEL { UnderGrad, Grad } ;
6:  enum HOUSING { Dorm, OffCampus };
7:  enum FOODPLAN { OneMeal, AllMeals, WeekEnds, NoMeals };
8:
9:  class student
10: {
11:    public:
12:       student():
13:          myStatus(FullTime),
14:          myGradLevel(UnderGrad),
15:          myHousing(Dorm),
16:          myFoodPlan(NoMeals)
17:       {}
18:       ~student(){}
19:       STATUS GetStatus();
20:       void SetStatus(STATUS);
21:       unsigned GetPlan() { return myFoodPlan; }
22:
23:    private:
24:       unsigned myStatus : 1;
25:       unsigned myGradLevel: 1;
26:       unsigned myHousing : 1;
27:       unsigned myFoodPlan : 2;
28: };
29:
```

LISTING 29.5   Continued

```
30:  STATUS student::GetStatus()
31:  {
32:     if (myStatus)
33:        return FullTime;
34:     else
35:        return PartTime;
36:  }
37:
38:  void student::SetStatus(STATUS theStatus)
39:  {
40:     myStatus = theStatus;
41:  }
42:
43:  int main()
44:  {
45:     student Jim;
46:
47:     if (Jim.GetStatus()== PartTime)
48:        cout << "Jim is part-time" << endl;
49:     else
50:        cout << "Jim is full-time" << endl;
51:
52:     Jim.SetStatus(PartTime);
53:
54:     if (Jim.GetStatus())
55:        cout << "Jim is part-time" << endl;
56:     else
57:        cout << "Jim is full-time" << endl;
58:
59:     cout << "Jim is on the " ;
60:
61:     char Plan[80];
62:     switch (Jim.GetPlan())
63:     {
64:       case OneMeal:  strcpy(Plan,"One meal"); break;
65:       case AllMeals: strcpy(Plan,"All meals"); break;
66:       case WeekEnds: strcpy(Plan,"Weekend meals"); break;
67:       case NoMeals:  strcpy(Plan,"No Meals");break;
68:       default :    cout << "Something bad went wrong! "<< endl;
69:                       break;
70:     }
71:     cout << Plan << " food plan." << endl;
72:     return 0;
73:  }
```

Output ▼

```
Jim is part-time
Jim is full-time
Jim is on the No Meals food plan.
```

Analysis ▼

On lines 4–7, several enumerated types are defined. These serve to define the possible values for the bit fields within the student class.

student is declared on lines 9–28. Although this is a trivial class, it is interesting because all the data is packed into five bits on lines 24–27. The first bit on line 24 represents the student's status, full-time or part-time. The second bit on line 25 represents whether this is an undergraduate. The third bit on line 26 represents whether the student lives in a dorm. The final two bits represent the four possible food plans.

The class methods are written as for any other class and are in no way affected by the fact that these are bit fields and not integers or enumerated types.

The member function GetStatus() on lines 30–36 reads the Boolean bit and returns an enumerated type, but this is not necessary. It could just as easily have been written to return the value of the bit field directly. The compiler would have done the translation. To prove that to yourself, replace the GetStatus() implementation with this code:

```
STATUS student::GetStatus()
{
    return myStatus;
}
```

No change whatsoever should occur in the functioning of the program. It is a matter of clarity when reading the code; the compiler isn't particular.

Note that the code on line 47 must check the status and then print the meaningful message. It is tempting to write this:

```
cout << "Jim is " << Jim.GetStatus() << endl;
```

that simply prints this:

```
Jim is 0
```

The compiler has no way to translate the enumerated constant PartTime into meaningful text.

On line 62, the program switches on the food plan, and for each possible value, it puts a reasonable message into the buffer, which is then printed on line 71. Note again that the switch statement could have been written as follows:

```
case  0: strcpy(Plan,"One meal"); break;
case  1: strcpy(Plan,"All meals"); break;
case  2: strcpy(Plan,"Weekend meals"); break;
case  3: strcpy(Plan,"No Meals");break;
```

The most important thing about using bit fields is that the client of the class need not worry about the data storage implementation. Because the bit fields are private, you can feel free to change them later and the interface will not need to change.

Programming Style

As stated elsewhere in this book, it is important to adopt a consistent coding style, although in many ways it doesn't matter which style you adopt. A consistent style makes it easier to guess what you meant by a particular part of the code, and you avoid having to look up whether you spelled the function with an initial cap the last time you invoked it.

The following guidelines are arbitrary; they are based on the guidelines used in projects done in the past, and they've worked well. You can just as easily make up your own, but these will get you started.

As Emerson said, "A foolish consistency is the hobgoblin of little minds," but having some consistency in your code is a good thing. Make up your own, but then treat it as if it were dispensed by the programming gods.

Indenting

If you use tabs, they should be three spaces. Be certain your editor converts each tab to three spaces.

Braces

How to align braces can be the most controversial topic between C++ programmers. Here are a few suggested tips:

- Matching braces should be aligned vertically.

- The outermost set of braces in a definition or declaration should be at the left margin. Statements within should be indented. All other sets of braces should be in line with their leading statements.

- No code should appear on the same line as a brace. For example,

```
if (condition==true)
{
    j = k;
    SomeFunction();
}
m++;
```

NOTE

As stated, the alignment of braces can be controversial. Many C++ programmers believe you should put the opening brace on the same line as the command it is associated with and the closing brace lines up with the command:

```
if (condition==true) {
    j = k;
    SomeFunction();
}
```

This format is considered harder to read because the braces don't line up.

Long Lines and Function Length

Keep lines to the width displayable on a single screen. Code that is off to the right is easily overlooked, and scrolling horizontally is annoying.

When a line is broken, indent the following lines. Try to break the line at a reasonable place, and try to leave the intervening operator at the end of the previous line (instead of at the beginning of the following line) so that it is clear that the line does not stand alone and that more is coming.

In C++, functions tend to be much shorter than they were in C, but the old, sound advice still applies. Try to keep your functions short enough to print the entire function on one page.

Structuring `switch` Statements

Indent switches as follows to conserve horizontal space:

```
switch(variable)
{
    case ValueOne:
        ActionOne();
        break;
    case ValueTwo:
        ActionTwo();
        break;
    default:
        assert("bad Action");
        break;
}
```

As you can see, the `case` statements are slightly indented and lined up. In addition, the statements within each case are lined up. With this layout, it is generally easy to find a case statement and easy to then follow its code.

Program Text

You can use several tips to create code that is easy to read. Code that is easy to read is generally easier to maintain.

- Use whitespace to help readability.
- Don't use spaces between object and array names and their operators (., ->, [ ]).
- Unary operators are associated with their operands, so don't put a space between them. Do put a space on the side away from the operand. Unary operators include !, ~, ++, --, -, * (for pointers), & (casts), and `sizeof`.
- Binary operators should have spaces on both sides: +, =, *, /, %, >>, <<, <, >, ==, !=, &, |, &&, ||, ?:, =, +=, and so on.
- Don't use lack of spaces to indicate precedence:

  (4+ 3*2).

- Put a space after commas and semicolons, not before.
- Parentheses should not have spaces on either side.
- Keywords, such as `if`, should be set off by a space: `if (a == b)`.
- The body of a single-line comment should be set off from the `//` with a space.
- Place the pointer or reference indicator next to the type name, not the variable name:

  ```
  char* foo;
  int& theInt;
  ```

  rather than

  ```
  char *foo;
  int &theInt;
  ```

- Do not declare more than one variable on the same line.

Naming Identifiers

The following are guidelines for working with identifier names:

- Identifier names should be long enough to be descriptive.
- Avoid cryptic abbreviations.

- Take the time and energy to spell things out.

- Do not use Hungarian notation. C++ is strongly typed and there is no reason to put the type into the variable name. With user-defined types (classes), Hungarian notation quickly breaks down. The exceptions to this might be to use a prefix for pointers (p) and references (r), as well as for class member variables (its).

- Short names (i, p, x, and so on) should be used only where their brevity makes the code more readable and where the usage is so obvious that a descriptive name is not needed. In general, however, you should avoid this. Also, avoid the use of the letters i, l, and o as variable names because they are easy to confuse with numbers.

- The length of a variable's name should be proportional to its scope.

- Be certain identifiers look and sound different from one another to minimize confusion.

- Function (or method) names are usually verbs or verb-noun phrases: `Search()`, `Reset()`, `FindParagraph()`, `ShowCursor()`. Variable names are usually abstract nouns, possibly with an additional noun: `count`, `state`, `windSpeed`, `windowHeight`. Boolean variables should be named appropriately: `windowIconized`, `fileIsOpen`.

Spelling and Capitalization of Names

Spelling and capitalization should not be overlooked when creating your own style. Some tips for these areas include the following:

- Use all uppercase and underscore to separate the logical words of `#defined` names, such as `SOURCE_FILE_TEMPLATE`. Note, however, that these are rare in C++. Consider using constants and templates in most cases.

- All other identifiers should use mixed case—no underscores. Function names, methods, class, typedef, and struct names should begin with a capitalized letter. Elements such as data members or locals should begin with a lowercase letter.

- Enumerated constants should begin with a few lowercase letters as an abbreviation for the enum. For example:
```
enum TextStyle
{
    tsPlain,
    tsBold,
    tsItalic,
    tsUnderscore,
};
```

29

Comments

Comments can make it much easier to understand a program. Sometimes, you will not work on a program for several days or even months. In that time, you can forget what certain code does or why it has been included. Problems in understanding code can also occur when someone else reads your code. Comments applied in a consistent, well-thought-out style can be well worth the effort. Several tips to remember concerning comments include the following:

- Wherever possible, use C++ single-line `//` comments rather than the `/* */` style. Reserve the multiline style (`/* */`) for commenting out blocks of code that might include C++ single-line comments.

- Higher-level comments are infinitely more important than process details. Add value; do not merely restate the code.

  ```
  n++; // n is incremented by one
  ```

  This comment isn't worth the time it takes to type it in. Concentrate on the semantics of functions and blocks of code. Say what a function does. Indicate side effects, types of parameters, and return values. Describe all assumptions that are made (or not made), such as "assumes n is nonnegative" or "will return –1 if x is invalid." Within complex logic, use comments to indicate the conditions that exist at that point in the code.

- Use complete English sentences with appropriate punctuation and capitalization. The extra typing is worth it. Don't be overly cryptic and don't abbreviate. What seems exceedingly clear to you as you write code will be amazingly obtuse in a few months.

- Use blank lines freely to help the reader understand what is going on. Separate statements into logical groups.

Setting Up Access

The way you access portions of your program should also be consistent. Some tips for access include the following:

- Always use `public:`, `private:`, and `protected:` labels; don't rely on the defaults.

- List the public members first, and then protected, and then private. List the data members in a group after the methods.

- Put the constructor(s) first in the appropriate section, followed by the destructor. List overloaded methods with the same name adjacent to each other. Group accessor functions together whenever possible.

29

- Consider alphabetizing the method names within each group and alphabetizing the member variables. Be certain to alphabetize the filenames in `include` statements.
- Even though the use of the `virtual` keyword is optional when overriding, use it anyway; it helps to remind you that it is virtual, and it also keeps the declaration consistent.

Class Definitions

Try to keep the definitions of methods in the same order as the declarations. It makes things easier to find.

When defining a function, place the return type and all other modifiers on a previous line so that the class name and function name begin at the left margin. This makes it much easier to find functions.

include Files

Try as hard as you can to minimize the use of `#include`, and thus minimize the number of files being included in header files. The ideal minimum is the header file for the class from which this one derives. Other mandatory includes are those for objects that are members of the class being declared. Classes merely pointed to or referenced need only forward references of the form.

Don't leave out an include file in a header just because you assume that whatever `.cpp` file includes this one will also have the needed include. And don't add extra ones to try to "help out" other included files.

TIP	All header files should use inclusion guards.

Using assert()

You learned about `assert()` earlier today. Use `assert()` freely. It helps find errors, but it also greatly helps a reader by making it clear what the assumptions are. It also helps to focus the writer's thoughts around what is valid and what isn't.

Making Items Constant with const

Use `const` wherever appropriate: for parameters, variables, and methods. Often, there is a need for both a `const` and a non-`const` version of a method; don't use this as an excuse to leave one out. Be very careful when explicitly casting from `const` to non-`const` and vice versa (at times, this is the only way to do something), but be certain that it makes sense, and include a comment.

Next Steps in Your C++ Development

You've spent four weeks working at C++, and you are likely to have the basics needed to be a competent C++ programmer, but you are by no means finished. There is much more to learn and many more places you can get valuable information as you move from novice C++ programmer to expert.

The following sections recommend a number of specific sources of information, and these recommendations reflect only personal experience and opinions. Dozens of books and thousands of articles are available on each of these topics, however, so be certain to get other opinions before purchasing.

Where to Get Help and Advice

The very first thing you will want to do as a C++ programmer will be to tap into one or more of the C++ communities on the Internet. These groups supply immediate contact with hundreds or thousands of C++ programmers who can answer your questions, offer advice, and provide a sounding board for your ideas.

The C++ Internet newsgroups (comp.lang.c++ and comp.lang.c++.moderated) are recommended as excellent sources of information and support. There are also sites such as http://www.CodeGuru.com and http://www.CodeProject.com. These two sites have hundreds of thousands of C++ developers come to them every month. They offer resources such as articles, tutorials, news, and discussions on C++. Numerous other such communities are available as well.

Also, you might want to look for local user groups. Many cities have C++ interest groups where you can meet other programmers and exchange ideas.

Finally, compiler vendors such as Borland and Microsoft have newsgroups that can be invaluable sources of information about their development environments and the C++ language.

Related C++ Topics: Managed C++, C#, and Microsoft's .NET

Microsoft's .NET platform is radically changing the way many of us develop for the Internet. A key component of .NET is the language C#, as well as a number of serious extensions to C++ called *Managed Extensions*.

C# is a natural extension of C++, and is an easy bridge to .NET for C++ programmers. A number of good books on C# are available, including *Programming C#* (O'Reilly Press), and of course, there is *Sams Teach Yourself the C# Language in 21 Days*, which follows a similar structure to the one used in this book.

As a programming language, C# has some differences from C++. For example, multiple inheritance is not allowed in C#; though the use of interfaces provides similar capabilities. In addition, C# avoids the use of pointers. This removes issues with dangling pointers and other such problems, at the price of making the language less capable of low-level, real-time programming. The final item worth mentioning on C# is that it uses a runtime and a garbage collector (GC). The GC takes care of freeing resources when they are needed so you, the programmer, don't have to.

Managed C++ is also from Microsoft and a part of .NET. In very simple terms, this is an extension to C++ that gives C++ the ability to use all the features of .NET, including the garbage collector and more.

DO	DON'T
DO look at other books. There's plenty to learn and no single book can teach you everything you need to know. **DO** join a good C++ user group.	**DON'T** just read code! The best way to learn C++ is to write C++ programs.

Summary

You learned more details about working with the preprocessor. Each time you run the compiler, the preprocessor runs first and translates your preprocessor directives such as #define and #ifdef.

The preprocessor does text substitution, although with the use of macros these can be somewhat complex. By using #ifdef, #else, and #ifndef, you can accomplish conditional compilation, compiling in some statements under one set of conditions and in another set of statements under other conditions. This can assist in writing programs for more than one platform and is often used to conditionally include debugging information.

Macro functions provide complex text substitution based on arguments passed at compile time to the macro. It is important to put parentheses around every argument in the macro to ensure the correct substitution takes place.

Macro functions, and the preprocessor in general, are less important in C++ than they were in C. C++ provides a number of language features, such as const variables and templates, that offer superior alternatives to use of the preprocessor.

You also learned how to set and test individual bits and how to allocate a limited number of bits to class members.

Finally, C++ style issues were addressed, and resources were provided for further study.

Q&A

Q If C++ offers better alternatives than the preprocessor, why is this option still available?

A First, C++ is backward-compatible with C, and all significant parts of C must be supported in C++. Second, some uses of the preprocessor are still used frequently in C++, such as inclusion guards.

Q Why use macro functions when I can use a regular function?

A Macro functions are expanded inline and are used as a substitute for repeatedly typing the same commands with minor variations. Again, however, templates usually offer a better alternative.

Q How do I know when to use a macro versus an inline function?

A Use inline functions whenever possible. Although macros offer character substitution, stringizing, and concatenation, they are not type safe and can make code that is more difficult to maintain.

Q What is the alternative to using the preprocessor to print interim values during debugging?

A The best alternative is to use watch statements within a debugger. For information on watch statements, consult your compiler or debugger documentation.

Q How do I decide when to use assert() and when to throw an exception?

A If the situation you're testing can be true without your having committed a programming error, use an exception. If the only reason for this situation to ever be true is a bug in your program, use assert().

Q When would I use bit structures rather than simply using integers?

A When the size of the object is crucial. If you are working with limited memory or with communications software, you might find that the savings offered by these structures is essential to the success of your product.

Q Can I assign a pointer to a bit field?

A No. Memory addresses usually point to the beginning of a byte. A bit field might be in the middle of a byte.

Q Why do style wars generate so much emotion?

A Programmers become very attached to their habits. If you are used to the following indentation:

```
if (SomeCondition){
    // statements
}    // closing brace
```

it is a difficult transition to give it up. New styles look wrong and create confusion. If you get bored, try logging in to a popular online service and asking which indentation style works best, which editor is best for C++, or which product is the best word processor. Then sit back and watch as ten thousand messages are generated, all contradicting one another.

Workshop

The Workshop provides quiz questions to help you solidify your understanding of the material covered and exercises to provide you with experience in using what you've learned. Try to answer the quiz and exercise questions before checking the answers in Appendix D, and be certain you understand the answers.

Quiz

1. Why would you use an assert?
2. What is the use of predefined macros such as __FILE__?
3. How many bit values could be stored in a two-byte variable?
4. How many values can be stored in five bits?
5. What is the result of 0011 1100 | 1111 1111?
6. What is the result of 0011 1100 & 1111 1111?

Exercises

1. Write the inclusion guard statements for the header file STRING.H.
2. Write an assert() macro that prints an error message and the file and line number if debug level is 2, prints a message (without file and line number) if the level is 1, and does nothing if the level is 0.

3. Write a macro `DPrint` that tests whether `DEBUG` is defined and, if it is, prints the value passed in as a parameter.

4. Write the declaration for creating a month, day, and year variable all stored within a single `unsigned int` variable.

Appendixes

APPENDIX A

Working with Numbers: Binary and Hexadecimal

You learned the fundamentals of arithmetic so long ago, it is hard to imagine what it would be like without that knowledge. When you look at the number 145, you instantly see "one hundred forty-five" without much reflection.

You generally see numbers in what is called the *decimal format*. There are, however, other formats that can be used for numbering. When working with computers, the two systems that come up the most are binary and hexadecimal. Understanding binary and hexadecimal requires that you re-examine the number 145 and see it not as a number, but as a code for a number.

Start small: Examine the relationship between the number three and "3." The number three is an idea; the numeral "3" is a squiggle on a piece of paper. The numeral is used to represent the number. The distinction can be made clear by realizing that three, 3, |||, III, and *** all can be used to represent the same idea of three.

In base 10 (decimal) math, you use ten symbols—the numerals 0, 1, 2, 3, 4, 5, 6, 7, 8, and 9—to represent all numbers. How is the number ten represented?

You can imagine that a strategy could have evolved of using the letter A to represent ten; or IIIIIIIIII could have been used to represent that idea. The Romans used X. The Arabic system, which we use, makes use of position in conjunction with numerals to represent values. The first (right-most) column is used for ones, and the next column (to the left) is used for tens. Thus, the number fifteen is represented as 15 (read "one, five"); that is, 1 ten and 5 ones.

Certain rules emerge, from which some generalizations can be made:

1. Base 10 uses ten digits—the digits 0–9.

2. The columns are powers of ten: 1s, 10s, 100s, and so on.

3. If the third column is 100, the largest number you can make with two columns is 99. More generally, with n columns you can represent from 0 to (10^n–1). Thus, with three columns, you can represent from 0 to (10^3–1) or 0–999.

Using Other Bases

It is not a coincidence that we use base 10; we have 10 fingers. You can imagine a different base, however. Using the rules found in base 10, you can describe base 8:

1. There are eight digits used in base 8—the digits 0–7.

2. The columns are powers of 8: 1s, 8s, 64s, and so on.

3. With n columns, you can represent 0 to 8^n–1.

To distinguish numbers written in each base, write the base as a subscript next to the number. The number fifteen in base 10 would be written as 15_{10} and read as "one, five, base ten."

Thus, to represent the number 15_{10} in base 8, you would write 17_8. This is read "one, seven, base eight." Note that it can also be read "fifteen" as that is the number it continues to represent.

Why 17? The 1 means 1 eight, and the 7 means 7 ones. One eight plus seven ones equals fifteen. Consider fifteen asterisks:

```
**********     *****
```

The natural tendency is to make two groups, a group of ten asterisks and another of five. This would be represented in decimal as 15 (1 ten and 5 ones). You can also group the asterisks as

```
********        *******
```

That is, eight asterisks and seven. That would be represented in base 8 as 17_8. That is, one eight and seven ones.

Converting to Different Bases

You can represent the number fifteen in base 10 as 15, in base 9 as 16_9, in base 8 as 17_8, in base 7 as 21_7. Why 21_7? In base 7, there is no numeral 8. To represent fifteen, you need two sevens and one 1.

How do you generalize the process? To convert a base 10 number to base 7, think about the columns: In base 7, they are ones, sevens, forty-nines, three-hundred forty-threes, and so on. Why these columns? They represent 7^0, 7^1, 7^2, 7^4, and so forth.

Remember, any number to the 0th power (for example, 7^0) is 1; any number to the first power (for example, 7^1) is the number itself; any number to the second power is that number times itself ($7^2 = 7 \times 7 = 49$); and any number to the third power is that number times itself and then times itself again ($7^3 = 7 \times 7 \times 7 = 343$).

A

Create a table for yourself:

Column	4	3	2	1
Power	7^3	7^2	7^1	7^0
Value	343	49	7	1

The first row represents the column number. The second row represents the power of 7. The third row represents the decimal value of each number in that row.

To convert from a decimal value to base 7, here is the procedure: Examine the number and decide which column to use first. If the number is 200, for example, you know that column 4 (343) is 0, and you don't have to worry about it.

To find out how many 49s there are, divide 200 by 49. The answer is 4, so put 4 in column 3 and examine the remainder: 4. There are no 7s in 4, so put a zero in the 7s column. There are 4 ones in 4, so put a 4 in the 1s column. The answer is 404_7.

Column	4	3		2	1
Power	7^3	7^2		7^1	7^0
Value	343	49		7	1
200 in base 7	0	4		0	4
Decimal value	0	$4 \times 49 = 196$	0	$4 \times 1 = 4$	

In this example, the 4 in the third column represents the decimal value 196, and the 4 in the first column represents the value 4. $196 + 4 = 200$. Thus, $404_7 = 200_{10}$.

Try another example. Convert the number 968 to base 6:

Column	5	4	3	2	1
Power	6^4	6^3	6^2	6^1	6^0
Value	1296	216	36	6	1

Be certain you are comfortable with why these are the column values. Remember that 6^3 = 6×6×6 = 216.

To determine the base 6 representation of 968, you start at column 5. How many 1296s are there in 968? There are none, so column 5 has 0. Dividing 968 by 216 yields 4 with a remainder of 104. Column 4 is 4. That is, column 4 represents 4×216 (864).

You must now represent the remaining value (968–864 = 104). Dividing 104 by 36 yields 2 with a remainder of 32. Column 3 is 2. Dividing 32 by 6 yields 5 with a remainder of 2. The answer therefore is 4252_6.

Column	5	4	3	2	1
Power	6^4	6^3	6^2	6^1	6^0
Value	1296	216	36	6	1
968 in base 6	0	4	2	5	2
Decimal value	0	4×216=864	2×36=72	5×6=30	2×1=2

864+72+30+2 = 968.

Binary

Base 2 is the ultimate extension of this idea. In base 2, also called *binary*, there are only two digits: 0 and 1. The columns are

Column	8	7	6	5	4	3	2	1
Power	2^7	2^6	2^5	2^4	2^3	2^2	2^1	2^0
Value	128	64	32	16	8	4	2	1

To convert the number 88 to base 2, you follow the same procedure: There are no 128s, so column 8 is 0.

There is one 64 in 88, so column 7 is 1 and 24 is the remainder. There are no 32s in 24 so column 6 is 0.

There is one 16 in 24 so column 5 is 1. The remainder is 8. There is one 8 in 8, and so column 4 is 1. There is no remainder, so the rest of the columns are 0.

Column	8	7	6	5	4	3	2	1
Power	2^7	2^6	2^5	2^4	2^3	2^2	2^1	2^0
Value	128	64	32	16	8	4	2	1
88_2	0	1	0	1	1	0	0	0
Value	0	64	0	16	8	0	0	0

To test this answer, convert it back:

```
1 * 64 =  64
0 * 32 =   0
1 * 16 =  16
1 *  8 =   8
0 *  4 =   0
0 *  2 =   0
0 *  1 =   0
          88
```

A

Why Base 2?

Base 2 is important in programming because it corresponds so cleanly to what a computer needs to represent. Computers do not really know anything at all about letters, numerals, instructions, or programs. At their core, they are just circuitry, and at a given juncture there either is a lot of power or there is very little.

To keep the logic clean, engineers do not treat this as a relative scale (a little power, some power, more power, lots of power, tons of power), but rather as a binary scale ("enough power" or "not enough power"). Rather than saying "enough" or "not enough," they simplify it to "yes" or "no." Yes or no, or true or false, can be represented as 1 or 0. By convention, 1 means true or yes, but that is just a convention; it could just as easily have meant false or no.

After you make this great leap of intuition, the power of binary becomes clear: With 1s and 0s, you can represent the fundamental truth of every circuit (there is power or there isn't). All a computer ever knows is, "Is you is, or is you ain't?" Is you is = 1; is you ain't = 0.

Bits, Bytes, and Nybbles

After the decision is made to represent truth and falsehood with 1s and 0s, *binary digits* (or bits) become very important. Because early computers could send eight bits at a time, it was natural to start writing code using 8-bit numbers—called bytes.

> **NOTE**   Half a byte (4 bits) is called a nybble!

With eight binary digits, you can represent up to 256 different values. Why? Examine the columns: If all 8 bits are set (1), the value is 255 (128+64+32+16+8+4+2+1). If none is set (all the bits are clear or zero), the value is 0. 0–255 is 256 possible states.

What's a KB?

It turns out that 2^{10} (1024) is roughly equal to 10^3 (1000). This coincidence was too good to miss, so computer scientists started referring to 2^{10} bytes as 1K or 1 kilobyte, based on the scientific prefix of kilo for thousand.

Similarly, 1024*1024 (1,048,576) is close enough to one million to receive the designation 1MB or 1 megabyte, and 1024 megabytes is called 1 gigabyte (*giga* implies thousand-million or billion). Finally, 1024 gigabytes is called a *terabyte*.

Binary Numbers

Computers use patterns of 1s and 0s to encode everything they do. Machine instructions are encoded as a series of 1s and 0s and interpreted by the fundamental circuitry. Arbitrary sets of 1s and 0s can be translated back into numbers by computer scientists, but it would be a mistake to think that these numbers have intrinsic meaning.

For example, the Intel 8086 chipset interprets the bit pattern 1001 0101 as an instruction. You certainly can translate this into decimal (149), but that number per se has no meaning.

Sometimes the numbers are instructions, sometimes they are values, and sometimes they are codes. One important standardized code set is ASCII. In ASCII, every letter and punctuation is given a seven-digit binary representation. For example, the lowercase letter "a" is represented by 0110 0001. This is not a number, although you can translate it to the number 97 in base 10 (64+32+1). It is in this sense that people say that the letter "a" is represented by 97 in ASCII; but the truth is that the binary representation of 97, 01100001, is the encoding of the letter "a," and the decimal value 97 is a human convenience.

Hexadecimal

Because binary numbers are difficult to read, a simpler way to represent the same values is sought. Translating from binary to base 10 involves a fair bit of manipulation of numbers; but it turns out that translating from base 2 to base 16 is very simple because there is a very good shortcut.

To understand this, you must first understand base 16, which is known as *hexadecimal.* In base 16, there are sixteen numerals: 0, 1, 2, 3, 4, 5, 6, 7, 8, 9, A, B, C, D, E, and F. The last six are arbitrary; the letters A–F were chosen because they are easy to represent on a keyboard. The columns in hexadecimal are

Column	4	3	2	1
Power	16^3	16^2	16^1	16^0
Value	4096	256	16	1

To translate from hexadecimal to decimal, you can multiply. Thus, the number F8C represents:

```
F * 256 = 15 * 256 = 3840
8 * 16 =              128
C * 1 = 12 * 1 =      12
3980
```

(Remember that F in hexadecimal is equal to 15_{10}.)

Translating the number FC to binary is best done by translating first to base 10, and then to binary:

```
F * 16 = 15 * 16 =   240
C * 1 = 12 * 1 =      12
252
```

Converting 252_{10} to binary requires the chart:

Column	9	8	7	6	5	4	3	2	1
Power	2^8	2^7	2^6	2^5	2^4	2^3	2^2	2^1	2^0
Value	256	128	64	32	16	8	4	2	1

There are no 256s.

$1\times128 = 128.\ 252{-}128 = 124$

$1\times64 = 64.\ 124{-}64 = 60$

$1\times32 = 32.\ 60{-}32 = 28$

$1\times16 = 16.\ 28{-}16 = 12$

$1\times8 = 8.\ 12{-}8 = 4$

1×4 = 4. 4–4 = 0

0×2 = 0

0×1 = 0

124+60+28+12+4 = 252.

Thus, the answer in binary is 11111100.

Now, it turns out that if you treat this binary number as two sets of four digits (1111 1100), you can do a magical transformation.

The right set is 1100. In decimal that is 12, or in hexadecimal it is C. (1×8 + 1×4 + 0×2 + 0×1)

The left set is 1111, which in base 10 is 15, or in hex is F.

Thus, you have

```
1111 1100
F    C
```

Putting the two hex numbers together is FC, which is the real value of 1111 1100. This shortcut always works! You can take a binary number of any length, reduce it to sets of four, translate each set of four to hex, and put the hex numbers together to get the result in hex. Here's a much larger number:

```
1011 0001 1101 0111
```

To check this assumption, first convert this number to decimal.

You can find the value of the columns by doubling. The rightmost column is 1, the next is 2, then 4, 8, 16, and so forth.

Start with the rightmost column, which is worth 1 in decimal. You have a 1 there, so that column is worth 1. The next column to the left is 2. Again, you have a 1 in that column, so add 2 for a total of 3.

The next column to the left is worth 4 (you double for each column). Thus, you have 4+2+1 = 7.

Continue this for each column:

```
1×1            1
1×2            2
1×4            4
0×8            0
1×16           16
0×32           0
1×64           64
1×128          128
1×256          256
0×512          0
0×1024         0
0×2048         0
1×4096         4096
1×8192         8192
0×16384        0
1×32768        32,768
Total          45,527
```

Converting this to hexadecimal requires a chart with the hexadecimal values.

Column	5	4	3	2	1
Power	16^4	16^3	16^2	16^1	16^0
Value	65536	4096	256	16	1

The number is less than 65,536, so you can start with the fourth column. There are eleven 4096s (45,056), with a remainder of 471. There is one 256 in 471 with a remainder of 215. There are thirteen 16s (208) in 215 with a remainder of 7. Thus, the hexadecimal number is B1D7.

Checking the math:

```
B (11) * 4096 =    45,056
1 * 256 =             256
D (13) * 16 =         208
7 * 1 =                 7
Total             45,527
```

The shortcut version is to take the original binary number, 1011000111010111, and break it into groups of four: 1011 0001 1101 0111. Each of the four then is evaluated as a hexadecimal number:

```
1011 =
1 x 1 =    1
1 x 2 =    2
0 x 4 =    0
1 x 8 =    8
Total      11
Hex:       B

0001 =
1 x 1 =    1
0 x 2 =    0
0 x 4 =    0
0 x 8 =    0
Total      1
Hex:       1

1101 =
1 x 1 =    1
0 x 2 =    0
1 x 4 =    4
1 x 8 =    8
Total      13
Hex =      D

0111 =
1 x 1 =    1
1 x 2 =    2
1 x 4 =    4
0 x 8 =    0
Total      7
Hex:       7

Total Hex:   B1D7
```

Hey! Presto! The shortcut conversion from binary to hexadecimal gives us the same answer as the longer version.

You will find that programmers use hexadecimal fairly frequently in advanced programming; but you'll also find that you can work quite effectively in programming for a long time without ever using any of this!

NOTE

One common place to see the use of hexadecimal is when working with color values. This is true in your C++ programs or even in other areas such as HTML.

APPENDIX B
C++ Keywords

Keywords are reserved to the compiler for use by the language. You cannot define classes, variables, or functions that have these keywords as their names.

asm	new	In addition, the following
auto	operator	words are reserved:
bool	private	
break	protected	and
case	public	and_eq
catch	register	bitand
char	reinterpret_cast	bitor
class	return	compl
const	short	not
const_cast	signed	not_eq
continue	sizeof	or
default	static	or_eq
delete	static_cast	xor
do	struct	xor_eq
double	switch	
dynamic_cast	template	
else	this	
enum	throw	
explicit	true	
export	try	
extern	typedef	
false	typeid	
float	typename	
for	union	
friend	unsigned	
goto	using	
if	virtual	
inline	void	
int	volatile	
long	wchar_t	
mutable	while	
namespace		

APPENDIX C
Operator Precedence

It is important to understand that operators have a precedence, but it is not essential to memorize the precedence.

Precedence is the order in which a program performs the operations in a formula. If one operator has precedence over another operator, it is evaluated first.

Higher precedence operators "bind tighter" than lower precedence operators; thus, higher precedence operators are evaluated first. The lower an operator's rank in Table C.1, the higher its precedence.

TABLE C.1   The Precedence of Operators

Rank	Name	Operator
1	Scope resolution	`::`
2	Member selection, subscripting, function calls, postfix increment and decrement	`. ->`
		`( )`
		`++ --`
3	`Sizeof`, prefix increment and decrement, complement, and, not, unary minus and plus, address-of and dereference, `new`, `new[]`, `delete`, `delete[]`, casting, `sizeof()`	`++ --`
		`^ !`
		`- +`
		`& *`
		`( )`
4	Member selection for pointer	`.* ->*`
5	Multiply, divide, modulo	`* / %`
6	Add, subtract	`+ -`
7	Shift (shift left, shift right)	`<< >>`
8	Inequality relational	`< <= > >=`
9	Equality, inequality	`== !=`
10	Bitwise AND	`&`
11	Bitwise exclusive OR	`^`
12	Bitwise OR	`|`
13	Logical AND	`&&`
14	Logical OR	`||`
15	Conditional	`?:`
16	Assignment operators	`= *= /= %=`
		`+= -= <<=`
		`>>=`
		`&= |= ^=`
17	Comma	`,`

APPENDIX D
Answers

Lesson 1, "Getting Started"

Quiz

1. Interpreters read through source code and translate a program, turning the programmer's code, or program instructions, directly into actions. Compilers translate source code into an executable program that can be run later.

2. Every compiler is different. Be certain to check the documentation that came with your compiler.

3. The linker's job is to tie together your compiled code with the libraries supplied by your compiler vendor and other sources. The linker lets you build your program in pieces and then link together the pieces into one big program.

4. Edit source code, compile, link, test (run), and repeat if necessary.

Exercises

1. This program initializes two integer variables (numbers) and then prints out their sum, 12, and their product, 35.

2. See your compiler manual.

3. You must put a # symbol before the word include on the first line.

4. This program prints the words Hello World to the console, followed by a new line (carriage return).

Lesson 2, "The Anatomy of a C++ Program"

Quiz

1. Each time you run your compiler, the preprocessor runs first. It reads through your source code and includes the files you've asked for, and performs other housekeeping chores. The compiler then runs to convert your preprocessed source code to object code.

2. `main()` is special because it is called automatically each time your program is executed. It might not be called by any other function and it must exist in every program.

3. C++-style, single-line comments are started with two slashes (`//`) and they comment out any text until the end of the line. Multiline, or C-style, comments are identified with marker pairs (`/* */`), and everything between the matching pairs is commented out. You must be careful to ensure that you have matched pairs.

4. C++-style, single-line comments can be nested within multiline, C-style comments:
   ```
   /* This marker starts a comment. Everything including
   // this single line comment,
   is ignored as a comment until the end marker */
   ```

   You can, in fact, nest slash-star style comments within double-slash, C++-style comments as long as you remember that the C++-style comments end at the end of the line.

5. Multiline, C-style comments can be longer than one line. If you want to extend C++-style, single-line comments to a second line, you must put another set of double slashes (`//`).

Exercises

1. The following is one possible answer:
   ```
   #include <iostream>
   using namespace std;
   int main()
   {
      cout << "I love C++\n";
      return 0;
   }
   ```

2. The following program contains a `main()` function that does nothing. This is, however, a complete program that can be compiled, linked, and run. When run, it appears that nothing happens because the program does nothing!

```
int main(){}
```

3. Line 4 is missing an opening quote for the string.

4. The following is the corrected program:

```
#include <iostream>
main()
{
    std::cout << "Is there a bug here?";
}
```

This listing prints the following to the screen:

```
Is there a bug here?
```

5. The following is one possible solution:

```
#include <iostream>
int Add (int first, int second)
{
    std::cout << "Add(), received " << first << " and " <<second<< "\n";
    return (first + second);
}

int Subtract (int first, int second)
{
    std::cout<< "Subtract(), received "<<first<<" and "<<second<<"\n";
    return (first - second);
}

int main()
{
    using std::cout;
    using std::cin;

    cout << "I'm in main()!\n";
    int a, b, c;
    cout << "Enter two numbers: ";
    cin >> a;
    cin >> b;

    cout << "\nCalling Add()\n";
    c=Add(a,b);
    cout << "\nBack in main().\n";
    cout << "c was set to " << c;
```

D

```
cout << "\n\nCalling Subtract()\n";
c=Subtract(a,b);
cout << "\nBack in main().\n";
cout << "c was set to " << c;

cout << "\nExiting...\n\n";
return 0;
}
```

Lesson 3, "Using Variables, Declaring Constants"

Quiz

1. Integer variables are whole numbers; floating-point variables are reals and have a floating decimal point. Floating-point numbers can be represented using a mantissa and exponent.

2. The keyword `unsigned` means that the integer will hold only positive numbers. On most computers with 32-bit processors, `short` integers are two bytes and `long` integers are four. The only guarantee, however, is that a `long` integer is at least as big or bigger than a regular integer, which is at least as big as a `short` integer. Generally, a `long` integer is twice as large as a `short` integer.

3. A symbolic constant explains itself; the name of the constant tells what it is for. Also, symbolic constants can be redefined at one location in the source code, rather than the programmer having to edit the code everywhere the literal is used.

4. `const` variables are typed. Therefore, the compiler can check for errors in how such variables are used. Also, they survive the preprocessor, and therefore the name is available in the debugger. Most importantly, using `#define` to declare constants is no longer supported by the C++ standard.

5. A good variable name tells you what the variable is for; a bad variable name has no information. `myAge` and `PeopleOnTheBus` are good variable names, but `x`, `xjk`, and `prndl` are probably less useful.

6. `BLUE = 102`

7.
   a. Good
   b. Not legal
   c. Legal, but a bad choice
   d. Good
   e. Legal, but a bad choice

Exercises

1. The following are appropriate answers for each:

   a. `unsigned short int`

   b. `unsigned long int` or `unsigned float`

   c. `unsigned double`

   d. `unsigned short int`

2. The following are possible answers:

   a. `myAge`

   b. `backYardArea`

   c. `StarsInGalaxy`

   d. `averageRainFall`

3. The following is a declaration for pi:
   ```
   const float PI = 3.14159;
   ```

4. The following declares and initializes the variable:
   ```
   float myPi = PI;
   ```

Lesson 4, "Managing Arrays and Strings"

Quiz

1. `SomeArray[0]`, `SomeArray[24]`

2. Write a set of subscripts for each dimension. For example, `SomeArray[2][3][2]` is a three-dimensional array. The first dimension has two elements, the second has three, and the third has two.

3. `SomeArray[2][3][2] = {0};`

4. 10×5×20=1000

5. This string contains 16 characters—the 15 characters you see and the null character that ends the string.

6. The null character that terminates the string.

Exercises

1. The following is one possible solution. Your array might have a different name, but should be followed by `[3][3]` in order to hold a 3-by-3 board.
   ```
   int GameBoard[3][3];
   ```

2. `int GameBoard[3][3] = { {0,0,0},{0,0,0},{0,0,0} }`

or

```
int GameBoard[3][3] = {0}
```

3. The following is one possible solution. This uses the `strcpy()` and `strlen()` functions.

```cpp
#include <iostream>
#include <string.h>
using namespace std;

int main()
{
    char firstname[] = "Alfred";
    char middlename[] = "E";
    char lastname[] = "Numan";
    char fullname[80];
    int  offset = 0;

    strcpy(fullname,firstname);
    offset = strlen(firstname);
    strcpy(fullname+offset," ");
    offset += 1;
    strcpy(fullname+offset,middlename);
    offset += strlen(middlename);
    strcpy(fullname+offset,". ");
    offset += 2;
    strcpy(fullname+offset,lastname);

    cout << firstname << "-" << middlename << "-"
         << lastname << endl;
    cout << "Fullname: " << fullname << endl;

    return 0;
}
```

4. The array is five elements by four elements, but the code initializes 4×5.

5. You wanted to write i<5, but you wrote i<=5 instead. The code will run when i ==
5 and j == 4, but there is no such element as `SomeArray[5][4]`.

Lesson 5, "Working with Expressions, Statements, and Operators"

Quiz

1. An expression is any statement that returns a value.

2. Yes, x = 5+7 is an expression with a value of 12.

3. The value of 201/4 is 50.

4. The value of 201%4 is 1.

5. Their values are myAge: 41, a: 39, b: 41.

6. The value of 8+2×3 is 14.

7. `if(x = 3)` assigns 3 to x and returns the value 3, which is interpreted as true. `if(x == 3)` tests whether x is equal to 3; it returns true if the value of x is equal to 3 and false if it is not.

8. The answers are

   a. False

   b. True

   c. True

   d. False

   e. True

Exercises

1. The following is one possible answer:

```
if (x > y)
    x = y;
else            // y > x || y == x
    y = x;
```

2. See exercise 3.

3. Entering **20**, **10**, **50** gives back a: **20**, b: **30**, c: **10**.

   Line 14 is assigning, not testing for equality.

4. See exercise 5.

5. Because line 6 is assigning the value of a-b to c, the value of the assignment is a (2) minus b (2), or 0. Because 0 is evaluated as false, the `if` fails and nothing prints.

Lesson 6, "Organizing Code with Functions"

Quiz

1. The function prototype declares the function; the definition defines it. The prototype ends with a semicolon; the definition need not. The declaration can include the keyword `inline` and default values for the parameters; the definition cannot. The declaration need not include names for the parameters; the definition must.

2. No. All parameters are identified by position, not name.

3. Declare the function to return `void`.

4. Any function that does not explicitly declare a return type returns `int`. You should always declare the return type as a matter of good programming practice.

5. A local variable is a variable passed into or declared within a block, typically a function. It is visible only within the block.

6. Scope refers to the visibility and lifetime of local and global variables. Scope is usually established by a set of braces.

7. Recursion generally refers to the capability of a function to call itself.

8. Global variables are typically used when many functions need access to the same data. Global variables are very rare in C++; after you know how to create static class variables, you will almost never create global variables.

9. Function overloading is the ability to write more than one function with the same name, distinguished by the number or type of the parameters.

Exercises

1. `unsigned long int Perimeter(unsigned short int, unsigned short int);`

2. The following is one possible answer:
```
unsigned long int Perimeter(unsigned short int length,
                            unsigned short int width)
{
  return (2*length) + (2*width);
}
```

3. The function tries to return a value even though it is declared to return `void` and, thus, cannot return a value.

4. The function would be fine, but there is a semicolon at the end of the `myFunc()` function's definition header.

5. The following is one possible answer:

```cpp
short int Divider(unsigned short int valOne, unsigned short int valTwo)
{
    if (valTwo == 0)
        return -1;
    else
        return valOne / valTwo;
}
```

6. The following is one possible solution:

```cpp
#include <iostream>
using namespace std;

short int Divider(
        unsigned short int valone,
        unsigned short int valtwo);

int main()
{
    unsigned short int one, two;
    short int answer;
    cout << "Enter two numbers.\n Number one: ";
    cin >> one;
    cout << "Number two: ";
    cin >> two;
    answer = Divider(one, two);
    if (answer > -1)
        cout << "Answer: " << answer;
    else
        cout << "Error, can't divide by zero!";
    return 0;
}

short int Divider(unsigned short int valOne, unsigned short int valTwo)
{
    if (valTwo == 0)
        return -1;
    else
        return valOne / valTwo;
}
```

D

7. The following is one possible solution:

```cpp
#include <iostream>
using namespace std;
typedef unsigned short USHORT;
typedef unsigned long ULONG;

ULONG GetPower(USHORT n, USHORT power);
```

```
int main()
{
    USHORT number, power;
    ULONG answer;
    cout << "Enter a number: ";
    cin >> number;
    cout << "To what power? ";
    cin >> power;
    answer = GetPower(number,power);
    cout << number << " to the " << power << "th power is " <<
      answer << endl;
    return 0;
}

ULONG GetPower(USHORT n, USHORT power)
{
    if(power == 1)
        return n;
    else
        return (n * GetPower(n,power-1));
}
```

Lesson 7, "Controlling Program Flow"

Quiz

1. Separate the initializations with commas, such as

   ```
   for (x = 0, y = 10; x < 100; x++, y++).
   ```

2. goto jumps in any direction to any arbitrary line of code. This makes for source code that is difficult to understand and, therefore, difficult to maintain.

3. Yes, if the condition is false after the initialization, the body of the for loop will never execute. Here's an example:

   ```
   for (int x = 100; x < 100; x++)
   ```

4. The variable x is out of scope; thus, it has no valid value.

5. Yes. Any loop can be nested within any other loop.

6. Yes. Following are examples for both a for loop and a while loop:

   ```
   for(;;)
   {
       // This for loop never ends!
   }
   while(true)
   {
       // This while loop never ends!
   }
   ```

7. Your program appears to hang because it never quits running. This causes you to have to reboot the computer or to use advanced features of your operating system to end the task.

Exercises

1. The following is one possible answer:

```
for (int i = 0; i< 10; i++)
{
    for ( int j = 0; j< 10; j++)
        cout << "0";
    cout << endl;
}
```

2. The following is one possible answer:

```
for (int x = 100; x<=200; x+=2)
```

3. The following is one possible answer:

```
int x = 100;
while (x <= 200)
    x+= 2;
```

4. The following is one possible answer:

```
int x = 100;
do
{
    x+=2;
} while (x <= 200);
```

5. counter is never incremented and the while loop will never terminate.

6. There is a semicolon after the loop and the loop does nothing. The programmer might have intended this, but if counter was supposed to print each value, it won't. Rather, it will print out only the value of the counter after the for loop has completed.

7. counter is initialized to 100, but the test condition is that if it is less than 10, the test will fail and the body will never be executed. If line 1 were changed to int counter = 5;, the loop would not terminate until it had counted down past the smallest possible int. Because int is signed by default, this would not be what was intended.

8. Case 0 probably needs a break statement. If not, it should be documented with a comment.

D

Lesson 8, "Pointers Explained"

Quiz

1. The address-of operator (&) is used to determine the address of any variable.

2. The dereference operator (*) is used to access the value at an address in a pointer.

3. A pointer is a variable that holds the address of another variable.

4. The address stored in the pointer is the address of another variable. The value stored at that address is any value stored in any variable. The indirection operator (*) returns the value stored at the address, which itself is stored in the pointer.

5. The indirection operator returns the value at the address stored in a pointer. The address-of operator (&) returns the memory address of the variable.

6. The `const int * ptrOne` declares that `ptrOne` is a pointer to a constant integer. The integer itself cannot be changed using this pointer.

   The `int * const ptrTwo` declares that `ptrTwo` is a constant pointer to integer. After it is initialized, this pointer cannot be reassigned.

Exercises

1.

   a. `int * pOne;` declares a pointer to an integer.

   b. `int vTwo;` declares an integer variable.

   c. `int * pThree = &vTwo;` declares a pointer to an integer and initializes it with the address of another variable, `vTwo`.

2. `unsigned short *pAge = &yourAge;`

3. `*pAge = 50;`

4. The following is one possible answer:

```
#include <iostream>

int main()
{
   int theInteger;
   int *pInteger = &theInteger;
   *pInteger = 5;

   std::cout << "The Integer: "
             << *pInteger << std::endl;

   return 0;
}
```

5. `pInt` should have been initialized. More importantly, because it was not initialized and was not assigned the address of any memory, it points to a random place in memory. Assigning a literal (9) to that random place is a dangerous bug.

6. Presumably, the programmer meant to assign 9 to the value at `pVar`, which would be an assignment to `SomeVariable`. Unfortunately, 9 was assigned to be the value of `pVar` because the indirection operator (`*`) was left off. This will lead to disaster if `pVar` is used to assign a value because it is pointing to whatever is at the address of 9 and not at `SomeVariable`.

Lesson 9, "Exploiting References"

Quiz

1. A reference is an alias, and a pointer is a variable that holds an address. References cannot be null and cannot be assigned to.

2. When you need to reassign what is pointed to, or when the pointer might be null.

3. A null pointer (0).

4. This is a shorthand way of saying a reference to a constant object.

5. Passing *by* reference means not making a local copy. It can be accomplished by passing a reference or by passing a pointer.

6. All three are correct; however, you should pick one style and use it consistently.

Exercises

D

1. The following is one possible answer:

```
#include <iostream>

int main()
{
    int  varOne = 1;      // sets varOne to 1
    int& rVar = varOne;
    int* pVar = &varOne;
    rVar = 5;             // sets varOne to 5
    *pVar = 7;            // sets varOne to 7

    // All three of the following will print 7:
    std::cout << "variable:  " << varOne << std::endl;
    std::cout << "reference: " << rVar   << std::endl;
    std::cout << "pointer:   " << *pVar  << std::endl;

    return 0;
}
```

2. The following is one possible answer:

```
int main()
{
    int varOne;
    const int * const pVar = &varOne;
    varOne = 6;
    *pVar = 7;
    int varTwo;
    pVar = &varTwo;
    return 0;
}
```

3. You can't assign a value to a constant object, and you can't reassign a constant pointer. This means that lines 6 and 8 are problems.

4. The following is one possible answer. Note that this is a dangerous program to run because of the stray pointer.

```
int main()
{
    int * pVar;
    *pVar = 9;
    return 0;
}
```

5. The following is one possible answer:

```
int main()
{
    int VarOne;
    int * pVar = &varOne;
    *pVar = 9;
    return 0;
}
```

6. The following is one possible answer. Note that you should avoid memory leaks in your programs.

```
#include <iostream>
int FuncOne();
int main()
{
    int localVar = FunOne();
    std::cout << "The value of localVar is: " << localVar;
    return 0;
}

int FuncOne()
{
    int * pVar = new int (5);
    return *pVar;
}
```

7. The following is one possible answer:

```
#include <iostream>
void FuncOne();
int main()
{
   FuncOne();
   return 0;
}

void FuncOne()
{
   int * pVar = new int (5);
   std::cout << "The value of *pVar is: " << *pVar ;
   delete pVar;
}
```

8. MakeCat returns a reference to the CAT created on the free store. There is no way to free that memory, and this produces a memory leak.

9. The following is one possible answer:

```
#include <iostream>
using namespace std;
class CAT
{
   public:
      CAT(int age) { itsAge = age; }
      ~CAT(){}
      int GetAge() const { return itsAge;}
   private:
      int itsAge;
};

CAT * MakeCat(int age);
int main()
{
   int age = 7;
   CAT * Boots = MakeCat(age);
   cout << "Boots is " << Boots->GetAge() << " years old";
   delete Boots;
  return 0;
}

CAT * MakeCat(int age)
{
   return new CAT(age);
}
```

D

Lesson 10, "Classes and Objects"

Quiz

1. The dot operator is the period (.). It is used to access the members of a class or structure.

2. Definitions of variables set aside memory. Declarations of classes don't set aside memory.

3. The declaration of a class is its interface; it tells clients of the class how to interact with the class. The implementation of the class is the set of member functions—usually in a related CPP file.

4. Public data members can be accessed by clients of the class. Private data members can be accessed only by member functions of the class.

5. Yes, member functions can be private. Although not shown in this chapter, a member function can be private. Only other member functions of the class will be able to use the private function.

6. Although member data can be public, it is good programming practice to make it private and to provide public accessor functions to the data.

7. Yes. Each object of a class has its own data members.

8. Declarations end with a semicolon after the closing brace; function definitions do not.

9. The header for a `Cat` function, `Meow()`, that takes no parameters and returns `void` looks like this:

   ```
   void Cat::Meow()
   ```

10. The constructor is called to initialize a class. This special function has the same name as the class.

Exercises

1. The following is one possible solution:

   ```
   class Employee
   {
       int Age;
       int YearsOfService;
       int Salary;
   };
   ```

2. The following is one possible answer. Notice that the `Get...` accessor methods were also made constant because they won't change anything in the class.

```
// Employee.h
class Employee
{
  public:
    int  GetAge() const;
    void SetAge(int age);
    int  GetYearsOfService() const;
    void SetYearsOfService(int years);
    int  GetSalary() const;
    void SetSalary(int salary);

  private:
    int itsAge;
    int itsYearsOfService;
    int itsSalary;
};
```

3. The following is one possible solution:

```
// Employee.cpp
#include <iostream>
#include "Employee.h"

int  Employee::GetAge() const
{
    return itsAge;
}
void Employee::SetAge(int age)
{
    itsAge = age;
}
int  Employee::GetYearsOfService() const
{
    return itsYearsOfService;
}
void Employee::SetYearsOfService(int years)
{
    itsYearsOfService = years;
}
int  Employee::GetSalary()const
{
    return itsSalary;
}
void Employee::SetSalary(int salary)
{
    itsSalary = salary;
}
```

D

```
int main()
{
   using namespace std;

   Employee John;
   Employee Sally;

   John.SetAge(30);
   John.SetYearsOfService(5);
   John.SetSalary(50000);

   Sally.SetAge(32);
   Sally.SetYearsOfService(8);
   Sally.SetSalary(40000);

   cout << "At AcmeSexist company, John and Sally have ";
   cout << "the same job.\n\n";

   cout << "John is " << John.GetAge() << " years old." << endl;
   cout << "John has been with the firm for " ;
   cout << John.GetYearsOfService() << " years." << endl;
   cout << "John earns $" << John.GetSalary();
   cout << " dollars per year.\n\n";

   cout << "Sally, on the other hand is " << Sally.GetAge();
   cout << " years old and has been with the company ";
   cout << Sally.GetYearsOfService();
   cout << " years. Yet Sally only makes $" << Sally.GetSalary();
   cout << " dollars per year! Something here is unfair.";
}
```

4. The following is one possible answer:

```
float Employee::GetRoundedThousands() const
{
    return Salary / 1000;
}
```

5. The following is one possible answer:

```
class Employee
{
  public:

    Employee(int age, int years, int salary);
    int  GetAge() const;
    void SetAge(int age);
    int  GetYearsOfService() const;
    void SetYearsOfService(int years);
    int  GetSalary() const;
    void SetSalary(int salary);
```

```
    private:
        int itsAge;
        int itsYearsOfService;
        int itsSalary;
    };
```

6. Class declarations must end with a semicolon.

7. The accessor `GetAge()` is private. Remember: All class members are private unless you say otherwise.

8. You can't access `itsStation` directly. It is private.

   You can't call `SetStation()` on the class. You can call `SetStation()` only on objects.

   You can't initialize `myOtherTV` because there is no matching constructor.

Lesson 11, "Implementing Inheritance"

Quiz

1. A v-table, or virtual function table, is a common way for compilers to manage virtual functions in C++. The table keeps a list of the addresses of all the virtual functions, and depending on the runtime type of the object pointed to, invokes the right function.

2. A destructor of any class can be declared to be virtual. When the pointer is deleted, the runtime type of the object will be assessed and the correct derived destructor invoked.

3. This was a trick question—there are no virtual constructors.

4. By creating a virtual method in your class, which itself calls the copy constructor.

5. `Base::FunctionName();`

6. `FunctionName();`

7. Yes, the virtuality is inherited and *cannot* be turned off.

8. `protected` members are accessible to the member functions of derived objects.

D

Exercises

1. `virtual void SomeFunction(int);`

2. Because you are showing a declaration of `Square`, you don't need to worry about `Shape`. `Shape` is automatically included as a part of `Rectangle`.
```
class Square : public Rectangle
{};
```

3. Just as with exercise 2, you don't need to worry about `Shape`.
```
Square::Square(int length):
    Rectangle(length, width){}
```

4. The following is one possible answer:
```
class Square
{
   public:
      // ...
      virtual Square * clone() const { return new Square(*this); }
      // ...
};
```

5. Perhaps nothing. `SomeFunction` expects a `Shape` object. You've passed it a `Rectangle` "sliced" down to a `Shape`. As long as you don't need any of the `Rectangle` parts, this will be fine. If you do need the `Rectangle` parts, you'll need to change `SomeFunction` to take a pointer or a reference to a `Shape`.

6. You can't declare a copy constructor to be virtual.

Lesson 12, "Polymorphism"

Quiz

1. A down cast (also called *casting down*) is a declaration that a pointer to a base class is to be treated as a pointer to a derived class.

2. This refers to the idea of moving shared functionality upward into a common base class. If more than one class shares a function, it is desirable to find a common base class in which that function can be stored.

3. If neither class inherits using the keyword `virtual`, two `Shapes` are created, one for `Rectangle` and one for `Shape`. If the keyword `virtual` is used for both classes, only one shared `Shape` is created.

4. Both `Horse` and `Bird` initialize their base class, `Animal`, in their constructors. `Pegasus` does as well, and when a `Pegasus` is created, the `Horse` and `Bird` initializations of `Animal` are ignored.

5. The following is one possible answer:

```
class Vehicle
{
    virtual void Move() = 0;
}
```

6. None must be overridden unless you want to make the class nonabstract, in which case all three must be overridden.

Exercises

1. `class JetPlane : public Rocket, public Airplane`

2. `class Seven47: public JetPlane`

3. The following is one possible answer:

```
class Vehicle
{
    virtual void Move() = 0;
    virtual void Haul() = 0;
};

class Car : public Vehicle
{
    virtual void Move();
    virtual void Haul();
};

class Bus : public Vehicle
{
    virtual void Move();
    virtual void Haul();
};
```

4. The following is one possible answer:

```
class Vehicle
{
    virtual void Move() = 0;
    virtual void Haul() = 0;
};
```

D

```
class Car : public Vehicle
{
    virtual void Move();
};

class Bus : public Vehicle
{
    virtual void Move();
    virtual void Haul();
};

class SportsCar : public Car
{
    virtual void Haul();
};

class Coupe : public Car
{
    virtual void Haul();
};
```

Lesson 13, "Operator Types and Operator Overloading"

Quiz

1. Yes. The const version would be used by the compiler for read operations while the non-const version would be used for writing. You can use this feature to customize behaviors for read and write. For instance, in a multithreaded environment, reading might be safe, whereas you might need synchronization for writing. This could improve performance at read times.

2. Assignment operators to allow "strDest = strSource;", operator+ to allow concatenation "strDest = strSource1 + strSource2;". operator+= to allow appends to the same string object "strDest += strAdd;", operator< to allow comparisons—this is useful when the string object is used by STL sort functions. operator== to enable comparisons between two string objects based on their contents, and other operators such as subscript operator[] to allow access to individual characters, and some conversion operators to allow easy conversion of a string to often-used types.

3. No. Bitwise operators such as &, !, ^ and | don't make sense even if a date stored is manipulated in bit format because no programmer would find any intuitive use for them.

Exercises

1. The prefix and postfix versions of the unary decrement operators can be declared as

```
CDate& operator -- ()
CDate operator -- (int)
```

2. Define operator== and operator< to suit the criterion:

```
bool CMyArray::operator== (const CMyArray& dest) const
{
    bool bRet = false;
    if (dest.m_nNumElements == this->m_nNumElements)
    {
        for (int nIndex = 0; nIndex < m_nNumElements; ++ nIndex)
        {
            bRet = dest [nIndex] == m_pnInternalArray [nIndex];
            if (!bRet)
                break;
        }
    }
    return bRet;
}

bool CMyArray::operator< (const CMyArray& dest) const
{
    bool bRet = false;

    if (m_nNumElements < dest.m_nNumElements)
        bRet = true;
    else if (m_nNumElements > dest.m_nNumElements)
        bRet = false;
    else    // equal lengths
    {
        int nSumArrayContents = 0;
        int nSumDestArrayContents = 0;

        for (int nIndex = 0; nIndex < m_nNumElements; ++ nIndex)
        {
            nSumArrayContents += m_pnInternalArray [nIndex];
            nSumDestArrayContents += dest.m_pnInternalArray [nIndex];
        }

        bRet = (nSumArrayContents < nSumDestArrayContents);
    }

    return bRet;
}
```

D

Lesson 14, "Casting Operators"

Quiz

1. `dynamic_cast`

2. Correct the function, of course. `const_cast` and casting operators in general should be a last resort.

3. True.

4. Yes, true.

Lesson 15, "An Introduction to Macros and Templates"

Quiz

1. Inclusion guards are used to protect a header file from being included into a program more than once.

2. `#define debug 0` defines the term debug to equal 0 (zero). Everywhere the word debug is found, the character 0 is substituted. `#undef debug` removes any definition of debug; when the word debug is found in the file, it is left unchanged.

3. The answer is 4 / 2, which is 2.

4. The result is 10 + 10 / 2, which is 10 + 5, or 15. This is obviously not the result desired.

5. You should add parentheses:
   `HALVE (x) ((x)/2)`

6. Templates are abstractions that are instantiated at compile time to take a concrete form. Macros are more like constants that substitute strings.

7. Template parameters correspond to the type to which the template should be instantiated to, whereas parameters in a (nontemplate) function indicate the fixed type of the object the function can take.

8. The standard template library is an important part of most C++ development environment and supplies the programmer with template classes and functions that solve many day-to-day computational problems, and keep him from reinventing the wheel.

Exercises

1. The macro ADD would be

```
#define ADD(x,y) (x + y)
```

2. The template version would be

```
template <typename T>
T Add (const T& x, const T& y)
{
    return (x + y);
}
```

3. The template version of swap would be

```
template <typename T>
void Swap (T& x, T& y)
{
    T temp = x;
    x = y;
    y = temp;
}
```

4.
```
#define QUARTER(x) ((x)/ 4)
```

5. The template class definition would look like:

```
template <typename Array1Type, typename Array2Type>
class CTwoArrays
{
private:
        Array1Type m_Array1 [10];
        Array2Type m_Array2 [10];
public:
        Array1Type& GetArray1Element(int nIndex){return m_Array1[nIndex];}
        Array2Type& GetArray2Element(int nIndex){return m_Array2[nIndex];}
};
```

D

Lesson 16, "An Introduction to the Standard Template Library"

Quiz

1. A deque. Only a deque allows constant time insertions at the front and at the back of the container.

2. A std::set or a std::map if you have key-value pairs. If the elements need to be available in duplicates too, you would choose std::multiset or std::multimap.

3. Yes. When you instantiate a `std::set` template, you can optionally supply a second template parameter that is a binary predicate that the `set` class uses as the sort criterion. Program this binary predicate to criteria that are relevant to your requirements. It needs to be strictly weak ordering compliant.

4. Iterators form the bridge between algorithms and containers so that the former (which are generic) can work on the latter without having to know (be customized for) every container type possible.

5. `hash_set` is not a C++ standard compliant container. So, you should not use it in any application that has portability listed as one of its requirements. You should use the `std::map` in those scenarios.

Lesson 17, "The STL `string` Class"

Quiz

1. `std::basic_string <T>`

2. Copy the two strings into two copy objects. Convert the copied strings each into either lowercase or uppercase. Return the result of comparison of the converted copied strings.

3. No, they are not. C-style strings are actually raw pointers akin to a character array, whereas STL `string` is a class that implements various operators and member functions to make string manipulation and handling as simple as possible.

Exercises

1. The program needs to use `std::reverse`:

```
#include <string>
#include <iostream>
#include <algorithm>

int main ()
{
    using namespace std;

    cout << "Please enter a word for palindrome-check:" << endl;
    string strInput;
    cin >> strInput;

    string strCopy (strInput);
    reverse (strCopy.begin (), strCopy.end ());
```

```cpp
    if (strCopy == strInput)
        cout << strInput << " is a palindrome!" << endl;
    else
        cout << strInput << " is not a palindrome." << endl;

    return 0;
}
```

2. Use `std::find`:

```cpp
#include <string>
#include <iostream>

using namespace std;

// Find the number of character 'chToFind' in string "strInput"
int GetNumCharacters (string& strInput, char chToFind)
{
    int nNumCharactersFound = 0;

    size_t nCharOffset = strInput.find (chToFind);
    while (nCharOffset != string::npos)
    {
        ++ nNumCharactersFound;

        nCharOffset = strInput.find (chToFind, nCharOffset + 1);
    }

    return nNumCharactersFound;
}

int main ()
{

    cout << "Please enter a string:" << endl << "> ";
    string strInput;
    getline (cin, strInput);

    int nNumVowels = GetNumCharacters (strInput, 'a');
    nNumVowels += GetNumCharacters (strInput, 'e');
    nNumVowels += GetNumCharacters (strInput, 'i');
    nNumVowels += GetNumCharacters (strInput, 'o');
    nNumVowels += GetNumCharacters (strInput, 'u');

    // DIY: handle capitals too..

    cout << "The number of vowels in that sentence is: " << nNumVowels;

    return 0;
}
```

D

3. Use function toupper:

```
#include <string>
#include <iostream>
#include <algorithm>

int main ()
{
    using namespace std;

    cout << "Please enter a string for case-conversion:" << endl;
    cout << "> ";

    string strInput;
    getline (cin, strInput);
    cout << endl;

    for ( size_t nCharIndex = 0
        ; nCharIndex < strInput.length ()
        ; nCharIndex += 2)
        strInput [nCharIndex] = toupper (strInput [nCharIndex]);

    cout << "The string converted to upper case is: " << endl;
    cout << strInput << endl << endl;

    return 0;
}
```

4. This can be simply programmed as

```
#include <string>
#include <iostream>

int main ()
{
    using namespace std;

    const string str1 = "I";
    const string str2 = "Love";
    const string str3 = "STL";
    const string str4 = "String.";

    string strResult = str1 + " " + str2 + " " + str3 + " " + str4;

    cout << "The sentence reads:" << endl;
    cout << strResult;

    return 0;
}
```

Lesson 18, "STL Dynamic Array Classes"

Quiz

1. No, they can't. Elements can only be added at the back (that is, the end) of a vector sequence in constant time.

2. 10 more. At the 11th insertion, you will trigger a reallocation.

3. Deletes the last element; that is, removes the element at the back.

4. Of type `CMammal`.

5. Via (a) the subscript `operator[]` (b) Function `at()`.

6. Random-access iterator.

Exercises

1. One solution is

```cpp
#include <vector>
#include <iostream>

using namespace std;

char DisplayOptions ()
{
    cout << "What would you like to do?" << endl;
    cout << "Select 1: To enter an integer" << endl;
    cout << "Select 2: Query a value given an index" << endl;
    cout << "Select 3: To display the vector" << endl << "> ";
    cout << "Select 4: To quit!" << endl << "> ";

    char ch;
    cin >> ch;

    return ch;
}

int main ()
{
    vector <int> vecData;

    char chUserChoice = '\0';
    while ((chUserChoice = DisplayOptions ()) != '4')
    {
    if (chUserChoice == '1')
        {
            cout << "Please enter an integer to be inserted: ";
            int nDataInput = 0;
            cin >> nDataInput;
```

D

```
            vecData.push_back (nDataInput);
        }
        else if (chUserChoice == '2')
        {
            cout << "Please enter an index between 0 and ";
            cout << (vecData.size () - 1) << ": ";
            int nIndex = 0;
            cin >> nIndex;

            if (nIndex < (vecData.size ()))
            {
                cout<<"Element ["<<nIndex<<"] = "<<vecData [nIndex];
                cout << endl;
            }
        }
        else if (chUserChoice == '3')
        {
            cout << "The contents of the vector are: ";
            for (size_t nIndex = 0; nIndex < vecData.size (); ++ nIndex)
                cout << vecData [nIndex] << ' ';
            cout << endl;
        }
    }
    return 0;
}
```

2. Use the std::find algorithm:
   ```
   vector <int>::iterator iElementFound = std::find (vecData.begin (),
                                              vecData.end (), nDataInput);
   ```

3. Derive from the code sample in the solution to exercise 1 to accept user input and print the contents of a vector.

Lesson 19, "STL list"

Quiz

1. Elements can be inserted in the middle of the list as they can be at either ends. No gain or loss in performance is due to position.

2. The specialty of the list is that operations such as these don't invalidate existing iterators.

3. `mList.clear ();`

   or

   `mList.erase (mList.begin(), mList.end());`

4. Yes, an overload of the `insert` function allows you to insert a range from a source collection.

Exercises

1. This is like exercise solution 1 for the vector. The only change is that you would use the list insert function as

   `mList.insert (mList.begin(),nDataInput);`

2. Store iterators to two elements in a list. Insert an element in the middle using the list's insert function. Use the iterators to demonstrate that they are still able to fetch the values they pointed to before the insertion.

3. A possible solution is

```cpp
#include <vector>
#include <list>
#include <iostream>

using namespace std;

int main ()
{
    vector <int> vecData (4);
    vecData [0] = 0;
    vecData [1] = 10;
    vecData [2] = 20;
    vecData [3] = 30;

    list <int> listIntegers;

    // Insert the contents of the vector into the beginning of the list
    listIntegers.insert (listIntegers.begin (),
                    vecData.begin (), vecData.end());

    cout << "The contents of the list are: ";

    list <int>::const_iterator iElement;
    for ( iElement = listIntegers.begin ()
        ; iElement != listIntegers.end ()
        ; ++ iElement)
        cout << *iElement << " ";

    return 0;
};
```

D

4. A possible solution is

```
#include <list>
#include <string>
#include <iostream>

using namespace std;

int main ()
{
    list <string> listNames;
    listNames.push_back ("Jack");
    listNames.push_back ("John");
    listNames.push_back ("Anna");
    listNames.push_back ("Skate");

    cout << "The contents of the list are: ";

    list <string>::const_iterator iElement;
    for (iElement = listNames.begin(); iElement!=listNames.end();
➡++iElement)
        cout << *iElement << " ";
    cout << endl;

    cout << "The contents after reversing are: ";
    listNames.reverse ();
    for (iElement = listNames.begin(); iElement!=listNames.end();
➡++iElement)
        cout << *iElement << " ";
    cout << endl;

    cout << "The contents after sorting are: ";
    listNames.sort ();
    for (iElement = listNames.begin(); iElement!=listNames.end();
➡++iElement)
        cout << *iElement << " ";
    cout << endl;

    return 0;
};
```

Lesson 20, "STL set and multiset"

Quiz

1. The default sort criterion is specified by std::less<>, which effectively uses operator< to compare two integers and returns true if the first is less than the second.

2. Together, one after another.

3. `size()`, as is the case with all STL containers.

Exercises

1. The binary predicate can be

```
struct FindContactGivenNumber
{
    bool operator()(const CContactItem& lsh,const CContactItem& rsh) const
    {
        return (lsh.strPhoneNumber < rsh.strPhoneNumber);
    }
};
```

2. The structure and the multiset definition would be

```
#include <set>
#include <iostream>
#include <string>

using namespace std;

struct PAIR_WORD_MEANING
{
    string strWord;
    string strMeaning;

    PAIR_WORD_MEANING (const string& sWord, const string& sMeaning)
        : strWord (sWord), strMeaning (sMeaning) {}

    bool operator< (const PAIR_WORD_MEANING& pairAnotherWord) const
    {
        return (strWord < pairAnotherWord.strWord);
    }
};

int main ()
{
    multiset <PAIR_WORD_MEANING> msetDictionary;
    PAIR_WORD_MEANING word1 ("C++", "A programming language");
    PAIR_WORD_MEANING word2 ("Programmer", "A geek!");

    msetDictionary.insert (word1);
    msetDictionary.insert (word2);

    return 0;
}
```

D

3. One solution is

```
#include <set>
#include <iostream>

using namespace std;

template <typename T>
void DisplayContent (const T& sequence)
{
    T::const_iterator iElement;

    for (iElement = sequence.begin(); iElement!=sequence.end(); ++iElement)
        cout << *iElement << " ";
}

int main ()
{
    multiset <int> msetIntegers;

    msetIntegers.insert (5);
    msetIntegers.insert (5);
    msetIntegers.insert (5);

    set <int> setIntegers;
    setIntegers.insert (5);
    setIntegers.insert (5);
    setIntegers.insert (5);

    cout << "Displaying the contents of the multiset: ";
    DisplayContent (msetIntegers);
    cout << endl;

    cout << "Displaying the contents of the set: ";
    DisplayContent (setIntegers);
    cout << endl;

    return 0;
}
```

Lesson 21, "STL `map` **and** `multimap`"

Quiz

1. The default sort criterion is specified by std::less<>.

2. Next to each other.

3. size ().

4. You would not find duplicate elements in a map!

Exercises

1. An associative container that allowed duplicate entries. For example, a `std::multimap`.

   ```
   std::multimap <string, string> multimapPeopleNamesToNumbers;
   ```

2. An associative container that allowed duplicate entries.

   ```
   struct fPredicate
   {
       bool operator< (const wordProperty& lsh, const wordProperty& rsh) const
       {
           return (lsh.strWord < rsh. strWord);
       }
   };
   ```

3. Take a hint from the very similar solved exercise for sets and multisets.

Lesson 22, "Understanding Function Objects"

Quiz

1. A unary predicate.

2. It can display data, for example, or simply count elements.

3. Because in C++ all entities that exist during the runtime of an application are objects. In this case, even structures and classes can be made to work as functions, hence the term *function objects*. Note that functions can also be available via function pointers—these are function objects, too.

D

Exercises

1. A solution is

   ```
   template <typename elementType=int>
   struct Double
   {
       void operator () (const elementType element) const
       {
           cout << element * 2 << ' ';
       }
   };
   ```

This unary predicate can be used as

```cpp
int main ()
{
        vector <int> vecIntegers;

        for (int nCount = 0; nCount < 10; ++ nCount)
                vecIntegers.push_back (nCount);

        cout << "Displaying the vector of integers: " << endl;

        // Display the array of integers
        for_each ( vecIntegers.begin ()            // Start of range
                 , vecIntegers.end ()                    // End of range
                 , Double <> () ); // Unary function object

        return 0;
}
```

2. Add a member integer that is incremented every time the `operator()` is used:

```cpp
template <typename elementType=int>
struct Double
{
    int m_nUsageCount;

    // Constructor
    Double () : m_nUsageCount (0) {};

    void operator () (const elementType element) const
    {
        ++ m_nUsageCount;
            cout << element * 2 << ' ';
    }
};
```

3. The binary predicate is:

```cpp
template <typename elementType>
class CSortAscending
{
public:
    bool operator () (const elementType& num1,
                        const elementType& num2) const
    {
        return (num1 < num2);
    }
};
```

This predicate can be used as

```
int main ()
{
    std::vector <int> vecIntegers;

    // Insert sample numbers: 100, 90... 20, 10
    for (int nSample = 10; nSample > 0; -- nSample)
        vecIntegers.push_back (nSample * 10);

    std::sort ( vecIntegers.begin (), vecIntegers.end (),
                CSortAscending<int> () );

    for ( size_t nElementIndex = 0;
          nElementIndex < vecIntegers.size ();
          ++ nElementIndex )
          cout << vecIntegers [nElementIndex] << ' ';

    return 0;
}
```

Lesson 23, "STL Algorithms"

Quiz

1. Use the `std::list::remove_if` function because it ensures that existing iterators to elements in the list (that were not removed) still remain valid.

2. `list::sort` (or even `std::sort`) in the absence of an explicitly supplied predicate resorts to a sort using `std::less<>`, which employs the `operator<` to sort objects in a collection.

3. Once per element in the range supplied.

4. `for_each` will return the function object, too.

Exercises

1. Here is one solution:

```
struct CaseInsensitiveCompare
{
    bool operator() (const string& str1, const string& str2) const
    {
        string str1Copy (str1), str2Copy (str2);

        transform (str1Copy.begin (),
                   str1Copy.end(), str1Copy.begin (), tolower);
```

D

```
            transform (str2Copy.begin (),
                    str2Copy.end(), str2Copy.begin (), tolower);

            return (str1Copy < str2Copy);
    }
};
```

2. Here is the demonstration. Note how `std::copy` works without knowing the nature of the collections. It works using the iterator classes only.

```cpp
#include <vector>
#include <algorithm>
#include <list>
#include <string>
#include <iostream>

using namespace std;

int main ()
{
    list <string> listNames;
    listNames.push_back ("Jack");
    listNames.push_back ("John");
    listNames.push_back ("Anna");
    listNames.push_back ("Skate");

    vector <string> vecNames (4);
    copy (listNames.begin (), listNames.end (), vecNames.begin ());

    vector <string> ::const_iterator iNames;
    for (iNames = vecNames.begin (); iNames != vecNames.end (); ++ iNames)
        cout << *iNames << ' ';

    return 0;
}
```

3. The difference between `std::sort` and `std::stable_sort` is that the latter, when sorting, ensures the relative positions of the objects. Because the application needs to store data in the sequence it happened, I would choose `stable_sort` to keep the relative ordering between the celestial events intact.

Lesson 24, "Adaptive Containers: stack and queue"

Quiz

1. Yes, by supplying a predicate.

2. operator <

3. No, you can only work on the top of the stack. So, you can't access the coin at the bottom.

Exercises

1. The binary predicate could be operator<:

```
class CPerson
{
public:
    int m_nAge;
    bool m_bIsFemale;

    bool operator<  (const CPerson& anotherPerson) const
    {
        bool bRet = false;
        if (m_nAge > anotherPerson.m_nAge)
            bRet = true;
        else if (m_bIsFemale && anotherPerson.m_bIsFemale)
            bRet = true;

        return bRet;
    }
};
```

D

2. Just insert into the stack. As you pop data, you will effectively reverse contents because a stack is a last in–first out type of a container.

Lesson 25, "Working with Bit Flags Using STL"

Quiz

1. No. The number of bits a bitset can hold is fixed at compile time.

2. Because it isn't one. It can't scale itself dynamically as other containers do, it doesn't support iterators in the way containers need to.

3. No. `std::bitset` is best suited for this purpose.

Exercises

1. No. `std::bitset` is best suited for this purpose.

```cpp
#include <bitset>
#include <iostream>

int main()
{
    // Initialize the bitset to 1001
    std::bitset <4> fourBits (9);

    std::cout << "fourBits: " << fourBits << std::endl;

    // Initialize another bitset to 0010
    std::bitset <4> fourMoreBits (2);

    std::cout << "fourMoreBits: " << fourMoreBits << std::endl;

    std::bitset<4> addResult(fourBits.to_ulong() +
➥fourMoreBits.to_ulong());
    std::cout << "The result of the addition is: " << addResult;

    return 0;
}
```

2. Call the flip function on any of the bitset objects in the preceding sample:

```cpp
addResult.flip ();
std::cout << "The result of the flip is: " << addResult << std::endl;
```

Lesson 26, "Understanding Smart Pointers"

Quiz

1. I would look at www.boost.org. I hope you would, too!

2. No, typically well programmed (and correctly chosen ones) would not.

3. When intrusive, objects that they own need to hold it; otherwise they can hold this information in a shared object on the free store.

4. The list needs to be traversed in both directions, so it needs to be doubly linked.

Exercises

1. `pObject->DoSomething ();` is faulty because the pointer lost ownership of the object during the copy step. This will crash (or do something very unpleasant).

2. There would be no slicing because `auto_ptr` transfers ownership of the object without having copied it.

Lesson 27, "Working with Streams"

Quiz

1. The insertion operator (`<<`) is a member operator of the `ostream` object and is used for writing to the output device.

2. The extraction operator (`>>`) is a member operator of the `istream` object and is used for writing to your program's variables.

3. The first form of `get()` is without parameters. This returns the value of the character found, and will return `EOF` (end of file) if the end of the file is reached.

   The second form of `get()` takes a character reference as its parameter; that character is filled with the next character in the input stream. The return value is an `iostream` object.

   The third form of `get()` takes an array, a maximum number of characters to get, and a terminating character. This form of `get()` fills the array with up to one fewer characters than the maximum (appending null) unless it reads the terminating character, in which case it immediately writes a null and leaves the terminating character in the buffer.

D

4. `cin.read()` is used for reading binary data structures.

   `getline()` is used to read from the `istream`'s buffer.

5. Wide enough to display the entire number.

6. A reference to an `istream` object.

7. The filename to be opened.

8. `ios::ate` places you at the end of the file, but you can write data anywhere in the file.

Exercises

1. The following is one possible solution:

```
#include <iostream>
int main()
{
    int x;
    std::cout << "Enter a number: ";
    std::cin >> x;
    std::cout << "You entered: " << x << std::endl;
    std::cerr << "Uh oh, this to cerr!" << std::endl;
    std::clog << "Uh oh, this to clog!" << std::endl;
    return 0;
}
```

2. The following is one possible solution:

```
#include <iostream>
int main()
{
    char name[80];
    std::cout << "Enter your full name: ";
    std::cin.getline(name,80);
    std::cout << "\nYou entered: " << name << std::endl;
    return 0;
}
```

3. The following is one possible solution:

```
#include <iostream>
using namespace std;

int main()
{
    char ch;
```

```
      cout << "enter a phrase: ";
      while ( cin.get(ch) )
      {
         switch (ch)
         {
           case '!':
              cout << '$';
              break;
           case '#':
              break;
           default:
              cout << ch;
              break;
         }
      }
      return 0;
}
```

4. The following is one possible solution:

```
#include <fstream>
#include <iostream>
using namespace std;

int main(int argc, char**argv)    // returns 1 on error
{
   if (argc != 2)
   {
      cout << "Usage: argv[0] <infile>\n";
      return(1);
   }

   // open the input stream
   ifstream fin (argv[1],ios::binary);
   if (!fin)
   {
      cout << "Unable to open " << argv[1] <<" for reading.\n";
      return(1);
   }

   char ch;
   while ( fin.get(ch))
      if ((ch > 32 && ch < 127) || ch == '\n'|| ch == '\t')
         cout << ch;
   fin.close();
}
```

D

5. The following is one possible solution:

```
#include <iostream>

int main(int argc, char**argv)    // returns 1 on error
{
    for (int ctr = argc-1; ctr>0 ; ctr--)
        std::cout << argv[ctr] << " ";
}
```

Lesson 28, "Exception Handling"

Quiz

1. An exception is an object created as the result of invoking the keyword throw. It is used to signal an exceptional condition, and is passed up the call stack to the first catch statement that handles its type.

2. A try block is a set of statements that might generate an exception.

3. A catch statement is a routine that has a signature of the type of exception it handles. It follows a try block and acts as the receiver of exceptions raised within the try block.

4. An exception is an object and can contain any information that can be defined within a user-created class.

5. Exception objects are created when the program invokes the keyword throw.

6. In general, exceptions should be passed by reference. If you don't intend to modify the contents of the exception object, you should pass a const reference.

7. Yes, if you pass the exception by reference.

8. catch statements are examined in the order they appear in the source code. The first catch statement whose signature matches the exception is used. In general, it is best to start with the most specific exception and work toward the most general.

9. catch(...) catches any exception of any type.

10. A breakpoint is a place in the code where the debugger stops execution.

Exercises

1. The following is one possible answer:

```
#include <iostream>
using namespace std;
class OutOfMemory {};
```

```
int main()
{
    try
    {
        int *myInt = new int;
        if (myInt == 0)
            throw OutOfMemory();
    }
    catch (OutOfMemory)
    {
        cout << "Unable to allocate memory!" << endl;
    }
    return 0;
}
```

2. The following is one possible answer:

```
#include <iostream>
#include <stdio.h>
#include <string.h>
using namespace std;
class OutOfMemory
{
  public:
    OutOfMemory(char *);
    char* GetString() { return itsString; }
  private:
    char* itsString;
};

OutOfMemory::OutOfMemory(char * theType)
{
    itsString = new char[80];
    char warning[] = "Out Of Memory! Can't allocate room for: ";
    strncpy(itsString,warning,60);
    strncat(itsString,theType,19);
}

int main()
{
    try
    {
        int *myInt = new int;
        if (myInt == 0)
            throw OutOfMemory("int");
    }
    catch (OutOfMemory& theException)
    {
        cout << theException.GetString();
    }
    return 0;
}
```

3. The following is one possible answer:

```cpp
#include <iostream>
using namespace std;
// Abstract exception data type
class Exception
{
   public:
     Exception(){}
     virtual ~Exception(){}
     virtual void PrintError() = 0;
};

// Derived class to handle memory problems.
// Note no allocation of memory in this class!
class OutOfMemory : public Exception
{
  public:
    OutOfMemory(){}
    ~OutOfMemory(){}
    virtual void PrintError();
  private:
};

void OutOfMemory::PrintError()
{
   cout << "Out of Memory!!" << endl;
}

// Derived class to handle bad numbers
class RangeError : public Exception
{
  public:
    RangeError(unsigned long number){badNumber = number;}
    ~RangeError(){}
    virtual void PrintError();
    virtual unsigned long GetNumber() { return badNumber; }
    virtual void SetNumber(unsigned long number) {badNumber = number;}
  private:
    unsigned long badNumber;
};

void RangeError::PrintError()
{
   cout << "Number out of range. You used " ;
   cout << GetNumber() << "!!" << endl;
}

void MyFunction();  // func. prototype
```

```
int main()
{
   try
   {
      MyFunction();
   }
   // Only one catch required, use virtual functions to do the
   // right thing.
   catch (Exception& theException)
   {
      theException.PrintError();
   }
   return 0;
}

void MyFunction()
{
      unsigned int *myInt = new unsigned int;
      long testNumber;

      if (myInt == 0)
         throw OutOfMemory();

      cout << "Enter an int: ";
      cin >> testNumber;

      // this weird test should be replaced by a series
      // of tests to complain about bad user input

      if (testNumber > 3768 || testNumber < 0)
         throw RangeError(testNumber);

      *myInt = testNumber;
      cout << "Ok. myInt: " << *myInt;
      delete myInt;
}
```

D

4. The following is one possible answer:

```
#include <iostream>
using namespace std;
// Abstract exception data type
class Exception
{
  public:
    Exception(){}
    virtual ~Exception(){}
    virtual void PrintError() = 0;
};
```

```cpp
// Derived class to handle memory problems.
// Note no allocation of memory in this class!
class OutOfMemory : public Exception
{
  public:
    OutOfMemory(){}
    ~OutOfMemory(){}
    virtual void PrintError();
  private:
};

void OutOfMemory::PrintError()
{
    cout << "Out of Memory!!\n";
}

// Derived class to handle bad numbers
class RangeError : public Exception
{
  public:
    RangeError(unsigned long number){badNumber = number;}
    ~RangeError(){}
    virtual void PrintError();
    virtual unsigned long GetNumber() { return badNumber; }
    virtual void SetNumber(unsigned long number) {badNumber = number;}
  private:
    unsigned long badNumber;
};

void RangeError::PrintError()
{
    cout << "Number out of range. You used ";
    cout << GetNumber() << "!!" << endl;
}

// func. prototypes
void MyFunction();
unsigned int * FunctionTwo();
void FunctionThree(unsigned int *);

int main()
{
    try
    {
        MyFunction();
    }
    // Only one catch required, use virtual functions to do the
    // right thing.
    catch (Exception& theException)
    {
```

```
        theException.PrintError();
    }
    return 0;
}

unsigned int * FunctionTwo()
{
    unsigned int *myInt = new unsigned int;
    if (myInt == 0)
        throw OutOfMemory();
    return myInt;
}

void MyFunction()
{
        unsigned int *myInt = FunctionTwo();
        FunctionThree(myInt);
        cout << "Ok. myInt: " << *myInt;
        delete myInt;
}

void FunctionThree(unsigned int *ptr)
{
        long testNumber;
        cout << "Enter an int: ";
        cin >> testNumber;
        // this weird test should be replaced by a series
        // of tests to complain about bad user input
        if (testNumber > 3768 || testNumber < 0)
            throw RangeError(testNumber);
        *ptr = testNumber;
}
```

D

5. In the process of handling an out-of-memory condition, a `string` object is created by the constructor of `xOutOfMemory`. This exception can be raised only when the program is out of memory, so this allocation must fail.

   It is possible that trying to create this string will raise the same exception, creating an infinite loop until the program crashes. If this string is required, you can allocate the space in a static buffer before beginning the program, and then use it as needed when the exception is thrown. You can test this program by changing the line `if (var == 0)` to `if (1)`, which forces the exception to be thrown.

Lesson 29, "Tapping Further into the Preprocessor"

Quiz

1. To test conditions at debug time. Assert can be a powerful way to validate variables and conditions that are supposed to be valid (such as the validity of a string pointer) without compromising the runtime performance of the application.

2. Use them in traces and logs to know which file contains the event you want to record.

3. Two bytes is 16 bits, so up to 16 bit values could be stored.

4. Five bits can hold 32 values (0 to 31).

5. The result is `1111 1111`.

6. The result is `0011 1100`.

Exercises

1. The inclusion guard statements for the header file `STRING.H` would be

```
#ifndef STRING_H
#define STRING_H
...
#endif
```

2. The following is one possible answer:

```
#include <iostream>

using namespace std;
#ifndef DEBUG
#define ASSERT(x)
#elif DEBUG == 1
#define ASSERT(x) \
            if (! (x)) \
            { \
      cout << "ERROR!! Assert " << #x << " failed" << endl; \
            }
#elif DEBUG == 2
#define ASSERT(x) \
            if (! (x) ) \
            { \
      cout << "ERROR!! Assert " << #x << " failed" << endl; \
      cout << " on line " << __LINE__  << endl; \
      cout << " in file " << __FILE__ << endl;  \
            }
#endif
```

3. The following is one possible answer:

```
#ifndef DEBUG
#define DPRINT(string)
#else
#define DPRINT(STRING) cout << #STRING ;
#endif
```

4. The following is one possible answer:

```
class myDate
{
  public:
    // stuff here...
  private:
    unsigned int Month : 4;
    unsigned int Day   : 8;
    unsigned int Year  : 12;
}
```

D

Index

How can we make this index more useful? Email us at indexes@samspublishing.com

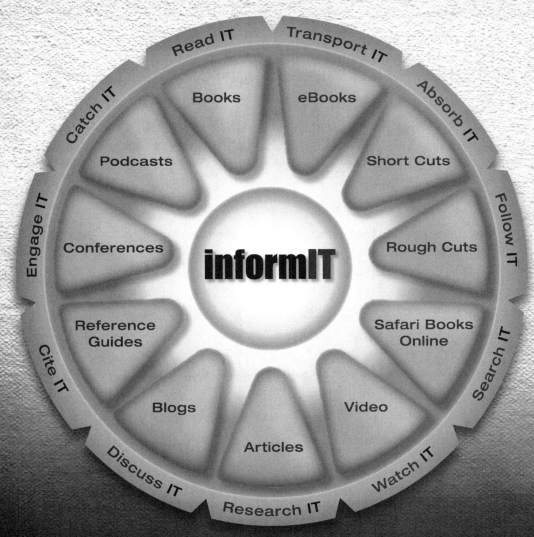

Safari Library
Subscribe Now!
http://safari.informit.com/library

Safari's entire technology collection is now available with no restrictions. Imagine the value of being able to search and access thousands of books, videos, and articles from leading technology authors whenever you wish.

EXPLORE TOPICS MORE FULLY

Gain a more robust understanding of related issues by using Safari as your research tool. With Safari Library you can leverage the knowledge of the world's technology gurus. For one flat, monthly fee, you'll have unrestricted access to a reference collection offered nowhere else in the world—all at your fingertips.

With a Safari Library subscription, you'll get the following premium services:

- **Immediate access to the newest, cutting-edge books**—Approximately eighty new titles are added per month in conjunction with, or in advance of, their print publication.

- **Chapter downloads**—Download five chapters per month so you can work offline when you need to.

- **Rough Cuts**—A service that provides online access to prepublication information on advanced technologies. Content is updated as the author writes the book. You can also download Rough Cuts for offline reference

- **Videos**—Premier design and development videos from training and e-learning expert lynda.com and other publishers you trust.

- **Cut and paste code**—Cut and paste code directly from Safari. Save time. Eliminate errors

- **Save up to 35% on print books**—Safari Subscribers receive a discount of up to 35% on publishers' print books.

THIS BOOK IS SAFARI ENABLED

INCLUDES FREE 45-DAY ACCESS TO THE ONLINE EDITION

The Safari® Enabled icon on the cover of your favorite technology book means the book is available through Safari Bookshelf. When you buy this book, you get free access to the online edition for 45 days.

Safari Bookshelf is an electronic reference library that lets you easily search thousands of technical books, find code samples, download chapters, and access technical information whenever and wherever you need it.

TO GAIN 45-DAY SAFARI ENABLED ACCESS TO THIS BOOK:

- Go to **http://www.samspublishing.com/safarienabled**
- Complete the brief registration form
- Enter the coupon code found in the front of this book on the "Copyright" page

If you have difficulty registering on Safari Bookshelf or accessing the online edition, please e-mail customer-service@safaribooksonline.com.

Operator precedence and associativity

Operator	Associativity	Operator	Associativity
`::`	Left to Right	`> >=`	
`++ -- () [].`	Right to Left	`== !=`	
`-> typeid()`		`& (Bitwise AND)`	
`const_cast`		`^`	
`dynamic_cast`		`|`	
`reinterpret_cast`		`&&`	
`static_cast ++ --`		`||`	
`+ - ! ~ (type)`		`c?t:f (ternary operator)`	
`* & sizeof new`		`=`	Right to Left
`new[] delete`		`+= -=`	
`delete[]`		`*= /= %=`	
`.* ->*`	Left to Right	`<<= >>=`	
`* / %`		`&= ^= |=`	
`+ - (Arithmetic plus and minus)`		`throw`	Not Applicable
`<< >>`		`,`	Left to Right
`< <=`			

Operators at the top of the table have higher precedence than operators below. In expressions beginning with arguments in the innermost set of parentheses (if any), programs evaluate operators of higher precedence before evaluating operators of lower precedence. In the absence of clarifying parentheses, operators on the same level are evaluated according to their evaluation order, as the table mentions.

For example: The unary plus (+) and unary minus (–) have precedence over arithmetic plus and minus. The & symbol that comes first is the address-of operator; the & symbol later is the bitwise AND operator. The * symbol that comes first is the pointer-dereference operator; the * symbol that comes later is the multiplication operator.

Operators that may be overloaded

`*`	`/`	`+`	`-`	`%`	`^`	`&`	`|`	`~`	`!`	`,`	`=`	`<`	`>`
`<=`	`>=`	`++`	`--`	`<<`	`>>`	`==`	`!=`	`&&`	`||`	`*=`	`/=`	`%=`	`^=`
`&=`	`|=`	`+=`	`-=`	`<<=`	`>>=`	`->`	`->*`	`[]`	`()`	`new`	`delete`		

Operators +, -, *, and & may be overloaded for binary and unary expressions. Operators ., .*, ::, ?:, and `sizeof` may not be overloaded. In addition, =, ( ), [ ], and `->` must be implemented as nonstatic member functions.

Standard Template Library (STL) containers

`vector`	Sequential container that implements a dynamic C++ array, with insertion at the back.
`list`	Sequential container that implements a double-linked list.
`deque`	Similar to a vector with insertion at the front and the back.
`set`	Associative container of unique keys.
`multiset`	Associative container of possibly duplicated keys.
`map`	Associative container of key-value pairs with unique keys.
`multimap`	Associative container of key-value pairs with possibly duplicated keys.
`stack`	Adaptive container that implements a last-in-first-out (LIFO) data structure.
`queue`	Adaptive container that implements a first-in-first-out (FIFO) data structure.
`priority_queue`	Adaptive container that implements an ordered queue where element of highest priority is at the top.